CW00547708

Microsoft® Flight Simulator® 5.1
The Official Strategy Guide

SECRETS OF THE GAMES® SERIES
COMPUTER GAME BOOKS

How to Order:

For information on quantity discounts contact the publisher: Prima Publishing, P.O. Box 1260BK, Rocklin, CA 95677-1260; (916) 632-4400. On your letterhead include information concerning the intended use of the books and the number of books you wish to purchase. For individual orders, turn to the back of the book for more information.

Microsoft® Flight Simulator® 5.1
The Official Strategy Guide

Nick Dargahi

PRIMA PUBLISHING

Secrets of the Games® and design is a registered trademark of Prima Publishing, a division of Prima Communications, Inc.

Prima Publishing™ is a trademark of Prima Communications, Inc. P™ is a trademark of Prima Publishing, a division of Prima Communications, Inc.

©1996 by Nick Dargahi. All rights reserved. No part of this book may be reproduced or transmitted in any form or by any means, electronic or mechanical, including photocopying, recording, or by any information storage or retrieval system without written permission from Prima Publishing, except for the inclusion of quotations in a review.

Microsoft Flight Simulator ©1983-1995 Microsoft Corporation. All rights reserved. Flight Simulator ©1983-1995 Bruce Artwick.

Microsoft, MS-DOS, and Windows are either registered trademarks or trademarks of Microsoft Corporation in the U.S. and/or other countries.

Flight Simulator is a registered trademark of Bruce Artwick.

Maps on pages 524–578 ©1996 Horizons Technology, Inc.

Project Editor: Dallas Middaugh
Technical Editors: Lynn Frances Guthrie and Patrick Shaffer

All products and characters mentioned in this book are trademarks of their respective companies.

Important: Prima Publishing, Inc., has made every effort to determine that the information contained in this book is accurate. However, the publisher makes no warranty, either express or implied, as to the accuracy, effectiveness, or completeness of the material in this book; nor does the publisher assume liability for damages, either incidental or consequential, that may result from using the information in this book. The publisher cannot provide information regarding game play, hints and strategies, or problems with hardware or software. Questions should be directed to the support numbers provided by the game and device manufacturers in their documentation. Some game tricks require precise timing and may require repeated attempts before the desired result is achieved.

ISBN: 0-7615-0155-X
Library of Congress Catalog Card Number: 95-68603

Printed in the United States of America
96 97 98 BB 10 9 8 7 6 5 4 3 2 1

Table of Contents

Acknowledgments

Much of the research and fact finding that went into this book was made possible by the efforts of many other individuals. In particular, David Wishnia assisted me with the preparation of the navigational data, and Patrick Shaffer, a navigational instructor for the U.S Navy, provided me with much insight on current navigation practices. Jack Yeazel compiled the frame rate results for Appendix A and graciously granted me permission to publish his findings. Hans van Wyhe, sysop on the CompuServe Flight Simulator forum, answered many questions about the program, and Phil Saitta of Microsoft provided me with much useful *Flight Simulator* related data. Anton Schwing, marketing manager at BAO (Bruce Artwick Organization), makers of *Flight Simulator*, was kind enough to keep me informed of the latest upgrades and add-ons for *Flight Simulator*. Cessna Aircraft, Learjet Corporation, and Schweizer Aircraft Co. were most gracious in sending me photographs, brochures, and other flight performance data for their featured aircraft in FS 5.1. Lynn Guthrie of Microsoft spent countless hours providing a quality technical review of this book, and her work is much appreciated.

The production staff at Prima Publishing also deserve mention for their work. My editors, Dallas Middaugh and Brett Skogen, took care of innumerable miscellaneous details. Marian Hartsough performed her customary magic on my graphics and also desktop published the manuscript.

Deeply missed will be Alec, my dog, who always watched over me while I was at work. To all my family, including Xenia Lisanevich, Kira and Milou Ivanovsky, and Ali, I owe everything. To Adriene goes my appreciation for all her support while I temporarily became a hermit.

Dedication

Alec, my dog, whose life was full of love

Introduction

With the release of *Flight Simulator 5.1*, the wizards at BAO, the primary developer of *Flight Simulator*, and Microsoft, their distributor, have teamed up to jointly produce the best flight simulator yet produced for the personal computer.

Make no mistake, *Flight Simulator 5.1* is a sophisticated flight simulation; it is not just a "game." Prior versions of *Flight Simulator*, for instance, have been used to train U.S. Navy pilots as well as countless other private pilots. In the near future, it may be possible to use PC-based flight simulations to help you qualify for your instrument flight rating license.

NEW HARDWARE REQUIREMENTS

Since *Flight Simulator* represents the state of the art in Personal Computer (PC) simulation technology, the program will tax the full power and resources of your PC. Currently, a Pentium-based CPU running at 120 MHz or 133Mhz with a PCI video card interface and PCI bus is the best hardware configuration to take full advantage of *Flight Simulator 5.1*'s capabilities (hereafter referred to as FS 5.1). Older 486 PCs using local bus video accelerator cards will run FS 5.1 adequately, but your frame rate[1] may be disappointing when using the dense scenery graphics modes. When Intel's new P6 becomes available in late 1995, FS 5.1 will run even smoother.[2]

The CPU, or Central Processing Unit, is commonly referred to as a "386," "486," or Pentium. The name PCI (Peripheral Connect Interface) refers to a new kind of expansion slot in the latest PCs, which allow super fast video cards to have faster

---

[1]Frame rate is a term used to describe the number of frames redrawn per second. A frame is a completely redrawn picture inside your cockpit view window.

[2]By smoother, I mean FS 5.1 will display more picture frames per second with faster processors.

access to the CPU. The speed at which a PC runs is measured in millions of cycles per second, or megahertz, and generally speaking, the faster the clock speed, the faster FS 5.1 will run. For example, FS 5.1 will run 50% to 80% faster on a 66 MHz 486 than on a 33 MHz 486, but it will run 300% faster on a 120 MHz Pentium then on a 66 MHz 486![3]

It is interesting to compare the technological evolution of CPUs with regard to transistor density. In 1986, the 386 CPU had 275,000 transistors, and when the 486 was introduced in 1989, it had 1 million transistors. In 1993, when the Pentium was introduced, it had 3.1 million transistors, and in 1995, the P6 has 6 million transistors. From this, you can see that transistor density is roughly doubling or tripling every 3 years. But does higher transistor density correspond to improved performance? If you look at performance comparison indices for these processors, the answer seems to be yes.[4] The Pentium is almost three times faster than a 486, and a P6 is expected to be twice as fast as a Pentium.[5]

The faster your computer, the more frequently the individual view "frames" will be drawn, so that the more frames per second your computer can draw, the better sense you have of smooth flight. With fewer frames per second being displayed, as for example on a 486/33 MHz microcomputer, you will have a choppy motion that is very irritating to watch and which doesn't allow you enough control to realistically fly your airplane. Furthermore, with slower machines, less scenery detail can be painted on the screen per frame without serious frame speed degradation, thus depriving you of the breathtaking new photo-realistic scenery that gives you the sensation of flying. Although a 386 or 486/33 MHz based PC will run FS 5.1 with the photo-realistic scenery, it is not satisfying because of the slow speed with which the screen frames are updated. Microsoft, however, has made FS 5.1 fully customizable so that you can switch off those features which bog down your machine. This makes it possible for slower 386 and 486 machines to run FS 5.1, minus the scenery enhancements, but fast enough so that your computer can still keep up with frequent screen updates to make the illusion of flying possible.

---

[3]The Pentium has a different internal architecture than the 486, and so the clock speed cannot be directly compared for measuring performance.

[4]Intel publishes iCOMP (Intel Comparative Microprocessor Performance) data on its world wide web site at http://www.intel.com. At this site, you can view charts and graphs that compare the relative performance of all the Intel-based microprocessors.

[5]For performance comparisons between the Pentium and P6, see the April 1995 issue of Byte Magazine on page 44.

FLIGHT SIMULATOR CHRONOLOGY

Commercial flight simulators have been with us for over 50 years, although computerized simulation trainers only became available in the late 1950's and early 1960's. Early simulators were very crude mechanical devices which could not offer the pilot any view outside of the cockpit. Primarily, these mechanical training devices were used to develop pilot skills with instruments, especially for flying airplanes under conditions where the pilot could not rely on outside geographical sources for determining the aircraft's position, speed, altitude, or attitude, because of weather or night flying conditions. The first use of simulators in ground training occurred during the late 1930's when the Army Air Corps decided to purchase Link Trainers to better prepare their pilots. The simulators were very successful in preparing the pilots for situations they might encounter while flying, and they offered two other benefits: they were less costly to operate than actually flying an airplane, and they offered a safe way to subject pilots to all kinds of situations without risking life or limb.

The early Link trainer was an enclosed cockpit which could rotate 360 degrees by means of a vacuum operated bellows, but offered no view out the windshield and was used primarily for instrument flight training. The Link simulator was connected to a map plotter on a nearby table, and an instructor would monitor the students progress as he tried to navigate by instruments alone. The instructor could communicate with the student in the cockpit, via a radio headset, and he also had direct control over all the cockpit instruments. Thus, with a twirl of a knob, the instructor could for example, simulate an instrument failure, or could challenge the student pilot to some unexpected event. After the training session was over, the student would get to look at the paper map on which his airplane's course was plotted, and could then take it home to evaluate his performance. A new paper map would be inserted on the map plotter for the next student.

By the end of the 1970's, simulation technology had become computerized. Computer graphics of outside scenery were projected on to the windshield, and cockpit capsules moved in three dimensions in response to the pilot-trainee's control movements. Unfortunately, these simulators were big, bulky and expensive, in part because they only ran on huge mainframe computers. With the advent of the cheap micro-processor in the late 1970's, computers became accessible to the average consumer. With this micro-electronic revolution taking place, it was only a matter of time before somebody developed a flight simulator that would run on a PC.

That time arrived in 1978 when Bruce Artwick, an electrical engineer and programmer with a pilot's license, decided to create a three dimensional flight simulator on the Apple II computer. This simulation met with instant success and became quite popular. Then, in 1981, Artwick was asked by Microsoft to produce a new version of Flight simulator for the newly introduced IBM PC. Microsoft told Artwick that they wanted a simulation that would show off the power and graphics capability of the PC. Thus was born version 1.05 of Microsoft's *Flight Simulator* program and it became a smash hit amongst computer buyers. Because of its ground breaking foray into new 3-D graphics routines, it pushed the envelope of the design limits of the original PC. In fact, for many years, the ultimate test of a computer's capability was the ability to run *Flight Simulator* without causing a system crash. If a system could pass muster and run *Flight Simulator*, it proved that the computer was beyond reproach—it could run any PC software without hardware conflicts.

Over the years, newer versions of *Flight Simulator* were released that improved the graphics, introduced color, and provided support for AT class PC's and 386's. When FS version 3.0 was released in June of 1988, it was substantially rewritten and offered many new features, including dual player mode via modem or direct connection via serial cable, new aircraft, and support for multiple windows so that you could see two different views simultaneously. For example you could view your plane from a "spot" or "track" plane and have it displayed in one window while watching your cockpit view and instrumentation in another window. FS version 4.0, introduced in September of 1989, offered experimental aircraft, the Sailplane, 16 color scenery, a customizable weather system including random weather patterns, custom 386 software drivers, dynamic scenery such as other aircraft and ground vehicles moving about, runway approach lighting systems for night flying, and air traffic control.

In 1993, *Flight Simulator* 5.0 was released. Unlike previous versions, this fifth generation *Flight Simulator* was completely rewritten, incorporating newer flight models, a new graphics engine with vastly improved 256 color photo-realistic scenery, photo-realistic flight instruments, and code specially written to take advantage of local bus Super VGA graphics cards, and 486 based PCs. Unfortunately, this version did not include worldwide navigational beacons and overseas airport refueling facilities, so it was impossible to realistically fly around the world.

COMMERCIAL FLIGHT SIMULATORS

Today's modern flight simulators are marvels to behold. Link, which is now called Singer-Link-Miles, still makes simulators today, but there are many other competitors, including CAE of Canada and Hughes-Rediffusion of England. Simulators must also come with software, or visual scenery that has been digitized, but you can buy a simulator from one company and equip it with scenery from another company. The visuals for many simulators are done by Evans & Sutherland and SPX-Wide (a division of Rediffusion), and represent a significant portion of the overall investment in the simulator system, since digitizing the scenery for airports around the world is quite costly. A commercial simulator can cost between $15 to $20 million, and operational costs for running it can hover around $500 to $800 per hour. Compared to the $250 million cost of a real Boeing 747, and hourly operating costs of $20,000 per hour, simulators are a real bargain.

Are commercial simulators realistic? Richard Cook, a pilot who works daily with simulators, describes a simulator experience he recently tried:

> "After the Schiphol 747 crash, I tried that flight in our 747-400 (simulator), with engine surges, engine fires, and engine separations happening going up through 3000 and 4000 feet after takeoff.[6] (I found) I was sweating, my leg was in pain from trying to keep the thing (flying) straight, and I was totally locked onto keeping that thing flying, while the fuel-dump took us closer to living. After 10 minutes of real knife edge stuff, my co-pilot said, 'There's the runway', and I looked up and knew where I was for the first time in 10 minutes. I got the thing on the ground (didn't have flap-asymmetry selected, unlike the real thing!), and was then TOTALLY unfit for work for 3 hours afterwards due to adrenaline-overload! Yes it's realistic, and a load of fun!"

The commercial simulator's realism is helped by the use of real cockpit instrumentation, with real switches, lights, gauges, knobs, and levers. Bumps and thumps during taxiing, and the raising and lowering of the landing gear are felt inside the cockpit, and routine noises emanating from various aircraft systems add to the illusion of being in a real cockpit. Air conditioning vents blow air on you, and every motion of the aircraft is implemented through hydraulic jacks, pistons, and control rods that move the cockpit so that you can actually feel the movement of the plane. In addition, highly detailed digitized scenery is projected onto the cockpit's windshields. The SPX-Wide system used on many commercial airline full flight simulators uses 3 projectors, with each projection screen displaying 800,000 pixels (picture elements), thereby giving a panoramic view area of 180 degrees (horizontal) by 40

---

[6]The 747 Schiphol disaster was attributed to an engine pylon separating from the wing. This crash, in Amsterdam, resulted in the loss of many lives on the ground, as the plane crashed into a crowded apartment building. More cracks on engine pylons were discovered on other 747's and as a result, Boeing issued an airworthyness directive for many older 747's to have their original engine pylons inspected and replaced.

degrees (vertical) inside the cockpit. Overall, by combining all three screens, the display resolution works out to 3000 horizontal by 800 vertical pixels.

Compared to this, FS 5.1 still has a long way to go to catch up with commercial flight simulators. The maximum display resolution of 640 horizontal by 400 vertical pixels at 256 colors with a field of view of only 20 degrees (for a single view direction) still is inferior to what commercial simulators are capable of doing. Even so, the improvement of FS 5.1 over FS 4.0, which had a maximum resolution of 640 horizontal by 340 vertical pixels with only 16 colors possible, is dramatic. With 240 additional colors and 60 extra lines of vertical resolution, FS 5.1's scenery is 16 times more realistic.

The power of the latest generation of microprocessors has given the flight simulation buff the best opportunity yet of experiencing the miracle of flight. Microsoft's latest *Flight Simulator* offering takes advantage of these new capabilities, and through some impressive software engineering brings you closer to what the million dollar simulators are doing today. With new super-scalar RISC (Reduced Instruction Set Computing) microprocessors such as the Power PC and Intel P6 on the horizon, many more exciting developments lie ahead in the world of flight simulation.

FLIGHT SIMULATOR'S NEW FEATURES

Outwardly, *Flight Simulator 5.1* resembles *Flight Simulator 5.0*. In fact, when you first start the program, you may think that *Flight Simulator 5.1* is more of a maintenance upgrade than a new program. However, there are many new features that significantly improve the simulation, and which make it well worth your while to upgrade. The next section lists the new FS 5.1 features that distinguish the program from the previous version 5.0.

Flight Simulator 5.1 New Features (Differences with FS 5.0)

Let's look at what's new in *Flight Simulator 5.1*:

- **CD-ROM Based Scenery:** With the advent of cheap CD-ROM drives, it was only natural that disk gobbling scenery for the world be put on compact disc. The CD-ROM version of FS 5.1 now includes extensive worldwide scenery so that you can fly over the seven continents, see mountains and other terrain, and visit cities around the world. In the FS 5.1 CD-ROM, each continent is broken up into sub-areas. The CD-ROM performance boosters in FS 5.1 are first used to determine which sub-area you're in. Then, the scenery for that sub-area is copied from the slow CD-ROM to the cache directory on your faster hard drive. Only when you move to a new sub-area does more scenery need to read in from the CD; up until that point, the scenery is all loaded into the program from the cache directory on your hard drive. After you exit the program, the cache is wiped clean. When you move into scenery areas that are covered by add-on discs, the program automatically loads the proper scenery files and will prompt you if necessary to load the new CD-ROM scenery disc. BAO has stated that the resolution of the world scenery in the CD version of FS 5.1 is 32 times better than that of the floppy disk based version of FS 5.1., which is a compelling enough reason to purchase the CD-ROM version.

- **Scenery Add-Ons:** You can now buy CD-ROM scenery add-ons that dramatically increase the available scenery for certain parts of the world. At the time of this writing, CD-ROM scenery was available for Las Vegas, Europe, and Hawaii. Floppy disk based scenery is available for the Caribbean, Japan, Paris, New York, Washington D.C., and San Francisco. There is also a large library of shareware scenery you can download from CompuServe's *Flight Simulator* Forum, America Online's *Flight Simulator* Forum, and from the Internet at ftp.iup.edu, in the flight simulator directory.

- **Scenery Manager:** A new scenery manager lets you easily select and load your scenery. You can change the priority of certain scenery areas, which gives you the power to choose which scenery you would prefer to use for a given area. Once you have done this, whenever you fly through your scenery areas, FS 5.1 will automatically load your preferred scenery files for you. What's more FS 5.1 can handle scenery in multiple subdirectories on multiple disks and CDs. In tests at BAO, Bruce Artwick was able to access 800 .bgl scenery files spread across 3 hard disks, a network drive, and a floppy! With new multiple CD-ROM players coming on the market, you can load more than one CD-ROM scenery add-on disc at the same time. Gone is the old 128 .bgl file limit in the \Scenery sub-directory that was the case for FS 5.0. This means that you can now build separate sub-directories to store unlimited amounts of scenery.

- **New Low Visibility-Hazing SVGA Video Driver:** FS 5.1 comes with a new SVGA video driver that allows you to modify visibility conditions. To load this special driver, under the Options/Preferences menu, click Display and choose for your Graphics Mode, SVGA 640x400 with Haze, or if you are running at a lower resolution, SVGA 320x200 with Haze. After doing this, you restart FS 5.1 and then select the World/Weather menu option, and click the Visibility button. You'll see a list box in which you can reduce visibility from 40 miles all the way down to 1/16 mile. Note that haze palettes are not included with older scenery add-ons such as San Francisco, Washington D.C, New York, Paris, and Europe I, so you won't be able to use the reduced visibility hazing features while using this scenery. The default CD-ROM scenery, as well as the Las Vegas and Hawaii scenery add-ons (or any new scenery created after 1995), have the new low visibility hazing palettes. (See the low visibility illustrations in the color insert.)

- **New Weather Manager Improvements—Low Visibility Hazing, Icing, New Cloud Types, Better Looking Clouds, Thunderstorm and In-Cloud Turbulence, Seasonal Color Changes:** The stunning new low visibility SVGA hazing drivers allow you to experience weather conditions that impair your cockpit view (see color insert). There are new broken cloud textures and thunderstorm visuals that you can create just by selecting the cloud type. You choose the cloud type by selecting the World/Weather menu option, which will open the Weather dialog box. If you click on the Clouds button, then click on the Create button, you'll find that there are now eleven different type of cloud types to choose from; e.g., user defined, cirrus, cirrostratus, cirrocumulus, altostratus, altocumulus, stratocumulus, nimbostratus, stratus, cumulus, and cumulonimbus. For each cloud type, you can click on the new icing feature, which allows you to create dangerous icing conditions that will rob the aircraft of lift, and you can specify the turbulence level. Also available is a new cloud thickness effect, which you can toggle on from the Options/Preferences/Display/Scenery Options dialog box. The cloud thickness will give you three dimensional clouds instead of the two dimensional clouds found in FS 5.0. Also, you can now experience in-cloud turbulence and thunderstorm (cumulonimbus) turbulence at two different intensities. Unfortunately, there are no rain showers yet. In addition, time and season changes are reflected in the color of the scenery. If you start the Oakland Approach 27R Landing Approach situation, and you select the World/Time and Seasons menu option, then change the season from winter to summer, you'll notice a change in the landscape from brown "winter" colors to greener "summer" colors. Other areas of the world have similar seasonal color changes.
- **More accurate 3-D textured coastlines:** Fractal generated coastlines, with white capped waves lapping at the shorelines, are more convincing than in the previous version.
- **Major redesigns of LA, Seattle, and Munich default scenery:** More buildings and other terrain features have been added.
- **Autopilot keyboard shortcuts:** New Autopilot keyboard shortcuts make the Autopilot much easier to use.

- **Frame Rate Counter and G-Meter:** Just press Shift Z four times to display your frame rate and acceleration meter in your view window. Your G meter tells you how many gravities (or units of 9.8 m/sec or 32 feet/sec) your aircraft is experiencing at the moment. This is useful for determining whether you are flying your aircraft within its performance envelope so that you are not overstressing the airframe.

- **More Realistic Texture Seeds for Urban, Suburban, Rural, and Water Scenery Areas:** FS 5.1 has new photo-realistic scenery seeds that are 1 km square, and which offer more convincing aerial views of the ground. The CD version covers the entire world so that you can now fly over desert areas, jungle foliage, farms, and other land textures. To view the textured water, you must click on the check box for Textured Water, found in the Scenery Options Display dialog box, which you open by selecting the Options/Preferences menu, then click on the Display button and then Scenery Options button. Note that the CD-ROM version of FS 5.1 has higher resolution scenery seeds than does the floppy disk version of FS 5.1.

- **Additional Navaids for the World:** FS 5.1 CD contains many, but not all, VOR/NDB navigational radio beacons for North America, South America, the Caribbean basin, the Pacific Ocean region, Australia, Europe, Africa, and Asia. However, don't be too disappointed if you can't find a favorite VOR/NDB station outside the USA. Microsoft only promises that the USA VOR/NDB database is complete. In all, there are 4,724 VOR/NDB radio stations built into FS 5.1 CD's database, and you can bring up a dialog box that lists the call letters, name and location of any VOR/NDB station that you have tuned in on your NAV radios. Range to station, DME (distance measuring equipment), and out of range indicators are accurate for each VOR station. It is important to note that the floppy disk version of FS 5.1 does not have the worldwide VOR/NDBs, or foreign airports that the FS 5.1 CD version has.

- **New World Wide Airports and Refueling Facilities:** The CD version of FS 5.1 contains 234 new airports around the world. Including the default scenery airports from the previous FS 5.0, there are now over 341 airports you can land at. Because the new airports are situated all over the world, you can now land and refuel the aircraft on realistic overseas flights.

- **Easter Eggs:** Scenery landmarks, such as the Pyramids of Egypt, the Vatican, the Taj Mahal, the Kremlin, Mt. Rushmore, and more have been placed in the CD version of FS 5.1 (see Chapter 14).

- **New Flying Models are available for each aircraft.** Mathematical description and flight characteristics have been completely upgraded and revamped. Stalls and spins, as well as landings and take offs, are modeled better than in the previous version 5.0. One example of this: you can now make true nose-high landings and keep the nose up to bleed off excess speed. Realism and reliability features, as found under the Sim menu, have been revamped. For example, when you set the reliability setting higher than 5 when flying the Cessna, you will still experience torque from the rotation of the propeller, but it won't radically turn your aircraft as was the case in FS 5.0. Also, the Damage from Aircraft Stress option has been reduced to a more tolerable level, so that your aircraft doesn't always break up with the smallest bump.

- **Flight Challenges:** The Quick Practice section of FS 5.0 has been replaced with a new menu option under the Options menu called Flight Challenges. These flight challenges offer you many different scenarios with two different levels of challenge, Basic and Advanced. Within each of these two levels, you have three difficulty levels to choose from. The challenges range from a simple flight from Chicago's Meigs airfield to a daredevil landing on the 50 yard line of the Los Angeles Coliseum. Each level of added difficulty brings on new problems, such as instrument failures and bad weather.

- **Improved Expanded/Extended Memory Support:** *Flight Simulator* will now run with as little as 500 Kb of conventional RAM, provided that you can allocate 2 Mb or more of expanded memory. A Simulator Info dialog box tells you how much memory FS 5.1 is using of each type, which is useful in determining whether the program is utilizing EMS memory (the more EMS memory used, the faster your frame rate will be).

Flight Simulator 5.0 and 5.1 Common Features

All the features described below are present in the newer FS 5.1 as well as the older FS 5.0. If you already know FS 5.0, you can skip this section. However, if you aren't familiar with FS 5.0, you might want to learn about the program's existing feature set:

- **Enhanced Photo Realistic Scenery** and instrumentation has been implemented in Super VGA 640x400 256 color mode using Photo-Realistic/Ray Tracing graphics technology. Included are real digitized high altitude photos of airports and cities around the country, where vegetation, streets, urban areas, parks, lakes, oceans, and other topography are realistically portrayed. Using Cyber-Graphics/Synth City graphics technology, buildings, bridges and other three-dimensional objects have realistic features. You can see windows that are lit in buildings, building ornaments and company logos, real roofs, shading and texture of building sides, etc. The city of Chicago has over 100 such Cyber-Graphic mapped buildings when you set the scenery to its densest setting. The airport around Meigs Field uses new Photo-Realistic scenery for a breathtaking view when landing or departing. Scenery expands with greater detail the closer you get. At night, airports and cities light up in a brilliant and colorful display of street lights, building lights, and airport runway lighting systems. The sky and clouds are absolutely stunning in the first realistic display of weather on a PC. There are now vanishing horizons for both the land and sky, with realistic gradient textures. Ground terrain is efficiently depicted with small repetitive graphic "seeds" that represent urban areas, forests, farm lands, mountains, coastline, swamps, tundra, prairies, snow, oceans, lakes, and rivers. Thus when a particular area is designated as a city, it uses the generic computer generated seed for cities.

- **Dynamic Scenery:** The Goodyear blimp, a hot air balloon, jet traffic, sailboats, and other moving scenery make your simulation experience more interesting.

- **True World-Wide Spherical Coordinate System:** This system, in latitude and longitude, replaces the older two dimensional North and West coordinate system.

- **Map Zooms Out To 160,000 Miles In Space** to allow a view of the entire planet.

- **New Learjet:** Aircraft included are the Cessna 182 Skylane RG (same as before), Learjet 35A (The Learjet 35A replaces the Gates-Learjet 25G), Schweitzer Skyplane 2-32, Sopwith Camel (both same as before).

- **Enhanced Instrument Panels & Controls For Each Aircraft:** The Cessna, Learjet, Sopwith Camel, and Schweitzer Skyplane come equipped with more realistic and authentic instrument panels. Many new engine controls and instruments give you added control and flexibility to monitor your aircraft's performance.

- **AutoPilot:** Autopilot capabilities include pitch and bank hold, ILS glide slope lock, ILS localizer hold, and ILS back course hold. The wing leveler, heading lock, altitude lock, and NAV 1 lock remain as they were in FS 4.0.

- **Dynamic Crash Graphics:** You can enable this feature if you want to see (and hear) your plane break apart when it crashes, thereby determining the cause of the accident.

- **Shadowing Effects:** Building & airplane shadows change with time of day and latitude/longitude position. Advanced real time ray tracing code gives photo-realistic scenery realistic shadows that match the 3-D folds of the terrain.

- **Accurate Portrayal Of Time & Seasons:** Polar regions experience 24 hour daylight or nightfall according to polar season. At night, stars become visible. Instead of the instant changes between night and day that were present in FS 4.0, FS 5.1 has richly colored, beautiful reddish-blue sunsets and sunrises that take place gradually.

- **Weather Generator:** You can create local weather areas with different weather from the global weather. Enhanced control over weather is now available, including the ability to create local weather fronts that move, as well as copying and pasting weather to other areas. You can customize wind layers, barometric pressure, temperature layers, and cloud layers.

- **Dual Player Mode:** Support is available for higher speed modems, as well as user definable modem strings.

- **More Realism & Reliability Options:** Jet Engine Flameout, instrument failures, out of fuel, airframe stress, etc., are all in FS 5.1.

- **Flight Challenges:** Specially created situations walk you through a basic familiarization with your airplane as well as teach you how to land the plane under varying conditions.

- **Jump to Airport Feature:** Easily put your airplane on the runway of any airport in the scenery areas without knowing the latitude or longitude of the airport. Also, your navigation and communication radios can be automatically set to the new location, without having to look up the frequencies in the airport sectional maps in the manual.

- **Set Exact Location:** You can precisely position your aircraft anywhere on Earth using the new latitude longitude coordinate system. You can even set your altitude and desired heading.

- **Expanded VOR/NDB Navigational Beacons for the USA/Europe:** Navaids are included for the entire USA and parts of Europe.

- **Land Me Feature:** You can now have the computer auto-land your plane at the nearest airport, in the event that you don't want to manually land your aircraft.

- **International Support:** Non-US pilots can convert US units of measurement to the metric system.

- **Digitized Aircraft & Instrument Sounds:** Sound Support is included for many industry standard sound cards. Engine pitch changes with throttle settings, airplane crashes are heard, and navigational instruments have their own distinctive sounds.

- **Video-Card Support** is available for many industry standard SVGA video accelerator chips.

- **Improved Mini-control:** On screen moveable indicator box is available for ailerons, elevator and rudder includes airspeed, and there is a throttle indication level. This is used for when the instrument panel is not on screen, as in full screen cockpit view.

- **Customizable Scenarios:** You can specify a start up situation, to include a particular aircraft, weather, location, realism & reliability, etc. Use them to create a situation you can return to over and over without having to create it from scratch.

- **Flight Photographs:** Capture screen shots of your 3-D view windows, map, or instrument panels to a PCX graphic file on disk that you can later print out.

ABOUT THE SCENERY

There are three types of scenery used in FS 5.1:

1. Older FS 4.0 Scenery (VGA 640x350 16 colors)
2. Cyber-Graphics/Synth City Style (Super VGA 640x400 256 colors)
3. Photo-Realistic/Ray Traced (Super VGA 640x400 256 colors)

The older scenery that was used in FS 4.0 employed simple polygon vector-draw routines that simulated 3-D buildings and other objects, and it filled in the ground terrain with various pattern fills. Although it was an improvement over previous flight simulators, it was 1988 graphics technology that was long overdue for an overhaul. You can still use FS 4.0 scenery in FS 5.1, which is a boon to the many arm-chair pilots who have designed their own add-on scenery using the Aircraft & Scenery Designer 4.0, or bought add-on scenery packages from other companies. However, you will not be able to utilize the newer graphics that are available in FS 5.1 while using the older scenery.

Cyber-Graphics/Synth City Style (for Synthesized City) is a newer technology graphics engine, developed by BAO (Bruce Artwick Organization), that is used in FS 5.1 to simulate city buildings, bridges, and other standard 3-D objects. The city buildings of Chicago off to the right of Meigs field are an example of Cyber-Graphics/Synth City Style. Cyber-Graphics/Synth City style differs from the previous FS 4.0 scenery in that you see many more features and details of individual buildings. For example, you can see lighted windows in skyscrapers, company logos on certain buildings, and building shadows that move according to the time of day (try checking out the Prudential building sign in Chicago with scenery density set to high). As such, this type of scenery is vector drawn; that is, each image's shape is mathematically described and then filled in with a texture and color. Vector drawn graphics are easily scaleable to any size, and form perfectly straight lines, smooth curves, round circles, and symmetrical ellipses. Thus, for example, you can see perfectly round wheels on the landing gear of FS 5.1's four aircraft, as opposed to the triangular shaped wheels of FS 4.0, and the appearance of the airplanes themselves is much more pleasing, with smooth curving fuselages, and wings, as opposed to the jagged polygon shaped surfaces of FS 4.0.

Cyber-Graphics/Synth City technology also allows highly detailed, complex, 256 color scenery such as sky shading and shadows, urban and suburban sprawl, coastlines, clouds, and oceans to be generated using a minimum of hard disk space storage. Using a new graphics technique called "seeding," a scenery area can be assigned a generic appearance, whether it be forests, suburbs, mountains, coastline, etc. An example of seeded scenery is the suburbs and ground terrain of Chicago, on top of which sit the Cyber-Graphics/Synth City style 3-D buildings. Seeded scenery such as this can be generated using just 700 bytes of data!

The Photo-Realistic/Ray Traced scenery is derived from actual high altitude photos of the ground taken by satellite and aircraft. The airport runway at Meigs Field, and the immediate airport vicinity are examples of Photo-Realistic/Ray Traced scenery. The satellite photo of Meigs Field has been texture mapped onto the ground, much like a decal is applied to a surface, but the ray tracing algorithm goes one step further: the photo or texture map can be wrapped around three dimensional topographical features such as mountains, valleys, or other ground contours. As a result of this contour mapping, the scenery looks three-dimensional. What is truly amazing about this, though, is that it is all done in "real time," rather than the many hours it would take using conventional ray tracing algorithms.

The term ray tracing itself refers to a computer graphics technique used to create complex 3-D images. Every pixel in a ray traced image is drawn to reflect a light ray from a source of light, and then is traced from the pixel to the viewer's eyes. Unfortunately, conventional ray tracing techniques can take many hours just to produce a single image. In FS 5.1, an advanced and speedy new real-time ray tracing algorithm, developed by BAO, breaks new ground with its speedy ray traced rendition of surface scenery. It allows simulated sunlight to produce the ground shadows and varying hues and colors of the terrain that produce the illusion of 3-D perspective and depth.

The actual photos of the ground are digitized into bitmaps broken up into many millions of pixels. Bitmaps are simply facsimiles of an original picture; that is, they copy each picture element and assign it a pattern and color, much like a PCX, BMP, GIF, or TIFF computer graphic. Unlike vector graphics, a bitmap is not easily scaleable, meaning that significantly resizing the bitmap causes it to become deformed and misshapen, much like bitmapped fonts become jagged and unreadable when you print them out in a font size that is much larger or smaller than the original bitmap font. With these new terrain bitmaps, the closer you fly to the ground, the less realistic the scenery will become because the individual pixel elements are expanded larger to the point where they become distorted.

The FS 5.1 scenery is a combination of the Photo-Realistic/Ray Traced and Cyber-Graphics technology. The Cyber-Graphics vector drawn buildings are super-imposed on the background bitmaps of the Photo-Realistic ground scenery to arrive at a pleasing synthesis of 3-D ground terrain with 3-D buildings and objects. It is a significant advance in PC based flight simulation graphics.

SO YOU WANT TO BE A PILOT?

Flight Simulator is already used by many schools as a basic training tool for students to learn the basics of aeronautics. The U.S. Navy, in fact, has used FS 4.0 for emergency situational training, but up till now, the Federal Aviation Administration (FAA) has refused to approve *Flight Simulator* as an official flight training device. The FAA claimed that PC based flight simulators did not have sufficient fidelity with an aircraft to ensure the development of the psychomotor skills and sense of coordination that are necessary to control an aircraft solely by reference to instruments. They also expressed other reservations: a flight simulator was required to have a course plotter, a means of recording flight path. Prior to *Flight Simulator* 3.0, there was no means to record your flight path. Also according to the FAA, prior to flying an aircraft you were supposed to perform a control check (verifying that the flaps, elevators, ailerons, and rudder are in working order), which could not be done on *Flight Simulator* 2.0. With *Flight Simulator* 3.0, this problem was addressed by implementing an on screen control position indicator (that could be moved around as needed when using your whole screen as a scenery window), and you could now actually see the wing flaps, ailerons, rudder, and elevators move in response to yoke/rudder movements that you made through an external view of your aircraft.[7]

There are various classes of pilot's licenses. At the bottom of the ladder is the Private Pilot license. Next is the Instrument rating which is a requirement for flying in bad weather. To fly non-airline type jobs, such as charters, towing banners, transporting cargo, etc., you will need to obtain the Com-

---

[7]You can see the airfoil surfaces move only on the Cessna while in spot view. Unfortunately, even in FS 5.1, this remains the case.

mercial Pilot's license. If, however, you relish the thought of becoming a passenger jet pilot, you will need to earn the Airline Transport Pilot (ATP) license, which is the penultimate pilot license. Or, if you prefer, you can become a Certified Flight Instructor (CFI) and teach others how to fly while getting paid for it.

To acquire a Private Pilot license, you must be at least 17 years old, log at least 40 hours flying time (55 is average), have 20 hours of supervised flight instruction and pass written and oral exams along with a practical check flight. You must also obtain a Third Class medical certificate, attesting that your vision is correctable, and that your heart, lungs and other aspects of your health are in good working order. This certificate must be renewed every two years.

If you want to obtain an Instrument rating, a requirement if you want to become a commercial pilot or airline transport pilot, you must log at least 125 hours flight time, which includes 50 hours of cross-country flying in addition to your student pilot time. You must also log 40 hours of instrument flight time, of which 20 hours can be performed in a ground trainer or simulator, and 15 additional hours must be accompanied by a certified instrument flight instructor. Additionally, for the Instrument rating license, you must pass a written test on aviation regulations and procedures and must perform a flight test for certification. Instrument ratings are becoming more and more common among private pilots because this type of rating is necessary for a pilot to fly safely and legally in bad weather, or conditions of low visibility. Without the instrument rating, you won't be able to get any legitimate flying job (although some South American drug cartels might be interested).

The Certified Flight Instructor (CFI) license allows you to legally teach others how to fly. This kind of license is often used by former airline pilots and others who like to fly and teach.

To obtain the commercial pilot's license, you must log 250 hours flying time, including 100 hours as pilot-in-command, along with 50 hours of cross-country flying. In addition, you must undergo 10 hours instrument instruction, or have an Instrument rating license with at least five hours of night flying logged. You must also pass the Second Class medical check, which is a more stringent physical exam than is the Third Class medical check, and renew this medical certificate each year. Finally, you will need to pass the Commercial Pilot Written Exam, which covers the myriad details about FAA rules and regulations.

The airline transport pilot (ATP) license requires that you be at least 23 years old, have the equivalent flying time that is required of the commercial license, and have an Instrument rating license. Furthermore, you must obtain a First Class medical certificate, a rigorous physical exam which is even more thorough than the Second Class exam, and renew it every six months. And then there are the written tests on airline rules, regulations, and the specific kind of plane being flown, including an oral exam and check ride for the aircraft in question. The typical total cost for the training that would qualify you for the ATP license can easily exceed $20,000 over two years. But for most people, it takes three years and more than $30,000 of schooling and training before they are able to qualify for an entry-level airline job. And usually, such beginning jobs would entail flying small commuter planes for regional carriers. After all this are you still interested?

THIS BOOK

This book is designed to explain to you some of the finer points of *Flight Simulator 5.1*. As a supplementary companion guide, it is not designed to replace the Microsoft manual, but to offer you insights and practical advice on how to fly the different kinds of airplanes offered in the simulation. In this book you will learn some of the basics of airplanes and engines, flight basics, learn how to read your instruments and understand how they work, perform some basic flight maneuvers, learn how to navigate using your aircraft's radio navigational equipment, and finally have an opportunity to try out some of your newly acquired skills in a specially prepared solo adventure.

Book Organization

This book is divided into four major parts, and concludes with some important reference appendices:

I.   The World of *Flight Simulator*
II.   Flight Academy: Ground School
III. Navigation & Aircraft Communication Systems
IV. Special Features and Add-Ons
Appendices

Part I: The World of *Flight Simulator*

The first four chapters cover how you control and customize the simulator. Chapter 1 is a get-your-feet-wet introduction to *Flight Simulator*, where you will experience your first solo flight and get to know how to use some of the simulator's controls. Chapter 2 amounts to a quick hands on tutorial of manipulating the 3-D windows and view systems, while Chapter 3 touches upon customizing the simulator's many options using the pull down menu system. Chapter 4 describes how the weather generator works and offers you an example of creating and editing your own weather.

If you are already familiar with FS 5.1, or feel that this is material you have already mastered in FS 5.0, you can skip Part I and proceed to Part II of the book. But you should glance through Chapter 4 to learn about the new low visibility weather generator that works in conjunction with the new SVGA hazing video driver.

Part II: Flight Academy: Ground School

The second part of the book deals with the actual airplane itself, and covers cockpit instrumentation, flight dynamics, and some fundamentals of airplanes and engines. Chapter 5 describes the operating principles of airplanes and engines, and Chapter 6 goes into some of the physics of flight, including a description of aerodynamic forces. Chapter 7 explains the operation and use of the cockpit instrumentation for the Cessna, Learjet, Sailplane, and Sopwith Camel. All the flight instruments and indicators are covered in detail, along with a brief description of how they work. Chapter 8 instructs you on how to perform some basic flight maneuvers, including the takeoff, climb, flying straight and level, the standard turn, the descent and landing. Chapters 9 through 11 focus on the operating characteristics of three FS 5.1 aircraft; the Cessna, the Learjet, and the Sailplane.

Part III: Navigation & Aircraft Communication Systems

The third part of the book gives you basic information on how to use the navigation and communication systems aboard your aircraft. Many illustrations and diagrams are offered as an aid to help you learn how to use the different systems.

Chapter 12 teaches you about Great Circle Navigation, and how to use the NAV/VOR/DME/ADF/NDB, and EFIS/CFPD instruments. Also covered is the operation of the Autopilot VOR Lock, and how the Instrument Landing Systems (ILS) works. Chapter 13 challenges you with an adventure situation, where you have a chance to fly around the world in the Learjet, and try your hand at radio navigation.

Part IV: Special Features and Add-Ons

This part of the book introduces special features found in FS 5.1, and shows you scenery and hardware add-ons you can buy that will enhance your enjoyment of the program. Chapter 14 delves into dual player mode, where you can link up with other FS 5.1 enthusiasts via modem; slew mode, where you can quickly move or rotate your aircraft in a special non-flight mode; and the maneuver and landing Analysis flight monitoring tools. Chapter 15 illustrates some of the add-on scenery and other products you can buy for FS 5.1.

Appendices

Appendix A covers the installation of *Flight Simulator* under DOS and Windows 95. Because *Flight Simulator* is so dependent on hardware speed, a brief performance comparison is also given for various PCs. You can use this data to compare your computer's frame rate with other similar computers, and in so doing, learn whether you are getting the best performance that you can out of FS 5.1. Appendix B offers you a quick look up guide for the various airports, VOR and NDB stations in FS 5.1, as well as navigational maps of the USA and the rest of the world. Using the material in this appendix, you can find the VOR/NDB call signs and radio frequencies, state by state, for the continental US and for other surrounding areas.

Appendix C provides a keyboard command summary for all the keyboard controls, along with a description of how the mouse works in yoke and slew modes.

The information found in this book will prove invaluable in your quest to master the latest and most sophisticated PC flight simulator on the market today.

P A R T

I

The World of
Flight Simulator

CHAPTER

1

Your First Solo Flight

In this chapter, you will take your Cessna Skylane 182RG out for its maiden flight. Don't worry, you don't need to know anything about flying; all you need are your sunglasses and a desire to see Chicago from the air. Landing will be accomplished via the Land Me feature, so you can sit back and enjoy the flight. You will take off from Meigs Field (along Chicago's Lake Michigan waterfront), then you'll take a leisurely flight over downtown Chicago. Once past Chicago, you will turn back and return to Meigs Field, whereupon the simulator's autopilot will land you safely without any intervention on your part. Along the way you will see the photo-realistic scenery around Meigs Field and the downtown skyscrapers of Chicago, including the Sears tower and the Prudential Building. While enjoying the picturesque view out the window, you'll also learn how to use some of the aircraft's instruments and controls.

If you are eager to fly or are already somewhat familiar with *Flight Simulator*, you can skip ahead to the section titled "Takeoff."

STARTING *FLIGHT SIMULATOR*

Assuming you have installed *Flight Simulator 5.1* (See Appendix A for instructions if you haven't done so) and you are currently in the Flight Simulator Directory, start up *Flight Simulator* by typing FS from the DOS prompt. (Windows 95 users can create a shortcut icon on their desktop of the FS5.com file.) If all goes well, you will see the Bruce Artwick Organization opening screen and then, a few moments later, the cockpit view should appear.

Using the Keyboard and Mouse to Open Menus and Select Commands

In *Flight Simulator*, you can choose menu commands, menu options, or other controls in one of two ways:

1. Using the Mouse: Aim the mouse pointer at the menu commands, menu options, or other controls and click the left mouse button.

2. Using the keyboard: Press [Alt] to highlight the pull down menus; to access any individual menu name, command, option, or other control, press the key matching the underlined letter. In some instances, there is a keyboard shortcut listed next to the command, so you can directly access the command from the keyboard without opening any menus.

After hearing a squeal of tires on pavement, you should be able to see the menu names that appear on the overhead menu bar. Aim the mouse pointer on the Options menu and click on it using the left mouse button and you should see a pull down menu appear as in Figure 1.1. If you are only using a keyboard, press [Alt] and then [O] to open the Options menu. The underlined letter "O" in the Options menu tells you the key you need to press in order to select that command. To close a menu using the mouse, all you need to do is click anywhere outside the menu; or using a keyboard, press either [Esc] or [Spacebar]. All other menu commands and options that have a single character underlined in their name, can be accessed from the keyboard by pressing that character on the keyboard (except the top menu bar commands, in which you need to first press [Alt]). In this book, when using the terms "select" or "click" we will mean that you select a command, using either the mouse or the keyboard.

Figure 1.1
The Options menu

➔ **Tip:** Clicking the right mouse button causes the mouse pointer to disappear, allowing you to use the mouse as the yoke control for piloting the airplane. To restore the mouse pointer, again click on the right mouse button. The left mouse button is used solely to select menus, commands, or aircraft controls by pointing the mouse pointer arrow on the object in question, then clicking.

Calibrating Your Joystick

If you have a joystick plugged into the game port of your PC, then you will need to configure and calibrate it before you can fly Flight Simulator. Some people prefer to use two joysticks in combination, one to control the ailerons/rudder and elevator, the second to control the throttle and brakes (or when using pedals as your second joystick, you can set the second joystick to control the rudder). But for now let's assume you are using a single joystick. Since FS 5.1 has no way of knowing beforehand where your joystick is centered, you will need to instruct the program as to its initial settings via a process known as calibration. If you didn't do this, your joystick might send the wrong signal to the program as to its true position, and you would have to fly a plane that chronically turns, climbs, or dives, even though your stick is apparently centered.

To set and calibrate your joystick, press $\boxed{\text{K}}$.

The sensitivity setting controls how much joystick movement will affect the aircraft. If you notice too much movement of the controls, you can come back and decrease the sensitivity. On the other hand, if you don't get enough movement of the controls you can increase the sensitivity. The null zone refers to that portion of the center of the joystick where the ailerons are centered. By adjusting the null zone sensitivity, you can find a comfortable zone where you can move your joystick slightly without causing the plane to bank. A wider null zone gives your joystick a looser feel, while a narrower zone gives your joystick a tighter feel. Too narrow a zone can be annoying since every joystick jitter can cause the plane to start turning. Click the Load Sensitivities Saved with Situation check box if you want to load these settings so you don't have to reset them each time you start the situation.

You can skip this section if you plan to fly your plane using the mouse or keyboard.

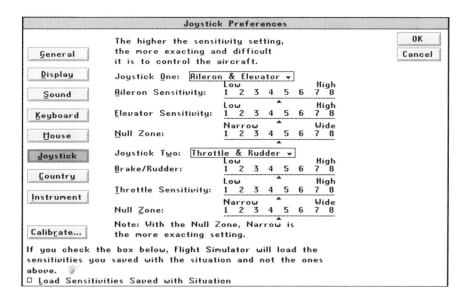

Figure 1.2
Setting Up and Calibrating Your Joystick 1

PRE-FLIGHT PREPARATION: LEARNING THE SIX BASIC FLIGHT INSTRUMENTS OF THE STANDARD INSTRUMENT CLUSTER

Let's now turn to your cockpit instrumentation and learn more about the six basic flight instruments that almost every aircraft uses.

The Three Pitot-Static Instruments

Take a moment to glance over your cockpit instruments and controls. It's better to do this now than later, when you are being fished out of Lake Michigan because you didn't know where your controls were located, or you didn't understand one of your flight instrument readings. There are six basic flight instruments; the first three to be discussed are the so called pitot-static instruments, because their measurements and displayed readings are derived from responses to air pressures in the pitot-static system. The pressure altimeter, the vertical speed indicator, and the airspeed indicator all calculate the amount of air pressure being rammed into the pitot tube. The pitot tube is a hollow cylindrical pipe mounted externally on the leading edge of the wing, nose, or tail of the aircraft. Each of these three instruments then compares the pitot tube pressure to the air pressure in a static chamber, where the air is not being subjected to any motive forces. The calculated pressure difference is displayed as the true airspeed in knots (nautical miles per hour in the air, not on the ground) on the airspeed indicator, rate of climb or descent in hundreds of feet per minute on the vertical speed indicator, and the altitude measured in feet over mean sea level (MSL) on the altimeter.

The Airspeed Indicator

Looking at your airspeed indicator, as shown in Figure 1.3, you can see that presently it registers 0 knots, but it can measure up to 210 knots.

The Altimeter

Your altimeter resembles a clock with 10 divisions instead of 12. For the large hand of the altimeter's "clock," each number marking represents 100 feet, although the smallest reading is in 50 foot increments. Since the large hand is almost over the 6, this means the aircraft is at 590 feet or so. Notice that this means you are approximately 590 feet above sea level, but not 590 feet above ground. Many pilots have crashed because of forgetting the crucial distinction between above ground level (AGL) and mean sea level (MSL).

The smaller hand of the altimeter's clock measures the altitude in thousands of feet, but since it has not reached the 1 yet, the altimeter shows that the aircraft is below 1,000 feet. If the small hand were to travel past the 1, then you would add to your altitude 1,000 feet for each number it passes.

The Vertical Speed Indicator

The vertical speed indicator lets you know how many hundreds of feet per minute you are descending or ascending at any given time. At present it shows no activity since you are motionless on the ground.

The Three Gyroscopic Instruments

The remaining three flight instruments, the attitude indicator, the turn indicator, and the heading indicator, are known as gyroscopic instruments because their readings are obtained from the inertial frame of reference of a spinning gyroscope. The gyroscopic instruments provide information about the aircraft's direction and attitude.

The Attitude Indicator

The attitude indicator, also known as the artificial horizon, tells you the airplane's attitude at all times. It shows the actual pitch and roll of the aircraft in relation to the ground. This gives the pilot an internal horizon inside the cockpit that serves as a reference point for flying the aircraft in any kind of weather, night or day. The brown colored portion of the attitude indicator's ball represents the ground, or horizon. The two white horizontal lines in the center of the scope represent the aircraft's wings. For example, if you bank the airplane to the left, the colored half of the horizon ball will rotate to the left. If you pull up the nose, the colored half of the ball will drop below the level of the wings, as indicated by the two white horizontal lines, thereby showing the aircraft nose is pitched upwards from the ground horizon. (Note: this doesn't necessarily mean you are climbing.)

The Turn Indicator

The turn indicator measures the turning rate of the aircraft. It also shows the amount of slip or skid the aircraft is experiencing in a turn. In auto-coordinated flight, you will not need to concern yourself with this instrument. However, if you fly with pedals simulating the rudder controls of a real aircraft, you must watch this gauge in order to make a stable turn.

Airspeed   Attitude/artificial
indicator   horizon   Altimeter

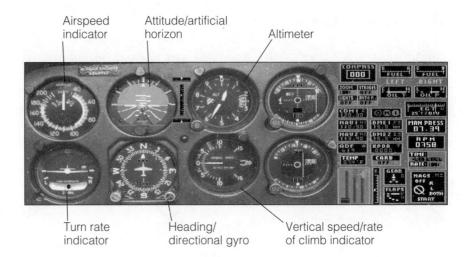

Figure 1.3 The Six
Primary Flight
Instruments of the
Standard Instrument
Cluster

Turn rate   Heading/   Vertical speed/rate
indicator   directional gyro   of climb indicator

The Heading Indicator

The last instrument, the heading indicator, or directional gyro, shows the compass heading the aircraft is currently on. It differs from the magnetic compass in that a highly accurate gyroscope provides a precise, instantaneous display of the course heading, even when the aircraft experiences pronounced accelerative forces like when climbing, diving, or turning. The main drawback of the directional gyro is it tends to drift away from an accurate compass reading over time due to precessional errors in the rotating gyroscope. From time to time, therefore, you must recalibrate the directional gyro so it agrees with the magnetic compass.

PRE-FLIGHT CHECKOUT: VIEWING YOUR AIRCRAFT EXTERNALLY THROUGH SPOT VIEW

While you are parked on the Meigs Field runway tarmac waiting to take off, you might as well try out some of the different viewing options. In FS 5.1, you can have up to two different view screens displayed simultaneously along with a map and your instrument panel. Each view screen can be independently controlled from the keyboard, and you can resize or move them at will using either the mouse or keyboard. If you'd like, you can have one view screen show your cockpit view, while another view screen might show your aircraft from behind. The map window might also be displayed at this time so you can keep an eye on your bearings.

Using Spot View

Let's inspect your airplane from outside the cockpit. Press ⑤ on the keyboard and you will see the scene change to an airport tower view of your airplane sitting at the end of the runway. Press ⑤ once more to obtain a spot view of your plane. Press ⑤ a third time, and you will return to your cockpit view. In spot view, you can look at your plane as if you were following it in a chaser plane at a discrete distance. By holding down [Shift] and pressing ⑦, ⑧, ⑨, ⑥, ③, ②, ①, ④ on the numeric keypad in succession, you will cycle through all possible angles from which to view your airplane (you can also do this in cockpit view to get a 360° view around your plane). If you want to zoom in or out with this spot view, press ⊞ or ⊟ on the main keypad and your spotting position will move closer or farther away to your airplane. If you want to return to your normal cockpit view, press ⑤ once more. Try experimenting to discover the vantage point you prefer.

In Figure 1.4, you can see the results of pressing [Shift] ⑦ combination. When you are finished, press ⑤ once more to return to cockpit view.

You can also call up a second view window that can display another view while simultaneously displaying the first view. Simply press [ ] once to call the window up. To close the second window, press [ ] twice quickly in succession. As with the first view window, you can choose which view you want to see from the tower, cockpit, track, or spot view options.

The more windows you have displayed, the slower the frame rate will be.

Open a second view window by pressing the [ ] key.

Call Up the Map View

To keep an eye on your ground location, you can call up a third window (in addition to the two available view windows), to display your airplane's position on a map. To open the map window, press [Num Lock] once (if several windows are overlapping, you may have to also press the apostrophe key to bring your map position to the foreground). To close the map, quickly press [Num Lock] twice. The map's magnification can be zoomed in or out by using ⊞ or ⊟ on the main keyboard. Your airplane's position is centered on a red cross hair in the middle of the map. The aircraft's nose always points toward the top vertical cross hair. As you turn, the map will rotate, showing that your aircraft is now facing a different direction.

Figure 1.4
External Spot View
of Your Airplane

Figure 1.5
The Map Window

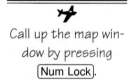

Call up the map window by pressing
[Num Lock].

If you find this confusing you can change the map display through the Display Preferences dialog box under the Options menu, and freeze the map in a north orientation. Then, regardless of your plane's heading, the map will always appear fixed (meaning it won't rotate). However, your airplane's cross hairs will move around as your position changes. Figure 1.5 shows the map zoomed out far enough to show the Meigs Field runway.

YOUR PRIMARY FLIGHT CONTROLS

Whether you are flying your airplane with just a keyboard, mouse, or joystick, your basic flight controls are controlled in the same way. The ailerons in the wings control your bank, or aircraft roll (left or right); the elevators determine the airplane's pitch angle (up or down); and the rudders affect which way the airplane is headed, or yawing (pivoting left or right). These wing surface controls are placed in the same general location on the Learjet, Schweizer 2-32 Sailplane, and Sopwith Camel.

Keyboard Yoke Control

On the numeric keypad, the [2] and [8] keys control the up and down elevators respectively, the [4] and [6] keys control the left and right ailerons along with the rudder, when flying in auto-coordinated mode.

Auto-Coordination

In FS 5.1, auto-coordination of your rudder and ailerons is essential if you are to make smooth coordinated turns. In real aircrafts pilots must coordinate any turns by using foot pedals, which are connected to the rudder, along with the aileron controls that are manipulated with the pilot's yoke. In this program, you can disable the auto-coordination mode and fly your plane using the rudders and ailerons as separate controls. When you do this, the [4] and [6] keys on the numeric keypad control only the left and right ailerons, and the [0] and [Enter] (also on the numeric keypad) now control left and right rudder movements, respectively. Turning off auto-coordination is very useful if you are using pedals in conjunction with a yoke. The pedals, which are connected to the rudders on a real airplane, are used to yaw the aircraft left or right. You might also want to switch off auto-coordination in order to perform some tricky aerobatic maneuvers. However, for ease of flying when learning *Flight Simulator*, you will want to keep auto-coordination turned on to lessen the complications of making smooth turns.

Mouse Yoke Controls

You can also fly your plane by using the mouse. To control your aircraft's pitch, move the mouse straight forward to lower the elevators (nose down), or straight backwards to raise the elevators (nose up). In auto-coordinated

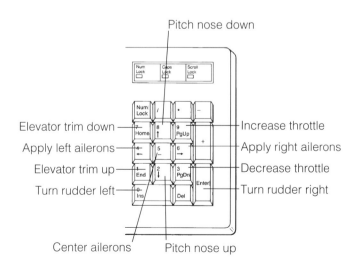

Figure 1.6
Keyboard Yoke and Throttle Controls on the Numeric Keypad

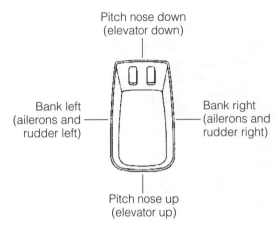

Pitch nose down
(elevator down)

Bank left
(ailerons and
rudder left)

Bank right
(ailerons and
rudder right)

Pitch nose up
(elevator up)

Figure 1.7
Mouse Yoke Controls

flight, moving the mouse left or right will cause the rudder and ailerons to move in a coordinated fashion that forces the plane to turn left or right respectively. But if you disable auto-coordination, the left/right mouse movements will control only the ailerons, and you will have to use ⎡0⎤ and ⎡Enter⎤ on the numeric keypad to move the rudder left or right.

Practice Moving Your Yoke

Let's practice moving the yoke, whether by keyboard, mouse, or joystick. You should note the main control position indicators on your instrument panel are lodged between the artificial horizon/attitude indicator. The vertical indicator in the center shows the current position of your elevators, the top horizontal indicator shows the ailerons position, and the lower indicator shows the rudder position.

Let's watch what happens outside your airplane when you move your controls. Press ⎡S⎤ two times till you are in spot view, then press ⎡+⎤ on the main keyboard once, so you can zoom in on the aircraft close enough to see the airfoil controls move.

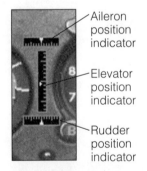

Aileron position indicator

Elevator position indicator

Rudder position indicator

Figure 1.8
The Control Position Indicators

Lower the Elevators and Watch them Move on Your Plane

Move your yoke all the way forward by repeatedly pressing ⎡8⎤ on the numeric keypad or by moving your mouse or joystick in the forward direction. Observe how the elevators move downward on your plane and how, simultaneously, the triangular pointer on the elevator control position indicator moves down, signifying that your elevators have been lowered. If you were flying, the nose of the aircraft would drop in response to this action. Return your elevators to the neutral (center) position by holding down and pressing ⎡2⎤ or by moving your mouse/joystick backward. This centered position is the most favorable for level flight. In some cases it may be necessary to trim your elevators at a different position in order to keep the nose of the aircraft level. This is where the elevator trim control comes in handy.

Elevator Trim

The elevator trim control allows you to remove the pressure you would have to make on the yoke to maintain a desired attitude. For example, if you were flying a real airplane, during flight you might have to pull back the yoke slightly and hold it in that position to maintain a level flight without gaining or losing altitude. After a while, you would get tired of holding the yoke against the pressure an outside airstream exerts on the elevators. To relieve this pressure and hold the yoke in its current position you would adjust the elevator trim control until it takes up the slack and you can release the yoke.

In the virtual reality world of Flight Simulator, the elevator trim control doesn't do you much good unless you are using a joystick type yoke. Because these input devices have springs, they exert a force on the stick that you must counteract. Joysticks act more like actual yokes in that there is a neutral or centered position where the stick will position itself once you let go. The keyboard has no such feedback, so if you release the elevators at a certain position they will remain fixed at that position.

To fly with the elevators slightly raised, you need to pull the joystick toward yourself. To release the pressure on the stick without changing the elevator setting, you must raise the elevator trim by pressing ⌈1⌉ or lower it by pressing ⌈7⌉ on the numeric keypad. Your plane will maintain its current attitude, even though you have now let go of your yoke and it has returned to its neutral or centered position.

Practice pulling the yoke back. The yoke causes your plane's nose to pitch up in response to raising the elevators. When you are done, return the elevators to the centered position.

Move the Ailerons/Rudder (Auto-Coordinated Mode)

Now move your yoke all the way left by pressing the ⌈4⌉ on the numeric keypad or by moving the joystick all the way to the left. You should see the ailerons moving in opposite directions on each wing. You should also see the rudder turning to the left. The rudder and aileron control position indicators should also show this movement. If you were flying, the aircraft would start banking to the left and the plane would be executing a left hand turn. Press ⌈5⌉ to center the rudder and ailerons, then repeat this maneuver for a right hand turn. Notice that the ailerons again are on opposite sides, one up and one down, but this time the rudder is pointing right.

Before proceeding to the next section, exit spot view and return to your cockpit view by pressing ⌈S⌉ once. Also make sure you have returned the ailerons/rudder controls to the centered position by pressing ⌈5⌉ on the

Center the ailerons/rudder by pressing ⌈5⌉ on the numeric keypad. Elevators must be centered manually.

numeric keypad (The $\boxed{5}$ key does not center the elevators. You will still have to manually center the elevator using the $\boxed{2}$ and $\boxed{8}$, or your mouse/joystick).

TAKEOFF

Since this is your first solo flight, you might be bewildered by the array of instrumentation and controls that sits before you. Don't worry if you haven't read the preceding warm-up section. You will be walked through a perfect takeoff, relax on a sightseeing tour of Chicago, and return for an exciting but safe dusk landing at Chicago's Meigs Field. Since this is your first solo flight, landing will be handled by the computer—you wouldn't want to risk a $75,000 airplane on its maiden voyage would you?

The end of this chapter includes a summary of all the steps to be performed for this flight.

The first thing you need to know before you can start rolling down the tarmac is what speed you must be traveling before you can rotate the aircraft. If you pull back on the yoke too soon, before the aircraft's stall speed, the aircraft will fail to leave the runway. Or it may lift up briefly, stall, and then crash. A stall is a condition where the smooth airflow over the wing is interrupted and the aircraft loses its lift. This can happen when the plane is not traveling fast enough for the airflow over the wings to create the forces of lift.

For the Cessna, the stall speed is 54 knots (54 nautical miles per hour is the equivalent of 62 miles per hour).[1] Therefore, you must accelerate the aircraft by pushing up the throttle to maximum and then wait until the aircraft has gained sufficient speed to pass 54 knots.

Turn on the Axis Indicator on Cockpit Windshield

To better see which direction your aircraft's nose is pointed with regard to the horizon, lets turn the Axis Indicator on. This is a little V-shaped pointer

---

[1] A nautical mile is based on the spherical coordinate system of degrees longitude and latitude that allows us to locate our geographical position on Earth. It is defined as the length that one minute of arc would take on a great circle all the way around the Earth. Since there are 60 minutes in each degree of arc, this means that there are 60 nautical miles in one degree of arc on a great circle. However, because the Earth is not a perfect sphere, the nautical mile varies at certain locations around the planet. By international agreement, the nautical mile has been fixed at 6076.115 feet. The standard English mile, from which we base our ground measurements of speed is founded upon the length of 5,280 feet. A nautical mile, then, is approximately 1.15 (or 15%) times longer than a standard mile.

in the center of your cockpit windshield that you can turn on or off. When you are flying straight and level, the top of the V should line up exactly with the horizon to let you know you are not gaining or losing altitude. This handy little device gives you the same information the artificial horizon/attitude indicator gives. But since you tend to look out the cockpit window, rather than at your instruments, it's a little bit eas-

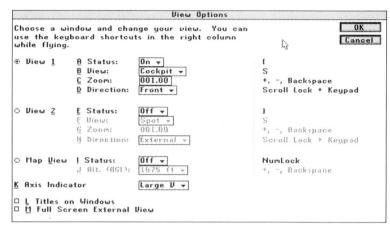

Figure 1.9
The Axis Indicator is selected from the View Options dialog box.

ier to use (however it does not tell you how steeply your plane is banking).

To turn on the Axis Indicator, follow these steps:

1. Pull down the Views menu.
2. Select the View Options command.
3. In the Axis Indicator list box select the Large V option.
4. Exit the View Options dialog box, and return to the simulator by pressing Esc twice, or clicking on the OK button.

Increase Throttle

Now that you're ready to go, increase the throttle to maximum by pressing and holding down 9 on the numeric keypad (or briefly press F4 once on the top function keypad). If you prefer using the mouse to increase the throttle, grab the throttle lever and drag it up to the top of its scale. Notice the pitch of the airplane rises as the engine revs up to its maximum thrust. Immediately, the airplane should begin to move and the airspeed indicator will show you are picking up speed. You will also see the propeller's rotations per minute (RPM) indicator increase along with a rise in manifold pressure, which is displayed above the RPM indicator. The manifold pressure tells you how much vacuum the engine is developing in the intake manifold. It is a direct indicator of engine power. It measures vacuum pressure in inches of mercury. The scale goes from 0" (0 percent power) all the way up to 29" (100 percent power).

The Manifold Pressure Gauge and RPM indicator.

Keep your plane centered on the runway as it takes off by using 0 for steering left, and Enter for steering right. Both keys are located on the numeric keypad.

Figure 1.10
Increasing the Throttle

—Manifold pressure gauge

—RPM

—Throttle lever

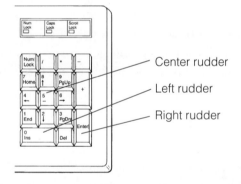

Figure 1.11 Steering
while on the runway is
accomplished by using
rudder controls located
on the numeric keypad.

— Center rudder

— Left rudder

— Right rudder

The Cessna will stall
at speeds of lower
than 54 knots. When
taking off, be sure to
rotate (i.e., apply up
elevator with ② or
by pulling back on
the yoke joystick)
after the aircraft
has passed this
speed.

Rotation When Airspeed Reaches 65 knots

To play it safe, you should rotate the aircraft only when the speed has reached 65 knots. This gives you an added margin of safety and will ensure that the plane does not stall on takeoff. To lift off, gently tap ② on the numeric keypad several times or pull back on the mouse/joystick, until the triangle pointer on the elevator control position indicator moves to the first mark above the center line. In a few moments, you should feel the entire plane lift off the runway, and shortly thereafter, the end of the runway should appear.

AFTER TAKEOFF

Soon after you have passed the runway threshold and have gained some altitude, ease back on the throttle. Move the throttle down (using ③ on the numeric keypad, or drag the throttle indicator via mouse) until the manifold pressure gauge gives a reading of 22.40" (it doesn't have to be exactly 22.40, just reasonably close). This corresponds to a throttle setting of approximately 75 to 80 percent. Doing so will ease the burden on the engine and it will also stabilize your rate of climb from 500 to 1,000 feet per minute.

Raise Landing Gear

To further streamline the airflow around the fuselage, thereby reducing drag and improving fuel economy, let's retract the landing gear. From the keyboard press the Ⓖ, or click on the Gear Up/Down Indicator on the control panel. You will see the gear indicator slide to the up position. You can view the gear being raised in spot view.

Climb to 1,500 Feet Altitude

During this phase of the flight, it is important to not put the plane into too steep a climb. If you do your airspeed will drop below 54 knots and the plane will stall and crash. This is where your six primary flight instruments help you figure out what is happening. As your airplane continues to ascend, as shown on the vertical speed indicator, try to keep your climb rate between 500 to 1,000 feet per minute by judicious application of the throttle. Watch the altimeter's long hand move around clockwise until it passes the 0. At this point you have reached 1,000 feet above MSL, and you should start thinking about leveling the plane off soon. The airspeed indicator will show you traveling at approximately 100 knots, and your compass heading should be due North at 0°.

Just before the long hand on the altimeter reaches 1,300 feet, begin to level the plane off by reducing throttle, and if necessary, lowering the elevators. If you have succeeded in leveling the plane, you will see the vertical axis pointer on the windshield line up with the horizon. Although there is a delayed effect, the vertical speed indicator needle should hover around the 0 mark, and the artificial horizon should show the wings are now lined up with the horizon semi-circle.

If you are running FS 5.1 at VGA 320 x 400 or 320 x 200 resolution, you will not see the manifold pressure gauge, or any other engine indicators on screen. If you press the Tab key it will bring up the sub panel from the main instrument panel. Press the Tab key again to return your view of the radio stack.

Warning: Don't let your speed drop below 54 knots, as measured on the airspeed indicator; otherwise the plane will crash.

Artificial horizon shows
the plane's nose is up

Altimeter shows
1,200 feet

Axis indicator above horizon
shows plane's nose is up

Airspeed
is 80 knots

Vertical speed
indicator shows
plane is climbing

Figure 1.12
The Six Flight
Instruments During
the Climb

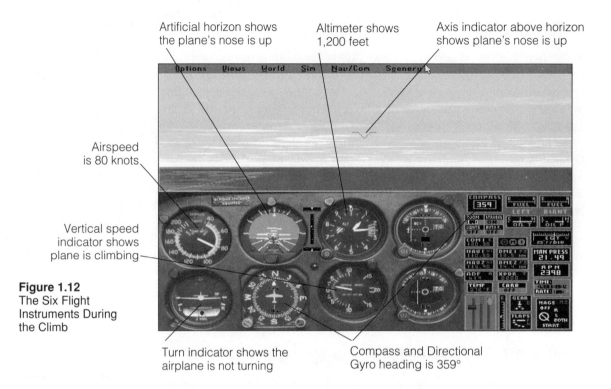

Turn indicator shows the
airplane is not turning

Compass and Directional
Gyro heading is 359°

*The vertical axis
V marker on the
cockpit windshield
lets you know where
the nose of the
airplane is actually
pointing. If you are
flying straight and
level, the top of the
V should precisely
line up with the
horizon edge.*

Bank Left Toward Chicago: Course Heading West (Between 240° and 280°).

Glance at your directional gyro and notice you are headed north. Since Chicago is on your left, to the east, you must begin banking the aircraft left if you are to fly through the downtown district. Gently tap the 4 on the numeric keypad several times, or move the mouse/joystick yoke control to the left until the plane begins turning. Carefully monitor this turn so you don't bank the plane too steeply. If you must, apply corrective steering to the right by applying right mouse/joystick movement, or by pressing the 6 on the numeric keypad. Watch the progression of the turn on the artificial horizon and the turn indicator. If the wings just line up on the L division marker on the turn indicator, you are performing a standard turn, whereby the airplane, if allowed to continue on its path, will make a complete 360° turn in 2 minutes.

Figure 1.13
Banking the Airplane
to the left, Enroute to
Chicago

Note Turn Indicator shows
wings on L marker,
indicating a standard turn
to the left.

Pointer on Directional
Gyro shows current
heading of 283°

Map display turned
on using [Num Lock]
and [-] to zoom out

Change course head-
ing to between 240°
and 270°. Call up the
map, if necessary, by
pressing [Num Lock].

When the directional gyro shows you are on a course heading of between 240° and 275° and you see the city of Chicago straight ahead, pull out of the turn by applying the right aileron/rudder. If you are having trouble finding your bearings, call up the map by pressing [Num Lock]. Zoom in and out of this view by using [+] and [-] on the main keyboard. When you are done, close the map by pressing [Num Lock] twice quickly.

When you see the skyline of Chicago's skyscrapers line up with your V-axis indicator on the cockpit windshield, you have completed your standard turn. The plane should be flying straight and level and the turn indicator should show your wings are horizontal. If you are on course, you should be headed towards downtown Chicago.

Pull out of your turn
by pressing [6], or
apply right joystick
pressure.

Buzzing Downtown Chicago

Try flying through some of the canyons of buildings, but take special care not to hit a building structure. You can see even more buildings if you select the Scenery/Scenery Complexity Menu Command, and in the dialog box

Turn up the scenery
density to see more
buildings downtown.

Figure 1.14
Full-screen spot view of your aircraft negotiating the downtown canyons of Chicago (Press S twice, then W)

Press the W key to summon up a full screen view. To return to the cockpit, press W again.

You can pause the simulation any time by pressing P. To resume flying, press P again.

that opens, choose Dense Scenery for the image complexity. With the scenery density turned up high, you should be able to see the Prudential Building, the Sears Building, and many other building landmarks.

If you are feeling a little adventurous, fly around the downtown area and take in the sights. Every so often, call up the spot view by pressing S twice. To return to the cockpit, press S once again.

Change the Time of Day/Pause the Simulation

Before turning home, for a change of pace, let's try flying at dusk. With Flight Simulator's awesome color capabilities, you are in for a real treat when viewing sunsets or sunrises.

Because you may not want to be distracted while flying, pause the simulation so there is no danger of crashing while you are fiddling with the controls. You can pause the simulation at any time by pressing P. On screen, you will see a pause message indicator informing you that all on-screen activity has been halted. While paused you can pull down menus, change your controls or views, alter the weather, and even change airplanes. To resume flying, press P once again.

To quickly change the time of day, all you need to do is set the digital clock on the instrument panel. To increase the hours, you must click the mouse pointer to the right side of the hours display on the digital clock. To move the clock back, you must click the mouse pointer to the left side of the

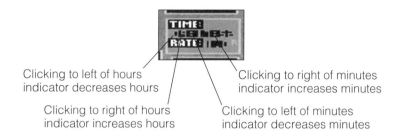

Clicking to left of hours
indicator decreases hours

Clicking to right of hours
indicator increases hours

Clicking to right of minutes
indicator increases minutes

Clicking to left of minutes
indicator decreases minutes

Figure 1.15
The 24-hour format
digital clock controls the
time of day and night.

hours display. You can hold down the mouse button to advance or reverse the time quickly, or you can click each individual number change.

Changing the minutes is accomplished in this way also.

Let's change the time of day to dusk by performing the following steps[2]:

1. First pause the simulator by pressing P.

2. Click on the right of the hours indicator and increase the time of day till it just begins to get dark.

3. Click on the left of the minutes indicator to decrease minutes until you see the sky gradually turn blue. If you have gone too far and it is again daylight, click the right of the minutes indicator until you see the sky turn red at dusk.

4. Click on the left of the minutes indicator, to reverse the time, and watch as the sky lightens as daylight returns.

5. Press P to cancel pause and resume flying the plane.

Change the time
to dusk.

It is fascinating to watch the darkening blue sky turn red, and the city lights slowly switch on as sunset approaches. In the distance you can see the blue glow of the Meigs Field runway lighting system.

NIGHT FLIGHT HOME

Now let's swing back to a course heading of 120° for the return trip home. Again, if you are lost and need to find your location, call up the map.

---

[2]Time is recorded in a 24 hour format, so that 1:00 p.m. becomes 13:00 and 1:00 a.m. becomes 1:00.

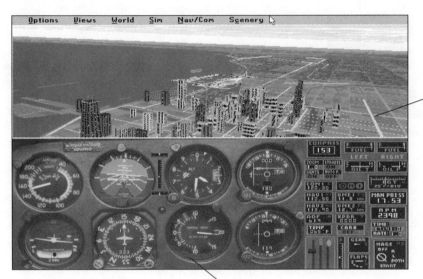

Runway of Blue-lighted Meigs Field

Figure 1.16
Dusk in Chicago, after changing the digital clock (simulator paused using P)

Instrument Panel is darkened due to nightfall. To turn on panel lighting, Press L.

Turn on Aircraft Lights

Come to a course heading of 120° for the return home.

Flight Simulator has four types of night flying lights: instrument panel lights, navigational lights, strobe lights, and landing lights. You can turn them all on or off by clicking the Lights indicator or pressing L. For individual manipulation, the instrument panel lights can be turned off and on by pressing Shift L; the navigation lights are controlled only by the Lights indicator, the strobe light is controlled by pressing O, and the landing lights by pressing Ctrl L. The navigation lights are located on your wings, and serve to identify your position to other aircraft while flying at night. The strobe is a tail mounted flashing light that acts as a beacon to other aircraft in your vicinity. The landing lights, which are like head lamps on an automobile, are used to illuminate the runway while taking off or landing at night.

Perform these steps in order to get acquainted with your lighting systems:

1. Turn on the landing lights by pressing Ctrl L. When you are on or over the runway, you will notice a spotlight beam that illuminates the ground in front of your airplane.

2. Make sure all lights are on by looking at the Lights indicator. It should say on. If you look at a spot view of your aircraft, you will see a green light under one wing, and a red light under the opposite wing.

3. Turn on the strobe light by pressing ⬚O⬚ (or click on STROBES control) . You should see a bright flashing strobe light on the tail.

Using the Land Me Command
for a Safe Touchdown at Meigs Field

Let's have Flight Simulator land our plane for us automatically. This will take some worry out of not being able to bring the airplane back in one piece. Land Me allows you to have an instructor take over the control of your airplane, and then land you at the nearest airport. Flight simulator will automatically pick the proper airport for landing.

Press ⬚X⬚ from the keyboard to engage Land Me. In a few seconds, you will see a message on-screen from your flight instructor informing you of what flight maneuvers are being performed. Sit back and relax while the Land Me instructor takes over. If you are interested in seeing what is going on outside your cockpit, press ⬚S⬚ twice to bring up the spot view. The Land Me instructor will return your plane to Meigs Field and execute a flawless textbook landing.

Press ⬚X⬚ to engage Land Me. To disengage Land Me, press ⬚X⬚ again.

SUMMARY

Summary of steps performed for your solo flight:

1. Turn on the Axis Indicator on Cockpit Windshield and release brakes by pressing ⬚.⬚.
2. Increase throttle to maximum (press and hold down ⬚9⬚ on numeric keypad, or drag throttle control to top) or press ⬚F4⬚.
3. Keep airplane centered on runway by using ⬚0⬚ to steer left and ⬚Enter⬚ (both are on the numeric keypad) to steer right. The mouse or the joystick also control left or right movement.
4. When aircraft passes 54 knots airspeed, rotate (apply up elevator) aircraft by gently tapping ⬚2⬚ on the numeric keypad (or pull back on yoke mouse/joystick), until the triangle pointer on the elevator control indicator moves to the first mark above the center line.
5. After lifting off and passing the runway threshold, move throttle back to 22" of manifold pressure by pressing ⬚3⬚, or dragging down the throttle control.
6. Climb rate should be 500 to 1,000 feet per minute on vertical speed indicator. Airspeed should be approximately 100 knots. Use throttle to adjust climb rate (⬚9⬚ key increases, ⬚3⬚ key decreases).

Tip: Watching the instructor's actions using the Land Me feature is very useful in learning how to properly land your airplane. To disengage Land Me at any time, press ⬚X⬚ again.

7. Raise landing gear by pressing ⒢ (or click on GEAR indicator).

8. Climb to 1,500 feet altitude mean sea level (MSL) then level off by reducing throttle.

9. Bank left toward Chicago by applying left ailerons (press ④).Your course heading will be west (between 240° and 280° on directional gyro). To straighten out a banking turn that is too steep, apply right ailerons (press ⑥). Move mouse/joystick left for banking turn to left. Move mouse/joystick right to return to level flight.

10. When Chicago skyline is lined up on the cockpit windshield's V-Axis indicator, fly straight and level. If you are lost, call up the map by pressing [Num Lock]. Zoom the map's magnification in and out by pressing the ⊕ and ⊖ keys on the main keyboard.

11. Buzz downtown Chicago.

12. Pause simulator by pressing ⒫.

13. Change time to dusk by clicking right side of hours on digital display until the sky turns red. To fine tune the appearance of dusk, click the right side of the minutes display to increase minutes and the left side of the minutes display to decrease minutes.

14. Resume simulation play by pressing ⒫ once again.

15. Swing back to a course heading of 120° for the return trip home. Use the map if necessary.

16. Turn on the aircraft navigation lights: Press ⒧ or click on LIGHTS control. (The instrument panel may be already on, due to changes you made in the clock. Therefore, to make sure everything is on, check the LIGHTS indicator to see if it is on.)

17. Turn on the landing lights: Press [Ctrl] ⒧.

18. Turn on strobe lights: Press ⒪.

19. Press ⓧ to engage the Land Me auto-land function.

20. Watch plane land by switching back and forth between spot and cockpit view (press ⒮ twice for spot view, then once more to return to cockpit view).

21. Pat yourself on the back.

Congratulations, you have completed your first solo flight! In this chapter, in addition to flying, you have learned how to use some of the simulator's most powerful features.

CHAPTER
2
Windows on Your World

This chapter introduces you to the different kinds of views possible in *Flight Simulator* and the various viewing options available under the Views menu. FS 5.1 offers not only a standard view from the cockpit, but also several external views. The external views, also known as tower, spot, and track view, and the internal cockpit view can be displayed on two separate three-dimensional windows. Each 3-D window's size attributes, direction of view, zoom or magnification factor, and placement on screen are controlled by you. Along with the two 3-D windows, there is a map window to chart the airplane's movement on a terrain map, and an instrument panel window, which can be moved but not resized. Both view windows and the map view can be displayed simultaneously, but only at the expense of slower CPU processor speed. Only one instrument panel may be displayed at a given time. However you can quickly jump between the available instrument panels by pressing Tab.

Under the Views menu, you can choose to disable or cover any instrument, instrument panel, or aircraft system for training purposes. If you need more visual cues as to your plane's attitude, you can include axis pointers on the cockpit windshield, and also display the name or title of your current view in each window. Using the Flight Photograph command, you can screen capture PCX formatted graphics of the entire screen, or of individual windows and instrument panels, and then save them to disk for later printing. All windowing menu options and commands are found in the View menu as shown in Figure 2.1.

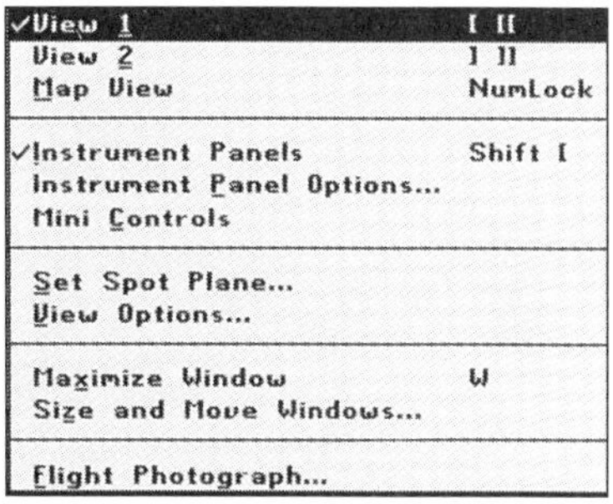

Figure 2.1 The Views menu

45

ACTIVATING A WINDOW

With up to three different windows on screen, (not including the instrument panel) you need to activate a window in order to let the simulator know which window you wish to move, resize, or zoom in on. To activate a window you can:

1. Click inside the window using the mouse.
2. Under the Views menu, select View 1, View 2, or Map View.
3. From the keyboard, press ⊞ to bring up the View 1 window, press ⊡ to bring up the View 2 window, or press [Num Lock] to bring up the Map View.
4. When the window has been activated you will see a thin white border gilding its edges.

To bring to the foreground a view or map window that is covered or concealed in the background, press ⸰. After you activate the window by clicking on it, a thin white border will appear around its edges.

RESIZING AND MOVING A WINDOW

Resizing and moving a window can be accomplished with either the mouse or the keyboard.

Resizing the Window Via the Mouse

Resizing the window using the mouse is the simplest and easiest way to manipulate the size of your window. To resize the window using the mouse:

- Click and drag the lower right corner of the window. The window, as pictured in Figure 2.2, will stretch and look distorted as it adjusts to its new size. If the window you wish to move is covered up by another window, press ⸰ to bring it to the foreground.

Figure 2.2
Resizing the window
via the mouse

Resizing the Window Via the Keyboard

To resize the window using the keyboard:

1. Pull down the Views menu and select Size and Move Windows.

2. In the Size and Move Windows dialog box, illustrated in Figure 2.3, click the button of the window you wish to resize.

3. When the window is displayed, press [Shift] in combination with the arrow cursor keys to resize it.

4. After finishing, press [Esc] to return to the Size and Move Windows dialog box, then click the OK button to return to the cockpit, or the Cancel button to cancel your resizing modification.

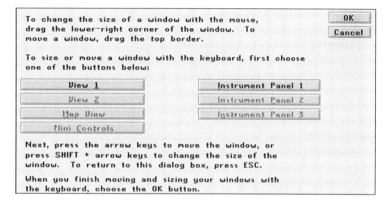

Figure 2.3
The Size and Move
dialog box

Moving a Window, Instrument Panel, or Mini-control Via the Mouse

When moving on-screen objects, you can move any window, instrument panel, or mini-control using the mouse by:

• Clicking and dragging the top edge of the window, instrument panel, or mini-control to move it to a new location. If the window you wish to move is covered up by another window, press ['] to bring it to the foreground.

Figure 2.4
Moving a window
via the mouse

Moving a Window, Instrument Panel, or Mini-control Via the Keyboard

To move a window, instrument panel, or mini-control using the keyboard, you must:

1. Pull down the Views menu and select Size and Move Windows. (See Figure 2.3).
2. In the Size and Move Windows dialog box, click the button of the window that you wish to move.
3. When the window is displayed, press one of the arrow cursor keys to move it.
4. After finishing, press [Esc] to return to the Size and Move Windows dialog box, then click the OK button to return to the cockpit, or the Cancel button to cancel the object's new placement.

Figure 2.5 Enlarging a window to full-screen

Enlarging a Window to Full-screen View

The View 1, View 2, and Map View windows can be enlarged to full screen by pressing [W], or by choosing Maximize Window from the View menu. These three windows can be quickly returned to their former size by once again pressing [W].

Full-screen External View Option

You can toggle between a full-screen spot or cockpit view at anytime by pressing [W]. To return to normal screen view, press [W] again.

If you would like the simulator to always display a full-screen view when you switch to tower or spot view, you can toggle on the M Full-screen External View option in the View Options dialog box.

ZOOMING THE MAGNIFICATION FACTOR OF A WINDOW

The zoom control is used to better view objects in your view and map windows. For example, you would use the zoom control to magnify and bring into close view a plane that is flying far away. Or, in map view you might be want to zoom in close to the ground so you can see local surface features.

Later, you might zoom to a higher altitude to see a broader view of your position in relation to the rest of the country.

The two view windows, and the map view can be zoomed in or out to various magnification factors by selecting and activating a window, then pressing ⊕ on the main keypad to zoom in, or ⊖ on the main keypad to zoom out. You can quickly restore normal 1x magnification by pressing ⌈Backspace⌋. Here are some other ways to zoom an activated window:

- Using the mouse
  1. Select the window you wish to zoom. When it is activated, you should see a thin white border around it.
  2. On the instrument panel, click the Zoom Indicator. To increase zoom, click to the right side of the numbers; to decrease zoom, click to the left side of the numbers.

Learjet Zoom Indicator

Cessna Zoom Indicator

- Using the keyboard
  1. Select the window you wish to zoom. When it is activated, you should see a thin white border around it.
  2. Press ⊕ on the main keypad to zoom in, or ⊖ on the main keypad to zoom out.

Figure 2.6
The Zoom Indicator zooms the active view or map window

- Using the View Options menu command
  1. Pull down the View menu.
  2. Select the View Options command.
  3. In the View Options dialog box, select the window you wish to zoom.
  4. In the list box for Zoom, type in the amount of zoom you want (you must type in numbers from the main keypad, not from the numeric keypad). If you want to zoom the Map View, select the Alt list box, and pull it down to display a list of altitudes you can choose from.
  5. Click the OK button.

Figure 2.7
Type in the zoom factor for the 3-D view windows

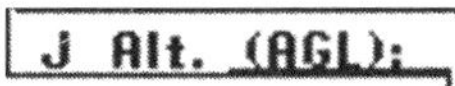

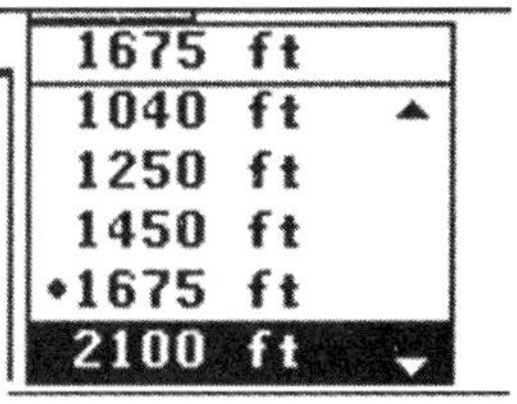

The view windows zoom factor ranges from 0.25 to 511; the map zoom, which is measured in terms of altitude, ranges from 200 feet to a whole earth view at 160,000 miles (257,440 kilometers).

J Alt. (AGL):	1675 ft
	1040 ft ▲
	1250 ft
	1450 ft
	♦1675 ft
	2100 ft ▼

Figure 2.8
Zooming for the Map View is performed by selecting the map altitude from the Alt pull down list box in the View Options dialog box.

To zoom any window, activate the window, then press ⊕ to zoom in or ⊖ to zoom out. Or you can click to the right or left of the zoom indicator numbers to increase or decrease zoom.

Whenever you type numbers into list boxes or other option text fields in Flight Simulator, you must use the number keys on the main keypad, not the numeric keypad. This is because the numeric keypad is used to control the plane, and using these keys could affect the way your plane flies when you return to the simulation.

Zooming With Finer Resolution

By using ⇧Shift in combination with ⊕ and ⊖ the zoom rate will give you a finer and narrower resolution change. Table 2.1 summarizes the zoom keyboard controls.

THE 3-D VIEW WINDOWS

The two 3-D view windows can be switched on from the keyboard using [for the first 3-D window, and] for the second 3-D window. To close the first 3-D window, you would press [twice quickly, and to close the second 3-D window, you would press] twice quickly. Table 2.2 summarizes these keyboard commands. Alternatively, you can pull down the Views menu and select View 1 or View 2 to turn these two view windows on or off. The selection of these two menu options is a toggle, that is when you first select them, you enable them (turn them on). A check mark will appear to the immediate left of the menu option, as is illustrated in Figure 2.1. When you select the menu option again, you will disable (turn off) the menu command, and the check mark will disappear.

Cycling Between Cockpit, Tower, Track, and Spot Views

There are four possible views out of each of your two 3-D windows: cockpit, tower, track, and spot. Cockpit view is a view from inside your airplane looking outside through one of nine possible view angles. Tower view gives you a fixed point perspective of your aircraft from inside the control tower of your scenario's startup airport. In tower view you cannot change the view direc-

Table 2.1 Zooming Keys	
Zoom	**Key**
Zoom In	⊕
Zoom In with Fine Resolution	⇧Shift ⊕
Zoom Out	⊖
Zoom Out with Fine Resolution	⇧Shift ⊖
Restore Normal Magnification	Backspace

Table 2.2 Turning Your Windows Off/On from the Keyboard

Window	Description	Opening Window from the Keyboard	Closing Window from the Keyboard
View 1	The first 3-D window	[I]	[I] [I]
View 2	The second 3-D window	[ ]]	[ ]] [ ]]
Map View	Navigational map	[Num Lock]	[Num Lock] [Num Lock]
Instrument Panels	Aircraft cockpit instrumentation	[Tab][1]	[Shift] [Tab][2]

To quickly restore normal magnification, press [Backspace].

tion since it is automatically set to track your airplane. In this view, you can watch the runways and airspace around the airport, while keeping an eye on your airplane. Track view lets you view your friend's plane while directly-connected via modem or serial cable in dual-player mode. Spot view gives you an external view of your airplane, as seen from the vantage point of a chase aircraft that is following your airplane.

To switch between cockpit, tower, and spot views from the keyboard, simply press [S]. The 3-D view that is currently active, as indicated by a white border around it, will cycle from cockpit to tower view on the first press of [S], then will cycle from tower to spot view, upon a second press of [S]. Pressing [S] again will cause you to return to the cockpit view. Track view is not accessible in the 3-D windows from the keyboard unless you are in dual-player mode.

You can also switch views, using the keyboard or mouse, by selecting View Options from the View menu, and pulling down the View list box to then choose from the available options. While in this dialog

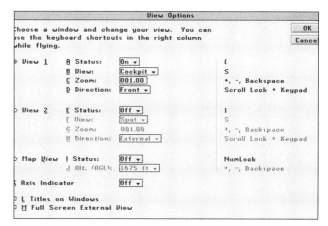

Figure 2.9
The View Options dialog box allows you to modify your view and map window options.

---

[1] This key brings up an instrument subpanel for the Learjet.
[2] This key combination is used to backtrack to a previous instrument subpanel.

3-D View	Description	Keyboard Command (Press S to Cycle Forward, Shift S to Cycle in Reverse Order)	Zoom Command	View Directions	Pan View
Table 2.3 The Four Possible Views Looking Out of the Two 3-D View Windows					
Cockpit	View out of aircraft's windshield	S	+ Zoom in − Zoom out	Shift + [7][8][9] [4][5][6] [1][2][3]	Up: Shift + Backspace Down: Shift + Enter Right: Ctrl + Shift + Enter Left: Ctrl + Shift + Backspace Return to no pan view (straight and level): Scroll Lock (or *) + keypad 8
Tower	Control tower observation of your plane	S	+ Zoom in − Zoom out	View changes automatically	No panning possible
Spot	View of your plane, as seen from a chasing spot plane	S	+ Zoom in − Zoom out	Shift + [7][8][9] [4][5][6] [1][2][3]	Up: Shift + Backspace Down: Shift + Enter Right: Ctrl + Shift + Enter Left: Ctrl + Shift + Backspace Return to no pan view (straight and level): Scroll Lock (or *) + keypad 8
Track (only available in dual player mode)	Track the other player's plane in dual player mode	S[3]	+ Zoom in − Zoom out	View changes automatically	No panning possible

Press S to quickly cycle between Cockpit, Tower, Track, and Spot views. (Track view is available in dual-player mode).

box, you can also set the zoom magnification factor and direction for each view window.

Changing the Viewing Direction Via the Keyboard

In both cockpit and spot views, you can choose one of nine different directions by pressing Shift in combination with 1, 2, 3, 4, 5, 6, 7, 8,

---

[3]Pressing S to switch to track view is only possible while in Dual Player Flight mode.

and $\boxed{9}$ from the numeric keypad, as seen in Figures 2.10 and 2.11. Along with choosing a directional view, you can also pan the view up by pressing $\boxed{\text{Shift}}$ and $\boxed{\text{Backspace}}$ at the same time, or down by pressing $\boxed{\text{Shift}}$ and $\boxed{\text{Enter}}$ at the same time. Table 2.3 displays the different view options available for the two 3-D view windows.

To change view directions in the Cockpit and Spot View windows, press $\boxed{\text{Shift}}$ in combination with $\boxed{1}$, $\boxed{2}$, $\boxed{3}$, $\boxed{4}$, $\boxed{5}$, $\boxed{6}$, $\boxed{7}$, $\boxed{8}$, or $\boxed{9}$ from the numeric keypad. To pan your view window up, press $\boxed{\text{Shift}}$ + $\boxed{\text{Backspace}}$ simultaneously. To pan your view down, press $\boxed{\text{Shift}}$ + $\boxed{\text{Enter}}$ simultaneously. To return to straight and level view, with no panning, press $\boxed{\text{Scroll Lock}}$ (or $\boxed{*}$ from the numeric keypad) + $\boxed{8}$.

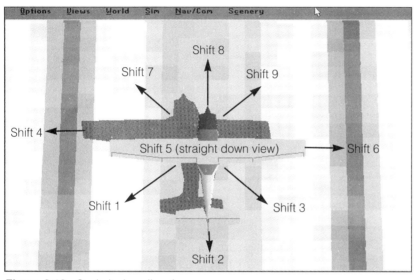

Figure 2.10 Cockpit view directions

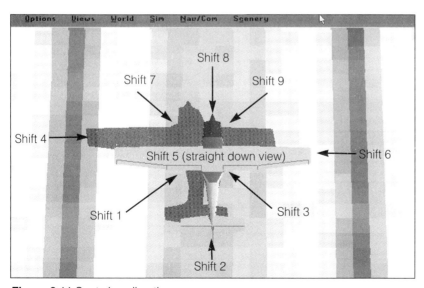

Figure 2.11 Spot view directions

Changing the Viewing Direction Via View Options Dialog Box

A second method of changing your view direction in both the cockpit and spot views is to set the view using the View Options command. To do this:

1. Open the Views menu.
2. Select the View Options command.
3. In the View Options dialog box, click open the Direction list box, and select the particular direction you want.

Panning the 3-D View

In the cockpit view only, you can pan the 3-D view window up and down, or left and right by using the keyboard.

   To pan up or down using the keyboard:

1. Press Shift + Backspace to pan your cockpit view up.
2. Press Shift + Enter to pan your cockpit view down.

You can also smoothly pan your view left or right in a 360° sweep around your aircraft by using the keyboard. To pan left or right:

1. Press Ctrl + Shift + Backspace to pan left.
2. Press Ctrl + Shift + Enter to pan right.

In all panning or view modes, press Scroll Lock or * then 8 (on the numeric keypad) to bringback a straight-ahead level view.

Table 2.4 Panning Keys	
Pan Direction	**Key Combination**
Up	Shift Backspace
Down	Shift Enter
Left	Ctrl Shift Backspace
Right	Ctrl Shift Enter
Return to Normal Level View	Scroll Lock, or * 8 (on numeric keypad)

Axis Indicator

If you have trouble determining exactly where your aircraft's nose is pointing, you can switch on the axis indicator which displays four dots, a small v, or a large V in the center of the cockpit windshield. The axis indicator is useful for establishing your plane's current pitch. To turn on the axis indicator:

1. Select the View Options command from the Views menu.
2. From the Axis Indicator list box, select one of the following options: Four Dots, Small V, Large V, or Off if you want to turn off the axis indicator.

Figure 2.12
Selecting the Axis Indicator in the View Options dialog box

Although the axis indicator shows the direction the nose is pointing, and its pitch in relation to the ground, it does not tell you what direction the airplane is flying in. This is because cross winds, and using certain yoke positions for your flight controls, can cause you to fly in a slightly skewed direction.

Titles on Windows

If you have trouble identifying which view you are currently looking at, you can have the simulation display the title of each view for all open windows. This is especially helpful when you are displaying more than one window. To turn on titles:

1. Select View Options from the Views menu.
2. Toggle on the Titles on Windows check box.

Customizing Spot View Using the Set Spot Plane Command

Although you can easily switch view directions for the spot view from the keyboard by using the Shift + 1, 2, 3, 4, 5, 6, 7, 8, and 9 numeric keypad combinations, you can customize viewing parameters with greater precision by using the Set Spot Plane command. Using this menu command, you can precisely set the spot plane's position, its exact altitude, and its distance from your plane. For aerobatic maneuvers, you can select whether your spot view is optimized for loops or for rolls, so you can better keep your airplane in view.

For more precise positioning control of your spot plane view, use the Set Spot Plane command under the Views menu to set altitude, precise viewing angle, and aerobatic viewing preferences. When you use the view dot slider in the Set Spot Plane dialog box, you are not limited to 15° view angle increments that the keyboard method constrains you to. Rather, you can specify any viewing angle from 0° to 360° around your plane.

Precision Placement of Spot Viewing Angle

To precisely specify which direction you want to view your aircraft from, perform the following steps:

1. Select the Set Spot Plane command under the Views menu.

2. In the View Direction box of the Set Spot Plane dialog box (pictured in Figure 2.13) click the mouse on the dot next to the aircraft, and drag it to the new viewing position. The dot, which turns red when selected, represents your spot plane and the direction it will view your plane.

Figure 2.13
Setting your spot
view angle for
viewing your plane

3. If you are using the keyboard, the dot can be moved by using the cursor arrow keys.

4. Click the OK button when you are finished.

```
                      Set Spot Plane
Choose the window you want for Spot view.        ┌──────┐
View:  View 1 ▾                                  │  OK  │
                                                 └──────┘
Choose how far away the spot plane is:           ┌──────┐
Distance (ft):  +000123                          │Cancel│
                                                 └──────┘
Altitude (ft):  +000016

Preference:        Transition:         View Direction
⊕ Roll             ⊕ Slow             ┌─────────────┐
○ Loop             ○ Fast             │             │
                                      │      ▲      │
Use the mouse or the arrow keys to    │    ──┼── ·  │
move the spot plane position in the   │      ▼      │
View Direction box.                   │             │
                                      └─────────────┘
Once you've set the spot plane position, choose the OK
button and then press the S key to cycle to Spot view.
```

Click and drag this dot to set your spot plane's viewing position. Using this control, you are *not* limited to the standard 15° viewing angles that are possible from the keyboard.

Setting the Spot Plane's Distance and Altitude

The spot plane's distance and altitude are set in the Distance and Altitude text entry boxes of the Set Spot Plane dialog box. Distance is the span which separates the spot plane from your plane, while altitude is the difference in altitude between the spot plane and your plane. Positive altitudes put the spot plane above your plane, and negative altitudes put the spot plane below your plane. Altitude can never be set such that your spot plane would be below ground level.

→ **Tip:** For an undocumented and interesting spot view from straight above looking down at your plane below, press (Shift) + (5) and then set the distance (in this case distance is the same as altitude) in the Set Spot Plane dialog box.

Looping or Rolling Preferences

These viewing preferences are used exclusively to optimize your spot view of aerobatic loops and rolls you perform in your plane.

Selecting Loop causes the spot plane to fly relative to one side of your wing in a horizontal plane. When your plane starts to loop the spot plane flies on in a horizontal direction, tracking one wing side of your aircraft. This allows you to stay on one side of your looping plane so you can watch the entire maneuver. Selecting Roll causes the spot plane to fly on the same heading on one side of your plane while it completes a full barrel roll.

Transition Slow/Fast

If you prefer to instantly jump between views while in spot view, select the Fast transition option in the Set Spot Plane dialog box. The Slow transition allows you to view the gradual panning between different viewing angles for a more thrilling 3-D effect.

MAP VIEW

The Map View, which is brought up in a separate window from the two 3-D windows, gives you a scrolling terrain map you can use for navigation purposes. The map can be zoomed from 200 feet all the way to a whole earth view at 160,000 miles (257,440 kilometers) by using the zoom indicator on screen or by activating the map then pressing + to zoom in, or − to zoom out (both keys are on the main keyboard, not the numeric keypad). Two red cross hairs at the center of the map define the location of the aircraft. The top vertical line of the cross hairs represents the aircraft's nose and the current direction the plane is traveling. You will notice the map is aircraft oriented so the map will rotate in response to changes in the aircraft's heading. If you find this confusing, you can always change the map display through the Display Preferences dialog box under the Options menu, and freeze the map in a north orientation. Then, regardless of your plane's heading, the map would always appear fixed (meaning it won't rotate), although your airplane's cross hairs would move around as your position changed. Figure 2.14 shows the map zoomed out to 200 feet altitude over the Meigs Field runway.

To change the map orientation:

1. Under the Options menu, select Preferences.
2. Click the Display button.
3. Click the Map Display Options button.
4. In the Map Display dialog box, select either North Oriented for a non-rotating map fixed in a north direction, Aircraft Oriented for a rotating map that has the aircraft's heading always pointing towards the top red cross hair, or North at High Altitude for a north oriented non-rotating map zoomed out to a high altitude.

The map can be viewed in aircraft orientation (the map rotates when the aircraft turns), or north orientation (the map moves, but does not rotate when the aircraft turns. Also north always points straight up). A third map orientation, north at high altitude, causes the map to display a north orientation but at high altitude for navigating long distances. All of these map viewing options are found in the Display Preferences command under the Options menu.

Figure 2.14
Map zoomed out to
200 feet altitude

Map is zoomed
to 200 ft above
ground level

Runway numbers show runway
heading. 36 signifies runway
faces 360° or 0° due north

This marker
represents
your plane

You can also zoom
the map by clicking
the zoom indicator

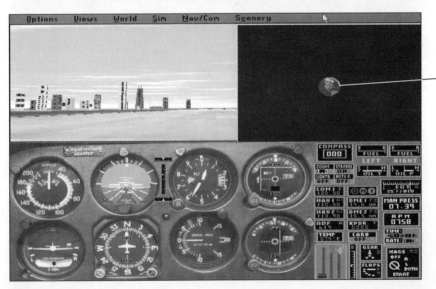

Orbital view of Earth,
160,000 miles in space

Figure 2.15
Map zoomed out to
160,000 miles

Map Display:	
	Aircraft Oriented
	North Oriented
	•Aircraft Oriented
	North at High Alt.

Figure 2.16 The Map
Display list box

MINI-CONTROLS

Enabling the mini-controls option (under the Views menu) causes a separate control position indicator window to be displayed on-screen. This indicator shows the position of your plane's elevators, ailerons, rudders, and throttle controls. It also displays the current airspeed. The mini-controls indicator is useful when you cannot see your instrument panel, like when flying with full-screen view for a 3-D window.

The mini-control window can be moved to any point on the screen by clicking and dragging the mouse pointer on the top of the window, or from the keyboard by using the Size and Move Windows command from the Views menu. (See earlier topic on moving windows using the keyboard in this chapter.) However, it cannot be resized.

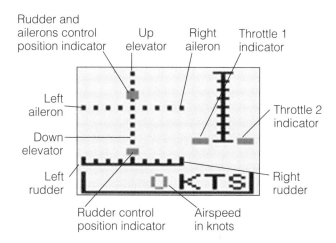

Figure 2.17
The Mini-control window

INSTRUMENT PANELS

FS 5.1 allows up to three different instrument panels, although at present only the Learjet is able to use more than one panel.[4] As mentioned earlier, the instrument panel can be moved on screen by dragging the top border of the panel with the mouse, or using the Size and Move Windows command via the keyboard, but it cannot be resized. Moving the instrument panel down is useful for when you want to make room to display a larger 3-D window or map on screen.

Instrument Subsections

FS 5.1 allows some aircraft to have additional instrument subsections displayed. Don't confuse instrument subsections with the three instrument panels—they are separate. Table 2.5 shows only the Learjet has instrument

---

[4]The Learjet's second instrument panel is the digital magnetic compass that you see displayed on the right cockpit windshield. There are no other instruments associated with this panel.

Table 2.5	Instrument Panels and Subsections that are Available for the Flight Simulator Aircraft			
	Cessna Skylane 182 RG	**Learjet 35A**	**Schweizer 2-32 Sailplane**	**Sopwith Camel**
Instrument Panel 1	No instrument subsections[5]	Instrument subsections available (Use Tab to cycle between)	No instrument subsections	No instrument subsections
Instrument Panel 2	None	Compass Center Post (No instrument subsections available)	None	None
Instrument Panel 3	None	None	None	None

✈

Press Tab to cycle between the instrument subsections on each instrument panel.

subsections and additional instrument panels available. To access the instrument subsections, simply press Tab, and to return to the normal instrument panel display press Tab again. The Learjet's instrument subsection displays engine monitoring devices, such as turbine speed gauges, engine switches, oil pressure, temperature gauges, fuel flow, and fuel capacity meters.

Switching Between the Three Instrument Panels

Switching among the three instrument panels is accomplished by first enabling the Tab On/Off option under the three Instrument Panel list boxes. At present, you cannot switch between other instrument panels using Tab, because none of the four basic aircraft have multiple panels you can fully use (The Learjet's second instrument panel consists of only one instrument—the compass center post).

Switching the Three Instrument Panels On/Off

Why would you want to turn any of these instruments, controls, or aircraft systems off? For training purposes you might want to simulate the failure of

---

[5]The Cessna has an instrument subsection only while in VGA or 320 x 200 mode, but not in Super VGA. This is because, at the lower resolutions, not all the instruments can be displayed simultaneously like they are in Super VGA. While using FS 5.1 at these lower resolution, press Tab to bring up the instrument subsections.

some part of the aircraft, and learn how to keep the aircraft under control. While instrument flying at night, you might lose your gyroscope, pitot-static, or vacuum system, thereby disabling most of your crucial altitude/attitude instruments. Or, you might experience a complete radio failure, or lose an entire instrument panel due to an electrical short circuit and be unable to navigate. What would you do under such circumstances? FS 5.1 gives you the tools to learn and test how you would react under emergency situations, all without risking your life.

Through the Instrument Panel Options command under the Views menu, you can:

- Switch any of the three instrument panels on or off.

- Turn any primary instrument from among the standard instrument cluster on or off.

- Turn any NAV/COM instrument on or off.

- Disable or enable any aircraft sub-system, including the pitot-static, vacuum, fuel, engine, and electrical systems.

To switch on or switch off any one of your three instrument panels, perform one of the following steps:

- Open the Instrument Panel Options dialog box from the Views menu and click the Instrument Panels option. This option is a toggle so you can turn it off by selecting it again. A check mark will appear beside the option name when the panel is on. No check mark will appear when the panel is off.

- To switch all instrument panels on or off, toggle the Master Switch (All Panels) check box switch, as is illustrated in Figure 2.18. If you are in the cockpit, press [Shift] + [[] on the keyboard. A check mark will appear beside the option name when the switch is on. No check mark will appear when the switch is off.

- To switch any individual panel on or off, select the appropriate panel from one of the three Instrument Panel list boxes, and select On or Off. If your aircraft does not have multiple panels, the Instrument Panel 2 and Instrument Panel 3 list boxes will be dimmed out.

The [Shift] + [[] combination is a toggle used to quickly turn on or off all instrument panels.

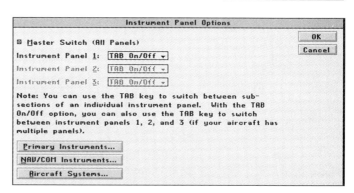

Figure 2.18 The Instrument Panel Options dialog box

How to Turn Off the Learjet's Compass Center Post (Instrument Panel 2)

To turn off the Learjet's compass center post:

1. While the Learjet's instrument panel is displayed on screen, select the Instrument Panels Options from the Views menu.
2. Select the Instrument Panel 2 list box, and highlight the Off option.
3. Click the OK button. When you return to the cockpit, the compass center post will be gone.

Covering or Disabling Instruments and Aircraft Systems

To cripple or cover any aircraft instrument or system, follow these steps:

1. Select the Instrument Panel Options command from the Views menu.
2. Choose the type of instrument or system you wish to cover or cause a malfunction to. In the Instrument Panel Options dialog box, shown in the previous figure, click on the

   • Primary Instruments button if you want to disable the airspeed indicator, attitude indicator, turn rate indicator, altimeter, vertical speed indicator, or heading indicator.
   • NAV/COM Instruments button if you want to disable the COM, NAV, Transponder, ADF, or magnetic compass.
   • Aircraft Systems button if you want to disable the entire pitot-static, vacuum, fuel, engine, or electrical systems.

3. Select the instrument or system you wish to incapacitate by clicking on the list box and selecting from among:

   • Operative
   • Inoperative
   • Covered

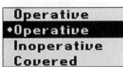

Figure 2.19
Options for disabling
the instruments and
subsystems

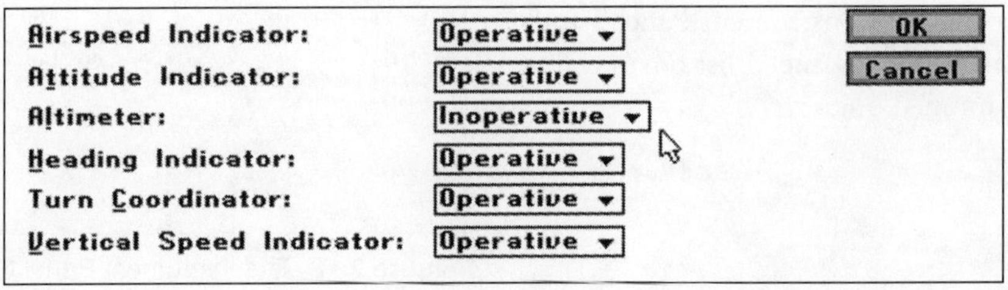

(See Figure 2.20 for an example of how to disable the altimeter).

Airspeed Indicator:	Operative ▾		OK
Attitude Indicator:	Operative ▾		Cancel
Altimeter:	Inoperative ▾	
Heading Indicator:	Operative ▾	
Turn **C**oordinator:	Operative ▾	
Vertical Speed Indicator:	Operative ▾	

Figure 2.20
The Primary
Instrument List boxes

Table 2.6   Aircraft Instruments and Systems

	Cessna Skylane 182 RG	Learjet 35A	Schweizer 2-32 Sailplane	Sopwith Camel
Primary Instruments				
Airspeed Indicator	X	X	X	X
Attitude Indicator	X	X		
Altimeter	X	X	X	X
Heading Indicator	X	X		
Turn Coordinator	X	X		
Vertical Speed Indicator	X	X	X	
NAV/COM Instruments				
COM	X	X	X	
NAV	X	X		
Transponder	X	X		
ADF	X	X		
Magnetic Compass	X	X	X	X
Aircraft Systems				
Pitot /Static	X	X	X	X
Vacuum	X	X		
Fuel	X	X		X
Engine	X	X		X
Electrical	X	X	X	

4. When you are finished, click OK to return to the Instrument Panel Options dialog box, then click OK again to return to the cockpit.

The instruments or aircraft systems will now be inoperative or covered.

Note that for some aircraft, not all the instruments and systems are available. Table 2.6 illustrates instruments and systems presently on the four default FS 5.1 aircraft.

SAVING YOUR FLIGHT PHOTOGRAPHS

Flight Simulator includes a screen shot utility that allows you to take pictures of your cockpit view. Through the Flight Photograph command under the Views menu, you can capture the whole screen, an individual 3-D window, the map view, or any individual instrument panel into a PCX graphic file that you name on your hard disk.

Let's try capturing a full-screen spot plane view of your plane as it is flying towards Chicago. Here's how to do this:

1. Take off from Meigs Field and head towards downtown Chicago, flying at a level 1,500 feet.
2. Press [S] twice to bring up spot view.
3. Select your viewing angle. For this example, use the right rear view, or from the keyboard, [Shift] + [3].
4. Press [W] to maximize the 3-D window to full-screen.
5. Pull down the Views menu, and select Flight Photograph.
6. In the Flight Photograph dialog box, pictured in Figure 2.21, click the Window list box, and select Whole Screen.
7. Type a file name, such as Chicapic, in the Filename text entry box. This is the name that the PCX graphic will be given.
8. Click the OK button, and quickly move your mouse to the top of the screen (or click the right mouse button to make the pointer disappear) to avoid having it mar your picture.
9. In a few seconds the screen will freeze and remain frozen until the screen capture is complete.
10. Exit *Flight Simulator.*

The screen capture will be saved in the C:\FLTSIM directory under the name you gave it. Now you can print your saved graphic using any graphics program capable of reading PCX type files.

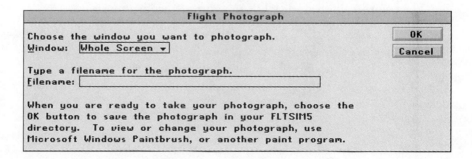

Figure 2.21
The Flight Photograph
dialog box

C H A P T E R
3

Simulation Controls

Flight Simulator has many menu options and commands that affect the way the simulator operates. This chapter introduces you to some of the main controls you access through the pull down menus. Each person has a unique set of preferences and through the simulator's ability to customize itself to your liking, you can modify the "off the shelf" default characteristics of the program till you are happy with the way the program runs.

SETTING YOUR PREFERENCES

Through the Preferences option under the Options menu, you can choose *Flight Simulator*'s default drivers. You may also choose the program's start up features. Within the Preferences dialog box, you will find buttons for:

- General Preferences
- Display Preferences
- Sound Preferences
- Keyboard Preferences
- Mouse Preferences
- Joystick Preferences
- Country Preferences
- Instrument Preferences

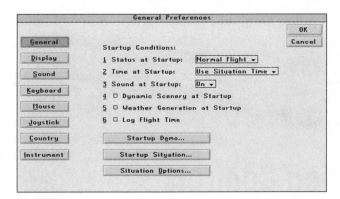

Figure 3.1
The General
Preferences dialog box

To bring up each Preference dialog box, click on the button's name. When you are finished with a particular preference box but still need to modify another preference, click on the Preference button you wish to activate, and it will open up the dialog box you wish. After completing all your selections, click the OK button.

Rebooting *Flight Simulator* When New Software Drivers Are Selected

Software drivers are special modules of computer code written so a particular device can work properly. For example, in Windows 95 most printers and SVGA cards have their own drivers that must be configured before they can work. Windows, or any program which uses a driver, must be told about the choice of drivers, and in many cases, must be restarted before the drivers can be used. This also happens in *Flight Simulator*; if you have modified any of the startup software drivers, you will be presented with a dialog box telling you to exit *Flight Simulator* and restart it for the changes to take effect. In this instance, click the Exit *Flight Simulator* and Restart button if you want *Flight Simulator* to exit and then restart the program automatically with the new drivers, or click the OK button if you are not yet prepared to do this.

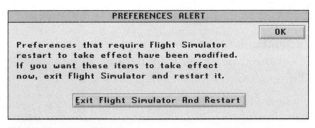

Figure 3.2 The Reboot dialog box pops up whenever you change software drivers in a Preference dialog box.

General Preferences

Under the General Preferences dialog box (shown in Figure 3.1) you can select your startup situation, startup demo, or various other startup aspects, including what options are saved or are loaded each time you restart the program or situation.

Status at Startup

Figure 3.3
Status at Startup

Using this list box, you can choose whether *Flight Simulator* starts up in normal flight mode, demo flight mode with sound, or demo flight mode without sound. You will probably always want to leave this selected on normal flight mode, since this mode is the only one you can fly the simulator in. In normal mode, the situation you have chosen in the Startup Situation button becomes the default opening situation (if you haven't selected a situation, FS 5.1 will default to Chicago's Meigs Field).

Use demo mode if you want an instant walk-through tour of flight simulator's capabilities. If you were a retailer selling *Flight Simulator*, for example, and you wanted to show what the program could do, you might want to leave the program perpetually on in demo mode.

Time at Startup

The Time at Startup list box offers you the choice of using your computer's clock as the basis for setting *Flight Simulator*'s clock, or the time you saved in a particular situation. If you want the program at startup to always match the time of day with your computer's clock, select Use System Time. If, on the other hand, you always like to fly at night and you want the situation time you have saved on disk to override the system clock, choose Use Situation Time.

Figure 3.4
Time at Startup

Sound at Startup

There are three options for enabling sound at startup:
- On (sound always on)
- Off (sound always off)
- See Situation File (sound on or off depending on what you had saved in the situation file)

Figure 3.5
Sound at Startup

Dynamic Scenery at Startup

The Dynamic Scenery at Startup check box tog-gle switches the dynamic scenery on or off at startup. Dynamic scenery consists of all moving objects like other airplanes, airport traffic, ground traffic, boats, hot air balloons, etc.

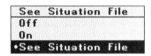

Figure 3.6
Scenery at Startup

Weather Generation at Startup

Toggling on Weather Generation at Startup enables the automatic weather generator to function. Toggling it off eliminates any random weather fluctuations.

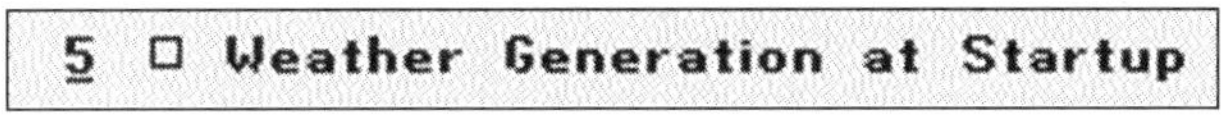

5 ☐ Weather Generation at Startup

Figure 3.7
Weather Generation at Startup

Log Flight Time

The Log Flight Time check box allows you to decide whether or not to keep track of all your flights in a special pilot's log. If toggled on at the end of every flight, a pilot's log will be displayed so you can record the number of hours flown at night or day. Under IFR rules you'll also need to record the date and the aircraft flown. Even if you toggle this feature off at startup, you can always turn it on manually from inside the program.

Figure 3.8
Log Flight Time

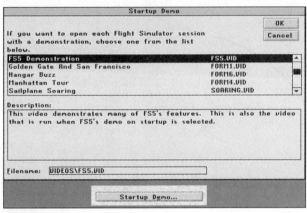

Figure 3.9
Startup Demo

Startup Demo

Press the Startup Demo button to select the startup demo *Flight Simulator* will show. You can record your own demo and then use this command to run it, instead of using the default FS 5.1 demo.

Startup Situation

The Startup Situation button allows you to select the default startup situation. Use this button to bring up a favorite situation you have previously created and saved as your default startup situation.

Figure 3.10
Startup Situation

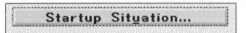

Situation Options

The Situation Options button brings up a dialog box with many different situation options you can save each time you start up a situation. You can save instrument panel and view window positions, aircraft, scenery, dynamic scenery, and the weather. You can also choose whether you want to load specific aircraft, scenery, keyboard sensitivities, mouse sensitivities, and joystick sensitivities.

Figure 3.11
Situation Options

Display Preferences

The Display Preferences dialog box presents you with many options that affect your display. This dialog box enables you to choose a performance mode, a different VGA or SVGA graphics driver, and set various options to make the scenery more interesting. You can also choose to degrade your image quality and increase your flicker rate in order to increase the frame rate for a smoother, less choppy image. Figure 3.12 illustrates the Display Preferences dialog box.

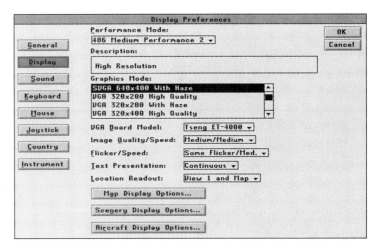

Figure 3.12
The Display
Preferences dialog box

Performance Mode

The Performance Mode simplifies the task of matching your computer's capabilities with the software's. In this list box, you choose the performance level best suited for your PC. The scenery options are then all automatically set up to maximize your PC's performance (except for VGA/SVGA card selection, and SVGA 640 x 400 display resolution selection). If you have a 486, you would choose 486 High Performance 1 or 2, or 486 Medium Performance 1 or 2. If you have a Pentium, select Pentium High Performance 1 or 2. In addition, there are six other performance options for 386-based PCs. For each performance mode, the High Performance mode uses a lower display resolution than Medium. The distinction between modes 1 and 2 for High and Medium is that mode 2 uses more scenery effects and increases the workload on your computer; however you get a nicer cockpit view. The tradeoff, as always, is frame rate speed and scenery complexity; the higher the frame rate, the more scenery options are turned off. Likewise, the higher the display resolution, the lower the frame rate.

When the setup for FS 5.1 was installed, it automatically determined the best performance mode for your computer. You don't need to change any of the other display settings (except VGA/SVGA Board Model, and SVGA 640 x 400 Graphics Mode) unless you want to customize the program's performance.

Table 3.1   Performance Modes for 486 and Pentium PCs

Performance Modes for 486 and Pentium PCs				
Performance Mode	Display Resolution Driver (with or without Haze)	Image Quality/ Speed	Flicker/Speed	Scenery Options
486 Max Performance	320 x 200 VGA	Low/Fast	Much Flicker/Fast	Very Sparse Scenery Density: uses simple polygon FS 4.0 type scenery, textured buildings off, textured aircraft off, shadows off, textured water off
486 Very High Performance	320 x 400 VGA	Medium/ Medium	Some Flicker/Medium	Very Sparse Scenery Density: uses simple polygon FS 4.0 type scenery, textured buildings off, aircraft textures off, shadows off, textured water off
486 High Performance 1	320 x 200 VGA	Low/Fast	Much Flicker/Fast	Very Sparse Scenery Density: textured buildings off, shadows off, textured water off
486 High Performance 2	320 x 200 VGA	Medium/ Medium	Much Flicker/Fast	Very Sparse Scenery Density: textured buildings off, shadows off, textured water off
486 Medium Performance 1	640 x 480 VGA 320 x 400 VGA	Medium/ Medium	Some Flicker/Medium	Very Sparse Scenery Density: ground shadows off, textured buildings off, textured sky off, textured water off, aircraft textures off
486 Medium Performance 2	320 x 400 VGA	Medium/ Medium	Some Flicker/Medium	Normal Scenery Density: ground shadow off, textured water on, textured aircraft on
Pentium High Performance 1	320 x 400 VGA	Medium/ Medium	Some Flicker/Medium	Dense Scenery: textured water on, textured aircraft off, ground shadows off
Pentium High Performance 2	640 x 480 VGA 320 x 400 VGA	Medium/ Medium	Some Flicker/Medium	Dense Scenery: textured water on, textured aircraft on

Graphics Mode

With the Graphics Mode list box, you can choose what display resolution *Flight Simulator* will use. The haze drivers are needed if you want to use the new visibility feature in FS 5.1. Note that if you select the Pentium High Performance 2 or the 486 Medium Performance 2 mode, you will still need to select the 640 x 400 SVGA mode with or without haze. This is because FS 5.1 defaults to the 320 x 400 VGA display resolution for these modes unless you have previously specified a SVGA graphics card under the VGA Board Model list box.

VGA Board

You should already have installed the correct VGA/SVGA display driver for *Flight Simulator*. If you want to change drivers, call up the VGA Board Maker list box to summon a list of the graphic accelerator chips and boards that are supported. If you don't know what board you have, try selecting VESA 1.2 compatible, since many board makers try to conform to this standard.

   To maximize your performance, always make sure you are using the correct video card driver for your particular computer. You can see the available options in Figure 3.13.

Image Quality/Speed

There is always a trade-off between image quality and speed. Lower quality images come with a faster display, medium quality images with a medium fast display, and high quality images with a slow display. Ordinarily, you don't need to change the settings in this list box because they are automatically set by the Performance Mode you selected for your PC.

Flicker/Speed

Flicker rate determines the rate at which multiple windows are repainted. If there is no flicker, each open 3-D scenery window gets repainted more often (the lower the flicker rate, the more frequent the view windows are refreshed; the higher the flicker rate, the less frequent the view windows are refreshed). The trade-off is, a low or nonexistent flicker rate decreases the speed scenery can be drawn (there are more frames per second to complete because of the low flicker rate). In essence, like image quality/speed, you make a call as to which trade-off you prefer. Ordinarily, you don't need to change the flicker rate because the changes are automatically set to the appropriate level for the Performance Mode you selected for your PC.

Figure 3.13
The VGA Board Model Choices

Text Presentation

The Text Presentation list box allows you to choose between having air traffic control messages scrolled across your screen horizontally in a continuous stream, or to have your messages displayed a single line at a time.

Location Readout

Your geographical coordinates can be displayed at the top of the screen using one of the following configurations:

- View 1 window (displayed only in the 3-D View 1 window)
- View 1 and Map (displayed in both 3-D View 1 and Map windows)
- Map (displayed only in the 3-D Map window)

To toggle on your on latitude/longitude screen coordinates, press Shift + Z twice.

Other Special Display Options

At the bottom of the Display Preferences dialog box, you can see three buttons which allow you to further customize your display options. The Map Display button allows you to change the way your on-screen map is displayed, the Scenery Display Options button lets you turn special scenery effects either on or off, and the Aircraft Display Options button lets you modify the appearance of your aircraft. Ordinarily, you don't need to make changes to these features, because they are automatically configured when you choose the Performance Mode for your PC.

Map Display Options

Your on screen map can be displayed in three forms:

- North Oriented where the map does not rotate and north is always facing toward the top of the display,
- North at High Altitude which is like North Oriented, except the aircraft is zoomed out to a high altitude so more landscape is covered, or
- Aircraft Oriented where the map rotates and the aircraft, which is represented by the center cross hair, is always pointed toward the top of the display.

Also in the Map Display Options dialog box, you can switch on ground textures in the map view. This allows you to see ground scenery in greater detail, which is helpful when you are trying to find runways at a distance.

Scenery Display Options

With a Pentium 120 or faster, you can take advantage of all the scenery display options as shown in Figure 3.14. You can choose ground scenery shadows, textured ground, textured buildings, sky texture for gradient hues that change for the time of day, wispy cloud and cloud thickness effects, gradient horizons, smooth transitions when panning or switching different views, and textured water.

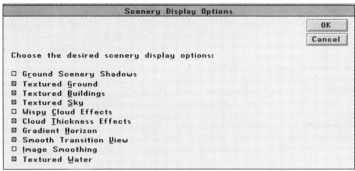

Figure 3.14
Scenery Display Options

Aircraft Display Options

The Aircraft Display Options dialog box, pictured in Figure 3.15, lets you modify the appearance of your aircraft.

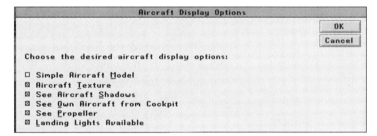

Figure 3.15
Aircraft Display Options

Sound Preferences

Although you don't need a sound card to play *Flight Simulator* (you can use the PC's built in speaker with less than desirable results), for best sound fidelity you should consider using a sound card. The Sound Preferences dialog box, shown in Figure 3.16, allows you to choose which sound card driver you want to use, the driver's hardware settings, and what kinds of sounds you want played back. There are three check boxes for Engine Sounds, Cockpit Sounds, and Navigation Sounds.

If you are easily tired by monotonous sounds, you might want to toggle off the Engine Sounds control, or you might consider sliding the Volume control to a lower setting. To move the Volume slide, click and drag it with the mouse, or with the keyboard press V, then the right cursor key to increase, or the left cursor key to decrease. You cannot, however, set the volume on your PC's built in speaker. On some cards, the Volume slide will be dimmed out, telling you the sound card's volume cannot be adjusted while in *Flight Simulator*. All is not lost in such a situation, though, because most cards have a dial on the back of the card which allows you to manually set the volume.

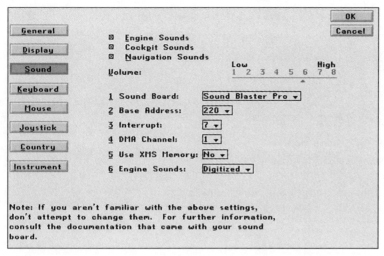

Figure 3.16
Sound Preferences
dialog box

Figure 3.17 Sound
Boards Supported
Under the Sound
Board List Box

```
Sound Blaster Pro/16/AWE 32
No Sound Device
PC Speaker
AdLib/PC Speaker
AdLib/Covox LPT1
AdLib/Covox LPT2
Sound Blaster Universal
•Sound Blaster Pro/16/AWE 32
Microsoft Windows S S
Thunderboard
Media Vision-Pro Audio Spectrum
```

The Cockpit Sounds check box, when switched on, allows you to hear warning horns when your aircraft is about to stall. It also enables crash sound effects, and beeps to alert you to messages from your friend while in dual-player flight.

The Navigation Sounds check box, when switched on, allows you to hear the marker beacons while using the ILS landing system.

In the event of problems with your sound card, more likely than not, it is because your hardware defaults are incorrectly set. You may have to reset the Base Address, Interrupt, or DMA Channel list box settings to match the configuration of your card. There is nothing to fear about doing this. Just check your documentation and setup on your PC to see if you can figure out what the correct settings are.

Note that the Adlib card does not support digitized sounds, so most sounds are shunted through the PC's tiny speaker.

If you have a sound card, the program can use XMS memory (extended memory above your conventional 640K) to temporarily store effects. To allow XMS memory to be used for sound, select Yes from the Use XMS Memory button.

The Engine Sounds list box is best set to Digitized for more authentic sounding noises. The Synthesized option sounds much worse because it uses frequency modulated (FM) synthesized tones to approximate the engine sounds. Digitized sounds more realistic because it uses real wave forms.

Keyboard Preferences

The three slider preference controls in the Keyboard Preferences dialog box, pictured in Figure 3.18, allow you to set the sensitivity for the keyboard yoke controls. The higher the sensitivity is set, the faster the controls react to your touch. Remember this comes at the expense of making your aircraft harder to control. Too low a sensitivity, on the other hand, tends to make the keyboard controls too sluggish and unresponsive.

To save your favorite sensitivity setting, toggle on the Load Sensitivities

Saved with Situation check box. But first make sure you save the sensitivity setting in a situation, by saving a situation *after* you have enabled the check box.

Mouse Preferences

There are four slider preference controls in the Mouse Preferences dialog box, illustrated in Figure 3.19. These allow you to set the sensitivity for the mouse yoke. Only the yoke controls for the ailerons and elevators are listed because the mouse is usually flown in auto-coordinated mode, and the rudder is automatically turned when you move the ailerons. In un-coordinated flight, the mouse would only control the ailerons and elevators, and you would use the keyboard to move the rudder. In such a situation, the sensitivity level for the rudder would be set in the Keyboard Preferences dialog box.

By adjusting the Yoke Null Zone width, you can find a comfortable zone where you can move your mouse slightly without causing the plane to bank, climb, or descend. The null zone refers to that portion of the center of the mouse where the ailerons remain centered. A wider null zone gives your mouse a looser feel, while a narrower zone gives your mouse a tighter feel. Too narrow a zone can be annoying since every mouse jitter can cause the plane to start turning. Click the Load Sensitivities Saved with Situation check box if you want to load your previously saved settings so you don't have to constantly reset them each time you start up the situation.

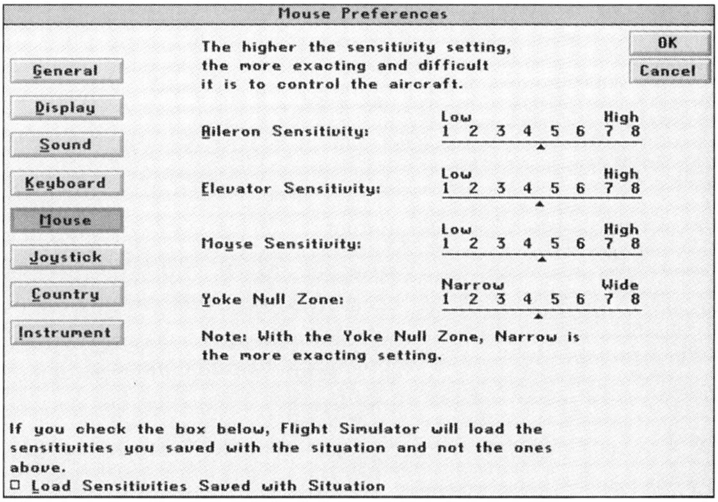

Joystick Preferences

If you have a joystick plugged into the game port of your PC, you need to configure and calibrate it

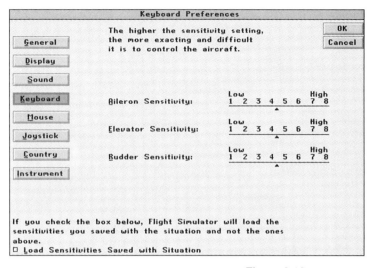

Figure 3.18
Keyboard Preference dialog box

Figure 3.19
Mouse Preferences dialog box

before you can fly *Flight Simulator.* Some people prefer to use two joysticks in combination, one to control the ailerons/rudder and elevators, the second to control the throttle and brakes (or when using pedals as your second joystick, you can set the second joystick to control the rudder). But for now let's assume that you are using a single joystick. Since FS 5.1 has no way of knowing beforehand where your joystick is centered, you will need to instruct the program as to its initial settings via a process known as calibration. If you didn't do this, your joystick might send the wrong signal to the program as to its true position, and you would have to fly a plane that chronically turns, climbs, or dives, even though your stick is apparently centered.

To set and calibrate your joystick, press K.

The sensitivity setting controls how much joystick movement will affect the aircraft. If you notice too much movement of the controls, you can come back and decrease the sensitivity. If you don't get enough movement of the controls, you can increase the sensitivity. The null zone refers to that portion of the center of the joystick where the ailerons are centered. By adjusting the null zone sensitivity, you can find a comfortable zone where you can move your joystick slightly without causing the plane to bank, climb, or descend. A wider null zone gives your joystick a looser feel, while a narrower zone gives your joystick a tighter feel. Too narrow a zone can be annoying because every joystick jitter can cause the plane to start turning. Click the Load Sensitivities Saved with Situation check box if you want to load these settings so you don't have to constantly reset them each time you start up the situation.

Country Preferences

Because *Flight Simulator* has now developed a huge international following, BAO/Microsoft decided to include worldwide support in the form of metric units of measurement and a spherical latitude/longitude coordinate system. In the Country Preferences dialog box, as shown in Figure 3.20, you can select the units of measurement you prefer from the following:

- U.S. System: Distances measured in miles, altitude in feet, weight in pounds.
- Metric (Alt feet): Altimeter is measured in feet. Distances and speed are measured in Systeme Internationale (SI) or mks units (mks-meters, kilograms, seconds) SI units represent the worldwide agreement on the adaptation of the metric system for standard measurements of time, mass, and length.
- Metric (Alt meters): Altimeter is measured in meters. Distances and speed are measured in SI or mks units.

Latitude is measured from 0° to 90° from the equator to the poles in both the northern and southern hemispheres of the Earth. Longitude is measured from 0° to 180° from the prime meridian in England in both the western and eastern hemispheres. Knowing your latitude and longitude is not enough to locate you if you don't specify the hemisphere you are in. For example, if you say that you are at 30° latitude, 90° longitude, another person trying to locate you would not know if you are at 30° degrees south of the equator, or 30° latitude north of the equator. To prevent confusion as to your correct latitude, or longitude, in *Flight Simulator* you must specify the proper hemisphere in the Country Preferences dialog box.

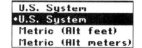

Figure 3.20
Units of measure

For example, to fly in the northern and eastern hemispheres, select the Northern option from the Latitude list box and the Western option from the Longitude box. Once you have specified these, whenever you type in coordinates using the World/Set Exact Location menu command, you don't need to prefix latitudes with an "N" nor do you need to prefix longitudes with a "W."

Instrument Preferences

Through the Instrument Preferences dialog box, illustrated in Figure 3.21, you can change your instrument gauges update rate to make them more realistic, make your panel display more legible, display indicated airspeed instead of true airspeed, and modify the number of frequencies your radios can receive.

Maximizing the gauge update rate causes your instruments to display changes in your airplane's attitude, speed, or position more quickly. But it will slow down the scenery display. You can choose between High, Medium, and Low update rates.

The numbered readings on the dials and gauges of the photo realistic instrument panel are not easily readable because of their small size. If you have trouble seeing these instruments, you can select Enhanced Readability from the Panel Display list box, and the photo realistic panel will be replaced by a new panel with more legible numbers. It's not as pretty, but it is easier to make out the dial markings.

If you are interested in super-realism, then you should toggle on the Display Indicated Airspeed check box. Your airspeed indicator will then show indicated airspeed instead of true airspeed. Indicated airspeed is the value read on the airspeed indicator, without regard to altitude or outside air density. True airspeed is the speed of an aircraft in undisturbed air. True airspeed has been corrected for air-density variations from the standard value at mean sea level (MSL). In the imaginary world of *Flight Simulator*, your airspeed indicator tells you the true airspeed at which you are traveling, despite the fact that your airspeed indicator can only give you accurate readings at

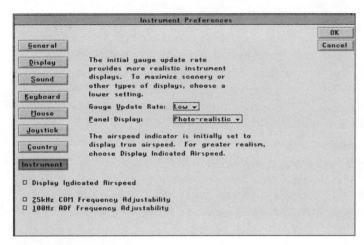

Figure 3.21
Instrument Preferences
dialog box

sea level. In the real world, however, the higher you go, the more air density drops. The reduced air pressure readings cause the pitot-static pressure system, from which the airspeed indicator derives its speed measurements, to show indicated airspeed (IAS).

The correction factor for true airspeed when flying at higher altitudes can be summarized by the following rule:

Add two percent to your indicated airspeed per thousand feet of altitude gained.

If you are showing an indicated airspeed of 100 knots at mean sea level (MSL), your true airspeed would also be 100 knots. But if you were at 5,000 feet, your true airspeed would be 110 knots (i.e. 5 x 2 percent = 10 percent, add 10 percent to 100 knots = 110 knots).

Additionally, in the Instrument Preferences dialog box, you can increase the number of radio channels to 725 by choosing to have a narrower 25 KHz COM Radio frequency channel separation. (For the same bandwidth, the narrower the channel width the more channels can be squeezed in the band). You can also modify the tuning parameters of the ADF Radio so it too has a narrower 500 Hz channel separation.

SOUND ON/OFF

Under the Sim menu, you can toggle all sound on or off by selecting the Sound command. Pressing Q accomplishes the same task. If you prefer, you can selectively turn off engine sounds, cockpit sounds, and navigation sounds in the Sound Preferences dialog box under the Options menu.

PAUSE

To completely pause the simulation, select the Pause command under the Sim menu. When you do this, you will see the word "pause" displayed on screen. During this time all simulation events are frozen. However, you can still access all the menus and controls you normally would be able to access while flying. You can also activate the pause function by pressing P. To resume play, press P again.

CRASH DETECTION

By disabling Crash Detection, you can practice flying your plane without fear of crashing. In this
mode, accidents or collisions are ignored. You can
open the Crash Detection dialog box by choosing
the Sim/Crash Detection menu option. There are
various other crash options which are self explana-
tory, as is illustrated in Figure 3.22.

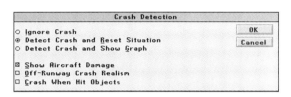

Figure 3.22
The Crash Detection
dialog box

SIMULATION SPEED

You can also affect the speed at which
Flight Simulator runs through the Simulation Speed command. This command
can be activated by selecting the Simulation Speed option from the Sim menu,
then choosing a rate from the Simulation Rate list box, shown in Figures
3.23 and 3.24.

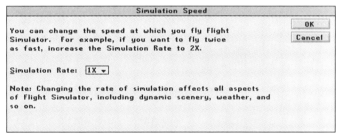

Figure 3.23
The Simulation
Speed dialog box

The simulation can be slowed to as much as ¼ times normal speed, or
increased to as much as 128 times normal speed. This is useful for long
cross-country or cross-oceanic trips where you want to speed up the simulation so you can quickly skip over the monotonous portions of the flight.

Normal simulator speed is 1x. Choosing a higher speed will change the
speed of your aircraft and increase the activity of the world around you.
Clouds and weather will whip by, and every motion you make using the
yoke controls becomes amplified. At high simulator speeds it is very easy to
slam into the ground in a fraction of a second, so exercise caution when
using this feature.

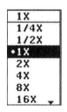

Figure 3.24
The Simulation
Rate list box

When using the autopilot you are limited to a maximum of four times
normal simulator speed. With the autopilot at four times normal speed, you
may notice a rocking of your wings, and other flight instability problems. If
left unattended, these problems can cause your airplane to crash. To regain
control, switch off your autopilot, and reduce simulator speed.

Learjet and Cessna Simulation Speed
Can Be Set On Screen or Via Keyboard

On both the Learjet and Cessna, you can adjust the simulation speed by
clicking on the Rate indicator just below the digital clock. To increase the

rate, click to the right of the number; to decrease the rate, click to the left of the number.

Unfortunately, the Sailplane & Sopwith Camel simulation speed must be set from the menu because there is no simulation rate control/indicator on their respective instrument panels. From the keyboard, you can press [R] followed by [+] on the main keyboard to increase speed, or [R] followed by [-] decrease simulator speed. The keyboard shortcut also works with the Learjet and Cessna.

SMOKE SYSTEM

To create puffs of smoke from the tail of the aircraft, press [I] or select the Smoke System option from the Sim menu. These smoke streams are visible from all views and help you track your plane's movement.

REALISM AND RELIABILITY

To create a more realistic flight, you can choose to have certain aircraft systems behave more as they would in the real world. You can also increase the degree of difficulty from easy to realistic and the aircraft reliability from unreliable to reliable using a sliding pointer. The more realistic a setting you choose for the flight controls, the harder it is to fly your plane. The more unreliable your aircraft, the greater the probability is that instruments and aircraft systems will catastrophically fail during flight.

Figure 3.25
Realism and Reliability
dialog box

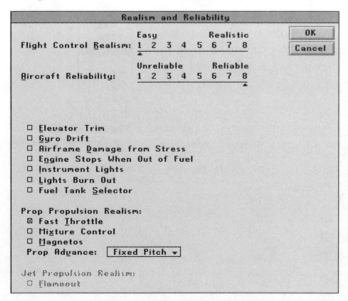

To choose a setting, open the Realism and Reliability dialogue box, then set the slide pointer. Using the mouse, click and drag the triangular shaped pointer to the difficulty level you want. From the keyboard, select the slider so the scale indicator turns red. Then either press the setting number from the main keyboard, or slide it by pressing the [←] or [→]. Figure 3.25 shows the Realism and Reliability dialog box.

Other realism options you can change are:

- **Elevator Trim:** The elevator trim is a small control surface on the elevators that relieves the pilot of continually applying pressure on the yoke. With this feature turned off, the program automatically trims the elevators when you are flying with the keyboard or mouse, but not when flying with spring back joysticks (the spring causes the joystick to return to the null zone, which should be where the controls are centered at the neutral position). Enabling this feature will cause the elevators to drift (the airflow over the elevators moves the elevators back to their centered position), and you will have to constantly compensate using the elevator trim control or applying more yoke pressure to correct the drift.

- **Gyro Drift:** With gyro drift enabled friction and gyroscope precession errors will cause your heading indicator/directional gyro to drift from the correct course heading. You will need to recalibrate the gyro by pressing D.

- **Airframe Damage from Stress:** Choosing this option will make your aircraft more sensitive to hard landings or aerobatic maneuvers with high gravity (G) forces. When the aircraft exceeds the manufacturer's performance specifications, the plane will suffer airframe damage that could cause a fatal crash.

- **Engine Stops When Out of Fuel:** With this option toggled on, you must pay attention to your fuel tank gauges. Otherwise, you may find yourself hitching a ride back to town.

- **Instrument Lights:** If you select this option, you must manually switch on your instrument lights at dusk in order to see your instrument panel. To turn on your instrument lights, press L.

- **Lights Burn Out:** Lights may randomly burn out on your instrument panel, thereby obscuring vital data from your view. Leaving your lights on during the day increases the probability of failure.

- **Fuel Tank Selector:** With this option enabled you must manually switch fuel tanks when they become empty. To display remaining fuel levels in multiple fuel tanks (including auxiliary tanks) bring up the Engine and Fuel dialog box

- **Prop Propulsion Realism:** This realism option is only available for the Cessna, although it may be available for other future propeller aircraft that will be with BAO's Flight Shop. You have two options:

  1. **Fast Throttle:** Increasing the throttle too fast can cause the engine to quit suddenly.

Figure 3.26
Prop Advance list box

Figure 3.27
The prop pitch and
throttle controls for the
Cessna

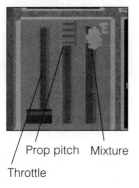

Prop pitch   Mixture

Throttle

2. **Prop Advance:** The Prop Advance list box controls how your propeller's pitch is governed by the simulation under different conditions. The basic idea is that there is a speed governor trying to keep your propeller spinning at a constant speed under varying speed and altitude conditions. There are three options under the Prop Advance list box:

- **Fixed Pitch:** The propeller's pitch is fixed. You cannot alter the prop pitch control.

- **Automatic:** The default setting is Automatic. FS 5.1 adjusts the prop pitch for you automatically as you set the throttle, thereby allowing you to maintain a constant RPM for different altitudes. This setting is the easiest to use, but not very realistic.

- **Manual:** With this option, you can manually override the speed governor, and advance or decrease the prop pitch control independently of the throttle. This option is for advanced users who understand the relationship between prop pitch, RPM, airspeed, and power settings for different altitudes. This setting is the most realistic of all choices.

3. **Jet Propulsion Realism:** Only available for the Learjet or other future jet aircraft. You have only one option:

4. **Flameout:** Jet aircrafts can lose engine thrust when combustion inside the engine falters. For example, volcanic ash deposited into the upper atmosphere can clog the jet engine's intake ports causing a catastrophic engine failure. Enabling this option will allow jet flameout failures to occur. When this happens, you must attempt to restart your engines by using the Starter Engine control to re-light your burners and spool up the compressor turbine blades.

CHOOSING YOUR AIRCRAFT

To select a different aircraft to fly:

1. Open the Options menu and select Aircraft.

2. In the Aircraft Selection dialog box, click on the name of the aircraft you wish to fly. In the description text box, you will see some text describing the type of plane you have chosen. In the Display window, you will see an image of the selected plane rotating in three dimensions, as is illustrated in Figure 3.28.

3. Click OK to return to the simulation.

You can also call up the performance specifications for any aircraft by doing the following:

1. Select the aircraft's name.
2. Click on the Performance Specs... button (Figure 3.28).
3. Click OK to return to the Aircraft Selection dialog box, and OK again to return to the simulation.

SELECTING YOUR SITUATION

Situations are files where ready-made scenarios are stored. You can create your own situations or use pre-existing situations. All your settings including plane type, yoke position settings, speed, altitude, location, weather, time of day, and season are stored in the situation file. In addition you can also save the instrument panel and view windows position and size on the screen, save any scenery density levels, along with keyboard, mouse and joystick sensitivity levels.

To Open a Situation

To open a situation:

1. Under the Options menu, select Situations.
2. In the list of situations that are displayed in the Situations dialog box, pictured in Figure 3.30, select the situation you want to load.
3. Click OK.

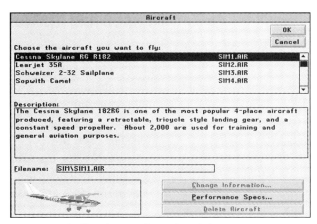

Figure 3.28 The Aircraft Selection dialog box

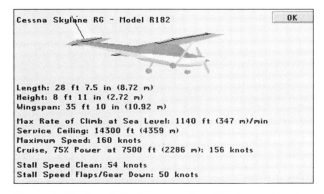

Figure 3.29 Aircraft Performance Specifications dialog box

Figure 3.30 Situations dialog box

TO SAVE A SITUATION

To save a situation:

1. Press the ⟨;⟩ key, or select Save Situation from the Options menu.

2. In the dialog box that follows, type in a descriptive title name of up to 30 characters and then press Enter.

3. The first eight characters of your title will then be displayed in the Filename text box as the proposed DOS file name for the situation. If this is OK, click the OK button, otherwise select the text box and give the situation a new file name of up to 30 characters (do not add a file extension, and you must use only characters that DOS will recognize for filenames). Figure 3.31 shows the Save Situation dialog box.

4. In the Description text box, type in any comments that will help you describe what the situation does.

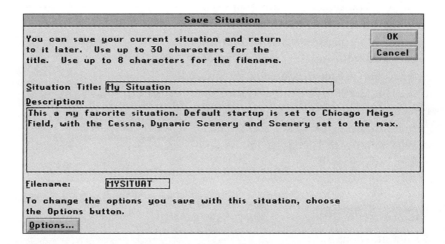

Figure 3.31
Save Situation dialog box

Changing the Options Stored in a Situation

To change the types of options stored with your situation:

1. In the Save Situations dialog box, shown in Figure 3.31, click the Options button. Select from the following list of options:

   • **Instrument Panel and View Windows Positions:** This saves the size and location of all instrument panels, 3-D view windows and maps. Next time the situation is opened, all windows will open to their last saved position.

   • **Aircraft:** The aircraft type is saved so when the situation is restarted, it will default to the last saved aircraft used in the situation.

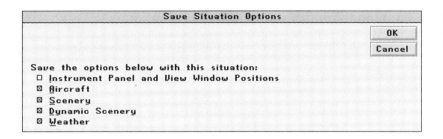

Figure 3.32
Situation Options
dialog box

- **Scenery:** The scenery density and scenery file(s) used are saved so when the situation is restarted, the scenery will look the same as when you last saved the situation.
- **Dynamic Scenery:** The dynamic scenery that is currently active, along with the dynamic scenery density, is saved in the situation file. Upon restarting the situation, the dynamic scenery is restored to the state it was last left in when the situation file was saved.
- **Weather:** Weather data is saved in the situation file. When the situation is restarted, you will experience the same weather that occurred when the situation was last saved.

To Delete a Situation

To delete a situation:

1. Open the Options menu and select Situations.
2. In the Situations dialog box, select the name of the situation you wish to delete.
3. Click the Delete Situation button. The situation will then be erased from your hard drive.

Resetting a Situation

To restart a situation from its initial conditions:

1. Press Ctrl + Print Screen, or select Reset Situation from the Options menu.
2. The simulator will reset itself to the beginning conditions of the currently active situation.

To store keyboard, mouse, and joystick sensitivities in a situation, you must first toggle on these check box items in the Situation Options dialog box, found under the Situations Option button in the General Preferences dialog box. Any changes made in this dialog box will affect all your situations, but any changes made in the Situation Options dialog box found under the Save Situation menu command, with the Options button, will affect only the current situation.

Changing the Information About a Situation

To change the description, filename, or title of a situation:

1. Choose Situations from the Options menu.
2. Select the situation you want to change.
3. Click the Change Information button.
4. Change any listed information.
5. Click OK to return to the Situations dialog box. Click OK to return to the simulator.

If you want to make a copy of a favorite situation and then modify it slightly without changing the original setup, give the situation a new filename, description, and title by using the Change Information option in the Situations dialog box.

Selecting a Startup Situation

To have *Flight Simulator* always load a particular situation upon startup:

1. Open the Options menu and select the Preferences menu item.
2. In the Preferences dialog box, click the Startup Situation button. The Startup dialog box will open, as pictured in Figure 3.33.
3. Select the startup situation.
4. Click OK to return to the Preferences dialog box.
5. Click OK to return to the simulator.

The next time the simulator starts up, it will load the situation you specified in the Startup Situations dialog box.

Selecting Situation Save/Load Options for All Situations

You can have various situation options be saved or loaded for all your situations by customizing the Situation Options dialog box, activated by clicking

Figure 3.33
The Startup Situation
dialog box

on the Situation Options button in the General Preferences dialog box. Do not confuse this dialog box with the Situation Options dialog box activated under the Save Situation command. When you toggle on the options in this dialog box, pictured in Figure 3.34, they apply to all situations.

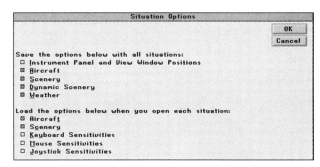

Figure 3.34
The Situation Options for the General Preferences dialog box

Reset All Joystick Controls, Including Trim Controls Before Resetting Situation

Remember to center all your joystick(s) and trim controls before resetting a situation. Otherwise, you must recalibrate them under Joystick Preferences (or by pressing K) when the situation restarts.

QUICK PRACTICE AND FLIGHT INSTRUCTION

As a learning aid, FS 5.1 includes a computer aided tutorial on flying. The Quick Practice feature, found under the Options/Entertainment menu, and illustrated in Figure 3.35, chooses four of the basic lessons (found under Flight Instruction) for a quick overview of taking off and landing.

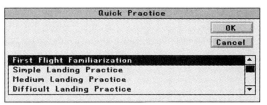

Figure 3.35
Quick Practice

The Flight Instruction command, located under the Options/Entertainment menu, offers a more comprehensive tutorial package. There are three lesson categories: Basic, Advanced, and Aerobatic. Each category has seven to 10 individual lessons that emphasize a particular flight maneuver. Figure 3.36 shows the lessons available for the Basic lesson category. If you prefer to watch a particular lesson before trying it yourself, have the flight instructor take command of the plane by toggling on Instructor Control. You can restart the lesson and take charge of the plane, while in Instructor Control, by pressing the Esc key. Otherwise, if you want to fly the lesson yourself select Student Control. The lessons can be executed in strict sequence if you click on the Lessons in Sequence button. To exit the lessons click the End Lesson button.

During Instructor Control mode, the instructor flies the plane and makes comments and suggestions in the message box. After the instructor finishes with the demonstration lesson, control is switched back to the student mode so you can try out what you've just learned. Later, you will get feedback on your performance.

While in Instructor Control mode during flight instruction, you can return control of the aircraft to yourself by pressing the Tab key.

Figure 3.36
Basic Lessons
Available under
Flight Instruction

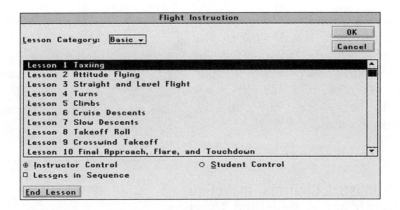

USING THE LAND ME COMMAND
TO AUTOLAND YOUR PLANE

The most difficult task in *Flight Simulator* is to land your airplane safely in one piece. Because most people cannot easily do this, FS 5.1 includes an autolanding autopilot for the default scenery areas. Land Me is activated by pressing X on the keyboard, or by selecting Land Me from the Options menu. When you do this, an instructor takes over control of the plane and tells you what actions he is performing in a message box on screen. By following along, and watching the controls, you can actually learn a great deal about how to properly land the airplane. You can disengage Land Me at any time by pressing X once again, or by selecting Land Me from the Options menu.

SETTING THE TIME AND SEASON

To set the time in *Flight Simulator*, you can adjust the digital clock on screen or call up the Set Time and Season dialog box using the Set Time and Season command from the World menu. Using the dialog box options, you can set the season, date, and enter the time of day you wish to fly, whether it be local time or Greenwich Mean Time (GMT). In addition, there is a Set Time of Day feature which allows you quickly jump right into a sunset or night flight without having to fiddle with the clock.

Upon booting up *Flight Simulator*, flight conditions are set to correspond to the exact time, day, and month that your computer's clock is currently showing. However, you can decide not to use your system clock. The startup preference for whether to use your system's time or situation time is found under General Preferences from the Options menu. If you do choose to base the simulator's clock on your system time, transition times for dawn, day, dusk, and night will be altered according to the latitude and longitude of your airplane and the Earth's inclination toward the sun. This means that for higher latitudes, you may be forced to endure 24 hours of daylight, or 24 hours of perpetual darkness, depending on the season.

You will experience new difficulties when changing seasons: icy runways in winter or reduced lift in summer, for example. The scenery will change to reflect the season; if you fly through Vermont in autumn, you will see the fall foliage take on new colors.

To change the season:

1. Select Set Time and Season from the World menu.

2. Open the Set Season list box, and select one of the following options:
   • Winter
   • Spring
   • Summer
   • Autumn
3. Click the OK button to return to the simulator.

The season you have selected will now be in effect. The outside temperature will be adjusted to reflect the season; the exact time of transition for dawn, day, dusk, and night will be varied according to season.

To set the date you wish to fly:

1. Select the Set Time and Season command from the World menu.

2. Click the Set Exact Date radio button. The rest of the text entry boxes for the Set Date portion of the dialog box will become active.
3. Enter the day of the month, from 1 to 31 (note that FS 5.1 will not allow you to enter incorrect entries, such as 29 for a non-leap year February).
4. Enter the month, from 1 to 12.
5. Enter the year.
6. Click OK to return to the simulator.

To select the part of the day you wish to fly:

1. Select the Set Time and Season command from the World menu.

2. Click the Set Time of Day radio button.
3. Open the Time of Day list box and choose from among the following:
   • Dawn
   • Day
   • Dusk
   • Night

To set the exact time from the cockpit:

1. To move the clock forward, click the mouse pointer to the right side of the hours display on the digital clock. To move the clock back, click the mouse pointer to the left side of the hours display

2. To change the minutes, click the pointer on the right of the minutes indicator to increase minutes. Click the pointer on the left of the minutes indicator to decrease the minutes.

To set the exact time using the menu:

1. Select the Set Time and Season command from the World menu.

2. When the Set Time and Season dialog box opens, as shown in Figure 3.37, click the Set Exact Time radio button.

3. Enter the local hour of day in 24-hour format (must be from 0 to 23), or enter the Grenwich Mean Time (GMT) hour. Local hour is the local time based on the current location of your aircraft, while GMT time is based on Greenwich, England time. Notice that entering information in the Local Hour text box will affect the entry for GMT Hour, and vice versa. If you move your aircraft to a different time zone, the GMT hour difference between the local hour will change.

4. Enter the minutes (must be from 0 to 60), either in local minutes, or GMT minutes.

5. Click the Reset Seconds to Zero if you want to reset the seconds portion of the clock.

6. Click the OK button to return to the simulator.

Figure 3.37
The Set Time and Season dialog box

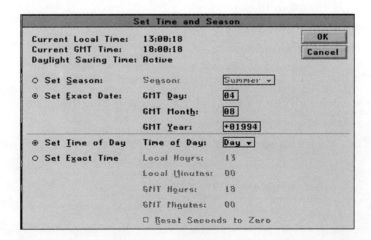

A CHANGE OF SCENERY

Using *Flight Simulator*'s Scenery Library command under the Scenery menu, you can run scenery from FS 4.0, FS 5.0, or FS 5.1. With the new Scenery Manager, power users of *Flight Simulator* can arrange the viewing priority of their existing scenery areas. Users can add new scenery areas, delete old scenery areas, and edit certain scenery options. Note that *Flight Simulator* automatically switches between scenery areas for any version 5.0 or 5.1 scenery you might have, including add-on scenery disks. To auto-switch between version 4.0 scenery areas, however, you must toggle on the Automatic Scenery Area Switching command in the Scenery Library dialog box.

    With the Scenery/Scenery Complexity menu command you can choose how much scenery is to be displayed. This function also allows you to make various other scenery modifications. The Scenery/Dynamic Scenery menu command allows you to reduce or increase the frequency with which moving scenery, such as other airplanes, boats, etc. appear in your field of view. Note that the Scenery Complexity and Dynamic Scenery settings have already been automatically set if you selected any performance mode, such as Pentium High Performance 2, or 486 Medium Performance 1.

> You don't need to use the Scenery/Scenery Library menu command to use add-on scenery you bought separately. Just install the scenery, and use the World/Airports command to select the add-on scenery area airports.

Adding New Scenery Add-ons

If you have purchased add-on scenery, first install the scenery from the CD-ROM or floppy disk, then start up FS 5.1. Once the scenery has been installed, you always use the World/Airport menu command to pick an airport in the add-on scenery area. You'll see the new add-on scenery area will have been added to the list of scenery areas found in the Airports dialog box. Therefore, you choose the name of the add-on scenery from the list box and then choose one of the airports that appears in the dialog box. Click the OK button and your aircraft will be placed at the airport in the add-on scenery area. The NAV radios will be pre-tuned to the local radio beacons. Remember, don't try installing commercial add-on scenery using the Scenery Library command.

Using the Scenery Manager to Search For and Add New Scenery

If you have scenery you didn't install via a setup program, then you must use the Scenery Manager to find it before you can use it. To open the Scenery Manager and search for a new scenery area:

1. Select the Scenery Library command from the Scenery menu. *Flight Simulator* will display a warning message stating that you shouldn't make

Figure 3.38
The Scenery Library
dialog box

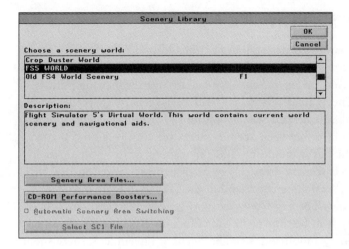

changes to the scenery unless you know what you are doing. Click OK to continue, and you'll see the Scenery Library dialog box, as shown in Figure 3.38.

2. In the Scenery Library dialog box, choose the type of scenery files you are looking for:[1]

   • Select FS5 World Scenery to use all FS 5.1 version scenery areas, including Japan and Caribbean scenery enhancements. Choosing this option makes all version 5 scenery areas available automatically, without having to individually select files.

   • Or select Old FS4 World Scenery for FS 4.0 type scenery.

3. If you want to auto-switch between version 4 scenery areas, be sure to toggle on the Automatic Scenery Area Switching check box. FS 5.1 automatically auto-switches all version 5.1 scenery areas.

4. Click the Scenery Area Files button. The Scenery Area Files dialog box will open, as shown in Figure 3.39.

5. Click the Scenery Area Search button. The Scenery Area Search dialog box will open, as shown in Figure 3.40.

6. Select the particular drive you wish to search from the pull down Drive to be Searched list, then click the Search Drive button. *Flight Simulator* will search your designated drive's directories until it finds the first scenery file with the file extension .BGL, and then it will display it in the dialog box.

---

[1] You can't edit or modify the Crop Duster World scenery type.

7. In the Scenery Area title box, type a title for the scenery area, such as Caribbean Scenery for the file CARIB10.BGL.

8. In the Scenery Area Type list box, select the scenery type according the following rules:

   • Global is the default scenery area for the world (outside regions and cities) and it includes all the generic scenery around the world. It has the highest layer level, and the lowest scenery priority.

   • Regional is the next layer, and includes the regional default scenery areas such as USA-Chicago. It has a lower layer level than Global, and a greater scenery priority than Global.

   • Local is the layer for scenery add-ons, such as Microsoft Caribbean, Microsoft Japan, BAO Las Vegas, etc. It has a lower layer level than Regional, and a greater scenery priority than Regional.

   • Scenery Builder Low and Scenery Builder High include the scenery areas you build. Scenery Builder Low has a lower layer level than Local, and a greater scenery priority than Local. Scenery Builder High has a lower layer level than Scenery Builder Low, and the highest scenery priority of all scenery types.

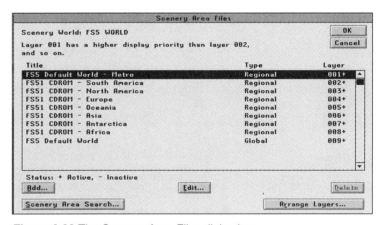

Figure 3.39 The Scenery Area Files dialog box

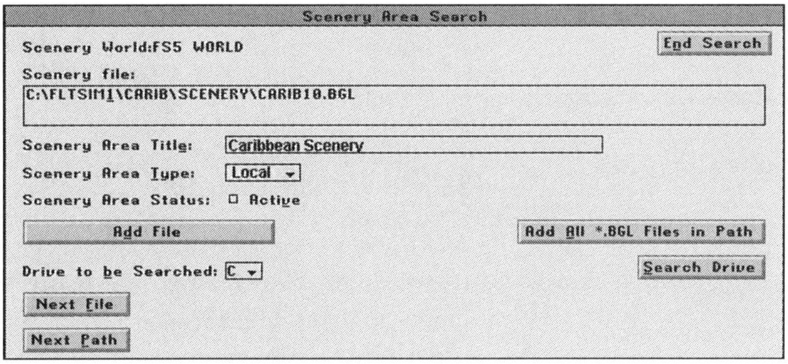

9. Click the Active check box for Scenery Active Status. If you don't do this, the scenery won't be active when you try to run it.

10. Click the Add File button to add the .BGL scenery file to your scenery file. Note: if you are adding a whole bunch of .BGL scenery files, as for example with Microsoft Japan, you need to add them one by one, or click the Add All *.BGL Files in Path button to load them all at once.

Figure 3.40 The Scenery Area Search dialog box

If you plan to modify the Japan or Caribbean add-on scenery areas, it's best to install each scenery add-on into a separate directory. Then, all files for a specific area will be easier to find. However, install New York and Paris add-on scenery directly into your Flight Simulator scenery directory.

You can't delete FS 5 world or crop duster world scenery.

11. To continue searching for other scenery files, click the Next File button to search for the next .BGL scenery file, or click the Next Path button to search the next directory path for scenery files on the same drive.

12. When you are finished, click the End Search button to return to the Scenery Area Files dialog box.

To add a new scenery area:

1. In the Scenery Library dialog box, click the Add button.

2. In the Add Scenery Area dialog box, type the path name and file names of the scenery files you want to add. For example, if you are adding all the files in the Japan scenery directory, you would type C:\japan\scenery*.bgl, then press the Enter key to continue.

3. In the Scenery Area title box, enter a title of up to 30 characters for the scenery.

4. Select the type of scenery from the Scenery Area Type list box. The types are defined in step eight of the previous section.

5. Give the scenery a priority layer number in the Scenery Area Layer box.

6. If you want to activate the scenery, click the Active check box.

7. Click OK to return to the Scenery Area Files dialog box.

To edit a scenery area:

1. In the Scenery Library dialog box, highlight the name of the scenery file you want to edit, then click the Edit button.

2. In the Edit Scenery Area dialog box you can change the path, title, type, layer, and status of the file.

3. Click the OK button to return to the Scenery Area Files dialog box.

To delete a scenery area:

1. In the Scenery Library dialog box highlight the name of the scenery file you want to edit, then click the Delete button.

2. Click the OK button to return to the Scenery Area Files dialog box.

Setting Scenery Priorities

Flight Simulator automatically arranges scenery in layers by scenery type. However you can change the scenery priority so a particular scenery area shows up over other areas.

To do this:

1. In the Scenery Library dialog box, click the Arrange Layers button. You'll see the Arrange Layers dialog box, as shown in Figure 3.41.

2. To have *Flight Simulator* auto-arrange the layers by scenery type, click the Auto Arrange button. However, if you want to manually arrange the layers, select a scenery area, then click the Raise Layer button to raise its priority, or the Lower Layer button to lower its priority. The layers are ranked in priority from one (the highest) down. A minus sign next to the scenery area means the scenery layer is not currently active and you won't be able to see it; a plus sign means it is active and will be visible.

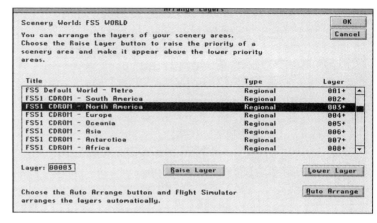

Figure 3.41 The Arrange Layers dialog box

3. Click the OK button to continue. The scenery areas will be re-arranged according to the layer priority you just specified. Note that the priorities for the scenery types are listed in step eight of the previous section.

Add-on CD-ROM Scenery Considerations

Older scenery add-ons, such as Microsoft New York, Microsoft San Francisco, and Microsoft Paris should be installed in the *Flight Simulator* scenery directory. If you installed FS 5.1 in the C:\FLTSIM5\ directory, you should install these older add-ons in the C:\FLTSIM5\SCENERY sub-directory. Running the setup program for each of these add-ons will install everything correctly, but you should ignore the message that states "Disabling Scenery not Found."

Also, before using Microsoft Japan, Microsoft Caribbean, and BAO Europe I scenery add-ons with FS 5.1 CD, you should copy the contents of the ADDONS directory on your CD-ROM to the SCENERY sub-directory on your hard drive for each add-on. From your CD-ROM, copy the contents of the ADDONS\JAPAN directory to the C:\FLTSIM5\JAPAN\SCENERY directory. Likewise, copy the contents of the ADDONS\CARIB\ directory to the C:\FLTSIM5\CARIB\SCENERY directory, and copy the contents of the ADDONS\EUROPE1\ directory to the C:\FLTSIM5\EUROPE1\SCENERY directory. There are some CD-ROM performance boosters and fixes that will make these scenery add-ons work better.

Each directory which contains add-on scenery area must have a SCENERY and TEXTURE sub-directory, containing the appropriate texture and .BGL scenery files.

> The lower the scenery layer number, the higher the priority it has for display.

You can install your CD-ROM scenery to run off your CD-ROM drive, instead of installing it on your hard disk. When you do this, however, you'll need to insert the CD-ROM containing the scenery before you use the World/Airports menu command to put your plane in the scenery area. Choosing the CD-ROM cache as your setup choice eases the hard disk space requirements, but it does increase the length of time to access scenery. Installing the scenery to hard disk is always faster than running it off your CD-ROM.

Note the performance boosters for the FS 5.1 CD monitor your aircraft's position and automatically load scenery from the CD-ROM drive to the cache directory on your hard disk. During setup, FS 5.1 automatically installs all of your CD-ROM performance boosters for the default scenery areas, and for add-on CD-ROM scenery. You can manually edit the way your performance boosters work by clicking on the Performance Boosters button in the Scenery Library, but be forewarned: this is not something most people are likely to want to do. Refer to the Microsoft manual for clinical details on this specialized surgery.

If you select Very Dense for the Image Complexity for Chicago, you will see over 60 buildings crowded into the downtown area!

The Wire Frame Polygons option affects only certain kinds of scenery and may or may not be visible, depending on what scenery you are using.

Adjusting Scenery Complexity

The scenery in FS 5.1 can be increased or decreased in display complexity by using the options found in the Scenery Complexity dialog box, pictured in Figure 3.42. Generally, the more complex the scenery, the slower your display frame rate will be. Each 3-D view window can have its scenery individually adjusted. This allows you to have one window display with a high degree of detail, while a second window might just show bare bones wire frame outlines.

To increase or decrease the number of buildings and other types of scenery:

1. Select Scenery Complexity from the Scenery menu.
2. Choose which 3-D View window you wish to apply the scenery modifications.
3. Open the Image Complexity list box and choose the level of complexity.
4. Click OK to return to the simulator.

To lower the graphics overhead on your PC, you can also switch off stars in the sky and runway approach lighting at airports. You can even display no scenery at all (Horizon Only). You can also display buildings and other objects as wire frame polygons. The Earth Pattern list box, which only works for FS 4.0 scenery, allows you to choose the texture pattern you want for the Earth's ground terrain.

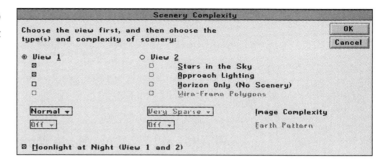

Figure 3.42
Scenery Complexity dialog box

Controlling the Density of Dynamic Scenery

Dynamic scenery refers to all scenery that moves, whether in the air, on the ground, or on the water. *Flight Simulator* has ground traffic, other aircraft, blimps, hot air balloons, and sailboats. You might want to reduce the density of dynamic scenery, however, if you have a slow 386, and you want to increase your display frame rate. If on the other hand, you like to see lots of dynamic scenery, and you have a fast Pentium, you can increase the density of dynamic scenery. Dynamic scenery customization options are located in the Dynamic Scenery dialog box, which is activated by selecting Dynamic Scenery from the Scenery menu. The various options, illustrated in Figure 3.43, can be applied selectively to each 3-D view window.

   To modify the dynamic scenery frequency settings:

1. Select the View 1 or View 2 window, depending on which view window you want to customize.

2. Open the Scenery Frequency list box, and select the frequency with which dynamic traffic appears.

3. Click the OK button.

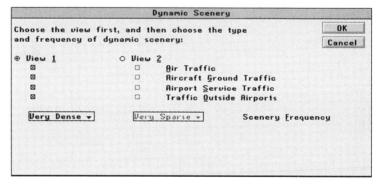

Figure 3.43
The Dynamic Scenery dialog box

You can also choose what kinds of dynamic scenery you wish to have displayed. Available options are:

• Air Traffic

• Aircraft Ground Traffic

• Airport Service Traffic

• Traffic Outside Airports

SETTING YOUR EXACT START LOCATION

You can specify your exact location by using the Set Exact Location command under the World menu. But before you do this, you need to understand how latitude and longitude coordinate systems work.

World Latitude/Longitude Maps

Flight Simulator relies in large measure upon the terrestrial latitude and longitude coordinate system. You will need to know where these lines fall on a map, so you can accurately locate yourself. The equator is defined as 0° latitude, while the prime meridian (which passes through Greenwich, England) is defined as 0° longitude. The latitude of a position is the angular distance measured from the equator northward or southward through 90°, and the direction of measurement is indicated by placing a prefix or suffix N (north) or S (south) next to the angular measure. Longitude is the angular distance measured from the prime meridian eastward or westward through 180°. The direction of movement is indicated by placing a prefix or suffix E (east) or W (west) next to the angular measure.

Each degree of latitude or longitude is subdivided into 60 minutes (60'), and each minute is further subdivided into 60 seconds (60"). For navigational purposes, a great circle that girdles the earth subtends 60 nautical miles for every degree of arc. A minute of arc therefore subtends one nautical mile. Along the great circle of the equator, therefore, the distance between 90°W and 91°W is exactly 60 nautical miles. Note the distance between 90°W and 91°W at a latitude of 45°N is no longer 60 nautical miles, because the circle at 45°N is not a great circle, as the longitude lines converge towards the poles. By the same token, the distance between 37°N and 40°N along the great circle of the Greenwich Meridian is 180 nautical miles (3° of arc x 60 nautical miles/degree = 180 nautical miles).

Moving Your Plane to Any Latitude/Longitude Coordinate

Moving your plane to any location on Earth is possible by using the Set Exact Location command. Here is how to do this:

1. Open the World menu, and select Set Exact Location.
2. In the Set Exact Location dialog box, shown in Figure 3.44, activate the Set Location of . . . list box and choose Aircraft.

Now you must choose which coordinate system you plan to use to precisely place the plane.

3. If you are using FS 4.0 north and east coordinates, select the Set Location with X/Z Coordinates. If you are using FS 5.1 type latitude/longitude coordinates, select Set Location with Latitude/Longitude.

4. Enter the coordinates by typing in the appropriate text boxes. For longitude/latitude, preface north coordinates with an "N," south coordinates with an "S," east coordinates with an "E," and west coordinates with a "W." For example, to enter 45° 55' 35" north latitude, 35° 28' 45" west longitude, type (with spaces or without spaces between numbers)[2]:

   N45 55 35 in the North/South text box

   W35 28 45 in the East/West text box

5. Enter the altitude you wish your plane to be in the Altitude text box.

6. Enter the course heading you want your airplane facing. If you are trying to place your airplane on a runway, you should remember runway numbers refer to compass headings. For example, Runway 32 faces 320° (±5°), runway 9 faces 90° (±5°), and so forth.

7. Click OK when you are satisfied with your position entries.

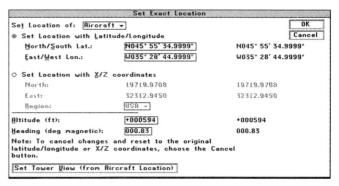

Displaying Latitude/Longitude Coordinates or Alternate FS 4.0 North and East Coordinates

Figure 3.44
The Set Exact Location dialog box

You can display your current position using FS 4.0's north and east coordinate system, and/or FS 5.1's latitude longitude coordinate system. To activate the display in your 3-D view windows and map window, press (Shift) + (Z). You can repeatedly press (Shift) + (Z) to cycle between displaying the two coordinate systems separately or simultaneously, along with the frame rate and G meter. To shut off the display, keep pressing (Shift) + (Z) until the display is turned off.

---

[2]Longitude and latitude are expressed in degrees, minutes, and seconds. There are 360 degrees in a great circle of the Earth, 60 minutes in a degree, and 60 arc seconds in a minute.

The Airports command is only available with FS 5.1 scenery. It will not work with FS 4.0 scenery.

HOW TO JUMP TO ANY AIRPORT

Included in FS 5.1 is the Airports menu command, which enables you to take off from any major airport in the default or add-on scenery areas. You can also choose to have your radios automatically tuned to local air traffic control. You should use this command only when your plane is on the ground because when you change locations, you may crash at the new airport location due to differences in altitude and airspeed.

To jump to any airport, perform the following steps:

1. Open the World menu, and choose Airports.
2. In the Airports dialog box, select the scenery area where the airport you wish to go to is located. You can see the default scenery areas for FS 5.1 CD in Figure 3.45.
3. Select the airport and click the OK button.

Your plane will now appear on the tarmac of the selected airport.

Figure 3.45
FS 5.1 CD Default Scenery Areas Available for the Airports Command

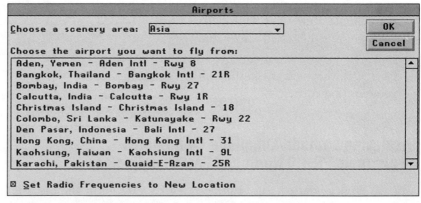

Figure 3.46 The Airports dialog box

Weathering the Weather

Using *Flight Simulator*'s powerful weather editor, you can micromanage local weather fronts or macromanage global weather. The automatic weather generator allows you to have your weather randomly determined or you can control individual aspects of weather such as wind, clouds, temperature, barometric pressure, and visibility. You can create a library of different weather scenarios by designing areas with specific kinds of weather and then copying and pasting them into other areas. Or you can copy and paste individual weather elements, such as a favorite thunderstorm or a pleasant wind shear, between weather areas.

CHOOSING WEATHER CONDITIONS

Weather is defined as the state of the atmosphere. It includes the temperature, precipitation, humidity, cloudiness, visibility, pressure, and winds. There are five factors which determine the weather for a given area. They are, in order:

- The *amount of solar energy* received because of the area's latitude. Higher latitudes near the North Pole, for instance, receive less solar energy than lower latitudes at the equator, which receive the most solar energy.
- The *elevation* of the area. Higher altitudes have lower temperatures and vice versa.
- The *proximity to large bodies of water*. Being close to water moderates temperature fluctuations and provides a more temperate climate. Coastal regions, for example, have milder winters and cooler summers than inland areas.
- The *number of storm systems*. Cyclones, hurricanes, and thunderstorms result from air-mass differences. The Earth's rotation causes air flow to deflect to the right of its direction in the Northern Hemisphere, and to the left in the Southern

Figure 4.1
The Coriolis effect, in which the Earth's rotation about its axis causes the flow of air and sea currents to be deflected to the right in the Northern Hemisphere, and to the left in the Southern Hemisphere.

Hemisphere. This is known as the Coriolis effect, named after the nineteenth century French mathematician G. Coriolis. Figure 4.1 illustrates this effect.

- The *distribution of barometric air pressure* over the land and nearest oceans. Barometric air pressure produces varying wind and air-mass patterns.

All of your weather modifications are performed by using the Weather command under the World menu.

Selecting Metric/US Measurement System

To change your units of measurements from metric to US, or vice-versa:

1. Select the Preferences command under the Options menu.
2. Click the Country button.

3. In the Units of Measure list box, choose:

- *US System* if you want temperature measured in Fahrenheit, distances measured in feet and miles, and weight measured in pounds.
- *Metric (Alt feet)* if you want temperature measured in Fahrenheit, distances measured in meters and kilometers (except for the altimeter which measures altitude in feet), and mass measured in kilograms.
- *Metric (Alt meters)* if you want all instruments and readings, including the altimeter, measured in metric units.

Creating Clouds/Thunderstorms

Clouds in the atmosphere form whenever the relative humidity, or moisture content, of an air mass exceeds 100 percent. Water vapor, always present in the atmosphere, is produced from the evaporation of water due to the sun's heating effect on the oceans and other bodies of water. Intermolecular dipole-dipole and London forces cause the water vapor molecules to bind together, and eventually cloud formation occurs.

Clouds can be hazardous to flying because they can obstruct your visibility for navigating. If clouds are cold enough, they can freeze on impact with your airplane, causing ice to build up on the body and wings. They can also cause turbulence and airframe damage. Warm clouds with temperatures greater than 32° Fahrenheit (0° Celsius) are generally safe. But cold clouds with temperatures below 32° Fahrenheit (0° Celsius) are to be avoided.

Types of Clouds

There are three basic shapes of clouds:

- *Cumulus Clouds* (from *cumulus* meaning heap in Latin) are cottony, billowing, puffball like clouds that form heaps of separated cloud masses with flat bottoms and cauliflower tops. Thunderstorms are cumuliform, and generally the air is turbulent around them.
- *Stratus Clouds* (from *stratus* meaning spread out in Latin) are flat, layered clouds that are much wider than they are thick. They form when upward air currents are relatively uniform over a wide area. Because of the smoother air currents, flying near stratus clouds causes less turbulence than cumulus clouds.
- *Cirrus Clouds* (from *cirrus* meaning curl in Latin) are wispy clouds that look like strands of hair.

Figure 4.2
Cumulus clouds

Figure 4.3
Stratus clouds
(layered)

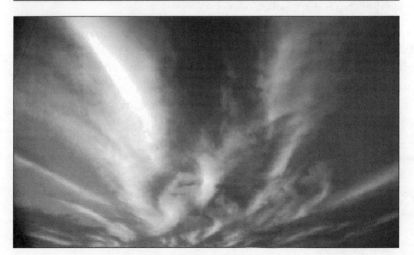

Figure 4.4
Cirrus clouds
(wispy curls)

Clouds formed at ground level are called fog. Clouds formed in the upper troposphere are referred to as cirrus clouds (also sometimes called cirrocumulus and cirrostratus), while clouds formed in the middle troposphere are called altostratus and altocumulus. Clouds formed in the lower troposphere are given the names stratus and cumulus. When precipitation falls from lower troposphere clouds, the clouds are called nimbostratus and cumulonimbus. Nimbostratus clouds are often produced by cyclones, while cumulonimbus clouds are associated with thunderstorms in which rainfall is brief but heavy. The term nimbus, first coined by the Romans, describes dark gray rain clouds, so a cumulous cloud with rain is called cumulonimbus.

Table 4.1 compares the different cloud shapes by describing their appearance and at what part of the atmosphere they typically form.

Under visual flying rules (VFR), you are allowed to fly your plane only when the visibility is more than three statute miles. Also, when flying near clouds, you must maintain a separation distance of at least 500 feet below, 1,000 feet above, or 2,000 feet horizontal distance from the cloud. If you have an instrument rating, these rules do not apply to you because you will have acquired the skills necessary to navigate under all conditions, including night and bad weather with zero visibility.

Thunderstorms

Thunderstorms form when the atmosphere is thermally unstable and large warm air currents, laden with moisture, rise upwards in the form of a towering cumulus cloud. When many such cumulus clouds merge, a cumulonimbus, or thunderstorm cloud, appears with its distinctive anvil-shaped top. Thunderstorms play an important role in the Earth's hydrological cycle because they transport large portions of surface heat and water vapor to the upper regions of the atmosphere. In many areas of the world, especially agricultural regions in the United States, Canada, and the Ukraine where corn and wheat are grown, most rainfall is produced by thunderstorms.

When a thunderstorm is brewing, katabatic wind downbursts (often called microbursts) from the cirrus anvil can produce downdrafts as strong as 6,000 feet per minute. Horizontal surface winds can be as strong as 45 knots (resultant horizontal shear is 90 knots because of the headwind to tailwind change for a traversing aircraft). Moderate to heavy rainfall occurs over broad regions below the base of the clouds and small hail and snowflakes may emanate from the interior of the cloud. Thunderstorms can produce violent windstorms, wind shear, tornadoes, large hailstones, heavy rainfall, and intense lightning. Because of this destructive potential, thunderstorms are extremely hazardous to aircraft—especially those landing or departing from airports. Many aircraft accidents, in fact, have been attributed to the wind

Table 4.1   Cloud Types in Flight Simulator 5.1

Shape	Cloud Type	Description	Atmospheric Shell Layer (L=0 to 10,000 ft; M=10 to 25,000 ft, L=25,000 to 50,000 feet)
Heap	Cumulus	There are three sub-types of cumulus clouds: cumulus of fair weather, swelling cumulus, and cumulus congestus. Puffball, cauliflower top appearance.	Cumulus of fair weather=L, swelling cumulus=LM, cumulus congestus=LMH
Layered Heaps	Stratocumulus	Low clouds appearing as soft, gray, roll shaped masses.	L
Layered Heaps	Altocumulus	Middle clouds consisting of a layer of large, ball-like masses that tend to merge together.	M
Layered Heaps	Cirrocumulus	High clouds composed of globular masses	H
Layered Heaps with Precipitation	Cumulonimbus	Massive clouds with great vertical development, rising in mountainous towers to great heights. Very unstable air masses are associated with them. Often called "thunderstorms." Avoid at all costs.	LMH
Layers	Stratus	Low clouds in a uniform layer, resembling fog. Often the base is no more than 1,000 feet high.	L
Layers	Altostratus	Middle clouds having a grayish or bluish, fibrous veil or sheet.	M
Layers	Cirrostratus	High clouds with a thin, milky white appearance that often resembles a tangled web.	H
Layers with Precipitation	Nimbostratus	Low, dark, shapeless cloud layer; nearly uniform. Typically a rain cloud.	LM
Wispy Curls	Cirrus	Detached high clouds with a delicate, fibrous appearance.	H

Table 4.2 Visual Flight Rules	
Minimum Flight Visibility for VFR	Minimum Distance from Clouds for VFR
3 statute miles (the controlled airspace only)	500 feet below cloud
	1,000 feet above cloud
	2,000 feet horizontal separation distance from cloud

shear associated with thunderstorms. Figure 4.5 shows some elements of a thunderstorm generated in *Flight Simulator* 5.0.

Wind Shear

What is wind shear? It is a change in wind direction or velocity that occurs with a change in altitude. When an airplane experiences a sudden reversal in wind direction, the airspeed of the airplane changes dramatically. At low speeds, such as during approaches and landings, you can stall the airplane because the airflow over the wings is insufficient. When this happens, there isn't enough lift and the airplane crashes.

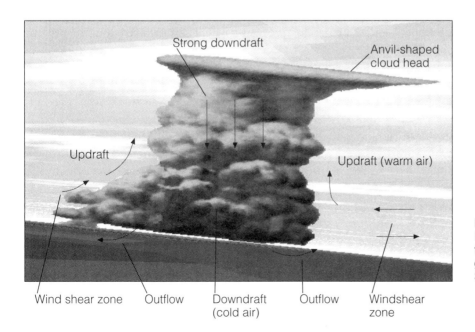

Figure 4.5
Elements of the thunderstorm generated in Flight Simulator

How does wind shear occur around thunderstorms? Let's use an example of an airplane flying towards a thunderstorm to describe what happens. In a thunderstorm, rain is pouring down the center, and air is rushing downward and fanning out at the surface. At the same time, a large amount of warm air is being sucked into the storm around the edges. The warm air is shearing past the cold air (shearing is a term used to describe the action of two bodies that move in opposite directions in parallel planes) and is moving above the cooler air that is coming out of the storm. If you were standing on the ground facing the storm, you would feel a strong cool breeze in your face. This is the cold air that is being pushed out of the storm that hits the ground and then is shunted outwards. But if you were to move vertically several hundred feet above where you stand, the wind would be in the opposite direction because it is the warm and humid air that is being drawn into the storm.

Suppose your airplane is flying towards the storm, which is between it and the airport. Your airspeed is 130 knots and the wind is nominally calm. When your plane approaches the storm, a warm air current updraft is encountered. This is no problem, because this is the air being sucked into the storm. The real trouble starts when you enter the interior of the storm. Here you run into the downdraft of the cold air and rain from the center. This translates into a 30 knot headwind, since this airflow is rushing outwards towards the edge or perimeter of the cloud. Your airplane's speed is suddenly 30 knots higher and you're climbing due to the extra lift. To stay cruising at the same altitude you may actually start to reduce thrust, and even point the nose down a little. But before things have settled down, you get the sudden change in tailwind. This suddenly and drastically reduces your airspeed by 60 knots (not 30 knots, because you have already reduced your airspeed at the center of the storm to compensate for the 30 knot headwind)! Consequently your lift drastically drops. In these circumstances, you are unlikely to have sufficient thrust to recover, so you get a complete stall due to lack of airflow over the wings. If you have enough altitude to recover, you can increase thrust and try to regain airspeed and lift.

Many airports around the country are now equipped with ground-based wind shear detecting devices. But these warning instruments have not been totally reliable. As a result, a new highly advanced Doppler radar system that can detect shifting wind patterns is being installed. Airborne wind shear radars that can be carried aboard an airplane are also being developed. In the not so distant future, the probability of encountering unexpected wind shear will be reduced to near zero.

The general rule for all pilots is to avoid thunderclouds. It's best to skirt around them by at least 20 miles to avoid turbulence. If you see lightning or spot large anvil shaped clouds, it indicates the probability of a severe thun-

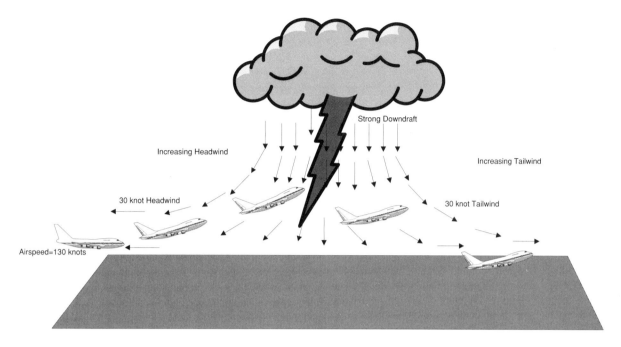

Figure 4.6
Thunderstorm
wind shear

derstorm. Never land or take off in the face of an approaching thunderstorm, and never attempt to fly under a thunderstorm even if you can see clear to the other side. Turbulence and wind shear under the storm (invisible to your eye) could be disastrous. If you must pass by a thunderstorm, it is preferable to fly on the upwind side of the storm's directional movement because it is less turbulent than the downwind side. Also, if you have to cross a thunderstorm's path, clear the top of the anvil cloud by at least 1,000 feet for each 10 knots of wind speed for the storm. If a thunderstorm is near the airport, airport operations will be suspended until the thunderstorm activity has passed. Many flight delays can be attributed to this phenomenon, especially at the busy Dallas-Ft. Worth airport in Texas, which is a central hub for many airline travelers in the United States.

Creating a Cloud Layer

To create a cloud layer or thunderstorm in *Flight Simulator*, you must make several decisions. Will the clouds appear locally or globally? What kind of clouds do you want? What will be the base and ceiling altitudes? What will the coverage area be? And what will the deviation factor (the randomness the clouds appear in) be?

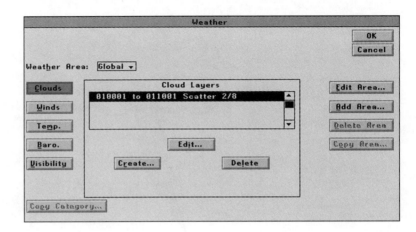

Figure 4.7
The Weather dialog
box showing the cloud
layer currently
available

Perform the following steps to create a Cloud Layer:

1. Select the Weather command option from the World menu.

2. In the Weather dialog box, from the Weather Area list box, choose either Global or the name of a local area you previously created.

3. Click the Clouds button, and you will see a list of cloud layers appear in the Weather dialog box, seen in Figure 4.7.

4. Click the Create button to add a new cloud layer. Keep in mind that you are only allowed to create two cloud layers and one thunderstorm layer per weather area.

5. In the Create Cloud Layer dialog box, illustrated in Figure 4.8, you must choose the type of cloud. If you pick one of the 10 pre-defined cloud types, as shown in Figure 4.9, you don't need to fill out any of the other options in the dialog box. You only make modifications to Base, Tops, Coverage, Deviation, Cloud Turbulence, and Icing, when you want to custom design your own cloud formations.

You can only create
two cloud layers and
one thunderstorm
layer per weather
area.

If you want to
experience a thun-
derstorm, choose
the Cumulonimbus
cloud type.

Type

FS 5.1 comes with 10 pre-defined cloud types you can pick from, as shown in Figure 4.9. The description for each cloud type was given in Table 4.1, but note that thunderstorms in FS 5.1 are now the cumulonimbus cloud type. You can also create your own custom cloud types by selecting User Defined in the list box, then enter your own cloud parameters for Base, Tops, Coverage, Deviation, Cloud Turbulence, and Icing.

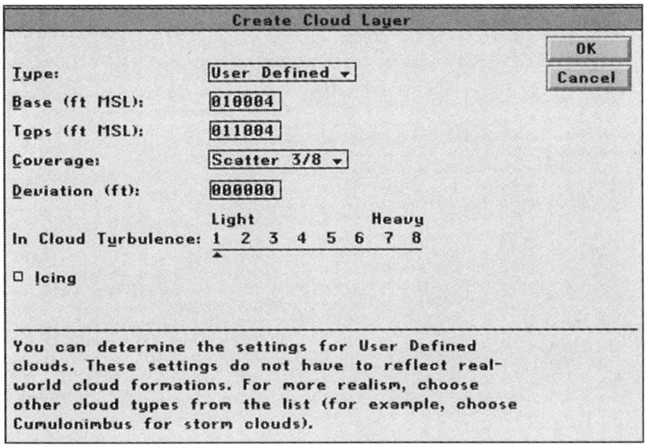

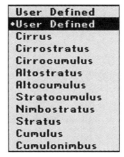

Figure 4.8 Create Cloud Layer dialog box

Figure 4.9 Cloud Types List Box. Pick your cloud type from one of the 10 available cloud types, or custom design your own when you select User Defined.

Base

The base refers to the bottom of the cloud and how far it is above mean sea level (MSL). If you are starting at Chicago's Meigs Field, which is at an altitude of 593 feet, and you want your clouds to appear 1,000 feet above the ground, you would enter 1,593 feet.

Tops

Tops refers to the ceiling top of the cloud. This can be any altitude above the base, or bottom of the cloud. For a cloud that is 3,000 feet tall, with a base altitude of 1,593 feet, you would enter 4,593 feet.

Coverage

In the Coverage list box, you can decide how extensively your clouds will blanket the sky. For clouds the coverage options are hazy, scattered, broken, or overcast. The fractional numbers appearing after the scattered and broken cloud layers indicate the fraction of sky covered by clouds.

Deviation

The Deviation list box controls *Flight Simulator's* randomness when creating your cloud layers. The deviation factor determines the top and base altitude of the cloud plus or minus a random number between 0 and the deviation value you enter. Primarily, this option allows you to create more realistic clouds that are not monotonously identical. Thus, if you enter a base value of 2,000 feet and a top value of 4,000 feet, and a deviation of 500 feet, the tops values would be increased by a random value between 0 and 500 feet, while the base value would be decreased by a random value between 0 and 500 feet.

Cloud Turbulence

New to FS 5.1, you can experience cloud turbulence on a scale of one to eight.

Icing

Also new to FS 5.1, you can create icing conditions inside clouds.

More Cloud and Icing Conditions Realism

With FS 5.1, you can make your clouds look more realistic if you select the Options/Preferences menu, click the Display button and the Scenery Display button, then toggle on Wispy Cloud Effects and Cloud Thickness Effects.

For more icing realism, such as loss of lift, increased weight, and control problems, you should increase the Flight Realism under Realism and Reliability for the Sim menu.

Creating Wind Layers

If you want to save your cloud layers for later use, you must save your changes in a situation.

Wind is defined as air in motion relative to the rotating surface of the Earth. Wind possesses both vertical and horizontal speed components, although typically the horizontal speed component is much larger than the vertical. Horizontal wind speeds usually average 31.25 mph (50 km/hr). However in the jet streams high up in the atmosphere, speeds in excess of 180 mph (300 km/hr) are not uncommon. Vertical wind speeds, on the other hand, typically are measured in only tenths of a kilometer per hour. When we talk about wind speed, it is almost always horizontal speed that is being referred to.

In *Flight Simulator*, wind directions are measured in terms of compass headings. A wind with a heading of 180° is from the south, a wind with a heading of 90° is from the east, and so on. This may be confusing to you, since you might assume that a compass heading of 90° means that the wind should blow east. However, this is not the case; by convention, wind always blows from the compass heading given.

Wind direction blows from a given compass heading.

The movement of air around the planet is largely the result of force imbalances due to large temperature variations, the Coriolis effect, and varied air pressure gradients around the Earth. Whenever there is warm mass of air, it tends to move in the direction of cooler air masses and the wind flow that results is an attempt to equalize the atmosphere's temperature.

The equatorial and polar regions have the largest temperature difference. This difference causes the winds to carry heat from the equator to the poles. As described before, the Coriolis effect, which is caused by the Earth's rotation, produces zero wind forces at the equator and maximum wind forces at higher latitudes near the poles.

Winds are classified into three types:

- **Planetary Winds:** trade winds and middle latitude westerlies
- **Secondary Winds:** sea breezes, monsoon winds, and cyclonic winds
- **Regional Anabatic and Katabatic Winds:** anabatic winds ascend vertically and are usually associated with geographic features like mountain ranges; katabatic winds descend vertically like microbursts (intense localized downdrafts that spread along the ground, causing wind shear). These winds are often the result of thunderstorm activity.

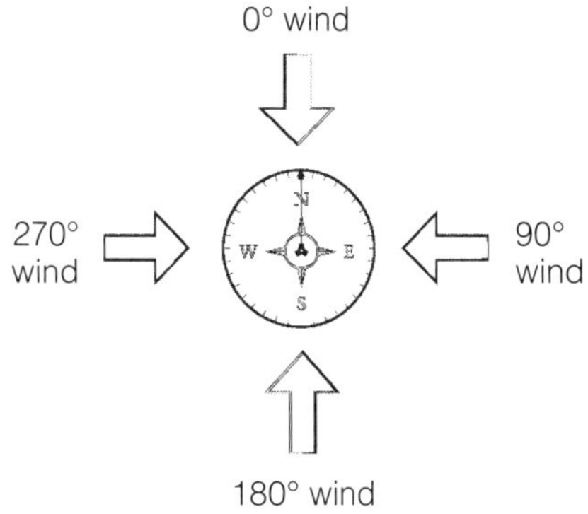

0° wind

270° wind

90° wind

180° wind

Figure 4.10
Wind Direction is based on compass heading. It blows from (not to) the given compass heading.

Winds at different altitudes can have different speeds and directions. At the boundaries or junctions of these wind layers, turbulence occurs. The wind that comes into frictional contact with the rotating Earth, for example, causes the most turbulence at altitudes of less than 3,225 feet. Above this altitude, winds are generally smooth except for wind layers that come into contact with the jet stream. The jet stream is a fast moving current of air in the upper atmosphere.

Clear air turbulence (CAT) is a serious concern for all flights since it can create passenger discomfort, and even cause injuries in severe instances. Turbulence is rated by four intensity levels, as described in Table 4.3.

You can create only three wind layers and one surface wind layer per geological weather area.

Creating a Wind Layer

To create a wind, follow this procedure:

1. From the World menu, select the Weather option.
2. In the Weather dialog box, from the Weather Area list box, choose either Global or the name of a local area you previously created.
3. Click the Winds button, and you will see a list of wind layers appear in the Weather dialog box.
4. Click the Create button to add a new wind layer. You can only create three wind layers and one surface wind layer per weather area.

Table 4.3   Clear Air Turbulence Rating Criteria

Intensity	Aircraft Reaction	Reaction Inside Aitcraft
Light	Slight erratic changes in altitude and attitude (pitch, yaw, roll). Slight bumps.	Passengers feel slight strain against seatbelts. Unsecured objects may move.
Moderate	Changes in altitude and attitude occur. Causes rapid bumps or jolts.	Passengers feel definite strains against seatbelts. Unsecured objects will move, and walking and food service are difficult.
Severe	Large, abrupt changes in altitude and attitude. Aircraft may be momentarily out of control.	Passengers are forced violently against seatbelts. Unsecured objects are thrown about. Walking and food service are all but impossible to perform.
Extreme	The aircraft is violently tossed about and is difficult to control. May cause structural damage to aircraft.	You don't want to know.

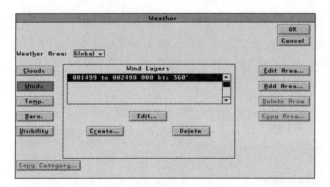

Figure 4.11 Available Wind Layers in the Weather Dialog Box

5. In the Create Wind Layer dialog box, you must choose whether you want a surface wind or a wind aloft, then you must select the type of wind, add the base (or bottom elevation) of the wind, enter the top (or ceiling altitude) of the wind, enter the speed and direction of the wind, and enter the turbulence factor, as shown in Figure 4.12.

Wind Aloft vs. Surface Winds

When you choose Surface Winds, the Base text box disappears and the Tops text box is replaced by the Depth text box. By definition, surface winds have no base or bottom, so all you need enter is the height above ground in the Depth text box. Winds Aloft are those wind layers above ground level.

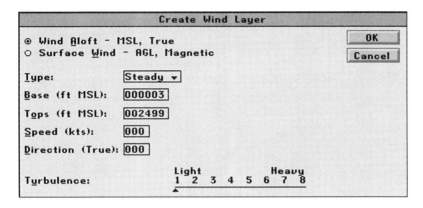

Figure 4.12
The Create Wind
Layer dialog box

Type

Select between Steady and Gusty winds.

Base

The base refers to the bottom of the wind layer and how far it is above mean sea level (MSL). If you are starting at Chicago's Meigs Field, which is at an altitude of 593 feet, and you want your wind to appear 1,000 feet above the ground, enter 1,593 feet.

Tops

Tops refers to the top of the wind layer. This can be any altitude above the base, or bottom of the wind layer. For a wind layer that is 3,000 feet tall, with a base altitude of 1,593 feet, enter 4,593 feet.

Speed

Enter the speed, in knots (nautical miles per hour) for the wind layer.

Direction

Enter the wind direction from your compass heading. Winds blowing from the south would be 180°, from the west would be 270° (see Figure 4.10). The wind direction is a source of confusion for many novice pilots; it is always measured from a particular compass heading (not in the direction of a heading).

Setting the Turbulence Factor

For a bumpier ride, slide the turbulence control to the Heavy side. But, if you get airsick easily, leave it on Light.

If you want to save your wind layers for later use, you must save your changes in a situation.

Adding Temperature Layers

The effect of increasing temperature causes the atmosphere to decrease in density (the mass per unit volume) for a constant air pressure. Conversely, lowering the temperature increases air density, also for a fixed air pressure. Thus, the density of air varies inversely with the air temperature.

$$Temperature \propto \frac{1}{Density}$$

Increasing air pressure increases air density, while decreasing air pressure decreases air density. Thus, the density of air is directly proportional to pressure.

$$Pressure \propto Density$$

In the atmosphere, both temperature and pressure decrease with altitude. However, air pressure drops more rapidly than temperature as altitude is increased; therefore air density decreases with altitude, despite the air density increase due to the temperature decrease.

Air Density Affects Airplane's Performance Characteristics

The density of the air, which is affected by altitude, barometric pressure, and temperature, has a significant influence over the airplane's handling characteristics. As air becomes less dense, it does four things:

1. Engine power is reduced because the engine takes in less air.
2. Propeller thrust is reduced because the propeller is less efficient in thin air.
3. Lift is reduced because thinner air exerts less force on the wings.
4. Drag is reduced because there is less air resistance on the fuselage.

The Effect of Temperature on the Airplane's Lift

If the temperature drops appreciably, the air density increases and lift increases. If the temperature increases, air density decreases and lift decreases. This means that if you are taking off on a very hot day, you won't be able to lift off as quickly as you would on a cold day. You must plan for using a longer length of runway. To maintain the same amount of lift, your airplane must be flown at a greater true airspeed on hot days than on cool days. Table 4.4 summarizes these results, and shows the effect on the aircraft's cockpit instrumentation. We will discuss the pitot-static system, which governs this instrumentation, in detail in Chapter 7.

Table 4.4	Temperature's Effect on Aircraft Lift and Pitot-Static System	
Temperature	**Aircraft Lift**	**Pitot-Static System**
Increases	Decreases	Altimeter shows you at a higher altitude than you really are; when your Airspeed Indicator shows IAS, you are really traveling faster than your Airspeed Indicator displays.
Decreases	Increases	Altimeter shows you at a lower altitude than you really are; when your Airspeed Indicator shows IAS, you are really traveling slower than your Airspeed Indicator displays.

You can add up to four different temperature layers per weather area, and create diurnal day/night temperature variations.

You can create up to four temperature layers per weather area; each layer must be at least 328 feet apart.

Temperature Variations with Altitude

Temperature drops by 3.5° Fahrenheit (2° Celsius) per 1,000 feet of increased altitude. In fact, this relationship helps to create stability in the atmosphere. Greater temperature variations than this can cause destructive atmospheric disturbances like thunderstorms, cyclones, tornadoes, typhoons, and hurricanes.

You can experience the temperature drop with increased altitude in *Flight Simulator* by entering slew mode (press Y), then increase your altitude by pressing F4. Notice that your temperature changes as your altitude increases.

Day/Night Temperature Variations

The diurnal temperature variation between night and day exists everywhere, but varies by region and season. During the day, when the sun's heating effect on the atmosphere is at a maximum, temperatures can vary from their night time lows by as much as 36° Fahrenheit (12.8° Celsius). By toggling on the Day/Night Variation Range check box, and entering a temperature differential in the text box, you can realistically simulate this diurnal temperature fluctuation. The variance must be between 0° and 36° Fahrenheit (0° to 20° Celsius).

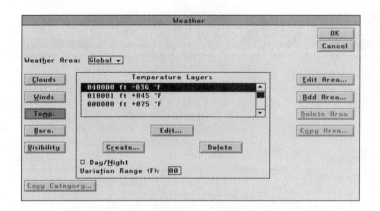

Figure 4.13
Temperature Layers
Available in the
Weather Dialog Box.

Creating a Temperature Layer

To create a temperature layer, follow these steps:

1. From the World menu, select the Weather command.

2. In the Weather dialog box, from the Weather Area list box, choose either Global or the name of a local area you have previously created.

3. Click the Temp button, and you will see a list of temperature layers appear in the Weather dialog box, as seen in Figure 4.13.

4. Click the Create button to add a new temperature layer. You are only allowed to create four temperature layers per weather area, and each temperature layer must be at least 328 feet (100 meters) apart.

5. In the Create Temperature Layer dialog box, enter the altitude above sea level where you want the temperature layer to appear and the daytime temperature, as shown in Figure 4.14.

If you want to save your temperature layers for later use, you must save your changes in a situation.

Figure 4.14
The Create Temperature
Layer dialog box.

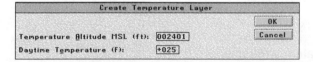

Temperature Altitude MSL

Enter the altitude above mean sea level (MSL) for the temperature layer. If you wanted to enter an altitude of 3,000 feet above Chicago's Meigs Field (altitude of 593 feet), for example, you would enter 3,593 feet.

Daytime Temperature

Type in the daytime temperature of the temperature layer. If you have toggled on the Day/Night Variation Range, the temperature will drop at night
by the number of degrees you have entered in the Variation Range text box.
To enter a negative temperature, press [–] on the main keyboard before typing in the temperature.

Barometric Pressure

Pressure, or force applied per unit area, is measured in inches of mercury,
Pascals (Newtons/meter squared), and millibars (1/100 of a Pascal). The
mercury barometer, invented by Evangelista Torricelli in 1643, measures the
height of a column of mercury due to the pressure the atmosphere exerts on
it. The greater the air pressure, the greater the height of the mercury column.
Mercury is measured in inches, or inches of Hg (Hg represents the element
Mercury on the Periodic Table of Elements). Atmospheric pressure can be
calculated by multiplying the height of the mercury column by the mercury
density and the acceleration due to gravity (this would give you the pressure
in pounds per square inch). Often meteorologists use the term "inches of
Hg" to express the atmosphere's pressure, rather than pounds per square
inch. At sea level, one atmospheric pressure equals 14.7 pounds per square
inch, or 29.9 inches of Hg. Expressed in metric units, one atmosphere of
pressure at sea level equals 101.3 kilopascals, or 1,013 millibars.

The international standard atmosphere (ISA) has been defined as an
atmospheric pressure of 29.92 inches of Mercury (29.92" Hg), or 1,013.2
millibars, at 59° Fahrenheit (15° Celsius). An inch of mercury is equivalent
to 33.8 millibars of pressure.

Atmospheric Pressure Decreases with Altitude

The standard decrease in pressure with increasing altitude is approximately
1" Hg per 1,000 feet, along with a 3.5° Fahrenheit drop in temperature per
1,000 feet. Table 4.5 lists the pressures of the standard atmosphere according
to different altitudes, temperatures, and air densities.

The Effect of Pressure Changes on Aircraft Performance

When air pressure increases, air density increases, and so does aircraft lift.
Conversely, if air pressure decreases, air density decreases, and so does lift.
Looking at Table 4.5, you can see that the density of air at 18,000 feet is

Table 4.5	Properties of Standard Atmosphere				
Standard Atmosphere					
Altitude (Feet)	Pressure (Inches Hg.)	Temperature (Celsius)	Temperature (Fahrenheit)	Density (slugs per cubic foot)	Density (g/cm^3)
0	29.92	15.0	59.0	0.002378	0.001226
1,000	28.86	13.0	55.4	0.002309	0.001190
2,000	27.82	11.0	51.9	0.002242	0.001155
3,000	26.82	9.1	48.3	0.002176	0.001121
4,000	25.84	7.1	44.7	0.002112	0.001088
5,000	24.89	5.1	41.2	0.002049	0.001056
6,000	23.98	3.1	37.6	0.001988	0.001025
7,000	23.09	1.1	34.0	0.001928	0.000994
8,000	22.22	-0.9	30.5	0.001869	0.000963
9,000	21.38	-2.8	26.9	0.001812	0.000934
10,000	20.57	-4.8	23.3	0.001756	0.000905
11,000	19.97	-6.8	19.8	0.001701	0.000877
12,000	19.02	-8.8	16.2	0.001648	0.000849
13,000	18.29	-10.8	12.6	0.001596	0.000823
14,000	17.57	-12.7	9.1	0.001545	0.000796
15,000	16.88	-14.7	5.5	0.001496	0.000771
16,000	16.21	-16.7	1.9	0.001448	0.000746
17,000	15.56	-18.7	-1.6	0.001401	0.000722
18,000	14.94	-20.7	-5.2	0.001355	0.000698
19,000	14.33	-22.6	-8.8	0.001310	0.000675
20,000	13.74	-24.6	-12.3	0.001267	0.000653

almost one half the density of air at sea level. Therefore, an airplane must fly at a greater airspeed at a higher altitude in order to maintain the same lift it would have at a lower altitude.

When the pressure changes, not only do your airplane's performance characteristics change, but your pitot-static flight instruments are adversely affected. Thus your measurements of altitude, airspeed, and rate of climb become inaccurate and must be corrected according to special charts and tables that are available. Table 4.6 summarizes these results. Note that in FS 5.1, your Airspeed Indicator is calibrated by default to show true airspeed (TAS). Real aircraft airspeed indicators display indicated airspeed (IAS), and you can change your FS 5.1 readout to IAS by selecting the Options/Preferences menu, then click the Instrument button, and then toggle on the Display Indicated Airspeed check box.

Your altimeter is set to show the correct altitude based on a standard atmosphere of 29.92 inches Hg. If the local barometric pressure differs from this pressure, your altimeter will give you an incorrect reading. You must, from time to time, calibrate your altimeter for local barometric conditions if you are to avoid becoming one of the fatality statistics classified as "pilot error."

You can test the effect of pressure on your altimeter. Lower the barometric pressure from 30.18 inches to 28 inches Hg and check your altimeter at Chicago's Meigs field. The altimeter's reading will jump from 590 feet to 2,560 feet; if you had been flying in low visibility with an uncalibrated altimeter, you would have crashed.

You can also manually calibrate your altimeter to any desired pressure level by choosing Calibrate Altimeter from the Sim menu, and then make your changes in the text entry box. Note that this does not change the barometric pressure for the atmosphere, it merely calibrates your altimeter for any specified pressure you enter.

To quickly calibrate your altimeter, press B.

Table 4.6 The Affects of Pressure on Aircraft Performance		
Barometric Pressure	**Aircraft Lift**	**Pitot-Static System**
Increases for lower altitudes	Increases	Altimeter shows you at a lower altitude than you really are; when your Airspeed Indicator shows IAS, you are really traveling slower than your Airspeed Indicator displays.
Decreases for higher altitudes	Decreases	Altimeter shows you at a higher altitude than you really are; when your Airspeed Indicator shows IAS, you are really traveling faster than your Airspeed Indicator displays.

Altering the Barometric Pressure

To change the barometric pressure, perform these steps:

1. Select the Weather menu option from the World menu.
2. In the Weather dialog box, from the Weather Area list box, choose either Global or the name of a local area that you have previously created.
3. Click the Baro button.
4. In the Barometric Pressure section of the Weather Dialog Box, enter the new barometric pressure either in the Pressure (in Hg) text box or the Pressure (millibars) text box.
5. If you want some random variation in pressure thrown in, select Drift.

If you want to save your barometric pressure for later use, you must save your changes in a situation.

Inches of Mercury

Enter the barometric pressure in inches of mercury. Allowed values are from 25 inches to 35 inches. The standard pressure at sea level is 29.92 inches.

Millibars

Enter the barometric pressure in millibars. Allowed values are from 847 millibars to 1,185 millibars. The standard pressure at sea level is 1,013.

Drift

Check this box to have *Flight Simulator* add some randomness to your barometric pressure.

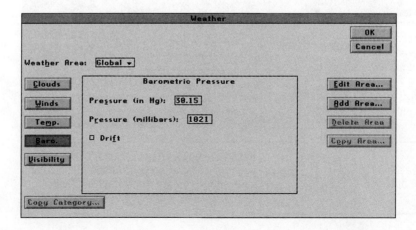

Figure 4.15
The Barometric
Pressure section of the
Weather dialog box

Reducing Your Visibility

For visual flight rules (VFR), you must have at least three miles visibility in controlled airspace, or one mile visibility outside controlled airspace. FS 5.1's new low-visibility feature is a terrific way to practice instrument flying. You can experiment with low-visibility as low as 1/16th of a mile and see if you can land the aircraft using the instrument landing system (ILS). In the insert, there are a few color pictures showing how to selectively reduce your visibility with hazing and fog.

Reducing Visibility

To reduce visibility, you must be running one of the graphics drivers in the Display Preferences dialog box (Options/Preferences/Display) that includes the words "with haze." For example, if you are running in SVGA mode, you must choose the SVGA with Haze driver, then restart FS 5.1 before you can use the low-visibility feature.

Once you have done this, you can change your visibility by doing the following:

1. Select the Weather menu option from the World menu.
2. In the Weather dialog box, from the Weather Area list box, choose either Global or the name of a local area that you have previously created.
3. Click the Visibility button, and you'll see the Visibility section of the Weather dialog box appear as in Figure 4.16.
4. Pull down the list box for Visibility and select the visibility you want from 1/16th of a mile to unlimited. Figure 4.17 shows the available visibility options.

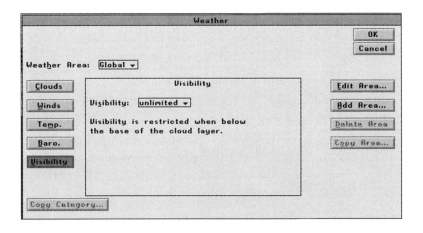

Figure 4.16
Visibility section of the Weather dialog box

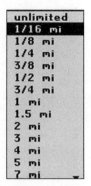

Figure 4.17
Visibility options

Note that if you are running an add-on scenery package prior to Las Vegas (e.g., San Francisco, Paris, New York, Washington D.C.), you won't be able use the low-visibility hazing features. This is because the older scenery was not designed with the appropriate color palettes. New scenery packages, like Hawaii, will support the new hazing palettes.

GLOBAL WEATHER AREAS

There are two types of weather areas in *Flight Simulator*: global and local. There is only one global weather area for a situation, and it affects the weather over the entire planet. Global weather does not pre-empt local weather, and you can have up to two local weather fronts in addition to the global weather. Since global weather applies to all regions of the Earth, you cannot edit a global area's coordinates, speed, course, width, or transition distance between other weather areas. When automatic weather is enabled, though, any other weather that you have created will not function.

Adding Weather to the Global Weather Area

To add clouds, wind layers, temperature gradients, and barometric pressure changes to the global weather area, first select the Weather menu from the World menu. Then choose Global from the Weather Area list box under the Weather dialog box. Finally, add each weather element, as is described earlier in this chapter.

Automatic Global Weather Generation

With automatic weather generation, you can have all weather randomly created for you. However, this will disable other weather that you may have created. The steps for switching on automatic weather generation globally are as follows:

1. Choose the Weather menu from the World menu.
2. In the Weather dialog box, from the Weather Area list box, select Global.
3. Click the Edit Area button.
4. Toggle on the Automatic Weather Generation check box in the Edit Weather Area dialog box. Notice that all other options are dimmed out. Remember you cannot edit the global weather area's coordinates, direction, or speed.

5. If you want to have clouds randomly generated, click on the Clouds check box. If you want to have wind layers automatically produced, click on the Winds check box.

CREATING AND EDITING LOCAL WEATHER AREAS

Local weather is weather that applies to a specific area of the Earth you determine. You can have only two local weather areas, in addition to your global weather; but the local weather pre-empts the global weather, except when automatic weather generation is turned on. For each area, you must define the coordinates, width, speed, course heading, and transition distance between other weather areas. Figure 4.18 shows the elements of a local weather area front that is moving from west to east, and is 10 miles long and 15 miles wide.

When automatic weather is enabled in the Global Edit Weather Area Dialog Box, all other weather options are temporarily disabled.

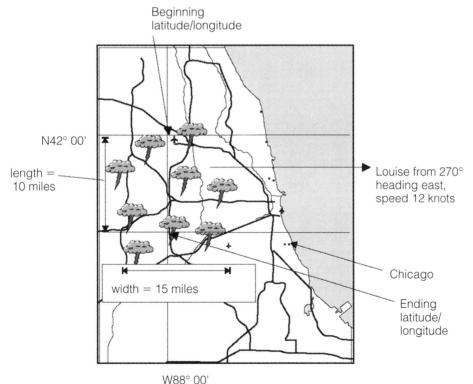

Beginning latitude/longitude

N42° 00'

length = 10 miles

Louise from 270° heading east, speed 12 knots

width = 15 miles

Chicago

Ending latitude/ longitude

W88° 00'

Figure 4.18
These are the latitude/ longitude coordinate lines that you need in order to properly locate the geographical area for your local weather area

Creating a Chicago Area Weather Front with Thunderstorms

 Let's create a 10 nautical mile long thunderstorm weather front, with a width of 15 nautical miles that approaches Chicago from the west, heading in a easterly direction at 12 knots:

1. Select the Weather menu from the World menu.
2. In the Weather dialog box, click the Add Area button.
3. In the Add Weather Area dialog box, type Chicago Area Weather in the Area Name text box.
4. Click on the Beginning Latitude text box, and type

N42 00 00

5. Click on the Beginning Longitude text box, and type

W88 00 00

6. Since you want to make the length of the weather front exactly 10 nautical miles long, in a vertical north-south line from the beginning coordinates, you will need to set your lower coordinate 10' (minutes of arc = nautical miles) lower than the 42° 00' 00" latitude previously given. In the Ending Latitude text box, type

N41 50 00

This latitude was calculated by subtracting ten minutes of arc from 42° (or 41° 60' which is equivalent to 42°).

7. Because the length of the front is in a north south orientation along a meridian, there is no change in longitude and in the Ending Longitude text box we type in the same longitude coordinate of

W88 00 00

8. Enter a width of 15 miles in the Width text box.
9. For the Transition text box, which controls the distance between adjacent weather areas, type in 5 miles.
10. Because your weather area is headed due east, enter a course heading of 270° in the Course text box. (Weather moves in the same direction as winds; that is from a given compass heading).
11. Type a speed of 12 knots for the weather area in the Speed text box. See Figure 4.19 for a view of what your dialog box should look like.
12. Click OK to exit the Add Weather Area dialog box. You will return to the Weather dialog box.

13. In the Weather Dialog box, select the Chicago Area Weather in the Weather Area list box.

14. Click the Clouds button.

15. Click the Create button, and the Create Cloud Layer dialog box will open.

16. In the Type list box, select Cumulonimbus.

17. Click OK to exit the Cloud Layer dialog box. Click OK once more to return to the simulation.

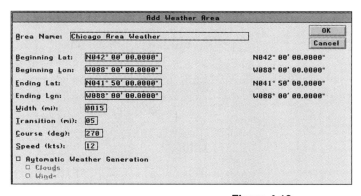

Figure 4.19
Completed entries for the Add Weather Area dialog box

Now if you look west, you should see thunderstorms approaching Chicago.

The next section describes the various options available in the Add Weather dialog box, as seen in Figure 4.19. Note that most of these features are dimmed out and unavailable when you select the global weather area; they are only used with creating local weather fronts.

If you want to reuse your weather area, you must save it in a situation.

Beginning Latitude/Longitude

The beginning latitude/longitude coordinates define one vertex of the weather front's line.

Prefix your latitude entry with a N if you are entering a northern latitude, or a S if you are entering a southern latitude. For example, typing N42 35 16 in the Beginning Latitude text box, will result in a latitude coordinate of N42° 35' 16" being entered. Longitude entries must be prefixed with a E if you are in the Eastern Hemisphere, or a W if you are in the Western Hemisphere.

Ending Latitude/Longitude

The ending latitude/longitude coordinates define the second set of coordinates needed to draw the weather's front line.

Width

The width of the weather front determines how far across the weather area is. Widths must fall between the range of 0 to 2,000 miles.

Transition

In this box, enter the transition distance you want between weather areas. If you want to fly from one weather system to another in a relatively short time, pick a low distance such as 5 miles. Valid transition distances range from 0 miles to 99 miles.

Course

Type in the course heading the weather area is moving in. This direction corresponds to wind direction; if the weather front is moving east, it is traveling from a course of 90°. If it is moving south, the course heading is from 0°.

Speed

Enter the speed, in knots, that the weather front is moving. Speeds can vary from 0 to 99 knots.

Automatic Weather Generation

This feature enables automatic weather generation of clouds or winds. It disables any other weather you may have created for this area.

Copying a Weather Area or Category

FS 5.1 allows only two local weather areas and one global weather area. Unfortunately, because each weather area can store only a limited number of weather categories, your repertoire of weather conditions is finite. For example, even though you have three weather areas (two local and one global), you can only have a maximum of nine different kinds of cloud layers, since only three cloud layers per weather area are allowed.

You can copy an entire category of weather from one weather area to another, but the destination weather area will have its own similar category erased when you do this. For example, if you have three wind layers that you like in one part of the country, and you want to copy them to another area, you would use the copy command to do this. However, when the three wind layers are copied, they will overwrite the three previous wind layers that you might have in the second area.

To copy a weather category:

1. Choose the Weather menu from the World menu.

2. In the Weather dialog box, select the Weather Area where the weather you wish copied is found.

3. Select the category of weather you wish copied, whether it be clouds, winds, temperatures, or barometric pressure.

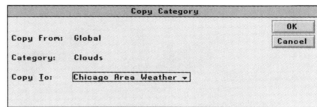

4. Click the Copy Category button, and you will be prompted to select the weather area where the weather is to be pasted, as shown in Figure 4.20.

Figure 4.20
Choosing which weather area the copied weather category is to be sent to

If you would like to copy an entire region's weather, including all wind, temperature, barometric pressures, and clouds, to another region, you would copy a weather area. Again, the second area's own weather will be overwritten when you do this.

To copy a weather area follow these steps:

1. Choose the Weather menu from the World menu.

2. In the Weather dialog box, select the Weather Area you wish to copy from.

3. Click the Copy Area button.

4. In the Copy Weather dialog box, select the Weather Area which is to be overwritten by the copied area, as is illustrated in Figure 4.21.

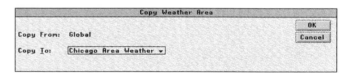

5. Click OK, once to return to the Weather dialog box, and once more to return to the simulator.

Figure 4.21
The Copy Weather dialog box

P A R T

II

Flight Academy: Ground School

C H A P T E R

5

Introduction to
Airplanes and Engines

This chapter introduces you to the basic airplane, its engine, and its associated equipment. It is important to have a basic knowledge of the airplane so you can understand how your airplane is affected by what you do. The main structural components of any airplane are the:

- Fuselage (or body)
- Wings
- Empennage (or tail section)
- Flight Controls and Airfoil Control Surfaces
- Landing Gear
- Engine

Figure 5.1 identifies these principal structural elements, as well as some other airplane components.

FUSELAGE, WINGS, EMPENNAGE

The fuselage houses the passenger cockpit, cargo, engine compartment, instruments, retractable landing gear, and other essential equipment. The engine is attached to the front of the fuselage in the engine compartment, but it is separated from the passenger compartment by a heat resistant steel firewall.

The wings produce the lift necessary for flight to occur and are considered an airfoil. Airfoils are surfaces on the airplane that produce some desired action when in motion. Beside wings, other examples of airfoils include: propeller blades, elevators,

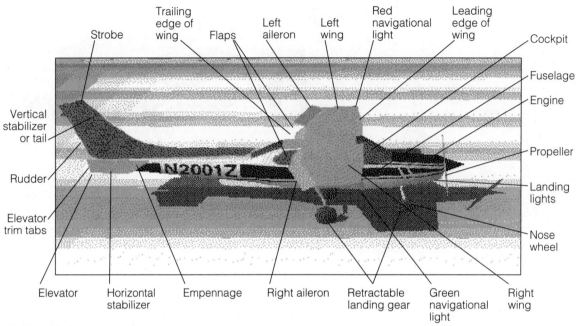

Figure 5.1
The basic structural components of the airplane

flaps, ailerons, rudders, trim tabs, spoilers, horizontal and vertical stabilizers, and slats. Attached to the trailing edge of the wing are the flaps, spoilers, ailerons, and trim tabs. On modern swept wing commercial aircraft, such as the Boeing 707, 727, 737, 747, 757, 767, and 777, there are lift devices on the front of the wings called leading-edge slats, which extend in conjunction with the flaps to further increase the lift of the wings.

There are two types of wings: semi-cantilever and cantilever. The semi-cantilevered wing is braced both externally by means of wing struts attached to the fuselage, and internally by spars and ribs. In the cantilever type wing, there is no external bracing; the stress is carried by internal wing spars, ribs, and stringers. Figure 5.1 shows the semi-cantilevered wing of the Cessna Skylane 182RG, while Figure 5.2 shows the Learjet's cantilevered wing. The fuel tanks in most modern aircraft today are integrated within the wing's structure.

The tail section of the airplane, or empennage, contains the airfoil surfaces nec-

Figure 5.2
Cantilevered wing of the Learjet

essary for pitch (up and down) and yaw (left and right) movements. It includes the fixed surfaces of the horizontal and vertical stabilizers. The empennage also includes all movable surfaces like the vertical and horizontal stabilizers, rudder, elevator, and trim tabs.

FLIGHT CONTROLS AND SURFACES

When you fly your airplane, you control its movement via a control stick, or wheel (also called the yoke) which moves the ailerons and elevator, and pedals which steer the rudder. In addition, there are other moveable wing surfaces like flaps, trim tabs, and spoilers. These moveable surfaces allow finer control over various aspects of flight. Small aircraft, such as the Cessna Skylane 182RG, the Schweizer 2-32 Sailplane, and the Sopwith Camel, have their flight control surfaces (otherwise known as "airfoil surfaces") controlled by means of cables, pulleys, and rods. For larger high speed jet aircraft, the airfoil surfaces are moved by hydraulic pistons. Such power assisted systems are necessary because of the vastly increased pressures needed to move the wing surfaces when traveling at high speeds. Usually there is an auxiliary power plant that runs off of the engine to provide hydraulic fluid throughout the plane at very high pressure. When the pilot moves a flight control, the movement is amplified and transmitted to the proper wing surface by means of high pressure hydraulic fluid through an elaborate network of hoses and pipes. Once the fluid reaches its destination, it moves a piston, and the piston in turn moves the wing surface.

Figure 5.3
Ailerons control aircraft roll (or bank) and are linked to the yoke by cables.

Ailerons

Ailerons, which means "little wing" in French, are two moveable wing surfaces located on the trailing edges of each wing near the outer tips. When they are deflected up or down, they change the wing's lift/drag characteristics and so enable the aircraft to roll about its longitudinal axis. Both ailerons are interconnected so they move in opposite directions of each other.

In *Flight Simulator*, the ailerons are usually moved together with the rudder

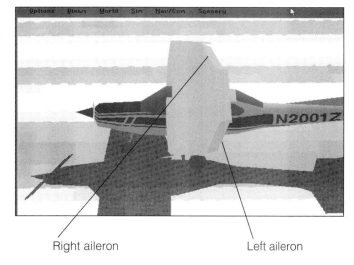

Right aileron   Left aileron

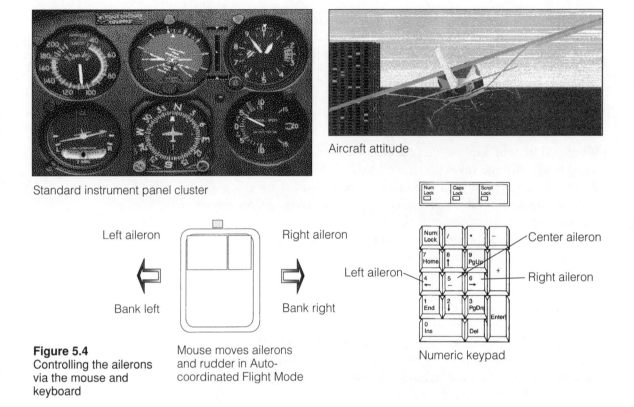

Standard instrument panel cluster

Aircraft attitude

Figure 5.4
Controlling the ailerons
via the mouse and
keyboard

Mouse moves ailerons
and rudder in Auto-
coordinated Flight Mode

Numeric keypad

in what is known as auto-coordinated mode. This mode enables you to make smooth turns without moving the rudder and ailerons separately. So if you move the yoke, stick, mouse, or keyboard controls to the right, the plane will make a right turn using the proper amount of rudder and aileron in concert together.

Wing Flaps

Extendible flaps on the inside trailing edges of the wings allow the wing to produce more lift, thereby permitting slower landing speeds and decreasing the required landing strip distance. In some cases, the extended flaps are used to shorten takeoff distance. The flaps can be extended in 10° increments, to a maximum of 40°. Each flap extension, however, increases both lift and drag.

The flaps must never be extended beyond the airplane's maximum flap extended speed (V_{fe}); to do so may result in damage to the flaps.

In *Flight Simulator*, you can adjust the flaps from the keyboard or by using the mouse, as is described in Figure 5.6.

Figure 5.5
Wing flaps permit slower landing speeds, and thus decrease required landing distances.

Rudder

Attached to the vertical stabilizer of the empennage, the rudder is used to control the airplane's yaw (left or right). Contrary to popular belief, the rudder by itself does not make the airplane turn (except on the ground). It is only when it is used in coordination with the ailerons, that it is possible for the airplane to make a smooth turn.

Moving the yoke left forces the rudder to the left, while moving the yoke to the right causes the rudder to move right. In auto-coordinated mode, moving the mouse left or right will also cause the ailerons to move the proper amount so that there is no slippage when making a turn. But in

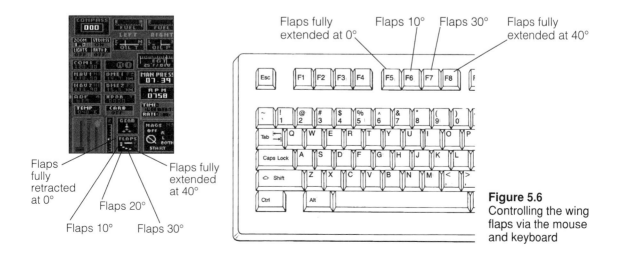

Figure 5.6
Controlling the wing flaps via the mouse and keyboard

uncoordinated flight (if you have rudder pedals or are flying in uncoordinated mode via the keyboard), you must set the rudder position independently of the ailerons when making turns. Figure 5.8 shows the keyboard and mouse controls for the rudder.

Right rudder applied

Figure 5.7
The rudder controls aircraft yaw (nose left or right movement) and is linked to foot pedals beneath the dashboard via cables.

Standard instrument cluster

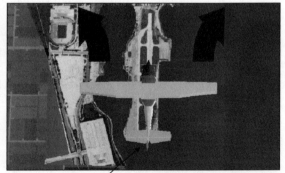

Rudder   Aircraft yaws left or right when rudder is moved left or right

Left aileron and rudder   Right aileron and rudder

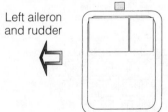

Center rudder

Right rudder

Left rudder

Figure 5.8
Controlling the rudder via the mouse and keyboard

Mouse moves ailerons and rudder in Auto-coordinated Flight mode

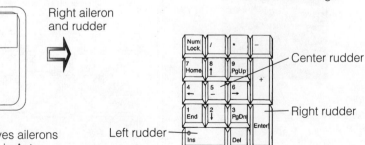

Numeric keypad

Elevator

The elevators are attached to the trailing edge of the horizontal stabilizer of the empennage. They act as airfoils to deflect the airflow up or down, thereby causing the nose of the aircraft to be pitched up or down. When you pull back on your yoke stick, the elevators go up, and the nose of your plane pitches upwards. When you push the yoke stick forwards, the elevators go down, and the nose pitches downwards.

Figure 5.10 illustrates the proper keyboard and mouse yoke movements for manipulating the elevator.

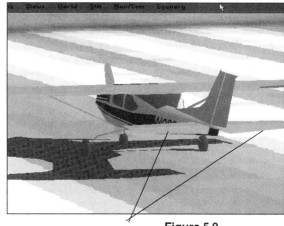

Elevators

Figure 5.9
The elevators control aircraft pitch (up or down movement), and are linked to the yoke by cables.

Elevator position indicator

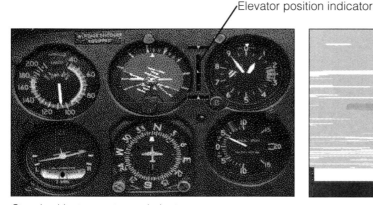

Standard instrument panel cluster

Aircraft climbing (Up elevator pitches nose up)

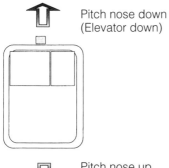

Pitch nose down
(Elevator down)

Pitch nose up
(Elevator up)

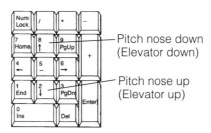

Pitch nose down
(Elevator down)

Pitch nose up
(Elevator up)

Figure 5.10
Controlling the elevator via the mouse and keyboard

Figure 5.11
The elevator trim tabs aid
the pilot in maintaining
level flight and are linked
to a lever via cables.

Elevator Trim Tabs

Trim Tabs

In addition to the primary flight control surfaces, there are secondary airfoil trim tabs, which help to maintain the aircraft's altitude while correcting for unbalanced aerodynamic forces on the plane. For example, if the pilot needs to pull the yoke back in order to keep the plane flying straight and level, he or she would quickly tire of keeping the pressure on the yoke indefinitely. The aerodynamic forces tend to force the elevator back to its neutral position. To prevent this, and relieve the pilot of constantly applying yoke pressure, the trim tab can be set to take up the slack.

Use elevator trim to make minor adjustments to nose pitch

Standard
instrument
panel
cluster

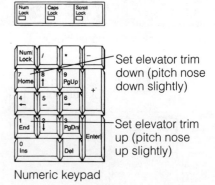

Set elevator trim
down (pitch nose
down slightly)

Set elevator trim
up (pitch nose
up slightly)

Numeric keypad

Figure 5.12
Controlling the elevator
trim tabs via the mouse
and keyboard

Elevator trim position indicator

Spoilers

The spoilers, found on most jets and gliders, are hinged wing panels mounted on the upper surface of each wing. Their purpose is to spoil, or disrupt, the flow of air over the wings, thereby reducing the lifting force of the wings. This allows the pilot to increase the rate of descent without increasing the airplane's speed. Spoilers are also used as a form of air braking, and if you have ever traveled on a commercial airliner and watched the wings during the descent phase of a flight, you may have noticed these panels deploying on top of the wing to slow the jet down.

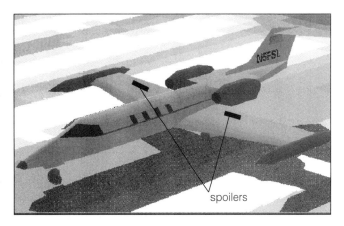

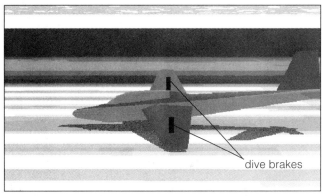

Figure 5.13 The glider and the learjet both have spoilers, which act as air brakes.

LANDING GEAR

The landing gear of the aircraft serves as its principal means of support whether on land or water. For amphibious water landings, special pontoons are mounted on each wheel. The pontoons allow the plane to hydroplane while landing or taking off and to float while stationary. Special ski landing gear can be mounted for snow bound areas, allowing operation on unimproved ice runways. Both pontoons and skis can have retractable wheels built into each wheel and strut assembly so the plane can operate on land, water, or ice, without changing landing gear.

Airplanes can have either a tailwheel or nosewheel that will help support the airplane on the ground and allow steering. Today, most modern airplanes are designed with a nosewheel and two main wheels mounted on either the wings or the fuselage. This landing gear arrangement is often called a "tricycle gear" since there are three wheels arranged in a triangular shape.

In *Flight Simulator*, the Cessna and Learjet have a tricycle landing gear, while the Sopwith Camel has a tailwheel type landing gear. The Schweizer 2-32 Sailplane has an unusual landing gear setup; there is a tailwheel and one center wheel mounted in the center of the fuselage along with a "tip wheel" on each wing tip. When the aircraft is at rest, you will notice that one wing

Figure 5.14
The Spoiler on/off indicator

tips onto the ground, and the wing tip wheel prevents it from rubbing or dragging on the runway.[1]

Retractable Landing Gear

Retractable landing gear, as found on the Cessna and Learjet, allows the plane to fly with reduced air drag. By retracting the landing gear into the wings and fuselage, the aircraft becomes more streamlined and offers less air resistance. This improves performance and fuel economy.

Because of the tremendous airflow pressures outside the aircraft, the retraction and extension of the landing gear cannot be performed by hand. Instead, hydraulic or electrically activated mechanisms force the landing gear up or down, and a locking device ensures that the gear is in place. A warning indicator informs the pilot when the wheels are down or stowed. In the event of a failure, a backup system is always provided to allow manual deployment of the landing gear. In the actual Cessna Skylane 182RG, there is an emergency hand-operated hydraulic pump that allows you to manually extend the landing gear in the event of a hydraulic system failure. But the landing gear cannot be retracted with the hand pump. The Learjet provides a manually controlled pneumatic system that blows the landing gear down with compressed air.

Nosewheel Steering

In both the Cessna and Learjet, the nosewheel can be steered by means of the rudder pedals. The linkage to the wheels can be via cables, push pull rods, or hydraulic fluid depending on the amount of force needed to turn the wheels. Large heavy aircraft utilize hydraulically assisted power steering because of the enormous forces needed to turn the wheel. The Learjet uses such power assisted steering via the rudder pedals.

Differential Wheel Brakes

When taxiing or landing, the wheel brakes are used for slowing, stopping, or steering the airplane. Differential brakes, found on both the Cessna and Learjet, are wheel brakes installed on each main landing wheel. They can be

---

[1]Notice that when you are on the ground, your out of airplane view in the Sailplane is tilted. This is because one of your wings is resting its tip wheel on the ground.

activated independently of each other by the pilot. The right-hand brake is controlled by applying pressure to the top of the right rudder pedal, while the left-hand brake is controlled by pressure applied to the top of the left rudder pedal. By judicious use of right or left brake pedal, you can steer the aircraft while on the ground during landing or taxiing. To apply both brakes, simply press on both toe pedals together.

Most small airplanes, such as the Cessna Skylane 182RG, have what is known as an "independent" brake system. In this system each brake has its own hydraulic fluid reservoir and is entirely independent of the airplane's main hydraulic system. The system operates much like conventional brake systems, with master cylinders, brake fluid reservoirs, fluid lines, and drum or disc brakes on each wheel. When the pilot applies toe pressure to a rudder pedal, the master cylinder builds up pressure through the movement of a piston inside a fluid filled cylinder. The brake fluid is then transmitted at high pressure through fluid lines to each brake assembly, where pistons force brake pads on the wheel's drum or disk surfaces. When parking, the brakes can be left on by employing a ratchet type locking device that maintains brake fluid pressure on the wheels.

AIRCRAFT ENGINES

The engine develops the power that gives the airplane forward motion, thereby generating the lift that enables it to fly. Engines are also commonly referred to as "powerplants" because they provide propulsion and they produce electrical power for the operation of electric motors, pumps, controls, lights, air conditioning, radios, and navigational instruments. In addition, engines provide hydraulic power necessary to pressurize the hydraulic system for the movement of the airfoil surfaces and landing gear. Furthermore, the engine furnishes heat for the crew members' and passengers' comfort and for de-icing the wings in cold weather. Also, the engine provides compressed air for pressurizing the cabin when flying above 8,000 feet.

The two most common types of internal combustion powerplants in use today are the reciprocating piston engine, and the turbine jet engine.

Reciprocating Piston Engines

The reciprocating piston engine gets its name because pressures from burning and expanding gases cause a piston in an enclosed cylinder to move up and down. The reciprocating motion of the piston is transferred into rotary motion by a crankshaft connected to the propeller.

To activate the brakes, press F11. For differential braking, the F11 function key applies the left brake, while the F12 function key applies the right brake. To set or release the parking brake, press Ctrl . simultaneously. For more realistic controls, you can buy rudder pedals that you hook up to your joystick port. Some pedals even have special toe fittings that allow you to individually control the left or right differential brake.

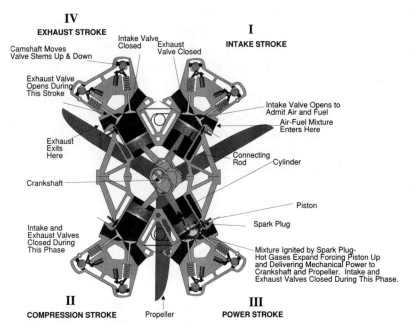

IV
EXHAUST STROKE

Camshaft Moves
Valve Stems Up & Down

Intake Valve
Closed

Exhaust
Valve Closed

I
INTAKE STROKE

Exhaust Valve
Opens During
This Stroke

Intake Valve Opens to
Admit Air and Fuel
Air-Fuel Mixture
Enters Here

Exhaust
Exits
Here

Connecting
Rod

Cylinder

Crankshaft

Piston

Intake and
Exhaust Valves
Closed During
This Phase

Spark Plug

Mixture Ignited by Spark Plug-
Hot Gases Expand Forcing Piston Up
and Delivering Mechanical Power to
Crankshaft and Propeller. Intake and
Exhaust Valves Closed During This Phase.

II
COMPRESSION STROKE

Propeller

III
POWER STROKE

Figure 5.15
The four-stroke cycle
of the reciprocating
piston engine

There are two principal means by which fuel is mixed with air into the cylinder of a reciprocating piston engine. The most common method of fuel mixing is called carburetion. In this method fuel is atomized, vaporized, and mixed with air in a mechanical device called the carburetor. Air and fuel are drawn into the cylinder by the suction of the piston moving down in the cylinder where it is then ignited by spark plugs. The other method of fuel mixing is called fuel injection. The fuel is injected under pressure by an electrical pump directly into the cylinders where it is vaporized and mixed with air. The fuel is precisely metered and controlled by a computer, along with the timing of the ignition by the spark plugs so that greater power, fuel economy, engine efficiency, and reliability can be achieved.

The reciprocating piston engine must go through four stages in order for complete combustion of the fuel to occur. This cycle is known as the "Four-Stroke Cycle" and is illustrated in Figure 5.15. When the piston moves downward, sucking in air and atomized fuel through the intake valve, it is in the intake stroke. After the piston reaches the bottom of its downward stroke, the intake valve closes and the piston begins to move upwards compressing the gaseous mixture of fuel and air. This is called the compression stroke. Just before the piston reaches the top of the cylinder on its way up, a spark plug over the cylinder head ignites the fuel mixture and an explosion of rapidly expanding hot gases ensues. The piston reaches the top of the cylinder head and, at the peak of the detonation, is forced downwards in what is called the power stroke. Both intake and exhaust valves are closed during this phase. The piston moves downward under great force and imparts momentum to the crankshaft, which in turn rotates the propeller. After this, when the piston reaches the bottom of the cylinder, the exhaust valve opens, and as the piston returns to the top of the cylinder, the gases are ejected into the atmosphere. This last stage is called the exhaust stroke.

With the Cessna's 6-cylinder (and six pistons), Lycoming Model O-540-L3C5D engine, each individual cylinder has its own four-stroke cycle, but staggered at even intervals so as to create a balanced power stroke. Two complete revolutions of the crankshaft are required for all the pistons to accomplish their four-stroke cycle.

Carburation, Air/Fuel Mixture Controls, Ignition Systems

Liquid fuel in all internal combustion engines must be vaporized into small particles and then mixed with air in precise quantities before combustion can occur. This process is called carbonation. The carburetor must sense the temperature, altitude, and other data to calculate how much fuel to mix at any given time. Because altitude affects the air/fuel ratio, a mixture control is provided for the pilot to manually control the carburetor's mixture ratios. The purpose of the mixture control is to prevent the mixture from becoming too rich (excess fuel) at high altitudes, due to the decreasing density (weight) of the air. Using the mixture control in conjunction with the Exhaust Gas Temperature (EGT) gauge, you can also lean the mixture (decrease amount of fuel mixed per mass of air) to conserve fuel and provide maximum fuel efficiency.

Air/fuel ratios are described by a ratio expression such as "12:1." What this means is that 12 pounds of air are being mixed with each 1 pound of fuel. Richer mixtures, where more fuel is being burned per mass of air, have lower ratios, for example 8:1. Leaner mixtures have higher ratios, e.g. 16:1, because less fuel is being mixed per quantity of air.

As altitude increases, the air fuel ratio decreases and the mixture becomes richer. At 18,000 feet, for example, the air is only half as dense as at sea level and a cubic foot of space contains only half as many molecules of air. Likewise, the engine cylinder drawing in air will contain only half as much air as the same cylinder at sea level. As a consequence, if you use the same amount of fuel at sea level that you use at 18,000 feet, the mixture will be much too rich and the engine will lose power or run roughly. Climbing higher and higher at the same throttle setting, the mixture becomes progressively richer because less oxygen is available the higher you go. Table 5.1 and Figure 5.16 summarize these results.

Using the mixture control you can counteract over-enriching the mixture by leaning the engine as you climb. How do you do this? By watching the EGT gauge

Figure 5.16
Air/fuel mixture gets richer with increasing altitude because of thinning atmosphere (fewer molecules of oxygen are available)

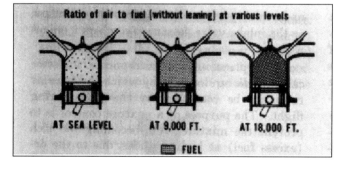

Ratio of air to fuel (without leaning) at various levels

AT SEA LEVEL   AT 9,000 FT.   AT 18,000 FT.

▨ FUEL

Table 5.1 Air–Fuel Mixture and Relationship with Altitude and EGT Temperature		
Air–Fuel Mixture	**Exhaust Gas Temperature (EGT)**	**Effect of Altitude**
Lean (less fuel per mass of air)	Temperature rises, engine gets hotter	Mixture leans with lower altitudes
Rich (more fuel per mass of air)	Temperature falls, engine gets cooler	Mixture is enriched with higher altitudes

(sometimes called the EGT Bug Needle) you can observe how hot the engine's exhaust is running. The exhaust gets hotter as you lean the engine, and cooler as you enrich it. The best fuel economy/power setting is found when you enrich the mixture 50° less than peak lean temperature. With aviation gas costing $2.50 a gallon, you should pay close attention to this fact! To properly lean your engine:

1. Lean the Mixture Control by dragging the control to the top until you establish what the peak EGT temperature is.
2. When the EGT needle reaches its highest temperature, enrich the Mixture Control by dragging the control to the bottom until the temperature has declined 50° below the peak EGT temperature. This is the recommended lean mixture setting, although the leanest (hottest) setting offers the best fuel economy.

Remember, be very careful not to over lean your engine, since too lean a mixture can damage the engine by over-heating. The following basic rules regarding changes to mixture settings should be followed at all times:

1. Always enrich the mixture before increasing the throttle.
2. Reset the mixture after any change in power/throttle settings or altitude.
3. Use full rich mixture for takeoff and climbing, unless the manufacturer recommends leaning at high altitudes to eliminate roughness and loss of power.

 In *Flight Simulator*, the Mixture Control is automatically adjusted for you, although you can switch this feature off under the Realism and Reliability menu command. To manually set the mixture perform these steps:

1. Select the Sim menu, and click on Realism and Reliability.

Table 5.2 Mixture and Exhaust Gas Temperature	
Mixture Description	**Exhaust Gas Temperature**
Recommended Lean	50° Rich of Peak EGT (50° cooler than peak lean temperature)
Best Fuel Economy	Peak EGT (hottest or peak lean temperature)

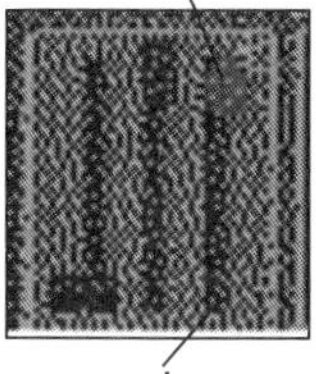

2. In the Realism and Reliability dialog box, locate the Prop Propulsion Realism area and toggle on the Mixture Control checkbox.

3. Click OK to return to the simulation. You can now manually adjust the Mixture Control.

The ignition system provides the spark which ignites the air/fuel mixture in the cylinders. On reciprocating piston engines, a magneto ignition system is used. This system has self-contained magneto generators driven by the engine, which supply electrical power to fire the spark plugs. Since the ignition system is so vital to the proper operation of the engine, the Federal Aviation Administration (FAA) requires modern airplane engines to have dual ignition systems that are completely separate from the rest of the plane's electrical system. Each ignition system has separate magnetos, cables, and spark plugs; in the event of one system failing, the engine may be operated until a safe landing is made. There is an ignition switch located on the instrument panel, which allows you to select the left or right magneto system, shut off the magnetos entirely, or operate the starter motor when starting the engine up.

Turbo-chargers

Many newer airplanes come equipped with turbo-charging systems to increase the power of the engine as well as allow high altitude operations. These superchargers are powered by the energy of the exhaust gas spinning a turbine blade and driving an air compressor that packs in more oxygen to each cylinder of the engine. This allows more air/fuel to be compressed into the cylinder for combustion, thereby increasing the maximum power the engine can produce. At high altitudes this is a very important feature, since the density of the air is much less and engine power decreases (despite leaning) because of the lack of oxygen.

Richer mixture

Leaner mixture

Figure 5.17
Mixture control

Figure 5.18
The Exhaust Gas Temperature Gauge (EGT). Each tick mark represents 25° Fahrenheit

Figure 5.19
Starter/magneto controls

Fixed Pitch Propellers vs. Constant Speed Propellers

The propellers transform the rotary motion of the engine into forward thrust for the airplane. Each blade of the propeller is a moving airfoil surface, and is thus essentially a rotating wing.

There are two kinds of propellers:

- Fixed-Pitch propellers
- Constant Speed propellers

The fixed pitch propeller has the blade pitch (blade angle) set to a constant angle which cannot be changed. These propellers are designed for operating best at one rotational per minute (RPM) and forward speed. The constant speed propeller, on the other hand, has a speed governor that regulates the blade pitch in order to maintain a constant engine RPM. In *Flight Simulator*, the Sopwith Camel comes equipped with a fixed pitch propeller while the Cessna Skylane 182RG has a constant speed propeller.

As mentioned previously, the constant speed propeller is an automatically controlled pitch propeller, with a governor that regulates the blade angle for a given engine RPM, altitude, and power setting. The purpose of having the blade's pitch adjusted is so a constant propeller speed can be maintained under varying engine loads. For example, if the engine RPM increases due to thinning air at higher altitudes, the speed governor increases the propeller's blade angle (increasing the air load) until the RPM has returned to a preset speed. The speed governor will respond automatically to small variations in RPM so a constant propeller speed is maintained at all times.

The propeller's blade angle affects the motion of the propeller through the airstream. When the blade angle is at a low pitch, as illustrated in Figure 5.20, the propeller slices through the air more easily, and a high RPM is maintained. A low propeller pitch is useful for obtaining maximum power on takeoff. When the blade angle is increased so it bites into the air more forcefully, the RPM is lowered. This is useful for flying at higher altitudes or at higher speeds where the approaching windstream tends to cause the propeller to windmill faster than you would like. By increasing the blade angle, the propeller's RPM will decrease and you can maintain a comfortable engine load.

The Prop Advance Control is initially set in *Flight Simulator* to automatic.[2] This means you don't need to pay any attention to the lever when you make changes in your throttle settings, altitude, or speed. However, if you want to manually advance or decrease the propeller's pitch, you must

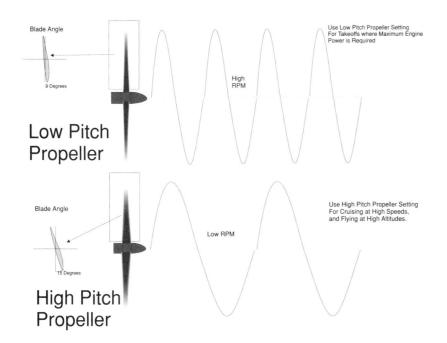

Blade Angle

9 Degrees

Low Pitch Propeller

High RPM

Use Low Pitch Propeller Setting For Takeoffs where Maximum Engine Power is Required

Blade Angle

15 Degrees

High Pitch Propeller

Low RPM

Use High Pitch Propeller Setting For Cruising at High Speeds, and Flying at High Altitudes.

Figure 5.20
Propeller blade angle vs. engine RPM

select Manual from the Prop Advance Control list box found in the Realism and Reliability dialog box. To do this:

1. Select the Sim menu, and click on Realism and Reliability.
2. In the Realism and Reliability dialog box, locate the Prop Propulsion Realism area and click open the Prop Advance list box.
3. Select Manual from among the three options of Automatic, Fixed Pitch, and Manual.
4. Click OK to return to the simulation. You can now manually adjust the propeller's pitch angle by sliding the Propeller lever up or down.

Low pitch angle/high RPM

High pitch angle/ low RPM

Figure 5.21
Prop pitch control

---

[2]The Propeller Control actually controls the propeller governor takes care of the dirty business of deciding the proper blade angle. Essentially, the setting you choose determines the maximum speed for the propeller; the governor won't let the prop pitch advance to allow a propeller speed faster than your setting

Table 5.3 Propeller Blade Angle and Engine RPM Relationship		
Pitch	**Effect on Engine RPM**	**Useful For**
Low blade angle	Higher RPM	Takeoffs, where maximum power is needed
High blade angle	Lower RPM	Cruising at high speed, or flying at high altitudes

When you slide the Propeller Control lever down, you increase the propeller's pitch and decrease the engine's RPM. If you slide the Propeller Control up, you decrease the propeller's pitch and increase the engine's RPM.

Manifold Pressure Gauge and the Tachometer

The two instruments that give you a measure of your engine's power output are the manifold pressure gauge and the tachometer. The manifold pressure gauge measures the amount of engine vacuum, or suction, the pistons are exerting on the incoming air/fuel mixture. It is measured in inches of mercury (Hg) below atmospheric pressure, and it ranges from 0" to slightly above 30". For most aircraft, there is a never exceed manifold pressure limit for any given RPM. If the manifold pressure limit is exceeded, severe stress on the engine cylinders to the point where structural failure could occur. For the Cessna, the manifold pressure averages around 29" to 31" Hg for most conditions.

The tachometer simply measures how many times the engine's crankshaft revolves per minute. It can range from 0 RPM all the way up to 3,000 RPM or more for piston powered engines. This instrument tells you whether your engine is rotating excessively fast, just right, or too slow. On the Cessna, typical cruising RPM is about 2,100 to 2,400 RPM.

Relationship Between Manifold Pressure and Engine RPM

As the throttle is increased, the power output of the engine increases and is indicated by an increase in manifold pressure. The Propeller Control, or Prop Advance, changes the pitch of the propeller blades and governs the RPM's of the engine, as indicated on the tachometer. Increasing the throttle further causes the manifold pressure to rise, and the pitch angle of the propeller blades is then automatically increased through the action of the speed

Maximum

Minimum

Figure 5.22
Throttle control

governor to hold down the speed of the propellers (as the blade angle increases to a higher pitch angle, the air load on the propeller increases and this increases the load on the engine and causes the RPM's to be held down to a constant level). Conversely, when the throttle is reduced, the manifold pressure falls and the pitch angle of the propeller blades is automatically decreased. This decrease in propeller pitch lightens the load on the engine, which is developing less power because of the reduced throttle setting, and the RPM remains constant.

Figure 5.23
Manifold pressure gauge and tachometer

Turbine (Turbojet)

Turbine jet engines use a different principle to produce thrust. A turbine inside the turbojet is driven by high speed exhaust gases; in turn this turbine spins a compressor turbine to compress the incoming air. After the incoming air is compressed, it becomes very hot and is forced into a combustion chamber where fuel is mixed and ignited by special burners. The resulting explosion of hot gas exits the rear of the engine, passing through the turbine that spins the compressors. The hot gas rushes out the rear of the engine at high velocity, creating great thrust for the aircraft.

Turbofan Jet

The favored type of engine for commercial jet aviation is the turbofan jet engine. This engine is a variation of the turbojet. It has a distinctively large, oversized low pressure compressor in the front of the engine, which creates a relatively cool and slow propulsive jet exhaust. Its advantages over the turbojet include reduced fuel consumption, better propulsive efficiency, and dramatically lower noise levels. This is an important consideration for airports that have restricted night flying because of neighborhood noise complaints. Jet aircraft equipped with turbofan engines can enjoy less restrictive flying schedules. In fact, to reduce noise and extend their useful life spans, many older aircraft, such as the McDonnell Douglas DC-9 (now called the MD-80 or Super 80) and Boeing 737, have had their turbojet engines replaced by the newer technology turbofan engines. Some aircraft, notably the Boeing 727, cannot be re-engined with these newer engines, and so have become obsolete. Due to these considerations, production of the turbojet engined Boeing 727 was discontinued in September 1984.

Figure 5.24
Operating principles of the Turbojet engine

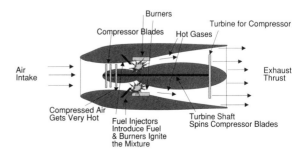

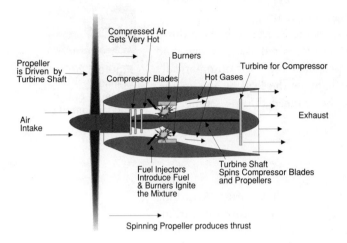

Figure 5.25
Operating principles of
the Turboprop engine

The two Garret AiResearch TFE731-2-2B turbofan engines used on the Learjet 35A are rated at 3,500 lbs of thrust each. Present day turbofan engines, such as the GE CF6-80C2, used on the Boeing 747, 767, and Airbus A310, and A330; produce thrust in the range of 50,000 to 60,000 lbs. Powerful new turbofan engines for the new twin engine Boeing 777 generate thrusts of nearly 100,000 lbs!

Modern turbofan jet engines are some of the most compact sources of power known to mankind, other than one-shot devices (meaning they can be used only once) such as explosives. These engines can be found in other diverse roles, for example driving air-cushion vehicles, powering warships, producing electrical power in power plants, driving pumps, and in general being used wherever high sustained power is required with the utmost reliability. Because there are fewer moving parts in a jet engine than in the reciprocating piston engine, the turbojet/turbofan powerplant is inherently more reliable than its piston powered counterpart. For example, the mean time between overhaul (TBO) can range from 1,400 hours for the Garrett turbofan jet engines, to 3,000 hours for the General Electric CFE 738 turbofan engine. The TBO applies only to the hot section of the engine core, and the TBO for the other parts of the engine can be as much as 6,000 hours before an engine rebuild is necessary! Compared to this, the 1,000 to 2,000 hours TBO for a piston powered reciprocating engine is not very appealing.

Turbo-prop

Another variance of the turbine jet engine, the turbo-prop engine has a turbine that also drives a propeller in addition to the compressor blades. The propeller in the turbo-prop engine supplies most of the engine's thrust. But some of the exhaust gas vented out the back of the engine contributes a portion of the overall thrust. Although the turbo-prop has a theoretical fuel efficiency advantage over most jet engines, problems remain with unacceptably high noise levels, particularly inside the cabin.

CHAPTER
6

Mastering Flight Basics

This chapter discusses the basic principles of flight. The actual physics and mathematical descriptions of flight dynamics are complex topics that go far beyond the scope of this book. However, a limited discussion on fluid dynamics, Bernoulli's Equation, and the fundamental aerodynamic forces is made so the reader can be de-mystified about how flight is possible. The chapter concludes with a brief overview of stalls and how to avoid them.

THE PHYSICS OF FLIGHT

For any discussion of aerodynamics, you must have a firm understanding of the nature of forces. The next section covers the application of Newton's Laws to the physics of flight.

Newton's Laws

Sir Isaac Newton, the brilliant seventeenth century English physicist and mathematician, formulated the basic concepts of mechanics (the laws of motion, action, and reaction) in 1687. He also discovered the law of universal gravitation, and invented calculus.

Newton's first law of motion was formalized by the following definition:

> *An object at rest will remain at rest and an object in motion will continue in motion with a constant velocity until it experiences a net external force.*

His second law of action defined force as follows:

> *The acceleration of an object is directly proportional to the resultant force acting on it and inversely proportional to its mass. $F = ma$*

His third law of reaction defines the interaction of forces, namely:

If two bodies interact, the force exerted by body 1 on body 2 is equal to and opposite the force exerted on body 2 to body 1.
$(F_{1-2} = -F_{2-1})$

According to the second law, force is thus defined as

$$F = ma$$

where F is defined in Newtons (or *kilogram-meters/second²*) or pounds (English unit of force is the lb which has units of *feet-slug/second²*), m is defined as mass in kilograms or slugs (English unit of mass is the slug), and a is the acceleration of the object in *meters/second²* or, in English units *feet/second²*.

Acceleration is defined as the change in velocity per unit time of an object, and it has the following derivation:

$$a = \frac{v_{final} - v_{initial}}{t_{final} - t_{initial}} = \frac{\Delta v}{\Delta t}$$

Δv is the difference between the final velocity and the initial velocity. Δt is the change in time from the initial time to the final time.

For an airplane to fly at a constant speed, according to Newton's first law of motion, the four forces of lift, weight, drag, and thrust must all cancel each other out. If the airplane is to climb, the force of lift must be greater than the force of weight. If the airplane is to descend, the force of lift must be less than the force of weight.

Figure 6.1
The four forces acting on the airplane

Likewise, to increase the airplane's speed, the thrusting force of the engines must be greater than the drag forces on the airplane. And to decrease the airplane's speed, the drag force must be greater than the thrust force.

The Four Basic Forces of Aerodynamics

The four forces of lift, weight, thrust, and drag affect your aircraft and must be balanced for stable flight to occur.

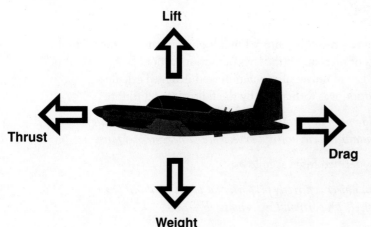

Lift

Thrust

Drag

Weight

Lift

Lift is an upward force on the wings which counteracts the opposing force of weight caused by the Earth's gravitational field on the mass of the airplane. Lift acts perpendicular to the relative wind in a vertical direction. There are two forces that create lift: the Bernoulli pressure differential on the upper and lower surfaces of the wing, and air deflection caused by the wing's angle of attack (the angle between the wind and the relative wind). A discussion of Bernoulli's Principle for fluids (or airflow, since air is considered a compressible fluid) follows later in this chapter. The lift must exactly counteract the opposite force of weight if the aircraft is to fly straight and level. Lift must be greater than the aircraft's weight in order to gain altitude, and less than the aircraft's weight in order to descend.

Greater lift is achieved if the wing travels faster through the air or if its angle of attack is increased. The angle of attack is the angle between the wing and the relative wind. Increasing the angle of attack increases lift but also deflects more air and increases induced drag. This induced drag at high angles of attack occurs because violent vortices form over the wing, creating more turbulence and disrupting the smooth flow of air over the wing.

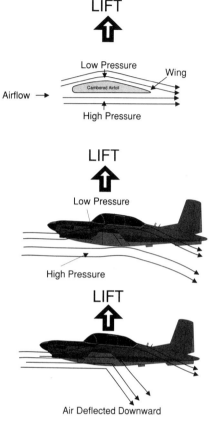

Figure 6.2
Forces creating lift

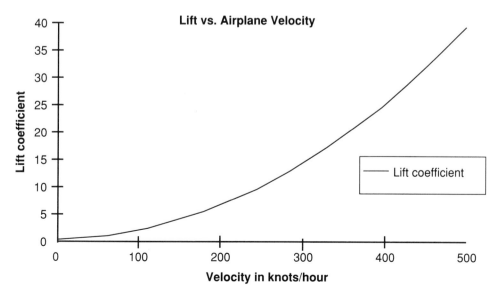

Figure 6.3
Lift is proportional to the square of the airplane's velocity.

Table 6.1 Required Takeoff Distance Increases on Hot Days					
Temperature (Fahrenheit)	60	70	80	90	100
Takeoff distance for the Learjet (feet), flaps set at 20 degrees	5020	5150	5560	6130	7370
Takeoff distance for the Cessna Skylane 182RG feet), flaps set at 20 degrees	790	855	925	975	1000

Lift is proportional to the square of the airplane's velocity, as is shown in the equation below and in Figure 6.4. An airplane traveling at 200 knots, for example, has four times the lift of an airplane traveling at 100 knots, if the angle of attack and other factors remain constant.

$$Lift \propto Velocity^2$$

You can also increase lift by extending the flaps. However, any extension of the flaps also increases parasitic drag and unless you apply more thrust, the aircraft will lose airspeed.

Lift also varies directly with the density of the air; the denser the atmosphere, the greater the lift. At an altitude of 18,000 feet, the density of air is 1/2 the density of air at sea level. To maintain its lift at a higher altitude, the airplane must fly at a greater airspeed. Also, on warm days, the air is less dense than on cold days. This means that to maintain the same amount of lift on a hot day, the airplane must travel at a greater speed than on a cold day. Furthermore, landings and takeoffs require longer runways on hot days than on cold days because of the decreased lift caused by the less dense hot air. A takeoff from Denver's Stapleton International Airport at an altitude of 5,871 feet will take a longer runway distance than from San Francisco International at an altitude of 11 feet.

Weight

Weight is the attractive force the Earth's gravitational field exerts on the mass of the airplane, its passengers, cargo, and fuel. It is diametrically opposed to lift and is mathematically described as

$$F = mg$$

where F is the Force of gravity, m is the mass of the airplane and its occupants, and g is the acceleration of gravity

$$g = 9.6 \; meters / second^2 = 32 \; feet / second^2$$

According to the above formula, the Cessna, with a weight of 3,122 lbs, has a mass of 97.56 slugs

$$m = \frac{F}{g} = \frac{3,122 \; lbs}{32 \; feet / second^2} = 97.56 \; slugs$$

In metric terms, the Cessna has a weight of 13,887 Newtons, and dividing out the acceleration of gravity (9.8 *meters / second*^{2}), we get a mass of 1,417 kilograms.

$$m = \frac{F}{g} = \frac{13,887 \; Newtons}{9.8 \; meters / second^2} = 1,417 \; kilograms$$

An aircraft has a center of gravity usually determined by the center of mass of the airplane. If an aircraft is loaded in an unbalanced way so too much weight is distributed in one place, the center of gravity (center of mass) can change and drastically effect the airplane's stability. This can cause an airplane to crash, and in fact, years ago a jetliner carrying a cargo of steer crashed because the cattle shifted around inside the plane and caused its center of gravity to be shifted too far forward. As a result, the jet lost its lateral stability and it nose dived into the ground.

Thrust

Thrust is the force applied by the engines causing forward motion of the airplane through the air. When applied, thrust causes the airplane to accelerate forwards, gaining speed until the counteracting force of drag equals that of thrust. In order for a constant speed to be maintained, thrust and drag must be equal, just as lift and weight must be equal to maintain a constant altitude.

To increase thrust, the throttle is pushed forward (or up on the FS 5.1 control panel), while to decrease thrust the throttle is pulled back (or down on the FS 5.1 control panel). Contrary to what you might think, increasing thrust does not translate into a direct increase in horizontal airspeed. Due to the airflow over the wings and tail, increasing the thrust tends to force the nose up causing the aircraft to ascend, as is illustrated in Figure 6.4. Similarly, decreased power causes the nose to lower and the aircraft to descend. This explains why you use the engine throttle settings to control your vertical speed (up and down ascending and descending velocity) in what is known as the Power/Pitch Rule:

Use the throttle power settings to make changes in vertical airspeed;
use the elevator pitch controls to make changes in airspeed.

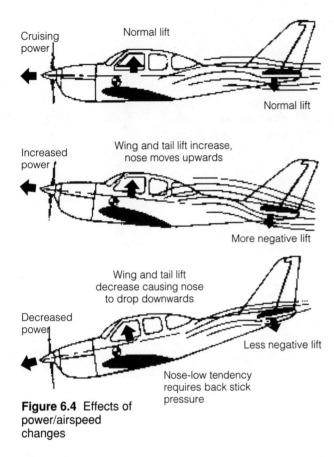

Figure 6.4 Effects of power/airspeed changes

Figure 6.5
Drag vs. speed chart

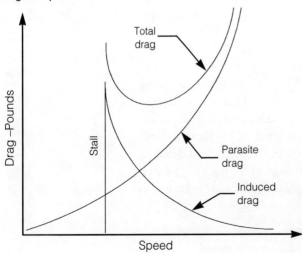

Drag

Drag is the force that retards forward motion of the aircraft. There are two types: parasitic drag and induced drag. Parasitic drag comes from the disruption and friction of the airflow over the surface of the airplane; induced drag comes from the turbulent vortices of air currents that are created whenever a wing moves through the airstream. With careful design of an aircraft, parasitic drag can be reduced. But induced drag is an inherent penalty of the wing's producing lift and it is always present in some form.

As illustrated in Figure 6.5, total drag is equal to the sum of parasitic drag and induced drag:

$$Total\ Drag = Parasitic\ Drag + Induced\ Drag$$

Furthermore, as can be seen in the figure, the faster the airplane travels, the greater the parasitic drag. Induced drag, on the other hand, decreases for greater aircraft speeds.

Bernoulli's Law for Pressure, Kinetic Energy, and Potential Energy

The study of fluids in motion is called fluid dynamics. A fluid is defined as having particles that easily move and change position. The particles can be compressible, as in a gas, or incompressible as in a liquid, but in both cases the particles are capable of flowing easily. The airflow over a wing and the flow of water through a pipe are examples of fluid dynamics.

To understand the physics of flight, one must understand Bernoulli's Equation and how it relates to the motion of a particle on a streamline. We will first use the example of fluid moving through a pipe to explain the general principles involved, then turn to the direct case of the streamlined flow of air around an airplane wing.

As fluid moves through a pipe of varying cross section and elevation, the pressure will change along the pipe. The Swiss physicist Daniel Bernoulli (1700–1782) discovered an expression that relates pressure to fluid speed and elevation. The equation he developed was derived from the laws of conservation of energy, as applied to an ideal fluid. Bernoulli discovered that if the velocity of a fluid (air) is increased at a particular point, the pressure of the fluid (air) at that point is decreased. The law derived for this observation is now called Bernoulli's Equation.

As applied to an airplane's wing, Bernoulli's Equation explains how lift occurs. Quite simply, the airplane's wing is designed to increase the velocity of the air flowing over the top of the wing. To do this, the top of the wing is curved, and the bottom of the wing is relatively flat. The air flowing over the top curved portion of the wing travels a farther distance than the air flowing over the flat bottom, hence it must flow faster. According to Bernoulli's Law, the airflow over the top of the wing, since it is faster, must have less pressure than the slower airflow underneath the wing. The higher pressure underneath the wing (associated with the slower speed airstream below the wing) pushes or lifts the wing up toward the lower pressure area above the wing (associated with the higher speed airstream above the wing).

To understand how Bernoulli's Equation works, consider the flow of

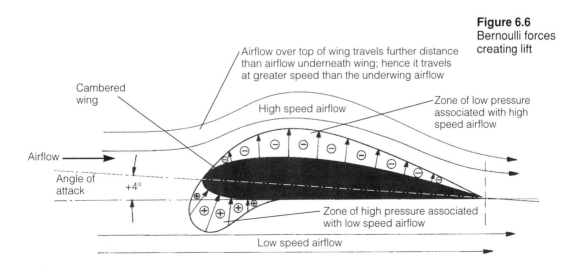

Figure 6.6
Bernoulli forces creating lift

Airflow over top of wing travels further distance than airflow underneath wing; hence it travels at greater speed than the underwing airflow

Cambered wing

High speed airflow

Zone of low pressure associated with high speed airflow

Airflow

Angle of attack   +4°

Zone of high pressure associated with low speed airflow

Low speed airflow

water through a pipe with different widths at each end, as illustrated in Figure 6.7. The force on the lower end of fluid is

$$F_1 = P_1 A_1$$

where P_1 is the pressure in Pascals (Newtons/meter^2) and A_1 is the area in meters^2 of the lower pipe end. The work, or energy input at the lower end of the pipe is

$$Work_1 = Force \times distance = F_1 \Delta x_1 = P_1 A_1 \Delta x_1$$

The force on the upper end of the fluid is

$$F_2 = P_2 A_2$$

where P_2 is the pressure and A_2 is the cross sectional area of the upper pipe end. The work, or energy used, at the top of the pipe is

$$Work_2 = F_2 \Delta x_2 = P_2 A_2 \Delta x_2$$

The volume of both shaded regions of fluid is the same, for example:

$$\Delta x_1 A_1 = Volume\ 1 = \Delta V$$

$$\Delta x_2 A_2 = Volume\ 2 = \Delta V$$

Since the two sections of fluid are trying to move in directions against each other, the net work done is:

$$Net\ Work = Work_1 - Work_2 = P_1 \Delta V - P_2 \Delta V = (P_1 - P_2) \Delta V$$

Kinetic Energy is defined as $\frac{1}{2} \times Mass \times Velocity^2$ or $KE = \frac{1}{2} mv^2$. The change in kinetic energy for the water in this system is

$$\Delta KE = \frac{1}{2} \Delta mv_2^2 - \frac{1}{2} \Delta mv_1^2$$

The potential energy of the system, which is defined as $\Delta U = Mass \times acceleration\ of\ gravity \times height\ above\ ground$, must take into account the two sections of water Δx_1 and Δx_2 and their respective distances above the ground. Since both volumes of water contain the same amount of mass, and the acceleration of gravity is a constant, this becomes

$$\Delta U = \Delta mgy_2 - \Delta mgy_1$$

By applying the work energy theorem in the form of

$$Work = Kinetic\ Energy + Potential\ Energy$$

or

$$Net\ Work = \Delta K + \Delta U$$

and plugging in the expressions for Net Work, Kinetic Energy and Potential Energy from the previously listed equations, we get:

$$Net\ Work = (P_1 - P_2)\Delta V = \frac{1}{2}\Delta m v_2^2 - \frac{1}{2}\Delta m v_1^2 + \Delta mgy_2 - \Delta mgy_1$$

If we then divide the above equation by ΔV, we get

$$(P_1 - P_2) = \frac{1}{2}\frac{\Delta m}{\Delta V}v_2^2 - \frac{1}{2}\frac{\Delta m}{\Delta V}v_1^2 + \frac{\Delta m}{\Delta V}gy_2 - \frac{\Delta m}{\Delta V}gy_1$$

Realizing that density is equal to mass divided by volume or

$$Density = p = \frac{mass}{Volume} = \frac{\Delta m}{\Delta V}$$

the equation then becomes:

$$(P_1 - P_2) = \frac{1}{2}pv_2^2 - \frac{1}{2}pv_1^2 + pgy_2 - pgy_1$$

Finally, rearranging the terms of the above equation we get:

$$P_1 + \frac{1}{2}pv_1^2 + pgy_1 = P_2 + \frac{1}{2}pv_2^2 + pgy_2$$

This is Bernoulli's Equation as applied to a non-viscous, incompressible fluid in a steady flow. It is often expressed as

$$P + \frac{1}{2}pv^2 + pgy = constant$$

Bernoulli's equation states that the sum of the Pressure (P) plus the energy per unit volume ($\frac{1}{2}pv^2$) plus the potential energy per unit volume (pgy) has the same constant value at all points along the stream line. This means that in Figure 6.7, the volume of fluid at the bottom of the pipe ($V = A_1\Delta x_1$) has the same value of P+$\frac{1}{2}pv^2$+pgy as the volume of water ($V = A_2\Delta x_2$) at the top of the pipe! This has important applications for the dynamics of flight as we shall soon see.

Consider the wing and the flow of air around it as illustrated in Figure

Bernoulli's Equation

Figure 6.7
Incompressible fluid
flowing through a pipe
of varying cross-
section.

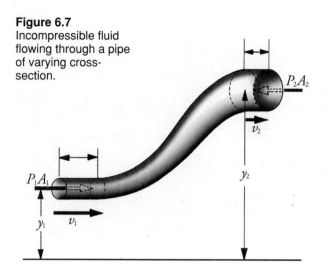

6.8. The shape of the airplane's wing is designed so that the upper surface is more curved than the lower surface. Air flowing over the upper surface follows a more curved path than air flowing over the lower surface. According to the Bernoulli principle of equivalence for all particles in a stream flow, the air flowing over the top of the wing must have the same Bernoulli constant as the air flowing over the bottom of the wing. This means that for both the top air flow and bottom air flow

$$P_1 + \frac{1}{2}\rho v_1^2 + \rho g y_1 = P_2 + \frac{1}{2}\rho v_2^2 + \rho g y_2$$

where P_1, v_1, and y_1 are the pressure, speed, and distance above ground for the air flow underneath the wing, and P_2, v_2, and y_2 are the pressure, speed, and distance above ground for the air flow above the wing. Since the top air flow needs to travel a more lengthy and circuitous route per unit time over the curved cambered portion of the wing than does the bottom air flow (they both arrive at the same time and at the same location on the trailing edge of the wing), the speed of the top air flow v_2 is greater than the speed v_1 of the airflow beneath the wing:

v_1 = speed of airflow under wing

v_2 = speed of airflow over top of wing

$v_2 > v_1$

Assuming for the sake of this argument that the distances above the ground y_1 y_2 have a negligible effect on the Bernoulli equation, you can see that in order for the two equations to balance, the pressure P_1 of the airflow underneath the wing MUST BE GREATER than the pressure P_2 of the airflow above the wing. The pressure being greater below the wing than above, causes a net upward force F on the wing, which is called dynamic lift. The faster the air flows over the wing, all things being equal, the greater the dynamic lift since the speed differential between $v_2 > v_1$ becomes much greater causing P_1 to be much greater than P_2.

It is a well known phenomenon that if you place a piece of paper on a table and blow across its top surface, the paper rises. This is because the faster air moving over the top surface causes a reduction in pressure above the paper and thus a net upward force. This is a simple example of the Bernoulli princi-

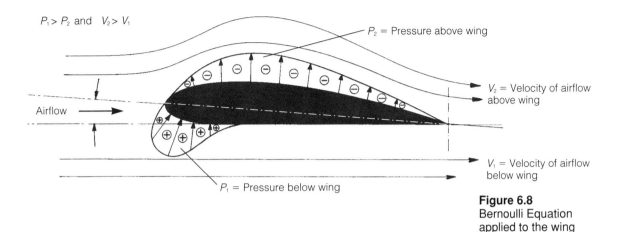

$P_1 > P_2$ and $V_2 > V_1$

P_2 = Pressure above wing

Airflow

V_2 = Velocity of airflow above wing

V_1 = Velocity of airflow below wing

P_1 = Pressure below wing

Figure 6.8
Bernoulli Equation applied to the wing

ples. By the same token, the roofs of buildings are often blown off by strong winds, hurricanes, or tornadoes because of the Bernoulli forces at work. This is because the rushing air over the outside surface of the roof causes a drop in outside pressure, and if the building is not well vented, the air pressure inside the building can build up and literally blow the roof off!

THE DANGER OF STALLS

A stall occurs when the smooth airflow over the airplane's wing is disrupted and the lift degenerates. It is important to realize that a stall can occur *at any airspeed, in any aircraft attitude, and with any engine power setting*. Without prompt corrective action, the airplane will crash into the ground. Fortunately, as an aid for armchair pilots, *Flight Simulator* has a visual stall warning indicator that appears on screen, warning you of an imminent stall situation. Figure 6.9 shows what a typical stall looks like. It also shows an illustration of the turbulent airflow over the wings that robs the airplane of its lift.

Figure 6.9
In the stall, smooth airflow is disrupted over the wing, causing loss of lift.

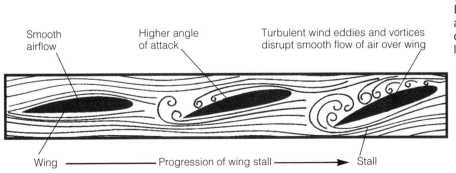

Smooth airflow

Higher angle of attack

Turbulent wind eddies and vortices disrupt smooth flow of air over wing

Wing ———————— Progression of wing stall ————→ Stall

Table 6.2 Stall Speeds for the Cessna, Learjet, Sailplane, and Sopwith Camel		
Aircraft	**V_{S0} Stall Speed with Landing Gear & Flaps Extended**	**V_{S1} Stall Speed with Flaps Retracted, Landing Gear Retracted**
Cessna Skylane 182RG	54 Knots IAS	50 Knots IAS
Learjet 35A	97 Knots IAS	No published info
Schweizer 2-32 Sailplane	Not applicable (no retractable landing gear or flaps)	48 Knots IAS
Sopwith Camel	Not applicable (no retractable landing gear or flaps)	50 Knots IAS

Stall Recovery

Here are the fundamental steps to follow in any stall recovery:

1. **Lower the pitch of the aircraft** so that the wing's angle of attack is decreased. Since the basic cause of the stall is always an excessive angle of attack for a given airspeed, lowering the airplane's nose by using the elevators (press the 8 key on the numeric keypad, or roll the mouse forwards, or push the joystick forwards) will remedy this problem.
2. **Increase throttle to maximum** (Press the F4 function key) This will increase the wing's speed and generate more lift.
3. **Resume straight and level flight** using ailerons, rudders, and elevators as necessary.

All aircraft manufacturers publish stall airspeed charts for different flight conditions. These charts tell you the minimum speed you can fly the aircraft before a stall will occur. You must never fly below these stall speeds, else your plane will lose all its lift and it will crash. There are two defined stall speeds:

V_{S0}: The stall speed or minimum flight speed at which the aircraft is controllable with the landing gear down, flaps extended to the 20° or 40° setting (landing configuration).

V_{S1}: The stall speed with or minimum flight speed at which the aircraft is controllable when the landing gear is up and the flaps are retracted to the 0° setting (clean configuration).

CHAPTER
7

Exploring the Cockpit

The cockpit of an airplane contains many instruments, displays, controls, and navigational equipment. This chapter discusses the cockpit instrumentation found on the Cessna Skylane 182RG, Learjet 35A, Schweizer 2-32 Sailplane, and Sopwith Camel. Since many of the controls and instruments are similar on the four planes, complete discussions on those instruments duplicating the Cessna's have been omitted. Therefore, if you are skipping ahead and reading the sections about the Learjet, Sailplane, and Sopwith Camel, and want a better explanation about a particular instrument or control, check the Cessna section in the first part of this chapter for more information. After reading this chapter, you should have a basic understanding of each control and instrument as it pertains to the operation of your aircraft.

UNDERSTANDING YOUR INSTRUMENTS
AND CONTROLS ON THE CESSNA

The photo-realistic Cessna instrument panel offers many new features over the previous *Flight Simulator 4.0* version. In addition to the throttle control, there is a carburetor mixture control, a propeller pitch control (speed governor), an Exhaust Gas Temperature (EGT) gauge, a manifold pressure indicator, and an outside digital temperature gauge. In the radio stack, there is a Distance Measuring Equipment (DME) indicator for the NAV 2 radio, and the autopilot has been enhanced. There are landing lights and you can now set the simulator's speed directly from the rate control underneath the digital clock.

All the instruments can be displayed without the photo-realism for easier readability or to speed up the simulation. If you find your flight instruments hard to read in

Figure 7.1
The Cessna's instrument control panel

the photo-realism mode, you can open the Instrument Preferences dialog box from the Options menu, and select the Panel Display list box to choose the Enhanced Readability option. In the same dialog box, you can also choose to have your instruments updated more frequently for added realism, but doing so slows down the simulation slightly. Figure 7.1 shows the Cessna's instrument panel.

Standard Instrument Cluster

There are six primary flight instruments in the standard instrument cluster. Based on their *modus operandi*, these instruments can be further divided into two categories: pitot-static instruments (pressure) and gyroscopic instruments. The pitot-static instruments include the following:

- Airspeed Indicator
- Altimeter
- Vertical Speed/Rate of Climb Indicator

The gyroscopic instruments include the:

- Artificial Horizon/Attitude Indicator
- Heading Indicator/Directional Gyro
- Turn Coordinator

Figure 7.2
The standard instrument cluster on the Cessna

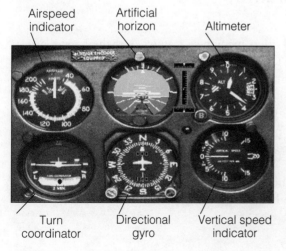

Airspeed indicator   Artificial horizon   Altimeter

Turn coordinator   Directional gyro   Vertical speed indicator

Figure 7.2 shows the standard instrument cluster for the Cessna.

Pitot-static Instruments

The pitot-static system takes impacted air pressure from a pitot tube (which is mounted face forward to the aircraft's direction of movement) and this dynamic pressure is ducted through the pitot line to the altimeter, airspeed indicator, and the vertical speed indicator. These instruments operate by measuring differences in air pressure to obtain their readings.

Airspeed Indicator

The airspeed indicator shows the aircraft's indicated airspeed (IAS)[1], and is calibrated in nautical miles per hour, or knots. The airspeed readings are obtained by measuring differences between ram air pressure from the pitot head and atmospheric pressure from the static vents. When the aircraft is parked on the ground, the pressure difference in the pitot-static system is zero; but when the aircraft is moving, pressure builds up and there will be a pressure difference that increases with speed. Note the IAS is not the same as your ground speed, since the airspeed readings are dependent on a hypothetical standard atmospheric air pressure at sea level. Air pressure depends on temperature, altitude, and weather. When these conditions change, the airspeed indicator will no longer show the aircraft's true airspeed (TAS). TAS is not the same as ground speed unless it is measured in still air.

Figure 7.3
The Airspeed indicator

Since air pressure is less at higher altitudes, the airspeed indicator gives you a slower reading for your speed than is actually the case.

As shown in Figure 7.3, the airspeed indicator in FS 5.1 is calibrated to show 5 knot increments. It reads from 40 knots all the way up to 220 knots. However the Cessna is not supposed to exceed 178 knots, as is shown by the red lined zone on the dial. Traveling faster than this speed, called the "never exceed" V-speed (V_{NE}), will cause structural damage to the airplane and possibly result in a crash. V-speeds are measured in IAS.

There are two types of airspeed defined for aviation purposes:

- *Indicated airspeed (IAS)* is the value read on the face of your airspeed indicator, uncorrected for changes in standard atmospheric conditions at sea level. Real aircraft airspeed indicators always display IAS because it is an accurate measure of airflow over the wings, with air density automatically taken into account.

- *True airspeed (TAS)* is the airspeed of the aircraft relative to undisturbed air, corrected for altitude, temperature, and barometric pressure conditions. In real aircraft, it is not displayed on your airspeed indicator. True airspeed increases with altitude because of the effects of the thinning atmospheric pressure. At higher altitudes, TAS is always greater than IAS. This means you will always travel faster than your airspeed indicator shows you to be traveling.[1] To calculate true airspeed from indicated airspeed, multiply the IAS by 1 plus 1.5 percent for every thousand feet of altitude. For example, if you are flying at 12,000 feet at a IAS of 200 knots, your true airspeed (TAS) will be 200 knots/hour $\times$ (1 + (12 (thousand feet) *0.015)) = 236 knots/hour.

Flight Simulator's airspeed indicator shows true airspeed (TAS), not indicated airspeed (IAS). You can change the airspeed indicator to show IAS by opening the Instrument Preferences dialog box under the Options menu, and toggling on the Display Indicated Airspeed check box.

---

[1]Exception: In FS 5.1, True Airspeed (TAS) is initially shown on the airspeed indicator.

In *Flight Simulator*, the airspeed indicator is initially set to show true airspeed (TAS), but you can change the altimeter's readings to show indicated airspeed (IAS). To do this, toggle on the Display Indicated Airspeed check box in the Instrument Preferences dialog box, which is found under the Options menu.

Federal aviation rules (FAR) prohibit flying your aircraft at high speeds below certain minimum altitudes. For the controlled airspace below 10,000 feet, you must limit your speed to less than 250 knots (288 mph). Around airports and terminal control areas, the speed limit drops to less than 200 knots (230 mph).

Each aircraft also comes with its own set of restrictions for flying at certain speeds (called *V-speeds*). The operating manuals for Cessna and Learjet, for example, show there are maximum speeds for flying with the landing gear extended. When these speeds are exceeded your aircraft will be damaged. Table 7.1 lists some of the airplane performance speeds and their descriptions.

Altimeter

The altimeter measures your altitude above mean sea level (MSL) by means of sampling the air pressure. At higher elevations, the air density and pressure is lower; at lower elevations, the density and pressure are higher. Unfortunately, due to variations in air temperature and barometric pressure, the air

Table 7.1 Description of Airspeed Limitation Speeds	
V speed (IAS)	**Description**
V_{S0}	Stalling speed with the landing gear down
V_{S1}	Stalling speed with the landing gear up
V_{LE}	Maximum landing gear extended speed
V_{LO}	Maximum landing gear operating speed
V_{FE}	Maximum flap extended speed
V_{NO}	Maximum structural cruising speed
V_{NE}	Never exceed speed; doing so will cause loss of airplane due to structural failure
V_A	Design maneuvering speed; do not make full or abrupt movements with your controls at this speed

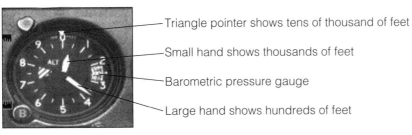

Triangle pointer shows tens of thousand of feet

Small hand shows thousands of feet

Barometric pressure gauge

Large hand shows hundreds of feet

Figure 7.4 The Altimeter

pressure can vary with a given altitude and so the altimeter can give erroneous readings. These non-standard conditions can result in altimeter differences as much as 2,000 feet between true altitude and indicated altitude! This is why, from time to time, you must calibrate your altimeter for the local barometric pressure in order to obtain accurate altitude measurements.

In *Flight Simulator*, the altimeter is read like a clock. The large hand shows hundreds of feet at mean sea level (MSL), and the small hand shows thousands of feet at MSL. Barometric pressure is shown in a small gauge on the outer right rim of the altimeter. The smallest increment on the altimeter is scaled at 50 feet for each tick mark.

There are several kinds of terms used to define altitude:

- AGL is altitude in feet above the ground.
- MSL is altitude in feet above mean sea level. Sea level is not the same as ground level. At Meigs Field, your altitude is 593 feet MSL, but your AGL is 0 feet.
- Indicated altitude is the altitude read on your altimeter. It tells you the altitude your aircraft is above mean sea level, but does not take into account non-standard atmospheric conditions which cause the altimeter to show false readings.
- True altitude is true height above sea level, corrected for standard atmospheric conditions.[2]
- Absolute altitude is the height above ground level (AGL) and is usually found on radio/radar type altimeters, which measure the time interval of a vertical signal bounced from the aircraft to the ground and back.

Most large terminal areas around the United States now require the installation of encoding altimeters. These special altimeters work in conjunction

To automatically calibrate the altimeter to current barometric pressure, press the B key. You can also manually calibrate the altimeter to any pressure by choosing the Sim/Calibrate menu, and then entering in the pressure level you want to set the altimeter at.

[2]See Chapter 4 for a table listing the Standard Atmospheric Conditions for different altitudes, temperatures, and pressures.

with the aircraft's transponder to send your altitude to Air Traffic Control (ATC), along with your identification or squawk code. ATC can then monitor your position and altitude on special computers to prevent any mid-air collisions from occurring.

Under visual flying rules (VFR), the federal aviation regulations (FAR) require you to fly at certain altitude levels when flying a particular course heading. These highways in the sky are called Victor airways, and for altitudes less than 29,000 feet you must travel at odd thousand foot increments plus 500 feet (e.g. 3,500, 5,500, 7500 feet) for course headings 0° to 179°. For course headings of 180° to 359°, you must fly at even thousand foot increments plus 500 hundred feet (e.g. 4,500, 6,500, 8,500 feet).

Under instrument flying rules (IFR), FARs require that for altitudes below 29,000 feet you fly at slightly different altitude levels. Below 29,000 feet for course headings of 0° to 179°, fly at any odd thousand foot increments (e.g. 1,000; 3,000; 5,000 feet). For course headings of 180° to 359°, fly any even thousand foot increments (e.g. 2,000, 4,000, 6,000 feet).

Vertical Speed/Rate of Climb Indicator

The vertical speed indicator tells you the rate at which your aircraft is climbing or descending. The display is calibrated in units of hundreds of feet per minute (FPM). The dial shows a reading of 0 to 10 up or down, signifying a climb or descent of 0 to 2,000 feet per minute. When the needle of the indicator is on the number 5 on the upper scale, you are climbing at the rate of 500 feet per minute. Because of delays in registering air pressure changes, this instrument should not be relied upon for instantaneous readouts of vertical speed.

Gyroscopic Instruments

The three gyroscopic instruments are so called because they are controlled by gyroscopes. Gyroscopes are rotating platforms able to detect changes in motion, whether by changes in velocity or attitude. The basic gyroscopic principle allows gyroscopes to retain their position in space regardless of

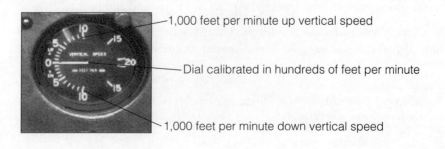

Figure 7.5
The Cessna's vertical speed/rate of climb indicator

1,000 feet per minute up vertical speed

Dial calibrated in hundreds of feet per minute

1,000 feet per minute down vertical speed

changes in velocity or position made by outside forces on the aircraft. By measuring the position of the gyroscope in relation to the aircraft, the gyroscopic instruments can make determinations as to the true aircraft orientation without any external visual references. Without the gyroscope, inertial navigation and all-weather precision flying would be impossible. Generally, the platter of the gyroscope is spun by engine vacuum, which sucks air past rotating vanes on the platter. Newer gyroscopes today, however, can be electrically operated for greater precision and accuracy.

Artificial Horizon/Attitude Indicator

The artificial horizon/attitude indicator shows the airplane's attitude at all times. It shows the actual pitch and roll of the aircraft in relation to the ground and provides a view of the natural horizon that otherwise may not be visible to the pilot.

A gimbal mounted gyroscope inside the artificial horizon retains its position in space regardless of the aircraft's attitude. By watching a colored ball that depicts the horizon, the pilot can determine whether the plane is rolling to the right or left or is pitched up or down. Note that it does not guarantee the aircraft is climbing or descending; for that you must use your vertical speed indicator, or stomach (for example, you aircraft could be pitched up while landing, but it is actually losing altitude). The bank index on the gauge shows markers for 10°, 20°, 30°, 60°, and 90°, telling you the aircraft's angle of bank. When the center horizontal bar representing your wings, is aligned with the top of the horizon (the horizon is represented by the lower colored half of the sphere) you are flying straight and level. Executing a 30° turn right causes the horizon to pivot to the left and the arrow pointer rotates toward the 30° marker. The wings will move above the horizon bar when climbing and below the horizon bar when descending.

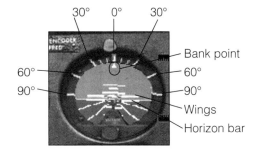

Figure 7.6
The artificial horizon/attitude indicator

Heading Indicator/Directional Gyro

The heading indicator, or directional gyro, is a compass that shows the aircraft's nose direction with greater accuracy than the ordinary magnetic compass. Because it is driven by a gyroscope, the heading indicator can quickly show changes in course—even when executing turns and other maneuvers that would ordinarily throw a magnetic compass off due to pronounced accelerative forces or vibrations. The disadvantage of the directional gyro is it tends to drift from the true course heading over time, due to the deviation caused by gyroscopic precession and internal friction. The chief cause of

Click here on the knob to manually calibrate the directional gyro.

Figure 7.7
Heading indicator/ directional gyro

error in the gyroscope is friction from the bearings, so many sophisticated inertial navigational systems go to great lengths to dampen the frictional effects. Gyroscopic precession errors are caused by the spin of the Earth, and for long flights can cause your readings to be inaccurate. Because of this tendency to drift, you must periodically calibrate the heading indicator to match the magnetic compass. In FS 5.1, you do this by pressing D. You can also manually calibrate the directional gyro by clicking the left knob at the bottom of the indicator. This has the effect of rotating the directional gyro's heading indicator left or right to match the magnetic compass heading.

In the directional gyro, the aircraft's nose always points toward the course heading. To ascertain your course, all you need do is examine what course number the nose of the airplane is currently pointing at. The numbers on the dial must be multiplied by 10 to obtain the correct reading. Thus a 3 represents 30°, while 33 represents a course heading of 330°. The dial is calibrated so that each tick on the scale represents 5°.

Turn Coordinator

The turn coordinator is often called the turn and bank indicator. This instrument has two functions: it measures turn rate and it measures the amount of slip or skid the aircraft has in making a turn. The aircraft wings on the turn indicator will bank whenever you make a turn. The "L" and "R" markers on the indicator show you where the wings must align if you are to make what is called a standard turn. A standard turn means the aircraft will complete a 360° turn in two minutes, coming back to its original course heading in that space of time. If you want to make a standard left turn with a turn rate of 3° per second (completing a 360° turn in two minutes), you would bank left until the wing tips on the dial match up with the "L" mark. If you had started on a course heading of 90°, after two minutes you would find your aircraft has made a complete 360° turn and would be again headed on a course of 90°.

The ball in the inclinometer at the bottom of the dial tells you whether your turn is coordinated or not. In an uncoordinated turn, the plane will slip or skid because of unbalanced centrifugal and horizontal lift forces as illustrated in Figure 7.9. If the ball stays in the center position during a turn, then all the forces are in balance. Fortunately, in FS 5.1's auto-coordinated mode (the default setup), you don't need to worry about coordinating your turns because the ailerons and rudders move together when you make a turn.

Figure 7.8
Turn coordinator

Left standard turn indicator

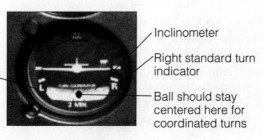

Inclinometer

Right standard turn indicator

Ball should stay centered here for coordinated turns

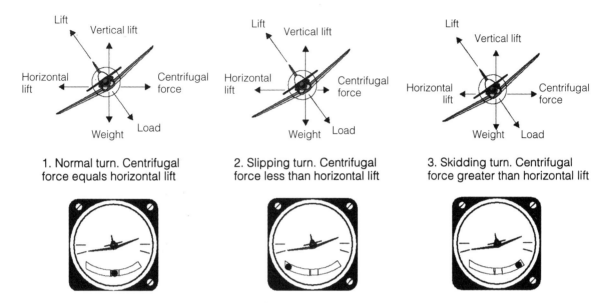

1. Normal turn. Centrifugal force equals horizontal lift

2. Slipping turn. Centrifugal force less than horizontal lift

3. Skidding turn. Centrifugal force greater than horizontal lift

Figure 7.9 Effects of coordinated turns, slips, and skids

Radio Stack

The radio stack contains all your communication and radio navigational aids. It consists of two NAV radios, one COM radio, two Distance Measuring Equipment (DME) indicators, an Automatic Dueltron Finder (ADF), and a transponder (XPDR). Each radio can be set from the keyboard, via the mouse, or even from the Nav/Com menu.

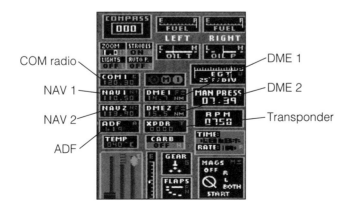

COM radio
NAV 1
NAV 2
ADF
DME 1
DME 2
Transponder

Figure 7.10
Radio stack

Changing the Frequency of the NAV, COM, and ADF Radios and XPDR Squawk Code Using the Mouse

To change the frequency settings for any of the radios using the mouse, follow these steps:

Figure 7.11
Changing radio
frequencies

1. To increase a frequency setting, first click on the part of the frequency you wish to change. The color of the numerals will change from red to yellow, indicating you can now tune in a different frequency. Note that you can't change individual digits for the NAV 1 and NAV 2 radios; you can change the fractional part of the frequency to the right of the decimal or change the integer part of the frequency to the left of the decimal point. For the ADF radio, you can select each digit separately but you cannot decrease the number (see Figure 7.11).

2. Click to the right of the numbers to increase the frequency or click to the left of the numbers to decrease the frequency, except for the ADF radio and the transponder (XPDR), in which you can only increase the digit and cycle it from 0 to 9.

Changing the Frequency of the NAV, COM, and ADF Radios and XPDR Squawk Code Using the Keyboard

Table 7.2 summarizes the keystrokes necessary to change the radio frequencies for the NAV 1, NAV 2, COM, and the ADF radios, and the transponder. To increase the ADF radio frequency you would press [A][+] (on the main keypad) to change the hundreds digit; for the tens digit, press [A][A][+]; for the ones digit, press [A][A][A][+]. To decrease the ADF radio frequency press [A][−] (on the main keypad) for the hundreds digit; for the tens digit, press [A][A][−]; for the ones digit, press [A][A][A][−].

Changing the Frequency of the NAV, COM, ADF Radios and Squawk Code for the XPDR Using the Nav/Com Menu

You can change the frequency for any of the radios by calling up the appropriate dialog box from the Nav/Com menu and entering the frequency in the listed entry text box.

To change the NAV 1 or NAV 2 radio frequencies using the menus:

1. Select Navigation Radios from the Nav/Com menu.

2. In the Navigation Radios dialog box, enter the new radio frequency you wish to tune into. There are two frequency boxes, one for each NAV radio.

Table 7.2 Changing the Radio Frequency and XPDR Squawk Code via the Keyboard	
Radio	**Keyboard Procedure**
ADF	First digit: Press Ⓐ followed by ⊞ to increase or ⊟ to decrease Second digit: Press Ⓐ Ⓐ followed by ⊞ or ⊟ Third digit: Press Ⓐ Ⓐ Ⓐ followed by ⊞ or ⊟
COM	For integer part of frequency to left of decimal point: Press Ⓒ followed by ⊞ to increase or ⊟ to decrease For fractional part of frequency to right of decimal point: Press Ⓒ Ⓒ followed by ⊞ or ⊟
NAV1	For integer part of frequency to left of decimal point: Press Ⓝ ① followed by ⊞ to increase, or ⊟ to decrease For fractional part of frequency to right of decimal point: Press Ⓝ Ⓝ ① followed by ⊞ or ⊟
NAV2	For integer part of frequency to left of decimal point: Press Ⓝ ② followed by ⊞ to increase or ⊟ to decrease For fractional part of frequency to right of decimal point: Press Ⓝ Ⓝ ② followed by ⊞ or ⊟
Transponder (XPDR)	For first digit (thousands): Press Ⓣ followed by ⊞ to increase, or ⊟ to decrease Second digit (hundreds): Press Ⓣ Ⓣ followed by ⊞ or ⊟ Third digit (tens): Press Ⓣ Ⓣ Ⓣ followed by ⊞ or ⊟ Fourth digit (ones): Press Ⓣ Ⓣ Ⓣ Ⓣ followed by ⊞ or ⊟

To change the COM radio frequency using the menus:

1. Select Communication Radio from the Nav/Com menu.

2. In the Communication Radio dialog box, enter the new radio frequency you wish to tune into.

Similarly, you can change the ADF frequency and XPDR squawk code in the ADF dialog box or the Transponder dialog box, both of which can be opened up from the Nav/Com menu.

NAV 1/NAV 2 Radio

The NAV 1 and NAV 2 radio receivers are used for navigation and tune in either very high frequency omni-directional range (VOR) or instrument landing systems (ILS) radio stations. Both radios receive up to 200 channels, between the frequencies of 108.00 and 117.95 MHz, with a channel separation of 50 KHz. VOR's transmit an omni-directional signal followed by a circular sweeping signal which your NAV radios receive and decode. The information is forwarded to the OBI indicators on your instrument panel, and you can then see which radius angle you are from the station. Each VOR station pulses out a radial signal for each of the 360° of arc around it. Using special navigational maps, you can plot where you are in relation to the VOR station. If you also are receiving DME signals through your NAV radios, your DME indicator will show you how far away the VOR station is from your current position. Your DME indicator will also tell you your ground speed in relation to the station. The NAV 1 radio is used in conjunction with the OBI 1 display and the DME 1 indicator, while the NAV 2 receiver is used with the OBI 2 display and the DME 2 indicator. If the NAV 1 and NAV 2 radios are tuned to two different VOR stations, it is possible to triangulate your position and obtain a precise "fix."

Unlike OBI 1, the OBI 2 does not have provision for an ILS glide slope. If you plan to tune in an ILS runway, do so on the NAV 1 radio.

Besides tuning in VOR and ILS stations, the NAV 1 radio is also used for the electronic flight instrument systems/command flight path display (EFIS/CFPD) advanced navigational graphics display system.

COM Radio

This communication radio transmits and receives voice signals between 118.00 and 135.95 MHz. The COM radio is used to communicate with Air Traffic Control and to tune in to the automatic terminal information service (ATIS) for current weather information. Each of the 360 available channels occupies a bandwidth of 50 KHz, although you can double channel capacity to 720 channels by toggling on the 25 KHz COM Frequency Adjustability check box found in the Instrument Preferences dialog box under the Options menu. By doing this, you halve the bandwidth of each channel from 50 KHz to 25 KHz, thus enabling your radio to squeeze in twice as many channels in the available bandwidth.

DME 1 and 2

Both DME 1 and DME 2 indicators can be toggled back and forth between displaying speed or distance to the VOR station. To do this merely click on

the DME indicator with the mouse, or from the main keyboard press F +
1 for DME 1, or press F + 2 for DME 2. You will see "KT" displayed in
the upper right corner of the DME when the aircraft speed in relation to the
VOR station is being measured in knots. On the other hand, when the
DME is displaying distance information, you will see "NM" signifying nautical miles to the VOR station and distance to the VOR station.

ADF

The automatic direction finder (ADF), is a navigational radio that tunes in
low frequency AM signals from 0 KHz to 999 KHz from AM commercial
stations as well as special non-directional beacon radio stations (NDB).
Essentially, the ADF calculates the relative bearing to the station
and displays it on the ADF bearing indicator. The bearing to the
NDB or AM broadcast station is relative to the nose of your aircraft, so to point your aircraft at the radio station you are currently
tuning in, just turn the airplane so that the needle on the ADF
bearing indicator is pointing straight up at the 0.

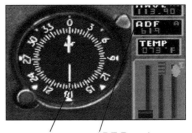

Figure 7.12
The ADF relative
bearing indicator and
radio receiver

ADF Relative   ADF Receiver
bearing
indicator

In FS 5.1, the ADF bearing indicator is not normally displayed
on the instrument panel. To call it up press Shift Tab, and it will
take the place of the OBI 2 display. If you prefer to use the menu
system, you can also switch on the ADF display by clicking on the
Activate ADF gauge in the ADF dialog box, which is opened by
selecting ADF under the Nav/Com menu.

Normally, the ADF radio can only tune in stations that are 1 KHz apart.
But if you toggle on the 500 Hz ADF Frequency Adjustability check box
found in the Instrument Preferences dialog box under the Options menu,
the ADF receiver will be able to tune in stations that are only 500 Hz apart
(500 Hz is exactly 1/2 of 1 KHz). This effectively doubles the number of
available channels. Figure 7.13 shows what the display looks like with the
addition of the extra digit to the right of the decimal point for setting the
increments of 500 Hz.

Figure 7.13
The ADF frequency
selection indicator
showing 500 Hz
channel separation

Transponder (XPDR)

Whenever you fly into a terminal control area (TCA), Air Traffic Control
will assign you a four digit special transponder squawk code that will identify
your aircraft to their computers. You must enter this code into your
transponder and then you can forget about it. Many transponders today are
required to have mode C capability, meaning they can take information
from an encoding altimeter, and when questioned by the ATC computer,
will broadcast this information. When coupled with radar, this gives the

Figure 7.14
Transponder

ATC computers a three dimensional fix on your aircraft for collision avoidance purposes. In an emergency, there are special squawk codes that can be used to alert the ATC to hijackings and mayday distress calls; 7500 indicates a hijacking, while 7700 alerts ATC to a distress or urgency condition.

Navigational Instruments

There are five additional navigational instruments that display important aircraft position information. They are:

- Magnetic Compass
- OMI Marker Lights
- Omnibearing Indicator 1 (OBI 1) with Glide Slope for ILS System.
- Omnibearing Indicator 2 (OBI 2)

Magnetic Compass

This is a standard magnetic compass that shows your current heading in digital form.

Figure 7.15
Magnetic compass

OMI Marker Lights

Figure 7.16
OMI marker lights

The outer (O), middle (M), and inner (I) marker lights are used in the instrument landing system (ILS) to give you a visual and audio cue as to the distance remaining to the runway. At approximately 4 to 7 miles from the runway, the blue outer marker light comes on and a 400 Hz audio signal sounds (two long beeps per second). At a distance of 0.67 miles (3,500 feet) or so, the yellow middle marker lamp comes on, and a 1300 Hz audio signal sounds (a long beep followed by a short beep). The inner marker, which may not be supported on some FS 5.1 runways, alerts you to the fact that you have less than 1,000 feet to the threshold of the runway.

Omnibearing Indicator with Glide Slope (OBI 1)

The omnibearing indicator 1 (OBI 1) is a navigational instrument used with the NAV 1 radio to tune in VOR and ILS stations. It also contains a glide slope indicator with moving cross hairs that is used with instrument landing systems to ascertain whether or not your aircraft is on the proper glide slope to the runway.

If you have tuned the NAV radio to a VOR station, and the DME indicator shows it is in range, you can figure out which VOR radial you are on

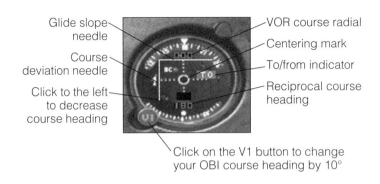

Glide slope needle

Course deviation needle

Click to the left to decrease course heading

VOR course radial

Centering mark

To/from indicator

Reciprocal course heading

Click on the V1 button to change your OBI course heading by 10°

Figure 7.17
Omnibearing Indicator with Glide Slope (NAV 1).

by clicking on the course heading of the OBI until the course deviation indicator (CDI) needle is centered. With the TO/FROM indicator showing TO, the top reading on the course heading displays the direction to the VOR station. To head toward the VOR station, fly your plane on the OBI course heading, making sure the the CDI needle is centered. When you pass directly over the VOR station, the needle will abruptly jump and the TO/FROM indicator will change to FROM.

To set the OBI 1 heading using the mouse, click to the right of the course heading to increase the reading and to the left of the course heading to decrease the reading. Using the keyboard to change the OBI 1 heading, press [V] and 1 followed by the [+] key to increase the readout, or [-] key to decrease the readout. You can also change the OBI 1 heading by directly entering it in the OBI Heading text box, found in the Navigation Radio dialog box which is accessed under the Nav/Com menu.

Omnibearing Indicator 2 (OBI 2)/Automatic Direction Finder (ADF)

Like the OBI 1, the OBI 2 tunes in VOR stations and allows you to see what radial direction the VOR station is in relation to your aircraft. The OBI 2 is used with the NAV 2 radio, but unlike the OBI 1, the OBI 2 does not contain a glide slope and so cannot be used with ILS equipped runways.

If you press the [Shift][Tab] keys simultaneously, you will disengage the OBI 2 indicator and replace it with the automatic direction finder (ADF) gauge. The ADF gauge tells you the relative bearing to an NDB or AM broadcast station in relation to the nose of your aircraft.

To set the OBI 2 heading using the mouse, click to the right of the course heading to increase the reading and to the left of the course heading to decrease the reading. Using the keyboard to change the OBI 1 heading,

Press [Shift][Tab] to replace the OBI 2 display with the ADF gauge.

Figure 7.18
Omni/Bearing Indicator
NAV 2/ADF

OBI 2 used with   ADF indicator used
NAV 2 radio   with ADF radio

press V and 1 followed by [+] to increase the readout, or [–] to decrease the readout. You can also change the OBI 2 heading by directly entering it in the OBI Heading text box, found in the Navigation Radio dialog box which is accessed under the Nav/Com menu.

Flight Instruments/Indicators

The remaining flight instruments and indicators supply information about the status of the aircraft.

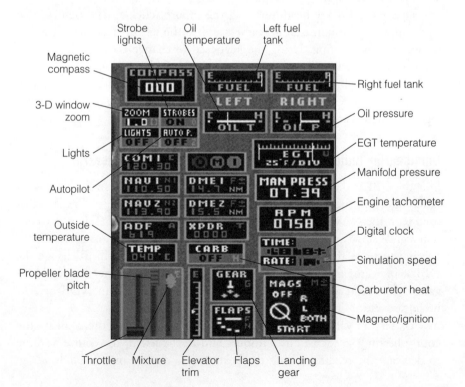

Figure 7.19
Flight instruments/
indicators

Zoom Indicator

The zoom indicator shows the current magnification or zoom factor of the selected 3-D view window. To increase magnification, press the ⊞ key. To decrease magnification, press ⊟. You can also click to the right of the zoom number to increase the zoom, or click to the left to decrease the zoom. Note the zoom indicator does not work with the Map window, although when the Map window is currently active, ⊞ and ⊟ will zoom the map in and out.

Lights

The lights switch, which turns on the instrument panel lighting and exterior navigational lighting for night flying, can be toggled on and off by clicking on it. Or, from the keyboard, press ⃞L. You can separately turn the instrument lights on or off by pressing ⃞Shift + ⃞L. To turn on only the landing lights for illuminating the runway, press ⃞Ctrl + ⃞L.

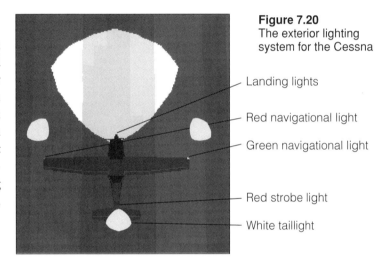

Figure 7.20
The exterior lighting system for the Cessna

Landing lights

Red navigational light

Green navigational light

Red strobe light

White taillight

Strobe

This indicator tells you whether the red flashing strobe is on or off. To turn the strobe on or off, click on the control or press ⃞O.

Autopilot

Using the autopilot, you can have the plane automatically level its wings or attitude, maintain a constant altitude, line up with a particular glide slope of an ILS runway or NAV 1/VOR radial, or you can choose a particular heading, approach, or back course. To engage or disengage the autopilot, click on it. From the keyboard, you can turn it on or off by pressing ⃞Z. You can switch the autopilot on or off by choosing Autopilot from the Nav/Com menu, and then selecting Connect in the Autopilot Switch list box. Note that turning the autopilot on or off doesn't mean the autopilot is engaged! To engage the autopilot you must also choose which feature you wish to engage, such as the altitude lock, heading lock, VOR lock, ILS lock, etc.

New Autopilot Keyboard Shortcuts

FS 5.1 introduces new keyboard shortcuts for engaging all the autopilot functions. You can see the keyboard equivalents for each autopilot function displayed below:

Key Combination	Autopilot Function
Z	Toggle autopilot on or off.
Ctrl V	Level the wings.
Ctrl T	Maintain present pitch and bank attitude.
Ctrl Z	Lock to present altitude.
Ctrl A	Lock to an ILS tuned on NAV 1 for a landing. Aircraft flies the glide slope and localizer descent profile for the selected ILS runway.
Ctrl N	Lock to a VOR radial tuned on NAV 1.
Ctrl H	Lock to your current magnetic course heading.
Ctrl O	Lock to the ILS localizer (but not the glide slope) tuned on NAV 1 for a landing.
Ctrl B	Lock to a back course of an ILS localizer tuned on NAV 1. This allows you to approach the runway from the opposite end for a landing.

These new autopilot hot keys greatly simply the task of flying your aircraft. For example, let's say you're flying the Learjet and you want to level off at 20,000 feet. As you approach 20,000 feet, you press Z to activate the autopilot. When you cross 20,000 feet, you hit Ctrl + Z to engage the altitude hold for this flight level. If you shut off the autopilot entirely, by pressing Z, and then descend to 15,000 feet, you'll find that when you again hit Z to activate the autopilot, the altitude hold has been disengaged and has reconfigured itself for your new altitude of 15,000 feet. To re-engage the altitude lock, for 15,000 feet simply press Ctrl + Z. Of course, you can accomplish all of this using the Autopilot dialog box, but you'll find the keyboard shortcuts are easier to use.

The same technique can be applied for leveling your wings, setting your course bearing, following a VOR radial (see Chapter 12), maintaining your current pitch and bank attitude, descending along an ILS glide slope for a landing, tracking an ILS localizer (helpful when you are trying to find an airport runway at night or in reduced visibility), or flying a back course (i.e. flying towards the opposite end of an ILS equipped runway).

Temp

Measures the outside temperature, also known as OAT (Outside Air Temperature Gauge). If you have selected US units of measurement in the Country Preferences dialog box, the reading will be in degrees Fahrenheit. Otherwise, the temperature gauge will show degrees Celsius. Remember the temperature will drop as you ascend to higher and higher altitudes.

Clock

The clock is used not only to tell time, but also to modify the time of day in FS 5.1. To set the time using the mouse, you must first click on the hours, minutes, or seconds portion of the display separately, then click to the right to increase the time or to the left to decrease the time. You can adjust the time in the Set Time and Season dialog box from the World menu.

Rate of Simulation

This indicator shows the current simulation speed. By clicking to the right of this number, you can increase the passage of time or if you click to the left you can slow down time. You can also modify the simulation's speed by entering it directly into the Simulation Speed dialog box from the Sim menu. This feature is very helpful for long boring transcontinental or transoceanic trips where you don't want to wait six hours to complete a trip. But be careful—speeding up the simulation makes your aircraft very difficult to control and very subtle movements of the controls can cause you to careen into the ground. Note that when using the autopilot, your rate of simulation is limited to four times normal speed.

When using the Autopilot, the rule of simulation is limited to four times normal speed.

Landing Gear Indicator

The landing gear indicator tells you the current position of your landing gear. When the wheels are down, the three wheel lights below the gear icon glow green; when the gear is being retracted, the wheel lights will briefly turn red before flickering out. The gear can be retracted or extended by clicking on the gear indicator or by pressing G.

Don't extend the landing gear when traveling faster than the V_{lo} (maximum airspeed when operating the landing gear). For the Cessna, this is 140 knots IAS.

Flaps Position Indicator

The flaps are used to create extra lift when landing or taking off. The flaps position indicator shows the current extension angle of the flaps. They can be deployed incrementally by 10° from a fully retracted position of 0° all the way to 40°. You deploy the flaps by clicking on the individual angle settings on the flaps position indicator. Or, from the keyboard you can use the [F5] through [F8] function keys. When the arm of the flaps position indicator points to the bottom dot, a flap position of 40° has been set; if the arm points to the upper dot, the flaps are fully retracted at 0°.

You must not fly faster than the V_{FE} (flap extension speeds), or else damage to the flaps will occur. For the flaps set to 30° or 40°, the V_{FE} is 95 knots IAS; for the flaps set to 20°, the VFE is 120 knots IAS; for the flaps set to 10°, the V_{FE} is 140 knots IAS.

Left Wing/Right Wing Fuel Tank Gauge

These fuel gauges tell you the current fuel supply remaining in your gas tanks. The left gauge is for the left wing fuel tank, while the right gauge is for the right wing fuel tank.

Oil Temperature Gauge

The oil temperature gauge tells you the oil temperature of the engine. Normal operating temperature is 100° Fahrenheit to 245° Fahrenheit (38° Celsius to 118° Celsius).

Oil Pressure Gauge

The oil pressure gauge alerts you to the oil pressure inside the engine. Normal operating pressure is 60 to 90 pounds per square inch (PSI).

Exhaust Gas Temperature (EGT) Gauge

The EGT measures the temperature of the engine exhaust gas exiting your engine cylinders. This temperature ranges up to 1,750° Fahrenheit. The EGT is used in conjunction with the manifold pressure gauge and the mixture control to fine tune the engine's cruise performance. When the engine runs hotter, usually it means you are running a very lean fuel mixture. If this happens, you should enrich the carburetor by increasing the mixture control. Watch the gauge to make sure you don't overheat your engine. Temperature is measured in 25° increments on the scale.

Manifold Pressure Gauge

The manifold pressure gauge tells you the amount of power your engine is developing. It measures the pressure difference between the atmosphere and the inside of the manifold chamber of the engine. The usual measurements are made in terms of inches of Hg (Mercury). The normal cruise speed operating range is 15 to 23 inches Hg, with a maximum of just over 29 inches of Hg at takeoff.

Tachometer

The engine speed is measured by the tachometer in rotations or revolutions per minute (RPM). Normal cruise operating range is from 2,100 to 2,400 RPM; at takeoff and other non-standard conditions, the RPM will stray outside this range.

Throttle, Propeller Control, and Mixture Control

The throttle sets the amount of power the engine develops. You can increase the power or speed of the engine, by dragging the throttle control up or down with the mouse. From the keyboard, you can also adjust the throttle by pressing the Function keys F1, F2, F3, and F4. F1 cuts engine power to idle, F2 decreases the engine power gradually, F3 increases engine power gradually, and F4 opens the throttle to its maximum setting.

The propeller control sets the propeller's blade angle so you can maintain an optimum RPM for the engine. At higher altitudes or at high speeds, the prop blade angle should be increased to avoid having the engine RPM exceed engine tolerances (push prop control lever down). For takeoffs and landings, or when flying at slow speeds, decrease the prop blade angle so the propeller will spin faster and develop more thrusting action (push prop control lever up).

Remember this simple rule:

Increasing the prop blade angle *decreases* RPM.

Decreasing the prop blade angle *increases* RPM.

To reduce RPM and increase the prop blade angle by using the mouse, drag the propeller control down; to increase RPM and decrease the blade angle, drag the lever up. From the keyboard, press Ctrl + F1 to increase the blade angle to its maximum setting (minimum RPM), or Ctrl + F2 to gradually increase it (gradually decrease RPM). To decrease the blade angle gradually (gradually increase RPM), press Ctrl + F3, or to increase it to its maximum setting (minimum RPM) press Ctrl + F4.

Because the atmospheric pressure declines as you go higher, the engine's air/fuel ratio tends to get too rich as less air is burned per unit of fuel. The mixture control allows you to manually adjust the air/fuel ratio, not only to compensate for altitude differences, but also to optimize fuel economy and engine performance. To enrich the air/fuel ratio by using the mouse, drag the mixture lever up; to lean the engine, drag the mixture lever down. From the keyboard, press [Ctrl] + [Shift] + [F1] to lean the engine to its highest air/fuel ratio, or press [Ctrl] + [Shift] + [F2] to gradually lean the engine. To gradually enrich the mixture, press [Ctrl] + [Shift] + [F3], or press [Ctrl] + [Shift] + [F4] to enrich it to its lowest air/fuel ratio. Generally, when taking off, you will want to set the mixture to rich so you don't encounter any sudden power drops or engine stalls. By default, in FS 5.1 the mixture control is automatically controlled and synchronized with the movement of the throttle. If you want to manually set the mixture, you must toggle on the Mixture Control check box in the Realism and Reliability dialog box under the Sim menu.

Carburetor Heat

The carburetor heat switch turns the carburetor heat on or off. You use the carburetor heat to prevent icing or to clear ice that has formed inside the engine, thus preventing ice-caused engine failure in cold weather. To toggle this control on or off, click on it with the mouse, or press [H].

Magnetos Switch

The magnetos switch specifies whether you have switched on the left, the right, or both magnetos for the engine's ignition system. As a precautionary back up, there are two separate magneto systems, each of which is able to supply electrical current to enable the spark plugs to fire. To change the magneto switch setting, click on the indicator, or press [M], plus [+] or [−], to cycle among Off, Right, Left, or Both. For added realism, you can choose to start your engines yourself by setting the magnetos to the Start position. But you must first toggle on the Magnetos check box in the Realism and Reliability dialog box, found under the Sim menu.

Control Position Indicators

The control position indicators tell you the current position of the ailerons, elevators, rudders, and elevator trim.

Ailerons Position Indicator

The ailerons are moveable hinged surfaces on the outside trailing edges of your wings. They control the rotational movement of banking or rolling.

Elevators Position Indicator

The elevators are moveable hinged control surfaces on the horizontal stabilizer (the tail wing). They control the up and down pitch of the aircraft's nose.

Rudders Position Indicator

The rudder is a hinged vertical control surface mounted on the trailing edge of the vertical stabilizer (the tail). It controls the rotational movement of yaw (left or right pivoting motion).

Elevator Trim Position Indicator

The elevator trim allows fine adjustment of the elevators and relieves the pilot of continually applying pressure on the yoke in order to maintain level flight. This hinged horizontal control surface is located on the elevator and looks like a miniaturized version of the elevator.

The elevator trim is activated from the numeric keypad by pressing [7] for nose down pitch movements and [1] for nose up pitch movements.

When you press [7] to pitch the nose down, the pitch trim indicator moves down; when you press [1] to pitch the nose up, the pitch trim indicator moves up.

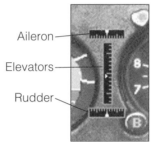
Aileron
Elevators
Rudder

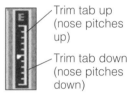
Trim tab up (nose pitches up)
Trim tab down (nose pitches down)

Figure 7.21
Yoke control position indicators and the elevator trim control position indicator

UNDERSTANDING YOUR INSTRUMENTS AND CONTROLS ON THE LEARJET

The Learjet comes equipped with a much more elaborate set of avionics than any of the other FS 5.1 aircraft. The six flight instruments of the standard instrument cluster are classified as electronic flight information systems (EFIS) avionics because they are microprocessor controlled. There are two instrument sub-panels associated with the FS 5.1 Learjet. The first instrument sub-panel shows the radio stack, and the second instrument sub-panel shows the engine monitoring gauges. Figure 7.22 illustrates both the Learjet's instrument sub-panels. To switch between each panel display, press [Tab].

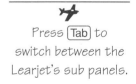
Press [Tab] to switch between the Learjet's sub panels.

Learjet radio stack subpanel 1

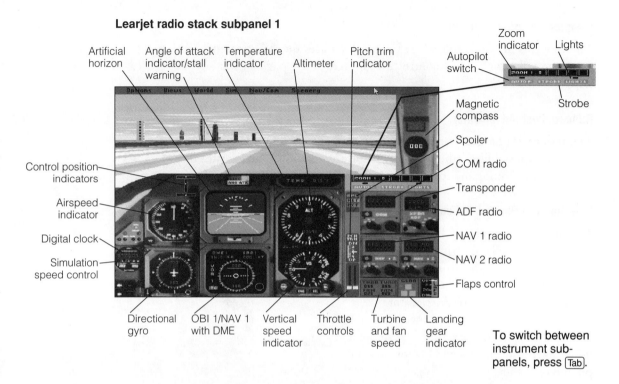

Artificial horizon

Angle of attack indicator/stall warning

Temperature indicator

Altimeter

Pitch trim indicator

Zoom indicator   Lights

Autopilot switch

Strobe

Magnetic compass

Spoiler

COM radio

Transponder

ADF radio

NAV 1 radio

NAV 2 radio

Flaps control

Control position indicators

Airspeed indicator

Digital clock

Simulation speed control

Directional gyro

OBI 1/NAV 1 with DME

Vertical speed indicator

Throttle controls

Turbine and fan speed

Landing gear indicator

To switch between instrument sub-panels, press Tab.

Learjet radio stack subpanel 2

Figure 7.22
The Learjet's two instru-ment panels. For more detail, see page 195.

Standard Instrument Cluster

The standard instrument cluster for the Learjet is similar to the Cessna's. However, because of the Learjet's superior thrust and agility, the instruments are specially tailored to measure different performance parameters.

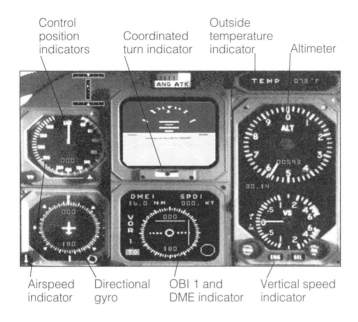

Figure 7.23
The standard instrument cluster for the Learjet

Airspeed Indicator

The airspeed indicator is calibrated to read true airspeeds (TAS), despite the fact that the display shows indicated airspeed (IAS).[3] The analog dial displays only speeds up to 450 knots, but the digital readout below can display speeds past this point.

The Learjet has a maximum cruise speed of 471 knots TAS (542 mph, 872 km/hr), however typical cruise speeds will vary for different altitudes. At 45,000 feet, for example, the Learjet cruises at 423 knots TAS (487 mph, 783 km/hr), while at 25,000 feet the Learjet cruises at 471 knots TAS (542 mph, 872 km/hr).

Typical landing approach speeds are 128 knots IAS, and the V_{SO} stall speed with the landing gear down is 97 knots IAS.

Figure 7.24
The airspeed indicator for the Learjet

Altimeter

The altimeter shows the aircraft's height above mean sea level (MSL). The display has a digital readout for an accurate account of your altitude and it

---

[3]For added realism, you can have the airspeed gauge display indicated airspeed (IAS), not true airspeed (TAS). To do this, go to the Instrument Preferences dialog box under the Options menu, and click on the Display Indicated Airspeed checkbox.

Figure 7.25
The altimeter for the Learjet

shows an analog display of your altitude in hundreds of feet. For example, when the digital display reads 4,500 feet, the analog hand on the altimeter covers the number 5 to tell that you are at 500 feet above 4,000 feet.

Just below the altimeter, the barometric pressure is displayed in digital form. Since your altimeter readings may be off due to non-standard atmospheric conditions, you should calibrate the altimeter from time to time by pressing B.

Since the Learjet routinely cruises at altitudes of over 45,000 feet, under FAR regulations you must fly IFR in one of the jet airways or "J" routes. These are special routes created above 18,000 feet for the purposes of creating safe aircraft separation distances monitored by air traffic control centers.

When you enter the airspace above 18,000 feet, the FAR regulations require you to fly at odd thousand foot increments (e.g., 21,000, 23,000, 25,000 feet) for course headings 0° to 179°; for course headings 180° to 359°, you must fly at even thousand foot increments (e.g. 18,000, 20,000, 22,000 feet). Above 29,000 feet different rules apply. For course headings 0° to 179°, fly at 4,000 foot intervals beginning with 29,000 feet (e.g. 29,000, 33,000, 37,000 feet); for course headings 179° to 359°, fly at 4,000 foot intervals beginning with 31,000 feet (e.g. 31,000, 35,000, 39,000 feet).

With only one engine operational, the Learjet has a service ceiling altitude of 25,000 feet (7,260 meters). This means the airplane cannot climb higher than this altitude on only one engine.

500 FPM up   1000 FPM up

6000 FPM down

Figure 7.26
The vertical speed/rate of climb indicator for the Learjet

Vertical Speed/Rate of Climb Indicator

The vertical speed indicator is calibrated to show vertical speeds in units of thousands of feet per minute. The scale registers speeds from 0 to 6, meaning speeds of 0 to 6,000 feet per minute up or down can be displayed.

On one engine, the Learjet can climb at a rate of 1,290 feet per minute. With two engines running, assuming maximum takeoff/landing weight at MSL and standard ISA atmospheric day conditions, the Learjet can climb at a rate of 4,340 feet per minute. With less fuel on board, the airplane is lighter and can climb faster.

Artificial Horizon/Attitude Indicator

The artificial horizon/attitude indicator shows the airplane's pitch, bank, and roll in relation to the horizon or ground. It provides a view of the natural horizon that may not otherwise be visible to the pilot.

By watching the lower half of the display that depicts the horizon, the pilot can determine whether the plane is rolling to the right or left, or if it's pitching up or down. The bank index on the display shows markers for 10°, 20°, 30°, 60°, and 90°, telling you the aircraft's angle of bank. When the center horizontal bar representing your wings, is aligned with the top of the horizon (the horizon is represented by the lower half of the display with the perspective lines vanishing into the distance), you are flying straight and level. Executing a 30° turn right causes the horizon to pivot to the left, and the arrow pointer to rotate towards the 30° marker. When climbing, the wings will move above the horizon bar; and when descending, the wings will move below the horizon bar. There are pitch indexes on the display which indicate 5°, 10°, 15°, and 20° angles for the nose of the airplane in relation to the ground. When the horizon just touches the uppermost horizontal line, for example, the airplane is climbing with the nose pitched up in a 20° ascent. Likewise, if the horizon touches the lowermost horizontal line, the nose is pitched down in a 20° descent.

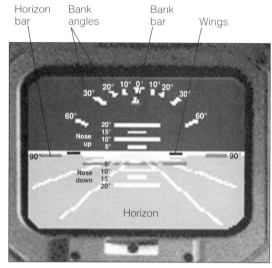

Figure 7.27
The artificial horizon/ attitude indicator for the Learjet

Turn Indicator

The turn indicator is located just below the artificial horizon. When the ball is centered in the inclinometer during a turn, the aircraft is executing a coordinated turn where all the lateral forces are in balance. If the ball moves to the left or right, however, the turn is uncoordinated and the airplane is skidding or slipping through the air. Since FS 5.1, by default, has your ailerons and rudders synchronized in auto-coordinated mode, you need not worry about making coordinated turns. But if you were flying in un-coordinated mode (which is switched on or off under the Sim menu), for example using pedals for your rudders and a yoke for your ailerons, you would try to keep the ball centered when making a turn.

Heading Indicator/Directional Gyro

With the Learjet, the heading indicator is output in digital form. The nose of your plane on the dial points to your current heading. At the bottom of the display, the reciprocal course heading (180° apart) is shown.

Because of the directional gyro's tendency to drift, you must periodically calibrate the heading indicator to match the magnetic compass. In FS 5.1, you do this by pressing the D key.

Figure 7.28
The heading indicator/ directional gyro for the Learjet

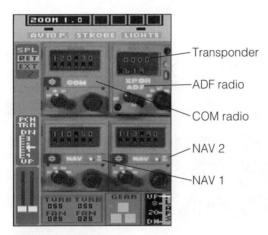

Transponder

ADF radio

COM radio

NAV 2

NAV 1

Figure 7.29
The Radio Stack for
the Learjet

Figure 7.30
The COM radio

Radio Stack and Navigational Instruments

Located on the first instrument sub-panel, the radio stack contains all your VOR/ILS/DME/ADF navigation radios as well as the COM communication radio used to call Air Traffic Control. You set the frequencies in much the same way as you do for the Cessna radios: to increase the frequency, click to the right of the numbers; to decrease the frequency, click to the left of the numbers. As listed earlier in this chapter, you can also use the keyboard and menu equivalents to change the frequencies.

COM Radio

Use the COM radio to call up Air Traffic Control or to display the automatic terminal information service (ATIS) weather report.

NAV 1 Radio/Omnibearing VOR 1 Display
and the NAV 2 Radio/Omnibearing VOR 2 Display

The NAV 1 radio is used with the omnibearing indicator 1 display, or OBI 1, to tune in VOR and ILS stations and display navigational information. The NAV 1 radio tunes in a VOR or ILS station for the OBI 1 display, while the NAV 2 radio tunes in a VOR or ILS station for the OBI 2 display.

In addition to displaying the VOR course radial your aircraft is currently on, the OBI 1 also contains a glide slope indicator with moving cross hairs that when used with instrument landing systems, tells you whether or not your aircraft is on the proper glide slope to the runway. A distance measuring equipment (DME) indicator on the display, shows the aircraft's current speed and distance to the VOR or ILS station.

A second OBI 2 display is provided so you can tune in a second VOR station, using the NAV 2 radio, and thus precisely fix your coordinates on a map. It is also equipped with a DME indicator for measuring speed and distance to the VOR station tuned on the NAV 2 radio. When plotted on a map, the intersection of the two VOR radials from both the OBI displays tells you the aircraft's exact position. Unlike OBI 1, the OBI 2 does not have provision for an ILS glide slope. If you plan to tune in an ILS runway, do so on the NAV 1 radio.

The omnibearing VOR 1 display is found on the first instrument sub-panel, while the second omnibearing VOR 2 display is found on the second instrument sub-panel along with the engine monitoring gauges. To switch between sub-panel displays to view the VOR 1 and VOR 2, press [Tab]. If you want the same instrument panel to remain on screen, you can press [Shift] + [Tab] to cycle between VOR 1, VOR 2, and the ADF gauge.

The Learjet's computerized OBI display is a little easier to use than the OBI for the Cessna. This is true because all the readouts for the DME, including both range and speed, are included on the same display as the OBI.

Besides tuning in VOR and ILS stations, the NAV 1 radio is also used for the electronic flight instrument systems/command flight path display (EFIS/CFPD) advanced navigational graphics display system. Using EFIS/CFPD, you can project special symbols onto the cockpit windshield that tell you where you should fly your aircraft. This display, which is called a "Heads Up Display" (HUD), is used on many military and commercial jet aircraft today.

To turn on the EFIS/CFPD and display red rectangles in the sky that point toward a particular VOR station:

1. First tune in a VOR or ILS station on your NAV 1 radio.

2. Select EFIS/CFPD Display from the Nav/Com menu.

3. In the dialog box that next opens up, click on the EFIS Master Switch.

4. Click on the Lock to VOR and Altitude check box.

5. Click on the Plot Intercepting Path check box.

6. Click OK, and exit the dialog box.

When you return to the cockpit, if you don't see the red rectangles at first, change your view angle, sweeping around in a 360° arc until they come into sight.

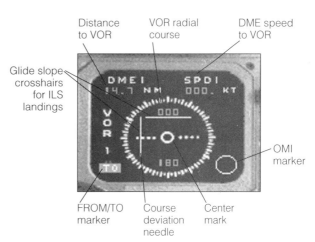

Figure 7.31
The NAV 1/VOR 1 display

ADF/Transponder (XPDR)

The automatic direction finder (ADF), is a navigational radio that tunes in low frequency AM signals from 0 KHz to 999 KHz from AM commercial stations as well as special non-directional beacon radio stations (NDB). Essentially, the ADF calculates the relative bearing to the station and displays it on the ADF bearing indicator. The bearing to the NDB or AM broadcast

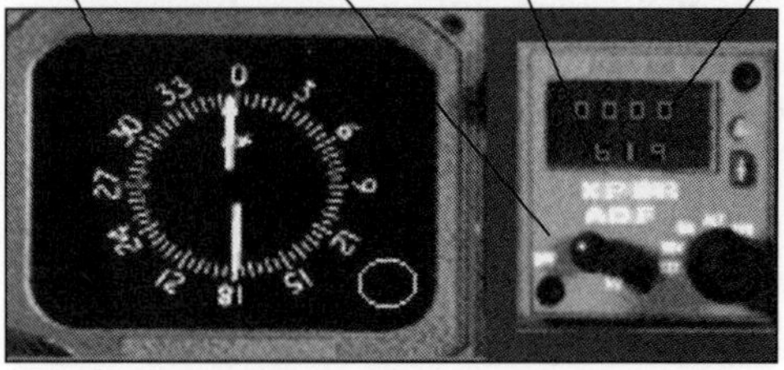

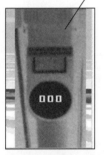

ADF course indicator   ADF radio   ADF radio frequency   Transponder squawk code

Figure 7.32
The Transponder (XPDR), ADF radio, and ADF course indicator

Click here and drag with mouse to move the compass to a different part of the screen.

Figure 7.33
The magnetic compass on the Learjet

You can easily move the magnetic compass using the mouse by clicking and dragging the top part of the compass.

station is relative to the nose of your aircraft. To point your aircraft at the radio station you are currently tuning in, just turn the airplane so the needle on the ADF bearing indicator is pointing straight up at the number 0.

The ADF course indicator is not normally displayed on the Learjet's instrument panel. To summon it on screen, press (Shift) + (Tab) to cycle between the VOR 1, VOR 2 and ADF course indicator.

The four digit transponder squawk code (XPDR) is entered in above the ADF frequency, as shown in Figure 7.32. The transponder sends out this radio code to the air traffic control computers, which allows them to get a three dimensional fix on your aircraft for collision avoidance purposes.

Magnetic Compass

As with the Cessna, the magnetic compass reports your plane's current course heading. The magnetic compass for the Learjet is located on a separate instrument panel mounted on a center post above the instrument panel. If you object to having this panel partly obscure your view out the window, you can turn it off by toggling off Instrument Panel 2 in the Instrument Panel Options dialog box found under the Views menu.

Engine Monitoring Instruments/Controls

All the Learjet's engine monitoring equipment is located on an instrument sub-panel. To display this sub-panel press (Tab).

Turbine and Fan Speed Gauges

In FS 5.1, there are two sets of turbine speed gauges (one digital, the other analog) for measuring the fan and turbine rotational speeds. None of the Learjet's engines display the precise RPM; rather they display the RPM as a

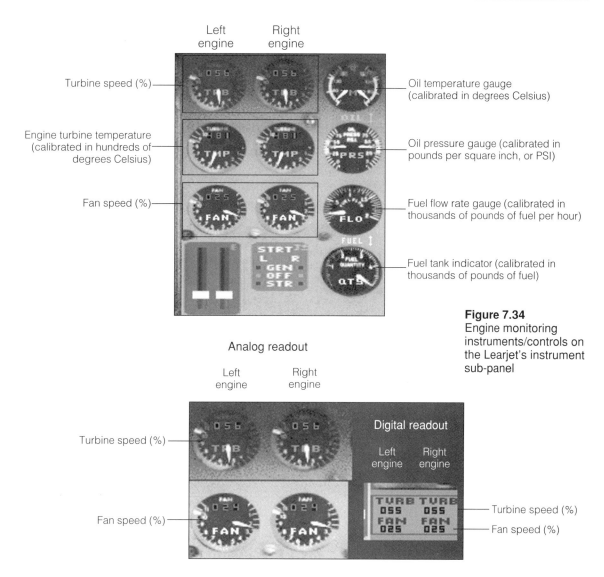

Figure 7.34
Engine monitoring instruments/controls on the Learjet's instrument sub-panel

Figure 7.35
Learjet's Fanjet engine speed gauges

percentage of maximum engine speed. Since the two Garrett AiResearch TFE731-2-2B engines are turbofan engines, there are separate instruments to monitor the speed of the low pressure frontal fan assembly and the turbine core section. Note the speeds for the turbine and fan are expressed as a percentage of maximum fan/turbine speed because they rotate at different speeds. The rotational speed for the turbine core of the engine runs around 30,000 RPM; while the fan runs at approximately 11,000 RPM. A reading of 56 on the turbine dial, for example, tells you that the engine is spinning at

Left engine   Right engine

Figure 7.36
Turbine temperature
gauge

56 percent of 30,000 RPMs, or 16,800 RPMs. On the other hand, a reading of 56 on the fan speed indicator tells you that the fan is spinning at 56 percent of 11,000 RPMs, or 6,160 RPMs.

Turbine Temperature Gauge

You will want to periodically monitor your engine core's temperature by observing the turbine temperature gauge. At average cruising speed, the temperature should hover around 799° Celsius. The dial indicates hundreds of degrees Centigrade, so if the needle points to the number 6, the engine's turbine core has a temperature of 600° Celsius.

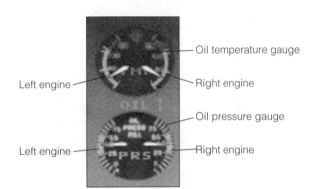

Oil temperature gauge

Left engine

Right engine

Oil pressure gauge

Left engine

Right engine

Figure 7.37
Oil temperature and
pressure gauges on
the Learjet. Pressure
dial is calibrated in
pounds per square
inch, or PSI.

Oil Temperature and Pressure

The current temperature of the engine oil is displayed on the oil temperature gauge in degrees Centigrade. There are two gauges, one for each engine. Normal operating temperature is 90° to 100° Celsius. Oil Pressure is shown on the oil pressure gauges below. Each engine has a separate gauge with normal operating pressure in the range of 38 to 91 pounds per square inch (PSI).

Fuel Flow

Your current fuel consumption, measured in thousands of pounds per hour, is displayed on the fuel flow meter. This gauge has two pointers, one for each engine. Each number on the scale represents 1,000 pounds. If the needle pointer is aiming at the number 0.5, it means that one engine is burning 500 pounds of fuel per hour. Average fuel consumption runs 400 to 600 pounds per hour for each engine, which when combined, equals a total fuel burn of 800 to 1,200 pounds of fuel per hour. Since each US gallon of fuel weighs 6.7 pounds, this translates to a fuel burn of between 119 to 179 gallons per hour.

Fuel Quantity

The current fuel remaining in the fuel tanks is displayed on the fuel quantity gauge. The dial is measured in thousands of pounds. If the needle rests on the number 4, it means 4,000 pounds of fuel remain in the tanks. The Learjet 35A can carry 6,198 pounds of fuel (925 US gallons, or 3,501 liters, or 2,811 kgs), which gives it a range of about 2,200 nautical miles (2,528 statute miles or 4,066 kilometers), or a flying time of about five hours and thirty-five minutes under optimum flying conditions (economy cruise at 394 knots).

Engine Start/Generator Switch

Because the Learjet is powered by twin fanjets which don't use sparkplugs, the engine start/generator switch replaces the magneto ignition system found on the Cessna. This switch tells you whether the left, right, or both fanjets are turned on. By clicking the STR switch, you can start the engines, and by clicking on the OFF switch, you can turn them off. From the keyboard, you can press J, then press + or – to cycle between OFF, STR, and GEN. The GEN, or generator setting is used to power the Learjet's electrical system from generators attached to the engines. Also use Ctrl Shift F1 to shut down engines and Ctrl Shift F4 to restart fuel flow.

Figure 7.38
Fuel quantity gauge (measured in thousands of pounds)

Throttle Controls/Thrust Diverters(Reverse Thrust)

The Garrett AiResearch TFE731-2-2B turbofan engines on the Learjet each have separate throttle controls. Each engine is rated at 3,500 pounds of thrust, and is equipped with electrically controlled and hydraulically operated thrust reversers (sometimes called thrust diverters) for slowing the aircraft on landings. The thrust reversers, which are pictured in Figure 7.41, shunt engine exhaust gases away from the rear of the engine, thereby enabling much of the engine's thrust to be converted into a braking action.

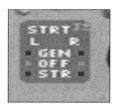

Figure 7.39
Engine start/generator switch on the Learjet

The throttle controls can be moved in tandem or can be moved individually. To choose the left engine throttle, press E + 1 then drag the left throttle control up or down. To choose the right engine throttle, press E + 2 then drag the right throttle control up or down. To move both throttles together, press E + 1 + 2, then drag the throttle levers up or down. The throttle levers can be moved via the mouse, the function keys F1, F2, F3, and F4, or by pressing 9 on the numeric keypad to increase the throttle, or 3 on the numeric keypad to decrease the throttle. F1 cuts engine power to idle, F2 decreases the engine power gradually, F3 increases engine power gradually, and F4 opens the throttle to its maximum setting.

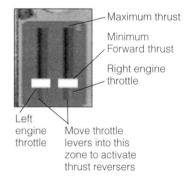

Maximum thrust

Minimum Forward thrust

Right engine throttle

Left engine throttle

Move throttle levers into this zone to activate thrust reversers

Figure 7.40
Throttle controls/thrust diverters for the Learjet

To apply the thrust reversers on landing, drag both throttle controls downward into the red zones. Full reverse thrust is achieved when the throttles are pushed down to the lowest possible setting. From the keyboard, you can activate the thrust reversers by pressing F1, then press 3 on the numeric keypad repeatedly, until the throttle levers move into the red zone.

Figure 7.41
Thrust diverters for the
Learjet (*Courtesy of
Learjet*)

Thrust reverse disengaged   Thrust reverse engaged

Other Instruments/Indicators

There are various other instruments and indicators used on the Learjet. They are listed as follows in this section.

Spoilers (SPL)

The spoilers are special flaps on the top surface of the Learjet's wings that act as air brakes. They can be used to slow the aircraft or prevent it from gaining too much speed when descending. After touchdown, you can extend the spoilers and flaps together along with activating the thrust reversers to quickly slow the aircraft. To deploy the flaps, click on the EXT button. To retract the flaps, click on the RET button. From the keyboard, press ⁄ to extend or retract the spoiler.

Retract
spoiler here

Extend
spoiler here

Figure 7.42
The spoilers control
on the Learjet

Flaps

The flaps are used to create extra lift when landing or taking off. The flaps position indicator shows the current extension angle for the flaps. They can be deployed incrementally from 0° to 8°, and from 20° to 40°. You deploy the flaps by clicking on the individual angle settings on the flaps position indicator. Or, from the keyboard you can use the F5 through F8 function keys. When the arm of the flaps position indicator points to the DN marker, the flaps are fully extended at 40°. If the arm points to the UP marker, the flaps are fully retracted at 0°.

The Learjet's flaps have only four settings as opposed to the Cessna's five flap settings:

UP: Flaps Fully Retracted Up to 0°

8: Flaps Set to 8°

20: Flaps Set to 20°

DN: Flaps Fully Extended Down to 40°

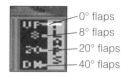

Figure 7.43
The flaps indicator/
control on the Learjet

You must not fly faster than the V_{FE} (flap extension speeds), or else damage to the flaps will occur. For the flaps fully down, the V_{FE} is 150 knots IAS, and for the flaps set to 20° the V_{FE} is 185 knots IAS.

Control Position Indicators

The position of the ailerons, rudders, and elevators are depicted on the control position indicators.

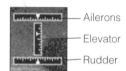

Figure 7.44
Control position
indicators on the
Learjet

Pitch Trim Indicator

The pitch trim is the Learjet's counterpart to the Cessna's elevator trim. Pitch trim is used to fine tune the aircraft's pitch (nose up or nose down angle). It also relieves the pilot of constantly applying pressure to the yoke to maintain level flight.

In FS 5.1, you will find this control most helpful when you are using a joystick/flightstick yoke because it enables you to fly at a level attitude without constantly pushing the stick forwards or backwards.

The pitch trim is activated from the numeric keypad by pressing [7] for nose down pitch movements, and by pressing [1] for nose up pitch movements.

Note the direction of movement of the Learjet's pitch trim indicator is the reverse of the Cessna's elevator trim indicator. When you press [7] to pitch the nose down, the pitch trim indicator moves up (on the Cessna it moves down), and when you press [1] to pitch the nose up, the pitch trim indicator moves down (on the Cessna it moves up).

Figure 7.45
Pitch trim indicator
on the Learjet

Angle of Attack/Stall Warning Proximity Indicator

The angle of attack indicator (ANG ATK) is a rectangular horizontal gauge that tells you how close you are to stalling the aircraft. A stall occurs when smooth airflow over the wings is disrupted, causing a loss of lift. The further

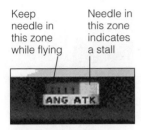

Keep needle in this zone while flying | Needle in this zone indicates a stall

Figure 7.46
Angle of attack/stall warning proximity indicator on the Learjet

Figure 7.47
Outside temperature gauge on the Learjet

Figure 7.48
Landing gear indicator on the Learjet

the needle moves to the right, the closer you are to a stall condition. When the needle enters the light colored zone on the right of the gauge, you are in danger of stalling and must take immediate action to prevent the airplane from crashing. Immediately lower the nose and increase thrust.

Although there is some relationship between a stall and the wing's angle of attack, a stall can occur at any speed, angle of attack, or engine setting; therefore this instrument should more aptly be called the stall proximity warning indicator.

Outside Air Temperature Gauge (OAT)

Measures the temperature outside the aircraft in degrees Fahrenheit. At higher elevations the temperature will drop.

Landing Gear

This indicator tells you the current position of your landing gear. When the wheels are down, the three wheel lights below the gear icon glow green. When the gear is being retracted, the wheel lights will briefly turn red before flickering out. The gear can be retracted or extended by clicking on the gear indicator, or by pressing G.

Don't extend the landing gear when traveling faster than the V_{LO} (maximum airspeed when operating the landing gear). For the Learjet this is 200 knots IAS.

Autopilot, Strobe, Lights, Zoom, Clock, and Simulation Speed Rate

The autopilot, strobe, lights, zoom, clock, and simulation speed rate controls are all similar to the Cessna's, with the exception of the landing lights. The Learjet has twin landing lights, one on each main landing gear. To turn on the autopilot, strobe, or lights, simply click on the indicator and it will light up. To turn off any control, click again and the light will blink out.

The zoom indicator allows you to change the magnification of the currently active 3-D view window, but it does not work with the Map view. To increase magnification, press +. To decrease magnification, press -. You can also click to the right of the zoom number to increase the zoom, or click to the left to decrease the zoom.

For a more complete description of each indicator and control, see the prior section on the Cessna's instrumentation.

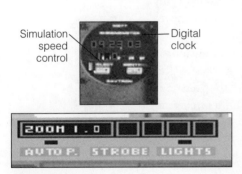

Simulation speed control | Digital clock

Figure 7.49
Autopilot, strobe, lights, zoom, clock, and simulation speed rate

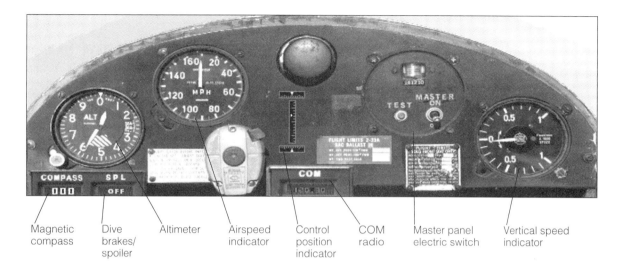

Magnetic compass   Dive brakes/ spoiler   Altimeter   Airspeed indicator   Control position indicator   COM radio   Master panel electric switch   Vertical speed indicator

Figure 7.50
Schweizer 2-32 sailplane's instrument panel

UNDERSTANDING YOUR INSTRUMENTS AND CONTROLS ON THE SCHWEIZER 2-32 SAILPLANE

Because the Schweizer 2-32 sailplane is used primarily for recreation, the cockpit instrumentation is kept simple. There are no engine controls, nor are there any navigational aids other than a simple magnetic compass. Only a radio, altimeter, airspeed indicator, vertical speed indicator, and dive brake control make up the instrumentation package for the sailplane.

Airspeed Indicator

The airspeed indicator measures the aircraft's indicated airspeed (IAS). However, in FS 5.1 the true airspeed (TAS) is actually displayed. The sailplane's maximum speed is about 158 miles per hour, so the dial is calibrated to read speeds of 20 mph to 160 mph.

Altimeter

Like the altimeter on the Cessna, this altimeter is read like a clock. The large hand shows hundreds of feet mean sea level (MSL), and the small hand shows thousands of feet MSL.

Vertical Rate of Climb Indicator

The vertical rate of climb indicator, which is calibrated in units of hundreds of feet per minute, tells you how fast up or down you are traveling. When the needle rests on the upper number 0.5, you know that the sailplane is climbing at the rate of 50 feet per minute.

Spoilers/Dive Brakes

The dive brakes, like the Learjet's spoilers, act to slow down the aircraft's rate of descent. To deploy these air brakes, click on the SPL indicator, or press ⌧.

Master/Test Switch

This switch activates the aircraft's electrical system, which is totally dependent on battery power.

COM Radio

The COM Radio is used to contact Air Traffic Control, or display the automatic terminal information service (ATIS) weather information. To change the frequency, see the instructions found earlier for the Cessna.

Magnetic Compass

This compass shows your aircraft's current heading.

Control Position Indicators

The position of the ailerons, rudders, and elevators are depicted on the control position indicators.

UNDERSTANDING YOUR INSTRUMENTS AND CONTROLS ON THE SOPWITH CAMEL

The walnut-faced control panel found on the Sopwith Camel is simple but practical. There are no sophisticated controls or instruments, but neverthe-

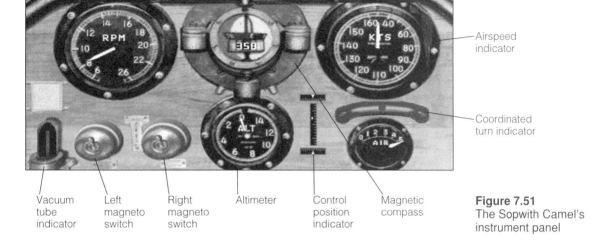

Vacuum   Left   Right   Altimeter   Control   Magnetic
tube   magneto   magneto   position   compass
indicator   switch   switch   indicator

Figure 7.51
The Sopwith Camel's
instrument panel

less, you still have much the same flight information displayed to help you
fly the plane.

Airspeed Indicator

The Sopwith Camel's airspeed indicator shows the plane's true airspeed
(TAS) in knots. Your aircraft speed will register if it falls within the range of
40 knots to 160 knots.

Altimeter

The altimeter measures the plane's altitude in feet, and is scaled in units of
thousands of feet. For an altitude of 4,000 feet, the needle would cover the
number 4 on the dial. The highest altitude the instrument can measure is
slightly over 14,000 feet, although practically speaking, the Sopwith Camel
would never fly that high.

Turn Indicator

The turn indicator is used to determine whether you are making a coordinated turn or not. Like the Cessna, unbalanced forces in a turn can cause
uncoordinated turns, meaning the airplane slips and skids through the air.

When this happens, the ball will roll to one side or the other, but if the turn is coordinated, the ball will stay centered. By default, FS 5.1 starts you out with your ailerons and rudders synchronized in auto-coordination mode. If you want more selective control over your turns, deselect the Auto-Coordination option under the Sim menu.

RPM Indicator

The engine's rotations per minute (RPM) indicator tells you how fast your engine is running, and is calibrated in hundreds of revolutions per minute. A reading of 16 on the scale thus shows an engine RPM of 1,600. For average cruising, the needle on the dial should hover around 2,200 RPMs.

Magnetic Compass

The magnetic compass tells you your plane's current compass heading.

Magneto Switches/Vacuum Tube

The two metal throw switches are used to turn the right and left magnetos on and off. Each magneto system generates electrical power for the spark plugs, and is independently redundant in case one should fail. To shut them off, click below each magneto switch; to turn them back on, click above the switch. When you have shut off both magnetos, the vacuum tube will cease to glow, telling you that your ignition system is without power.

Control Position Indicators

The position of the ailerons, rudders, and elevators are depicted on the control position indicators.

C H A P T E R

8

Basic Flight Maneuvers

This chapter introduces you to the basic ground and flight maneuvers of taxiing, taking off, climbing, flying straight and level, making turns, and landing. But because flight planning is such an important part of flying, you will also be introduced to Automatic Terminal Information Service (ATIS). ATIS helps with flight planning by notifing you about weather information, air traffic control, and the checklists.

Before starting this chapter, make sure *Flight Simulator* is properly configured to work with your computer, display card, keyboard, sound card, and mouse or joystick. After starting FS 5.1, you should see the tarmac of Chicago's Meigs Field Runway 36 out of the cockpit window of your Cessna Skylane 182RG airplane. In the background, you should hear the steady drone of your engines idling.

If you want to take off right away, you can skip the next section on taxiing and go directly to the take-off.

TAXIING

Before practicing how to taxi around the runway, you will want to familiarize yourself with the flight controls and how they operate. Hopefully, you will have studied the keyboard layout for the numeric keypad and will know which keys move the ailerons, elevators, rudders, and throttle setting. If you don't already know how to operate your controls, take a moment now to review this material. A quick reference for the keyboard commands can be found on the inside covers of this book. To use the mouse as your control yoke, you must click the right mouse button so the cursor disappears from the screen. At this point, any movement of the mouse will be translated into movements of the ailerons, elevators, and rudders. To disengage the mouse/yoke, simply press the right mouse button once again and the mouse pointer will reappear.

Mouse users can switch back and forth between mouse/yoke control and normal mouse control by clicking on the right mouse button.

Looking out the cockpit window for a 360° panoramic view.

Enlarge any view or map window by pressing W.

Panoramic View

Next, spend a few moments practicing how to use your 360° field of view by looking out the windows. Your initial view out the window is the front view. Press Shift and 9 on the numeric keypad to see out your right front window. Holding down Shift, press the numeric keypad keys 6, 3, 2, 1, 4, 7, and 8 to cycle through all possible views that make up your field of vision. Press Shift + 9 to return to the front cockpit view.

The Map Window

To better orient yourself while on the ground, bring up the map window by pressing Num Lock. Zoom in and out of the map view by pressing + and − on the main keyboard till you get a good view of your immediate surroundings. The cross in the map window represents your airplane, and when you move, the map will scroll accordingly. To remove the map, press Num Lock twice in succession, but for now keep it open.

Flight Simulator allows you to see any of your view or map windows full screen. Simply press W once to enlarge the window to full screen, and press W again to reduce the window to its normal size. Try this by pressing W, then press − (on the main keyboard) several times until you have the entire Meigs Field runway environs in view.

For this exercise in taxiing, follow the path illustrated in Figure 8.1 and then return to your starting position on Runway 36. Notice you will make a left turn off the main runway onto a small turnoff runway, then you'll make another left turn and taxi straight until you see the turnoff for the main runway where you started from. When you reach this turnoff, turn left and you will be back again on Runway 36. All you need to do at this point is make a 90° left turn and you will be back to your original starting position.

Flight Simulator 5.1 has painted runway guides off the main runways to help keep your plane from running off the pavement or crashing into

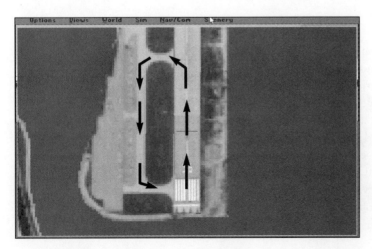

Figure 8.1
The map window open to full-screen, showing the taxi path you should take

some ground object. To stay out of trouble make sure your plane follows the runway guide. Don't veer to the left or right of the guide, just stay right on top of it and you'll be fine.

Whenever taxiing off the main runway, follow the painted runway guides!

Practice Turning, Starting and Stopping while Taxiing

Before taxiing, see if your parking brakes are on by looking at the lower left hand corner of your cockpit window. If it says "Parking Brake," then you must release the parking brake by pressing `.`. To begin taxiing, press `9` on the numeric keypad seven times. The airplane will begin to roll down the runway as the tachometer shows the engine speed increasing to between 1,055 and 1,155 RPMs. Steer the aircraft by pressing `0` on the numeric keypad to steer left, and by pressing `Enter` on the numeric keypad to steer right.

Stopping the airplane is accomplished by pressing `.` on the main keyboard to engage the wheel brakes. You should also cut the throttle by pressing `3` on the numeric keypad until the engine is again idling at 451 RPM. Press `.` and hold down `3` to stop the plane now. After the airplane has come to a complete halt, press `.` again to release the brakes and then press `9` seven times to allow the airplane to start rolling again.

How to Pivot your Airplane 180° While Stationary

By using *Flight Simulator*'s differential brakes, you can pivot your airplane 180° while stationary on the ground. A differential brake system allows you to apply different braking pressures on each wheel. This allows you to lock one wheel in place, while allowing the other to rotate freely. Note this technique is not recommended for all of your turning because it causes the locked wheel to skid and can damage your landing gear. It is better to turn the aircraft by first increasing the throttle until you begin to move, then use the nose wheel steering to turn the aircraft (on the numeric keypad, to turn left press `0`, to turn right press `Enter`).

To perform a 180° pivot left, follow these steps:

1. Press `F11` to apply the left differential brake.

2. Increase the throttle by pressing `9` on the numeric keyboard until you start moving (1055 to 1155 RPM). You may have to press `F11` several times to re-engage the differential. Your airplane will begin to rotate left, while staying in place.

The differential brakes: Press F11 for the left differential brake and press F12 for the right differential brake.

To perform a 180° pivot right, follow these steps:

1. Press F12 to apply the right differential brake.
2. Increase the throttle by pressing 9 on the numeric keypad until you start moving (1055 to 1155 RPM). You may have to press F12 several times to re-engage the differential brake. Your airplane will begin to rotate right, while staying in place.

Taxi Around Meigs Field and Return to the Takeoff Position on Runway 36

Now that you've had some practical experience stopping and turning the aircraft while on the ground, let's try taxiing back to the beginning of Runway 36. Allow the aircraft to roll forward and look for the runway turnoff to the left; make sure your speed does not become excessive. When you see the turnoff, press . to slow the aircraft, then press 0 on the numeric keypad to pivot left. If you pass the runway turnoff, don't worry, simply stop the airplane and apply the left differential brake (F11) to rotate the aircraft left and head back (see the previous section on pivoting the airplane 180°). Look for the painted runway guides, as illustrated in Figure 8.2, and follow the line veering off to the left.

Follow the runway guide until you reach the turnoff for Runway 36. Make a left turn, applying the brake (.) and left rudder (0) to precisely maneuver your plane. Don't be afraid to come to a complete stop and survey your position via the map window. You can always pivot the aircraft in place, using the differential brakes, and point it in the right direction.

Don't worry if you have trouble taxiing around the airport. These movements take much practice. If you get stuck or too frustrated, simply press Ctrl + Print Screen and the simulator will reset itself.

Figure 8.2
Follow the painted runway guides and stay right on top of them, or your plane may crash or get mired in the mud. In this figure, you will want to stay with the left guide.

Painted runway guides

ATIS AND AIR TRAFFIC CONTROL

Before taking off, you should obtain weather information for your area by tuning in the local Automatic Terminal Information Service (ATIS) radio station on your COM radio. You will also need to request takeoff clearance from Air Traffic Control. The next two sections discuss how the ATIS and Air Traffic Control work.

The following information appears on your screen:

Scrolling ATIS Message On-Screen	Explanation
Chicago O'Hare Information Charlie	ATIS station identification. Each ATIS message is assigned a letter from A to Z, which is read as "Alpha," "Bravo," "Charlie," etc. When the message contents are updated, the letter is changed, alerting you to the fact that the ATIS message is a new one.
1500 Zulu	1500 (3:00 P.M.). Coordinated Universal Time. Note that this time is not local time, but Greenwich Mean Time (GMT) in England, and it is expressed in 24-hour format.
Weather:	Weather Conditions
Measured Ceiling 10,000	Clouds are found at up to 10,000 feet
Visibility 10	Visibility is 10 miles
Temperature +075 F	Temperature is 75° Fahrenheit
Winds 90 at 10	Wind direction 90° at 10 knots. Winds blow west from 90° to 270°.
Altimeter 30.15	Barametric air pressure is 30.15 inches of Hg.
Landing and Departing Runway 09R	Landing and departing on Runway 09 Right. Runway numbers are always described by the direction the runway is facing. For example, Runway 09R means the runway faces due east at 90° (±5°). The "R" tells you there are two runways facing this direction; but you must use the one on your right. If ATIS tells you that you are "Landing and departing Runway 27L," it means that you must go to the opposite end of the runway to take off or land on a compass heading of 270° (±5°), or due west.
Advise Controller on initial contact you have Charlie	Contact Air Traffic Control for permission to land or take off. Tune your COM radio to the airport's control tower frequency for clearance.

To see the ATIS message scroll across your screen while at Chicago's Meigs Field, tune your COM radio to a frequency of 135.40 MHz. This will tune in the ATIS station for Chicago's O'Hare International Airport.

You must request take off or landing clearance from Air Traffic Control whenever you take off or land.

To request Air Traffic Control clearance:

1. Toggle on the Air Traffic Control option from the Nav/Com menu. If it is on, you will see a check mark next the menu name.
2. From the Nav/Com menu, select Communications Radio.
3. In the Communications Radio dialog box, click the Send Message button. The Air Traffic Control dialog box should open.
4. If you are taking off, click the Request to Take off button. If you are landing, click the Request to Land button.
5. Follow the instructions from the tower, and set your four digit transponder squawk code to the code that Air Traffic Control specifies.
6. Go through your takeoff checklist.

BEFORE TAKEOFF, PERFORM THE TAKEOFF CHECKLIST

Before taking off, you should go through the takeoff checklist to make sure everything is in order. Very briefly move all your controls, checking that the ailerons, elevators, and rudders all move. Examine your other instruments, being sure to check the following items as shown on Table 8.1.

After going through this checklist, you will be ready for takeoff.

TAKING OFF

For this section of the chapter, you will need to have your Cessna aircraft poised for takeoff at the very beginning of Runway 36. If your aircraft is not in takeoff position, simply press the [Ctrl] and [Print Screen] keys and the simulation will reset itself.

Next, read the Takeoff Checklist for the Cessna, as outlined in Table 8.2. This table is a handy reference guide for taking off. When you are sure you understand what needs to be done, proceed to the next section.

Performing the Checklist

Make sure the wing flaps are fully retracted and the carburetor heat is turned off. Increase the throttle to its maximum setting. Watch as the aircraft begins to move slowly down the runway. Align the Cessna on the center of the runway using [0] on the numeric keypad to steer left, and [Enter] on the numeric

Table 8.1   Before Takeoff Checklist

Item	Indicator/Control	Action
1	Parking Brake	Set (press [Ctrl] [.])
2	Ailerons, rudder, elevator, elevator trim	Check operation, then center as indicated on control position indicators
3	Mixture	Set to rich (move lever up)
4	Fuel quantity	Check left and right tanks are full
5	Throttle	1700 RPM
6	Magnetos	Perform magneto check: Set engine to 1700 RPM with parking brake engaged. Move ignition switch first to R position and note RPM. Next move switch back to BOTH position to clear the other set of spark plugs. Then move switch to the L position, note RPM, and return the switch to the BOTH position. RPM drop should not exceed 175 RPM on either magneto or show greater than 50 RPM differential between magnetos.
7	Carburetor heat	Off
8	Propeller	Cycle from high to low pitch (meaning low RPM to high RPM). Return pitch to low setting for maximum RPM (i.e., move Prop Pitch Lever to top).
9	Oil pressure and temperature	Gauge Indicators Centered
10	Throttle	800–1000 RPM
11	Strobe lights	Set by pressing [O]
12	COM radio	Set to local ATIS frequency
13	Directional gyro	Press [D] to Calibrate
14	Altimeter	Press [B] to Calibrate
15	Autopilot	Off
16	Wing flaps	Set to 0°
17	Parking brakes	Release by pressing [.] on main keyboard

Table 8.2   Takeoff Checklist

Item	Indicator/Control	Action
1	Wing flaps	0° for normal runway 20° for soft runways or short field takeoff (flaps settings greater than 20° not allowed for takeoff)
2	Carburetor heat	Cold (off)
3	Throttle	Set to 29" Hg, 2400 RPM
4	Prop pitch control	Move to highest RPM setting (slide prop pitch control lever UP) for lowest propeller pitch angle
5	Mixture	Full rich (move mixture level to top)
6	Elevator control	Lift Nose Wheel at 55 knots IAS (Press ⏌2⏌ or pull back on yoke)
7	Airspeed indicator	Climb airspeed should be 80 knots IAS (Flaps at 0°) or 70 knots IAS (Flaps at 20°)
8	Wheel brakes	Apply momentarily when airborne and prior to retracting landing gear. This will stop wheel from rotating and prevent any rubbing as it is retracted into the wheel well. Press ⏌.⏌.
9	Landing gear	Retract landing gear. Press ⏌G⏌.
10	Wing flaps	For short field takeoff/soft runways where flaps are set to 20°, retract slowly once airborne and after reaching 70 knots IAS.

To quickly center the steering wheel, press ⏌5⏌ on the numeric keypad.

keypad to steer right. These keys control the left and right movement of your steering wheel on the ground. In auto-coordination mode (the default mode in this case), the ailerons are linked with the rudders, so you also steer with ⏌4⏌ and ⏌6⏌, or the mouse. To quickly center the ailerons, rudders, or steering wheel, press ⏌5⏌ on the numeric keypad.

With your throttle set to maximum, your speed will increase very rapidly, as shown on the airspeed indicator. Strong crosswinds often make a controlled takeoff difficult, so you may have to counteract this drift by carefully moving the ailerons and rudders (press ⏌4⏌ and ⏌6⏌ on the numeric keypad). Try not move the ailerons/rudders excessively (this will cause you to zigzag down the runway) and do not hesitate to abort the takeoff if you run into trouble. To abort the takeoff, decrease the throttle by pressing ⏌3⏌ on the numeric keypad. Then apply the brakes repeatedly by pressing ⬚ on the main keypad.

The normal takeoff ground roll distance is about 1,215 feet for the Cessna. But to gain sufficient altitude to clear a 50 foot obstacle at the end of the runway, you need at least 2,310 feet of horizontal distance. Meigs Field, with its 3,948 foot runway, gives you ample room to takeoff and land.

As soon as you have lifted off (you will know this because your wings will start to rock if you make any slight motions left or right), apply the wheel brake momentarily by pressing ⬚ on the main keypad, then retract the landing gear by pressing ⬚G⬚. Since the wheels are still spinning furiously from the takeoff, you will want to slow them before stowing them in the wheel well. Try to keep your airspeed around 70 to 80 knots during the climb by applying a light touch to the elevators (⬚8⬚ and ⬚2⬚ on the numeric keypad).

If possible, always lift off into the wind because the headwind adds to your takeoff speed and reduces your takeoff distance. Figure 8.3 shows the screen as the plane takes off.

At a speed of 55 knots, press ⬚2⬚ once or twice (or pull back on your joystick/mouse slightly) to pull your nose up. This act is called "rotation," and each aircraft has a different rotation speed.

Taking Off With a Crosswind

Crosswinds are winds that cross the runway in a semi-perpendicular angle. To successfully take off with a crosswind, you must switch off auto-coordination and then use your ailerons to correct the aircraft's tendency to yaw to the left or right. Auto-coordination, you will remember, links your ailerons and rudders together. If you leave this option on when trying to correct a crosswind force, your rudder will interfere. Figure 8.4 shows what happens to your airplane when a crosswind blows across the runway.

To take off with a crosswind present:

Figure 8.3
Taking off (spot view)

1. Switch off auto-coordination under the Sim menu.
2. Create a surface crosswind blowing from 270° with a speed of 15 knots. To do this, pull down the World menu and select Weather. In the Weather dialog box, click the Winds button, and the click the Create button. In the Create Wind dialog box, click the Surface Winds radio button, and then enter a speed of 15 knots and a course heading of 270°. Click OK to exit all the dialog boxes and return to the simulator.

Switch off auto-coordination while taking off with a crosswind.

Effects of the Crosswind on Takeoff

**No Correction
Plane Blown Off Runway**

**Proper Correction
Ailerons Applied Into Wind
& Plane Stays on Course**

Figure 8.4
When taking off with a crosswind present, the airplane skips to the left. By applying ailerons in the direction of the wind, you can have better control during takeoff.

3. Tune in the ATIS frequency to listen for the weather report. The wind direction should be given. If the report says "winds 270 at 15," you will know that a wind is blowing at 15 knots from your 270° compass heading (the wind is blowing east from 270° to 90°).

4. Apply full ailerons into the direction of the wind. Since you are facing 0° due north, and the wind is blowing from 270° (eastward), you will turn your ailerons all the way left (press 4 on the numeric keypad until the control position indicator shows the aileron at the far right). Figure 8.4 shows the correct procedure for taking off in a crosswind, but note you are viewing the aircraft from the front, so the wind direction looks like it's coming from the right, when it is actually coming from the aircraft's left.

5. Use the rudder to steer left and right. Before taking off, however, move the rudder in the direction of the wind. This will prepare the airplane for what is yet to come. For this example, apply left rudder by pressing 0.

6. Increase the throttle to maximum by pressing F4.

7. Steer down the center of the runway, correcting any zigzag movements with the rudder (0 and Enter keys on the numeric keypad).

8. At an airspeed of 50 knots, center the ailerons and rudders with 5. This will prevent your plane from tipping over once it leaves the ground.

9. After passing 55 knots, raise the nose (apply the up elevator by pressing 2).

Your plane may soar in an awkward direction just after it leaves the ground. But you should now be able to stabilize the airplane into a level climb.

Later in this chapter, you will find information on how to land with a crosswind.

CLIMBING

Climbing is often defined as the transition between takeoff and flying straight and level at cruising altitude. The Cessna performs normal climbs at 610 feet per minute. Climbs that require quick ascents, such as when clearing mountains or obstacles rapidly, can be performed at a maximum rate of 1,040 feet per minute at MSL.

Table 8.3 Normal and Maximum Climb Rates for the Cessna at Mean Sea Level		
Climb Type	**Feet per Minute**	**Airspeed**
Normal climb	610	90 to 100 knots IAS
Maximum climb	1,040	90 knots IAS

Both the normal rate of climb and the maximum rate of climb numbers are affected by altitude, aircraft speed, and weather. Due to thinner air, the rate of climb decreases at higher altitudes. At 8,000 feet, for example, the normal rate of climb falls to 455 feet per minute.

To achieve a normal climb, increase the throttle and apply up elevator. Use the elevator sparingly; the engine should take over most of this responsibility.

To climb, follow these steps:

1. Increase the throttle and apply the up elevator (press [2] on the numeric keypad or pull back on the mouse/yoke) to initiate the climb. Watch as the vertical speed indicator creeps upwards. You can fine tune your climb rate by moving the throttle (use [9] and [3] on the numeric keypad) and by making small adjustments to the elevator trim ([7] and [1] on the numeric keypad).

2. For a normal climb, adjust throttle and propeller control until airspeed is 90 to 100 knots, 25 inches of Hg, with 2,400 RPM. The vertical speed indicator should show approximately 600 feet per minute rate of ascent. For a maximum rate of climb, increase throttle and propeller control until 29 inches of Hg is developed at 2,400 RPM. Use full rich mixture and watch that your airspeed stays around 87 to 90 knots, with a vertical rate of climb of 1,040 feet per minute at MSL, or 455 feet per minute at 8,000 feet.

Figure 8.5 shows the screen during a normal climb. Note the vertical speed indicator shows a vertical speed of around 600 feet per minute and the airspeed is hovering around 90 knots.

Figure 8.5
The Normal Climb. Note the vertical speed indicator shows a vertical speed of around 600 feet per minute and the airspeed is hovering around 90 knots.

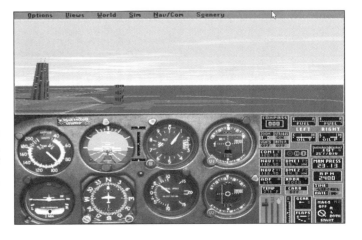

Table 8.4   Minimum Climb Checklist for the Cessna

Item	Indicator/Control	Action
1	Airspeed indicator	90 to 100 knots IAS
2	Vertical speed indicator	At sea level, temperature 60° F, normal rate of climb is 610 feet per minute.
3	Throttle and propeller controls	Set engine power to 25 inches Hg and 2400 RPM using prop control and throttle. Adjust both controls as necessary. (Sliding the prop pitch control down slightly often increases engine power.)
4	Mixture	Full rich (move mixture lever to top)

Table 8.5   Maximum Climb Checklist for the Cessna

Item	Indicator/Control	Action
1	Airspeed indicator	90 knots IAS at sea level to 87 knots at 20,000 feet
2	Vertical speed indicator	At MSL, maximum rate of climb is 1,040 feet per minute. At 8,000 feet, maximum rate of climb is 455 feet per minute.
3	Throttle and propeller control	Set engine power to 29 inches Hg and 2400 RPM using prop control and throttle. Adjust both controls as necessary. (Sliding the prop pitch control down slightly often increases engine power.)
4	Mixture	Full rich (move mixture lever to top)
5	Propeller	Lowest pitch angle (move lever up)

Use the throttle to make changes in your climb rate. Don't use the elevators to climb.

Tables 8.4 and 8.5 detail the climbing procedures for both the normal and maximum climb.

Your plane will enter a stall if your airspeed is too low (below 55 knots at mean sea level), or if your rate of climb is too high (see Figure 8.6). *Flight Simulator* reacts to this condition by sounding an audible warning and by displaying a stall indication message on the right side of the cockpit windshield. The best way to recover from this situation is to lower the nose to regain flying speed and lift.

If you keep continuing to climb, eventually the atmosphere will thin to the point where there is not enough sufficient lift to support your plane. This also constitutes a stall situation and you must descend to a lower altitude to regain lift.

Furthermore at higher altitudes, the manifold pressure gauge will indicate a loss of power. This is because the total air pressure in the manifold is decreased, due to the less dense air. We will come back to this topic in the next chapter. During prolonged climbs, the throttle must be continually advanced if constant power is to be maintained.

Figure 8.6
External view of a stall

CRUISING STRAIGHT AND LEVEL

After your climb has been completed, you will want to enter the cruise phase of your flight. To make the transition to a straight and level flight, reduce the throttle and lower the elevators as necessary. Be sure to start the leveling off process well before your desired cruising altitude because it takes time to stabilize the aircraft.

At higher altitudes, the Cessna's engine will lose power as indicated on the manifold pressure gauge.

Leveling Off From the Climb

To level off the aircraft and exit the climb, reduce your throttle. Use the elevator trim to make any last minute adjustments to nose pitch. The general rule of thumb is to start leveling off approximately 50 feet below the desired altitude for each 500 feet per minute rate of climb.

For example, if you were climbing at a rate of 1,000 feet per minute, you would start your level off at 100 feet below the altitude you wish to establish.

Normal Cruise

Normal cruising does not require full throttle. In fact, flying straight and level usually is performed using only 55 to 75 percent of the engine's rated horsepower. The throttle, propeller pitch control, and mixture control all influence the amount of power the engine produces. In addition, altitude and temperature also affect the power setting needed for a level cruise. Therefore, you must adjust your throttle, propeller pitch, and mixture settings for different altitudes in order to achieve straight and level flight. Table 8.7 illustrates cruise airspeeds vs. altitude for various power settings in the range of 75 percent. If you wanted to cruise at 75 percent power at an altitude of 6,000 feet, you would need to travel at an airspeed of 154 knots. To achieve this, manipulate your throttle, propeller, and mixture controls until you see 23 inches of Hg on your manifold pressure gauge, with a propeller RPM of 2,100. Notice that, in the table, the higher you travel the faster your cruise speed must be. This fits in with the aerodynamic theory predicting that as the atmosphere thins at higher elevations, less lift is generated by the wings of an airplane. Therefore, to maintain level flight and generate the same amount of lift, the plane must have a higher forward velocity.

A good power setting for cruising at 4,000 feet and below can be found when the engine is set to 2,400 RPM with 22.5 inches Hg of manifold pressure (75 percent of engine power). To achieve this:

1. Reduce the RPM through the propeller control by pressing Ctrl + F2 until you get 2,400 RPM.

2. Next, reduce the throttle by pressing F2 until you get 22.5 inches Hg of manifold pressure.

3. Adjust elevator trim as necessary for level flight by pressing 7 and 1 on the numeric keypad.

See Table 8.6 for a summary of the steps to be performed for cruising straight and level.

Figure 8.7
Cruising straight and level in the Cessna

EXECUTING TURNS

The turn is used to change the aircraft's heading. You make turns by banking the wings of the aircraft, using the ailerons and rudders in combination. It is often necessary to apply the elevators to maintain altitude.

The artificial horizon and the turn indicator are used to obtain information about the turn. The artificial horizon tells you how much of a bank angle your wings are making with the ground; the turn indicator tells you if you are mak-

Table 8.6   Cruise Checklist for the Cessna

Item	Indicator/Control	Action
1	Throttle	17 to 25 inches Hg, 2100 to 2400 RPM
2	Mixture	Lean to hottest EGT temperature, then enrich by 50° (slide mixture control down to lean, up to enrich)
3	Propeller pitch	Set RPM to 2400 by adjusting propeller pitch up or down as needed.
4	Vertical speed indicator	0 feet per minute
5	Elevator trim	Adjust up or down as necessary (Press ⑦ or ① on the numeric keypad)
7	Artificial horizon	Horizontal flight is displayed when the shaded horizon is centered on the gull wing marker in center of dial. Roll pointer should also be centered on 0° roll marker.

Table 8.7   Cruise Airspeed Varies by Altitude for the Cessna

Altitude (feet)	Engine Power as %	Airspeed in Knots TAS
2,000	76	148
4,000	78	153
6,000	75	154
8,000	73	154
10,000	70	154
12,000	62	155

ing a standard coordinated turn. The standard turn is defined as a turn that takes the aircraft two minutes to pivot 360° in a circle. If you ever get lost in a cloud with zero visibility, for example, you could use the turn indicator to help you make a standard turn and head out of the cloud from whence you came. This precision instrument helps you make tightly controlled turns.

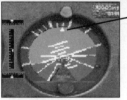

20° marker

Artificial horizon bank angle shows 20°. Triangular pointer is lined up with 20° marker.

Shallow turn (20°)

30° marker

Artificial horizon Bank angle shows 30°. Triangular pointer is lined up with 30° marker.

Medium turn (30°)

60° marker

Artificial horizon bank angle shows 60°. Triangular pointer is lined up with 60° marker.

Steep turn (60°)

Figure 8.8
The Shallow, Medium, and Steep Turns
(Includes Artificial Horizon showing Bank Angles)

Turns are divided into three classes:

- Shallow turns have a bank angle of less then 20°. Without any action on your part, the aircraft's wings will level themselves unless some force is used to maintain the bank.

- Medium turns are those turns with a bank angle of 20° to 45°. The plane will continue to turn without any additional application of the ailerons.

- Steep turns have a bank angle of more than 45°. At this angle, the plane will continue to bank ever more steeply unless some counteracting aileron pressure is applied.

The Standard Turn

In all turns where you plan to maintain your altitude, you will have to apply a little up elevator (2 on the numeric keypad, or pull back on the mouse/yoke). If you are flying in auto-coordinated mode, turning is made easier since the simulation takes over the responsibility of synchronizing the ailerons and rudders. On the other hand, if you are flying in non-coordinated mode with rudder pedals and a joystick (or just from the keyboard), you must use the turn indicator to make coordinated turns. When the wings in the turn indicator align with the L (left) or the R (right) markers, the plane will make what is known as a standard turn. This means that in two minutes, the plane will complete a 360° turn and be headed once again in the same direction. In a standard turn, the plane will turn at a rate of 3° per second.

To make a standard turn, follow these steps:

1. In auto-coordinated mode, apply the right aileron to turn right (press ⑥ on the numeric keypad or move the mouse/yoke right), or the left aileron to turn left (press ④ on the numeric keypad or move the mouse/yoke left). If you are flying in non-coordinated mode, to make a right turn, apply the right aileron with the right rudder (press ⑥ and ⏎Enter on the numeric keypad), or to make a left turn, apply the left aileron with the left rudder (press ④ and ⓪ on the numeric keypad).

Figure 8.9 Executing a standard right turn while maintaining altitude

2. As you move your controls, watch your turn indicator to see that the airplane wings stays lined up with either the L or R marker. In un-coordinated mode, you must move your ailerons and rudders together so the moving ball in the turn indicator's inclinometer stays centered.

3. For level flight, apply a little up elevator (press ② or pull back on the mouse/yoke). Make sure your plane is flying horizontally with respect to the horizon by checking the artificial horizon.

Figure 8.10 Executing a right turn while climbing

4. Observe your heading and the time on the clock. In exactly two minutes, the plane should have completed the turn and be back on its original heading.

Figures 8.9 through 8.11 illustrate what your instrument panel would look like when executing various turns.

Figure 8.11 Executing a left turn while descending

Coming Out of the Turn

To exit medium or steep turns of 20° or greater:

1. Apply reverse aileron pressure to counteract the turn. If you are turning left, apply right aileron (⑥ on the numeric keypad or right mouse/yoke movement). If you are turning right, apply left aileron (④ on the numeric keypad or left mouse/yoke movement).
2. When the plane is level, press ⑤ on the numeric keypad to center the ailerons.

To exit shallow turns of less than 20°:

Center the ailerons by pressing ⑤ on the numeric keypad.

After you finish your turn, make sure the artificial horizon is level with the wings at the center of the dial and that the vertical speed indicator is at 0. This will ensure the aircraft is flying straight and level.

To exit the shallow turn, neutralize the ailerons by pressing ⑤ on the numeric keypad. To exit medium or steep turns, apply reverse aileron pressure, then center the ailerons when the plane is level by pressing ⑤.

How to Come Out of a Turn to a Predetermined Heading

To come to a desired heading, you must roll out of the turn at the right time. The standard rule of thumb for doing this is as follows:

$$Rollout\ Angle° = \frac{Bank\ Angle°}{2}$$

For example, suppose you are turning right with a bank angle of 20° and you want to come to a course heading of 90°. Using the above formula, you can figure that your rollout angle will be:

$$\frac{20°}{2} = 10°$$

Thus you begin the rollout from the turn when you reach 80° and by the time the rollout has been completed, you will be on a course of 90°.

DESCENDING AND LANDING

Landing the plane is the most difficult aspect of flying. Even in the simulated world of *Flight Simulator*, learning how to land is not simple. This section will teach you the essential principles and steps you need to perform to land. But do not expect to master them the first time around. You will need to practice descending and landing many times, as the procedures and skills needed are involved and tricky.

Fortunately, FS 5.1 includes two features to help teach you how to land properly:

- Land Me: A *Flight Simulator* instructor will take over the operation of your plane and land it for you. You can then watch and learn how to land the plane. Press [X] to activate. At any time, you can disengage Land Me by pressing [X] once again.
- Flight Instruction: If you select the Options/Flight Instruction menu option, you'll see a dialog box with a bunch of lesson situations. Lesson 10 guides you through a perfect landing at Meigs Field. Without any intervention on your part, the Cessna will land by itself on the runway and you can see how it is done.

The *Lesson 10: Final Approach, Flare, and Touchdown* situation is good for learning how to make your final approach. However, it does not place you far enough away from the runway so you can plan your descent properly. To better learn how to perform the complete descent and landing operation, *Flight Simulator* includes another excellent flying mode, called Oakland 27R-Landing Approach.

To quickly land your plane using FS 5.1s Land Me feature, press [X]. An instructor will take over your plane and land it at the nearest airport. You can take over at any time by again pressing [X].

Oakland 27R-Landing Approach

After starting up *Flight Simulator*, select the Options menu and then click on the Situations command. In the Situations dialog box, click on the lower scroll bar button arrow until you see the Oakland 27R-Landing Approach situation in the list box. Once Oakland 27R-Landing Approach is selected, you are ready to start the simulator by clicking on the OK button.

Planning Your Landing

You will need to make preparations for the descent and landing before leaving cruising altitude. Pause the *Flight Simulator* program by pressing [P]. This will freeze the simulation until you have time to plan your approach.

Press [P] to Pause *Flight Simulator* in order to plan your landing.

Check Weather and Runway Condition Information

Tune in to ATIS on your COM radio by clicking on the frequency selector to 135.40 MHz. The ATIS message will soon scroll across your windshield, giving you helpful information in planning your approach and landing.

Cross-check Your Instruments

While the simulator is still paused, take a few moments to scan your instruments.

- Start with the altimeter. Your altitude is 1,490 feet above mean sea level (MSL), which means you are actually 1,477 feet above ground level (AGL), since Oakland Airport is 13 feet above MSL. Do not confuse AGL with MSL, as the results could be fatal! For example, at higher elevation airports, your altimeter MSL readings may tempt you to think you have plenty of altitude above the ground. In reality you may be plummeting toward the ground.

- Next check your airspeed indicator reading of 100 knots along with your engine speed of approximately 2,400 RPM developing 22.5 inches Hg on the manifold pressure gauge (your readings may vary from this, because it depends on when you pressed the pause button at startup).

- Observe the turn and bank indicator, artificial horizon, and vertical speed indicator. These instruments confirm that you are flying straight and level.

- Your directional gyro should show that you are on a course of 276°. Since Oakland 27R-Landing Approach is oriented on a course of 270° (remember, you multiply the runway number by 10 to obtain the proper course heading) you will have to correct your heading by 6°.

- Looking at your other miscellaneous controls and instruments, note that your flaps are set to 10°, the landing gear is extended, the temperature is 64° Fahrenheit, your COM radio is tuned to 135.40 MHz, and the VOR 1 is tuned to 109.9 MHz which is the ILS frequency for runway 27R. VOR 2 is tuned to Concord VOR.

Starting the Descent

Before resuming the simulation, perform these preliminary steps:

1. Tune your NAV 2 radio to 116.8 MHz. You will want to use your Distance Measuring Equipment 2 indicator (DME 2) to gauge how far you are from the airport. At the start of this situation, your VOR 2 radio was tuned to Concord VOR, which shows a distance of over 20 miles to Concord on your DME 2. After retuning the radio, your DME 2 indicator should display a distance of about 3.3 miles.

2. Turn the Axis Indicator on. Under the Views menu, select View Options, and in the dialog box that follows turn on option K Axis Indicator Large V. When you are done, click the OK button to return to

the simulation. This V-shaped marker on your cockpit windshield helps you point your aircraft in the right direction. It also tells you whether your nose is pointed into the ground or above the ground.

3. Make sure the landing gear is down (the gear indicator light should glow green).

4. Enrich the fuel mixture by pushing the mixture knob all the way up.

5. Turn carburetor heat on.

6. Reduce the throttle to about 1/4 of the full setting (press ③ on the numeric keypad to lower the throttle).

7. Lower the elevators a notch by pressing ⑧ on the numeric keypad a few times.

Calculating the Rate of Descent

In order to touchdown on the runway, you need to calculate your rate of descent (vertical speed) you need to maintain. First calculate how much time you have before reaching the runway by using the following formula:

$$Time\ to\ Runway\ in\ Minutes = \frac{Distance\ to\ Runway}{Airspeed}$$

Since the DME 2 indicator shows you to be 3.3 miles from the runway, and your airspeed is 100 knots (1.66 nautical miles per minute), you will cross the threshold of the runway in 2.16 minutes. You must decrease your altitude from 1,490 feet MSL within two minutes. This requires a rate of descent of 745 feet per minute, as is illustrated by the following formula:

$$Vertical\ Speed = \frac{Altitude}{Time\ to\ Runway\ in\ Minutes}$$

Note the vertical speed indicator doesn't show your instantaneous vertical velocity; it shows your vertical velocity after some delay (it takes time for the air pressure to move the needle). So you will need to fudge your vertical speed somewhat. Try using a vertical speed of 1,500 feet per minute until you achieve the desired glide path.

When to Start Your Descent in the Cessna

For the Cessna, it is convenient to remember that your descent should begin five miles out per thousand feet above the airport. For example, if you are landing at an airport that is 2,000 feet above MSL and your cruising altitude is 10,000 feet, you would start your descent 40 miles away (i.e., 10,000 feet − 2,000 feet = 8,000 feet, and 8(000) × 5 = 40 miles).

A general rule of thumb for all descents in the Cessna is to start your descent five miles out per thousand feet above the airport elevation.

Figure 8.12
Pause the simulation so you can take your time completing the landing preparations.

Resuming the Descent

Now you are ready to continue with the descent. Your screen should look like Figure 8.12

1. Press P to resume the simulation.

2. Immediately reduce engine speed to 1,878 RPM with a manifold pressure of about 12.83 inches Hg (press 3 on the numeric keypad to lower throttle or 9 to increase throttle).

3. Use the elevators to lower your pitch until your vertical speed indicator shows a downward movement (press 8 on the numeric keypad). When the vertical indicator settles on 1,500 feet per minute, you must again readjust your elevators upward with 2 on the numeric keypad. This will stabilize your descent and prevent it from becoming steeper.

4. Use the elevator trim to fine tune your nose pitch (press 7 on the numeric keypad to lower the nose, or 1 to raise the nose).

5. Apply the ailerons, if needed to line up your nose with the runway (press 4 on the numeric keypad to turn left, or 6 to turn right). The axis indicator should be lined up with the beginning of the runway.

6. At 500 feet altitude, raise the nose slightly (press 2 on the numeric keypad) until your vertical speed stabilizes at 500 feet per minute.

Table 8.8 shows the general descent checklist for the Cessna.

Use a vertical speed of 1,500 feet per minute as your initial rate of descent for the Oakland 27R-Landing Approach, until you reach 500 feet on your altimeter, then level off to a vertical speed of 500 feet per minute.

Table 8.8 Descent Checklist for the Cessna		
Item	**Indicator/Control**	**Action**
1	Throttle	Decrease engine RPM as necessary to obtain 500 feet per minute rate of descent. Use throttle to control vertical speed, not horizontal speed.
2	Vertical speed indicator	500 feet per minute
3	Airspeed indicator	Hold speed to 133 Knots IAS
4	Mixture	Enrich mixture to full if below 5,000 feet, otherwise enrichen as required
5	Carburetor heat	On to prevent carburetor icing
6	Wing flaps	Set flaps at 0 to 10° below 140 knots IAS

Final Approach and Landing

At a distance of 1.6 miles from the runway, your altitude should be 200 feet, and the middle marker alarm will sound. When this happens, you will see a blue M appear on the OMI marker indicator and a beeping sound will ensue. Figure 8.13 illustrates what your screen should look like.

Figure 8.13
The terminal descent

Final Approach

- At a distance of 1/2 mile from the runway (monitor the DME 2 indicator for closing distance), your altitude should be around 180 feet MSL.
- Increase throttle (press 9 on the numeric keyboard) to decrease vertical speed between 200 and 500 feet per minute. Do not use your elevators to adjust your descent rate. Increasing or decreasing engine thrust will accomplish the same thing.
- Your airspeed should be around 60 to 75 knots.
- If the landing approach is going according to plan, you should be on the

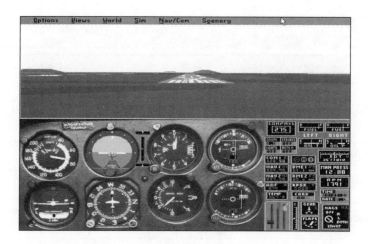

Figure 8.14
Final approach
to Oakland

correct glide path to the runway. Check that your vertical speed is between 200 and 500 FPM again. If your rate of descent is too high, increase the throttle by pressing ⑨ on the numeric keypad. If you start climbing, decrease the throttle by pressing ③.

- Make sure the axis indicator on your cockpit windshield is aimed at the head of the runway. Adjust your pitch angle if it is too low by pressing ②on the numeric keypad. If it is too high press ⑧ on the numeric keypad. Left and right course corrections can be made by applying left and right ailerons (press ④ on the numeric keypad to turn left, or ⑥ to turn right).

Figure 8.14 shows what your screen should look like on the final approach to Oakland.

Landing

- After crossing the runway threshold, pick your touchdown point just beyond the runway numbers.
- At 20 to 30 feet above the ground, flare the plane (pull back on the yoke by gently applying up elevator—gently tap ② on the numeric keypad once or twice). By performing the flare maneuver, you will be trying to create a controlled stall onto the runway.
- Reduce throttle to idle.
- As the airplane descends in the final moments, gently keep the nose up so the main wheels hit first. Then, when touchdown occurs, gently lower the nose (press ⑧ on the numeric keypad) and cut the engines (press ③ on the numeric keypad repeatedly or press F1).

Figure 8.15
Performing a flare
while landing at
Oakland

- Apply the brakes (repeatedly press ⌊.⌋) until the airplane rolls to a halt.

Figure 8.15 shows a spot view of the airplane performing the flare maneuver while landing at Oakland.

Don't be discouraged if you crack up your plane on your first try. Reset the simulation by pressing ⌊Ctrl⌋ + ⌊Print Screen⌋, and you can practice some more.

Table 8.9 shows the general landing checklist for the Cessna.

Landing with a Crosswind

Winds that cross the runway in a perpendicular direction present some difficulties when landing. These crosswinds, as they are called, can be successfully dealt with when landing by using one of two landing techniques:

- Crabbing Method: The airplane is slightly turned to face the direction of the wind when landing. Although easier for the pilot to maintain during final approach, it requires a high degree of skill to remove the crab prior to landing because the wheels of the plane must be quickly aligned with the runway to avoid sideways skidding.

- Wing Low Method: The airplane faces the runway when landing, but lowers one wing in the face of the oncoming crosswind. This method is recommended in most cases.

In both the crabbing and wing low methods, auto-coordination must be turned off so that you can independently work the ailerons and rudders.

Switch off auto-
coordination while
trying to land with a
crosswind.

Table 8.9   Landing Checklist for the Cessna

Item	Indicator/ControlEvent	Action
1	Seat backs, seatbelts	Most upright position, seatbelts secure
2	Throttle	Reduce throttle (press ③ on numeric keypad) to 1836 RPM with 12 to 14 inches of Hg manifold pressure
3	Airspeed indicator	Below 140 knots
4	Landing gear	Gear down, press Ⓖ. Check to see that green indicator light is illuminated.
5	Mixture	Full rich (move mixture lever up)
6	Propeller	Pitch set to low blade angle, highest RPM setting (move propeller control up)
7	Carburetor heat	On
8	Airspeed indicator	Reduce airspeed to 70–80 knots IAS (with flaps UP or at 10°), or 66 knots IAS (with flaps full down)
9	Flaps	Set flaps to 30° (press F7), or as desired.
10	Airspeed indicator	Reduce airspeed to between 65 and 75 knots IAS
11	Elevator trim	Adjust nose pitch angle (press ⑦ and ① on numeric keypad)
12	Vertical speed indicator	Reduce vertical speed to 200–500 feet per minute by increasing the throttle with ⑨
13	Altimeter	Watch that you maintain on altitude reading of 120 to 250 feet AGL (above ground level). For example, when landing at Meigs Field, make your landing approach to the runway at about 800 to 850 feet MSL (which is 200 to 250 feet above ground level).
14	Pick touchdown point just beyond runway numbers	Aim nose of aircraft for touchdown just past the runway numbers
15	Flare	Flatten out your approach at 20 to 30 feet above AGL
16	Touchdown	Main wheels first, then gently lower nose wheel to the ground
17	Throttle	Reduce to idle (press F1)
18	Brakes	Apply brakes (press ⟨.⟩ on main keyboard). For maximum braking power, retract the flaps (press F5), and apply full up elevator (press ⑧ on numeric keypad)
19	Taxi off runway	Use differential braking (F11 left brake, F12 right brake) with steering control (⓪ - right, Enter - left) to navigate and make turns on runways. Increase throttle to 1055-1100 RPMs to begin taxiing.
20	After landing checklist	Retract flaps, switch off carburetor heat, turn off lights, turn magnetos to OFF position, set parking brake (press Ctrl .)

Auto-coordinationlinks your ailerons and rudders together; if you leave this option on when trying to correct a crosswind force, your rudders will interfere.

Crabbing Method

The crabbing method is executed by establishing a heading, called a crab, toward the crosswind. The airplane's direction of movement, even though the nose direction is slightly askant to the runway heading, is in a straight line towards the runway. The crab angle is maintained until just prior to touchdown, when the pilot must quickly realign the nose of the plane with the runway to avoid sideways skidding of the wheels. Figure 8.16 illustrates the crosswind landing using the crabbing method.

Figure 8.16
Crosswind landing using the crabbing method

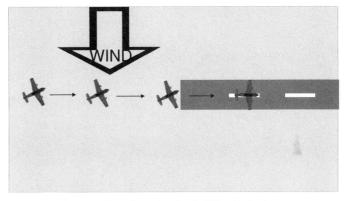

Crosswind Landing using the Crabbing Method

To fly using the crab approach keep your wings level using the aileron controls, but aim your nose slightly in the direction of the oncoming crosswind.

Wing Low Method

The wing low method is preferred for landing the plane in a crosswind. The pilot banks the wings of the airplane in the direction of the crosswind. To use this method, you must align the airplane's nose with the runway heading and then lower the wing that faces the crosswind. The amount of lowering depends on the force of the crosswind, but generally the stronger the wind, the lower you will want the wing to be. When one wing is lowered, however, the airplane will want to

Figure 8.17
Crosswind landing using the wing low method.

Crosswind Landing Using the Wing Low Method

turn in the lowered wing's direction. To counteract this, you must also simultaneously apply opposite rudder pressure to prevent turning into the wind and drifting off course from the runway heading.

For example, if the crosswind has a direction of 90° (blowing from east to west) and you are on a heading of 0°, you must apply the right aileron (press 6 on the numeric keypad) and simultaneously apply the left rudder (press Ins on the numeric keypad) to counteract the tendency of the aircraft to turn right when you bank right. This will allow you to maintain your course heading of 0° while landing with the crosswind.

CHAPTER
9

Flying the Cessna

This chapter contains a short history of the Cessna Skylane, and also includes actual performance data that will aid you in planning your flights.

CESSNA SKYLANE HISTORY

Cessna Aircraft Company, which is now a subsidiary of General Dynamics Corporation, was started by the late Clyde V. Cessna in 1911. Incorporated in 1927, the company has designed and built over 177,553 aircraft at its Wichita, Kansas factory. The company's aircraft include 7,500 Model 152s; 35,773 Model 172 Skyhawks; 1,159 Cutlass RGs; 19,812 Model 182 Skylanes; 2,102 Model 182 Skylane RGs; 2,400 Citation Jets; and various other models.

The Cessna Skylane 182RG II had its design origins in the 1949 Cessna Model 170A, which was an all metal, 145 horsepower (hp), four seat taildragger. In 1952 the Cessna 180, a derivative of the 170A, was introduced and it sported a larger 225 hp engine, although the same airframe was used. Tricycle landing gear replaced the tail-dragger wheel in 1956, when the Cessna 182 was introduced. The name "Skylane" was added to the 182 when a new deluxe version was offered in 1958. The deluxe version included full instrumentation and radio equipment as standard equipment.

The 1958 Skylanes continued to retain the basic airframe of the 170A and 182. However, in 1962, the airplane was redesigned with a sportier body that also included a new rear window and larger cabin. The new airframe for the 182 enjoyed much success and was retained over the years. In fact, today's Skylane is much the same as that of the 1962 model, except for internal structural and equipment changes.

Figure 9.1
1984 Cessna Skylane
182 RG II (*Photo
courtesy of the Cessna
Aircraft Company*)

Production of the Cessna Skylane RG series of aircraft was suspended on December 31, 1987. In all there were 2,102 Skylane RG aircraft produced; this number was surpassed by its fixed-gear brother, the Cessna Skylane, which had a production run of over 19,812. Cessna has found it more economical to produce larger cargo and commercial aircraft such as the Caravan Model 208 and the Cessna Citation Business Jets, and so has closed a chapter on one of aviation's most popular personal aircraft.

CESSNA PERFORMANCE

This next section includes performance tables, specifications, and charts that will prove useful to you in flying the Cessna. Please note: these tables, charts, and figures are to be used only with Microsoft's *Flight Simulator 5.1*, and are not be used for real flying purposes. In many cases, the numbers will not jibe with FS 5.1's flight data due to inaccuracies in the flight model.

In *Flight Simulator*, true airspeed (TAS) is what is shown on your air-

Figure 9.2
Retractable landing gear Cessna Skylane 182RG II (*Photo courtesy of the cessna aircraft company*)

speed indicator. On real aircraft however, indicated airspeed (IAS) is shown on the airspeed indicator. Since the airspeed indicator bases its readings on static and dynamic air pressure, IAS does not tell you your true airspeed, due to varying air pressure differences at different altitudes and temperatures. At MSL TAS and IAS are approximately the same, but at high altitudes IAS is always less than TAS. For example, in the FS 5.1 Skylane, if you had changed your airspeed indicator to show IAS instead of TAS[1], and you were traveling at 14,000 feet with an IAS of 70 knots, your TAS (or ground-speed), would be more like 110-120 knots.

The V-speeds, the maximum and minimum speeds you must obey while flying the Skylane, are expressed in IAS. Therefore, if you want to fly realistically, you should choose IAS for your airspeed indicator.

---

[1]To have the airspeed indicator show IAS instead of TAS, go to the Instrument Preferences dialog box, found under the Options menu. There, click the check box for IAS Airspeed.

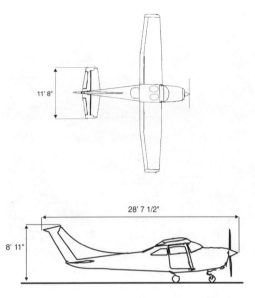

Figure 9.3
Aircraft dimensions

Setting the Optimum Air/Fuel Mixture

The Exhaust Gas Temperature (EGT) gauge is used to determine how the throttle mixture is affecting engine performance. At higher altitudes, the air/fuel mixture gets richer due to the rarefied atmosphere. Therefore you must lean the engine, or reduce the air/fuel ratio by using the mixture control as you go higher. To determine the optimum mixture setting, slide the mixture control up and down until you see the EGT needle move as far to the right as possible. When this happens, the engine is running at its hottest temperature and leanest mixture setting. For better engine performance, you should enrich the mixture (slide the mixture control down) by about 50° cooler as measured by the EGT gauge. This means the needle should move about two notches to the left.

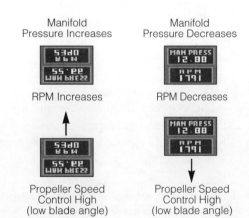

Figure 9.4 The effect of air/fuel mixture ratio on EGT temperature. Propeller speed control (propeller blade pitch) and its affect on manifold pressure and RPM

Table 9.1   Cessna Performance Specifications

Speed		
	Maximum	160 knots
	Cruise 75% power at 7,500 feet	156 knots
Cruise Range and Time		
	50% power at 12,000 feet; 88 gallons useable fuel	1,100 nautical miles
Rate of Climb		
	At Sea Level	1,040 FPM
	At 8,000 feet	455 FPM
Certified Maximum Operating Altitude		
	Maximum Ceiling Altitude	14,300 feet
Takeoff Performance		
	At Sea Level	
	Ground Roll	820 feet
	Total distance over 50-ft obstacle	1,570 feet
	At 4,000 feet	
	Ground Roll	1,101 feet
	Total distance over 50-ft obstacle	2,174 feet
	At 7,000 feet	
	Ground Roll	1,391 feet
	Total distance over 50-ft obstacle	2,897 feet
Landing Performance		
	At Sea Level	
	Ground Roll	600 feet
	Total distance over 50-ft obstacle	1,320 feet
	At 4,000 feet	
	Ground Roll	678 feet
	Total distance over 50-ft obstacle	1,443 feet
	At 7,000 feet	
	Ground Roll	738 feet
	Total distance over 50-ft obstacle	1,545 feet
Stall Speed		
	Flaps up, power off	54 knots
	Flaps down, power off	50 knots
Maximum Weight		
	Ramp	3,112 lbs.
	Takeoff or Landing	3,100 lbs.
Standard Empty Weight		
		1,784 lbs.
Fuel Capacity		
		88 gallons
Engine		
	Avco Lycoming O-540-J3C5D flat six	235 hp (175 kw)

Table 9.2   Cessna Airspeed Limitations

V speed	Speed	Knots TAS	Knots IAS	Explanation
V_{NE}	Never exceed speed	175	178	Do not exceed this speed under any circumstance.
V_{NO}	Maximum safe structural cruising speed	155	157	Do not exceed this speed except in smooth air, but only with caution.
V_A	Maneuvering speed	111	112	Do not make full or abrupt movements of the rudder, ailerons, or elevator.

Table 9.3   Mixture and Exhaust Gas Temperature

Mixture Description	Exhaust Gas Temperature
Recommended lean	50° rich of peak EGT (50° cooler than peak lean temperature)
Best fuel economy	EGT (hottest or peak lean temperature)

Note you must first activate the propeller control and mixture control in *Flight Simulator* by clicking on the Propeller Control Manual setting, and the Mixture Control check box, under the Realism and Reliability dialog box, found under the Sim menu.

Propeller Speed Control and Mixture Relationship to Engine Power

The propeller speed control adjusts the pitch of the propeller's blade angle. When the blade angle is high, the RPM of the propeller decreases because the propeller is "biting" larger slices of air. When the blade angle is low, the RPM of the propeller increases because the propeller is slicing through the air more easily. At higher altitudes, the air is thinner and the propeller can spin faster than is good for the engine. You can use the propeller control to slow down the propeller. Simply slide the control down to reduce RPM. Note that engine power, as shown on the manifold pressure gauge, changes when you make alterations to the propeller's blade angle. Engine power generally decreases as you slow down the RPM (slide the prop lever down), and increases as you speed up the RPM (slide the prop lever up). See Figure 9.4 for an illustration of this principle.

The mixture control also affects engine power. If you slide the lever up, thereby enriching the air/fuel ratio, you will notice that the engine's power, as shown on the manifold pressure gauge, goes up. On the other hand, if you slide the lever down, thereby leaning the air/fuel ration, you will notice that manifold pressure goes down.

To set the engine's power setting you will need to combine movements of the mixture control and propeller speed control and observe their results on the manifold pressure gauge.

To set engine power:

1. Set the mixture control to Recommended Lean, as shown on the EGT gauge.

2. Adjust the propeller speed control until you achieve the RPM and manifold pressure you want.

3. Set engine throttle.

Be careful when increasing the throttle to its maximum setting, because you may overboost the engine. Normal engine operation almost never requires full throttle except on takeoff.

Table 9.4 shows the time, fuel, and distance to climb to a given altitude from mean sea level (MSL). You can see that, for example, if you wanted to climb from sea level to 10,000 feet, it would take 6.1 gallons of fuel and you would travel 30 nautical miles.

Table 9.4 Time, Fuel, and Distance to Climb			
Density Altitude: From Mean Sea Level To	Time (Minutes)	Fuel Burned (Gallons)	Distance Traveled (nautical miles)
2,000	3	1.0	5
4,000	6	2.0	10
6,000	9	3.1	15
8,000	12	4.4	21
10,000	18	6.1	30

Table 9.5 Cessna 182 RG Cruise Performance

RPM	Manifold Pressure	Max Power	2,000 ft Altitude Knots TAS	Gallons/Hr	Max Power	4,000 ft Altitude Knots TAS	Gallons/Hr	Max Power	6,000 ft Altitude Knots TAS	Gallons/Hr
2,400	23"	76%	148	13.6	78%	153	14.0			
	21"	67%	141	12.0	69%	145	12.4	71%	150	12.7
	19"							61%	141	11.1
2,300	23"	72%	146	13.1	75%	150	13.5	77%	155	13.9
	21"	64%	138	11.5	66%	143	11.9	68%	147	12.2
	19"									
2,200	23"	69%	143	12.5	71%	148	12.9	74%	152	13.3
	21"	61%	136	11.0	63%	140	11.4	65%	145	11.7
	19"									
2,100	23"	66%	140	11.8	68%	145	12.2	70%	149	12.6
	21"	58%	133	10.5	60%	137	10.9	62%	142	11.2
	19"	50%	124	9.1	51%	129	9.5	53%	133	9.8
	17"									

RPM	Manifold Pressure	Max Power	8,000 ft Altitude Knots TAS	Gallons/Hr	Max Power	10,000 ft Altitude Knots TAS	Gallons/Hr	Max Power	12,000 ft Altitude Knots TAS	Gallons/Hr
2,400	23"									
	21"	73%	154	13.1						
	19"	63%	146	11.5	65%	150	11.8			
2,300	23"									
	21"	70%	152	12.6						
	19"	61%	143	11.1	63%	148	11.4			
2,200	23"									
	21"	67%	149	12.1						
	19"	58%	141	10.6	60%	145	10.9			
2,100	23"									
	21"	64%	146	11.5						
	19"	55%	137	10.1	57%	142	10.4			
	17"	47%	127	8.7	49%	131	9	50%	136	9.3

Manifold Pressure and its Relationship to Altitude and Power

In normally aspirated engines without turbochargers, manifold pressure decreases about one inch per thousand feet of elevation gain. If your engine power shows 23 inches of manifold pressure at 2,000 feet, climbing to 3,000 feet without adjusting your controls will reduce manifold pressure to 22 inches.

Table 9.6 shows a standard atmosphere table for engine performance. Note that maximum engine power drops by about 4 percent per thousand foot increase in altitude.

The maximum available manifold pressure can be expressed as follows in FS 5.1:

$$Manifold\ pressure = Barometric\ pressure - \frac{Altitude}{1000} - 0.5$$

The 0.5 in the above equation represents induction system loss. You might get different results due to non-standard atmosphere temperature deviations.

Table 9.6 Standard Atmosphere Table for Engine Performance			
Altitude (Feet)	**Barometric Pressure**	**Temp (F)**	**Max Available Power**
Mean Sea Level	29.92"	59°	100%
1,000	28.86"	55.4°	97%
2,000	27.82"	51.9°	93%
3,000	26.82"	48.3°	90%
4,000	25.84"	44.7°	86%
5,000	24.90"	41.2°	83%
6,000	23.98"	37.6°	80%
8,000	22.22"	30.5°	74%
10,000	20.58"	23.3°	69%
12,000	19.03"	16.2°	64%
15,000	16.89"	5.5°	56%
20,000	13.75"	-12.3°	46%

Above 7,900 feet a non-turbocharged engine is incapable of producing 75 percent power, so it can be run full throttle and with full propeller pitch.

Refueling and Range

The Cessna Skylane 182RG II has a maximum range of 1,100 nautical miles (1,265 statute miles) when flying at a cruise speed of 136 knots, 50 percent power. At this speed and power setting, the 88 gallon fuel tank can keep the plane aloft for over 9.3 hours. This does not include the Skylane's 45-minute reserve. When flying at higher power settings, range is considerably reduced.

In *Flight Simulator*, you can have your aircraft serviced and refueled by landing at an airport with a refueling facility, as indicated in the airport directory. To refuel and have the aircraft serviced, locate the fuel rectangle (displayed by a yellow border with the letter "F" inside it) and then taxi your airplane inside the rectangle. Almost immediately, your aircraft will be refueled and serviced and you can resume flying. You can also manually add fuel to your tanks by adjusting the fuel quantity in the Engines and Fuel dialog box under the Sim menu.

Engine Failure

If an engine failure occurs during takeoff, the most important thing to do is abort the takeoff and stop the airplane on the remaining length of runway. If the engine fails after takeoff, promptly lower the nose to maintain airspeed. Airspeed above 55 knots IAS means your airplane can still generate enough lift to fly; if you allow the speed to fall below this minimum, the plane will crash. The best glide speed, if you are trying to prolong your time in the air, is 83 knots IAS. If you have enough altitude to make a 180° turn back to the airport, do so. Otherwise, look for the nearest flat field or highway to land on.

If you have enough altitude, follow these steps to restart your engine:

1. Maintain airspeed of 83 knots IAS.
2. Turn carburetor heat on.
3. Enrichen the fuel mixture.
4. Restart the engine by turning the master magneto switch OFF, then to BOTH, (or START position, if the propeller has stopped).

Figure 9.5 shows the maximum glide at the optimum glide airspeed of 83 knots IAS. Note that if you are at 10,000 feet, you have approximately 17 miles ground distance in which to find an airport to land at.

If you increase your propeller pitch angle (drag the middle knob all the way down on your engine control), you can increase your glide distance by as much as 20 percent with your engine out. This presents less of the propeller blade to the windstream, thereby reducing drag.

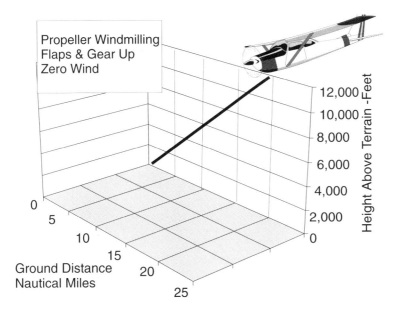

Maximum Glide Distance at 83 Knots IAS

Figure 9.6
Maximum glide chart for the Cessna

CHAPTER
10

Flying the Learjet

In this chapter, you will learn more about the Learjet 35A and its performance characteristics. Information is also provided on how to turn the Learjet while on the ground, and how to fly with an inoperable engine. With the knowledge you obtain from this chapter, you can make realistic mission planning profiles for trips around the world.

   Regardless of the aircraft you are currently flying, whether on the ground or in the air, you can fly the Learjet at any time by following these steps:

1. Select the Options menu, and click on the Aircraft command.
2. Next, in the Aircraft dialog box, highlight Learjet 35A and then click the OK button. The Learjet instrument panel will then be displayed.

LEARJET HISTORY

Learjet, Inc. was originally founded in 1960 by Bill Lear, Sr. as the Swiss American Aircraft Company (SAAC). In 1962, the company was transferred to Kansas and renamed the Lear Jet Corporation. Gates Rubber Company bought out a 60 percent majority stake in the company in 1967 and the company was subsequently renamed Gates Learjet Corporation. Following a 1987 acquisition by Integrated Acquisition Inc., the company was renamed Learjet Corporation, and all manufacturing was moved from Tucson, Arizona, to Wichita, Kansas. The most recent change in company ownership was completed in 1990 when Canada's Bombardier Group took over Learjet's line of credit.

Figure 10.1
The Learjet 35A
(*Courtesy of Learjet*)

The Lear 23 was the first Learjet produced. It was one of the world's first light, twin-turbojet powered business jets. Next came the Learjet 25G which, as most *Flight Simulator* buffs will tell you, was the original Learjet for Microsoft *Flight Simulator* (first introduced with FS 3.0 in 1988). With the introduction of a new turbofan in the late 1960s, Learjet embarked on a new research and development program to design a more technologically advanced business jet, the Learjet 35A. The Learjet 36A, which was produced later, is a variant of the Learjet 35A but with a much greater range. The first flight of the turbofan Learjet 35A occurred on January 4, 1973. The $3 million dollar Learjet 35A, with its distinctive fuel tank pods on the wing tips, soon became a resounding success, selling more than 720 aircraft over the years. Learjet now makes four newer jets: the Lear 31A, the Lear 55B, the Lear 55C, and the Lear 60.

Today there are over 1,700 Learjets of all types in operation around the world. They are flown by the US Air Force, the US government, 20 countries around the world, multi-national corporations, and countless other private companies.

The Learjet 35A is an all-metal, pressurized, low wing monoplane. It flies

Figure 10.2
The Learjet 35A
(*Courtesy of Learjet*)

at a maximum altitude of 45,000 feet at a speed of 471 knots (542 mph, or approximately nine miles per minute), and climbs at nearly a mile a minute. The cabin has room for eight passengers and two crew members, and offers a maximum height of 52 inches and a maximum width of 59 inches. At the rear of the cabin is the baggage compartment, which has approximately 40 cubic feet of space and, 500 pound storage capacity. Inside, the cabin has many amenities including swivel seats, a three place divan, folding tables, a refreshment cabinet with ice chest, hot and cold beverage service, running water, a warming oven, an audio-visual entertainment center, and a private toilet.

The Learjet 35A has been engineered for superior reliability and strength. The fail-safe fuselage exceeds most operational requirements and has been tested for metal fatigue by pressurizing and de-pressurizing the cabin through 50,000 continuous cycles from sea level to 50,000 feet and back again without a single problem. This is the equivalent of 100 years of normal flying. The windshield is also fail-safe tested for bird strikes, and with its one inch thickness, is designed for an unlimited life. Each main landing gear puts two tires on the pavement, adding an extra measure of safety during takeoff and landing.

Figure 10.3
Learjet interior
(Courtesy of Learjet)

PERFORMANCE AND MISSION PLANNING

This section includes performance tables, specifications, and diagrams that will prove useful to you in flying the Learjet. Please note, this information is to be used only with Microsoft's *Flight Simulator* 5.1, and should not be used for real flying purposes. In many cases, the numbers will not match the FS 5.1 Learjet's flight model. But even if some of the data is off, you will still gain some useful insights into the aircraft you wouldn't ordinarily have.

Operating Speeds

As noted in previous chapters, true airspeed (TAS) is different from the indicated airspeed (IAS) ordinarily shown on your airspeed indicator. Your airspeed indicator relies upon outside static and dynamic ram air pressures in the pitot-static system to determine airspeed. At higher elevations, the airspeed indicator shows you to be traveling *slower* than you actually are because of the more rarefied atmospheric pressure. True airspeed is defined

Figure 10.4
Learjet 35A cockpit

to mean your airspeed, corrected for this altitude error, and is approximately equivalent to ground speed in the absence of any wind.

On the real Learjet, airspeed is displayed as *indicated air speed* (IAS). Airspeed on the FS 5.1 airspeed indicator, on the other hand, is displayed as *true air speed* (TAS). You can change the FS 5.1 display to show IAS, for more realism, by toggling on the Indicated Airspeed check box in the Instrument Preferences dialog box, found under the Options menu.

You may wonder what the difference between TAS and IAS means to you. On the real Learjet your IAS airspeed, as measured on the airspeed indicator, *will never show more than 350 knots or so even though you may actually be traveling at 471 knots (542 mph) TAS!*

In the FS 5.1 Learjet, because the analog portion of the dial only shows speeds up to 400 knots, a special digital readout has been added to show the TAS airspeeds above 400 knots. Naturally, if you choose to display IAS airspeed on your dial, you won't need the digital display.

Maximum operating speed from sea level to 8,000 feet is 300 knots IAS. Above 8,000 feet, your speed should not exceed 350 knots IAS (471 knots

Table 10.1   Performance Specifications*

Weight Limits	
Maximum Ramp Weight	18,500 lbs.
Maximum Takeoff Weight	18,300 lbs.
Maximum Landing Weight	15,300 lbs.
Approximate Standard Empty Weight	10,022 lbs.
Useful Load	7,981 lbs.
Approximate Fuel Capacity	6,198 lbs.
Takeoff Field Length	4,972 feet
Landing Distance	3,075 feet
Landing Approach Speed	128 knots IAS (147 mph, 237 km/hr)
Stall Speed (Landing Configuration)	97 knots IAS (112 mph, 180 km/hr)
Rate of Climb	
Two Engine	4,340 feet per minute
Single Engine	1,290 feet per minute
Single Engine Service Ceiling	25,000 feet
Maximum Cruise Speed	
39,000 Feet	471 knots TAS (542 mph, 850 km/hr)
41,000 Feet	453 knots TAS (521 mph, 839 km/hr)
43,000 Feet	441 knots TAS (508 mph, 817 km/hr)
Range	2,196 Nautical miles (2,525 miles, 4,670 km)
Maximum Operating Altitude	45,000 feet
Passenger Seating Capacity	Up to ten
Power Plant	
Type	Garrett TFE 731-2-2B
Number	2
Takeoff Thrust (Sea Level)	7,000 lbs. (3,500 lbs./engine)
Exterior Dimensions	
Length	48 feet 8"
Height	12 feet 3"
Wing Span	39 feet 6"
Wing Area	253.3 square feet
Wing Sweep	13°
Wheel Base	20 feet 2"
Range	2,196 Nautical miles (2,525 miles, 4,670 km)

*This data not for flight planning purposes; use only with Microsoft *Flight Simulator*

TAS). Note while flying in regulated airspace, Federal Aviation Regulations prohibit flight speeds of more than 250 knots TAS (288 mph) below 10,000 feet mean sea level (MSL) or 200 knots TAS (230 mph) below 2,500 MSL.

Overspeed Warning System, Overspeed Dangers, and Mach Numbers

When flying the Learjet, you shouldn't fly with full throttle because you can easily exceed the Mach maximum operating (Mmo) speed which is Mach 0.81. When this happens, you'll activate the overspeed warning system. If you ignore this and don't immediately reduce speed, supersonic shock waves will travel back on the wings until they reach the ailerons. Because the aircrafts ailerons are linked mechanically to the yoke, your yoke will shake and move violently from side to side (actually, since there is no feedback mechanism for your yoke, you won't feel a thing, but your aileron control indicators will fluctuate back and forth wildly).

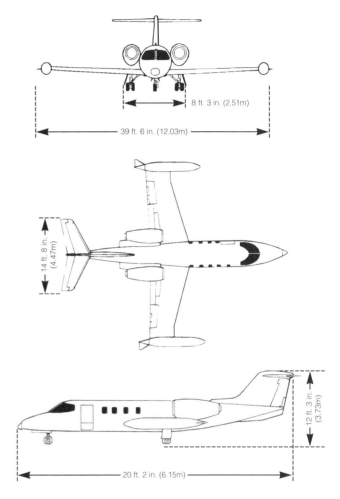

Figure 10.5
Aircraft dimensions

If you are caught in an overspeed situation, you must regain control of the aircraft by performing the following: reduce the throttle and gently pull back on the yoke. Don't yank back on the yoke because it will cause too much stress to the wings and make the controls shake even more. If this doesn't work, try lowering the landing gear to reduce speed. The landing gear on a Learjet is designed to withstand the forces of gear down at high speed with only minimal damage.

Mach speeds refer to the ratio of a given velocity v and the speed of sound v_s so that:

$$Mach\ Number = \frac{v}{v_s} .$$

Table 10.2 Airspeed Limitations*	
Maximum Operating Speeds	**Speed**
Sea Level to 8,000 Feet	300 knots IAS
8,000 Feet to 24,000 Feet	350 knots IAS
Above 24,000 Feet	0.81 Mach
Flap Extension Speeds	
Flaps 8 Degrees	200 knots IAS
Flaps 20 Degrees	185 knots IAS
Flaps 40 Degrees	150 knots IAS
Landing Gear Operating and Extending Speed	
Maximum Speed Extending Gear	200 knots IAS
Maximum Speed Retracting Gear	200 knots IAS
Maximum Speed Operating Gear	260 knots IAS

The speed of sound can be determined through the following formula:

$$v_S = 38.9432 \sqrt{\frac{5}{9}(T_{Fahrenheit} - 32F°) + 273.15}$$

Where $T_{Fahrenheit}$ is the temperature in degrees Fahrenheit and v_s is the speed of sound measured in knots. Use this formula to convert between Fahrenheit and Celsius:

$$T_{Fahrenheit} = \frac{9}{5} T_{Celsius} + 32F°$$

Note that *Mach 1* is the speed of sound, *Mach 2* is twice the speed of sound, and Mach 0.81 is 81percent of the speed of sound. Since the speed of sound increases for higher temperatures and decreases for lower temperatures, a *Mach 0.81* at sea level is not the same as a Mach 0.81 at 40,000 feet. For example, when the temperature is 66° Fahrenheit (18.89° Celsius) the speed of sound at mean sea level (MSL) is 666 knots (767 mph), so Mach 1 = 666 knots. But at 40,000 feet, if the temperature has dropped to −62° Fahrenheit (−52.22° Celsius), Mach 1 would drop to 579 knots (666 mph).

---

*This data not for flight planning purposes; use only with Microsoft *Flight Simulator*

What does this mean to you? In a nutshell, the Learjet must travel at slower TAS at higher altitudes than at sea level for a given Mach 0.81. For example, at sea level the Learjet can safely travel at Mach 0.81 which is 0.81 x 666 knots (speed of sound at sea level 68 Fahrenheit) = 540 knots (621 mph) TAS. But at 40,000 feet, the Learjet's Mach 0.81 speed limit becomes 0.81 × 579 knots (speed of sound at 40,000 feet −62 Fahrenheit) = 469 knots TAS. Therefore, the Learjet's maximum airspeed has declined from 540 knots at sea level to 469 knots at 40,000 feet!

Cost of Operating the Learjet

The cost of operating a Learjet is pretty reasonable when when compared to other business jets in its class. The most costly item in the equation is fuel, which runs $400 an hour. You must also consider the expense of maintenance and scheduled inspections. These costs rise steeply the longer you own the jet. Assuming an average of 400 hours a year utilization for the first year, the maintenance and repair budget will come to $68 per hour of flight. These costs will rise to $400 per hour in the fourth year. Of course, when you throw in insurance and the salaries of the pilot and co-pilot, it becomes quickly apparent that the Learjet is an expensive investment for getting around. But when money is no object, the Learjet will get you there no matter what. And it will land you on short unimproved airstrips that no commercial jetliner could possibly attempt.

Pivoting the Learjet on the Ground

You can pivot the Learjet while on the ground, but it requires the use of your differential brakes. This technique is not recommended for most turning because you can damage the tires if you brake one wheel so that it skids. Normal turns can be accomplished by using the nose wheel steering via the rudder controls. If you have pedals, such as with the CH Pro Pedals, you

The term Mach is named in honor of Ernst Mach (1838–1916), a brilliant Austrian physicist who studied the action of bodies moving through gases at high speeds.

Table 10.3 Hourly Cost of Operation	
Fuel	$400.00
Maintenance	$68.00
Miscellaneous	$40.00
Total Per Hour	$458.00
Total Per Nautical Mile	$1.21

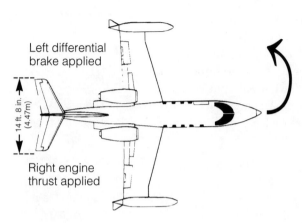

Left differential
brake applied

14 ft. 8 in.
(4.47m)

Right engine
thrust applied

Figure 10.6
Pivoting the Learjet left
using only the right
engine and the left
differential brake

steer the aircraft by using the right and left pedals. But from the numeric keypad, use [0] to turn left and [Enter] to turn right.

If you really want to pivot the aircraft in place, you must apply the differential brake on the wheel that is on the same side of the turn direction, and apply engine throttle on the opposite engine side from which the turn is being made. To illustrate this technique, observe Figure 10.6 to see how the Learjet is pivoted to the left. Notice that to turn left, the right engine throttle is increased and the left differential brake is applied. Turning to the right would be the exact opposite of this; you would increase the left engine throttle and apply the right differential brake.

Here is a summary of the actions to take when pivoting left or right for the Learjet while on the ground:

To pivot left:

1. Press [F11] to apply the left differential brake. You will see the word "BRAKE" on the lower left corner of the cockpit window when the brake is on.

2. Increase the right engine throttle by pressing [E] and [2] (on the main keyboard) then [9] (on the numeric keypad) until you start moving (or you can simply drag the right throttle up by using the mouse). Since it has tendency to release itself every few moments, you may have to press [F11] repeatedly to re-engage the differential brake while you are adjusting the throttle Your airplane will begin to rotate left, while staying in place.

3. To stop the plane, press [.] and reduce the left engine throttle (simply press [3] on the numeric keypad you don't need to press [E] and [2] this time).

To pivot right:

1. Press [F12] to apply the right differential brake.

2. Increase the left engine throttle by pressing [E] and [1] (on the main keyboard) then [9] (on the numeric keypad) until you start moving (or you can simply drag the right throttle up by using the mouse). You may have to press [F12] repeatedly to re-engage the differential brake while you adjust the throttle. Your airplane will begin to rotate right, while staying in place.

3. To stop the plane, press [.] and reduce the left engine throttle (simply

press ③ on the numeric keypad you don't need to press Ⓔ and ① this time).

Takeoff Performance

Tables 10.4 and 10.5 show some of the Learjet's takeoff performance statistics. Using Table 10.4, you can estimate the length of runway needed for a takeoff under various conditions. For a takeoff at a temperature of 70 Fahrenheit at sea leve, the 14,000 pound Learjet needs a runway of at least 2,950 feet. But under the same conditions, a fully loaded 18,000 pound Learjet would need a runway of at least 5,150 feet. When taking off at Meigs Field (runway length of 3,947 feet), the 14,000 pound Learjet barely clears the end of the runway. Obviously, you shouldn't even takeoff from Meigs Field with a fully loaded 18,000 pound Learjet. Although the FS 5.1 flight model should theoretically assume a weight of 18,000 pounds, for the purposes of simplifying the program, the Learjet's characteristics were slightly tweaked to allow it to takeoff with an implied weight of 15,000 to 16,000 pounds.

Table 10.5 gives you the safe takeoff speeds for the Learjet with different flap settings. For a shorter takeoff distance and slower takeoff speed, you can set the flaps to 20°, although you can also takeoff with the flaps set to 8°.

Flaps should be set to 8 or 20 on takeoff.

Climb Performance

Under full thrust with a maximum rate of climb of 4,340 feet per minute, the climb from sea level to a 45,000 foot cruise altitude for the 14,000 pound Learjet takes about 19 minutes and covers 121 nautical miles. Using Table 10.6, you can see how much fuel is burned and the distance covered to achieve this climb and climbs, to other intermediate altitudes.

Cruise Performance

After the Learjet has achieved a straight and level cruising speed, you may want to know what its true airspeed and fuel flow are for various altitudes. For example, if you wanted to know what the true airspeed would be for a cruising Learjet at an altitude of 45,000 feet, you would look up the row for 45,000 feet in Table 10.7 and see that the Learjet travels at 423 knots TAS (487 mph) and burns 954 pounds of fuel per hour (142 gallons per hour). The indicated airspeed (IAS) on your airspeed indicator would be around 350 knots.

Table 10.4   Takeoff Performance

	60° F (16° C)	70° F (21° C)	80° F (27° C)	100° F (38° C)
18,300 lb. Learjet	Takeoff Distance (Feet)	Takeoff Distance (Feet)	Takeoff Distance (Feet)	Takeoff Distance (Feet)
Runway Altitude				
Sea Level	5,020	5,150	5,560	7,370
2,000 Feet	5,630	5,960	7,110	Not possible
4,000 Feet	6,700	7,120	9,350	Not possible
6,000 Feet	8,785	10,100	Not possible	Not possible
8,000 Feet	Better not try it	Better not try it	Better not try it	Not possible
17,000 lb. Learjet	Takeoff Distance (Feet)	Takeoff Distance (Feet)	Takeoff Distance (Feet)	Takeoff Distance (Feet)
Runway Altitude				
Sea Level	4,340	4,350	4,760	7,090
2,000 Feet	4,810	5,020	5,690	7,930
4,000 Feet	5,575	5,950	7,560	Not possible
6,000 Feet	6,750	8,080	10,580	Not possible
8,000 Feet	9,880	8,800	Not possible	Not possible
16,000 lb. Learjet	Takeoff Distance (Feet)	Takeoff Distance (Feet)	Takeoff Distance (Feet)	Takeoff Distance (Feet)
Runway Altitude				
Sea Level	3,800	3,800	4,160	5,085
2,000 Feet	4,205	4,400	4,900	6,590
4,000 Feet	4,810	5,120	5,895	9,070
6,000 Feet	5,810	6,400	8,385	Not possible
8,000 Feet	7,870	8,800	11,245	Not possible
15,000 lb. Learjet	Takeoff Distance (Feet)	Takeoff Distance (Feet)	Takeoff Distance (Feet)	Takeoff Distance (Feet)
Runway Altitude				
Sea Level	3,325	3,340	3,640	4,410
2,000 Feet	3,680	3,850	4,265	5,255
4,000 Feet	4,190	4,420	4,995	6,965
6,000 Feet	4,940	5,330	6,565	8,835
8,000 Feet	6,000	6,880	8,190	Better not try it.
14,000 lb. Learjet	Takeoff Distance (Feet)	Takeoff Distance (Feet)	Takeoff Distance (Feet)	Takeoff Distance (Feet)
Runway Altitude				
Sea Level	2,910	2,950	3,175	3,825
2,000 Feet	3,210	3,350	3,700	4,540
4,000 Feet	3,640	3,900	4,325	5,660
6,000 Feet	4,275	4,620	5,370	6,680
6,000 Feet	5,060	5,600	6,340	Better not try it.

Table 10.5 Takeoff Speeds (Knots IAS)		
Weight (Lbs.)	**20° Flaps**	**8° Flaps**
	Takeoff Speed (Knots)	**Takeoff Speed (Knots)**
18,300	137	142
14,000	127	125
13,000	125	125

Descent Performance

The Learjet can safely descend at speeds of 3,000 to 4,000 feet per minute. However, even with this high rate of vertical speed, the Learjet will still take about 14 to 16 minutes to descend from 45,000 feet to sea level. Furthermore, if you are planning to land, you must begin your descent no later than 109 nautical miles from the airport! Table 10.8 shows the descent performance for the Learjet.

Landing Performance

The normal landing distance for a 14,000 pound Learjet landing at sea level with an outside temperature at 70° Fahrenheit is 2,900 feet. In the FS 5.1 Learjet, you should be able to just barely land at Chicago's Meigs Field (3,947 feet length). You have only 1,000 feet of spare runway to land on so don't squander precious real estate by overshooting your approach.

Table 10.9 shows some of the different landing distance requirements for the Learjet at different altitudes and temperatures. Notice as the temperature gets colder, the landing distance gets shorter; as the temperature gets hotter, the landing distance gets longer. Likewise, as the altitude increases, the landing distance requirement also increases. This is in accordance with an aerodynamic theory that predicts as the air density gets lower (i.e. higher altitude, hotter temperatures), the lifting forces on the airplane decrease. The airplane must make up for this loss of lift by flying faster and taking a longer distance to land.

For the landing approach the flaps should be set to 8° or 20°. Be sure not to extend the flaps when traveling at speed in excess of 200 knots. Also, the gear should be lowered only when the indicated airspeed is below 200 knots. Your vertical speed should be under 500 feet per minute when landing. If you land at a little over 500 fpm, you will probably loosen a few

For a landing approach descent from 45,000 feet to sea level, you should start your descent no later than 109 nautical miles from the airport.

Table 10.6 Time, Fuel, and Distance to Climb*	
Sea Level To:	**Aircraft Weighs 14,000 Lbs.**
25,000 Feet	
Time (Minutes)	5.4
Fuel (Lbs.)	235
Distance (Nautical Miles)	27
30,000 Feet	
Time (Minutes)	7.1
Fuel (Lbs.)	289
Distance (Nautical Miles)	39
35,000 Feet	
Time (Minutes)	9.2
Fuel (Lbs.)	348
Distance (Nautical Miles)	53
37,000 Feet	
Time (Minutes)	10.2
Fuel (Lbs.)	370
Distance (Nautical Miles)	59
39,000 Feet	
Time (Minutes)	11.3
Fuel (Lbs.)	369
Distance (Nautical Miles)	67
41,000 Feet	
Time (Minutes)	12.9
Fuel (Lbs.)	426
Distance (Nautical Miles)	77
43,000 Feet	
Time (Minutes)	15.2
Fuel (Lbs.)	467
Distance (Nautical Miles)	92
45,000 Feet	
Time (Minutes)	19.4
Fuel (Lbs.)	545
Distance (Nautical Miles)	120

*This data not for flight planning purposes; use only with Microsoft *Flight Simulator*

Table 10.7 Cruise Performance*	
Cruise Altitude	**Aircraft Weights 14,000 Lbs.**
25,000 Feet	
Knots TAS	471
Fuel flow (lbs./hr.)	2007
30,000 Feet	
Knots TAS	469
Fuel flow (lbs./hr.)	1759
35,000 Feet	
Knots TAS	463
Fuel flow (lbs./hr.)	1487
37,000 Feet	
Knots TAS	462
Fuel flow (lbs./hr.)	1425
39,000 Feet	
Knots TAS	459
Fuel flow (lbs./hr.)	1320
41,000 Feet	
Knots TAS	453
Fuel flow (lbs./hr.)	1204
43,000 Feet	
Knots TAS	441
Fuel flow (lbs./hr.)	1085
45,000 Feet	
Knots TAS	423
Fuel flow (lbs./hr.)	954

fillings in your teeth and give your passengers something to think about. For realistic airframe stress damage when landing or even during flight, you can toggle on the Airframe Damage From Stress check box in the Realism and Reliability dialog box, found under the Sim menu.

When you get close to the airport, lower the flaps all the way and check to see that your landing gear is fully extended (the green landing gear light should be lit). Under no circumstances should you allow your airspeed to fall below 128 knots IAS (147 mph). Remember the aircraft's stall speed in the

For more realism when landing, you can toggle on the Airframe Damage From Stress check box in the Realism and Reliability dialog box.

*This data not for flight planning purposes; use only with Microsoft *Flight Simulator*

Table 10.8   Normal Descent

Descending at 3,000 Feet Per Minute @ 350 Knots IAS Down to 10,000 Feet			
Descending at 3,000 Feet Per Minute @ 250 Knots IAS from 10,000 Feet to Sea Level			
From Altitude to Sea Level (Feet)	Time (Minutes)	Fuel (Lbs.)	Distance (Nautical Miles)
45,000	16.4	285	109
43,000	15.7	278	104
41,000	15.0	271	99
39,000	14.4	262	94
37,000	13.7	252	88
35,000	13.0	241	83
33,000	12.4	228	78
30,000	11.3	205	70
25,000	9.7	158	57

Table 10.9   Landing Distance

14,000 lbs. Learjet	60° F (16° C)	70 ° F (21° C)	80° F (27° C)	100° F (38° C)
Runway Altitude	Landing Distance (Feet)	Landing Distance (Feet)	Landing Distance (Feet)	Landing Distance (Feet)
Sea Level	2,870	2,900	2,930	2,995
2,000 Feet	3,005	3,035	3,065	3,130
4,000 Feet	3,115	3,145	3,180	3,250
6,000 Feet	3,265	3,300	3,335	Have life insurance?

Table 10.10   Landing Speeds (Full Flaps)

Aircraft Weight (Lbs.)	Landing Speed (Knots)
13,000	119
14,000	123
15,000	127

landing configuration is 97 knots IAS (112 mph).

Keep in mind the Learjet is very heavy and when you are landing you will want to bring the speed down to less than 150 knots IAS, otherwise you will have difficulty stopping the plane.

Coping with Engine Failure

Before dealing with any engine failure, you must immediately switch off Auto-Coordination under the Sim menu. With only one engine operative, the aircraft is experiencing a torque force that creates aerodynamic instability. To counteract this torque imbalance you will need to fly the plane with the ailerons and rudders independently applied. When auto-coordination is on, you cannot do this, since the ailerons and rudders are synchronized to move together.

Many pilots erroneously believe that if an aircraft has two engines, it will continue to operate at least half as well with only one engine working. This is not so. In any multi-engine aircraft, the loss of an engine causes a 70 percent to 90 percent reduction in performance. When one engine fails, not only does the remaining engine have to carry the full burden of the aircraft's forward thrust, but drag is increased because of asymmetric thrust. For example, in the Learjet the maximum rate of climb with both engines operating is 4,340 feet per minute. With only one engine functioning the rate of climb drops to 1,290 fpm. This is a performance loss of over 70 percent!

Figure 10.7 illustrates the asymmetric and unbalanced engine thrust forces at work when either the right or left engine fails.

The correct way to deal with a loss of an engine is to turn your rudders in the direction of the still operative engine, and bank the wings of the aircraft at least 5° onto the good engine. The amount of aileron and rudder pressure needed will vary, but you should first apply rudder to counteract the

To deal with an engine failure on the Learjet, you must switch off Auto-Coordination under the Sim menu. The ailerons and rudders must each be used independently to achieve stable flight, and this can only be done if you are flying in uncoordinated flight mode.

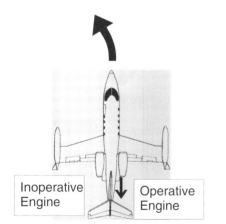

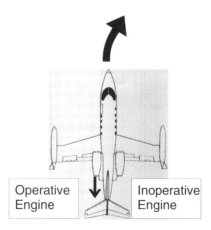

Unbalanced Forces Created During Single-Engine Operation

Figure 10.7
Unbalanced forces created during single-engine operation

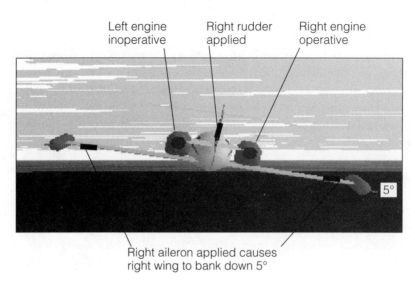

Left engine inoperative | Right rudder applied | Right engine operative

5°

Right aileron applied causes right wing to bank down 5°

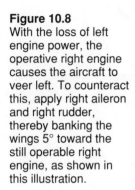

Figure 10.8
With the loss of left engine power, the operative right engine causes the aircraft to veer left. To counteract this, apply right aileron and right rudder, thereby banking the wings 5° toward the still operable right engine, as shown in this illustration.

yawing tendency of the jet to turn left or right. After stabilizing the yaw, apply the ailerons. Figure 10.8 illustrates the proper V_{mc} technique for flying the Learjet on one engine.[1]

The in-cockpit view is illustrated in Figure 10.9. You will notice from the position of the throttle levers that the left engine is not operating. To counteract the yawing forces to the left, the right rudder was applied, as shown by the lower control position indicator. Also, a 5° bank angle to the right (toward the still operative right engine) was achieved by applying the right aileron, as indicated by the upper control position indicator and by the artificial horizon (note the bank angle pointer is less than 10°).

The next section summarizes the procedure to take when flying with only one engine operating.

To stabilize the Learjet when an engine failure occurs:

1. Switch off Auto-Coordination under the Sim menu.

2. Determine which engine has failed by looking at your engine turbine and

---

[1]The V_{MC} is defined as the minimum airspeed with the critical engine inoperative at which the airplane is controllable. It does not assume that the aircraft can climb or hold its present altitude. It only means that a particular course heading can be maintained, using the rudder and ailerons to overcome the asymmetrical yawing forces caused by the still operable engine.

fan speed indicators. If necessary, call up your engine instruments by pressing Tab.

3. Turn the rudder (0-Yaw Left, Enter-Yaw Right, both are located on the numeric keypad) toward the direction of the still operative engine until the aircraft's yawing (left-right turning motion) is stopped.

4. Apply the ailerons (4-Left Aileron, 6-Right Aileron, both are located on the numeric keypad) in the direction of the still operative engine to trim and stabilize the aircraft.

5. Using the ailerons (4-Bank Left Wing Down, 6-Bank Right Wing Down, both are located on the numeric keypad), bank the wings down by 5° in the direction of the still operative engine. Note the bank angle on the artificial horizon indicator. The arrow pointer should hover between the 0° and 10° pitch markers.

You can practice flying with one engine by merely reducing the thrust on one of the engines.

Aileron control position indicator shows right aileron applied

Rudder control position indicator shows right rudder applied

Artificial horizon shows 5° bank angle towards the still operating engine

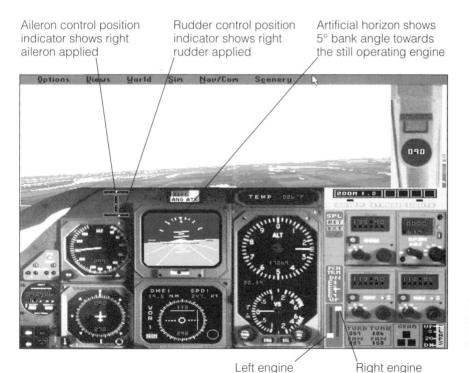

Figure 10.9
In the cockpit of the Learjet with the left engine inoperative

Left engine inoperative (throttled down)

Right engine operative (throttled up)

Range and Refueling Requirements

The Learjet's fuel tank capacity of 6,198 pounds (2,811 kg or 925 gallons) of fuel allows the aircraft to have a maximum range of 2,196 nautical miles (2,525 statute miles or 4,062 km). When flying nonstop at this range, however, the Learjet can only carry four passengers and two crew members (normal passenger load is eight). Figure 10.10 shows some of the mission capabilities for the Learjet. Note the missions indicated with an arrow are flights that may be accomplished by the Learjet in the opposite direction to the arrow only with favorable wind conditions. If there is a strong headwind, the range of the aircraft is diminished and the mission will have to be scrubbed until weather conditions permit.

For a typical 575 statute mile trip, the Learjet 35A can complete the voyage in 1-1/2 hours on about 200 gallons of fuel. Since aviation fuel has a density of about 6.7 pounds per gallon, this translates to 1,340 pounds of fuel. Fuel flow and quantity is measured in pounds. The Learjet burns around 938 to 1,252 pounds of fuel per hour (140 to 187 gallons per hour). As you can see from these figures, fuel costs can be enormous. With fuel averaging about $2.25 per gallon, the cost of operating the jet per hour is $400. Table 10.10 gives you the Learjet's fuel burn, airspeed, and altitude performance data that are useful for planning a long range mission.

The Learjet 35A's high fuel efficiency, when compared to other business jets, comes in part from the higher cruise altitude which it can operate from. The 35A is certified to cruise at 45,000 feet, more than a mile above most commercial passenger jets and above the 100 mph jet stream headwinds. Butting into such wind for lower flying jets causes ground speed to drop from 500 mph to 400 mph, and this causes lower fuel efficiency. Flying at this higher altitude, due to the thinner air, the Learjet can fly faster and with lower drag and air resistance friction.

If you want the engines to stop when they run out of fuel, toggle on Engine Stops When Out of Fuel in the Realism and Reliability dialog box.

Fuel Realism on the Flight Simulator Learjet

By default, *Flight Simulator* allows you to fly the Learjet with unlimited fuel. For greater simulation realism, you can choose to have your engines stop when they are out of fuel. To do this:

1. Select the Sim menu.
2. Click on the Realism and Reliability menu option.
3. Toggle on Engine Stops When Out of Fuel.
4. Click OK to return to the simulation.

Table 10.11   Long-Range Cruise Performance

Distance (Nautical Miles)	Cruise Altitude (Feet)	Time to Travel (Hrs:Min)	Fuel Burned (Lbs.)	Speed (Knots TAS)
200	35,000	0:45	744	266
400	41,000	1:14	1,182	324
600	43,000	1:41	1,620	356
800	43,000	2:10	2,063	369
1,000	43,000	2:39	2,528	377
1,200	43,000	3:07	3,009	385
1,400	43,000	3:35	3,509	390
1,600	45,000	4:05	4,020	391
1,800	45,000	4:34	4,549	394
2,000	45,000	5:02	5,089	397
2,200	45,000	5:30	5,648	400
2,400	45,000	5:58	6,207	402

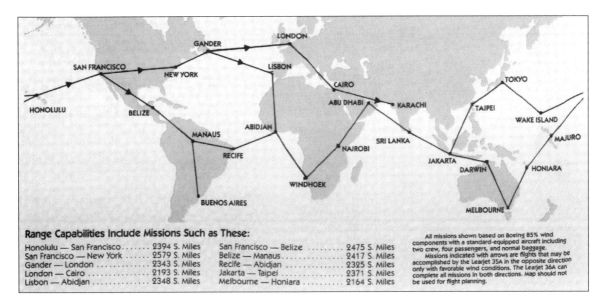

Range Capabilities Include Missions Such as These:

Honolulu — San Francisco....... 2394 S. Miles	San Francisco — Belize .... 2475 S. Miles
San Francisco — New York ...... 2579 S. Miles	Belize — Manaus.............. 2417 S. Miles
Gander — London .... 2343 S. Miles	Recife — Abidjan .... 2325 S. Miles
London — Cairo .... 2193 S. Miles	Jakarta — Taipei .... 2371 S. Miles
Lisbon — Abidjan .... 2348 S. Miles	Melbourne — Honiara .... 2164 S. Miles

All missions shown based on Boeing 85% wind components with a standard-equipped aircraft including two crew, four passengers, and normal baggage.
Missions indicated with arrows are flights that may be accomplished by the Learjet 35A in the opposite direction only with favorable wind conditions. The Learjet 36A can complete all missions in both directions. Map should not be used for flight planning.

Figure 10.10 Range capability for the Learjet 35A carrying four passengers and two crew members. (This data *not* for flight planning purposes; use only with Microsoft *Flight Simulator*) *(Courtesy of Learjet)*

Toggle on Engine
Stops When Out of
Fuel and press ⊡ to
save the Learjet sit-
uation with the lim-
ited fuel option. Then
each time you reset
the situation, limited
fuel will be enabled.

If you want don't want to keep resetting the Engine Stops When Out of Fuel check box each time you fly the Learjet, remember to save the situation and give it a name so you can reload it from disk. Then each time the simulation resets itself, either by your crashing the plane or by your pressing the Ctrl and Print Screen keys, the Learjet situation will start up with limited fuel enabled.

C H A P T E R

11

Flying the Sailplane

This chapter discusses the history, performance characteristics, and gliding techniques of the Schweizer 2-32 Sailplane. You will also learn how to best take advantage of thermal and ridge currents to gain altitude. Please note: all of the tables, charts, and information are for use with Microsoft's *Flight Simulator*; they are not to be used for real flight planning purposes.

SCHWEIZER SAILPLANE HISTORY

Since 1930, the Schweizer Aircraft Corporation has produced over 2,000 Sailplanes. The first glider, constructed by the Schweizer brothers in 1929, was the Model SGP 1-1, of which only one was completed. During the war years Schweizer was asked to produce metal training gliders for the US Air Corps training program, so they created the TG 2 and the TG 3, of which 171 Sailplanes were created. In the post-war period, Schweizer began to market a new series of Sailplanes. This series culminated in the popular 2-22 (1945), the 1-26 (1954), the 2-32 (1962), and the 2-33 (1967). The first digit in the serial number identifier for each Schweizer Sailplane tells you the number of seats and the second number tells you the chronology of the firm's design sequence.

The SGS 2-32 is an all-metal, two seat high performance sailplane that has won world and national records in glider competitions. It has a large, roomy, cockpit and in the two seat version, has dual flight controls.

Figure 11.1
Schweizer 2-32
Sailplane *(Courtesy
of Schweizer Aircraft
Corporation,
copyright 1993)*

FUNDAMENTALS OF THERMAL SOARING

A thermal is a rising air current caused by the sun's heating of the surface. As the air expands from the heat radiated by the Earth, it becomes lighter than the surrounding atmosphere. The air then rises like a hot air balloon, which by itself is nothing but an enclosed thermal.

Different kinds of surfaces absorb heat at different rates. Dark surfaces, in general, get hotter than light ones; smooth surfaces get hotter than rough ones. Blacktop highways, runways, and parking lots are both smooth and dark and thus generate vigorous thermals. Sandy beaches, dry river beds, and smooth deserts are also good sources of thermals. On the other hand, vegetation, forests, and green fields do not get as hot because they exude moisture and their large surface area dissipates much heat. Flying over forests and green fields usually means the Sailplane will sink; flying over bare brown fields means that the Sailplane will experience lift.

Thermals cannot be seen by the naked eye. However, studies have shown them to be bubble shaped. The air is warmed by the ground, swells, breaks free of the ground, and then rises like bubbles in boiling water. Cooler air then moves in from the sides to replace the warm air and there is a delay while a new bubble forms.

If the surface is hot enough the air bubbles will be produced more rapidly. The net result is the formation of a roughly cylindrical column of warm air that extends from the surface and occasionally penetrates the stratosphere at 60,000 feet. Most soaring, however, is done in the range of ground level to 8,000 feet.

The basic idea for thermaling is you try to find thermals and ride them up to higher altitudes. You can circle up them or perform figure eights, but in all cases you want to remain inside the thermal. Knowing that darker land masses absorb more heat than lighter colored land, you can head for those areas that have a high probability of generating thermals.

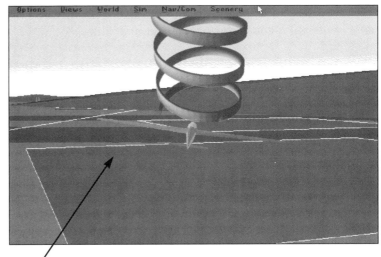

Brown field causes thermal updrafts

Figure 11.2
Thermal soaring. The brown fields are where the thermals are. In thermal soaring, circle upwards to take advantage of rising hot air.

FUNDAMENTALS OF RIDGE SOARING

Ridge soaring is another Sailplane technique used for gaining altitude. In ridge soaring, you fly the Sailplane parallel to the upwind slope, crabbing into the wind as necessary. The wind, which is shoved upward by the contour of mountains, cliffs, and hills, provides an upward lift for the Sailplane. When you notice the glider is no longer gaining altitude, you simply reverse direction and retrace your path parallel to the slope. Make sure that when you turn, you always turn away from the ridge (into the wind), and that you do not fly over the ridge. Essentially, you will be performing figure eights on one side of the ridge.

Note that with the ridge lift technique, you can never fly more than a few hundred feet over the ridge. With thermal soaring there is no such limit. Another gliding technique used, called wave soaring, offers tremendous amounts of lift but it is a complex topic that goes beyond the scope of this book.

Figure 11.3
Ridge soaring

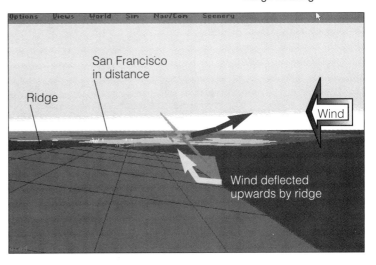

San Francisco in distance

Ridge

Wind

Wind deflected upwards by ridge

All the current soaring altitude records were accomplished using the wave soaring method.

SCHWEIZER 2-32 SAILPLANE PERFORMANCE

Figure 11.4 shows the Schweizer 2-32 Sailplane's overall dimensions; Table 11.1 gives its physical specifications.

Figure 11.4
Schweizer 2-32
sailplane dimensions

Table 11.1 Schweizer 2-32 Sailplane Specifications	
Length	26 feet, 9 inches
Wingspan	57 feet
Height	9 feet
Wing Area	180 square feet
Aspect Ratio	18.05
Gross Weight	1,340 lbs
Standard Empty Weight	830 lbs
Maximum Useful Load	490 lbs
Wing Loading	7.44 lb/square feet
Maximum Operating Speed	150 mph
Stall Speed (Single Seater)	48 mph
Maximum L/D	34 at 59 mph
Minimum Sink (Single Seater)	2.1 feet per second at 50 mph
Landing Gear	Non-retracting wheels in underbelly. Hydraulic brakes included.

CONTROLS

The Schweizer 2-32 sailplane has an altimeter, airspeed indicator, magnetic compass, dive brakes (called spoilers or SPL), a COM radio, master electrical switch, control position indicators, and a vertical speed indicator. The airspeed indicator shows speeds in statute miles per hour, unlike most other airspeed indicators which are calibrated to display knots. The dive brakes, like the spoilers on the Learjet, are moveable airfoils located on the top of the wing. When deployed they act to slow the aircraft's rate of descent, and they can be used to slow the aircraft's horizontal velocity as well.

OPERATIONAL PLACARD

Every glider carries an operations limitation placard. It is there to inform the pilot of the glider's safe minimum operating characteristics. The placard also states the safe maximum glide speed, the maximum aerotow and ground launch speeds, maximum gross weight permissible, maximum maneuvering, the wind gust limit, and balance and load factors. On the FS 5.1 Sailplane, you can barely discern the placard below the master electrical switch (above and to the side of the COM radio).

TAKEOFF

Normally, the Schweizer 2-32 Sailplane must be towed up to an altitude that can enable it to glide. In *Flight Simulator*, you can start one of the built in soaring situations or you can create your own. To create your own soaring situation, simply fly the Cessna to any location where you want to soar, then select the Sweizer 2-32 Sailplane as your aircraft under the Options menu. Or you can move your Sailplane to whatever location you choose by entering slew mode. To enter slew mode, press [Y], then press [F4] to gain altitude, or [F1] to descend (if your function keys are on the left, press [F2] to ascend and [F10] to descend). To freeze all slewing motion, press [5] on the numeric keypad.

IMPORTANT SPEEDS

The Sailplane's stall speed when fully loaded is 48 mph. In level flight, the Sailplane has a minimum sink rate of 2.1 feet at 50 mph.[1] Do not fly the Sailplane lower than the minimum stall speeds. When spiraling in thermals, be careful not to fly at less than 55 mph for a 30° bank, or 57 mph for a 45° bank. If you do so, you run the danger of stalling the aircraft. Also, be sure not to exceed 150 mph when descending because this is the maximum speed that is safe for the airframe.

Best Glide Speed is at 55 Miles per Hour

Table 11.4 reveals the Sailplane's sink rate for various speeds. The sink rate is the number of feet the glider falls per second at a given speed in the absence of a thermal. In the table, the sink rate has been calculated per mile from various performance charts. You can see that the slowest, or best, sink rate is to be found when the glider is traveling at 55 mph. From this information you

---

[1]The Microsoft manual is in error. The sink rate for the sailplane is 2.1 feet per second at 50 mph., not 58 mph.

Table 11.2 Maximum Stall Speed When Banking or Spiralling in Thermals	
Bank Angle	**Speed in Miles Per Hour**
30°	55
45°	57

Table 11.3 Maximum Speeds for the Schweizer Sailplane	
Description	**Speed in Miles Per Hour**
Maximum Glide Speed, Dive Brakes Off	150
Maximum Glide Speed, Dive Brakes On	158

can figure out how many miles you can glide before having to land. Use the following formula:

$$Distance\ in\ Miles\ =\ \frac{Altitude}{Feet\ of\ Altitude\ Lost\ per\ Mile}$$

At a speed of 55 mph and an altitude of 5,000 feet, you would look at the table and find your rate of sink. For 55 mph there is 344 feet of altitude lost per mile. Plugging all this information into the formula, we arrive at:

$$14.53\ miles = \frac{5,000\ feet\ Altitude}{344\ feet\ /\ mile}$$

So at 5,000 feet you have 14.53 miles to find an airstrip to land on. Otherwise, you might end up in some cow pasture. If you must land in a field, be sure to look for one without a bull penned inside.

Table 11.4 Glide Performance: Altitude Lost vs. Distance and Speed												
Speed (mph)	35	40	45	50	55	60	65	70	75	80	85	90
Minutes Required to Fly One Mile	1.71	1.50	1.33	1.20	1.09	1.00	0.92	0.86	0.80	0.75	0.71	0.67
Feet of Altitude Lost Per Mile	448	393	365	351	**344***	346	353	366	382	401	422	446

III

Navigaton and Aircraft Communication Systems

CHAPTER

12

Great Circle Route Planning and Radio Navigation

This chapter discusses great circle navigation, and the use of your navigation and communication radio equipment. You must understand how radio navigation works in order to travel from point to point in the *Flight Simulator* world. *Flight Simulator 5.1* CD now includes all the VOR/NDB radio beacon stations for the continental USA, including Hawaii, Alaska, and most parts of Canada; in all, over 3,237 stations! Many VOR/NDBs are included for other parts of the world as well. For example, there are 418 VOR/NDBs for the entire Pacific Ocean region from the South Pacific to the North Pacific, extending west to the Far East, and there are 159 VOR/NDBs for Asia. In Africa, there are 116 VOR/NDBs, and for Europe, there are 475 VOR/NDBs. In South America, Central America, and the Caribbean basin, there are 236 new VOR/NDBs. Using these beacons you can now navigate trans-oceanic flights and refuel your aircraft, something that was not possible before with *Flight Simulator 5.0*.

If you have purchased the floppy disk version of *Flight Simulator 5.1*, then you will unfortunately not have all the worldwide VOR/NDBs, nor will you have the worldwide airports which you will need if you want to fly and refuel the aircraft for trans-oceanic flights. Only FS 5.1 CD has the necessary worldwide airport facilities and Navaids (i.e., "navigational aids") stored on the CD-ROM, and what's more, you'll need to have the CD inserted into your CD-ROM player while you use FS 5.1, because the program needs to access the CD-ROM while flying into different scenery areas. FS 5.1 stores only those Navaids that are close by to your aircraft's current location in a special cache on your hard disk. When you exit the program, the cache is wiped clean.

Before jumping into the science of navigating your aircraft, let's first learn about air traffic control, and the use of your communication radios.

AIR TRAFFIC CONTROL

Radio communication with air traffic control (ATC) is vital to establishing safe operating conditions in the air and on the ground. When talking on the radio, concise phraseology and clarity of expression are crucial to getting messages across accurately. To prevent miscommunication, special radio communication procedures and phrases have been uniformly adopted.

Voice Contact Procedure

To contact a given FAA facility, control tower, or other airplane follow this format:

1. Name of contact facility, tower, or plane being called.
2. Your full aircraft identification using the phonetic alphabet to identify single letters and numbers.
3. Your message

   Example:

   "NEW YORK RADIO, CESSNA THREE ONE SIX ZERO FOXTROT, REQUEST TRAFFIC ADVISORY"

In *Flight Simulator*, you don't need to send messages to ATC using this terminology. You can request clearance to land or takeoff by summoning up the Air Traffic Control dialog box and clicking on the Request to Take off or the Request to Land buttons. The simulator will then take care of sending the message for you. To send a message to ATC, follow these steps:

1. Click on the Air Traffic Control option under the Nav/Com menu.
2. Select the Communication Radio menu command.
3. In the Communication Radio dialog box, click on the Send Message button.

4. In the Air Traffic Control dialog box, click on the Request to Land or Request to Take off radio buttons.

Figure 12.1 shows the Air Traffic Control dialog box.

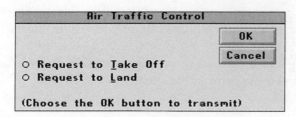

Figure 12.1
The Air Traffic Control dialog box

Table 12.1	Phonetic Alphabet		
Character	Pronounced	Character	Pronounced
A	Alpha	S	Sierra
B	Bravo	T	Tango
C	Charlie	U	Uniform
D	Delta	V	Victor
E	Echo	W	Whiskey
F	Foxtrot	X	X-Ray
G	Golf	Y	Yankee
H	Hotel	Z	Zulu
I	India	0	Zero
J	Juliett	1	Wun
K	Kilo	2	Too
L	Lima	3	Tree
M	Mike	4	Fo-wer
N	November	5	Fife
O	Oscar	6	Six
P	Papa	7	Seven
Q	Quebec	8	Ait
R	Romeo	9	Niner

Use of Numbers

Normally numbers are spoken by speaking each number separately. There are exceptions to the above rule, however. Figures indicating hundreds and thousands are spoken like this:

9,000	"Niner-Thousand"
500	"Fife-Hundred"
14,500	"Wun-Fo-wer-thousand-fife-hundred"

Course headings are always spoken with three digits of bearing.

Course Heading 005°   "Zero-Zero-Fife"

Also, time is stated in 24 hour format with four digits.

06:45   "Zero-Six-fo-wer-fife"

COM RADIOS

The COM radio is used to tune in ATIS weather reports, and the Air Traffic Control. It has 360 channels on frequencies between 118.00 and 135.95 MHz, with 50 kHz channel separation. You can make the radio capable of receiving more than 720 channels by selecting the 25 kHz COM Frequency Adjustability check box in the Instrument Preferences dialog box under the Options menu. For a list of airport control tower and ATIS frequencies, see appendix B.

NAVIGATION

In FS 5.1, to navigate using radio beacons, you need to have charts that show the locations and frequencies of VOR/NDB stations on your intended path. In appendix B, you will find navigational maps for the entire USA, and for the rest of the world. However, due to size constraints and other factors, the included maps in this book only list the names of the VOR stations for the USA, and omit frequencies and magnetic course information. In order to navigate using these maps, you will have to first look up the radio frequency and latitude/longitude points for these radio beacons (you locate them first on the map, then look them up in the alphabetical VOR/NDB listings, also in Appendix B). Then, you figure out the desired magnetic course to fly between each beacon, using the techniques described in this chapter.

You can easily purchase the real map sectionals, as they are called, for the USA by going to your local airport's pilot shop. Or, if you prefer, you can buy each aeronautical chart directly from the US. Department of Commerce's National Oceanic and Atmospheric Administration (NOAA) for $6.00, plus shipping and handling. To see the coverage area for some of the sectionals in the USA, see the bibliography at the end of this book, under the maps and sectionals section. There are also enroute low altitude charts, and IFR high altitude charts for cross country navigation (see bibliography for coverage areas) and these charts can be ordered for approximately $9.00, plus shipping and handling. In addition, if you want maps of other parts of the world, the Department of Defense Mapping Agency publishes aeronautical charts through the NOAA. Particularly interesting are the North Pacific Route Charts, and the North Atlantic Route Charts, which show all the navigational beacons and waypoints for trans-oceanic flights.

To order the NOAA map catalog, or to place an order,
contact the NOAA at:
NOAA Distribution Branch, N/CG33
National Ocean Service
Riverdale, Maryland 20737-1199
Telephone and FAX orders are also accepted
by the NOAA Distribution Branch:
General Information and Individual Orders: 301-436-6990
FAX Orders: 301-436-6829

In general, aeronautical navigation falls into the following categories:

Pilotage: Navigation by following visual landmarks. Limited to daytime flight with good visibility.

Dead Reckoning: Deduced or "ded." reckoning based on computations of speed. Limited to daytime flight with good visibility.

VOR: Very High Frequency Omnirange Radio Beacons. Maximum range of 80 miles in FS 5.1. (In reality, high powered VOR stations can be received as far as 130 nautical miles away).

NDB: Low Frequency Non-Directional Radio Beacons. Maximum 75 mile day range, 200 mile night range.

ILS: Instrument Landing System Radio Beacons. 18 mile range extending from runway.

Loran C: Long Range Low Frequency Radio Navigation. Semi-global coverage. 1,200 mile range by day, 2,300 miles by night.

Omega: Very Low Frequency Radio Navigation. Global Coverage.

GPS: High Frequency Radio Navigation. Using the Global Positioning System's Navstar satellites, a GPS receiver can determine its position, speed, and altitude worldwide.

Inertial Navigation: Using gyroscopes, accelerometers, and computers, inertial navigation equipment can internally determine the airplane's position, without input from outside sources.

Celestial Navigation: Tracking the Stars, Sun and Moon Using Optical Methods. This method has fallen into disuse in favor of more reliable electronic navigational aids.

In *Flight Simulator*, there are only three radio navigation aids available to you.[1] They are as follows:

- VOR
- NDB
- ILS

Latitude/Longitude

Any discussion of navigation must include the topic of coordinate systems. The principal means of determining your position on the spherical earth is to use the latitude/longitude coordinate system. This coordinate system is the foundation for all navigational methods, including the VOR/NDB, Loran C, Omega, Global Positioning Satellite system (hereafter called GPS), and celestial navigation.

Lines of longitude, also known as meridians, run north and south, connecting the North Pole and the South Pole. They are numbered in angular degrees from 0° to 180° east and west of the prime meridian, which runs through Greenwich, England. Each longitude line forms what is known as a great circle; that is, it contains a plane that cuts through the center of the earth. All great circles circumscribe the Earth, and their circumferences are approximately the same (because the Earth has an oblate spheroid shape and is not perfectly symmetrical, the circumference of a great circle can vary slightly from other great circles).

Lines of latitude, also called parallels, run east and west, parallel to each other. They too, are numbered in angular degrees, from 0° to 90° north and south of the equator. However, only the equator latitude line forms a great circle; the other latitude lines get smaller as they get closer to the poles.

You can quickly display your current latitude and longitude on-screen by pressing (Shift)(Z) twice. You can also change your aircraft's position to any latitude/longitude coordinate by using the World/ Location menu command.

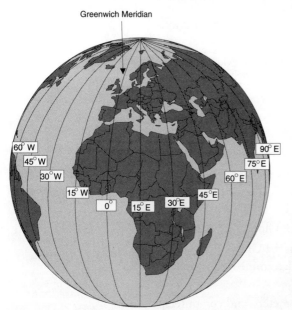

Figure 12.2
Lines of longitude

[1]You can simulate the GPS satellite radio system by displaying your latitude/longitude coordinates on screen. Press (Shift)(Z) twice.

As mentioned in earlier chapters, each degree of arc is divided into 60 minutes of arc, and each minute of arc is in turn divided into 60 arc seconds, so there are 3600 arc seconds in one degree. Since a degree of arc is equivalent to 60 nautical miles on a great circle around the earth, each minute of arc is equal to 1 nautical mile, and each second of arc is equal to 1/60 nautical mile. But this distance relationship only applies to the equator, lines of longitude, and great circles. As you get closer to the poles, the lines of longitude converge, and thus you cannot use the distance ratio of 60 miles/degree of arc for measuring distances between two longitude points not on the equator.

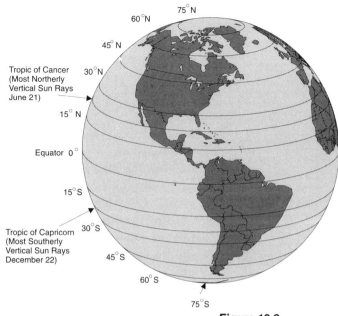

Figure 12.3
Lines of latitude

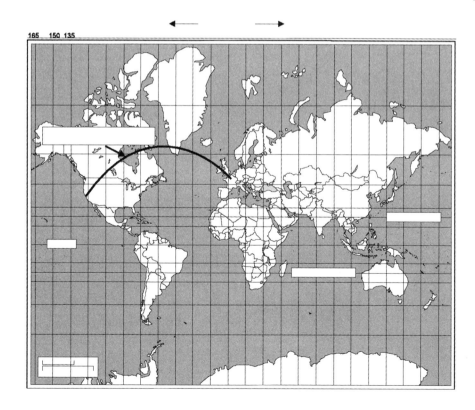

Figure 12.4
Mercator projection of the Earth showing latitude/longitude lines

Because great circle paths are the shortest routes between any two points on the Earth, let's first learn a little bit more about them, then skip straight to the mathematical formula that is used to calculate the distance between any two locations on earth.

Great Circle Tracks

The intersection of a plane and the surface of a sphere is a circle; but if the plane passes through the center of a sphere, the intersection of the plane and the sphere is a great circle, otherwise the intersection is known as a small circle. Obviously, the circumference of a great circle is equal to the circumference of the sphere it intersects, while the circumference of a small circle is smaller. Great circles form the shortest and most direct surface path between any two locations on Earth. On a globe, a great circle track between Paris and San Francisco would look like a circle that circumscribes the Earth, and which directly joins Paris and San Francisco, as is illustrated in Figure 12.5.

On a Mercator map, a great circle track appears curved, and looks longer than the straight line distance between two locations. However, because the Mercator projection purposely distorts the size of the higher latitudes, the curved great circle course is still the shortest path. Mercator maps are not generally used in aviation, because of this distortion of great circle tracks. You can see the curved great circle track in the Mercator map of Figure 12.4.

A Gnomonic Projection of the Earth, otherwise known as a great circle chart, is a type of map which is convenient for navigation because it depicts great circle paths as straight lines. You can see an example of this in Figure 12.6. Most general aviation maps are gnomonic projections of the Earth (or Lambert conformal conics), although for polar regions, other kinds of map projections are used (such as transverse Mercators).

Figure 12.5
A Great Circle Track represents the shortest path between any two locations on Earth.

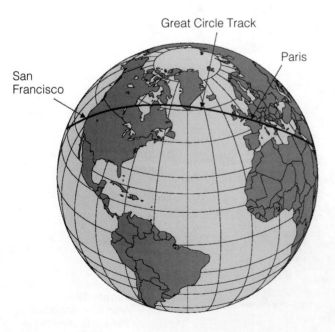

Great Circle Track

Paris

San Francisco

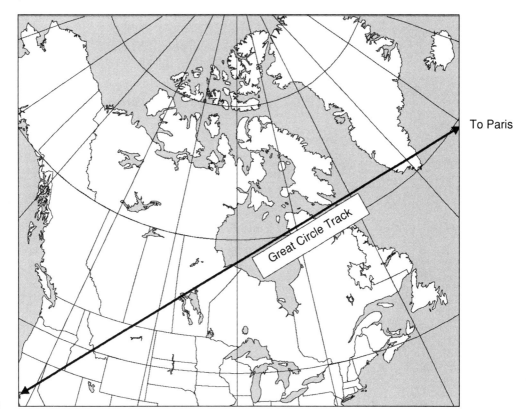

Figure 12.6
On a Gnomonic map (Great Circle Chart), Great Circle Tracks are shown as straight lines.

Calculating Great Circle Distances Between Two Locations

If the longitude and latitude of two locations are known, the great circle distance between them can be easily calculated, using one of the following three equations:

$$\textit{Distance in Nautical Miles} = 60 \times \cos^{-1} [[\sin(\textit{Lat}_1) \times \sin(\textit{Lat}_2)] + [\cos(\textit{Lat}_1) \times \cos(\textit{Lat}_2) \times \cos(\textit{Long}_1 - \textit{Long}_2)]]$$

or

$$\textit{Distance in Statute Miles} = 69.094 \times \cos^{-1} [[\sin(\textit{Lat}_1) \times \sin(\textit{Lat}_2)] + [\cos(\textit{Lat}_1) \times \cos(\textit{Lat}_2) \times \cos(\textit{Long}_1 - \textit{Long}_2)]]$$

or

$$\textit{Arc Distance in Degrees} = \cos^{-1} [[\sin(\textit{Lat}_1) \times \sin(\textit{Lat}_2)] + [\cos(\textit{Lat}_1) \times \cos(\textit{Lat}_2) \times \cos(\textit{Long}_1 - \textit{Long}_2)]]$$

where

$Distance =$ The distance between the two places in statute miles, nautical miles (multiply statute miles by 1.15 to obtain nautical miles), or arc distance measured in degrees.

$Lat_1 =$ The latitude of the first place (must be entered in decimal degrees). Enter South Latitudes (Southern Hemisphere) as a negative number.

$Long_1 =$ The longitude of the first place (must be entered in decimal degrees). Enter East Latitudes as a negative number.

$Lat_2 =$ The latitude of the second place (must be entered in decimal degrees). Enter South Latitudes (Southern Hemisphere) as a negative number.

$Long =$ The longitude of the second place (must be entered in decimal degrees). Enter East Latitudes as a negative number.

$\cos^{-1} =$ Arc Cosine Function (Inverse Cosine)

You must have a scientific calculator that has trigonometric functions and inverse trigonometric functions. Also, you must make sure that the calculator is being run in degree display mode, not radian display mode. Radians are arc measurements made in units of PI, and cannot be used in this formula.

Note that the variables Lat_1, $Long_1$, Lat_2, and $Long_2$ must be entered in decimal degree form; you cannot enter them as a normal latitude/longitude coordinate. To convert a latitude or longitude to decimal format, follow this formula:

$$Convert\ latitude\ or\ Longitude\ to\ Decimal\ Degree = HHH + \frac{MM}{60} + \frac{SS}{3600}$$

where

$HHH =$ Degrees of Latitude or Longitude
$MM =$ Minutes of Latitude or Longitude
$SS =$ Seconds of Latitude or Longitude

When performing any of the calculations listed here, make sure your calculator is displaying results in degree form, *not* radians.

For example, to convert a starting longitude coordinate of W132° 55' 15" to decimal degree format, add

$$132° + \frac{55'}{60} + \frac{15"}{3600} = 132.9208°.$$

You would then use 132.9208° as your input for the variable $Long_1$ in the above listed distance equation.

This conversion of the latitude/longitude coordinates is greatly simplified if you have a scientific calculator that converts degrees in the hour-minutes-seconds format to the decimal hours format. On a Hewlett Packard Scientific Calculator 22S, for example, you would use the H-HMS function by entering the latitude or longitude as HHH.MMSS, where the HHH represents the hours, the MM represents the minutes, and the SS represents the seconds. Thus to convert W132° 55' 15", you would enter 132.5515 in the calculator, and then press the H-HMS button, and on the menu display, select HM, to convert the longitude to decimal hour format.

EXAMPLE PROBLEM: Calculate the distance between San Francisco International Airport (N37° 37' 07" latitude, W122° 22' 32" longitude) and Paris' Orly Airport (N48° 43' 30" latitude, E02° 22' 54" longitude).

SOLUTION: After performing the decimal degree conversions, San Francisco has a decimal degree coordinate of N37.6186° latitude, W122.3756° longitude. Paris has a decimal degree coordinate of N48.7250° latitude, and E2.3817° longitude. Plugging these numbers into the equation:

VARIABLE	VALUE	DESCRIPTION
$Lat_1 =$	37.6186	Decimal Latitude SF
$Long_1 =$	122.3756	Decimal Longitude SF
$Lat_2 =$	48.7250	Decimal Latitude Paris
$Long_2 =$	-2.3817	Decimal Longitude Paris (Notice that a negative sign was added because Paris has an Eastern Longitude)
$Distance =$	5,578.89 statute miles, 4,844.60 nautical miles, or 80.7433° arc measure	Total Air Miles, or Distance, between SF and Paris

Accuracy and Significant Figures for Great Circle Distances

The great circle distance is only as accurate as the precision and accuracy of the two latitude/longitude coordinates from which you are measuring. The following general rules will be of use in determining the degree of accuracy to be expected when dealing with angles in trigonometry.

1. Latitude/longitude coordinates expressed to the nearest 30 minutes (30') will give you results accurate to only two significant figures (i.e., if

measuring the distance between San Francisco and Paris, and your best measured latitude/longitude coordinate for S.F. is N37° 30', W122° 30, and for Paris is N49° 00', E02° 30', the great circle distance can only have two significant figures, meaning that the calculated distance will be 5,600 statute miles, or 4,800 nautical miles.)[2]

2. Latitude/longitude coordinates expressed to the nearest 5 minutes (5') will give you results accurate to only three significant figures (i.e., your accuracy for the great circle distance for S.F-Paris is now 5,580 statute miles, or 4,850 nautical miles).

3. Latitude/longitude coordinates expressed to the nearest minute (1') will give you results accurate to four significant figures (i.e., the great circle distance for S.F.- Paris is now 5,579 statute miles, or 4,845 nautical miles).

4. Latitude/longitude coordinates expressed to the nearest 6 seconds (6") will give you results accurate to five significant figures (i.e., the great circle distance for S.F.- Paris is now 5,578.9 statute miles, or 4,844.6 nautical miles).

Magnetic Heading

The magnetic compass is the mainstay of all navigational methods, and its basic operating principle remains unchanged from the compasses used by ancient mariners. A compass contains a magnetized needle that is allowed to rotate in a horizontal plane. Because the Earth acts as a huge magnet, there are magnetic flux lines of force connecting its two magnetic poles. These lines of force flow from the South Pole, bending around the Earth before returning into the North Pole. The direction and magnitude of these lines of force are what determine the size and shape of the Earth's magnetic field. The needle on the compass, being magnetized, is attracted by the magnetic poles of the Earth, and orients itself along the Earth's magnetic flux lines, as is illustrated in Figure 12.7.

---

[2]Even though your calculator will show other digits after the "6" for the 5,600 statute miles, or after the "8" for the 4,800 nautical miles, you must discard these digits that follow, and round up to only two significant digits. You do this by counting from the left, two digits, then rounding up the second digit if the third digit is five or greater. Thus, for example, if your calculated Great Circle distance were 325.55 miles, you could only claim 330 miles as your distance, because if you have only two significant figures, you would count from the left most digit, two digits, then round the second digit up by one if the third digit is 5 or greater.

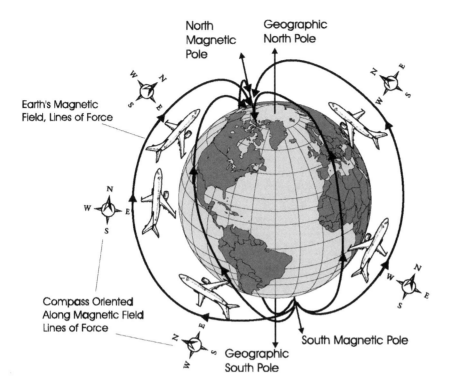

Figure 12.7
The Earth's magnetic field causes magnetic compass needles to line up in the direction of the field's lines of force.

Variation

Since the magnetic poles of the Earth do not coincide with the geographic poles, a compass needle in line with the Earth's magnetic field will not indicate true north, but magnetic north. The angular discrepancy between true north and magnetic north is called variation, and this variation has different values for different parts of the Earth. Figure 12.8 shows the isogonal variation lines plotted on a Mercator projection of the Earth. Along each isogonal line, the magnetic variation remains the same.[3] Note that because the Earth's magnetic poles are shifting by about 10 miles a year, the isogonic lines of variation are not fixed, and must be replotted periodically on navigational charts.

Also in Figure 12.8, you can see that the North Magnetic Pole is located over Canada, and that there are some lines of 0°, or no magnetic variation, which are called the agonic lines. As you move west past the Great Lakes, your compass north will shift eastward from the Earth's geographic north pole, while if you move east past the Great Lakes, your compass north will shift westward. The exact number of degrees your compass north will shift

---

[3] The term isogonal, sometimes called isogonic, means having equal angles.

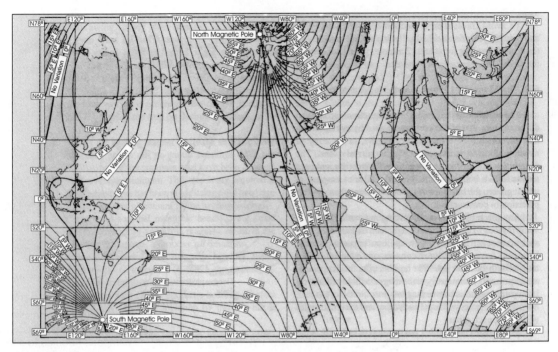

Figure 12.8
Isogonic Chart:
Worldwide magnetic
variation angles are
plotted along
isogonal lines.

can be determined by looking at the figure. Thus, Denver has about a 11°
east magnetic variation from true north, meaning that if you were flying and
your compass showed a reading of 0° (or due north), you would be actually
flying on a true course of 11 degrees, with regard to the geographic north
pole. Likewise, if you were flying on a compass heading of 259° over Denver,
your true course would be 270° (see figure 12.9).

Figure 12.9
True Heading is
different from Magnetic
Heading. Example:
Flying a compass
heading of 259° over
Denver with E11°
Magnetic Variation,
your True Heading
would be 270°.

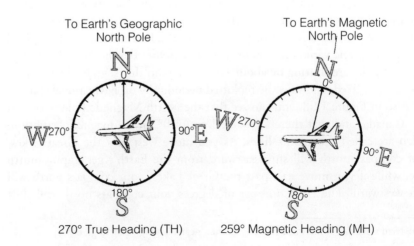

Deviation

Aircraft and ships have magnetic fields of their own that can cause a compass to deflect from magnetic north. This phenomena is known as deviation, and it must be accounted for when determining course headings. If the compass needle points east of the magnetic pole, the deviation is easterly; if the needle points west of the magnetic pole, the deviation is westerly. In *Flight Simulator*, deviation is not modeled in the simulation, so you don't need to account for this kind of compass error.

Magnetic Heading (MH), True Heading (TH)

An aircraft's heading, or azimuth angle, is expressed in degrees clockwise from north, either as a true heading (TH), or as a magnetic heading (MH). When the angle your aircraft is flying is measured clockwise from the Earth's geographic north pole, it is called a true heading. However, when the angle is measured from the Earth's magnetic pole, it is called magnetic heading. Both angles are illustrated in Figures 12.9 and 12.10.

On most navigational maps, the courses are usually printed as magnetic courses, meaning that you just fly the aircraft on the given compass heading as it appears on your magnetic compass or directional gyro. When you use these navigational charts, you needn't bother with worrying about where true north is.

Where you do need to worry about true north and magnetic variation is when you calculate your own great circle courses. The great circle course azimuth is always calculated as a true heading. You then need to convert this true heading to magnetic heading in order to fly the proper great circle track using your compass. The next section teaches you how to do this.

Great circle courses are measured from true north, not magnetic north. Before flying a great circle track, you must first convert the true heading to magnetic heading; only then can you use your magnetic compass or directional gyro to fly the course given.

Conversion of True Heading to Magnetic Heading

To convert from true heading to magnetic heading, follow these steps:

1. If your magnetic variation is east, you subtract the variation angle for the area from your true course to arrive at your magnetic heading.

   Or

2. If your magnetic variation is west, you add the variation angle for the area to your true course to arrive at your magnetic heading. You can easily remember both these rules by the following memory aid:

   "East is Least, and West is Best."

So subtract for east variations, and add for west variations!

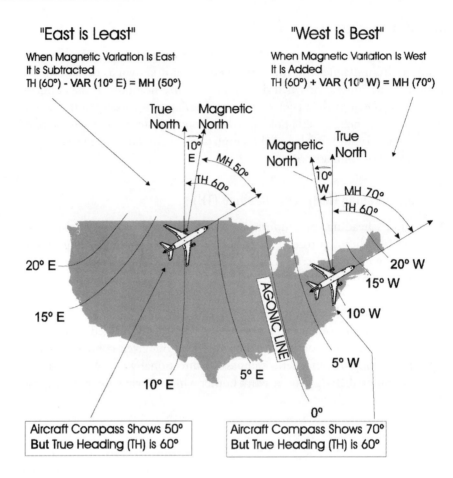

Figure 12.10
Calculating Magnetic
Heading from True
Heading using
Magnetic Variation
Lines

Let's look at an example of converting true heading to magnetic heading, using the magnetic variation chart. Examining Figure 12.10, we see that the aircraft on the left is flying over a 10° E magnetic variation line on a true course heading of 60°. What is the magnetic heading that this aircraft needs to fly using its compass? Well following the rule, "East is Least," you subtract 10° E VAR (variation) from 60° TH (true heading) to get 50° MH (magnetic heading). So to fly on this course, you would turn the aircraft until your directional gyro or compass reads 50°.

Now let's look at what happens when the aircraft is flying over a west magnetic variation line. In Figure 12.10, you can see that the aircraft on the right wants to fly on a 60° TH. Since the aircraft is over a 10° W magnetic variation line, you use the rule "West is Best." Thus, you add 10° W VAR to the 60° TH to obtain 70° MH. So to fly the aircraft on a true course of 60°, you would need to turn the aircraft to a compass reading of 70°.

Determining Great Circle Courses from Two Latitude/Longitude Points

To understand how great circle course angles are computed, it is helpful to understand some of the spherical trigonometry involved. A spherical triangle is that part of the surface of a sphere bounded by three arcs of great circles. There are three sides to the triangle; the sum of the arc lengths of these sides is less than 180°. The sum of the three interior angles is between 180° and 540°. The following rules apply to spherical triangles:

1. The sum of any two sides is greater than the third side.
2. If two sides are equal, the angles opposite are equal.
3. If two angles are equal, the sides opposite are equal.
4. If two sides are unequal, the angles opposite are unequal.
5. If two angles are unequal, the sides opposite are unequal, and the greater side is opposite the greater angle.

The solution of the spherical triangle is made by using Napier's analogies and the law of sines, but the derivation, proofs, and application are far beyond the scope of this book. Just to give you a basic idea of how it works; if you know the lengths of two sides of a spherical triangle (i.e., 90° − the latitudes of two cities; this is often called the *colatitude*), and the angle between them (i.e., the difference in longitude between the two cities), you can calculate the inside angles of the triangle. The inside angles are then converted to true heading, and then to magnetic heading, which is the great circle course you fly using your compass.

To compute your magnetic course heading, given two longitude/latitude points, you must perform the following procedures:

1. Compute the azimuth angle *C* of the terrestrial triangle.
2. Convert the azimuth angle *C* to a true heading.
3. Convert the true heading to a magnetic heading. Your magnetic heading is the initial great circle compass heading to take at departure, but this angle changes along your route.

The next few sections teach you how to perform the above steps. However, before we begin, let's first define the terrestrial triangle and have a look at it.

The Terrestrial Triangle

The terrestrial triangle, which is used for computing great circle headings, is the special case of a spherical triangle whose vertices are any two points and the North Pole (or South Pole). Figure 12.11 shows one such terrestrial triangle, where *P* is the North Pole, *1* is the point of departure, and *2* is the

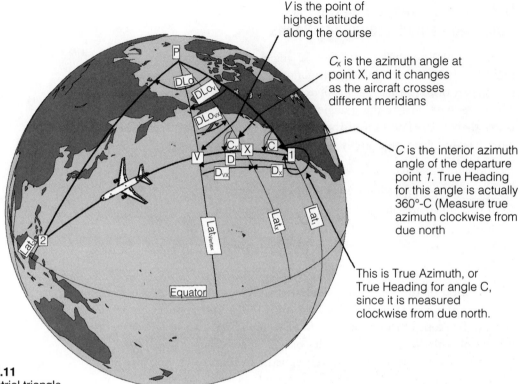

V is the point of highest latitude along the course

C$_x$ is the azimuth angle at point X, and it changes as the aircraft crosses different meridians

C is the interior azimuth angle of the departure point *1*. True Heading for this angle is actually 360°-C (Measure true azimuth clockwise from due north

This is True Azimuth, or True Heading for angle C, since it is measured clockwise from due north.

Figure 12.11
The terrestrial triangle is a spherical triangle which has as its vertices any two points and the North Pole (or South Pole)

destination. In this diagram, the distance *D* is the arc length between the arrival and destination points. Notice that the great circle track along *D* is not a straight line, but that it reaches a maximum latitude, called the vertex *V*, and then falls away. Note that the vertex *V* does not have to be between point *1* and point *2*.

Calculating the Azimuth Angle *C* of the Terrestrial Triangle

The interior angle *C*, the azimuth angle, is the great circle heading at the point of departure, and this is the angle we wish to calculate. It is crucial that you understand that the azimuth angle *C* is not the same at some arbitrary point *X* along the great circle track *D*; rather it changes as your aircraft crosses different meridians! So, in order to fly a great circle track, you need to subdivide your path into 300 nautical mile segments, called rhumb lines, and recompute the angle *C* at waypoints separated by 300 miles.

To find *C*, measured in degrees, use this formula (make sure your calculator is running in degree mode, not radian mode):

$$C = \tan^{-1} \left(\frac{\sin DLo}{(\cos Lat_1 \tan Lat_2) - (\sin Lat_1 \cos DLo)} \right)$$

In the equation above, Lat_1 is the latitude of your departure point *1* and Lat_2 is the latitude of your destination point *2*. If the latitude of the destination point is in the opposite hemisphere from that of the departure point, then you treat Lat_2 as a negative quantity (example if Lat_1 = N45° and Lat_2 = S15°, then set Lat_2 = −15°, or if Lat_1 = S15° and Lat_2 = N45°, set Lat_2 = −45°).

The angle *DLo* is the difference of longitude of the departure point *1* and destination point *2*, which can be calculated by using the following formula:

$$DLo = | Long_2 - Long_1 |$$

except if

$$DLo > 180° \text{ then } DLo = 360° - | Long_2 - Long_1 |$$

The absolute sign in the above equation $||$ is used to change any negative numbers to a positive number (i.e., $|-45°| = 45°$). As with latitudes, treat $Long_2$ as a negative quantity if $Long_1$ is in the opposite hemisphere.

EXAMPLE PROBLEM: Find *DLo* between San Francisco and Paris.

SOLUTION: Since San Francisco has a western longitude at W122° 26', and Paris has an eastern longitude at E2° 20', they are in opposing hemispheres. Therefore, after converting to decimal longitude and changing the sign of $Long_2$ so that it is negative, we have $Long_1 = 122.43°$ (SF) and $Long_2 = -2.33°$ (Paris). Therefore:

$$DLo = | Long_2 - Long_1 |$$
$$DLo = | -2.33° - 122.43° | = 124.76°.$$

EXAMPLE PROBLEM: Find *DLo* between Rio de Janeiro and Sydney, Australia.

SOLUTION: Since Rio de Janeiro has a western longitude at W43° 10', and Sydney has an eastern longitude at E151° 12', they are in opposing hemispheres. Therefore, converting to decimal longitude and changing the sign of $Long_2$ so that it is negative, we have $Long_1 = 43.17°$ (Rio de Janeiro) and $Long_2 = -151.2°$ (Sydney). Therefore:

$$DLo = | Long_2 - Long_1 |$$
$$DLo = | -151.2° - 43.17° | = 194.37°.$$

But since *DLo* > 180°

$$DLo = | Long_2 - Long_1 | = 360° - 194.37° = 165.63°.$$

You must convert negative arctan results to positive angular equivalents. Therefore if $C<0°$, you must add 180° to it so that it becomes the positive angular equivalent.

There is one other important thing to remember. The tan function is a periodic function that repeats itself every 180°. Your calculator can only return arctan values of C that fall between ±90°, even though $\tan(-45°) = \tan 135°$. You must convert C to its equivalent positive C angle. To do this, if you obtain a negative value of C, just add 180° to obtain its positive counterpart.

$$\text{If } C < 0° \text{ then } C_{\text{positive tan angle equivalent}} = C + 180°$$

Converting Azimuth Angle to True Azimuth (True Heading)

Once you have obtained your interior azimuth angle C (and made sure that it is positive), you must convert this angle to a true azimuth, which is the same thing as a true heading (TH). The true azimuth is measured clockwise from due north of point 1 to the intersection of the great circle track between 1 and 2, as shown in Figure 12.11. Note that if you were traveling from point 2 to point 1, your interior azimuth angle C would be located at point 2, and your true heading would be measured clockwise from due north at point 2.

Hemisphere and Direction of Flight Ambiguity Rules

To resolve the ambiguities involved in determining true headings, because of the direction of your travel and the hemisphere you are in, we will present some rules for you to follow below.

Ambiguity Rules:

1. If you are traveling from east to west in the Northern Hemisphere:

$$C_{\text{True Heading}} = 360° - C$$

2. If you are traveling from west to east in the Northern Hemisphere:

$$C_{\text{True Heading}} = C$$

3. If you are traveling from west to east in the Southern Hemisphere:

$$C_{\text{True Heading}} = C + 180°$$

4. If you are traveling from east to west in the Southern Hemisphere:

$$C_{\text{True Heading}} = 180° - C$$

Converting True Heading to Magnetic Heading

Now that you have your true heading, you need to convert this to a magnetic heading before you can fly the great circle track using your compass. To do this, you must add your west magnetic variation ("west is best"), or subtract your east magnetic variation ("east is least") from your true heading.

$$C_{Magnetic\ Heading} = C_{True\ Heading} - East\ Magnetic\ Variation$$

or

$$C_{Magnetic\ Heading} = C_{True\ Heading} + West\ Magnetic\ Variation$$

You can find your magnetic variation for most any city by looking up the nearest VOR station in Appendix B. For locations that are not listed in Appendix B, you can look up the magnetic variation for the nearest isogonal line in the Isogonic Chart of Figure 12.8. Then, factor in the distance from your location to the isogonal line. For example, if you are located midway between a 5°E and a 10°E isogonal line, use 7.5°E as your magnetic variation.

Consult the VOR station list in Appendix B to find your magnetic variation for any departure city, or use the Isogonic Chart of Figure 12.8.

Examples: Great Circle Azimuth Calculations

The following great circle example calculations will help you understand how to plot your own azimuth angles for your trips.

EXAMPLE PROBLEM: Calculate the initial magnetic heading for a great circle flight from San Francisco to Hawaii, and from Hawaii to San Francisco. Use only nearest degree measurements.

SOLUTION: From San Francisco (N37° W122°)to Hawaii (N21° W158°):

$$C = \tan^{-1} \left(\frac{\sin DLo}{(\cos Lat_1 \tan Lat_2) - (\sin Lat_1 \cos DLo)} \right)$$

$$= \tan^{-1} \left(\frac{\sin |W158° - W122°|}{(\cos N37° \tan N21°) - (\sin N37° \cos |W158° - W122°|)} \right)$$

$$= -73° \text{ but since } C < 0 \text{ add } 180°$$

$$C = 107°$$

Because the arctan function only returns values between $+90°$ and $-90°$, we will need to convert the $-73°$ into its positive counterpart; to do this simply add $180° + (-73°) = 107°$ (because $\tan -73° = \tan 107°$). Now to convert $C = 107°$ to a true course heading, we note that the flight is in the Northern

Hemisphere, and that it is from east to west. Therefore we use the Ambiguity Rule 1 to determine true heading:

$$C_{True\ Heading} = 360° - C = 360° - 107° = 253°$$

Since San Francisco has a E17° magnetic variation, to get your magnetic heading to Hawaii, you subtract 253° − 17° = 236°. So to fly to Hawaii, your initial great circle compass heading should be C=236°.

Traveling the reverse direction, from Hawaii to San Francisco, we have

$$C = \tan^{-1}\left(\frac{\sin DLo}{(\cos Lat_1 \tan Lat_2) - (\sin Lat_1 \cos DLo)} \right)$$

$$= \tan^{-1}\left(\frac{\sin |W122° - W158°|}{(\cos N21° \tan N37°) - (\sin N21° \cos |W122° - W158°|)} \right)$$

$$= -55°$$

Remember that, in the above equation, you must take the absolute value of DLo such that

$$DLo\,|W122° - W158°| = |-36°| = 36°$$

Because this flight is in the Northern Hemisphere and is from west to east, you use Ambiguity Rule 2:

$$C_{True\ Heading} = C = 55°$$

However, you'll still need to correct for magnetic variation. The magnetic variation for Honolulu is E11°, so you'll subtract 55° −11° = 44°. Thus your initial great circle compass heading from Hawaii to San Francisco is $C = 44°$.

> EXAMPLE PROBLEM: Calculate the initial magnetic heading for a great circle flight from New York's JFK airport to London's Heathrow, and from Heathrow back to JFK. Use nearest minutes measurement.
>
> SOLUTION: First convert New York's JFK (N40° 38' W73° 46') and London's Heathrow (N51° 29' W000° 28') coordinates to their decimal equivalents. Then plug these coordinates into

$$C = \tan^{-1}\left(\frac{\sin DLo}{(\cos Lat_1 \tan Lat_2) - (\sin Lat_1 \cos DLo)} \right)$$

$$= \tan^{-1}\left(\frac{\sin |W00.47° - W73.77°|}{(\cos N40.63° \tan N51.29°) - (\sin N40.63° \cos |W00.47° - W73.77°|)} \right)$$

$$= 51.34°$$

Because this flight is in the Northern Hemisphere and is from west to east, you use Ambiguity Rule 2:

$$C_{True\ Heading} = C = 51.34°$$

However, you'll still need to correct for magnetic variation. The magnetic variation for JFK is W12°, so you'll add 51.34° + 12° = 63.34°. Thus your initial great circle compass heading from JFK to Heathrow is C = 63.34°.

Returning from Heathrow to JFK,

$$C = \tan^{-1}\left(\frac{\sin DLo}{(\cos Lat_1 \tan Lat_2) - (\sin Lat_1 \cos DLo)} \right)$$

$$= \tan^{-1}\left(\frac{\sin |W73.77° - W00.47°|}{(\cos N51.29° \tan N40.63°) - (\sin N51.29° \cos |W73.77° - W00.47°|)} \right)$$

$$= 72.09°$$

Since this trip is in the Northern Hemisphere, and is from east to west, we use Ambiguity Rule 1:

$$C_{True\ Heading} = 360° - C = 360° - 72.09° = 287.91°$$

To correct for variation, we note that Heathrow's magnetic variation is W4°, so we add 287.91° + 4° = 291.91°. Thus the initial great circle compass heading from Heathrow to JFK is 291.91°.

EXAMPLE PROBLEM: Calculate the initial magnetic heading for a flight from Rio de Janeiro to Sydney, Australia, and from Sydney back to Rio. Use coordinates to nearest degree.

SOLUTION: Solution: From Rio de Janeiro (S23° W43°)to Sydney (S34° E151°), the azimuth angle *C* is

$$C = \tan^{-1}\left(\frac{\sin DLo}{(\cos Lat_1 \tan Lat_2) - (\sin Lat_1 \cos DLo)} \right)$$

But since $DLo = |-E151° - W43°| = 194° > 180°$

$$DLo = 360° - |-E151° - W43°| = 360° - 194° = 166°$$

$$= \tan^{-1}\left(\frac{\sin (166°)}{(\cos S23° \tan S34°) - (\sin S23° \cos 166°)} \right)$$

$$= 14°$$

Now to convert *C*=14° to a true course heading, we note that the flight is in the Southern Hemisphere, and that it is from west to east. Therefore we use Ambiguity Rule 3 to determine true heading:

$$C_{True\ Heading} = C + 180° = 14° + 180° = 194°$$

Since Rio de Janeiro has a W21° magnetic variation, to get your magnetic heading to Sydney, you add 194° + 21° = 215°. To fly to Sydney, your initial great circle compass heading would thus be $C = 215°$. This course will take you over the Antarctic polar region. Of course, after crossing the polar regions, your azimuth angle C will be totally different from your initial angle at departure.

Traveling the reverse direction, from Sydney to Rio de Janeiro, we have

$$C = \tan^{-1}\left(\frac{\sin DLo}{(\cos Lat_1 \tan Lat_2) - (\sin Lat_1 \cos DLo)} \right)$$

But since $DLo = |-W43° - E151°| = 194° > 180°$

$$DLo = 360° - |-W43° - E151°| = 360° - 194° = 166°$$

$$= \tan^{-1}\left(\frac{\sin(166°)}{(\cos S34° \tan S23°) - (\sin S34° \cos 166°)} \right)$$

$$= 15°$$

Because this flight is in the Southern Hemisphere and is from east to west, you use Ambiguity Rule 4:

$$C_{True\ Heading} = 180° - C = 180° - 15° = 165°$$

You'll still need to correct for magnetic variation, though. The magnetic variation for Sydney is E12°, so you'll subtract 165° + 12° = 153°. Thus, your initial great circle compass heading from Sydney to Rio de Janeiro is $C = 153°$, which again brings you over the Antarctic polar region.

Calculating the Magnetic Heading between VOR/NDB Stations

The same techniques you learned in the previous section can be applied to calculating magnetic headings between VOR/NDB stations. By using this method, you can fly between any VOR/NDB station plotted on the maps in Appendix B. In effect, you can fly anywhere in the world, and create your own flight plans, all without any additional maps!

Let's see how this is done for a trip between Seattle and Portland.

EXAMPLE PROBLEM: Find the magnetic course heading between Seattle and Portland.

SOLUTION: In Appendix B, look up Figure B.1, which is a map index for the USA. On this map, you can see that the Seattle-Portland area is covered by Map 4. So turn to Map 4 in Appendix B, and find Seattle and Portland. You can see that Seattle has its own VOR station, as does Portland. Next, look up the latitude/longitude points for the two VOR stations in the VOR station list for the USA, also in Appendix B. You'll also want to write down the magnetic variation for Seattle, which is your departure point. Following the procedure from the previous section, where Seattle's coordinates are N47° 26' W122 18' with a magnetic variation of E22°, and Portland's coordinates are N45° 35' W122° 36', we first convert the coordinates to decimal equivalents and then solve for C:

$$C = \tan^{-1}\left(\frac{\sin DLo}{(\cos Lat_1 \tan Lat_2) - (\sin Lat_1 \cos DLo)}\right)$$

$$= \tan^{-1}\left(\frac{\sin|W122.6° - W122.3°|}{(\cos N47.43° \tan N45.583°) - (\sin N47.43° \cos|W122.6° - W122.3°|)}\right)$$

$$= -6.477°$$

Since $C < 0°$, we add 180° so that $C = 173.5°$ (we need to express C as a positive angle, and since $\tan(-6.477°) = \tan 173.5°$, this is the angle C's positive angular equivalent).

Next, to convert C to a true heading, we note that the flight is from east to west (because Seattle is slightly east of Portland); therefore we use the following Ambiguity Rule 1 for east-west flights:

$$C_{True\ Heading} = 360° - C = 360° - 173.5° = 186.5°$$

and finally, converting to magnetic heading

$$C_{Magnetic\ Heading} = C_{True\ Heading} - East\ Magnetic\ Variation$$
$$= 186.5° - E22°$$
$$= 164.5°$$

So, when you take off from Seattle, you turn to a compass heading of 165° (round off 164.5° to 165°), and you're on your way to Portland!

Establishing Great Circle Waypoints
Every 300 Nautical Miles (Rhumb Lines)

This section demonstrates the mathematical formulas you use to compute great circle waypoints, so that you can fly 300 mile rhumb line approximations of a great circle track.

It's important to realize that the true course heading C that you computed in the previous section is only good at the point of departure. Great circle tracks do not maintain constant headings, so you must break a great circle into legs of up to 300 nautical miles, and then recompute the angle C for each new 300 nm segment (called rhumb lines).

To do this:

1. First calculate the initial great circle azimuth angle C between points *1* and *2*, using the equation

$$C = \tan^{-1}\left[\frac{\sin DLo}{(\cos Lat_1 \tan Lat_2) - (\sin Lat_1 \cos DLo)}\right]$$

2. Next calculate the latitude of the vertex Lat_{Vertex} at point V of the great circle. This point is the highest latitude that the great circle crosses, and it is always greater than or equal to Lat_1 or Lat_2 of your departure and arrival points. Note that the vertex doesn't have to be between points *1* and *2*, so your great circle track from point *1* point *2* may not go through the vertex.

$$Lat_{Vertex} = \cos^{-1}(\cos Lat_1 \sin C)$$

If the azimuth angle C is greater than 90°, the vertex is located away from point *1* in the opposite direction to point *2*. If this is the case, you follow this rule:

$$Lat_{Vertex} = -Lat_{Vertex}$$

3. Find the difference of longitude (DLo_v) of the vertex V and the point of departure *1*.

$$DLo_v = \sin^{-1}\left[\frac{\cos C}{(\sin Lat_{Vertex})}\right]$$

If the initial course angle C is less than 90°, the vertex is toward point *2*, but if C is greater than 90°, the vertex is in the opposite direction. This is important because you need to know which direction that DLo_v is measured from point *1* to the vertex V, so that you can add or subtract DLo_v as needed in your computations that follow.

4. Calculate the latitude for each of the waypoints X along great circle track D, measured from either side of the vertex V using

$$Lat_X = \sin^{-1}(\sin Lat_{Vertex} \cos D_{VX})$$

where D_{VX} is measured in 5° increments and is the distance between the vertex V and waypoint X along great circle track D. Thus, once you know what Lat_{Vertex} is from step 2, you create latitude waypoints on either side of the vertex by increasing D_{VX} in 5° increments until you pass through points *1* and *2*.

5. Now calculate the distance in longitude from the vertex *V* for each of the latitude waypoints you found in the previous step along great circle path *D*.

$$DLo_v = \sin^{-1}\left(\frac{\sin D_{VX}}{(\cos Lat_X)} \right)$$

6. Calculate the new azimuth angle that you need to turn your aircraft at each new waypoint X using this formula:

$$C_X = \cos^{-1}(\sin Lat_X \sin DLo_{VX})$$

7. Finally, pair the latitude longitude coordinates of the great circle waypoints you just calculated with the azimuth angles C_X. To obtain the actual longitudes, be sure to add $DLo_{VX} \pm$ longitude of your departure point, depending on which direction east or west you are traveling.

EXAMPLE PROBLEM: Find the latitude/longitude coordinates of waypoints between S.F. (N37° W122°) and Hawaii (N21° W157°) that are approximately 300 nautical miles apart. Then calculate the true course heading and magnetic course heading to Hawaii for each waypoint. By flying each 300 mile rhumb line segment, and turning your aircraft at each waypoint to the new magnetic course heading, you will fly the equivalent of a great circle track from S.F. to Hawaii:

SOLUTION: Following the step by step description above:

1. Calculate azimuth angle C at San Francisco departure:

$$C = \tan^{-1}\left(\frac{\sin DLo}{(\cos Lat_1 \tan Lat_2) - (\sin Lat_1 \cos DLo)} \right)$$

$$C = \tan^{-1}\left(\frac{\sin |W158° - W122°|}{(\cos N37° \tan N21°) - (\sin N37° \cos |W158° - W122°|)} \right)$$

$C = -73°$ but since $C < 0$ add 180°

$C = 108°$

Note that the true heading would be $360° - C = 253°$, and you would subtract 17° for the magnetic variation in SF to obtain a magnetic heading of 236°.

2. Find the latitude of the vertex V:

$$Lat_{Vertex} = \cos^{-1}(\cos Lat_1 \sin C)$$
$$= \cos^{-1}(\cos 37°\sin 107°) = 40°$$

Because the azimuth angle C is greater than 90°, the vertex is away from point 1 in the direction opposite from point 2. Thus, we use the rule:

$$Lat_{Vertex} = -Lat_{Vertex} = -40°$$

3. Find the difference in longitude between the vertex V and San Francisco:

$$DLo_v = \sin^{-1}\left(\frac{\cos C}{(\sin Lat_{Vertex})} \right)$$

$$= \sin^{-1}\left(\frac{\cos 107°}{(\sin -40°)} \right) = 27°$$

The longitude of the vertex, since it is away from point 1 in the opposite direction of point 2, is W122° − 27° = W95°.

4. Calculate the latitude of waypoints X_n along D, measured in 5° increments, starting from San Francisco (i.e., start $D_{VX_1} = 27°$, $D_{VX_2} = 32°$, $D_{VX_3} = 37°$, $D_{VX_4} = 42°$, $D_{VX_5} = 47°$, $D_{VX_6} = 52°$):

$$Lat_X = \sin^{-1}(\sin Lat_{Vertex}\cos D_{VX})$$
$$Lat_{X_1} = \sin^{-1}(\sin -40°\cos 27°) = -35° = N35°$$
$$Lat_{X_2} = \sin^{-1}(\sin -40°\cos 32°) = -33° = N33°$$
$$Lat_{X_3} = \sin^{-1}(\sin -40°\cos 37°) = -31° = N31°$$
$$Lat_{X_4} = \sin^{-1}(\sin -40°\cos 42°) = -29° = N29°$$
$$Lat_{X_5} = \sin^{-1}(\sin -40°\cos 47°) = -26° = N26°$$
$$Lat_{X_6} = \sin^{-1}(\sin -40°\cos 52°) = -23° = N23°$$

5. Now calculate the difference in longitude between the vertex V and the location X_n of the above waypoints, and then calculate the longitude position:

$$DLo_{VX} = \sin^{-1}\left(\frac{\sin D_{VX}}{(\cos Lat_X)} \right)$$

$$DLo_{VX_1} = \sin^{-1}\left(\frac{\sin D_{VX_1}}{(\cos Lat_{X_1})} \right) = \sin^{-1}\left(\frac{\sin 27°}{(\cos -35°)} \right) = 34°; \; Long_{X_1} = Long_{Vertex} + DLo_{VX_1} = W95° + 34° = W129°$$

$$DLo_{VX_2} = \sin^{-1}\left(\frac{\sin D_{VX_2}}{(\cos Lat_{X_2})} \right) = \sin^{-1}\left(\frac{\sin 32°}{(\cos -33°)} \right) = 39°; \; Long_{X_2} = Long_{Vertex} + DLo_{VX_2} = W95° + 39° = W134°$$

$$DLo_{VX_3} = \sin^{-1}\left(\frac{\sin D_{VX_3}}{(\cos Lat_{X_3})}\right) = \sin^{-1}\left(\frac{\sin 37°}{(\cos -31°)}\right) = 45°; \; Long_{X_3} = Long_{Vertex} + DLo_{VX_3} = W95° + 45° = W140°$$

$$DLo_{VX_4} = \sin^{-1}\left(\frac{\sin D_{VX_4}}{(\cos Lat_{X_4})}\right) = \sin^{-1}\left(\frac{\sin 42°}{(\cos -29°)}\right) = 50°; \; Long_{X_4} = Long_{Vertex} + DLo_{VX_4} = W95° + 50° = W145°$$

$$DLo_{VX_5} = \sin^{-1}\left(\frac{\sin D_{VX_5}}{(\cos Lat_{X_5})}\right) = \sin^{-1}\left(\frac{\sin 47°}{(\cos -26°)}\right) = 55°; \; Long_{X_5} = Long_{Vertex} + DLo_{VX_5} = W95° + 55° = W150°$$

$$DLo_{VX_6} = \sin^{-1}\left(\frac{\sin D_{VX_6}}{(\cos Lat_{X_6})}\right) = \sin^{-1}\left(\frac{\sin 52°}{(\cos -23°)}\right) - 59°; \; Long_{X_6} = Long_{Vertex} + DLo_{VX_6} = W95° + 59° = W154°$$

6. Calculate the azimuth angles for each waypoint. We get:

$$C_X = \cos^{-1}(\sin Lat_{Vertex}\sin DLo_{VX})$$

$$C_{X_1} = \cos^{-1}(\sin Lat_{Vertex}\sin DLo_{VX_1}) = \cos^{-1}(\sin -40°\sin 34°) = 111°; \; C_{TrueHeadingX_1} = 360° - 111° = 249°$$

$$C_{X_2} = \cos^{-1}(\sin Lat_{Vertex}\sin DLo_{VX_2}) = \cos^{-1}(\sin -40°\sin 39°) = 114°; \; C_{TrueHeadingX_2} = 360° - 114° = 246°$$

$$C_{X_3} = \cos^{-1}(\sin Lat_{Vertex}\sin DLo_{VX_3}) = \cos^{-1}(\sin -40°\sin 45°) = 117°; \; C_{TrueHeadingX_3} = 360° - 117° = 243°$$

$$C_{X_4} = \cos^{-1}(\sin Lat_{Vertex}\sin DLo_{VX_4}) = \cos^{-1}(\sin -40°\sin 50°) = 120°; \; C_{TrueHeadingX_4} = 360° - 120° = 240°$$

$$C_{X_5} = \cos^{-1}(\sin Lat_{Vertex}\sin DLo_{VX_5}) = \cos^{-1}(\sin -40°\sin 55°) = 122°; \; C_{TrueHeadingX_5} = 360° - 122° = 238°$$

$$C_{X_6} = \cos^{-1}(\sin Lat_{Vertex}\sin DLo_{VX_6}) = \cos^{-1}(\sin -40°\sin 59°) = 123°; \; C_{TrueHeadingX_6} = 360° - 123° = 237°$$

7. Pairing the waypoint coordinates, we get:

Rhumb Line Approximation of Great Circle Track S.F. to Hawaii: Coordinates and Headings							
Waypoint X_N	S.F.	X_1	X_2	X_3	X_4	X_5	X_6
Lat/Long	N37° W122°	N35° W129°	N33° W134°	N31° W140°	N29° W145°	N26° W150°	N23° W154°
True Heading	$C = 253°$	$C_{X_1} = 249°$	$C_{X_2} = 246°$	$C_{X_3} = 243°$	$C_{X_4} = 240°$	$C_{X_5} = 238°$	$C_{X_6} = 237°$
Magnetic Heading (MH)	$= C$ -17°E MH = 236°	$= C_{X_1}$ -16°E MH = 233°	$= C_{X_2}$ -15°E MH = 231°	$= C_{X_3}$ -16°E MH = 227°	$= C_{X_4}$ -14°E MH = 226°	$= C_{X_5}$ - 14°E MH =224°	$= C_{X_6}$ -13°E MH =224°

It is important to realize that you still need to convert the true heading C_x for each waypoint above to the magnetic heading (MH), if you are to use your compass to fly the course. Therefore, you must consult the isogonic magnetic variation chart of Figure 12.8, to determine what the variation is for each of the waypoints, then subtract the variation from C_x to get your compass heading. The last row of the table on the previous page shows the proper magnetic headings for each waypoint X_n.

In conclusion, if you fly from San Francisco to point X_1, and then to X_2, X_3, X_4, X_5, X_6, and finally on to Hawaii, you will be flying 320 nautical mile rhumb line approximations of the great circle track from S.F. to Hawaii.

Distance to the Visible Horizon

If you've ever wondered how far you can see to the visible horizon for a given altitude, you can use this formula:

$$Distance\ to\ the\ Visible\ Horizon = 1.17 \times \sqrt{Altitude\ (feet)}$$

Thus, if you are at 40,000 feet, you should be able to see as far as 234 nautical miles all around you.

Pilotage

The most basic method of navigation is called pilotage. In this method you navigate using only a chart and fly from one visible landmark to another. The flight must be conducted during the day at comparatively low altitudes so that landmarks can be easily seen. Because pilotage relies upon line of sight recognition of landmarks, poor visibility in bad weather, or night flying is ruled out. Its main advantage over all other navigational methods is that it is easy and requires no special skills or equipment. Aside from not being able to fly under conditions of low visibility, the pilotage method's main drawback is that you often cannot fly a direct course and must follow a zigzag route from landmark to landmark. For example, if you fly from San Francisco to Los Angles using the coastline to orient yourself, your route will not be the most direct or shortest because of the curvature of the coast.

Use visible landmarks to navigate using the pilotage method.

When flying under the pilotage method, use highways, railways, coastlines, major power transmission lines, aqueducts, rivers and lakes as visual references to be checked against your chart. Be very careful when flying over large stretches of water or land that have no reference points to check with on your map. You can easily become disoriented and get lost. For this reason, pilotage should not be relied upon exclusively to navigate the aircraft.

Dead Reckoning

Dead reckoning refers to the technique of navigation by computations based on airspeed, course heading, wind direction and speed, ground speed, and elapsed time. Most VFR (visual flying rules) flying is based on a combination of dead reckoning and pilotage. During the course of a flight, the airplane's position is calculated by dead reckoning, and then corrected for errors by visually checking for nearby landmarks.

To effectively use dead reckoning, you must know what the wind speed and direction is. Knowing your aircraft speed and course heading, you can then plot your aircraft's motion on a map using vectors to correct for the amount of deviation caused by the wind.

Let's see how dead reckoning works. In Figure 12.12 you can see that an airplane flying at an airspeed of 120 knots in calm air will have a groundspeed of exactly 120 knots. At the end of one hour, your aircraft will have covered 120 nautical miles. But, if there is a tailwind of 20 knots in the direction of the aircraft's heading, the speed of the aircraft over the ground will jump to 140 knots, even though the airspeed indicator may still show only 120 knots. This is because the wind carries the airplane allowing with it, boosting its speed by 20 knots. Likewise, if there is an opposing headwind of 20 knots, the aircraft's groundspeed will fall to 100 knots, though the airspeed indicator may still show an airspeed of 120 knots.

Armed with this information, if you were planning a flight with an airspeed of 120 knots, and knew that there was a tailwind of 20 knots, you would know that by the end of 1 hour you will have traveled not 120 nautical miles, but *140* nautical miles. This is because the aircraft's true groundspeed was boosted by the 20 knot windspeed.

If the wind is blowing *perpendicular* to the aircraft's heading (called a crosswind), then not only will the aircraft speed change but also its heading will deviate from

Using the dead reckoning method, you can compute your position by deducing where it should be after a given amount of time, based on the aircraft's speed and direction, corrected for wind drift.

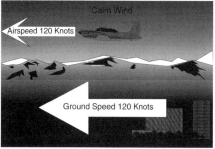

No Wind

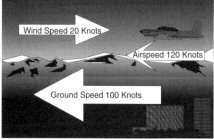

20 Knot Headwind

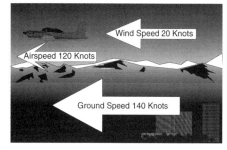

20 Knot Tailwind

Figure 12.12 Airspeed vs. groundspeed

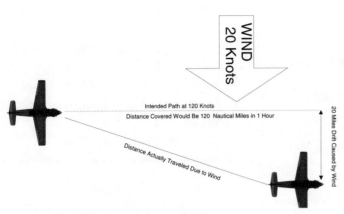

Figure 12.13 Effect of wind in one hour

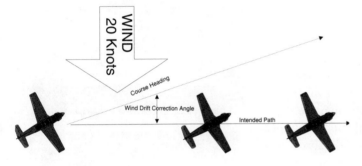

Figure 12.14 Correcting wind drift by turning into the wind

your intended path. Figure 12.13 shows the effect of a 20 knot cross-wind on the aircraft after 1 hour. As you can see, the plane is blown off course by 20 miles from its intended destination.

To correct this drift, you turn the aircraft's nose in the direction of the wind, as illustrated in Figure 12.14. If the crosswind is from the right, the airplane will drift to the left, and you must therefore head the airplane sufficiently to the right to counteract the wind. If the wind is from the left, you must turn the airplane to the left, or slightly into the wind. This technique of turning into the wind to correct your course is called "crabbing."

Radio Navigation Using VOR/NDB Stations

The next section discusses how the VOR and NDB radio beacons work, and how they are used to navigate in *Flight Simulator*.

VOR (Very High Frequency Omnirange Radio Beacons)

The over 1,200 VOR radio beacons in the United States form the backbone of aeronautical radio navigation today. Transmitting signals in the VHF band between 108 MHz and 118 MHz, these ground based stations provide reference points from which aircraft equipped with special VOR radios can situate themselves. Some of the advantages of VOR radios are:

- Static Free Reception in all kinds of weather.
- Course Radials provide precise heading information for navigation.
- When receiving two or more VORs, a coordinate fix, or line of position, can be determined quickly.

VORs do have some drawbacks. They are strictly line-of-sight, meaning that their signal can be blocked by the curvature of the Earth, or by mountains.

Because of this, VOR's do not provide worldwide coverage and are therefore useless for transoceanic voyages.

There are three classes of VORs. The T (Terminal) VOR has a normal usable range of 25 nautical miles at altitudes of 12,000 feet and below. It is used for short range purposes adjacent to airports or in terminal areas for instrument approaches. The L (Low Altitude) VOR sends out signals for 40 nautical miles at altitudes of 18,000 feet and below. The H (High Altitude) VOR transmits for 100 nautical miles between 14,500 and 17,999 feet, and 130 nautical miles between 18,000 and 45,000 feet. In Flight Simulator, the VOR range is limited to 80 miles, although in the real world VOR night time coverage can extend as far as 200 miles. Appendix B lists all the VOR stations that are found in Flight Simulator 5.1.

Figure 12.15 shows a map of the VOR installations for the United States.

How VOR Navigation Works

Each VOR station sends out a signal that can be segmented into radials in all 360 degrees of the compass. The signal is rotated electronically at 1800 RPM, and its beam flashes out in a circular pattern, much like a lighthouse. There are two components to the signal; one which is in phase with magnetic north, the other which is out of phase to a varying degree in all other

> ✈
> The VOR range in FS
> 5.1 is limited to 80
> nautical miles.

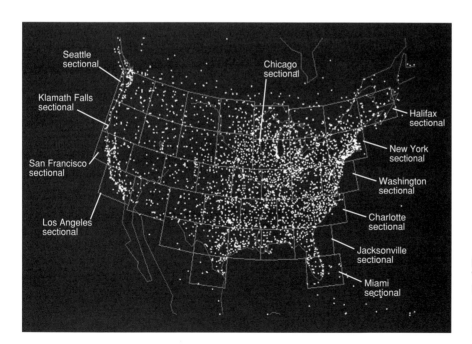

Figure 12.15
VOR stations for the
United States
*(Courtesy of Terry
Carraway and Tom
Canafax)*

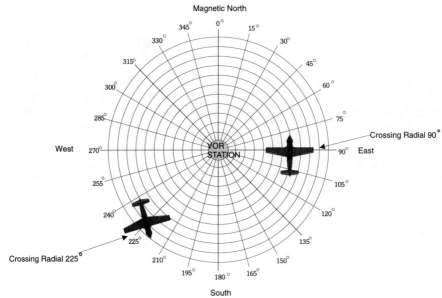

Figure 12.9 VOR radials

Only the NAV 1/OBI 1 radio can be used with *both* VOR and ILS radio beacons. The NAV 2/OBI 2 can *only* be used with VOR stations.

directions. All the VOR receiver does is measure the phase difference of the two signals and then calculate the correct radial direction to display on the OBI (Omni-Bearing Indicator).

Setting the NAV Radios

The NAV 1 radio is used in conjunction with the OBI 1 display, while the NAV 2 radio is used with the OBI 2 display. Note that the NAV 1/OBI 1 radio can be used to tune in VOR *or* ILS stations, but that the NAV 2/OBI 2 radio can be used *only* with VOR stations.

To tune in a VOR station, first look up the VOR frequency on your chart for the VOR station you wish to use. Then click on the integer portion of the NAV radio frequency indicator to adjust the frequency. Click on the right hand side above the decimal to increase the frequency, or click on the left of the numbers to decrease the frequency. For the fractional part of the frequency, click on the right to increase the frequency, and to the left, above the decimal point, to decrease. If you prefer to use the keyboard, see Appendix C for a list of the keyboard strokes necessary to adjust the radio frequency.

VOR stations broadcast their signals with a power output of 200 watts and, in the frequencies *between 108.0 MHz to 112.0 MHz*, have their frequency assignments set to *even* tenth decimals to avoid conflict with ILS stations. Thus, for example, VOR stations can have frequencies of 109.0, 109.2, 109.4, etc., while ILS stations are assigned *odd* tenth decimals, such as 109.1, 109.3, 109.5, etc. *Above 112.0 MHz,* the frequency assignment may be either even or odd tenth decimals, as for example Chicago's O'Hare International VOR which is set to 113.9 MHz.

Using the OBI Azimuth Display

The OBI azimuth display is used to project the VOR radial the aircraft is currently on. It also displays the deviation from the radial on a CDI (Course Deviation Indicator Needle), so that you can determine whether you are to the right or left of the specified VOR radial.

To determine the VOR radial you are currently on, follow these steps:

1. Using the NAV radio, tune in the VOR station by entering the proper frequency. (From the keyboard press N 1 followed by the + or − key)
2. Click the course indicator, or click on the *V* button to adjust the course until the CDI needle is centered. (From the keyboard, press V 1 followed by the + or − keys. To increment by tens of degrees, press Shift followed by the + or − keys.)
3. If the TO/FROM indicator shows *TO*, then you are on the radial shown by the *bottom* course indicator, and if you wanted to fly towards the VOR, you would turn the aircraft to the course heading shown on the top course indicator. If the TO/FROM indicator shows *FROM*, you are on the radial shown by the top course indicator. Note that this does *not* mean you are headed toward or away from the VOR station!

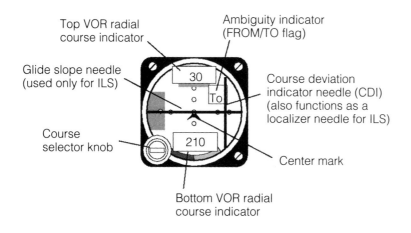

Top VOR radial course indicator

Ambiguity indicator (FROM/TO flag)

Glide slope needle (used only for ILS)

30

To

Course deviation indicator needle (CDI) (also functions as a localizer needle for ILS)

Course selector knob

210

Center mark

Bottom VOR radial course indicator

Figure 12.17 The OBI azimuth sisplay

VOR stations between 108 MHz and 112 MHz are tuned to even tenths on the frequency dial, while ILS stations on this band are tuned to odd tenths on the frequency dial. Above 112.0 MHz, VOR stations can have even or odd tenth decimals.

To select OBI 1, press V 1; to select OBI 2, press V 2. Follow this by pressing the + or − key to increase or decrease the course heading. To adjust the OBI course indicator in *tens of degrees* from the keyboard, hold down the Shift key and press the + or − keys to increase or decrease the course heading.

In the previous procedure for determining the VOR radial, if you are using the NAV 2/OBI 2, simply replace the [N][1] keystrokes with [N][2], and the [V][1] keystrokes with [V][2].

In the following example, you will learn how to tune in a VOR radial and see it displayed on your OBI indicator.

1. Start up FS 5.1 so that you are on the ground at Chicago's Meigs Field.

2. Select Chicago's O'Hare VOR by tuning in 113.9 MHz on the NAV 1 radio. Use the mouse to click on the frequency selector, or from the keyboard, press [N] followed by the [+] or [-] key to increase or decrease the integer portion of the frequency. Next, press [N][N] followed by the [+] or [-] key to increase or decrease the fractional portion of the frequency.

3. With the mouse, click the OBI display's course indicator until you see the CDI needle centered and the *TO* flag is lit. With the keyboard, press [V] followed by the [+] or [-] key to increase or decrease the course indicator.

4. When the CDI needle is centered and the *TO* flag is lit, your VOR radial is displayed on the *lower* course indicator as 119°. This is the direction *from* the VOR station to your plane, as measured from 0° magnetic north. The *top* course indicator showing a compass direction of 299° tells you the heading you would need to take if you wanted to fly *directly to* the O'Hare VOR station. If the *FROM* flag is lit, then simply reverse the course headings shown on the top and lower indicators so that the top reading is your direction from the VOR station, and the lower reading is your direction to the VOR station.

5. The DME 1 indicator shows that the Chicago O'Hare VOR station is exactly 15.5 nautical miles from your present location.

The TO/FROM Indicator

Also called the ambiguity indicator, the TO/FROM flags on the OBI tell you whether the displayed heading on the *top* course indicator will take the aircraft *TO* or *FROM* the station. It does *NOT* tell you whether the aircraft is heading to or from the station, as Figure 12.18 illustrates. When *TO* is displayed, the *top* course indicator shows the heading you would need to take to travel straight to the VOR station. When *FROM* is displayed, the *top* course indicator tells you the radial *from* the VOR station to your aircraft you are currently on.

Note that the *Microsoft Flight Simulator 5.1 Manual*, on page 142, incorrectly depicts the TO/FROM ambiguity flags. The top CDI indicator should display the FROM flag, and the needle should be to the right. The bottom CDI indicator should display the FROM flag, and the needle would then be correct.

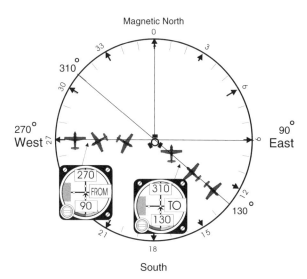

Figure 12.18
To/from ambiguity indicator and the relationship to the VOR station

TO/FROM Ambiguity Indicator and the Relationship to the VOR station

The Course Deviation Indicator (CDI)

The CDI, or course deviation indicator, is a needle that moves left and right on the OBI to tell you whether you are within 10° of a selected radial. When the needle deflects right, it tells you that you are to the *left* of the selected course radial (you need to turn right to get back on the radial). When the needle deflects left, it tells you are to the *right* of the selected course radial (you need to turn left to get back on the radial). Full needle deflection to the right or left, tells you that you are off from the displayed course indicator radial by *more* than 10°, in which case you need to adjust the course indicator setting until the needle is again centered.

There are several horizontal dots on either side of the center mark on the OBI. Each dot indicates a horizontal displacement from course of 200 feet per nautical mile. For example, at 30 nautical miles from the VOR station, one dot deflection means that the air-

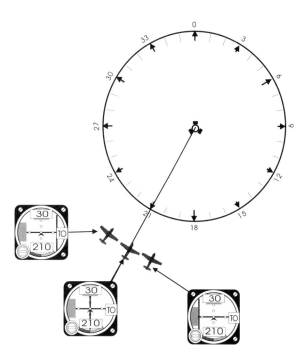

Figure 12.19
CDI Needle Deflection and relationship to course radial

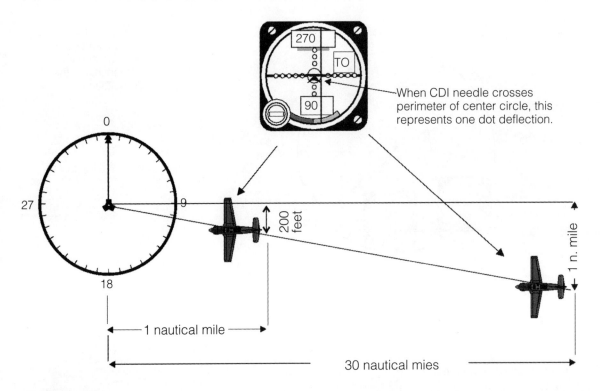

When CDI needle crosses perimeter of center circle, this represents one dot deflection.

Figure 12.20
When the CDI needle deflects by one dot on the scale, the Aircraft is off the VOR radial centerline by 200 feet for each mile from the VOR station.

craft is approximately 1 nautical mile off the side of the displayed course radial. Figure 12.20 shows how this works.

As you pass directly over a VOR station, the needle will fluctuate from side to side, and the *TO/FROM* indicators will change flags.

Understanding the DME Indicator

The DME, or Distance Measuring Equipment tells you the distance to the VOR station from your present location. It can also tell you your speed in relation to the VOR station. Note that the distance to the VOR station is measured in slant *range form; that is the distance from your plane directly to the VOR station.* This distance is *not* the same as your horizontal distance to the VOR station. For example, when flying directly over a VOR station at 6,000 feet, your DME distance is approximately *one nautical mile*, even though you are passing right over it.

By the same token, the DME speed is *not* the same as your ground speed. If you are traveling parallel to a VOR station, for example, your speed is measured in terms of how fast you are moving *towards* or *away* from the VOR station.

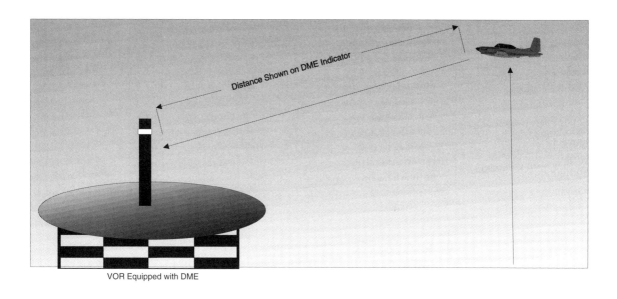

Figure 12.21
The DME indicator shows the diagonal distance to the VOR station, not the ground distance

When combined with the VOR radial information, the DME, makes it possible for you to know the exact geographic position of your aircraft.

To toggle between speed and range displays on the Cessna DME, press [F] followed by the [+] key.

Press [F] followed by the [+] key to toggle the Cessna DME indicator between speed and range displays.

Setting the Autopilot VOR Lock

The autopilot can be used to lock in a particular VOR station and fly the airplane towards it. This allows you to devote your attention to other important activities, such as looking out your window at the pretty scenery.

To set your autopilot to lock onto a VOR station via the menu, follow these steps:

1. Tune in the VOR station you want on the NAV 1 radio (This only works on the NAV 1 radio).

2. Select Autopilot from the Nav/Com menu.

3. In the Autopilot dialog box, click on the NAV 1 (Heading Hold) check box.

4. Select the Autopilot Switch list box, and highlight Connected.

5. Click OK to return to the simulation.

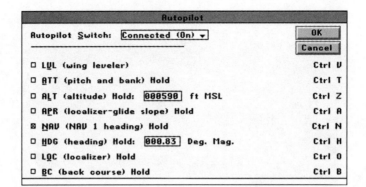

Figure 12.22
Using the autopilot to
lock onto a VOR radial

6. Keep the CDI needle centered by clicking on the course indicator. From the keyboard you can press [V] followed by the [+] key to increase the course, or the [-] key to decrease the course.

7. If you want to shut off the autopilot at any time, press [Z], or click on the autopilot indicator.

Alternatively, you can lock onto a VOR radial by using just keyboard commands:

1. Tune in the VOR station you want on the NAV 1 radio (this only works on the NAV 1 radio).

2. Press [Z] to activate the autopilot.

3. Press [Ctrl][N] to activate the VOR Lock.

4. Keep the CDI needle centered by clicking on the course indicator. From the keyboard you can press [V] followed by the [+] key to increase the course, or the [-] key to decrease the course.

5. If you want to shut off the autopilot at any time, press [Z], or click on the autopilot indicator.

Your airplane will now automatically follow a direct course for the VOR station you selected (as long as the CDI needle is centered!).

While in the Autopilot dialog box, you can also set the autopilot to lock in a particular altitude lock, and automatically level the wings for you. Just click on the autopilot check box options you want engaged, or press the keyboard shortcut, as displayed on the right side of Figure 12.22.

Using EFIS/CFPD for VOR and Altitude Tracking

Using the EFIS (Electronic Flight Information System)/CFPD (Command Flight Path Display), you can project the path to the VOR station on your cockpit windshield. To do this follow these steps:

1. Select EFIS/CFPD Display from the
    Nav/Com menu.

2. Next click on the EFIS Master Switch.

3. Toggle on the Lock to VOR 1 and Altitude
    Tracking radio button.

4. Select the Altitude (Feet Above Ground
    Level) text box and type in 5000. This will
    be the altitude in feet at which the CFPD
    display will appear.

5. Toggle on the Plot Intersecting Path check
    box.

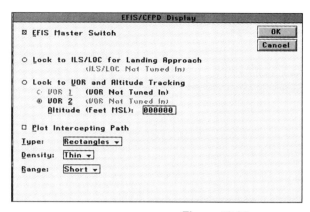

Figure 12.23
EFIS/CFPD dialog box

6. Choose Rectangles for the Type list box, although you can also choose
    telephone poles, or a yellow brick road.

7. Click the OK button.

When you return to the simulation, you will see bright red rectangles
showing you the way to the VOR station. All you need to do is fly through
them, one by one, until you reach the VOR station.

Using the VOR Tracking Method

VOR tracking is a technique used to navigate towards a VOR station, correcting for unknown wind drift forces. To track inbound towards a VOR
station, follow these steps:

1. On the NAV 1 radio, tune in the VOR station you want to home in on.

2. Click on the OBI course indicator until the CDI needle is centered and
    the *TO* flag is lit.

How to use the
EFIS/CFPD head-up
display to show VOR
radials.

CFPD
rectangles

Figure 12.24
Fly through the CFPD
red rectangles to get to
the VOR station

The VOR tracking
Method

3. Turn the aircraft until its course heading, as indicated on the directional gyro, is the same as is displayed on the OBI course indicator.

4. As you fly towards the VOR station, observe the CDI for deflection to the left or right. If the CDI deflects left, it means there is a crosswind from the *right*. If the CDI deflects right, it means there is a crosswind from the *left*.

5. Turn 20° *toward* the CDI needle. If the needle is on the left, turn your plane to a course heading 20° left of its present heading. If the needle is on the right, turn your plane to a course heading 20° right of its present heading.

6. When the CDI needle centers, reduce the drift correction by 10° and note whether this drift correction keeps the CDI needle centered. If not, reduce or increase the drift correction as necessary.

7. Keep the CDI needle centered, and soon you will fly over the VOR station, as will be indicated when the needle makes a full deflection from side to side, and the *TO/FROM* flag changes.

Figure 12.25
VOR tracking

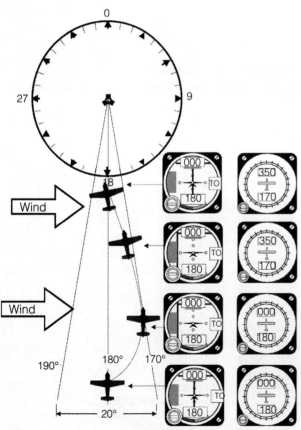

Figure 12.25 illustrates the technique of VOR tracking.

Using Two VORs to Get a Position Fix

Because Flight Simulator provides two NAV radios and corresponding OBIs, you can tune in two different VOR stations and obtain a position fix. By plotting on a navigational map the intersection of the two VOR radials you are currently on, you can accurately determine your coordinates. The procedure is quite simple and is illustrated in Figure 12.26. To simplify matters, in order to use this method, you should have *both FROM* indicators lit, and you should obtain your course radials from the *top* of each OBI course indicator.

Use both NAV 1/OBI 1 and NAV 2/OBI 2 navigational radios to get a position fix from two separate VOR stations.

Let's try to fix our position on the runway at Meigs Field. Follow these steps and then examine Figure 12.26 to check out your results:

1. Tune in your VOR 1 radio to DuPage VOR on a frequency of 108.4 MHz. Set with the mouse, or press N followed by the + or − key for the integer part of the frequency and N N followed by the + or − key for the fractional part of the frequency.

2. Adjust the course indicator on OBI 1 until the CDI needle is centered and the FROM flag is lit. Click to the right or left of the course indicator with the mouse, or press V followed by + or − key. (To adjust the course in increments of 10°, press Shift + or −.) If you have done this correctly, your top course indicator should read 92°.

3. Tune in VOR 2 to Joliet VOR on a frequency of 112.3 MHz. Use the mouse to set the frequency or, from the keyboard, press N 2 followed by the + or − key for the integer part of the frequency and N N followed by the + or − key for the fractional part of the frequency.

4. Set the OBI 2 course heading so that the CDI needle is centered and the FROM flag is lit. Click the OBI 2 course indicator with the mouse, or press V 2 followed by the + or − key. (Use Shift + or − to increment by 10°.) If you have done this correctly, your top course indicator on OBI 2 should read 58°.

5. Now, using the map shown in Figure 12.26, plot a line from DuPage VOR on radial 92° and then plot a second line from Joliet on radial 58°. Where the two lines intersect is where your plane is located.

This is the basic method of fixing your position using two VOR stations.

Non Directional Beacon Navigation (NDB)

The NDB, or Non-Directional Beacon station, is an older navigational system that can be used as a backup for the VOR/OBI instruments. It consists of many low frequency transmitters, operating on a frequency of 200-415 kHz, with a maximum power of 2,000 watts. With a maximum range of 75 nautical miles by day, and up to 200 miles by night, the NDB station still has not outgrown its usefulness. Its primary disadvantage is that it is susceptible to storm interference and it is not as accurate as the VOR system. In Flight Simulator you tune in an NDB station by using the ADF radio, and then consult the ADF indicator to see which direction the NDB station is in relation to your aircraft.

How NDB Works

How does it work? The NDB sends out an omnidirectional signal that radiates out in all directions. The NDB's electromagnetic waves consist of two

How non-directional beacon navigation works.

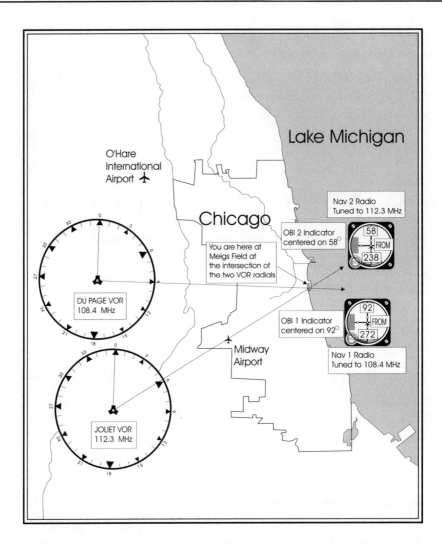

Figure 12.26
Using two VORs to fix your position.

components: fluctuating magnetic fields and fluctuating electric fields that are always oriented 90° with respect to each other. The magnetic field propagates outwards from the transmitter as concentric circles, while the electric field propagates outwards in radials. When the signal is received by your ADF radio, it rotates a loop antenna to determine which direction improves the signal's strength. According to Lenz's Law of Physics, the *maximum* signal strength in the loop, will occur when a magnetic force field enters *perpendicular* to the plane of the loop. This occurs when the antenna is rotated so that the plane of the loop points in the direction of the electromagnetic wave emanating from the transmitter tower. As the loop is rotated, it rotates the needle on the ADF gauge thereby showing the direction of the NDB station.

If you want to head directly for the NDB station, all you would do is re-orient the aircraft so that the arrow points to the 0° mark.

In *Flight Simulator*, the ADF gauge is not normally displayed. In order to use it, you must replace the OBI 2 indicator with the ADF dial. To do this, simply press Shift Tab.

Setting the ADF Frequency

Flight Simulator 5.1 now includes an option for allowing your ADF radio to tune in increments of 500 Hz, and to tune in frequencies higher than 999 kHz (theoretically, you can now tune in AM broadcast stations on 540 kHz to 1610 kHz!). Normally, each NDB is separated by a frequency of at least 1 kHz, so by allowing a 500 Hz separation, the number of receivable stations is increased.

To have your ADF radio tune in NDB stations with 500 Hz selectivity, follow these steps:

1. Open the Instrument Preferences dialog box under the Options menu.
2. In the Instrument Preferences dialog box, toggle on the 500 Hz ADF Frequency Adjustment check box.
3. Click the OK button to return to the simulator.

Your ADF radio will now have four integer digits and one fractional digit for the frequency selection.

Tuning in ADF frequencies with 500 Hz separation is a little bit different from the method used for the ordinary ADF radio. With the mouse, you select the *first two digits*, then click to increase. If you want to decrease the digits, you *must* use the keyboard's − key, you cannot use the mouse alone. The third digit of the frequency can be set individually by clicking on it followed by the + or − key. The fourth *and* fractional fifth digit are set together. Click on these last two digits, followed by the + or − key.

To tune in a frequency using the keyboard alone, follow these steps:

Tuning in Frequencies with 500 Hz separation on the ADF radio

1. Press A followed by the + or − keys to adjust the first two digits.
2. Press A A followed by the + or − keys to adjust the third digit.
3. Press A A A followed by the + or − keys to adjust the fourth and fractional fifth digits.

ADF (Automatic Direction Finder)

The ADF, or Automatic Direction Finder, gauge shows you the bearing, relative to the nose of the aircraft, to the NDB station. The ADF display has a 360° scale and a needle pointer. The compass scale is read just like that of the directional gyro, with each number multiplied by 10 to obtain the bear-

Don't confuse the ADF gauge's course markings with your aircraft's current heading.

ing. For example, a reading of 9 on the scale means 90°, and a reading of 27 means 270°.

To navigate using an NDB station, you must first look up the station's frequency and enter it on the ADF radio. If you are in range of the NDB, your ADF gauge will then show the direction towards the station. Don't confuse the ADF gauge's course markings with your aircraft's current heading, for they are not the same. The needle pointer only points to the *relative bearing* of the NDB station in relation to your aircraft's nose. Thus, if your airplane is heading south on a course of 180°, and your ADF pointer is aimed at *9*, it means that the NDB station is off to the *right* by 90° from your present heading.

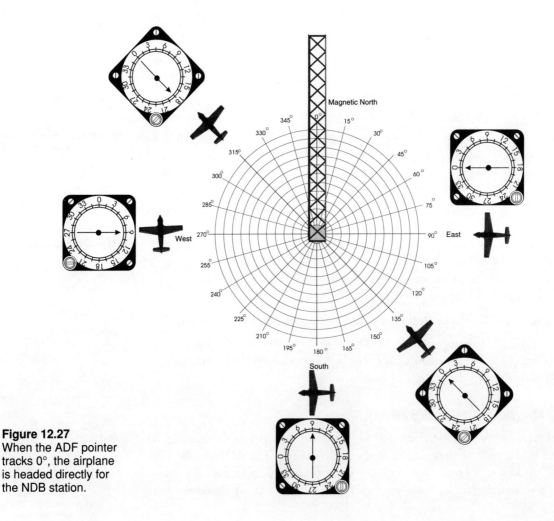

Figure 12.27
When the ADF pointer tracks 0°, the airplane is headed directly for the NDB station.

Note that when the pointer tracks 0°, the airplane is homed in on the station. If you keep flying with the needle pointing at 0°, eventually you will pass over the station.

Using the ADF Homing Method

ADF homing is a navigational technique used to fly the aircraft towards an NDB station. Follow these steps to use the ADF homing method:

1. Tune in a desired NDB station on your ADF radio.
2. Bring up the ADF gauge, by pressing [Shift][Tab].
3. Turn the aircraft until the azimuth needle moves to the 0° position on the ADF gauge.
4. If crosswinds start blowing you off course, turn the airplane until you again have the needle centered on 0°.

When the needle suddenly jumps to 180°, you will have crossed over the NDB station below, and be headed on an outbound path. If you want to continue traveling straight *away* from the NDB station, keep the azimuth needle pointed on 180°. However, with the NDB station behind you, be aware that turning the aircraft left and right will make the azimuth needle move in the opposite direction.

The disadvantage of the ADF homing method is that, in the presence of a crosswind, your path to the NDB station will not be the most direct or straight. You will in essence be flying a curved route, as is illustrated in Figure 12.28.

The ADF Homing Method

The Instrument Landing System

The ILS, or Instrument Landing System, offers a means of safely landing your aircraft in conditions of poor visibility. Each ILS ground station is situated next to major runways, and can be tuned in by your NAV radios. The CDI needle on

WIND

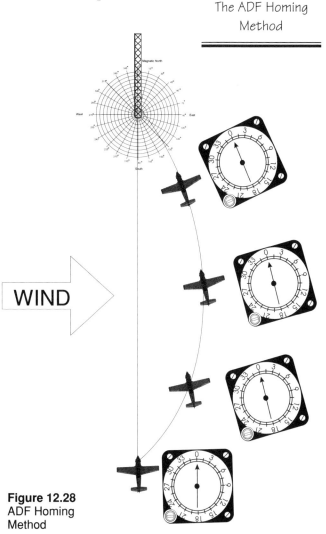

Figure 12.28
ADF Homing Method

the OBI indicator is joined by a second needle, the *glide slope needle*, to offer both vertical *and* horizontal range indications for the proper glide slope to the runway.

The ILS has four main components:

- Localizer Radio Course
- Glide Slope Radio Course
- VHF Marker Beacons
- Approach Lights for the Runway

The ILS system consists of marker beacons, approach lights, and the localizer/glide slope radio course.

The localizer and glide slope transmitters together provide a radio beam that the aircraft "rides" down to the runway. Using cross hair needles on the OBI indicator, the pilot can follow the precise glide angle necessary to reach the runway. Three additional VHF radio marker beacons, located at precise distances from the runway threshold, give the pilot range information. The outer marker warning comes on about 4–7 miles from the runway, while the middle marker warning comes on about 3,250 feet from the runway. There is an additional inner marker warning that some ILS runways come equipped with that comes on when the runway is 1,000 feet off.

In addition, many ILS stations have DME equipment so that your DME indicator can tell you how far away the runway is.

Using the Localizer and Glide Slope For Your Landing

Each runway that is equipped with an ILS has a localizer transmitter, a glide slope transmitter, and at least two OMI radio marker beacons. The localizer transmitter furnishes horizontal guidance information to the OBI localizer needle (same as the CDI needle for the VOR) causing it to move left or right when the aircraft is off the runway centerline. For vertical guidance information, the glide slope transmitter sends out a signal that allows a special glide slope needle on the OBI to move up and down, thereby indicating the aircraft's vertical position with respect to the proper glide slope. When both needles converge in the center of the OBI indicator, the aircraft is on the proper course for the runway.

Localizer

Located off the runway on a centerline, the localizer radiates a fan shaped radio field with an angular width of 3° to 6°, as seen in Figure 12.29. The localizer beam extends out for about 18 miles from the runway threshold and is transmitted on frequencies between 108.10 MHz to 111.95 MHz with a power of about 100 watts. All ILS localizer frequencies are assigned *odd* tenth

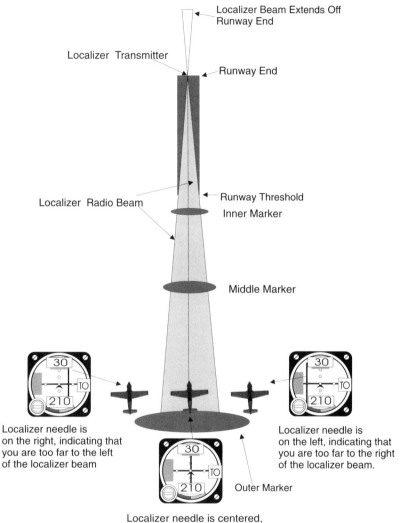

Figure 12.29
Localizer and Glide Slope on the OBI indicator.

decimals, so that an ILS station could use, for example, 108.10, 108.30, 108.50 MHz, etc., frequencies.

Notice that the localizer needle on the OBI is the same as the CDI needle, and it serves the same function of showing horizontal deviation. In Figure 12.29, you can see that if the needle is deflected to the right, your plane is too far to the *left* of the runway. Likewise, if the needle is deflected to the left, your plane is too far to the *right* of the runway.

The Localizer gives horizontal guidance.

The Glide Slope gives vertical guidance.

Rotation of the course indicators on the OBI has no effect on the operation of the localizer needle.

Glide Slope

The glide slope UHF (Ultra High Frequency) transmitter sends out radio beam that radiates diagonally upward from the ground. The angle which the glide slope makes with the ground is about 3°, which gives it a very gradual slope. In fact, at the middle marker distance of 3,250 feet to the runway, the glide slope is only 200 feet above the ground. At the outer marker distance of 4 to 7 miles from the runway, the glide slope is only 1,400 feet above the ground. The beam itself is transmitted on a frequency between 329.15 MHz and 335 MHz, with a power of only 5 watts. Don't worry though, in Flight Simulator, the NAV radio automatically tunes in the proper glide slope frequencies for you when you tune in an ILS station.

On the OBI, the glide slope needle moves up and down to show whether the plane is deviating from the glide slope. If the needle is above the centerline, your airplane is *too low*, and you must regain some altitude. If the needle is below the centerline, your aircraft is *too high*, and you will therefore need to shed some altitude. Of course, if the glide slope needle is smack in the middle of the center mark, your airplane is right on the money.

What the OMI Marker Beacons Tell You

In an ILS approach, the VHF OMI marker beacons provide the pilot with distance information to the runway. There are three markers; the Outer, Middle, and Inner. Each VHF marker sends out a cone shaped radio beam straight up into the air on the approach to the runway. When the airplane

Figure 12.30
Glide Slope OBI indicator for various glide slopes.

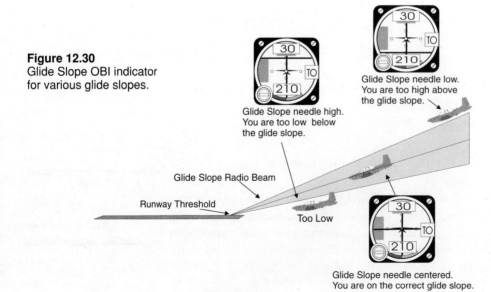

Glide Slope needle high. You are too low below the glide slope.

Glide Slope needle low. You are too high above the glide slope.

Glide Slope Radio Beam

Runway Threshold

Too Low

Glide Slope needle centered. You are on the correct glide slope.

Plate 1 Cessna instrument panel

Plate 2 Learjet instrument panel

Plate 3 Sailplane instrument panel

Plate 4 Sopwith Camel instrument panel

Plate 5 Learjet instrument panel illuminated for night flying. New landing lights illuminate the runway. The downtown Chicago skyline is seen in the distance.

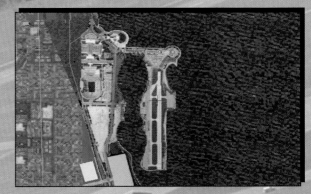

Plate 8 Photorealistic view of Meigs Airport, Chicago

Plate 6 Default startup

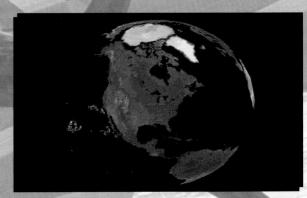

Plate 9 The FS 5.1 Map view of the Earth

Plate 7 The Cessna over Chicago

Plate 10 New Scenery Seed texture for urban and rural areas

Plate 11 New SVGA Haze Driver, with visibility set to ten miles

Plate 12 New SVGA Haze Driver, with visibility set to five miles

Plate 13 New SVGA Haze Driver, with visibility set to one mile

Plate 14 Photorealistic satellite view of New York area (*Microsoft New York scenery add-on*)

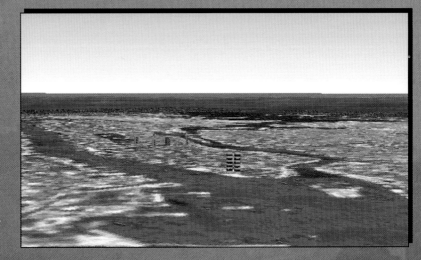

Plate 15 Photorealistic view of Manhattan (*Microsoft New York scenery add-on*)

Plate 16 Statue of Liberty fly-by (*Microsoft New York scenery add-on*)

Plate 17 World Trade Towers fly-by in Manhattan (*Microsoft New York scenery add-on*)

Plate 18 The bridges and skyline of New York City at dusk (*Microsoft New York scenery add-on*)

Plate 19 Photorealistic satellite view of Paris (*Microsoft Paris scenery add-on*)

Plate 20 View of the Seine River in Paris at dusk (*Microsoft Paris scenery add-on*)

Plate 21 Nighttime downtown view of Paris, with the Eiffel Tower in the distance (*Microsoft Paris scenery add-on*)

Plate 22 The Eiffel Tower in Paris (*Microsoft Paris scenery add-on*)

Plate 23 The Louvre museum in Paris with Notre Dame in the distance
(*Microsoft Paris scenery add-on*)

Plate 24 A view of the Alps (*BAO Europe I scenery add-on*)

Plate 25 Innsbruck Airport, Austria (*BAO Europe I scenery add-on*)

Plate 26 Schiphol Airport, Amsterdam, Netherlands
(*BAO Europe I scenery add-on*)

Plate 27 The Strip, Las Vegas (*BAO Las Vegas scenery add-on*)

Plate 28 Hoover Dam, Lake Mead (*BAO Las Vegas scenery add-on*)

Plate 29 Mirage Hotel, Las Vegas (*BAO Las Vegas scenery add-on*)

Plate 30 Canadian Air jet flying over Las Vegas with new urban scenery visible in background (*BAO Las Vegas scenery add-on and BAO Flight Shop add-on*)

Plate 31 The Strip, Las Vegas (*BAO Las Vegas scenery add-on*)

Plate 32 Kona, the Big Island (*Microsoft Hawaii scenery add-on*)

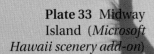

Plate 33 Midway Island (*Microsoft Hawaii scenery add-on*)

Plate 34 Volcano eruption of the Big Island of Hawaii (*Microsoft Hawaii scenery add-on*)

Plate 35 Kuaii
(*Microsoft Hawaii
scenery add-on*)

Plate 36 Kahului Airport
approach, Maui (*Microsoft
Hawaii scenery add-on*)

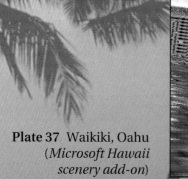

Plate 37 Waikiki, Oahu
(*Microsoft Hawaii
scenery add-on*)

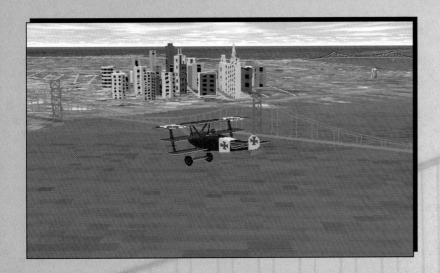

Plate 38 Red Baron over San Francisco (*BAO Flight Shop add-on*)

Plate 39 Austrian Air 707 over San Francisco (*BAO Flight Shop add-on with BAO S.F. scenery add-on*)

Plate 40 AerLingus jet flying over Chicago (*BAO Flight Shop add-on*)

Plate 41 KLM 747 over New York (*BAO Flight Shop add-on*)

Plate 42 Midway Commuter Turboprop over Chicago (*BAO Flight Shop add-on)*

Plate 43 American Airlines DC-10 (*BAO Flight Shop add-on)*

Plate 44 WWII bomber
(*BAO Factory Shop add-on*)

Plate 45 Ultra-Light
over Coney Island (*BAO
Flight Shop add-on*)

Plate 46 Tower Air
Traffic Control for
Windows (*BAO Tower*)

Table 12.2 Aircraft Marker Beacons			
Marker Designation	Typical Distance to Runway Threshold	Audible Signal in Cockpit	OMI Light Indicator Color
Outer	4 to 7 nautical miles	Continuous dashes (400 Hz)	Blue
Middle	3,250 to 3,750 feet	Continuous alternating dot-dash (1300 Hz)	Amber
Inner	1,000 feet	Continuous (6/second)	White

The OMI marker beacons warn you how far you are from the runway.

passes over the "cone," it causes the OMI indicator in the cockpit to sound off with a distinctive signal and colored light. All OMI beacons operate on a frequency of 75 MHz, with a power output of 3 watts.

Table 12.2 lists the standard distance designation, sound signal, and light color for each marker. Note that many ILS systems do not have an Inner Marker, just the Outer and Middle.

Figure 12.31 illustrates the ILS Marker Beacons in greater detail, while Figure 12.32 shows the limits of ILS glide slope and localizer coverage.

Figure 12.31
ILS Marker Beacons and Glide path

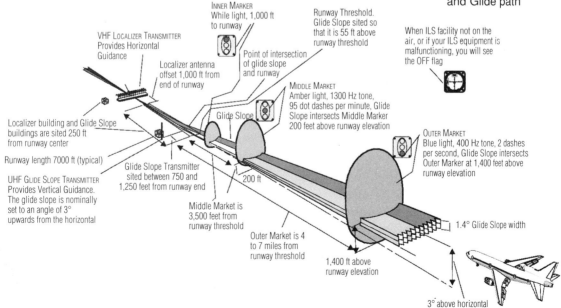

Figure 12.32
Normal limits of ILS coverage

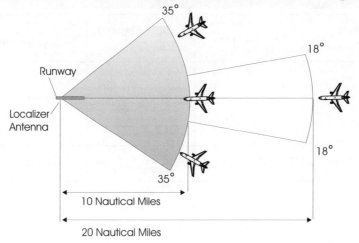

Normal Limits of ILS Localizer Coverage

Horizontal width of Localizer beam is 10° either side of the course along a radius of 18 nautical miles from the antenna, and 35° either side of the course along a radius of 10 nautical miles. The same area and range applies to a back course, at the opposite end of the runway.

Normal Limits of ILS Glide Slope Coverage

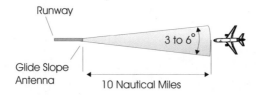

Getting Guidance From the Approach Lighting Systems

When landing at an ILS equipped runway, there are approach lighting systems to help the pilot discern the runway orientation, distance to the end of the runway, and the correct glide path. There are three separate approach lighting systems in common use with ILS equipped runways:

- **REIL:** Runway End Identifier Lights
- **VASI:** Visual Approach Slope Indicator

- **MALSR:** Medium Approach Lighting System with Runway Alignment Indicator Lights

In addition, there are airport beacon lights, which help you spot the airport from among the bright lights of the city.

REIL (Runway End Identifier Lights)

The REIL, or Runway End Identifier Lights, are mounted on each side of the runway's end. Green lights denote the beginning of the runway, and red lights mark the end of the runway, giving a visual cue as to how much runway length is left.

VASI (Visual Approach Slope Indicator)

The Visual Approach Slope Indicator lights give the pilot descent guidance information during the approach to the runway. The FS 5.1 VASI configuration consists of rows of colored lights on each side of the runway. The lighted bar colors of the lights tell you if your approach is too high, just right, or too low. When the upper and lower lights are both *white*, you are too high. If the upper row is *white* and the lower row is *red*, you are on the correct glide slope. If you are too low, however, both lights are *red*.

MALSR (Medium Intensity Approach Lighting System with Runway Alignment Indicator Lights)

MALSR, or the Medium Intensity Approach Lighting System, are runway lights that resemble tracer shells being fired at the runway. You will see these strobe lights at most major airports.

Airport Beacons

FS 5.1 now includes flashing beacon lights which help you locate the airport at night from among the many bright lights of the city. Airport beacons, which operate from dusk until dawn, flash a bright light which alternates between green and white. They are clearly marked on the sectionals and airport maps as a star shaped symbol.

Using EFIS/CFPD for Landings

The EFIS/CFPD display can be used to project a path to the runway on your cockpit windshield. Using the NAV 1 radio, you tune in the ILS station where you wish to land, then activate the CFPD display. You can have rectangles, telephone poles, or a yellow brick road show you the exact glide path to the runway in zero visibility.

The flashing REIL lights are installed at the end of runway.

VASI lights tell you if you are on the correct glide path to runway.

MALSR consists of a row of flashing strobe lights that resemble tracer shells being fired at the runway, along with steadily burning horizontal roll guidance lights just before the runway.

Airport Beacons are marked as star shaped symbols on the Airport maps and sectionals that come with the FS 5.1 manual.

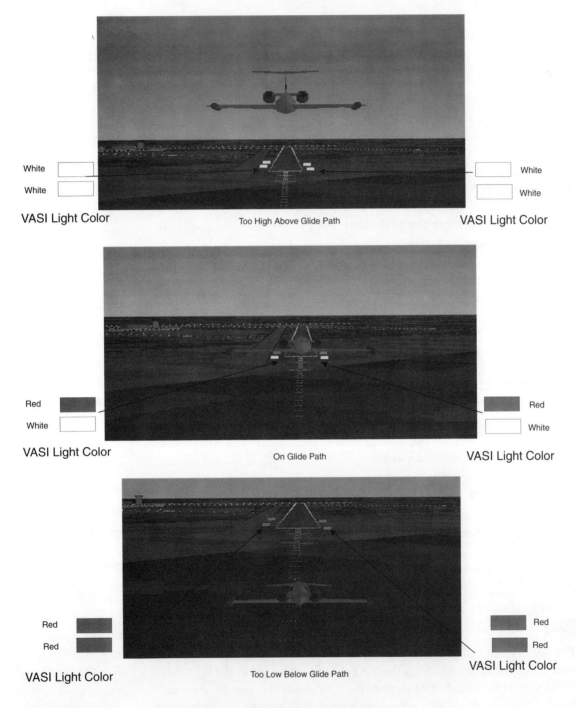

White

White

VASI Light Color

White

White

VASI Light Color

Too High Above Glide Path

Red

White

VASI Light Color

Red

White

VASI Light Color

On Glide Path

Red

Red

VASI Light Color

Red

Red

VASI Light Color

Too Low Below Glide Path

Figure 12.33
VASI approaches

*"Red over White, You're all Right
Red over Red, You're Dead"*

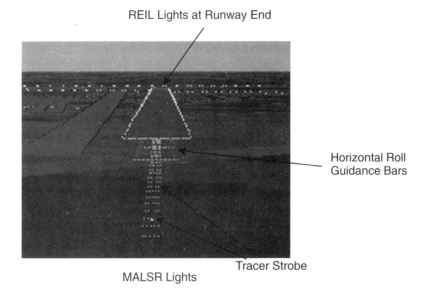

REIL Lights at Runway End

Horizontal Roll
Guidance Bars

Tracer Strobe

MALSR Lights

Figure 12.34
MALSR lights

To setup EFIS/CFPD for ILS landings follow this procedure:

1. First, tune in the ILS station on your NAV 1 radio.
2. Next, select the EFIS/CFPD Display command from the Nav/Com menu.
3. In the EFIS/CFPD dialog box, click on the EFIS Master Switch check box.
4. In the same dialog box, click on the Lock to ILS for Landing Approach radio button.
5. Click the Plot Intercepting Path check box and choose the type of graphic you wish. You can pick from rectangles, telephone poles, and a yellow brick road.
6. Click the OK button.

When you return to the simulation, you will see a computer generated glide slope path to the runway, as is pictured in Figure 12.35.

OTHER NAVIGATIONAL AIDS IN THE REAL WORLD

Today, there are various other navigational systems in use around the world. The Omega, Loran C, GPS (Global Positioning System), and inertial naviga-

CFPD
rectangle

Figure 12.35
EFIS Rectangles are
displayed on cockpit
windshield showing
glide slope to ILS
runway.

tion systems, are used for long range navigation. Ultimately, however, the satellite based GPS navigation system will replace all other navigational methods. In fact, the Department of Transportation foresees the day when GPS will replace the *entire* VOR/NDB radio beacon network. With the advent of the high accuracy differential correction-GPS, the ILS and MLS (Microwave Landing System that is proposed to replace the ILS in the late 1990s) may well be rendered obsolete. A brief description of each system is given in the next section.

LORAN

Loran C (for Long Range Navigation) is a long-range hyperbolic navigation system that has a coverage area of 1,200 miles by day, and 2,300 miles by night. Expanded and improved over the years since its first introduction in 1957, Loran C now covers most regions of the northern Atlantic and Pacific Oceans, along with the Mediterranean. Night time skywaves are receivable over most of the northern hemisphere (except the Indian Ocean). The system operates by having a master station transmit a pulse at a frequency of 100 kHz, which then triggers the slave stations to emit a radio pulse. By recording the unique time differences between the master pulse and the slave pulse, a Loran C receiver can plot a line of position and thus fix its coordinates. Loran C is still used in much of the world, but with the advent of GPS, its usefulness may soon be outlived.

OMEGA

One of the major disadvantages of terrestrial based navigation systems such as VOR/NDB and Loran C, is that they do not truly offer worldwide coverage. For most of the world, in fact, there is no coverage at all. The Loran C range falls off after about 1,200 miles by day (2,300 miles by night), and the range for VOR/NDB stations is at most 200 miles. Because of this, in 1947, the US Navy began a research and development program to develop a low frequency radio navigation system that could achieve worldwide coverage. By 1960, the last technical hurdles were overcome and the Omega system, as it is called, was put into operation.

The Omega system consists of eight stations located 5,000 to 6,000 miles apart, transmitting on the VLF (very low frequencies) band on a frequency of 10 to 14 kHz. The low frequency radio waves are propagated very long distances with very little loss of signal or distortion, except for unusual atmospheric conditions or when there is sunspot activity. These frequencies can also penetrate the surface layers of ocean water, enabling submerged submarines to receive the signal.

By comparing phase differences in signals from four or more Omega stations, an Omega equipped aircraft can plot its position within 1 nautical mile by day, and 2 nautical miles by night anywhere in the world. Omega service is scheduled to last until the year 2005, even though the military use of it ended in 1994. After 2005, the last civilian users of the service are expected to make the transition to GPS.

GPS (Global Positioning System)

The GPS, or Navstar Global Positioning System, is a satellite based navigation system that is operated by the Department of Defense. The system consists of a constellation of 24 satellites distributed in three orbits containing 8 satellites each. Each satellite will orbit the earth at an altitude of 10,900 nautical miles, with a period of 12 hours. For precise latitude and longitude determination, at least 3 satellites signals must be received by the GPS receiver. For precise altitude determination, a fourth satellite signal is needed.

When fully operational, the GPS system will be capable of achieving worldwide accuracy of less than 18 meters (60 feet) in latitude and longitude, and less than 28 meters (92 feet) in altitude. But because the system was designed for the US military, the best accuracy will be reserved for the armed forces (available to the military only, this service is called PPS, or Precise Positioning Service). Commercial services will have to subscribe to a

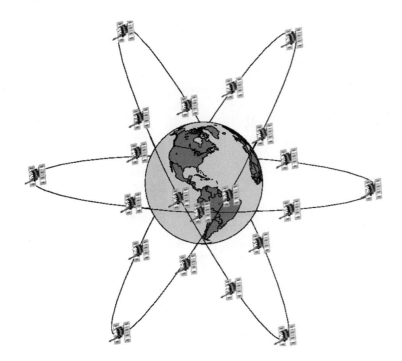

Figure 12.36
GPS: Global Positioning System Satellites in Orbit Around the Earth. Using triangulation techniques, a civilian GPS receiver on the surface can determine its horizontal position to less than 100 meters (328 ft) and less than 156 meters (514 ft) vertical accuracy. U.S. Military GPS receivers have better accuracy: less than 18 meters (60 ft) horizontal and less than 28 meters (92 ft) vertical displacement.

degraded GPS signal that provides accuracy of about 100 meters (330 feet) for latitude and longitude, and 156 meters (514 feet) in altitude. However, there are new Differential GPS (DGPS)services coming on line that will not rely on PPS, and which working in conjunction with GPS satellites, will offer 4 to 20 meter continuous accuracy. DGPS is a system in which differences between observed and calculated GPS signals are broadcast to users using radio beacons on the ground. The local ground based corrections to the satellite GPS signals allow greater precision in position determination.

In *Flight Simulator 5.1*, you can simulate having a GPS receiver by activating your latitude/longitude display. To do this, press ⦗Shift⦘⦗Z⦘ twice.

GPS-The Wave of the Future

Press ⦗Shift⦘⦗Z⦘ twice to display your GPS latitude/longitude coordinates.

GPS, as presently envisioned, is the most accurate and reliable navigational system ever invented by humankind. To see why this is so, compare the benefits of GPS over all other systems.

- **GPS provides worldwide coverage;** Loran C does not, VOR/NDB stations do not, and Omega is only accurate to 1 nautical mile.
- **GPS is more accurate** than Loran, VOR/NDB, or Omega.

- **GPS signals are not affected by bad weather.** Rain, electrical thunderstorms, and other weather can wipe out Loran C, and interfere with the VOR/NDB signal.
- **Differential Correction GPS can be used in place of ILS.**[4] In the future, with differential correction of the GPS signal, a pilot could land at virtually any airport in the world blindfolded.

GPS-How Does it Work?

GPS works by having each satellite transmit a signal on a frequency of 1575.42 MHz and 1227.6 MHz and then having a ground or airborne receiver compare the time differences of the transmissions of at least three of the satellites to determine its position. If a fourth satellite is in a line of sight with the receiver, then an additional position fix can be obtained that tells you your altitude. In order to be as precise as possible, all the satellites and the GPS receiver must have their internal clocks synchronized. There are four atomic clocks on board each satellite which keep time, accurate to one second in every 70,000 years! Each clock measures time in nanoseconds (a nanosecond is *one-billionth* of a second or 10^{-9} seconds), and if a clock should stray by *one-thousandth of a second*, the resulting position fix could be off by 186 miles! Due to relativistic time dilation effects, the clocks must be also be corrected to account for time differences caused by the motion of the satellites. As Einstein explained in his theory of relativity, a clock in a fast moving vehicle will count time more slowly than a clock in a stationary frame of reference.

So how exactly does the GPS receiver know how to fix its position? Well, if you know when the signal left the satellite and you calculate how long the signal takes to reach the receiver, you can calculate the distance by using the formula

$$distance = time \times c$$

where c is the speed of light, or 186,000 miles per second.[5] The satellite sends out a special code that tells the receiver when the signal was first sent, so all the receiver needs to do is calculate the distance from the above formula.

---

[4]Differential GPS Correction is a land based way of improving the basic accuracy of the GPS fix. A ground station broadcasts a "differential" coordinate correction to the GPS receiver, thereby allowing it to narrow the accuracy of its position fix down to a few meters or less. Eventually, this system may replace the instrument landing systems currently in use.

[5]All electromagnetic waves propagate through a vacuum at the speed of light.

In addition, each receiver has a special almanac database that predicts where each satellite is scheduled to be at any given time. Since the motion of orbital bodies is *very* precise, the receiver knows the exact coordinates of every satellite.

But now that the GPS receiver knows the distance to one satellite, how does it figure out where on earth it is? To understand how this is done, let's see step by step what the GPS receiver does.

First, the GPS receiver tunes in the *first* satellite that it needs for the position fix. This satellite is approximately 11,000 miles out in space, and if you were to tie one end of a string to the satellite and pull it in every possible direction, the free end of the string would trace an imaginary sphere of radius 11,000 miles.

This of course, covers quite a bit of area, so the GPS receiver must narrow its position down by locating a *second* satellite. Using the same distance determination, a line of position, or LOP, is drawn on the intersection of the two imaginary spheres for each satellite. The intersection of two spheres, as any geometry student will tell you, is a circle. Therefore, the GPS receiver has narrowed down its position to somewhere on a circle, which is the precise intersection for the two imaginary spheres.

Next, a *third* satellite is tuned in by the GPS receiver to draw a third imaginary sphere. With the intersection of all three spheres, there remains only two points where the GPS receiver can be. But which point is correct? The GPS computer makes a determination based upon what is logically possible, and this result is then displayed in latitude/longitude form on its display.

With the addition of a *fourth* satellite, the GPS receiver can now make a third dimensional fix, and thus obtain its altitude. Furthermore, from this additional information, the GPS receiver can also calculate its speed in relation to the ground.

Inertial Navigation Systems

All the electronic navigation systems discussed so far, including the GPS, are dependent on electromagnetic waves transmitted by external transmitters. The inertial navigation system was developed during the 1950's by the US Navy to offer an independent means of position determination that was not subject to external disruption or interference during wartime. First deployed on ballistic missile submarines, inertial navigation systems have decreased in size and cost to the point that today, most commercial jetliners have them installed as standard equipment.

Inertial navigation works by calculating movements of the aircraft based on sensed accelerations in known spatial directions. Two accelerometers are stabilized by a system of three gyroscopes so that they are constantly maintained on a plane tangential to the earth's surface. One accelerometer measures movements in a north-south direction, while the other accelerometer measures movements in a east-west direction. Both accelerometers are only sensitive to horizontal movements of the aircraft; they do not care about altitude changes. By using Newton's laws of motion,

$$Distance = \frac{1}{2}\ at^2 = \int_0^t ax\ dx$$

where a = acceleration in *feet / second²* (or *meter / second²*) and *t* = time in seconds, the accelerometers detect the amount of acceleration in each direction, and then add and subtract the distance that is traveled to the plane's known starting location. This process is known as integration ($\int_0^t ax\ dx$ where *t* = time in seconds, *a* = acceleration, and *x* is a dummy variable), and it occurs second by second.

Due to gyroscopic precession and other errors, inertial navigation systems do not offer 100% accuracy. On long trans-oceanic flights, they can be off by 20 miles or more, with the average drift being about 1.5 nautical miles per hour of flight.

CHAPTER
13

Around the World in 80 Hours

This chapter will teach you how to fly an around-the-world flight that will start in San Francisco, and go to Honolulu, Wake Island, Guam, Manila, Bangkok, Calcutta, Karachi, Kuwait City, Cairo, Rome, Paris, London, Keflavik, Goose Bay, New York, Chicago, and return to the San Francisco Bay Area, where you will land at Oakland International Airport. The flight will be broken up into 17 separate segments or *legs*. At the end of each leg, you'll land the aircraft, refuel, and depart for the next leg of the flight. If you accelerate time, using the simulator's rate of speed control, you can accomplish each leg in just under an hour.

Because calculating course bearings for an around-the-world trip can be a cumbersome time consuming chore, this chapter will make use of maps and tables that pre-plot the waypoints and magnetic course bearings for you. All you need to do is look at the tables and accompanying maps, and fly the indicated magnetic headings using your compass. If you drift off course from a given waypoint, you can correct your heading by using a special correction angle formula that will bring you back on track. We will return to this topic later in this chapter.

Note that you must be using FS 5.1 CD to complete this flight.

FLYING THE LEARJET

Flying around the world in the Learjet 35A is a pleasure. This jet is very fast, and can cruise comfortably at high altitudes. Unfortunately the limited range of 2,196 nautical miles for this Learjet, does not allow it to fly all great circle paths around the world. You can see some of the allowable range capabilities for flights around the world in Figure 10.10 of Chapter 10. Note that the missions indicated with arrows are flights that may be accomplished by the Learjet in the opposite direction only with favorable wind conditions. Thus, for example, the flight from San Francisco to Hawaii should not be attempted if there is a strong headwind; to do otherwise would risk running out of fuel.

For our flight around the world, we will cruise at an average altitude of 43,000 feet. For maximum fuel efficiency, the exact altitude is determined by the distance of the particular flight segment you are flying, which you can see listed in Table 13.1.

Don't fly the Learjet with full throttle. It's very easy to fly faster than 0.81 Mach at 45,000 feet (471 knots TAS), which will cause the Overspeed warning to light, and possibly result in the loss of control of the aircraft.

FLYING FROM WAYPOINT TO WAYPOINT

To fly around the world using the tables in this chapter, you must look up each waypoint, and see what the magnetic course heading is for the next waypoint. You then fly the aircraft at the given altitude, on the magnetic heading that is listed. Then, when you reach the next waypoint's longitude location, you check to see how far off course you are in terms of degrees and minutes of latitude, either north or south of the predicted waypoint destination. After calculating your drift, you compensate by adding or subtracting a few degrees to the compass heading listed for the next waypoint. This will get you to the next waypoint, whereupon you repeat the process of determining your drift and then compensate for it by adding or subtracting a few degrees for the subsequent waypoint. Finally, you should arrive at the airport that is listed, where you then land, refuel, and takeoff for the next leg of your trip.

The trip around the world is broken up into 17 segments as shown in Table 13.1. You can fly any segment out of order; thus if you want skip the rest of the world but simply fly from London to New York, you would turn to the London to Keflavik section, and fly that segment before flying the Keflavik to Goose Bay, and Goose Bay to New York segments.

You can fly any of the flight segments in this chapter out of order.

Flying the Reverse Direction

If you want to fly the reverse paths of any of the listed flight segments in this chapter, you can do so by flying the given magnetic course headings minus 180° (if the resultant angle is less than 0°, then you add 180°). For example, if instead of flying from San Francisco to Honolulu, you wanted to fly from Honolulu to San Francisco, you would use Table 13.2, but reverse the order of the waypoints and subtract 180° from each magnetic course heading. Note that the course heading you use for the reverse direction is from the row above your departure waypoint; for example to fly from Honolulu to

BITTA, you use the entry for BITTA, or 211° − 180° = 31°. From BITTA to BRADR, you would take the heading of 224° for BRADR and fly on a heading of 224° − 180° = 44°. Keep in mind that when traveling the reverse direction, only the magnetic course heading is changed; the OBI course headings for interception of VOR radials does not change.

During your flight you should always keep the GPS latitude/longitude display on screen (press [Shift] + [Z] twice). Watch the longitude numbers very closely, and then pause the simulation when you reach the longitude of the next waypoint on your course. At the waypoint, you look at your latitude display and determine how far north or south of the waypoint you are, then you calculate the error correction to your magnetic heading to the next waypoint. On east to west flights, if you are too far north of the waypoint, you turn the aircraft a few degrees left of the magnetic course heading. By the same token, on an east to west flight, if you are too far south of the waypoint, you fly the aircraft a few degrees right of the magnetic course heading. The next section explains how to calculate the number of degrees to turn left or right in correcting your drift.

You can fly the reverse paths of any of the flight segments in this chapter by using the listed magnetic course heading minus 180°.

Correcting Your Compass Heading When You Are Off Course

You will find that, despite your best effort at flying the indicated magnetic bearing, your aircraft will drift off course from its expected waypoint destination. When this happens, you *must* correct your heading to the next waypoint to account for this error! If you don't, the accumulated errors will build up until you are no longer flying the given great circle track.

There are two principal rules of thumb you follow when calculating your how far off course you are:

1. One degree of latitude is equal to sixty nautical miles, and one minute of latitude is equal to one nautical mile:

$$1° = 60 \ nautical \ miles$$

$$1' = 1 \ nautical \ miles$$

2. If you are one nautical mile off north or south of your track after flying 60 nautical miles, you are one degree off track:

$$\frac{1 \ nautical \ mile \ deviation \ north \ or \ south}{60 \ nautical \ miles \ traveled \ on \ track} = 1°$$

You must correct your heading at each waypoint to account for your aircraft's drifting off course.

Let's use an example to demonstrate how these rules are applied. Our hypothetical aircraft is flying on a magnetic course of 234° from waypoint 1, located at N29° 06' W145° 37', to waypoint 2 located at N26° 31' W150° 27', as illustrated in Figure 13.1. The pilot wishes to end up at waypoint 3,

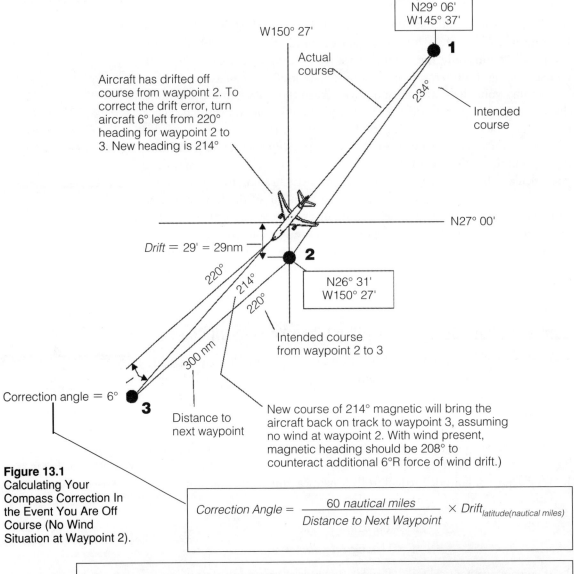

N29° 06'
W145° 37'

W150° 27'

Actual course

234°

Intended course

Aircraft has drifted off course from waypoint 2. To correct the drift error, turn aircraft 6° left from 220° heading for waypoint 2 to 3. New heading is 214°

N27° 00'

Drift = 29' = 29nm

220°

214°

220°

N26° 31'
W150° 27'

Intended course from waypoint 2 to 3

300 nm

Correction angle = 6°

3

Distance to next waypoint

New course of 214° magnetic will bring the aircraft back on track to waypoint 3, assuming no wind at waypoint 2. With wind present, magnetic heading should be 208° to counteract additional 6°R force of wind drift.)

Figure 13.1
Calculating Your Compass Correction In the Event You Are Off Course (No Wind Situation at Waypoint 2).

$$Correction\ Angle = \frac{60\ nautical\ miles}{Distance\ to\ Next\ Waypoint} \times Drift_{latitude(nautical\ miles)}$$

Corrected Magnetic Heading = Intended Magnetic Course ± Course Correction ± Wind Drift Correction
No wind at waypoint 2 = 220° − 6°L − 0° = 214°
wind at waypoint 2 = 220° − 6°L − 6°L = 208°

which is a distance of 300 nautical miles from waypoint 2. The desired course from waypoint 2 to waypoint 3 is 220°.

After the aircraft reaches the meridian of W150° 27', the pilot notices that his aircraft's latitude is N27° 00'. This means that his aircraft is off course by 29' since N27° 00' − N26° 31' = 29'. Using Rule 1 above, this means that the aircraft is 29 nautical miles north of its intended course, since 29 minutes of latitude = 29 nautical miles.

Using Rule 2, the pilot can figure out the number of degrees he must turn the aircraft left at waypoint 2 to compensate for the effects of the wind upon his aircraft's course. Since the distance to the next waypoint 3 is 300 nautical miles, we can develop the following proportional relationship:

$$\frac{29 \ nautical \ miles \ deviation \ north}{300 \ nautical \ miles \ traveled \ on \ track} = \frac{5.8 \ nautical \ miles \ deviation \ north}{60 \ nautical \ miles \ traveled \ on \ track} = 5.8 \times 1° = 5.8°$$

which is good for a no wind situation at waypoint 2. If there were wind still present at point 2, then not only would the pilot have to correct 5.8° left to compensate for the error in his track, but he would also have to crab his airplane to account for the wind drift at waypoint 2, else he would still be blown off track at waypoint 3.

Assuming that no wind is present, according to Rule 2, the pilot should turn 5.8° left at waypoint 2 (we shall assume no-wind for the examples to follow, as well as for the around the world flight). We can summarize Rule 2 in an easy to use formula, as shown below:

$$Course \ Correction \ Angle = \frac{60 \ nautical \ miles}{Distance \ to \ Next \ Waypoint} \times Drift_{latitude(nautical \ miles)}$$

where the Drift distance, in nautical miles, is measured north or south of the latitude for the waypoint whose longitude meridian the aircraft is crossing.

$$Drift_{latitude(nautical \ miles)} = minutes \ north \ or \ south \ of \ waypoint$$

In the above example, the correction angle would be computed like this:

$$Course \ Correction \ Angle = \frac{60 \ nautical \ miles}{Distance \ to \ Next \ Waypoint} \times Drift_{latitude(nautical \ miles)}$$

$$= \frac{60 \ nautical \ miles}{300 \ nautical \ miles} \times 29 \ nautical \ miles$$

$$= 5.8$$

So, after arriving at waypoint 2, the pilot's new magnetic course bearing will be 220° − 5.8° = 214.2°, since he must turn the aircraft left to compensate for the north drift of 29 miles. To simplify matters, round off 5.8° to 6°. Thus, the pilot turns the aircraft to 214° to get the aircraft back on course so that it will arrive at waypoint 3 (assuming no wind drift at waypoint 2).

Corrected Magnetic Heading = Intended Magnetic Course ± Course Correction ± Wind Drift Correction

$$= 200° - 6°L - 0°$$

$$= 214°$$

Note that if the pilot were 29 miles south of waypoint 2, then he would have had to turn the aircraft 6° right to compensate. Thus the course would have been 220° + 6° = 226° (assuming no wind drift at waypoint 2).

Note too, that if the aircraft were traveling from west to east in the opposite direction, than the direction of the correction angle would be reversed. That is, if the aircraft were north of the waypoint, it would turn right to compensate, and if it were south, it would turn left.

Factoring in the Effects of Wind Drift on Course Heading

If there is wind present at waypoint 2, then you must not only account for the course correction angle, but you must also counteract the effects of the wind. To do this, you must figure out the angle by which you were blown off course from the previous waypoint 1, and then crab (or turn) your aircraft by an additional angular amount as follows:

Corrected Magnetic Heading = Intended Magnetic Course ± Course Correction ± Wind Drift Correction

Thus, in the previous example, if there were the same wind at waypoint 2 that existed at waypoint 1 (in other words, wind blowing from left to right across the plane's path) the pilot would figure out the wind drift using this formula:

$$\frac{Wind\ Drift}{Correction\ Angle} = \frac{60\ nautical\ miles}{Distance\ from\ Previous\ Waypoint} \times Drift_{latitude(nautical\ miles)}$$

$$= \frac{60\ nautical\ miles}{300\ nautical\ miles} \times 29\ nautical\ miles$$

$$= 5.8°$$

where the Drift was previously calculated to be 29 nautical miles, and the distance from waypoint 1 to waypoint 2 is 300 nautical miles. We know that the wind is blowing 5.8°, or when rounded up, 6° right (6°R) since the aircraft was blown off course from left to right. The correction angle would be in the *opposite direction*, and therefore be 6° left (6°L). Crabbing the aircraft 6°L *in addition to the previously calculated course correction angle* of 6°L, will bring the aircraft back on course to waypoint 3.

To summarize, when wind is present at waypoint 2, the corrected magnetic heading would be 220° − 6° − 6° = 208°.

Corrected Magnetic Heading = Intended Magnetic Course ± Course Correction ± Wind Drift Correction

$$= 200° - 6°L - 6°L°$$
$$= 208°$$

Use the Autopilot to Refine Course Heading

The Autopilot is very useful if you want to get your aircraft flying on a given heading to the exact degree. To do this, select the Nav/Com menu, then choose Autopilot. In the Autopilot dialog box, select the Connected (On) option for the Autopilot Switch, then click the HDG (Heading) check box. In the Heading text box, type in the magnetic course bearing, then click the OK button to return to the simulation.

Note that while the Autopilot is engaged, your simulation speed is limited to 4x normal. However, once the aircraft is on the desired heading, you can disengage the Autopilot, and then accelerate time as desired.

DESCENDING FROM ALTITUDE AND FINDING THE AIRPORT

After coming in range of the airport's VOR beacon, which you tune in on your NAV 1 radio using the frequency listed in the tables, you must determine the proper course heading to the airport. To do this, you use the OBI and center the CDI needle with the TO flag lit. You then take the course heading displayed on the top of the OBI, and turn your aircraft to this compass heading. This will put you on course to the airport.

Even though, at 43,000 feet altitude, your descent should start at 109 nautical miles from the airport, you will start your descent at 80 miles out, and use a steeper descent rate to compensate. When you arrive at the airport, you may have to fly descending circles to reduce excess altitude. On the other hand, if you find that you are descending too rapidly, just maintain 5,000 feet AGL until you see the airport. You'll have to adjust your vertical speed using a descent rate of approximately 3,000 fpm, with an airspeed of 250–300 knots.

Follow this descent procedure when you first come into range of the airport VOR(assuming you've already tuned in the proper VOR frequency):

1. Use the OBI to determine what radial the airport VOR is located on. Press $\boxed{V}\boxed{+}$ to change the course selector on the OBI until the CDI needle is centered and the TO flag is lit. Then turn the aircraft to the

compass heading shown on the top course indicator on the OBI, since this is the direction to the airport VOR station.

2. Reduce throttle to 60%.

3. Extend spoilers to bring airspeed down to between 250-300 knots.

4. Retract spoilers when airspeed falls below 250 knots. Extend again, if airspeed exceeds 300 knots.

5. Use elevator trim to adjust pitch so that your descent rate hovers around 3,000 fpm on your vertical speed indicator.

6. When you get to within 7 or 8 miles of the airport, as shown on your DME (note: some airport VOR's are not equipped with DME), you should see the airport below.

Don't forget to lower your landing gear and flaps on the approach. The time to descend from 45,000 feet to sea level should be about 12 to 16 minutes of unaccelerated time, depending on your descent rate.

REFUELING FACILITIES

You must refuel the aircraft each time you land at an airport. All the airports on this round-the-world flight have refueling facilities, which are identified by a yellow square which has the character "F" inside it. To refuel the aircraft, move it inside the square and come to a complete stop. After a moment, the aircraft will be refueled and repaired, should any damage have occurred on the flight.

Finding the Refueling Quadrangle

Finding the yellow refueling square can be tricky after you land, especially if the surrounding terrain masks the color yellow. This was especially true for Kuwait airport, because the square was hard to make out against a washed out background of brown.

Usually the fuel quadrangle is located near a runway, but how exactly do you find it when you can't see it? The best way, I discovered, was to open the map window to full screen (press [Num Lock] then press [W]) and then zoom in to a 1.3 mile altitude view (select Views/View Options menu, then in the View Options dialog box, click the Map View radio button, and select 1.3 mi from the Alt list box). You still won't be able to see the fuel quadrangle if it is off the edge of your map, so what you need to do is taxi down the runway, keeping an eagle eye out for the yellow box. It will eventually pop into view on the map if you travel down the length of each runway.

TIME OF FLIGHT AND ACCELERATION OF TIME

To spare you the long hours of boredom over the vast expanse of ocean and land, you can accelerate time up to 16×, 32×, 64× as needed, but realize that you can't fly faster than 4× with the autopilot. So if you accelerate time to 32× and take over manually, you have to be very careful not to make sudden movements of the controls, because you can lose control of the aircraft and crash.

In 1983, businesswoman-pilot Brooke Knapp of California, set a new speed record of 50 hours, 22 minutes total elapsed time for a flight around the world in a Learjet 35A.

If you accelerate time to about 64× between waypoints, and reduce time to 1x at waypoints and airports, the entire trip around the world will take about 17 hours of your real time. If you flew the trip without accelerating time, you could do it in 57 hours and 14 minutes of your real time. However, if you were flying the real Learjet 35A, the whole trip would take about 80 hours because you would have to take into account the time to refuel the aircraft, rest, and taxi to and from the terminals.

Table 13.1 shows the time of flight and mileage for each flight segment of the round-the-world flight.

Save situations as necessary for each leg. This way you can fly the entire flight a few hours each day, and come back again at a later time to continue the flight.

Also use the VOR/OBI indicator, and tune the NAV radio to the VOR station nearest the destination airport. This will allow you to find the airport once you near the area. In the case where you need to use an NDB station, you turn on the ADF gauge (press Shift Tab until it appears on your instrument panel), then tune in the frequency on your ADF radio. Note that the maximum range for either type of beacon is 80 nautical miles.

REALISM AND RELIABILITY
FOR FUEL CONSUMPTION

To make your flight more realistic, your aircraft engine should run out of fuel when your tanks run dry. To enable this, you must select the Sim/Realism and Reliability menu option, then click on the Engine Stops When Out of Fuel check box.

If you want the Learjet's fuel tank to empty the next time you fly it, you should save your flight in a situation. For, example, after enabling the fuel realism, you fly from San Francisco to Honolulu. After completing the flight, you save the situation, and exit the program. The next evening, you decide to resume your round-the-world flight from where you left off in Honolulu. Simply open the previously saved situation, and voila, you needn't reset the fuel realism again.

Table 13.1 Time of Flight and Mileage for Round the World Trip				
Flight Segment	**Time of Flight (Unaccelerated Time)**	**Nautical Miles**	**Statute Miles**	**Cruising Altitude**
S.F. to Honolulu	5h 30m	2,086	2,401	45,000 feet
Honolulu to Wake Island	5h 15m	2,003	2,305	45,000 feet
Wake Island to Guam	3h 45m	1,371	1,578	43,000 feet
Guam to Manila	3h 50m	1,384	1,593	43,000 feet
Manila to Bangkok	3h 07m	1,137	1,258	43,000 feet
Bangkok to Calcutta	2h 40m	868	999	43,000 feet
Calcutta to Karachi	3h 25m	1,199	1,380	43,000 feet
Karachi to Kuwait	3h 15m	1,225	1,410	43,000 feet
Kuwait to Cairo	2h 55m	976	1,123	43,000 feet
Cairo to Rome	3h 35m	1,296	1,492	43,000 feet
Rome to Paris	2h 00m	632	727	43,000 feet
Paris to London	1h 00m	174	200	35,000 feet
London to Keflavik	3h 13m	1,123	1,293	43,000 feet
Keflavik to Goose Bay	3h 45m	1,319	1,518	43,000 feet
Goose Bay to New York	3h 15m	1,161	1,336	43,000 feet
New York to Chicago	2h 10m	709	816	43,000 feet
Chicago to Oakland (via Denver/Salt Lake City)	4h 34m	1,705	1,962	45,000 feet
TOTAL	**57h 14m**	**20,368**	**23,443**	

SAN FRANCISCO TO HONOLULU

We'll start the round the world trip in San Francisco, and go through all the necessary steps for a successful flight. After you've completed this leg, you can fly the other segments on your own, referring only to the maps and tables for the waypoints. If you get stuck in another part of the world, just re-read the instructions for the S.F.-Honolulu flight, and you'll figure out where you went wrong.

Keep in mind that the S.F. to Hawaii flight, a distance of 2,086 nautical miles, is at the limit of the Learjet's range. You must be very careful to fly the given route, and not waste fuel.

Follow these steps for the S.F. to Honolulu flight segment:

1. Select the World/Airports menu, then in the dialog box that opens, choose USA-San Francisco as your scenery area. From the list of airports, pick San Francisco Intl. Runway 28R, then click the OK button to return to the simulation.

2. Select the Options/Aircraft menu option, then pick the Learjet as your aircraft choice. Click OK to return to the simulation.

3. For added fuel realism, let's allow the engines to stop when they run out of fuel. Select the Sim/Realism and Reliability menu option, then click on the Engine Stops When Out of Fuel check box. Click OK to return to the simulation.

4. Using the Sim/Engine and Fuel menu command, make sure you top off your Left, Right, Left Aux(iliary), and Right Aux(iliary) fuel tanks to 100%. You need every ounce of fuel to get to Hawaii, and if you just refuel at the S.F. fuel quadrangle, you won't get 100% capacity for each tank.

5. Because the aircraft is so heavily laden with fuel (aircraft weighs about 18,000 lbs!), you'll need to take off with full flaps and your takeoff distance will be about 8,785 feet for a temperature of 60°. Lower Flaps to 40°, then advance throttle to maximum. When you reach a speed of 137 knots, you can rotate the aircraft with the elevator (Keypad ②) to lift off.

6. After takeoff, retract flaps to 0°, and raise the landing gear.

7. Turn the aircraft to a heading of 237° and climb to 45,000 feet cruising altitude. Reduce throttle shortly after completing the climb.

8. You can use the Autopilot to fly the aircraft to altitude and on the 237° heading. If you like, you can increase the simulation speed to 4x normal; to increase speed, press ⓡ followed by ⊞ two times; to reduce speed to normal 1x, press ⓡ followed by ⊟ two times. You can see the rate of speed displayed on the clock.

9. Activate the GPS latitude/longitude on-screen display by pressing Ⓢⓗⁱᶠᵗ Ⓩ two times.

10. Look up your first waypoint BEBOP in Table 13.2 and Figure 13.2. You'll note that distance from S.F. to BEBOP is 130 miles and that the magnetic heading is 237°. Keep the aircraft flying on a course of 237°. Once you are at 45,000 feet, you can disengage the Autopilot and increase the simulation speed (press ⓡ then the ⊞ key repeatedly) to 64x. Keep a steady hand, and don't allow your aircraft to climb, descend or turn.

11. Since the longitude of BEBOP is W125° 00' 00", you want to keep flying until the aircraft crosses W125° 00' 00". Once you arrive at W125° 00' 00" on your GPS display, reduce simulation speed to 1x normal (press R then the – key repeatedly), and pause the simulation (press P). Note your latitude. Compare this latitude with the latitude of BEBOP, which is N37° 00' 00". For every degree of latitude you are north or south of BEBOP, you are 60 nautical miles off course. For every minute of latitude north or south, you are 1 nautical mile off course. For example, if your aircraft's latitude reading shows N37° 40' 42", it means that you are 40' 42" too far north, which is the equivalent of 40.75 nautical miles north of BEBOP. To simplify things, you can round off the seconds to the nearest degree (i.e., 40' 42" rounded off is 41'), so that your drift is 41 nautical miles.

12. Since you now know how far off course you are, you must apply the course correction rule. From Table 13.2 and Figure 13.2, you can see that the distance to the next waypoint BAART is 99 miles, therefore using example drift of 41 nautical miles and using the formula below, we get (assuming no wind present at BEBOP):

$$Course\ Correction\ Angle = \frac{60\ nautical\ miles}{Distance\ to\ Next\ Waypoint} \times Drift_{latitude(nautical\ miles)}$$

$$= \frac{60\ nautical\ miles}{99\ nautical\ miles} \times 41\ nautical\ miles$$

$$= 25°$$

At BEBOP, the magnetic bearing to BAART, the next waypoint, is 236°. Since your drift in this example is 41 nautical miles north and your flight is from east to west, to compensate, you must turn the aircraft left by 25°. Therefore you subtract the correction angle (assuming no wind present at BEBOP):

$$Corrected\ Magnetic\ Heading = Intended\ Magnetic\ Course \pm Course\ Correction \pm Wind\ Drift\ Correction$$

$$= 236°_{Bebop \to Baart} - 25° - 0°$$

$$= 211°_{Bebop \to Baart}$$

So turn the aircraft to 211° magnetic, and fly to the next waypoint BAART. Note that the correction angle is very large for this particular example because the waypoint distance between BEBOP and BAART is so small. If the waypoint distance were 300 nautical miles (such as for example between BLUFF and BAKON), the correction angle would be only 8°.

13. Look up the longitude of the next waypoint BAART, which is W126° 56'. Increase simulation speed to 64x and watch your longitude display until it shows W126° 56', then reduce simulation to 1x, and pause the simulation.

14. Compare your aircraft's current latitude with the latitude of BAART (N36° 27'). Calculate your drift distance, and repeat step 12. Remember to add the correction angle if you are south of the waypoint BAART, and subtract the correction angle if you are north (assume no wind conditions in your calculations).

15. Repeat steps 13 and 14 for the waypoints that follow, until you arrive at the next to last waypoint BITTA before Honolulu, at W155° 28.7'.

16. At BITTA, pause the simulation and tune your NAV 1 radio to 114.8 MHz, which is the VOR for Honolulu International Airport (HNL). Make sure that your OBI 1 is displayed on the cockpit instrument panel (press [Shift] [Tab] until you see it). Even though you're out of range at the moment, as you near Honolulu, you'll watch the OBI and DME until they switch on, letting you know that you are within 80 nautical miles.

17. While still at BITTA, figure out your drift distance, then compensate for it by subtracting the correction angle (if north of BITTA), or adding the correction angle (if south of BITTA) to 211°. Then resume the simulation and fly the new heading with correction angle till you are in range of the HNL VOR.

18. When the OBI flags light up, click the course indicator until the TO flag is lit and the CDI needle is centered. Note the top course indicator reading. This is the compass heading you need to fly to get to Honolulu International.

19. Turn the aircraft to the compass heading shown on the top course indicator of the OBI. If the CDI needle moves, re-center it with the [V][1][+] or [V][1][-] keys (or if you are using the NAV2/OBI2, press [V][2][+] or [V][2][-]), then re-read the top course indicator and turn your aircraft to match this new heading.

20. Begin your descent; extend the spoilers, and reduce throttle to 60%. Keep your descent rate to 3,000 fpm, and your airspeed to between 250 and 300 knots. If you descend too fast before getting to the airport, just maintain 5,000 feet altitude until you arrive.

21. When you see the runway, extend the landing gear, retract the spoilers, adjust the throttle as needed to keep speed over 127 knots, align the Learjet with the runway, and extend the flaps to 40°.

22. Land and refuel the aircraft on the yellow fuel rectangle.

Table 13.2   San Francisco to Hawaii

Waypoint/ VOR/Airport	Latitude	Longitude	Magnetic Bearing to Next Waypoint	Distance to Next Waypoint (nm)
San Francisco VOR 115.8 MHz	N37° 37.0'	W122° 22.0'	237°	130
BEBOP	N37° 00.0'	W125° 00.0'	236°	99
BAART	N36° 27.7'	W126° 56.0'	234°	140
BLUFF	N35° 38.6'	W129° 38.1'	233°	300
BAKON	N33° 41.9'	W135° 13.3'	231°	343
BILLO	N31° 10.7'	W141° 17.4'	227°	257
BEATS	N29° 06.8'	W145° 37.3'	226°	300
BANDY	N26° 31.8'	W150° 27.4'	224°	219
BRADR	N24° 32.6'	W153° 50.9'	224°	108
BITTA	N23° 31.7'	W155° 28.7'	211°	190
Honolulu, Hawaii VOR 114.8 MHz	N21° 18.5'	W157° 55.8'		

The entire trip from S.F. to Honolulu would take 5 hours and 30 minutes if you flew it in real time. With time acceleration, you can accomplish the flight in less than an hour.

HONOLULU TO WAKE ISLAND

The trip from Honolulu to Wake Island, a U.S. Territory, is much the same as from San Francisco to Honolulu. You fly the indicated magnetic headings for each waypoint, and then compensate for your deviation from the given great circle track. The distance between Honolulu and Wake is 2,003 nautical miles, so again- you'll have to be very careful not to waste fuel in order to arrive safely.

Pay careful heed to the fact that your longitude readout between waypoint FROTH and DUSKI will change from West longitude to East longitude.

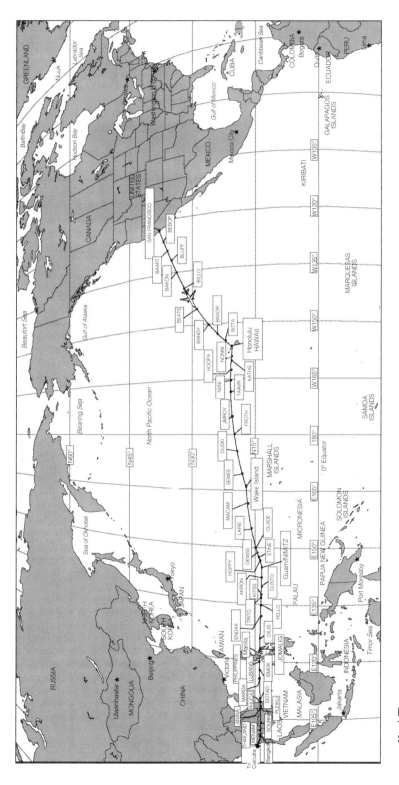

Figure 13.2
The Waypoints for the flight between San Francisco and Bangkok.

Table 13.3   Honolulu to Wake Island

Waypoint/ VOR/Airport	Latitude	Longitude	Magnetic Bearing to Next Waypoint	Distance to Next Waypoint (nm)
Honolulu, Hawaii VOR 114.8 MHz	N21° 18.5'	W157° 55.8'	258°	175
NONNI	N21° 13.7'	W161° 03.0'	234°	21
KATHS	N21° 04.8'	W161° 23.4	263°	81
HOOPA	N21° 07'	W162° 50'	262°	122
NIIMI	N21° 11.9'	W165° 00'	260°	280
TAAVR	N21° 14.0'	W170° 00'	260°	280
JMROY	N21° 07.2'	W175° 00'	258°	281
FROTH	N20° 51.5'	W180° 00'	255°	283
DUSKI	N20° 24.0'	E175° 00'	256°	285
SEWEE	N19° 47.7'	E170° 00'	254°	195
Wake Island VOR 113.5 MHz	N19° 17.1'	E166° 37.7'		

WAKE ISLAND TO GUAM

The trip from Wake Island to Guam, another U.S. Territory, is only 1,371 nautical miles. Therefore the most efficient cruise altitude is at 43,000 feet, not 45,000 feet. Follow the procedure for flying between waypoints, as described for the S.F. to Honolulu flight.

GUAM TO MANILA

Guam to Manila, in the Philippines, is an air distance of only 1,384 nautical miles. Your cruise altitude should be 43,000 feet. When you fly over the JOMALIG VOR in this segment, you will know because the OBI gauge will show your To/From flag alternate from one to the other.

Table 13.4   Wake Island to Guam

Waypoint/ VOR/Airport	Latitude	Longitude	Magnetic Bearing to Next Waypoint	Distance to Next Waypoint (nm)
Wake Island VOR 113.5 MHz	N19° 17.1'	E166° 37.7'	251°	386
MACAM	N17° 50.9'	E160° 00'	251°	297
LARIE	N16° 35'	E155° 00'	251°	364
OLADE	N15° 10.7'	E150° 00'	251°	63
DEWSS	N14° 52.5'	E148° 58.9'	251°	81
STINE	N14° 28.0'	E147° 38.2'	248°	80
HOPPY	N14° 01.2'	E146° 20.5'	248°	100
Guam/NIMITZ VOR 115.3 MHz	N13° 27.2'	E144° 43.9'		

Table 13.5   Guam to Manila

Waypoint/ VOR/Airport	Latitude	Longitude	Magnetic Bearing to Next Waypoint	Distance to Next Waypoint (nm)
Guam/NIMITZ VOR 115.3 MHz	N13° 27.2'	E144° 43.9'	274°	100
AKRON	N13° 37.3'	E143° 01.7'	274°	77
GUSTO	N13° 44.7'	E141° 43'	274°	63
KITSS	N13° 50.1'	E140° 38.7'	274°	37
TRITO	N13° 53'	E140° 00'	273°	292
YELLO	N14° 10'	E135° 00'	271°	291
ENDAX	N14° 15.0'	E130° 00'	273°	233
DILIS	N14° 31'	E126° 00'	273°	209
JOMALIG VOR 116.7 MHz	N14° 43.6'	E122° 24.1'	261°	82
Manila, Philippines VOR 113.8 MHz	N14° 30.6	E121° 01.0'		

MANILA TO BANGKOK

Manila to Bangkok, Thailand is 1,137 nautical miles distance. Your cruise altitude should be 43,000 feet, and you'll fly over Vietnam and Cambodia before reaching Thailand. The terminal area takeoff procedure for Manila is a little complicated because you need to turn the aircraft to the LUBANG VOR after traveling 39 miles from the airport. You'll do this by using the OBI display to show you when you are crossing the 85° radial from LUBANG, as indicated by the CDI needle on the OBI. This intersection point between Manila Airport and the LUBANG VOR 85° radial is the place where you will then turn the aircraft towards LUBANG on a course of 265°.

Follow these steps for your Manila departure:

1. Make sure your NAV 1 radio is tuned to Manila VOR at 113.8 MHz. Also, check to make sure the correct OBI 1 indicator is displayed on screen (press [Shift][Tab] to change instruments).

Table 13.6	Manila to Bangkok			
Waypoint/ VOR/Airport	**Latitude**	**Longitude**	**Magnetic Bearing to Next Waypoint**	**Distance to Next Waypoint (nm)**
Manila, Philippines VOR 113.8 MHz	N14° 30.6	E121° 01.0'	206° for 39 miles till you cross the 85° radial on your OBI for LUBANG VOR (117.5 MHz), then turn to 265° for 36 miles to cross LUBANG VOR	39 + 36 = 75
LUBANG VOR 117.5 MHz	N13° 51.69'	E120° 6.99'	274°	98
ISMOK	N13° 56.9'	E118° 26.2'	273°	259
MARDA	N14° 07.3'	E114° 00'	268°	233
DOTAD	N13° 59.7'	E110° 00'	268°	56
PHUCAT	N13° 59.0'	E109° 00'	273°	60
PLEIKU	N13° 59.0'	E108° 00'	268°	35
ANINA	N13° 59.0'	E107° 25'	261°	84
SOURN	N13° 45.5'	E106° 00'	274°	187
MENAM	N13° 57.4'	E102° 47.5'	271°	125
Bangkok, Thailand VOR 115.9 MHz	N13° 59.7'	E100° 39.2'		

2. After taking off from Manila, fly on a course of 206° for 39 miles, as shown on your DME indicator.

3. Shortly before reaching the 39 mile mark, tune in the LUBANG VOR at 117.5 MHz, and adjust the course indicator on the OBI 1 till it shows 85° with the FROM flag lit.

4. When the CDI needle on the OBI crosses the center mark, turn the aircraft to a compass heading of 265°, and fly for another 36 miles till you cross the LUBANG VOR.

5. After crossing the LUBANG VOR, turn to 274° and fly the rest of the waypoints as shown in Table 13.6.

BANGKOK TO CALCUTTA

Bangkok to Calcutta, India is 868 nautical miles distance. Your cruise altitude should be 43,000 feet.

CALCUTTA TO KARACHI

Calcutta to Karachi, Pakistan is 1,199 nautical miles distance. Your cruise altitude should be 43,000 feet.

KARACHI TO KUWAIT

Karachi to Kuwait City, in Kuwait, is 1,225 nautical miles distance. Your cruise altitude should be 43,000 feet. This trip is not as direct as it could be,

Table 13.7 Bangkok to Calcutta				
Waypoint/ VOR/Airport	Latitude	Longitude	Magnetic Bearing to Next Waypoint	Distance to Next Waypoint (nm)
Bangkok, Thailand VOR 115.9 MHz	N13° 59.7'	E100° 39.2'	312°	161
LIMLA	N15° 49.1'	E98° 35.8'	307°	152
BAGO	N17° 20'	E96° 30'	306°	317
TEBOV	N20° 25'	E92° 00'	304°	238
Calcutta, India VOR 112.5 MHz	N22° 38.7'	E88° 27.3'		

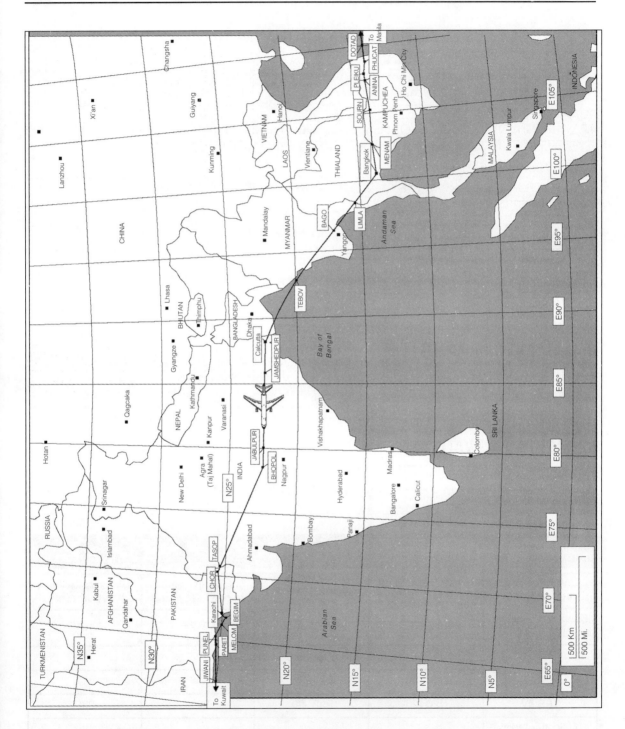

Figure 13.3 Waypoints for the flight between Bangkok and Karachi.

Table 13.8   Calcutta to Karachi

Waypoint/ VOR/Airport	Latitude	Longitude	Magnetic Bearing to Next Waypoint	Distance to Next Waypoint (nm)
Calcutta, India VOR 112.5 MHz	N22° 38.7'	E88° 27.3'	273°	133
JAMSHEDPUR VOR 115.4 MHz	N22° 48.7'	E86° 10.2'	275°	332
JABULPUR	N23° 11.6'	E80° 03.4'	273°	150
BHOPOL	N23° 17.2'	E77° 20.5'	288°	377
TASOP	N25° 13.3'	E70° 48.0'	289°	59
CHOR	N25° 32.0'	E69° 46.0'	255°	148
Karachi, Pakistan VOR 112.1 MHz	N24° 54.5'	E67° 10.5'		

Table 13.9   Karachi to Kuwait

Waypoint/ VOR/Airport	Latitude	Longitude	Magnetic Bearing to Next Waypoint	Distance to Next Waypoint (nm)
Karachi, Pakistan VOR 112.1 MHz	N24° 54.5'	E67° 10.5'	220°	16
BEGIM	N24° 43'	E67° 00'	311°	33
MELOM	N25° 05'	E66° 32'	285°	65
PUNEL	N25° 20'	E65° 23'	285°	95
PARET	N25° 27.2'	E64° 51.5'	263°	168
JIWANI	N25° 03.75'	E61° 47.75'	271°	77
EGPIC	N25° 08.8'	E60° 23.0'	271°	353
SHARJAH, Dubai Intl. Airport	N25° 19.8'	E55° 31.2'	296°	96
ORSAR	N26° 04.5'	E53° 57.5'	301°	127
IMDAT	N27° 40.0'	E51° 13.0'	294°	66
KUVER	N28° 09.4'	E50° 06.0'	297°	39
TESSO	N28° 28.9'	E49° 27.6'	243°	90
Kuwait City, Kuwait VOR 115.5 MHz	N29° 13.1'	E47° 58'		

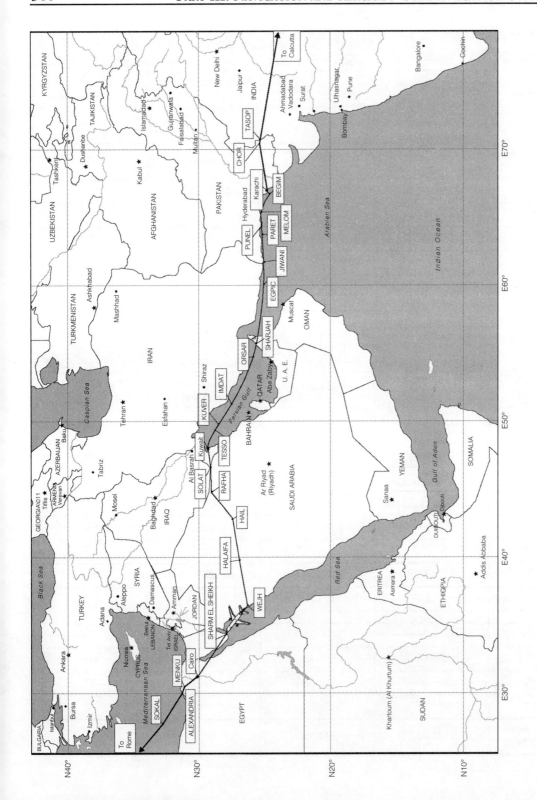

Figure 13.4 Waypoints for the flight between Karachi and Cairo.

since you will be avoiding the airspace over Iran and Afghanistan. However, to avoid trouble, this is the route most commercial traffic takes over the Persian Gulf.

Refueling at Kuwait Airport is tricky, because you must find the fuel rectangle amidst a sea of brown sand. I found the fuel rectangle in the middle of the 33R runway, on the left (as you are facing 330°).

KUWAIT TO CAIRO

Kuwait to Cairo, Egypt is 976 miles distance. Your cruise altitude should be 43,000 feet. Upon landing at Cairo, you might want to take a side trip to visit the Great Pyramids and Sphinx, just outside city limits.

CAIRO TO ROME

Cairo to Rome, Italy is 1,296 nautical miles distance. Your cruise altitude should be 43,000 feet. Landing at Rome's Fiumicino Airport is a little complicated, since you'll use your ADF radio and ADF gauge to tune in the NDB at Fiumicino to home in on the airport. What you'll do is, after passing over the OSTIA VOR, open the ADF gauge on the instrument panel (press [Shift][Tab] until you see it on-screen), then tune in the Fiumicino NDB at 345 kHz on your ADF radio. If you then turn the aircraft so that

Table 13.10 Kuwait to Cairo				
Waypoint/ VOR/Airport	Latitude	Longitude	Magnetic Bearing to Next Waypoint	Distance to Next Waypoint (nm)
Kuwait City, Kuwait VOR 115.5 MHz	N29° 13.1'	E47° 58'	265°	70
SOLAT	N29° 09.5'	E46° 38.0'	276°	129
RAFHA	N29° 37.2'	E43° 29.9'	214°	163
HAIL	N27° 25.5'	E41° 41.0'	244°	142
HALAIFA	N26° 26.0'	E39° 16.1'	263°	151
WEJH	N26° 10.7'	E36° 29.3'	312°	115
SHARM EL SHEIKH	N27° 58'	E34° 23'	307°	206
Cairo, Egypt VOR 112.5 MHz	N30° 09'	E31° 25'		

Table 13.11 Cairo to Rome				
Waypoint/ VOR/Airport	Latitude	Longitude	Magnetic Bearing to Next Waypoint	Distance to Next Waypoint (nm)
Cairo, Egypt VOR 112.5 MHz	N30° 09'	E31° 25'	314°	82
MENKU	N31° 05.5'	E30° 17.0'	285°	20
ALEXANDRIA	N31° 11.2'	E29° 56.9'	302°	148
SOKAL	N32° 36.0'	E27° 37.0'	303°	150
METRU	N34° 00'	E25° 09'	314°	164
PALEOCHORA	N35° 13.4'	E23° 41.0'	300°	469
CARAFFA	N38° 45.3'	E16° 22.2'	309°	204
PONZA VOR 114.6	N40° 54.7'	E12° 57.5'	313°	59
OSTIA VOR 114.9 MHz	N41° 48'	E12° 14.2'	Tune in Fiumicino NDB and Use ADF Gauge to Head for Fiumicino Airport.	<10 nm
Rome, Italy: Fiumicino NDB 345 kHz	N41° 52.8'	E12° 11.9		

the ADF needle remains centered squarely on the 0° mark, you'll arrive in a short time at the airport.

ROME TO PARIS

Rome to Paris, France is 632 nautical miles distance. Your cruise altitude should be 43,000 feet. Now navigating gets a bit easier because you can use the VORs in Europe, instead of waypoints. After arriving at COULOMMIERS VOR station, you have a choice of landing at Orly Airport in Paris, or Charles de Gaulle Airport, also in Paris. If you choose to fly to Orly from COULOMMIERS, than you should take a magnetic course heading of 260°, whereas if you fly to de Gaulle, you should fly a magnetic heading of 307°.

PARIS TO LONDON

Paris to London, England, where you will land at Heathrow Airport is only 174 nautical miles. This trip is the shortest hop of all your flights, and so you

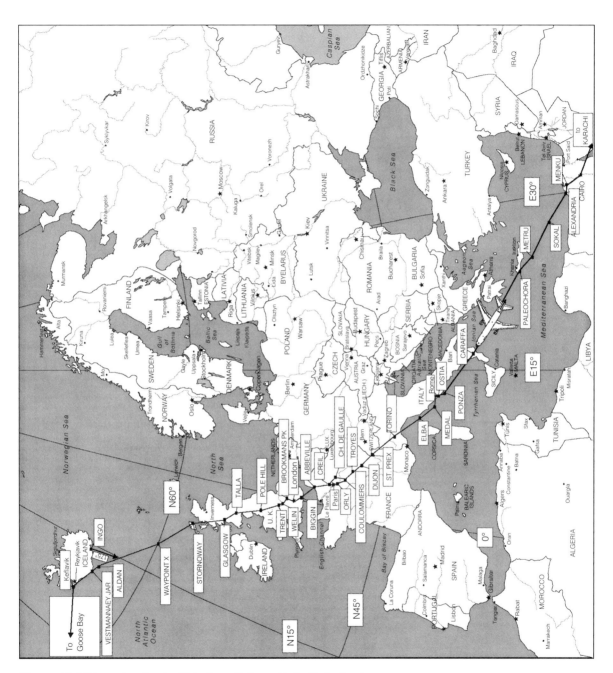

Figure 13.5 Waypoints for the flight from Cairo to Keflavik, Iceland.

Table 13.12   Rome to Paris

Waypoint/ VOR/Airport	VOR/NDB Freq.	Latitude	Longitude	Magnetic Bearing to Next Waypoint	Distance to Next Waypoint (nm)
Rome, Italy OSTIA VOR	114.9 MHz	N41° 48.2'	E12° 14.2'	291°	41
MEDAL		N42° 02'	E11° 24.0'	312°	59
ELBA VOR	114.7 MHz	N42° 43.8'	E10° 23.7'	321°	171
TORINO VOR	114.5 MHz	N44° 55.4'	E07° 51.6'	331°	111
St. PREX VOR	113.9 MHz	N46° 28.2'	E06° 26.9'	312°	74
DIJON VOR	113.5 MHz	N47° 16.2'	E05° 05.8'	325°	74
TROYES VOR	116.0 MHz	N48° 15.0'	E03° 57.8'	316°	52
COULOMMIERS VOR	112.9 MHz	N48° 50.6'	E03° 00.8'	307° to de Gaulle Airport	17.8
				260° to Orly Airport	25
Paris, France Orly VOR Charles de Gaulle VOR	111.2 MHz 112.15 MHz	N48° 43.7' N48° 59.9'	E02° 23.2' E02° 37.4'		

Table 13.13   Paris to London

Waypoint/ VOR/Airport	VOR/NDB Freq.	Latitude	Longitude	Magnetic Bearing to Next Waypoint	Distance to Next Waypoint (nm)
Paris, France Orly VOR	111.20 MHz	N48° 43.7'	E02° 23.2'	11°	31.4
Charles de Gaulle VOR	112.15 MHz	N48° 59.9'	E02° 37.4'	357°	15.7
CREIL VOR	109.20 MHz	N49° 15.3'	E02° 30.9'	340°	44
ABBEVILLE VOR	116.60 MHz	N50° 08.1'	E01° 51.3'	321°	100
BIGGIN VOR	115.10 MHz	N51° 19.8'	E00° 02.1'	296°	30
London, England Heathrow Airport VOR	113.60 MHz	N51° 29.2'	W00° 28'		

should climb to only 35,000 feet. You have a choice of taking off from Orly Airport, or Charles de Gaulle Airport. If you take off from Orly, you should take a magnetic course of 11° to fly over the CREIL VOR station. On the other hand, if you take off from Charles de Gaulle, you should take a magnetic course heading of 357° to fly over the CREIL VOR station.

LONDON TO KEFLAVIK

Although you could fly all the way from London to Goose Bay, you should play it safe and refuel at Keflavik, Iceland, before proceeding on to Goose

Table 13.14   London to Keflavik

Waypoint/ VOR/Airport	VOR/NDB Freq.	Latitude	Longitude	Magnetic Bearing to Next Waypoint	Distance to Next Waypoint (nm)
London, England Heathrow Airport VOR	113.6 MHz	N51° 29.2'	W00° 28'	43°	22.1
BROOKMAN'S PARK VOR	117.5 MHz	N51° 44.9'	W00° 06.3'	319°	45
WELIN		N52° 14.8'	W00° 51.2'	333°	109
TRENT		N53° 03.2'	W01° 40.2'	345°	44
POLE HILL VOR	112.1 MHz	N53° 44.6'	W02° 06.2'	344°	114
TALLA VOR	113.8 MHz	N55° 29.9'	W03° 21.2'	308°	43
GLASGOW VOR	115.4 MHz	N55° 52.2'	W04° 26.8'	346°	151
STORNOWAY VOR	115.1 MHz	N58° 12.4'	W06° 11.1'	323°	159
WAYPOINT X		N61° 00'	W12° 34'	322°	183
INGO VOR (INGO is not a waypoint; but a VOR radio cross check which enables you to check whether you are on course)	112.4 MHz			When you cross the 175° radial from INGO on your OBI, at W15° Longitude, you are on course	125
ALDAN		N62° 57.9'	W18° 45.9'	321°	49
VESTMANNAEYJAR NDB	375 kHz	N63° 24'	W20° 13.1'	320°	71
Keflavik, Iceland VOR	112.00 MHz	N63° 59.1'	W22° 36.3'		

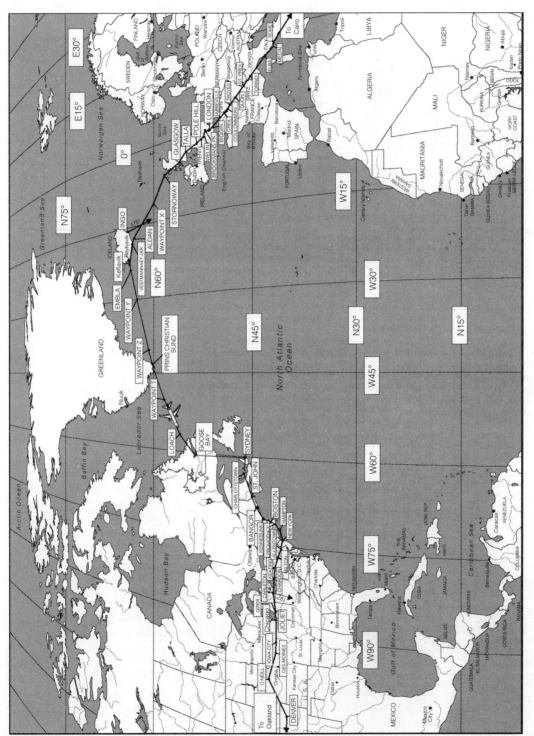

Figure 13.6 Waypoints for the North Atlantic Crossing Between London and New York.

Bay, Canada. The distance between London and Keflavik is 1,123 nautical miles, so you'll want to cruise at 43,000 feet. Note that after reaching Waypoint X, you should tune in the INGO VOR at 112.4 MHz. Although INGO is not a waypoint on your course, it serves as a cross check to make sure your aircraft is on course. The intersection of the 175° radial from INGO and your course represents a waypoint, even though you don't actually fly over INGO. But how do you determine where this intersection point is? What you do is adjust the OBI course indicator till it reads 175°, and wait until the FROM flag lights up. Then you watch the CDI needle till it crosses the center mark. If you are on course, the CDI needle will center itself when you cross W15° longitude, as shown on your latitude/longitude display.

Also, when you near Iceland, you'll need to switch on your ADF gauge, and determine which direction you need to fly. After tuning the ADF radio to the VESTMAANEYJAR NDB, instead of flying the magnetic course heading shown in the table, you can just as well get there by turning the aircraft so that the ADF needle is lined up with the 0° mark. This will point your plane directly towards the NDB. Upon crossing the VESTMAANEYJAR NDB, your ADF needle will spin 180° around, letting you know that you have just overflown the beacon.

KEFLAVIK TO GOOSE BAY

The distance between Keflavik and Goose Bay is 1,319 nautical miles, so you'll want to fly at an altitude of 43,000 feet.

GOOSE BAY TO NEW YORK

Goose Bay to New York is 1,161 nautical miles, so you will want to fly at 43,000 feet. Because your next waypoint after Goose Bay is Sydney, Canada, and Sydney lies on almost the same meridian as Goose Bay, you will fly the Learjet on a true course of 180° from Goose Bay. However, due to the extreme magnetic variation in this region (26°W), your course will have to be 206° magnetic variation (180°+26°=206°).

Table 13.15   Keflavik to Goose Bay

Waypoint/ VOR/Airport	Latitude	Longitude	Magnetic Bearing to Next Waypoint	Distance to Next Waypoint (nm)
Keflavik, Iceland VOR 112.00 MHz	N63° 59.1'	W22° 36.3'	278°	120
EMBLA	N63° 28.2'	W26° 58.9	276°	87
WAYPOINT Y	N63° 00'	W30° 00'	277°	307
WAYPOINT Z	N61° 00	W40° 00'	269°	110
PRINS CHRISTIAN SUND NDB 372 kHz	N60° 03.5'	W43° 09.8'	275°	245
WAYPOINT T	N58° 00'	W50° 00'	270°	275
LOACH	W55° 31.0'	W57° 01'	252°	175
Goose Bay, Canada VOR 117.30 MHz	N53° 20.3'	W60° 22.0'		

Table 13.16   Goose Bay to New York

Waypoint/ VOR/Airport	VOR/NDB Freq.	Latitude	Longitude	Magnetic Bearing to Next Waypoint	Distance to Next Waypoint (nm)
Goose Bay, Canada VOR	117.30 MHz	N53° 20.3'	W60° 22.0'	206°	431
SYDNEY VOR	114.90 MHz	N46° 09.2'	W60° 03.4'	289°	122
CHARLOTTETOWN, PRINCE EDWARD ISLAND VOR	114.10 MHz	N46° 12.4'	W62° 58.7'	271°	130
ST. JOHN VOR	113.50 MHz	N45° 24.4'	W65° 52.3'	277°	132
BANGOR, MAINE VOR	114.80 MHz	N44° 50.5'	W68° 52.4'	241°	113
KENNEBUNK VOR	117.10 MHz	N43° 25.5'	W70° 36.8'	212°	66
BOSTON VOR	112.70 MHz	N42° 21.5'	W70° 59.4'	224°	43
PROVIDENCE VOR	115.60 MHz	N41° 43.5'	W71° 25.8'	234°	63
HAMPTON VOR	113.60 MHz	N40° 55.1'	W72° 19.0'	272°	61
New York, JFK Airport VOR	115.90 MHz	N40° 38.0'	W73° 46.3'		

Table 13.17   New York to Chicago

Waypoint/ VOR/Airport	VOR Freq.	Latitude	Longitude	Magnetic Bearing to Next Waypoint	Distance to Next Waypoint (nm)
New York, JFK Airport VOR	115.9 MHz	N40° 38.0'	W73° 46.3'	287°	77
ALLENTOWN VOR	117.5 MHz	N40° 43.6'	W75° 27.3'	298°	58
MILTON VOR	109.2 MHz	N41° 01.4'	W76° 39.9'	289°	68
KEATING VOR	116.0 MHz	N41° 12.9'	W78° 08.6'	289°	138
CHARDON VOR	112.7 MHz	N41° 31.0'	W81° 09.8'	284°	107
CARLETON VOR (Note: CARLETON is not a waypoint. Use the 197° radial from CARLETON VOR to determine where to turn for the leg to GIPER)	115.7 MHz	N/A	N/A	After passing the 197° radial on your OBI from the CARLETON VOR, turn to 269°	126
GIPER VOR	115.4 MHz	N41° 46.1'	W86° 19.1'	262°	91
JOLIET VOR	112.3 MHz	N41° 32.8'	W88° 19.1'	20°	44
Chicago O'Hare Airport VOR	113.9 MHz	N41° 59.3'	W87° 54.2'		

NEW YORK TO CHICAGO

New York to Chicago is only 709 nautical miles. Your cruise altitude should be 43,000 feet. After you reach CHARDON VOR, you should tune in the CARLETON VOR, as indicated in Table 13.17. However, CARLETON VOR is not a waypoint on your flight path; instead at the intersection of the 197° radial from CARLETON to the 284° track from CHARDON, you turn the aircraft to a course of 269°. How do you determine where this intersection is? Well, after leaving CHARDON on a course of 284°, you tune in CARLETON at 115.7 MHz, and then adjust the top course indicator on the OBI till it reads 197°. Then, wait until the CARLETON VOR comes into range, and when the FROM flag lights up, watch the CDI needle until it crosses the center cross hair mark. At this exact moment, you should turn the aircraft to a new compass heading of 269°, and then fly on till you reach the GIPER VOR.

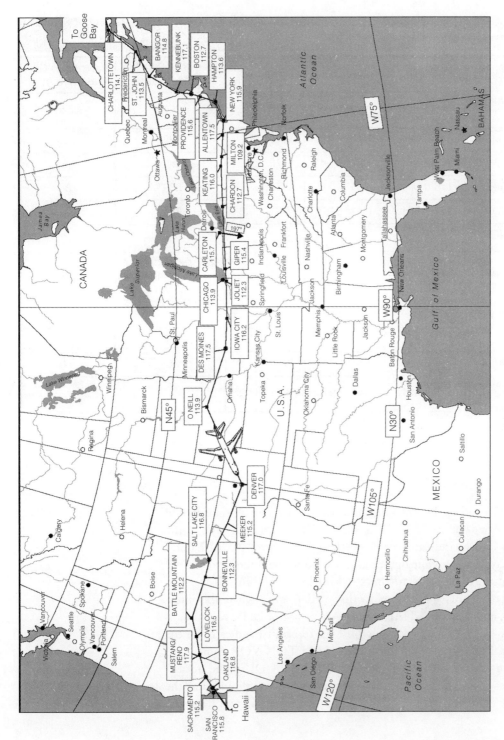

Figure 13.7 Waypoints for the flight from New York to Oakland

Table 13.18   Chicago to Oakland

Waypoint/ VOR/Airport	VOR Freq.	Latitude	Longitude	Magnetic Bearing to Next Waypoint	Distance to Next Waypoint (nm)
Chicago O'Hare Airport VOR	113.9 MHz	N41° 59.3'	W87° 54.2'	200°	44
JOLIET VOR	112.3 MHz	N41° 32.8'	W88° 19.1'	268°	148
IOWA CITY VOR	116.2 MHz	N41° 31.1'	W91 37'	263°	92
DES MOINS VOR	117.5 MHz	N41° 26.3'	W93° 39'	280°	234
O NEILL VOR	113.9 MHz	N42° 28.2'	W98° 41.2'	232°	323
DENVER VOR	117.0 MHz	N39° 48.0'	W104° 53.2'	265°	141
MEEKER VOR	115.2 MHz	N40° 04'	W107° 55.5'	270°	192
SALT LAKE CITY VOR	116.8 MHz	N40 51.0'	W111° 58.9'	249°	81
BONNEVILLE VOR	112.3 MHz	N40° 43.7'	W113° 45.5'	250°	145
BATTLE MOUNTAIN VOR	112.2 MHz	N40° 34.15'	W116° 55.3'	233°	80
LOVELOCK VOR	116.5 MHz	N40° 07'	W118° 34.7'	219°	61
MUSTANG/RENO VOR	117.9 MHz	N39° 31.9'	W119° 39.4'	218°	110
SACRAMENTO VOR	115.2 MHz	N38° 26.6'	W121° 33.1'	200°	54
Oakland Intl. Airport VOR	116.8 MHz	N37° 43.6'	W122° 13.5'		

CHICAGO TO OAKLAND
VIA DENVER AND SALT LAKE CITY

This route is not the most direct to Oakland, California. Instead, you will fly from Chicago to Denver, where you fly over the Rocky Mountains and see the new Denver International Airport, and then proceed on to Salt Lake City, where you can fly over the Great Salt Lake. Next, you'll fly to Mustang/Reno, on to Sacramento, and finally land at Oakland International, across San Francisco Bay from San Francisco International Airport. Total flight distance is 1,705 nautical miles.

FLYING OTHER GREAT CIRCLE ROUTES

For other great circle routes around the world, you can use the pre-printed waypoints in aviation charts, or calculate your own track using the method described in Chapter 12. You can also download shareware navigation software to calculate your great circle waypoints. There are two programs that are useful for doing this:

- WinPlanner for Windows: You can download Antoine Becker's WinPlanner for Windows (see Chapter 15 for a description of the program) from the CompuServe Flight Simulator Forum, Library 2. Note that you will have to download special shareware .BGL files that contain waypoints and VORs for the regions of the world not covered by the default scenery in FS 5.1 CD.
- FSPLAN: Also on the CompuServe Flight Simulator Forum, John Trindle's FSPLAN is a DOS program that will calculate waypoints (called WINS) for great circle tracks you specify.

In addition, the new Flight Shop add-on from BAO comes with a flight planner that allows you to create flight plans automatically from the Navaids found in FS 5.1CD (complete with air traffic control instructions). Because there are few Navaids over the oceans, or in other countries, you can import into Flight Shop new waypoints/Navaids from text files you create or obtain (visit CompuServe's Flight Simulator Forum Libraries to obtain free Navaids for the rest of the world). The flight planner will generate magnetic headings for each Navaid along the flight path you specify. Note that waypoints imported into the program must have a "phantom" VOR frequency assigned to them to work properly. Just add any acceptable VOR frequency you like for these waypoints and they will act like normal VOR stations.

I have found, however, that the easiest way to plan great circle flights is to purchase the Department of Defense Enroute High Altitude Charts for the regions of the world you will be flying. In these charts, all the waypoints are printed, along with the magnetic bearings to fly between each waypoint. In addition, all the VOR/NDBs are plotted, and you don't have to hassle with any calculations for magnetic variation, since the course headings take them into account for the region. The maps are fairly inexpensive; for example, you can order map sets for the entire Pacific region, including India, Thailand, Japan, Australia, Guam, Hawaii, etc., for $9.50 total. The entire European continent maps go for $8.75. You can order the maps for overnight delivery from Aviation Services in Del Mar, California at 619-755-1190, or toll free at 800-869-7453. The same maps can also be obtained from the U.S. Department of Commerce's National Oceanic and Atmospheric Administration (NOAA) in Riverdale, Maryland at 301-436-6980, or at FAX 301-436-6829, but allow several weeks for delivery.

P A R T

IV

Special Features and Add-ons

C H A P T E R

14

Special Features

This chapter guides you through the many special features available under the Options/Entertainment and Options/Flight Analysis menus. You will learn how to quickly move the aircraft from place to place using a special non-flight mode called slewing. You'll also learn how to use the logbook. Under the Options/Entertainment menu, you can fly in dual-player mode with a friend via modem or direct link serial cable; or you can try your hand at formation flying, crop dusting, or some quick practice maneuvers. The flight review tools under the Options/Flight Analysis menu allow you to analyze your flight maneuvers and landings, record and play back videos of your flights, get instant video replays of the last 50 seconds of flight, and plot your course trajectory for later perusal. Using the special slewing controls, you can quickly move the airplane from place to place or rotate it in 3-D.

ENTERTAINMENT

There are four options available under the Entertainment menu option accessed from the Options menu. They are:

- Dual-player
- Formation Flying
- Crop Duster
- Quick Practice

Inside the Dual-player, Formation Flying and Quick Practice dialog boxes, there are multiple selections you can choose from. In the next section we will touch upon some of these, as well as how to use the dual-player mode.

377

Dual-player Mode Via Direct Link or Modem

Flight Simulator can link another player into the simulation using a second computer hooked up to your computer via a serial cable or by modem and a telephone line. If you are hooking up the computers directly via serial cable, you must use a null-modem cable. This cable is a special type of serial cable that crosses the internal wires a certain way. It differs from other serial cables, so don't expect a normal serial cable to allow you to communicate directly. You can buy a null-modem serial cable from almost any computer store, and it shouldn't cost more than $10 or $15. Just ask for a DB25 nullmodem serial cable. The DB25 refers to a rectangular connector that has 25 pins; both ends of the null-modem cable should have female connectors—that is empty sockets you can connect to the male prongs on the computer's serial COM port.

When hooking up two computers, use only a null-modem serial cable.

Specifying Dual-player Preferences

When you select the Dual-player option from the Options/Entertainment dialog box, a communications dialog box will open up. In this dialog box, shown in Figure 14.1, you can:

- Select the other plane's color. This is the color that your computer will give to your flying companion's plane on your computer. It is not the color that your flying companion will see for his/her plane.
- Select Auto-pilot Lock to Other Plane.
- Have your ADF gauge always track the other plane (ADF Track Other Plane, ADF Tracking checkboxes), or have the ADF and DME track the other plane (ADF Track Other Plane, ADF and DME Tracking). See later in this chapter for more details on how to use this feature.

Figure 14.1
Dual-player dialog box

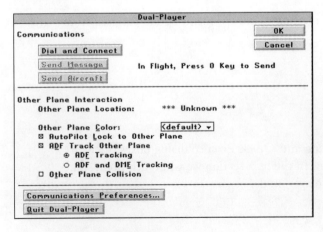

- For more realism, allow the other plane to crash into you or you to crash into it (Other Plane Collision checkbox).
- Set your modem's communications parameters (Communications Preferences button).
- Send a message to the other player, if you are already connected (Send Message button). During flight, press [0] to send a message.
- Send information about your aircraft to your flying companion's computer (Send Aircraft button).

Setting the Communications Parameters

Click on the Communications Preferences button to bring up the Dual-player Communications Preferences dialog box, pictured in Figure 14.2. In this window, you must select the COM port your modem or serial cable is hooked up to (COM 1 through COM 4 are available), the baud rate (The use of the term "baud rate" is really a misnomer here; it should be called bits per second. It refers to the speed with which your computer is allowed to communicate.) You must also enter the telephone number of the person you wish to call. If you are expecting someone to call you to link up via modem, you would then click the Wait for Ring checkbox.

When linking up two computers, make sure you set the data transmission rate (baud rate) to the same number for both computers. Use the maximum transmission speed you can for the available hardware. For direct null-modem serial cable hook-up (computer to computer, no telephone line) you can use a baud rate of 57,600 bits per second (bps). For high speed 28,800 bps modems (called V.34 modems), you can try using 19,200 bps; 38,400 bps; 57,600 bps; or if those higher speeds don't work, 4,800 or 2,400 bps.[1] If you have a slower speed 2,400 bps modem, use the 2,400 bps setting; if you have a 14,400 bps modem, try using the 9,600 bps setting (your 14,400 bps modem might have a data buffer; if so try using speeds higher than 9,600 bps).

The rest of the options in the Dual-player Communications Preferences dialog box allow you to customize your modem's operation. If you have an error correcting, data compression capable high speed modem, you must have these features turned off. *Flight Simulator* will not work with data compression or error correction turned on in your modem. To turn off data compression and error correction, type in the following characters after the modem initialization string:[2]

&Q0 (be sure to use a zero and not the "O" character)[3]

According to Microsoft, *Flight Simulator* runs most efficiently at speeds lower than 9,600 for modem connections. However, choose 57,600 bps for direct null-modem serial cable connection from computer to computer.

---

[1]Some 28,800 bps modems are able to use the 38400 bps, or 57600 bps baud rates, even though they can physically transmit at only 28,800 bps. Thus you might try these higher speeds to see if they work with your V.34 28,800 modem. The reason why you can use a higher speed than your modem can physically transmit, is that the modem has a buffer that allows it to absorb data from the computer; when the buffer is full, the modem tells the computer to wait before sending the next chunk of data. The modem will continue to send the data over the telephone at 28,800 bps, its maximum transmission speed, but with the buffer always filled with data, the modem is never left waiting for the computer to send data.

[2]A "string" is a term used with computers to describe a series of characters or numbers.

[3]Note that the AT modem commands used in this chapter work with Practical Peripherals modems, but these commands will have functional equivalents that may be coded differently for your own modem. Consult your modem manual, and just replace the &Q0 command with whatever &xx command your modem uses instead.

You must turn off data compression and error correction in your modem for dual-player mode to work. Consult your modem manual to see what your modem commands are for these two functions, then replace the &Q0 command with the appropriate command string.

Your modem initialization string should look like this:

AT&F&C1&D2X4Q0V1S0=0&Q0

Table 14.1 lists what the individual modem commands in the above listed modem initialization string when using a Practical Peripherals modem. If your modem uses different command strings, don't worry, just look up the functional equivalents in your modem manual and then substitute them in the string listed above.

Establishing the Modem Connection

Using modems you can fly *Flight Simulator* with a friend no matter how far away they live. You can see their plane fly and they can see your plane fly. You can even send messages to each other that will appear on screen.

If you are placing the call, here are the steps to follow when connecting up via modem:

1. Under the Options menu, select Entertainment.
2. In the Entertainment dialog box, choose Dual-player, and then click OK.
3. In the Dual-player dialog box that next opens, click on the Communications Preferences button.
4. Pull down the COM Port list box, and select the COM port your modem is currently using.
5. Pull down the Baud Rate list box, and choose your modem's maximum baud rate. If you have a 28,800 bps modem, try using 19,200 or faster. Make sure your friend is using the same baud rate.
6. Your friend must now click the Wait for Ring checkbox.

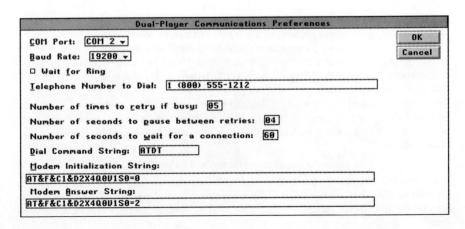

Figure 14.2
Dual-player
Communications
Preferences

Table 14.1 Modem Command Summary for Practical Peripherals Modems	
AT Modem Command	**Function Description**
AT	Attention modem, listen for commands to follow
&F	Load Hayes compatible factory default modem settings
&C1	Track data carrier of external modem to see if it is on. Report the results back.
&D2	Monitor data terminal ready line (DTR) and if off, hang up the telephone
X4	Modem sends a message to *Flight Simulator* if a proper connection has been made (i.e., "connect 9600")
Q0	Modem sends a message to *Flight Simulator* such as "OK," "busy," or "ring"
V1	Makes messages appear as words rather than as number codes
S0=0	Disables auto-answer mode for your modem. (Your AA light on an external modem should be snuffed out.)
S0=2	Turn auto-answer mode on for your modem. You can now receive modem calls. (Your AA light on an external modem should be lit.)
&Q0	Turn off error correction, data buffering, and data compression
L2	Medium modem speaker volume
M1	Modem speaker on until other modem answers
ATDT	Tone dial a telephone number (eg., ATDT 8437060).

7. Since you are placing the call, type in the telephone number of your friend. If the call is long distance, be sure to type **1** before the area code.

8. Click the OK button to return to the Dual-player dialog box.

9. Click the Dial and Connect button to have the modem connect you to your friend's computer.

You should now hear a dial tone as your modem dials your friend's computer. If all goes well, your friend's computer will pick up the line and answer with a harsh screech. Your computer will retort with an even harsher

Flight Simulator works best with external modems that have hardware "handshaking" serial cables. If you have an internal modem, you don't have any serial cables and don't need to worry about this.

static like sound and you should soon be connected. If something goes wrong you need to adjust the baud rate, disconnect error correction or data compression on your modem (or your friend's modem), or perhaps send a different modem string to properly initialize your modem. You might have to enter &Q0 after the modem initialization string to disable your modem's error correction and data compression (or substitute whatever command string on your modem you use for shutting off data compression/error correction) before the connection can be made to work.

When the connection is complete, you will see the message, "V5.10 User Connected!" on your screen. At this point, your computer will exchange latitude/longitude aircraft position coordinates and you will soon be able to send messages to your friend.

To quit dual-player mode and hang up the modem, select the Options/Entertainment/Dual-player menu command, then in the Dual-player dialog box, click the Quit Dual-player button.

Direct Connect Using a Serial Null-modem Cable

The link up procedure for a serial cable direct connection, computer to computer, is slightly different than the modem setup.

Follow these steps:

1. Under the Options menu, select Entertainment.

2. In the Entertainment dialog box, choose Dual-player, and then click OK.

3. In the Dual-player dialog box that opens next, click on the Communications Preferences button.

4. Pull down the COM Port list box, and select the COM port the null-modem serial cable is currently using on the first computer. On the second computer, select the COM port the second computer is using.

5. Pull down the Baud Rate list box, and choose the fastest speed of 57,600 bps.

6. Check to make sure that the Wait for Ring checkbox is toggled off for both computers.

7. Erase all the text in the Modem Initialization String text box for both computers. To do this, select the text box and press [Backspace] until the box is cleared of all text; then press [Enter]. (You must do this, otherwise the Direct Connect button will not appear in the Dual-player dialog box.)

8. Click the OK button to return to the Dual-player dialog box.

9. Click the Direct Connect button, and the program will begin the connection procedure. (The Direct Connect button will replace the Dial and Connect button.)

To quit dual-player mode select the Options/Entertainment/Dual Player menu command, then click the Quit Dual-player button.

When the connection is complete, you will see the message, "V5.10 User Connected!" on your screen. At this point, your computer will exchange latitude/longitude aircraft position coordinates and you will soon be able to send messages to your friend.

How to Send and Receive Messages in Dual-player Mode

You can send text messages that will appear on their screen to your friend. To do this, press 0 on the main keyboard. Type in the message in the message text box that pops open, then press Enter to send the message.

Messages sent to you by your friend will appear on top of the instrument panel. If you have sound turned on, you will hear an audible beep each time you receive a new message.

How to Find Your Friend's Plane in Dual-player Mode

It is often difficult to locate your friend's plane while in dual-player mode. To remedy this, *Flight Simulator 5.1* includes the following multi-player utilities:

- *Send Aircraft:* Before choosing any of the other multi-player utilities, you should click this button in the Dual-player dialog box. *Flight Simulator* will send information about your aircraft to your friend's computer so both aircraft can be displayed accurately.

- *Track View:* Displays your friend's aircraft on your cockpit windshield, no matter where they are. Press S to cycle between cockpit, tower, track, and spot views. This view is only available in dual-player mode. Using your second 3-D view window, you can have both your cockpit view and the track view of the other aircraft on screen simultaneously.

- *Other Plane Color:* Change your friend's aircraft color, as it is displayed on your screen. Go to the Dual-player dialog box and pull down the Other Plane Color list box. Choose a distinctive color you can readily identify.

- *Airports:* Place both aircraft at the same airport using the Airports menu option under the World menu.

- *Other Plane Location:* In the Dual-player dialog box, you can see the latitude/longitude coordinates of your friend's current aircraft position. Use the Set Exact Location command under the World menu to match these latitude/longitude coordinates for your plane. You don't need to use this option if you use the Airports command listed previously.

- *Quick Catch Up:* Press Ctrl and Spacebar to quickly catch up to the other plane. Make sure you are both on the ground or in the air simultaneously, otherwise you will crash.

To send messages, press 0 on the main keyboard, then type your message and press Enter.

If your sound is turned on, new messages are accompanied by an audible beep.

- *ADF Track Other Plane:* Clicking on this option checkbox in the Dual-player dialog box allows you to track your friend's aircraft on your ADF gauge as if the other plane were an NDB radio beacon. To also have your DME indicator show the distance to your friend's plane, click the ADF and DME Tracking checkbox. Make sure that your ADF gauge is displayed on your instrument panel. If it is not, press (Shift) and (Tab) to switch between the OBI 2 and ADF gauge. With this feature enabled, the ADF needle will show you the direction of the other airplane in relation to your aircraft's nose. If the needle points to 9 (90°), for example, your friend's plane is directly to your right. To aim your aircraft toward your friend's plane, turn the aircraft until the needle is centered on 0 (0°).

- *Auto-pilot Lock to Other Plane:* Both you and your friend should each click on this checkbox in the Dual-player dialog box to have the auto-pilot fly toward the other plane. Make sure you are both flying at approximately the same altitude and that the Altitude Lock (ALT) checkbox in the Auto-pilot dialog box is toggled on.

Tip: Use (Spacebar) to instantly catch up with the lead plane in formation flying.

Formation Flying

The Formation Flying option allows you to follow a second computer generated airplane in one of several different modes you can select. The second airplane often performs rather reckless flight maneuvers that are aerobatic in nature, so you will need some experience and practice to keep up. Just follow the smoke puff contrails of the plane in front of you.

Crop Duster

The Crop Duster option gives you the opportunity to try your hand at spraying a field with insecticides. You are scored by how many blocks, or acres, of land you can spray within a given time frame. The entire field is broken up into 64 acres, each acre you successfully cover with spray turns black. You can see how you are doing by looking at your score card displayed on the right side of the cockpit window, or you can call up the map and see how many squares are black. The remaining green squares need to be sprayed before your time is up. To start spraying, press (I). Press (I) again to stop spraying.

FLIGHT REVIEW

Flight Simulator includes special tools to give you feedback on your maneuvers, landings, and crashes. Using a course plotter, FS 5.1 allows you to track

Sprayed   Unsprayed   Count-   Number of
area   area   down   squares
                               timer   sprayed

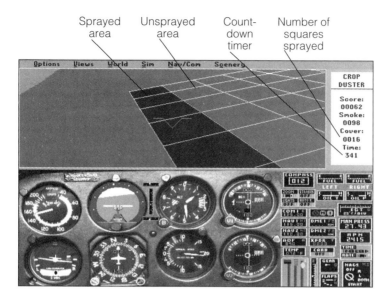

Figure 14.3
Crop dusting

your aircraft's course and see how close to a particular path you were flying. There is also a video recorder for taping flights, and an instant replay camera for recording the last 50 seconds of flight.

Using these tools helps you improve your flying abilities by analyzing the flight maneuvers afterward.

To see all your flight review options, select the Flight Analysis command from the Options menu. You will see the Flight Analysis dialog box open up, as pictured in Figure 14.4.

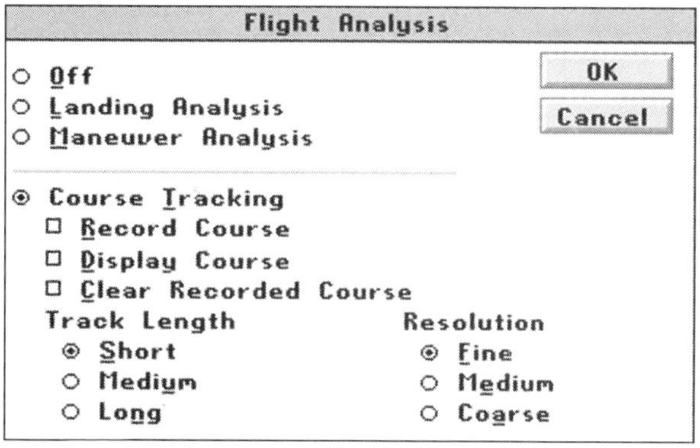

Figure 14.4
Flight Analysis
dialog box

Landing Analysis

Landing Analysis reports your landing speed and flight path to the runway. It is only activated when your airplane comes within 100 above the runway.

To activate Landing Analysis:

1. Select the Flight Analysis command from the Options menu. The Flight Analysis dialog box will open.

Flight Analysis

○ Off
○ Landing Analysis
○ Maneuver Analysis

⊙ Course Tracking
  ☐ Record Course
  ☐ Display Course
  ☐ Clear Recorded Course
  Track Length   Resolution
    ⊙ Short   ⊙ Fine
    ○ Medium   ○ Medium
    ○ Long   ○ Coarse

[OK]
[Cancel]

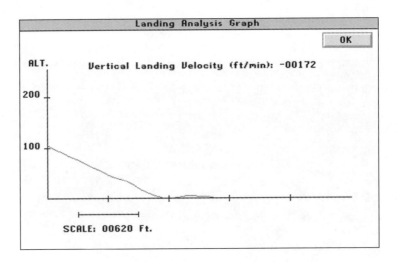

Figure 14.5
Landing analysis

2. Toggle on the Landing Analysis radio button.

3. Click the OK button to return to the simulation.

Maneuver Analysis

To display a two-dimensional path of your airplane's flight maneuvers, select Maneuver Analysis in the Flight Analysis dialog box. Maneuver Analysis differs from Landing Analysis in that course recording begins the moment you leave the Flight Analysis dialog box. To end the Maneuver Analysis and bring up the report, press ⟨\⟩. A graph showing your flight path is then displayed.

To activate Maneuver Analysis:

1. Select the Flight Analysis command from the Options menu. The Flight Analysis dialog box will open.

2. Toggle on the Maneuver Analysis radio button.

3. Click the OK button to return to the simulation.

You can turn off Maneuver or Landing Analysis by toggling on the Off radio button in the Flight Analysis dialog box.

Electronic Flight Information System (EFIS) Navigational Situations

Flight Simulator comes with four situations that use the advanced Electronic Flight Information System (EFIS) cockpit display. Each scenario starts you off in a landing approach with the EFIS/CFPD (Command Flight Path Display) projecting rectangles on your cockpit windshield leading to the airport. To follow the correct glide path or course, you must keep your plane flying through each rectangle. Note in the Chicago Learjet Cruise to O'Hare scenario, the CFPD rectangles do not lead you directly to the runway. Once you have the airport in sight, you need to veer to the left or right to land on one of the parallel runways.

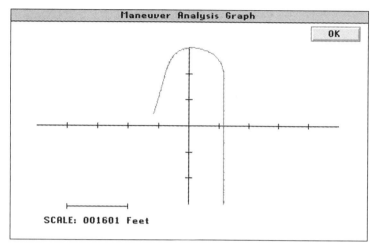

Figure 14.6
Maneuver analysis

The following EFIS navigational situations are available:

• San Francisco 28L ILS Approach

• Stormy approach to Oakland

• Learjet Cruise to O'Hare

• Stormy Approach to Oakland

To fly any of these EFIS situations, use the Options/Situations menu command then select one of the situations above.

Recording and Playing Back Videos of Your Flights

You can record and playback videos of your flights, or of others, by using *Flight Simulator*'s built in video recorder.

To play a video:

1. Select Video Recorder from the Options menu.

2. In the Video Recorder dialog box, highlight the name of the video you want to play.

3. Click the Play Selected Video button.

4. Click the OK button to start the video. To end video playback, press Esc.

To record a video, follow these steps:

1. Select Video Recorder from the Options menu.

2. Click the Record New Video button.

3. In the Record New Video dialog box, choose the recording interval you

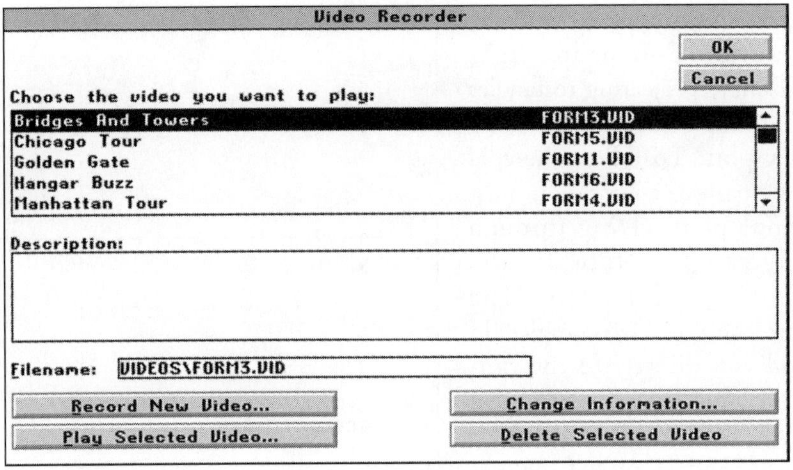

Figure 14.7
The Video Recorder
dialog box

want. You can choose between one second or five second intervals. Choosing one second intervals gives you a smoother and more accurate video because you are recording one frame every second; the five second recording interval will be jerkier, but will offer a longer video recording time.

4. Click the OK button. The Video Recorder is now on and you can see a status report on the lower left corner of the screen.

5. To stop recording, press ⌐. You will see a Stop Video Recording dialog box.

6. Type a title for your video, then click one of the following buttons:

   - Save Video: Saves your video with the title you gave it.
   - Cancel: Returns to the simulator and resumes video recording.
   - Review: Reviews your video.
   - Discard Video: Returns to *Flight Simulator* without saving the video.

Course Tracking

Using the Course Tracking option you can record the course you flew and display it in your 3-D view window 1 and Map window (but not the 3-D view window 2). The length of the plotted track can be displayed in Short (five line segments), Medium (15 line segments), or Long (30 line segments), and the resolution can be set to Fine, Medium, or Coarse. For short flights, use Fine resolution, while for longer flights use Medium or Coarse. Since memory for course tracking is limited, when you run out of memory, the oldest part of your course is erased.

You can simultaneously record and view your course as it is being tracked. To do this, simply click on both the Record Course checkbox and the Display Course checkbox. To clear a previously recorded course, click the Clear Recorded Course checkbox. You can see the various Course Tracking options in Figure 14.4.

Instant Replay

Using Instant Replay, you can play back the last 50 seconds of flight at any time. To do this follow these steps:

1. Select Instant Replay from the Options menu.
2. In the Replay Final Seconds dialog box, type in the number of seconds you want to have replayed in the Replay Final Seconds text box. You can enter from 1 to 50 seconds.
3. Choose the Replay Speed. Enter a percentage of normal speed. One hundred percent is normal speed, 200 percent is twice normal speed, 50 percent is half normal speed.
4. Click the Repeat Replay check box if you want to have the instant replay repeated indefinitely in a loop. Press (Esc) to stop the instant replay loop.
5. Click the OK button to start the replay of the last few seconds of your flight.
6. After the replay has finished (if it hasn't, you can press (Esc) to stop it), click the OK button in the Instant Replay dialog box, then press (P) to resume flight.

USING THE LOGBOOK

To keep track of your flight time, the aircraft you flew, and the type of flying involved, you can use *Flight Simulator's* logbook. To create a new logbook:

1. Select the Logbook command from the Options menu.
2. In the Standard Pilot Logbook dialog box, click the Create Logbook button.
3. In the Create Logbook dialog box that next opens, click OK to accept the proposed name for the new logbook. If you want to change the name, simply type a new name in the text box. After clicking OK, you will be returned to the Standard Pilot Logbook dialog box.
4. Select the logbook you wish to use and then toggle on the Log Flight Time checkbox.

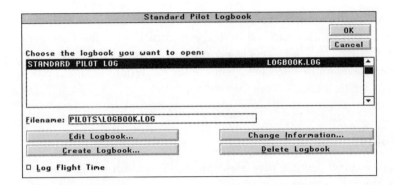

Figure 14.8
Creating your first
logbook

Figure 14.9
Editing the Standard
Pilot Logbook

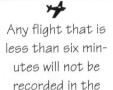

Any flight that is
less than six min-
utes will not be
recorded in the
logbook.

Your logbook is now open and will record your current flight. If you prefer to have the logbook always on, go to the General Preferences dialog box under the Options menu, and click on the Log Flight Time checkbox. Then, whenever you start up *Flight Simulator*, the logbook will always be on.

Other options in the Standard Pilot Logbook allow you to add new entries, review and edit the logbook, delete entries, change the name of a logbook, delete a logbook, or create other logbooks. In fact, you can create a logbook for each person in your family or you can create a separate logbook for each airplane.

SLEWING AROUND THE *FLIGHT SIMULATOR* WORLD

Slewing is a special non-flight mode that allows you to quickly move from point to point in the *Flight Simulator* world. In addition to actually moving the aircraft in 3-D (called *translation*), you can also re-orient the plane to any attitude (called *rotation*). This mode is extremely useful for re-positioning your aircraft anywhere in the *Flight Simulator* world. In addition, you can easily view scenery out of your cockpit window and move the aircraft to vantage points you could not ordinarily attain in regular flight.

The slewing controls will only work when you enter slew mode. To enter and exit slew mode press ⓨ.

There are two types of slewing motion: translation and rotation. These are described in the next section, along with a list of keyboard and mouse slewing controls.

Translation

Translation is the movement that occurs when you move your plane from one location to another. You can translate the aircraft up and down, left and right, or backward and forward using the translation slew keys. With the mouse, you can only translate backward or forward by rolling the mouse backward or forward.

Rotation

Rotation is the revolving, or turning motion that occurs around one of the plane's axes. Unlike translation, during rotation the plane's position in space does not change. There are three axes of rotation:

- Yaw: Refers to the rotation about the aircraft's vertical axis. When you change the course heading left or right, you are yawing.
- Roll: Refers to the rotation about the aircraft's longitudinal axis. For example, when the wings bank left or right, this is considered a roll movement.
- Pitch: Refers to the rotation about the aircraft's lateral axis. Pitching causes the plane's nose to go up or down.

Figure 14.10 shows the three rotational movements possible in slew mode.

Using the keyboard, you can affect all the rotational slew movements. With the mouse, however, you can only yaw the aircraft left or right by moving the mouse left or right.

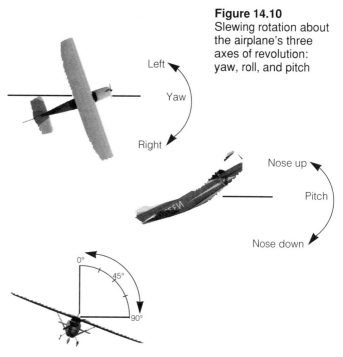

Figure 14.10
Slewing rotation about the airplane's three axes of revolution: yaw, roll, and pitch

Slewing Translation Using the Keyboard

The following keys allow you to translate the aircraft while in slew mode:

SLEW TRANSLATION	KEY (FUNCTION KEYS ON TOP)	KEY (FUNCTION KEYS ON LEFT)
Up or Down in Altitude		
Up Slowly	Q	Q
Up Quickly	F4	F2
Down Slowly	A	A
Down Quickly	F1	F10
Freeze	5	5
Forward & Backward		
Forward	8	8
Backward	2	2
Freeze	5	5
Sideways		
Left	4	4
Right	6	6
Freeze	5	5

Slewing Rotation Using the Keyboard

The following keys allow you to re-orient the aircraft's pitch, bank (roll), and heading (yaw) while in slew mode:

SLEW ROTATION	KEY (FUNCTION KEYS ON TOP)	KEY (FUNCTION KEYS ON LEFT)
Pitch		
Nose Up Slow	9 (on main keyboard)	9 (on main keyboard)
Nose Up Fast	F5	F1
Freeze	F6	F5
Nose Down Fast	F8	F9
Nose Down Slow	0 (on main keyboard)	F7
Bank (Roll)		
Left	7	7
Right	9	9
Freeze	5	5

SLEW ROTATION	KEY (FUNCTION KEYS ON TOP)	KEY (FUNCTION KEYS ON LEFT)
Heading (Yaw)		
Left	1	1
Right	3	3
Freeze	5	5

Other keyboard slewing functions include the following:

Z   Toggle Position Display Between On/Off/Latitude-Longitude/North-East Coordinate Systems

Spacebar   Reset Aircraft Orientation so it is level:

           Heading: North
           Pitch: 0°
           Bank: 0°

Using the Mouse to Slew

While in slew mode, the mouse can also be used to move the plane. First enter slew mode by pressing Y. Then to activate the mouse, press the right mouse button so the mouse pointer disappears. To move forward, move the mouse forward; to move backward, move the mouse backward. To rotate the plane left or right, roll the mouse left or right; but notice the plane is merely rotating in place and not moving from its present position. To stop all motion, click the left mouse button. To make the mouse pointer reappear, click the right mouse button.

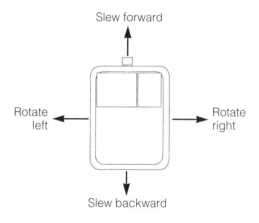

Figure 14.11 Using the mouse to slew

Slew forward

Rotate left   Rotate right

Slew backward

SIMULATOR INFORMATION

The Simulator Information dialog box is a new feature of *Flight Simulator* that gives you vital memory management information about your computer. In this dialog box, you can learn how much conventional and expanded (EMS) memory is being allocated to *Flight Simulator*. It also tells you what simulator files are being used.

Figure 14.12 Simulator information dialog box

```
                        Simulator Info
                                                        ┌────────┐
                                                        │   OK   │
                                                        └────────┘
Flight Simulator Version:  5.0                          ┌────────┐
                                                        │ Cancel │
Situation:                 Meigs Takeoff Runway 36      └────────┘
Situation Filename:        SITUATIO\FS5.STN

Aircraft:                  Cessna Skylane RG R182
Aircraft Filename:         SIM\SIM1.AIR

Scenery:                   FS5 World Scenery


                           USED          FREE
Conventional Memory (K)    00596         00044
EMS Memory (K)             0002016       0001376
XMS Memory (K)             0000608       0002464

EMS Handles                00021         00043
XMS Handles                00035         00029

Disk Space Available (K)   0016608
```

EASTER EGGS

Flight Simulator 5.1 CD has some Easter Eggs in the form of scenery landmarks. Since some of this scenery is not easily found, the latitude/longitude points for them have been provided in the table below:

Table 14.2   FS 5.1 CD Easter Egg Scenery

Scenery Landmark	Latitude	Longitude
Big Ben in London, England	N51° 29' 47.00"	W000° 07' 15.00"
Champs Elysees and Arc de Triomphe in Paris, France	N48° 52' 35.62"	E002° 17' 31.47"
Eiffel Tower in Paris, France	N48° 52' 12.56"	E002° 16' 48.52"
Hot Air Balloon NW of Seattle, Washington	N47° 56' 52.96"	W122° 26' 56.24"
Kremlin and Red Square in Moscow, Russia	N55° 45' 02.43"	E037° 38' 58.41"
Leaning Tower of Pisa in Pisa, Italy	N43° 43' 51.53"	E010° 24' 00.56"
Los Angeles Coliseum	N34° 00' 51"	W118° 16' 49"
Mt. Rushmore SW of Rapid City, South Dakota	N43° 51' 94.52"	W103° 25' 23.29"
Sphinx and Pyramids in Cairo, Egypt	N29° 57' 56"	E031° 08' 29.03"
St. Louis Gateway Arch in St. Louis, Missouri	N38° 36' 46.84"	W090° 10' 28.90"
Sydney Opera House in Sydney, Australia	S33° 46' 03.42"	E151° 10' 54.28"
Taj Mahal in Agra, India	N27° 07' 51.64"	E078° 03' 20.79"
Vatican and Vatican City in Rome, Italy	N41° 53' 54.81"	E012° 28' 33.65"

CHAPTER

15

Scenery Enhancements and Add-Ons

In this chapter you will learn about some of the amazing add-on products and accessories available for FS 5.1. The list presented is by no means complete; only a representative sample is presented. Prices are shown as suggested retail. Don't be discouraged by some of the prices you see; in most cases, the street price is much lower. If you shop around and compare prices, you can find terrific deals.

PURCHASING ADD-ON SCENERY DISKS

Probably the most interesting aspect of FS 5.1 is its new photo-realistic scenery. You can now buy special scenery, on CD-ROM or floppy disk, that contains photo-realistic detailed scenery for certain parts of the world.

There are several photo-realistic scenery packages available right now. They are listed below in chronological order:

- Mallard/BAO San Francisco Scenery (1993)
- Mallard/BAO Washington, D.C. Scenery (1993)
- Microsoft Paris Scenery (1993)
- Microsoft New York Scenery (1993)
- Microsoft Japan Scenery (1994)

- Microsoft Caribbean Scenery (1994)
- BAO Europe I (1995)
- BAO Las Vegas (1995)
- Microsoft Hawaii (1995)

You can see color examples of the Paris, New York, Europe I, Las Vegas, and Hawaii scenery in the color insert for this book. The most recent scenery add-ons, Las Vegas, Caribbean, and Hawaii, have the new hazing palettes built in so you can take advantage of the new low visibility features found in FS 5.1.

Mallard's San Francisco Scenery

Because Mallard is no longer in business, BAO has acquired the rights to the San Francisco scenery, but BAO has not resumed production of this scenery package just yet. You can still purchase older copies from Flight Sim Central (listed later in this section). San Francisco's photo-realistic scenery offers great visual detail. Fly over prominent buildings of the metropolitan areas and all of the major bridges like the Golden Gate, San Mateo, and Oakland Bay Bridges. You'll takeoff and land at San Francisco International, Oakland, Alameda Naval Air Station and other airports complete with runways, taxiways, main buildings, lighting, and Navaids. The landscape is incredible to look at; as you fly, the cities, fields, mountains, and San Francisco Bay unfold beneath you. The topography looks three-dimensional with shadows moving according to latitudinal and longitudinal position as the seasons, weather, and time of day change. You can fly over photo-realistic scenery from Vallejo in the North Bay all the way down to San Jose in the South Bay. Other points of interest include Marin, southern Napa Valley, San Francisco, Oakland/Berkeley East Bay Hills, Concord/Walnut Creek, and the Santa Cruz mountains. A note of warning: this scenery gobbles up 18 MB of hard disk space and can slow your frame rate to a crawl if you don't have a super-charged system. Price is $22.95.

Mallard's Washington, D.C. Scenery

As with the San Francisco scenery, Mallard's Washington D.C. scenery has been acquired by BAO, and currently it is not being produced anymore (Flight Sim Central still has some copies left). The Washington D.C. scenery package offers the same photo-realism as the San Francisco scenery. Fly over the US Capital and over the Mall, and take in the sights of the Washington D.C. area. Hard disk requirements are 18MB, and your frame rate can suffer unless you have a fast system. Price is $22.95.

Microsoft Paris Scenery

The airports in the Paris add-on scenery replace the default scenery airports and offer many more airport buildings and runway visual aids. The Eiffel Tower, the Chaillot Palace, River Seine, Louvre Museum, Tuileries Gardens, Notre Dame, the Arc de Triomphe, the Arche de la Defense, and the George Pompidou Center are all parts of the scenery. Most of Paris is covered with a synthetic town texture, which places streets and boulevards not really at the right place. But if you go to the Map view and zoom out, you'll see a photo-realistic view of Paris. The farther you fly from the center of Paris, the less realistic the scenery becomes. If you fly after dark, you will know why they call Paris the "City of Lights," as the Eiffel Tower lights, beautiful glowing windows of Notre Dame, and street lights along the Champs-Elysees brighten the night sky. Price is $34.95.

Microsoft New York Scenery

Microsoft's New York scenery add-on starts at the eastern tip of Long Island at Montauk point, which is about 100 nautical miles from Manhattan, and extends south and west into New York City, finally ending up in New Jersey. If you zoom your Map view out, you'll eventually see a photo-realistic view of New York; but close to the ground, it's strictly synthetic scenery. Even though the manual states that there are only 14 airports, in reality there are 24 airports included: including one that is a heliport only, one a grass strip, and one that includes a seaplane base. Be sure to read the README.NYC file included on the disk, because there is a complete airport listing with runway descriptions, ATIS, ILS frequencies, and elevations. You'll also discover some of the special scenery not mentioned in the manual, such as the World Fair Grounds and Yankee Stadium. Most of the good scenery, however, is on Long Island, where you'll find the big bridges, Central Park, most of the bigger skyscrapers, Ellis Island, and the Statue of Liberty. This area also includes the major airports, such as La Guardia and Kennedy, plus interesting sites like Coney Island (with two roller coasters) and Shea Stadium. Price is $34.95.

Microsoft Japan Scenery

In the Microsoft Japan Scenery, you'll find Mount Fuji, the Ginza District of Tokyo, palaces, and lots of detailed synthetic scenery for the major islands of Japan. Most of the Navaids and airports are present, so you can enjoy navigating around Japan. Price is $34.95.

Microsoft Caribbean Scenery

Microsoft Caribbean is all synthetic scenery, no photo-realistic imagery here. But it has many other features, such as water colors showing varying water depth, reefs, and beautifully rendered islands. There are many scenery objects, like cranes and large docks in the ports, and Freeport in the Bahamas has a huge oil refinery. Other objects to be found include forts, radar balloons, the radar telescope at Arecibo, volcanoes, and stadiums. Each island has a reasonable level of detail. But be sure to visit Miami, which has plenty of big buildings downtown, plus a bustling harbor, and Miami beachfront hotels. To see mountains, check out the Dominican Republic, which has a mountain range just west of Santo Domingo that rises to 10,128 feet. Old forts are to be found in Nassau, the Bahamas, and St. Georges Harbor in Grenada. Price is $34.95.

BAO Europe I

Europe I by BAO, is the first in a series of European scenery add-ons. It covers the central European countries of Austria, Germany, Switzerland, and the Netherlands, using synthetic scenery techniques. Included are over 100 airports, and many scenic cities such as Berlin, Amsterdam, Munich, Vienna, and Geneva. You can explore through the winding Alps, absorb the beautiful mountain lakes, or try landing at the difficult mountain resort of Innsbruck. All major roads, waterways, lakes, cities, mountains, and numerous landmarks combine to give you a very realistic flight over Europe. Europe I occupies only a sparse 6 MB of hard disk space, regardless of whether you install it from CD-ROM or floppy disk. Price is $29.95.

BAO Las Vegas

The new Las Vegas scenery from BAO is especially impressive for its photo-realism. The terrain is mapped using photo-realistic imagery, except for the urban part of Las Vegas which is rendered in synthetic scenery style. It offers nine new airports and covers more than 4,000 square miles of the Nevada landscape around Las Vegas. Based on satellite images, combined with aerial and ground-based photos, Las Vegas also includes famous scenery landmarks, like the famous Las Vegas strip, casinos, hotels, Hoover Dam, Lake Mead, Lee Canyon, and Mount Charleston. The 3-D mountain ranges are exceptionally beautiful, and you'll have a blast flying around Lake Mead. Be forewarned though, Las Vegas consumes 18 MB of precious hard disk space, whether you install it from CD-ROM or floppy disk. Price is $37.95.

Microsoft Hawaii

Although the Microsoft Hawaii scenery add-on was not available in time for review, you can see the color preview images in the insert are stunning. The ocean coastlines shimmer and the islands' jungle foliage looks verdant and lush. What's more, the volcano on the big island of Hawaii even erupts! Pricing is expected to be $34.95.

You can order any of the above scenery software at:

Flight Sim Central
1440 Quarry Road
Dept. 495-M
Mt. Juliet, TN 37122-7904
Telephone   800-477-7467
             615-754-8750
Fax   615-754-4138
Modem   615-754-5676
CompuServe 72662,3123
Internet   72662.3123@compuserve.com

For information about Microsoft scenery products contact:

Microsoft
One Microsoft Way
Redmond, Washington
Telephone 206-882-8080
USA Toll Free 800-426-9400

For information about BAO scenery products contact:

BAO
2004 Fox Drive, Suite G
Champaign, IL 61820
Telephone   217 -356-0188
Fax   217-356-7895

SCENERY SHAREWARE

Many *Flight Simulator* enthusiasts all over the world have created their own custom FS 5.1 scenery. Much of this scenery is available free as "shareware" and can easily be downloaded from bulletin boards and online services all over the world. The Flight Simulator Forum on CompuServe has an extensive library of scenery covering many parts of the world, as does the ftp.iup.edu site on the Internet. For more information, consult the section later in this chapter on Other Resources.

OTHER SHAREWARE SOFTWARE

Along with shareware scenery software, there are many shareware programs and utilities that allow you to get the most out of *Flight Simulator*. For a small fee, you can license these programs and obtain the full use of certain restricted features. These programs can be found on many on-line services, such as CompuServe's Flight Simulator Forum and on the Internet.

Because the list of free programs is so numerous, it is not possible to describe them all here. However, two programs worth mentioning are:

- Final Approach 5.0 for Windows: A utility for creating, printing, and viewing instrument approach plates for use with PC-based flight simulators.
- WinPlanner 1.2a for Windows: Navigational utility for planning your flights.

Final Approach 5.0 for Windows

Most modern flight simulators have reached a level of realism that makes the use of real world instrument approach plates (IAPs) almost a necessity.

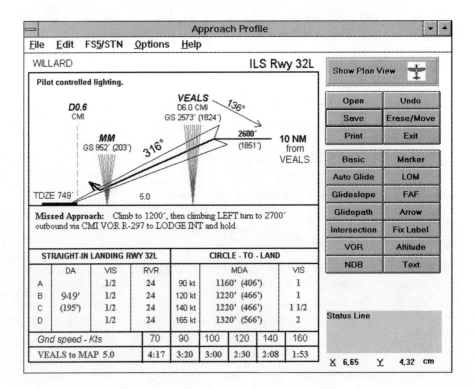

Figure 15.1
Profile View of Final Approach 2.2 for Windows

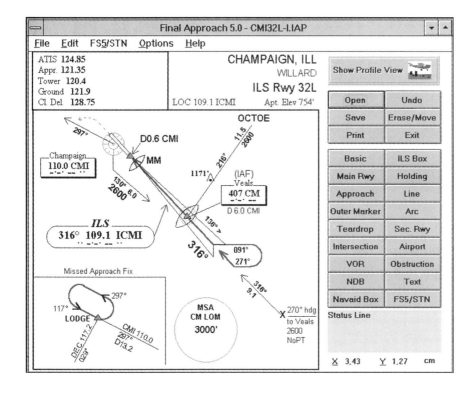

Figure 15.2
Plan View of Final
Approach 5.0 for
Windows

Unfortunately, only a few charts generally are included with these programs. The same is true for most of the currently available scenery disks and add-ons.

What's more, countless user-created scenarios and adventures are waiting to be downloaded from bulletin board systems and online services all around the world. Again, these sometimes excellent productions would strongly gain in interest and usability if their designers had found a way to include digitized instrument approach plates with their files.

With Final Approach you can display and design your own instrument approach plates right on screen. You may also generate vectorized hard copies in the highest resolution available on your printer.

Unlike scanned IAPs, the plates you design with Final Approach can be easily distributed because they require extremely little disk space (generally below 1K).

Final Approach was first released as shareware in 1993. The program quickly gained an enormous popularity among *Flight Simulator* users. Two years after its initial release, the program totals over 6,000 downloads from CompuServe's Flight Simulator Forum alone and more than 1,600 approach plates are available free of charge in the same forum. According to the author, users from 36 countries worldwide are working with the program. Even the scenery designers at BAO used Final Approach to create the approach plates for their Europe I Scenery manual!

The latest version, 5.0, brought an abundance of new features. All limitations on the number of symbols and elements to place on a chart have been removed. The plate header now allows for multiple frequencies and a field for the clearance frequency has been added. To support the new *Flight Simulator* 5.1 visibility features, minimum visibility and runway visual range (RVR) tables have been added. Multiple options allow each plate to be displayed and printed in the format you prefer; symbology may adhere to the NOS, Jeppesen or Lufthansa standard, or even be a mix of all three. Timing table speeds may be individually selected, visibility and RVR fields may be displayed in the US or the European metric system. Final Approach 5.0 can display and print the approach plates in black and white or color.

The latest version of Final Approach can easily be linked to *Flight Simulator 5.1*. Based on the airport coordinates for any given approach plate, Final Approach calculates an initial approach position and transfers the relevant data to an FS 5.1 situation file. Provided you have the appropriate scenery installed, simply load that situation in FS 5.1 and you'll find yourself set-up for the desired approach, some 10 miles out of the airport, flying at the required altitude and heading. Even your radios have been pre-tuned with the correct communication and navigation frequencies!

An evaluation version of Final Approach is available from CompuServe's Flight Simulator Forum (GO FSFORUM) Library 2 (General Aviation) as FINALA.ZIP.

If you want to use the program after the usual 30 day shareware evaluation period, you are required to register it. In exchange for a relatively small fee, you receive a license key that provides the program with complete functionality to fly and entitles you to free upgrades to future shareware versions.

You can contact the author at:

Georges Lorsche
5, Rue des Violettes
L-3447 Dudelange
Luxembourg/Europe
CompuServe: 100041,211
Internet: 100041.211@compuserve.com

English, French, and German commercial versions are available from Colorado Technologies, Paris. Telephone (+33) (1) 4859 2850, Fax (+33) (1) 4859 2812.

Flight Planner 1.2a and Weather Wizard

Antoine Becker created Flight Planner 1.2a for Windows and Weather Wizard to help *Flight Simulator* pilots navigate and manage weather. Flight Planner can help plan your flights for you, and can use the Navaids built into FS 5.1 to plot and create waypoints for your journey. Each waypoint can be a VOR/ NDB station, and the magnetic course bearing and distance to the next waypoint is calculated and displayed in your route summary. Your course trajectory can be printed out in columnar form, or printed out on a map, as is shown in the accompanying figures. Flight Planner can also import and read the FS 5.1 .BGL files containing the navigational data for the different scenery areas. You can import any VOR/NDBs or airports found in these .BGL files and when you buy new add-on scenery, you can add to your navigational database the new VOR/NDBs and airports found in the new scenery's .BGL files.

With a new program called Weather Wizard, you can:

- Manage Sets of Weather Stations
- Manage Sets of Weather Data From the Stations
- Import Weather Server Text Files (like AWX Forum in CompuServe)
- Write FS 5.1 Situation Files with the Following Data:

    departure area weather and location

    enroute area weather

    arrival area weather, including icing and visibility

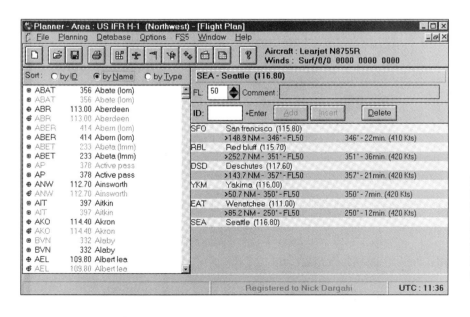

Figure 15.3
Flight Planner 1.2a for Windows. This program can plot the magnetic bearings and list VOR/NDB Navaids, between any two airports you specify.

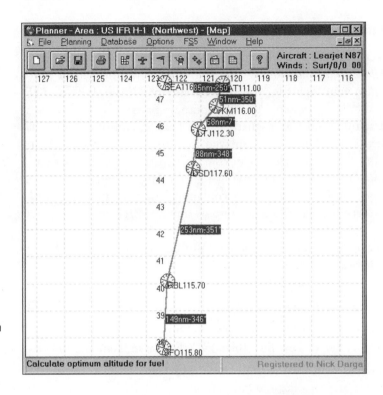

Figure 15.4
Flight Planner 1.2a can plot your course visually on a map you can print out.

You can download an evaluation copy of Flight Planner and Weather Wizard from the CompuServe Flight Simulator library. For more information, contact:

Antoine Becker
CompuServe: 100440,1120
Internet 100440.1120@compuserve.com

Warning Note
Shareware scenery created for FS 5.0 may be incompatible with the new scenery for FS 5.1 CD. Also, shareware aircraft created for FS 5.0 may also wreak havoc with FS 5.1.

Where to Find Free Scenery and Airplanes

There are many scenery shareware files and aircraft available for free on CompuServe's Flight Simulator Forum, America Online's Flight Simulator Forum, and the ftp.iup.edu Internet site. There are so many kinds of aircraft and so much scenery that have been contributed over the years, it is impossible to list them all here. Be forewarned though. The new FS 5.1 might have problems importing aircraft created for FS 5.0. Also, shareware scenery created for FS 5.0 may conflict with the new global scenery for FS 5.1 CD.

Not to despair however. BAO's Flight Shop, which will come with some new aircraft for FS 5.1, will also allow you to design your own custom planes (see the color insert for some examples of aircraft created with Flight Shop).

ADD-ON FS 5.1 PRODUCTS

The next section lists some of the hardware add-ons you can purchase separately for FS 5.1.

CH Products

CH Products is a leading US manufacturer of precision analog joysticks for the home and industry.

The CH Virtual Pilot is a true, professional flight yoke that mounts easily to your desk via clamps. You plug it directly into your joystick port and voila, you are ready to go. The yoke features aileron and elevator control via the yoke, aileron and elevator trim tabs, fire buttons mounted on the wheel, and a throttle lever. You can use the Virtual Pilot in place of a joystick for Microsoft's *Flight Simulator 5.1*. Remember—you must clamp it to a table, and your keyboard will have to be placed to the side.

With its built in springs, the yoke has a realistic amount of travel and tension in comparison to a real yoke.

The Virtual Pilot Pro is an extended version of the Virtual Pilot. It comes with all the features of the Virtual Pilot, but it also offers four-way 3-D view controls, along with flap and landing gear controls.

The CH Pro Pedals complement the Virtual Pilot perfectly. These pedals give you realistic forward and backward pedal motion for flying as well as for driving games. For flying, Pro Pedals work as rudders and toe brakes. The Pro Pedals come equipped with a special cable attachment that allows you to use your existing game port in conjunction with your Virtual Pilot or Virtual Pilot Pro yoke. The only problem you need to be aware of is, after you install the pedals, you'll need to edit the Fs5.ini file and delete the DEVICE=STICK2.FSO line (see installation instructions for CH Products in Appendix A).

The Flightstick Pro, an IBM compatible joystick, works with all standard analog joystick ports and lets the FS 5.1 pilot choose 3-D views, activate flaps, landing gear, brakes, and trim controls.

Suggested retail prices are as follows:

CH Virtual Pilot	$109.95
CH Virtual Pilot Pro	$129.95
CH Pro Pedals	$139.95
CH Flightstick Pro	$ 99.95

Figure 15.5
CH Virtual Pilot Pro

Figure 15.6
CH Pro Pedals

To order, contact:

CH Products
970 Park Center Dr.
Vista, CA 92083
Telephone 619-598-2518

Colorado Spectrum

Colorado Spectrum produces the innovative Mouse Yoke, which uses your existing mouse and transforms it into a realistic aircraft style yoke. Priced less than leading analog joysticks, the Mouse Yoke provides precision movements, a realistic yoke feel, and user friendly installation. To install it, you simply clamp the Mouse Yoke to a table and slip the mouse under an elastic "seat belt" on top of the device. The yoke's shaft then drives the mouse ball, translating yoke movements into corresponding mouse signals. Pushing forward on the yoke is equivalent to moving the mouse forward on the desk, and turning the yoke right is the same as moving the mouse to the right. The Mouse Yoke is the first product to receive Microsoft *Flight Simulator*'s new "Seal of Approval," and it works on both MS-DOS and Macintosh systems.

Notebook owners the world over will rejoice now that Colorado Spectrum's Notebook Gameport is out. For the first time, you can hook up your joystick to your notebook and fly your flight simulation programs while on the road or traveling on an airliner. The Notebook Gameport connects to your notebook's nine pin serial port. You then hook up your joystick directly to the Gameport and, if you have a mouse too, you can hook it up to the

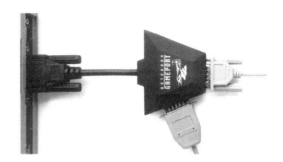

Figure 15.8
Colorado Spectrum's
Notebook Gameport

Figure 15.7
Colorado Spectrum's
Mouse Yoke

pass through serial mouse port. The four-axis Gameport also supports joy-stick and rudder pedals simultaneously.

The Mouse Yoke sells for a suggested retail price of $34.95, while the Notebook Gameport sells for a suggested retail price of $54.95

To order, contact:

Colorado Spectrum
748 Whalers Way E-201
Fort Collins, CO 80525
Telephone 303-225-1687
USA Toll Free 800-238-5983

ThrustMaster

ThrustMaster specializes in making flight controls for air combat simula-tions. Their unique Mark I and Mark II flight control systems can also be used with *Flight Simulator*, however. They also make rudder pedals, a spe-cialized game card controller, flight sticks, and a basic cockpit with fiber-glass shell.

The Mark I Flight Control System is a four button, four-way hat switch joystick, that allows you to switch views, weapons, and other vital simulator functions.

The Mark II Weapons Control System is a fully programmable hands on

Figure 15.9
ThrustMaster Rudder
Control System (pedals)

Figure 15.10
ThrustMaster Mark II
Weapons Control System

throttle and stick (HOTAS) version of the Mark I Flight Control System. With six buttons and a three-way switch, the Mark II can be programmed for a total of 12 independent functions. Since it has a new U-PROM chip, you can re-program the buttons on the Mark II for any current or future flight simulator.

The Rudder Control System is constructed out of gold anodized aluminum and ABS plastic, and works with software supporting external rudder pedal input.

The ACM Game Controller Card virtually eliminates joystick drift in all simulations. Speed adjustability allows the user to dial in the card to match the computer's speed exactly. You can adjust the card to any speed from 4.77 MHz to 66 MHz.

ThrustMaster's new F-16 flight sticks are the state of the art in joystick technology. The F-16 FLCS is fully user configurable, has four four-way switches, four buttons, dual state trigger, macros and repeating keystrokes, and advanced configuration software. The F-16 TQS, which requires the F-16 FLCS, is also fully user configurable, offers a thumb trackball, fore/aft throttle movement, radar range and antenna roll switches, dogfight switch, and a throttle tension adjustment wheel.

ThrustMaster's F-16c Cockpit allows you to experience the thrill of flying in a mock up of an F-16c cockpit. Using your computer in conjunction with the ThrustMaster control panels, you can fly your simulations with extra realism.

Suggested list prices are as follows:

Mark I Flight Control System	$ 99.95
Mark II Weapons Control System	$149.95
Rudder Control System	$149.95
ACM Game Card	$ 39.95
F-16 FLCS	$199.95
F-16 TQS	$199.95
F-16c Cockpit Basic Unit	$695.00

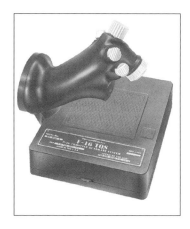

Figure 15.12
ThrustMaster F-16 TQS

Figure 15.11
ThrustMaster F-16
FLCS

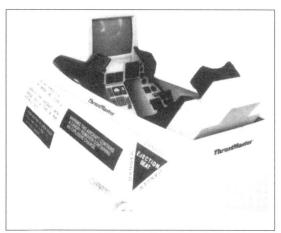

Figure 15.13
ThrustMaster Cockpit

Switch Control Module and Switch Kit $ 449.00
External Fiberglass Skin $975.00
Seat Pads $199.00
Shoulder Harness $ 99.00

To order, contact:

ThrustMaster, Inc.
10150 S.W. Nimbus Ave.
Suite E7
Portland, OR 97223
Telephone 503-639-3200

ThunderSeat Technologies

ThunderSeat Technologies makes various flight simulation products, including a virtual reality chair, yokes, and other cockpit controls and instrumentation. Here's what some people have to say about ThunderSeat:

> *"The perfect computer pilot enhancement-realistic sensation of flight has never been this comfortable or this inexpensive."*
>
> —Hugo Fuegen, CEO, Bruce Artwick Organization,
> Creators of Microsoft Flight Simulator 5.1

> *"A must have item for your cockpit ... ThunderSeat will raise your level of realism to a new dimension!"*
>
> —Jon Solon, Program Manager,
> Aerospace Simulation Software, Microsoft Corporation

The ThunderSeat Pro Virtual Reality Chair is a seat that contains a special sub-woofer type of sonic transducer built into its base. This sonic transducer generates an omni-directional low frequency sound that rumbles through the air chamber hidden inside. The ensuing resonance amplifies the sound waves until the entire chair becomes a radiating speaker. With the resultant air and bone conduction, the user not only hears the sound but feels it as well. In essence, all the vibratory sensations of flight, including engine noise, landing, and takeoff, are felt by the person seated in the chair. The same type of tactile feedback system is used in real F-16 Flight Simulators. Due to its unique design, an ordinary stereo amplifier can power the ThunderSeat; all you need to do is hook up your PC's sound card to the stereo.

The YM-2 Yoke Module includes not only a yoke, but also switches and buttons enabling you to control up to 39 separate aircraft functions. Aircraft controls on the right side of the panel include a four position flap switch, landing gear, parking brake, and rotary trim switch. The left side has a total of 23 other aircraft function controls including a four position magneto/ignition switch and an assortment of appropriate rocker and push-button type aircraft switches. The function of all the switches on the front panel can be easily changed by software so you can customize the controls to your program. A special batch file loaded into the program is provided for FS 5.1. From that point on, every time FS 5.1 is started, the correct functionality of all switches is loaded automatically. The YM-2 connects to your PC by means of the parallel port and features a full travel, aluminum yoke with baked enamel finish. An optional yoke shaker system to give the user full-motion feedback will be available in early 1996 and will be designed to work with FS 5.1 stalls, hard landings, and other maneuvers generating appropriate yoke movement.

The YM-1 features the same precision yoke mechanism as the YM-2, but without any of the front panel switches. The YM-1 can be upgraded to the YM-2. Both the YM-1 and YM-2 are housed in a heavy duty steel case designed to hold any monitor. An integrated steel tray puts your keyboard at your fingertips.

The King Air Style Yoke is molded from an actual King Air Yoke, and features a two way rocker switch on the left stalk for up and down trim control. There is also a built-in trackball on the right stalk that allows you to tune the radios and perform all other mouse controlled actions without taking your hands off the controls. An actual Beechcraft quartz chronometer is also available.

The 3-Lever Power Quadrant for single engine aircraft mates to the YM-2 Yoke Module and offers controls for throttle, propeller speed, mixture, cowl flaps, carburetor heat, and fuel tank selection. Other Power Quadrants available include a 2-Lever Learjet with Reverse Thrust and Spoiler Extend/Retract Controls, and 6-Lever 310R engine controls for a Light Twin Piston Powered Engine.

The ThunderFlight Rudders are all steel and perfect for flying tricky crosswind landings in un-coordinated mode in FS 5.1. Designed to duplicate control forces found in actual aircraft, the ThunderFlight Rudders are the only ones on the market with a "Progressive Loading" resistance feature. Progressive loading refers to the increased force required to press the rudder pedal to its full extreme, thus simulating the progressive movement of the aircraft's rudder into the slipstream.

The View Control Module allows you to quickly adjust your cockpit view by flipping an eight- position rotary switch. Push-button control of zoom in and zoom out is also included.

Suggested retail prices are as follows:

ThunderSeat Ace	$159.95
Aces II Ejection Seat	$695.00
YM-2 Yoke Module	$995.95
YM-1 Yoke Module	$349.95
Beechcraft King Air Yoke with Trackball	$395.00
3-Lever, High Performance Power Quadrant	$395.95
Single Lever, Power Quadrant	$150.00
ThunderFlight Rudders	$349.95
Side Consoles	$119.95
Fresnel Lens	$219.95
Retractable-Tactical Keyboard Holder	$ 64.00

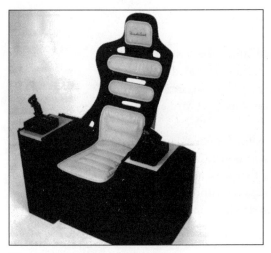

Figure 15.14 ThunderSeat

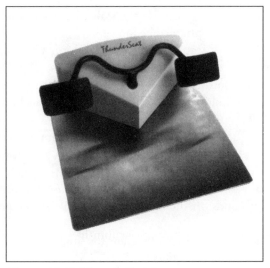

Figure 15.15 ThunderPedals

Figure 15.16 YM-2 with 3-Lever
Power Quadrant

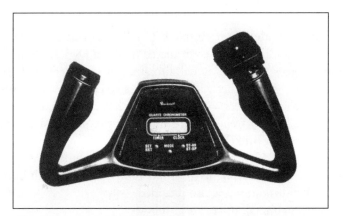

Figure 15.17 King Air Style Yoke

To order, contact:

ThunderSeat Technologies
6330 Arizona Circle
Los Angeles, CA 90045
Telephone 310-410-0022
USA Toll Free 800-884-8633

FLY IT Simulation Products

The FLY IT General Aviation Control Panel replaces the keyboard with real aircraft switches, knobs, and levers that feel and operate like they do in the real aircraft. This panel supports FS 5.1, and takes the simulation experience to a more serious level.

The FLY IT Military Control Panel allows the fighter pilot of Spectrum Holobyte's Falcon 3.0 F-16, FA 18 and MIG 29 to see and operate all aircraft systems, flight controls, armament, navigation, and communications. Two vacuum-formed ABS panels contain membrane switch panels. Extending from the left and right sides of the control panel are joystick consoles.

With the Personal Motion Simulator, you can experience 13° of roll and pitch movements as you move your yoke. Since there are no hydraulics, there is little danger of pinching your body on catch points.

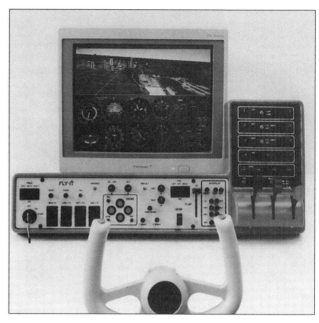

Figure 15.18 FLY IT Simulators General Aviation Control Panel

For a more elaborate setup, the Personal Trainer Motion Flight Simulator gives you a Pentium 90, set-up with a control panel, and a motion simulator all configured and ready to go.

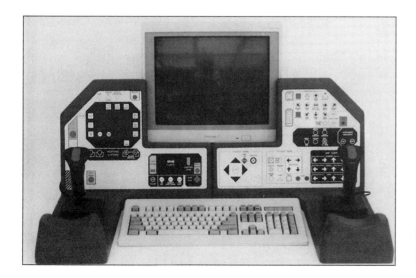

Figure 15.19
FLY IT Simulators
Military Control Panel

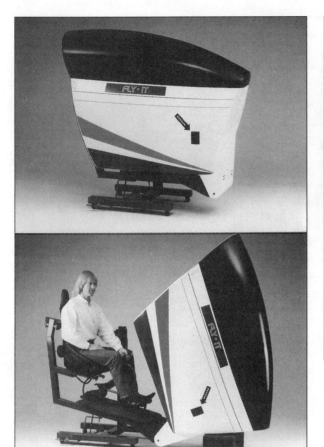

Figure 15.21 FLY IT Personal Simulator

Figure 15.20 FLY IT Commercial Simulator

The high end Commercial Motion Simulator is a top of the line motion platform, that comes with a Pentium and virtual reality like cockpit hood. Again, since movements are generated by the pilot, there is no machinery to cause injury.

Prices are as follows:

General Aviation Control Panel with Epic Game Card	$ 595.00
Military Control Panel with Epic Game Card	$ 495.00
Personal Motion Simulator	$2,690.00
Personal Trainer Motion Flight Simulator (with Pentium 90)	$9,900.00

Commercial Motion Simulator(with
   Pentium, 23" Diagonal projected
   screen,and sound system) $36,900.00

To order, contact:

FLY IT Simulators
3042 Highland Drive
Carlsbad, CA 92008
Telephone 800-983-3744

Flightmaster Computer Flight Simulator Control

The Flightmaster control consists of a yoke, throttle, trim control, rudder pedals, and brakes under the toes of the rudder pedals. Some of its key features include:

- Keyboard is placed on top of the unit for easy access to keyboard commands.
- Yoke rotates 90° on roll axis, and travels three inches on pitch axis.
- Yoke is spring-loaded on both axes.
- Elevator trim relieves yoke pressure.
- Trim pointer assures perfect calibration.
- Fire button is located under left thumb.
- Rudder pedals travel three inches and are spring-loaded.
- Brakes are under toes of rudder pedals.
- Unit plugs directly into your game card.
- Lifetime warranty on parts and labor.
- Thirty-day money back guarantee.

Flightmaster sells for a suggested retail price of $199.95, while the heavy duty aluminum base Flightmaster IV sells for $799.95 (The Flightmaster IV rudder and pedal assembly are also made of aluminum. In addition, you can order a Hobbs clock and key for an additional $99.95).

   To order, contact:

Flightmaster
300 SE 5th Street, #400
Grand Prairie, Texas 75051
Telephone 214-264-3652

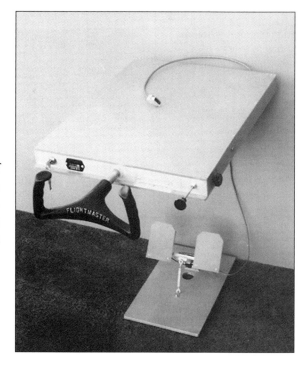

Figure 15.22
Flightmaster IV Yoke
and Pedals

The Tools You Need to Create the Flight Experience You've Been Waiting For!

*F*light Simulator™ *Flight Shop* is the new power program for power pilots. This advanced aircraft design and flight adventure editor for Microsoft® *Flight Simulator*™ 5 gives you the tools you need to create the ultimate flight experience.

As a power pilot, the first thing you'll need is an aircraft unlike any other, one that's exclusively yours. With the aircraft factory of *Flight Shop* you'll find only one limitation—your imagination. You'll be able to design, construct, paint and test fly your own aeronautical masterpieces from hang gliders to stealth bombers. Or, if you just can't wait

to get into the air, a variety of ready-to-fly aircraft is included. You can even use downloadable aircraft designs from various B.B.S.'s like *CompuServe*®.

The adventure features of *Flight Shop* let you customize your own flight experiences, setting goals, including random events and visual feedback.

The aircraft factory and pilot adventure editor will give you a ride that will require more than a seat belt. Only BAO can bring you *Flight Shop*, the power package for power pilots. Go ahead—take a power trip!

Flight Simulator Flight Shop puts the tools in your hands.

- Flight Simulator Flight Shop *is fully compatible with* Microsoft Flight Simulator version 5.0 or later.
- Take-off on one of the pre-compiled adventures included in the program.
- Share custom adventures with friends on various B.B.S.'s.
- The paint shop feature lets you add your own personal graphics.

Easy-to-use (window-based) aircraft factory lets you design your own plane.

Create your own flight plan and send it to the built-in Flight Service Station (FSS) for a ATC controlled flight.

In the Flight Dynamics Editor you specify the flying characteristics.

Figure 15.23
Flight Shop allows you to create new aircraft and custom flight plans for FS 5.1.

Flight Shop from BAO

Flight Shop, created by BAO, makers of FS 5.1, is a program that allows you to build, customize, and paint your own planes. Also included is a flight dynamics editor that allows you to specify the flying characteristics of your aircraft. You can also create your own flight plans and send it to the built-in flight service station (FSS) for an Air Traffic Controlled (ATC) flight. (See the color insert in this book for examples of Flight Shop created aircraft).

To order, contact:

BAO
2004 Fox Drive, Suite G
Champaign, IL 61820
Telephone 217-356-0188
Fax 217-356-7895

Tower from BAO

Tower is a new Air Traffic Control (ATC) simulation program developed by BAO. Based on FAA and Transport Canada's professional training simulation software, Tower is a stand alone program that does not need *Flight Simulator* to run.

From the the control towers of major metropolitan and international airports, you can simulate being an Air Traffic Controller. Pan your photo-realistic view 360° around the tower, and use local and ground control radar to help you guide aircraft traffic in and out of the airport. You can simulate all kinds of conditions, weather, and levels of traffic at any time of the day. Watch as airplanes (superimposed on the photo-realistic scenery) take off, taxi, land, fly patterns, or abort takeoffs. Simulated pilots speak back to you using digitized sound files. Tower is expected to include a special communication mode with FS 5.1, using the dual-player feature, so you can give Air Traffic Control instructions to FS 5.1 pilots.

"Tower is not all that different from our professional training version of this product," says Hugo Feugen, CEO of BAO. In fact, a variant of Tower is now being used to train Air Traffic Controllers.

Tower will be available for Windows at a suggested retail price of $69.95. To order, contact:

BAO
2004 Fox Drive, Suite G
Champaign, IL 61820
Telephone 217-356-0188
Fax 217-356-7895

Figure 15.24
Tower Air Traffic Control Simulation from BAO

Tracon for Windows

Wesson International has produced Tracon, a unique Windows-based Air Traffic Control simulation that interfaces with FS 5.1. You can link the program via a null-modem serial cable computer to computer for a direct connection, or you can use your modem to communicate with a friend. The program works with a sound card, so the Air Traffic Controller speaks in a digitized voice to the aircraft. You have a choice of several airports, and can choose the number of aircraft you want to handle at any given time. The program scores your ability to handle different Air Traffic Control challenges, so you won't be bored too quickly.

To order, contact:

Wesson International
Telephone 512-328-0100
Fax 512-328-7838

Figure 15.25
Tracon Air Traffic
Control Simulation for
Windows

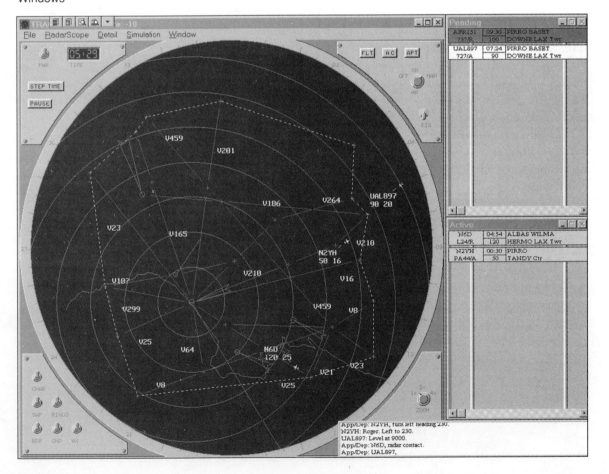

Wagner Computer Products' Microflight Simulator

For the serious *Flight Simulator* enthusiast, Wagner Computer Products provides the Microflight Simulator. This simulator allows precision flight control responsiveness and realism. This micro-processor controlled device includes an aluminum yoke, rudder pedals with toe brakes, and a console that serves as the control device for Microsoft's *Flight Simulator*. The Microflight simulator is connected to your PC via one of your COM serial ports. Trim and other flight control commands are automatically dispatched from the console to the computer via the serial port. All nine of your available 3-D View angles can be instantly selected by means of a rotary switch. There are also individual controls for your NAV/COM radios, flaps, mixture control, throttle, carburetor heat, landing gear, lights, OBI indicators, transponder, and magnetos.

The Microflight Simulator has a suggested retail price of $3,995.00. To order, contact:

Wagner Computer Products, Inc.
Oswego Road
Pleasant Valley, NY 12569
Telephone 914-677-3794

OTHER RESOURCES

For Flight Simulation buffs, there are many excellent sources of information: online commercial services, the Internet, and magazines. The next section briefly describes each resource.

Figure 15.26
Wagner Computer
Products' Microflight
Simulator

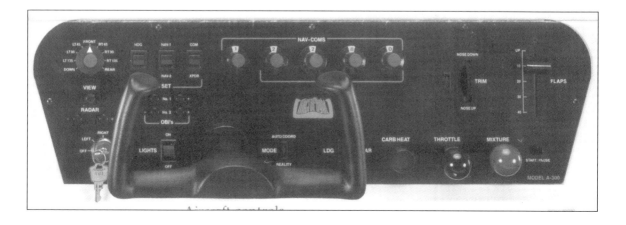

CompuServe Flight Simulator Forum

The CompuServe Flight Simulator Forum is a terrific source of information on the latest developments in Flight Simulation. There are topics on air combat, scenery design, aircraft design, general aviation, Air Traffic Control, hardware, space simulations, and software libraries to download files from. If you have some scenery or aircraft, or some important message you would like to share with other *Flight Simulator* enthusiasts, you can easily post your files to the forum's message center or library.

To best use the CompuServe network, you really need to use the CompuServe Information Manager (CIM). This program greatly simplifies the task of navigating the labyrinthine passages of the network and removes the burden of having to remember what commands to type each time you log on. If you are running Windows, CIM for Windows is strongly recommended. CIM allows you to paste, cut, and copy text back and forth from CompuServe to any of your Windows applications.

To access *Flight Simulator* Forum on CompuServe, type GO FSFORUM. Once there, you can browse through the different message groups and see what there is in the libraries. If you have questions that you want to direct to a Microsoft representative, you can type GO MICROSOFT HOME, and bring up the Microsoft Home Forum. There, if you click on the Simulation message board you can post questions, or go to the Simulation library, where you can find material related to Microsoft's simulator products.

Figure 15.27
CompuServe
Information Manager
for Windows

CompuServe now provides full access to the Internet, and you can surf the Internet with any world wide web browser, using their Internet Dialer software.

CompuServe's US monthly service fee is $9.95, which entitles you to five free hours of connect time for the extended services. For the basic services (including news, weather, e-mail messaging, electronic encyclopedia, shopping) there is no connect time charge; but for the forums (including the Flight Simulator Forum), there is an hourly connect time fee of $2.95 per hour.

To contact CompuServe, call 614-529-1340, or call toll free in the USA 800-848-8990.

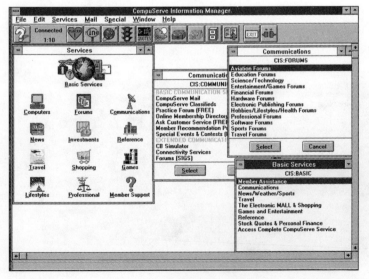

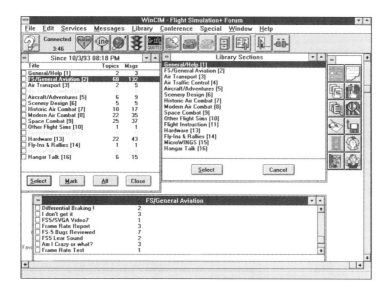

Figure 15.28
CompuServe Flight
Simulator Forum

America Online Flight Simulator Forum

America Online has a good flight simulator forum, with many libraries of interesting scenery files and other goodies you can download. The cost of the service is $9.95 per month for five hours of online connect time, with additional hours at $2.95 per hour. America Online now offers a web browser and full access to the Internet.

To access the Flight Simulator Resource Center, use the keyword Flight Sim.

To learn more about America Online, call 800-827-6364 for sales information. If you want technical support, call 800-827-3338, or 703-448-8700.

Prodigy's Games Bulletin Board

The Prodigy Online service has a games bulletin board that caters to flight simulator aficionados. Unfortunately, they don't yet have an online library where you can download files. To get to the flight simulator BBS, jump Games bbs, and then select the topic of Flight Simulators. Once there, you can scroll through many messages about *Flight Simulator*, or leave questions or comments that you have about the program.

Prodigy costs $9.95 per month, and online connect charges are $2.95 an hour, with the first five hours free. To contact Prodigy, call 800-PRODIGY.

The Internet

On the Internet, you can download interesting scenery files, aircraft, and other goodies at ftp.iup.edu. If you are using file transfer protocol (ftp) software, log on as anonymous and type in your e-mail address as your password. Once you have logged onto the site, you then change directories to the flight simulator directory, where you'll find sub-directories of flight simulator related files categorized by subject.

Some world wide web browsers will allow you to access the ftp site directly. This is much easier than using ftp software, so if you have access to the world wide web, try typing in the following web universal resource locator (URL) address:

ftp://ftp.iup.edu

However, even if you can't get into the ftp.iup.edu site, you can also visit a flight simulator world wide web page located at:

http://macwww.db.erau.edu/www-virtual_lib/aviation/flightsim.html

There you'll find all kinds of flight simulator related resources.

Another good FS web resource is located at:

http://www.infonet.net/showcase/wceo

Flight Simulator Internet Mailing List

There is also an e-mail newsletter sent out on the Internet you can join. To receive this free newsletter, send e-mail to mailserv@grove.iup.edu and in the subject field of your e-mail type *Subscribe flight-sim*. You should start to receive periodical mailings of the newsletter almost immediately.

Internet USENET Newsgroups

The USENET newsgroups are another valuable source of information about *Flight Simulator*. In particular, if you subscribe to the newsgroup comp.sys.ibm.pc.games.flight-sim or rec.aviation.simulators, you can keep abreast of all the latest *Flight Simulator* gossip.

MicroWINGS Magazine

If you want to join an organization devoted to aerospace simulation, then MicroWINGS is the one for you. MicroWINGS bills itself as the International Association for Aerospace Simulations and they have members from

Figure 15.29 MicroWINGS Magazine

all over the world. Once you join, you receive six issues a year of MicroW-INGS Magazine and are entitled to free Dallas/Fort Worth scenery for FS 5.1 (you pay the shipping and handling for the scenery).

The membership fee is $49 per year. Canada and Mexico add $6 postage surcharge. All other countries add $18 postage surcharge. To order, contact:

> Robert M. MacKay
> President
> MicroWINGS, Inc.
> 381 Casa Linda Plaza #154
> Dallas, TX 75218
> Telephone 214-324-1406
> CompuServe e-Mail ID 71641,2321
> America Online MICROWINGS
> Internet e-mail fltsim@microwings.com
> World Wide Web: http://www.microwings.com

Full Throttle: The Microsoft *Flight Simulator* Pilot's Journal

Figure 15.30
Full Throttle Magazine

Full Throttle Magazine is a journal focusing on specialized *Flight Simulator* tips and tricks. In every issue, Full Throttle teaches you proven techniques for increasing your system's efficiency and enhancing your *Flight Simulator* skills. You find fully illustrated articles that help you uncover all the secrets Microsoft built into *Flight Simulator.*

One year's subscription for six issues costs only $29. To order, contact:

> Full Throttle
> The Cobb Group
> P.O. Box 35160
> Louisville, KY 40232-9719

PC Pilot Magazine

PC Pilot Magazine is a British based *Flight Simulator* periodical that is published six times yearly. They review all kinds of software and hardware of aerospace simulation products for the PC. Subscription for 1 year in the UK and Northern Ireland is £23.70, but costs slightly more for other countries.

To order, contact:
Douglas McKay
PC Pilot Magazine
P.O. Box 118 Witney
Oxfordshire OX8 8LT
United Kingdom
Telephone (please phone only between 9-6:30 pm UK time): 44 (0)1869-324167
Fax: same as above
CompuServe e-Mail: 100561,3102
Internet: 100561.3102@compuserve.com

Figure 15.31
PC Pilot Magazine

FAA CERTIFIED FULL-MOTION SIMULATORS

SimuFlite, a company located at the Dallas-Ft. Worth Airport in Texas, offers full-motion simulators of business jets you can rent on an hourly basis.

They have a special program for non-pilots called the JetPilot, which puts you in the cockpit of a Learjet (other popular business jets are offered as well) for only $200 per hour. You can bring one guest at no additional charge.

No previous flying experience is required. A briefing before your flight will familiarize you with enough of the basics to allow you to get the most out your simulator time.

During the simulation, you sit at the controls for one full hour in an FAA certified Level C full motion simulator, getting the feel of flying a real corporate jet. Afterward, a videotape of your flight and a flight certificate are yours to keep.

Over 40 worldwide destinations are offered, including Dallas, Hong Kong, and San Francisco.

Figure 15.32 FAA approved Level C business jet full-motion simulators can be rented for $200 per hour at SimuFlite at the Dallas, Ft. Worth Airport in Texas.

The JetPilot schedule is offered on a reservation basis only, and is as follows:

Friday   12 noon - 12 midnight
Saturday 8 am - 12 midnight
Sunday   8 am - 12 midnight
Monday   9 am - 12 midnight

At other times of the week, the SimuFlite center is used for aviation training of pilots who go there for recurrent training, or recertification of their FAA license.

For more information, contact:

SimuFlite Training International
2929 W. Airfield Drive
Box 619119
Dallas-Ft. Worth Airport, TX 75261
Telephone 214-456-8054
Toll Free 800-527-2463

Figure 15.33 SimuFlite simulators use the same instrumentation as found in the real Learjet.

APPENDIX

A

Windows 95 Installation Tips and Frame Rate Comparison Guide

This appendix helps you properly configure and install FS 5.1 as a DOS application under Windows 95, and concludes with a frame rate comparison guide so you may better know what the performance of the program is like with various hardware platforms.

The next section guides you through the installation of FS 5.1 regardless of whether you are using Windows 95 or not. If you have already installed FS 5.1 under Windows 95, but would like some tips on how to get it to run as a DOS application in Windows, skip ahead to the section titled "Running *Flight Simulator* Under Windows 95."

INSTALLATION IS A SNAP

If you are not using Windows 95, you can install FS 5.1 like any other DOS application: run the Setup.com program from the DOS prompt.

However, if you are running Windows 95, you can install FS 5.1 by one of the following methods:

- Open the Control Panel (use the Start menu, select Settings, and in the pop-up menu, choose Control Panel), then double click the Add/Remove Programs icon. The Add/Remove Programs will automatically search your floppy drive and CD-ROM for the Setup.com file; when it finds it, you will be prompted to continue. Follow the instructions on-screen to start Setup.com.

- Use the Explorer or My Computer to open a window that shows the contents of your floppy drive or CD-ROM drive from which you will be installing FS 5.1. Then double click on the Setup.com file.

427

- Exit Windows 95 (use the Start menu, select Shutdown, and choose Restart the Computer in MS DOS Mode) and run the Setup.com program from the DOS prompt.

  The installation itself is simple, with self-explanatory instruction screens to help guide you through every step. Before you begin, however, you must know these things about your hardware setup:

- Do you have a 486 or better PC? Pentiums are recommended for best performance. *Flight Simulator* will run on older 386's, but with much degraded performance and loss of program features.

- Do you have enough hard disk space free for the installation of *Flight Simulator*? If your hard drive has 32 KB clusters (32,768 bytes/cluster), which is typical for Windows 95 formatted gigabyte drives, the save load time disk space requirement is 12.9 MB, and the save disk space requirement is 9.57 MB. If your hard drive has 8 KB clusters (8,192 bytes/cluster), the save load time disk space requirement is also 12.9 MB. You can check to see what your cluster size is by running CHKDSK (a DOS utility) on your hard drive. CHKDSK will report to you the size of the "allocation" unit, which is the same thing as your cluster size.

  Although the program files need only 12.9 MB, the setup program checks for 20 MB of free hard disk space so there is enough room for the cache files (created on the fly when you run FS 5.1). If you don't have enough room, it is time to do some hard disk housekeeping.

- What kind of video card do you have? VGA or Super VGA?

- If you have a Super VGA card, do you know the name of your card's manufacturer and the type of video accelerator chip used inside?

- Do you have a Microsoft compatible mouse installed?

- What kind of sound card, if any, do you have installed?

- Do you have a joystick, flightstick, yoke, or pedals installed?

- How much random access memory (RAM) do you have installed? *Flight Simulator* will run with 2 MB of RAM, but 4 MB or higher is recommended along with the use of an expanded memory manager such as EMM386 (Windows 95 users don't need to worry about this). For DOS 6.22 users, FS 5.1 will run better if you use the following RAM memory parameter in your config.sys file:

  DEVICE=C:\DOS\EMM386.EXE RAM H=255 D=64

- Do you have at least 500 KB of conventional RAM free after booting your computer? If you don't have an expanded memory manager loaded, such as EMM386 (Windows 95 users can disregard this, since the memory manager is built in), you will need 560 KB of free conventional memory.

- Have you loaded DOS into high memory? (Windows 95 users can ignore this.) When running FS 5.1 from the DOS prompt, you should load DOS into high memory above 640 KB (This is known as 256 KB of extended or "high" memory), so you can improve the performance of the program. In your config.sys, DEVICE=HIMEM.SYS

  DOS=HIGH, UMB will do this for you.

If you already know the answers to these questions, then proceed with the installation as outlined in the next section.

Simply insert your FS 5.1 installation floppy disk 1 into your drive and type:

A:\Setup

Or, if you are installing the FS 5.1 CD-ROM, substitute the drive letter for your CD-ROM drive so the setup command from the DOS prompt looks something like this (assuming for this example that your CD-ROM is assigned the drive letter "E"):

E:\Setup

1. If you are running the setup program under Windows 95, you'll see a Performance Note message screen warning that you will achieve better performance if you run FS 5.1 in MS-DOS mode. Don't worry, just press any key to continue with the installation. Follow the steps below:

2. In the initial setup screen, you'll have the option of changing the Mode, Display, Keyboard, Mouse, and Sound configurations. Select the Mode option, then press [Enter].

3. In the Mode configuration dialog box that opens, select the performance option recommended for your computer hardware. If you are running a Pentium workstation, then you should select either the Pentium High Performance High Resolution or Pentium High Performance Medium Resolution option. There are other options available for slower 486 and 386 computers, and if you select one of these, FS 5.1 will use lower display resolutions, simpler scenery, and make other changes to the program (essentially lessening the graphics burden) in order to speed up your frame rate. When you have made your selection, press the [Enter] key.

4. You'll see a Display Selection Note warning that before proceeding, you'll need to know what kind of VGA or SVGA video card or video chip you are using. Press [Enter] to continue, or [Esc] if you are unsure and want to exit the installation.

5. You should already know what kind of video display card you have; select your particular VGA/SVGA board card or video chip from the scrolling

list (see Figure 3.19 in Chapter 3 for a listing of high-end cards for the 486/Pentium performance mode; note that changing your performance mode also changes the kinds of video card/chip drivers available in the scrolling list). If you aren't sure of which card/chip you have, try using the VESA 1.2 Compatible option. This is a graphics standard that most SVGA card manufacturers have agreed to adopt, and your card should theoretically work under this driver. However, for optimum speed, you should try to identify which manufacturer makes your display card, and then select it from the list that appears on screen. Press the [Enter] key to continue.

6. After choosing your video card/chip, you'll be returned to the main setup screen. If you don't want haze effects, you can skip to step 8, however, if you want to have haze effects, you'll need to change your Display resolution. Make sure the current option for Display is highlighted, then press the [Enter] key.

7. You'll see a Performance Note warning, telling you that modifying the display type will change your performance mode you choose in step three. In the Display Modes list box, select the kind of display you have,

---

Video card notes:

VESA 1.2 compatibility: Some VESA 1.2 drivers are not fully implemented. Function 7 and modes 100h or 101h must be implemented for FS 5.1 to work in SVGA mode. If FS 5.1 does not properly display using the VESA driver, reinstall the program using the Standard VGA display option (you'll need to select a 386 or 486 Low Resolution performance mode in step 3 above, before you can choose a Standard VGA video card).

SVGA 320 x 200 mode: Although this mode may run 10 percent to 20 percent faster than VGA 320 x 200 mode, some graphics cards do not support this mode. If your screen flashes or does not display at all, select VGA 320 × 200 mode.

ATI Mach 64 cards: Older ATI Mach 64 cards may need a BIOS upgrade. BIOS version .15, dated 1994/6/10 or newer, is required.

The Stealth 64 DRAM card: This card does not support 640 × 400 VESA mode directly; it needs a little help to work correctly with FS 5.1. Use FS 5.1's VESA 1.2 driver, and also download UVBE5A.ZIP from CompuServe's Flight Simulator Forum, Library 13 (hardware). UVBE5A.ZIP is a BIOS patch that will allow the Stealth to handle 640 × 400 mode. That in combination with the VESA 1.2 driver in FS 5.1 should work fine for you.

whether it is VGA or SVGA, and whether you want Haze effects or not. For example, if you have a SVGA card, choose SVGA 640 × 400 256 Colors with Haze. At this point, after you make your selection, you may or may not be asked to again choose your video card/chip that you already selected in step five. If this happens, just repeat your selection. Press Enter to continue.

8. Upon returning to the main setup screen, check to make sure your Mode and Display selections are correct. Change them again if necessary.

9. In the main setup screen, under Keyboard, you have the option of choosing a keyboard with function keys on the top (default), or for older keyboards, on the side. Leave this alone if your function keys are on top.

10. In the main setup screen, under Mouse, you have the option of choosing No Mouse or Microsoft Compatible Mouse (default). Leave this alone if you have a Microsoft Mouse already installed.

Sound card installation notes:

Windows 95, Windows NT, Windows 3.1: Don't use the PC Speaker sound when using FS 5.1 under Windows 95, Windows NT, or Windows 3.1, because you'll experience problems. Avoid this by choosing No Sound Device from the sound board list.

Media Vision-pro Audio Spectrum sound cards: You must install the Media Vision driver (MVSOUND.SYS) before running FS 5.1. If you still get poor results, you may need to disable direct memory access (DMA) sharing with your card. To run Pro Audio Spectrum cards as Sound Blaster compatible, you must have a SET BLASTER=A220 I7 D1 H5 P330 T6 in your autoexec.bat file. Additionally, you need the appropriate Media Vision driver MVSOUND.SYS or PA3D.SYS installed in the config.sys file.

Gravis Ultrasound sound card: You need to have the SBOS or MEGAEM Sound Blaster emulation drivers loaded prior to running FS 5.1.

Loading sound into XMS memory: Sound files are loaded into extended memory (XMS) for storage and quick playback. Certain memory configurations can cause this memory to be moved, resulting in noisy sounds or system crashes. If this occurs, from the Options/Preferences/Sound menu in FS 5.1, change the Use XMS Memory option to No. FS 5.1 will use extra conventional memory for this setting, but it will resolve sound playback problems that occur using XMS memory.

---

11. If you have a sound card, you should select Sound on the main setup screen, then press [Enter] so that you can install the appropriate sound driver.

12. In the Sound setup screen, choose from the list of sound boards which board you have installed in your system. If you don't know, select Auto-detect.

13. Returning to the main setup screen, make sure all the remaining choices for your keyboard and mouse are correct for your system. If they are not, select the item in question and press [Enter] to change it. Otherwise, highlight Install *Flight Simulator* and press [Enter] to continue.

14. You may see an additional warning screen for your Sound Blaster selection, but for now, press any key to continue.

15. The setup program next asks you whether you agree to install *Flight Simulator* in the target drive/directory it has chosen for you. If you don't like this drive/directory choice, select Change Target Directory.

16. When you are finished making your drive/directory choice, select Install *Flight Simulator*, and press the [Enter] key.

17. Setup will now ask you whether you want to save hard disk space and take longer to load scenery, or whether you want to consume more hard disk space (22 MB), but save time loading scenery (note the program files by themselves take only about 12.9 to 15 MB of disk space; it is the scenery cache files created on the fly that take up extra room. You need to reserve disk space for these cache files when they are needed). The installation program will begin to decompress the files from the floppy disk or CD-ROM, and install the program files to your hard disk.

18. If you are installing from floppy disk, after the setup program has finished with the first diskette, it will prompt you to remove disk 1 and insert disk 2. Be sure to press the [Enter] key after you have put in disk 2. Again, the program will continue with the process of decompressing files. Continue this process for the other installation disks.

19. If all goes well, and the program has successfully copied all its files to your hard disk, you will see the initial setup screen information dialog box. Click OK to proceed on.

20. A dialog box will appear asking you whether you want sound to be audible. The default is for sound to be On, so if that is what you want, click the OK button.

21. The Sound Setup screen will appear, in which you are asked to select your sound card from a list, customize the volume level, set the base memory address, modify the direct memory access (DMA) channel, choose whether or not you want to use XMS memory (see previous

installation notes for step 12), and if you want your engine sounds digitized.

Many sound cards conflict with other cards such as scanner cards, modem cards, SCSI cards, and thus don't work unless they are configured differently than their default setting programmed in at the factory. Because the FS 5.1 program has no way of checking how your sound board is configured on your PC, you must give it some vital information to make it work properly. Don't worry if you don't know the answers to these questions, you can continue with the installation and figure this out later. After installing the program and finding your sound card doesn't work, just select the Sound button from the Preferences dialog box found under the Options menu, and tinker with the settings until you get it right. Of course. it would be better if you knew what the proper settings are before doing this. But have no fear, you aren't going to destroy your computer or sound card. By the way, choose Digitized Engine Sounds if you can, because it sounds much better than the synthesized version. Click OK to proceed on. Also, if you have problems with XMS memory lockups, select No for Use XMS Memory.

22. The next setup screen asks you whether you want to have dynamic scenery and automatic weather generation start up by default each time FS 5.1 begins. Dynamic scenery includes other planes, blimps, hot air balloons, ground traffic, boats, and other moving objects. If you have a 486 33MHz or slower PC, you probably won't want to toggle these features on because it will slow down the simulation too much. If you want to switch dynamic scenery on later, you can do so inside the program by toggling on the options as found in the Dynamic Scenery dialog box under the Scenery Menu. Likewise you can turn automatic weather generation on by bringing up the Weather dialog box under the World menu, and toggling on the Automatic Weather Generation list box found in the Edit Weather Area dialog box. Click OK to proceed on.

23. The next setup screen prompts you to choose the startup situation that FS 5.1 defaults to when initially booting up. For now choose Normal Flight mode. Click OK to proceed.

24. If you want to have FS 5.1 automatically record your flight hours in a logbook, click the Log Flight Time checkbox. Click OK to proceed on.

25. You can use one or two joysticks with FS 5.1 and you can even use pedals to control the rudders, and a separate yoke to control the ailerons, elevators, throttle, and brakes, just like real cockpits. If you have such a setup, you can customize the second joystick (or pedals) to control the Throttle Only, the Throttle and Brakes, the Rudder Only, or the Throttle and Rudder. Once you've switched on your joysticks in the

Figure A.1
After deleting the
DEVICE=STICK2.FSO
in your fs5.ini file,
the following buttons
and switches will work
on the CH Products
Virtual Pilot Pro
Yoke Stick.

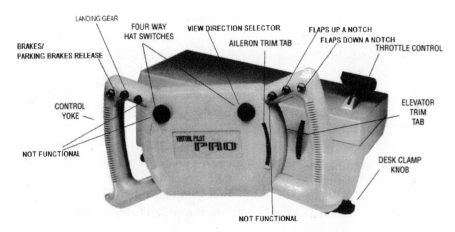

CH Products The Virtual Pilot Pro

Preferences dialog box, you will not be able to override the joysticks via the mouse or keyboard flight controls, with one exception: when flying the Learjet, once you've landed you can close the throttles and then press the [F2] or keypad [3] key a few times to engage the thrust reversers, and press the [F1] (cut throttle) or keypad [9] key to disengage them (you can also nudge the joystick throttle forward a bit).

Joystick installation notes:

- CH Products:

  In order to use the hat switches and buttons on the Virtual Pilot Pro, you'll need to edit your fs5.ini file using any text editor (the fs5.ini file is in your Fltsim5 directory). After completing the installation of FS 5.1, in the fs5.ini file delete the DEVICE=STICK2.FSO line, then save the file. This will allow the hat switches to activate the functions shown listed in Figure A.1.

  If you have the CH Products Virtual Pilot Pro Yoke, Joystick 1 should be set to Aileron and Elevator.

  If you don't have the rudder pedals, set Joystick 2 to Throttle Only.

  However, if you also have CH Products Pro Pedals rudder pedals, set Joystick 2 to Throttle and Rudder.

- ThrustMaster: Edit the fs5.ini file and change the DEVICE=STICK2.FSO to DEVICE=TM_STIK.FSO, then save the file. In the Joystick Preferences dialog box, set Joystick 1 to Ailerons and Elevators; and if you have the RCS pedals, set Joystick 2 to Rudders Only.

- Colorado Spectrum Notebook Gameport: A driver is included for use with the appropriate joystick. To use this driver, type the following line in your fs5.ini file:

  DEVICE=CS_STIK.FSO

  Note the gameport driver NG.EXE from Colorado Spectrum must be installed for this to work.

- Other joystick drivers: The following drivers exist: STICK2.FS0 and CS_STIK.FSO. If no joystick driver is specified in the DEVICE= line in the fs5.ini file, the CH Products driver is the default. STICK2.FSO supports a generic two-button joystick. But as mentioned earlier, it will not allow the CH Pro Pedals to work.

26. In the next dialog box, press the Run *Flight Simulator* button if you wish to fly the simulator now. You can also press the Exit to MS-DOS button if you want to come back to the program later or, if you plan on installing Add-on Scenery or other Add-on software, you can press the Install Add-on button.

27. If you are installing Add-on scenery software, insert the floppy disk containing the Add-on scenery or software into your floppy drive. In the Setup Add-On dialog box, select the floppy drive and press ⌨Enter to begin the installation process. If you have a CD-ROM Add-on scenery disk, insert the CD-ROM disk and select the drive letter which corresponds to your CD-ROM, then press ⌨Enter.

RECONFIGURING YOUR SETUP OPTIONS IF YOU DECIDE TO LATER ADD A NEW SYSTEM COMPONENT

If you buy a new sound card, video card, joystick, or flightstick/rudder combination, you can always go back into the setup to change the FS 5.0's settings. You can do this without reinstalling the entire program from your floppy disk or CD-ROM. There are two ways to do this: one from inside the program, the other from outside the program, using the Setup.com file in your Fltsim5 directory.

To reconfigure your setup options while inside the *Flight Simulator* program:

1. Pull down the Options menu and select Preferences.

2. Click on the Display button, the Joystick button, the Sound button, or the Mouse button to make changes in any of these settings. Follow the instructions inside each dialog box, then click the OK button to exit Preferences.

3. If the program needs to reboot itself, it will prompt you with the Preferences Alert dialog box. Click the Exit *Flight Simulator* and Restart button, and when the program restarts your new setup options will take effect.

To reconfigure your setup options while outside the *Flight Simulator* program run the Setup.com file in your Fltsim5 directory (you can do this from the DOS prompt, or you can run the setup program from within Windows 95 by just double clicking on the Setup.com icon):

1. Run Setup.com.
2. You will see a setup dialog box asking you to accept the system configuration choices as currently displayed. If you want to make a change in the current Mode, Display, Keyboard, or Mouse, or Sound settings, highlight the selection and press the Enter key.
3. After you are satisfied with your choices for the display, keyboard, and mouse, select the Install *Flight Simulator* item and press Enter.
4. *Flight Simulator* will next prompt you with some of the same setup screens you saw when you first installed the program. At the end of this, press the Run *Flight Simulator* button if you wish to fly the simulator now. Otherwise press Exit to MS-DOS, if you want to come back to the program later.

RUNNING FLIGHT SIMULATOR UNDER WINDOWS 95

Although you can run *Flight Simulator* as a DOS application in Windows 95 (only with full-screen, not in a MS-DOS sub-window), it is not recommended. You will lose some video performance because Windows will slow down *Flight Simulator* by creating more demands on your CPU. Figure on at least a 10 percent frame rate loss with a Pentium, and a 15 percent to 25 percent frame rate loss on a 486 66MHz.

Quick and Easy Configuration Under Windows 95

There are two steps to configuring FS 5.1 to run painlessly under Windows 95:

1. It's best to run *Flight Simulator* under Windows 95 without an autoexec.bat and config.sys. Just rename these two files and restart your machine (Windows 95 has built in 32 bit drivers for most of the device drivers you load using your autoexec.bat and config.sys files, so it doesn't really need to boot up with these files). Be sure not to delete these two files, but rather rename them with distinctive names such as autoexec.bak

and config.bak. Later, if you find your computer won't boot properly, or you have some DOS real mode driver or 16 bit driver needed for your hardware and Windows 95 doesn't have a built in 32 bit driver equivalent, you can easily rename these two files back to their original names, then reboot to enable them again (if this is your situation, it would be better for you to create a DOS or Windows 95 floppy boot disk, and start *Flight Simulator* from the boot disk). Note you can still run FS 5.1 with your autoexec.bat and config.sys enabled, as long as you have at least 500 KB free of RAM. The only reason to remove these two files is that Windows will then configure itself to run with maximum conventional memory.

2. To have Windows 95 automatically configure FS 5.1 to run properly, create a shortcut for Fs5.com and then drag this shortcut on to your desktop. To do this: select the Fs5.com file either in the Explorer, or in a directory window for the Fltsim5 directory, then click and hold down the right mouse and drag the icon over to your desktop. When you release the right mouse button, you'll see a pop-up menu appear; select the Create Shortcuts Here menu option and an icon for *Flight Simulator* will appear on your desktop.

From now on, if you click on this shortcut icon, *Flight Simulator* will start up!

Advanced Windows 95 Setup

If you need a more advanced setup under Windows 95, it is possible to customize the shortcut icon you created on the desktop for Fs5.com to include special MS-DOS drivers you may need. To do this:

1. Click the right mouse button on the shortcut you created for Fs5.com and select Properties.

2. In the Properties dialog box, click on the Program tab, then click the Advanced option button.

3. In the Advanced Program Settings dialog box, click the MS-DOS mode checkbox.

4. Click the Specify a New MS-DOS Configuration radio button, and you can then type in a custom config.sys and autoexec.bat file for *Flight Simulator*. As shown in Figure A.2, you'll probably need to include DOS=HIGH,UMB and DEVICE=EMM386.EXE RAM and DEVICE=HIMEM.SYS in your config.sys, and load a mouse driver such as lh mouse.com in your autoexec.bat. Also, you should add any additional drivers, (i.e. Sound Blaster) needed for your computer to boot properly. Click OK when you are done.

To quickly configure FS 5.1 under Windows 95, rename your autoexec.bat and config.sys files, reboot your machine, and create a shortcut icon for Fs5.com on your desktop.

If you get an XMS memory error message when starting Flight Simulator in Windows 95, go through the Flight Simulator Setup, and in the Sound Setup, change Use XMS Memory to No.

5. Click the Memory tab, and check to see if the memory is set to auto, as shown in Figure A.3. Click OK, to finish.

Now, when you double click the shortcut icon for Fs5.com, your machine will reboot, shell out to DOS, run your custom autoexec.bat and config.sys, and then start *Flight Simulator*. When you exit *Flight Simulator*, Windows 95 will reboot the machine and start up normally again.

Note this advanced setup for Windows 95 is a real hassle because of the rebooting process. It is much preferable, and easier to setup *Flight Simulator* as a shortcut icon, without the custom MS-DOS autoexec.bat and config.sys changes. Before you do the advanced setup, first try dragging the shortcut icon for Fs5.com onto your desktop, then try starting the program. You may find that it works without any fine tuning.

Task Switching in Windows

While in SVGA display mode, you can't switch back to Windows from within *Flight Simulator* using the familiar [Alt] + [Esc] key task switcher key combination.

Figure A.2 Advanced Configuration for Flight Simulator under Windows 95 Note you probably won't need to do this because you can just create a shortcut to Fs5.com on your Windows 95 desktop. (see text for more details).

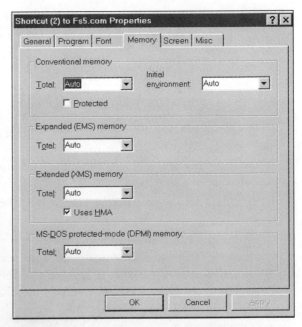

Figure A.3 Advanced Memory Configuration for Flight Simulator in Windows 95

Some people have had some success in task switching by using VGA, or VESA 1.2 drivers for FS 5.1. But task switching is not possible for SVGA resolutions. (You can [Ctrl] + [Alt] + [Delete] out of FS 5.1, then when presented with the Task List window, click the Cancel button to return to Windows 95. But once back in Windows, if you try to return to FS 5.1 by clicking on the task bar icon for the FS 5.1 MS-DOS icon, you will get an error message.)

STARTING FLIGHT SIMULATOR

To start *Flight Simulator* from DOS:

1. If you are using the CD-ROM version of FS5.1, insert the CD into your CD-ROM drive. Make sure you always keep the FS 5.1 CD in your CD-ROM drive because *Flight Simulator* needs to download scenery data from the disc when you fly into different scenery areas.
2. From the DOS prompt, change to your Fltsim5 directory on your hard disk, type Fs, and then press [Enter]. The program will load, and you should see a cockpit and view of Runway 36 at Meigs Field in Chicago.

To start *Flight Simulator* from within Windows 95:

1. If you are using the CD-ROM version of FS 5.1, insert the CD into your CD-ROM drive. Make sure you always keep the FS 5.1 CD in your CD-ROM drive because *Flight Simulator* needs to download scenery data from the disc when you fly into different scenery areas.
2. Click on the shortcut icon you created for Fs5.com. The program will load and you should see a cockpit and view of Runway 36 at Meigs Field in Chicago.

FRAME RATE COMPARISON GUIDE

FS 5.1 depends heavily on having a fast CPU and video card. The higher the frame rate, or number of frames per second redrawn on your screen, the better FS 5.1 runs. You can quickly check your frame rate by pressing [Shift] + [Z] four times until you see the frame rate displayed on-screen.

The two hardware components that affect speed are the central processing unit (CPU—sometimes called 486 or Pentium) and the video card. The best way to gauge the speed of hardware used with FS 5.1 is to compare the frames per second each CPU and video card combination can produce.

In order to obtain a common reference point by which equipment can be judged equally, you need to use standard tests that use a similar FS 5.1

setup. In the previous edition of this book a program called Frame.zip, found in the CompuServe *Flight Simulator* Forum, was used. Unfortunately, this program, though useful for FS 5.0, could not be used for testing the frame rate in FS 5.1 because of the addition of new SVGA haze display features. So, to address this problem, CompuServe member Jack Yeazel devised a series of tests using situations found in the Options/Situations menu. These situation sallow you to conduct your own comparison tests.

Here's how Mr. Yeazel conducted his tests. First he made sure FS 5.1 was setup with SVGA Haze, all scenery display options were turned on (under the Options/Preferences/Display menu), and the Scenery Quality/Speed was set to Low/Fast, and Flicker/Speed was set to Much/Fast. Mr. Yeazel then started the following situations and recorded the frame rate for each one:

- Meigs Takeoff, Dense Scenery
- Meigs Takeoff, Medium Scenery
- Meigs Takeoff, Runway 36
- Meigs Takeoff, Fast Graphics

Figure A.4 graphically illustrates the frame rate results for various CPU and video card combinations. In the figure, the longer the bar, the greater the frames per second, and the better FS 5.1 will run. Also, there are four bars for each computer type. This is because four measurements were taken, one for each of the above situations. The Meigs Takeoff, Dense Scenery situation tests your computer's ability to draw complex objects such as the cybergraphics buildings. On the other hand the Meigs Takeoff, Fast Graphics situation tests your computer's ability to draw simple objects so as to maximize your frame rate. The acronyms for the CPU descriptions have the following meanings: VLB stands for VESA Local Bus, SVGA represents a Super VGA Video Card, and PCI stands for Peripheral Connect Interface, which is the new bus architecture for Pentiums and Power PCs.

Examining Figure A.4 more closely, you can see the best frame rate performance was found with PCI Pentium 120 MHz PCs, which achieved around three times the frame rate of an older 486 66MHz PC. That is to say, the Pentium 120 achieved 19 frames per second for dense scenery vs. 4.6 frames per second for the 486. You'll also note that, for those computers running *Flight Simulator* as a DOS application under Windows 95, the frame rate can drop by as much as 25 percent[1]! This Windows 95 performance degradation was more pronounced on older 486 PCs than it was for

---

[1]This result was taken from a 486 66 Mhz machine running a beta of Windows 95. Your actual frame rate loss should be much lower with the release version of Windows 95.

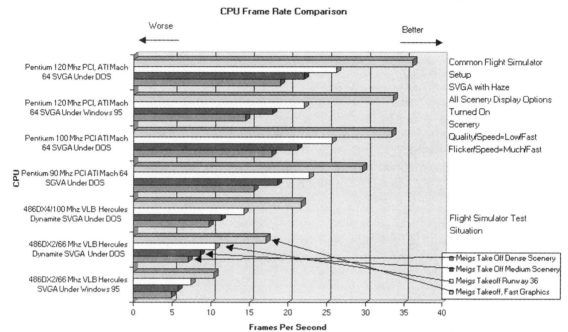

Figure A.4
Flight Simulator Frame
Rate Results for
Various CPUs

Pentiums, and was also greater when dense scenery was selected. Due to the fact these tests were run on a late beta build of Windows 95 (this book went to press before Windows 95 was released), the Windows 95 frame rate results in Figure A.4 are worse than you will get with the release version of Windows 95. Microsoft has run tests with the release version, and they claim a frame rate loss of only 15 percent for a 486 66MHz PC and a loss of only 10 percent for a Pentium, while running under Windows 95 protected mode.

In late 1995, Pentium 133 MHz PCs are slated to be released, and Intel's new P6 chip is expected to ship, with even greater frame rates being promised. With the advent of RISC chips, such as the Motorola Power PC 604, it will be possible in the near future to run *Flight Simulator* even faster, using Windows NT.

OPTIMIZING YOUR FRAME RATE WITH EXPANDED MEMORY

As mentioned earlier, you'll get the highest frame rate if you run FS 5.1 from the DOS prompt, not from within Windows 95. But your frame rate also depends on having plenty of expanded memory. *Flight Simulator* has a hard time running in conventional memory alone; if you have enough expanded memory, it will configure itself to run more efficiently. Therefore, if you are booting from DOS, you should make an effort to load the EMM386.EXE driver (along with HIMEM.SYS and DOS=HIGH,UMB) in your config.sys file. Under DOS 6.22, you can use the Memmaker utility (just type Memmaker while in the DOS directory) to properly setup up enough expanded memory. You will have a much easier time of setting up expanded memory, if you have at least 8MB of RAM, although you can get by with 4 MB of RAM.

Under Windows 95, if you start *Flight Simulator* as a DOS application (i.e. click on the shortcut icon for Fs5.com), Windows will automatically allocate as much expanded memory as needed. But, depending on your PC and FS 5.1 graphics situation setup, you can take a hit of 10 percent to 25 percent in your frame rate, due to Windows' high graphical overhead.

A P P E N D I X

B

VOR/NDB Station List, Airports Directory, and Navigational Maps

Appendix B contains FS 5.1 CD Navaid listings, navigational maps, and a worldwide airport facilities listing. All of these materials are useful for navigating the Flight Simulator world. You will find a complete listing of all the VOR/NDBs in the FS 5.1 CD. The CD also contains maps depicting all the VOR Navaids for the USA and VOR/NDBs for the rest of the world (NDBs are not shown on the USA maps because of space constraints). The VOR/NDB Navaid listings for the rest of the world are sorted by region, and include the following areas:

- USA/Canada
- South America/Central America/Caribbean Region Ocean
- Western Pacific Ocean
- Eastern and Southern Pacific Ocean
- Asia
- Africa
- Europe
- North Atlantic Ocean

Please be advised that all the information in this chapter is to be used only with FS 5.1. Please do NOT use any data found in this book for real navigational purposes because some of the data can quickly become obsolete, or is, in some cases wrong!

   WARNING, ALL OF THE INFORMATION IN THIS APPENDIX IS TO BE USED ONLY WITH FLIGHT SIMULATOR. DO NOT USE FOR REAL NAVIGATIONAL PURPOSES.

HOW TO READ THE VOR/NDB STATION LIST

The VOR/NDB station list is sorted by state/country/location and then alphabetically by name. Under each listing you will find the station's three to four letter identifier, the station type (VOR or NDB), frequency, latitude/longitude coordinates, altitude, and magnetic variation. Some VOR/NDB stations don't have altitudes or magnetic variations listed because this information was not available in the FS 5.1 Navaid database.

Using the information in this file, you can plot a flight path using stations you know exist along your route. For example, if you wanted to fly from Seattle to San Francisco, you would consult Map 3, Map 2, and Map 1 in this appendix (see USA Map index, Figure B.1), then write down the names of the VOR stations along your route. Next, look up the VOR stations in the USA/Canada Navaid table that match your intended path, and write down the frequency, latitude/longitude, and magnetic variation for each station. Finally, figure out the magnetic course heading from one VOR station to the next VOR station (using the techniques found in Chapter 12), and then fly!

Of course, if you have the real aeronautical charts (available from the NOAA — see bibliography), you don't really need the table because you can consult the VOR/NDB listings directly on the map, and see the already calculated magnetic bearings printed on the map.

The USA/Canada Navaid table contains some VORs and NDBs outside of the continental USA. These additional Navaids, such as in Cuba and the Caribbean, have more extensive VOR/NDB listings in the regional Navaid tables that follow the USA/Canada table. The FS 5.1 floppy disk version does not contain the additional Navaids.

State/Country	VOR/NDB Name	Ident.	Type	Freq.	Latitude		Longitude		Altitude	Mag Var

USA/CANADA NAVAIDS

Alabama

State/Country	VOR/NDB Name	Ident.	Type	Freq.	Latitude		Longitude		Altitude	Mag Var
	ALEXANDER CITY	DER	NDB	382.00	N32°	52.75'	W85°	57.68'		
	ANDALUSIA	UIA	VOR	110.20	N31°	18.57'	W86°	23.53'	331	E00°
	BESSEMER	BEQ	NDB	368.00	N33°	18.71'	W86°	55.38'		
	BLOOD (LOM/NDB)	BLOO	NDB	365.00	N31°	49.81'	W86°	06.32'		
	BOGGA (LOM)	BOGG	NDB	211.00	N33°	32.06'	W85°	55.84'		
	BOLL WEEVIL	BVG	NDB	308.00	N31°	20.21'	W85°	58.99'		
	BRANTLEY	XBR	NDB	410.00	N31°	33.70'	W86°	17.57'		
	BROOKWOOD	OKW	VOR	111.00	N33°	14.37'	W87°	15.00'	649	E00°
	CAHABA	CAQ	VOR	114.90	N32°	20.69'	W86°	59.49'	160	E02°
	CAIRNS	OZR	VOR	111.20	N31°	16.14'	W85°	43.58'	298	E02°
	CALERA	AOA	NDB	215.00	N33°	07.10'	W86°	46.03'		
	CAPSHAW	CWH	NDB	350.00	N34°	46.42'	W86°	46.73'		
	COLE SPRING	CPP	NDB	230.00	N34°	22.07'	W86°	49.43'		
	COLUMBUS	CSG	VOR	117.10	N32°	36.91'	W85°	01.05'	629	E01°
	DECATUR	DCU	VOR	112.80	N34°	38.89'	W86°	56.36'	590	W01°
	ENTERPRISE	EDN	VOR	116.60	N31°	17.76'	W85°	54.19'	367	E00°
	EUFAULA	EUF	VOR	109.20	N31°	57.01'	W85°	07.83'	278	E02°
	FAYETTE	FDF	NDB	204.00	N33°	42.87'	W87°	48.81'		
	FENIX (LOM)	FENI	NDB	355.00	N32°	27.11'	W85°	02.51'		
	FORT PAYNE	FTP	NDB	426.00	N34°	31.26'	W85°	40.40'		
	GADSDEN	GAD	VOR	112.30	N33°	58.58'	W86°	05.01'	560	E02°
	GRAGG-WADE	GGY	NDB	338.00	N32°	51.19'	W86°	36.66'		
	GREENE CO	GCV	VOR	115.70	N31°	05.87'	W88°	29.16'	298	E05°
	GREENSBORO	EOG	NDB	417.00	N32°	36.14'	W87°	39.78'		
	HAMILTON	HAB	VOR	110.40	N34°	11.70'	W88°	00.75'	810	E02°
	HANCHEY	HYE	NDB	221.00	N31°	22.01'	W85°	38.99'		
	HANCHEY	HEY	VOR	110.60	N31°	22.44'	W85°	39.16'	298	E02°
	JUDD	JUY	NDB	264.00	N31°	18.26'	W86°	23.44'		
	LAWSON	AWS	NDB	335.00	N32°	17.59'	W85°	01.39'		
	LOWE	LOR	NDB	269.00	N31°	21.61'	W85°	44.61'		
	MARRA (LOM)	MARR	NDB	245.00	N32°	18.69'	W86°	30.63'		
	MC DEN (LOM/NDB)	BH	NDB	224.00	N33°	30.67'	W86°	50.73'		
	MONROEVILLE	MVC	VOR	116.80	N31°	27.62'	W87°	21.16'	416	E04°
	MONTGOMERY	MGM	VOR	112.10	N32°	13.34'	W86°	19.18'	268	E03°
	MUSCLE SHOALS	MSL	VOR	116.50	N34°	42.41'	W87°	29.48'	580	E01°
	OPOLE (LOM)	OPOL	NDB	423.00	N32°	30.55'	W85°	26.23'		
	PERSIMMON	PRN	NDB	359.00	N31°	51.05'	W86°	36.86'		
	POLLK (LOM/NDB)	POLL	NDB	344.00	N32°	16.18'	W86°	55.65'		
	REDSTONE	HUA	NDB	287.00	N34°	41.90'	W86°	41.28'		
	ROCKET	RQZ	VOR	112.20	N34°	47.82'	W86°	38.03'	1,200	E02°
	ROEBY (LOM)	ROEB	NDB	394.00	N33°	36.45'	W86°	40.72'		
	RUCKR (LOM/NDB)	RUCK	NDB	212.00	N31°	13.53'	W85°	48.95'		
	SARATOGA	ARF	NDB	296.00	N34°	15.17'	W86°	13.41'		
	SPRING HILL	XNE	NDB	281.00	N31°	41.06'	W85°	58.46'		
	SUMMERDALE	ESU	NDB	204.00	N30°	29.96'	W87°	43.54'		
	SYLACAUGA	SCD	NDB	284.00	N33°	10.45'	W86°	19.09'		
	TALLADEGA	TDG	VOR	108.80	N33°	34.50'	W86°	02.56'	531	E02°
	TROY	TOI	VOR	110.00	N31°	51.80'	W86°	00.65'	390	E00°
	TUSCALOOSA	TCL	VOR	117.80	N33°	15.53'	W87°	32.21'	370	E03°
	TUSKE (LOM)	TUSK	NDB	362.00	N33°	09.49'	W87°	40.22'		
	TUSKEGEE	TGE	VOR	117.30	N32°	29.09'	W85°	40.15'	488	E02°
	VULCAN	VUZ	VOR	114.40	N33°	40.21'	W86°	53.98'	751	E02°
	WILCOX CO	IWE	NDB	350.00	N31°	58.82'	W87°	20.21'		
	WIREGRASS	RRS	VOR	111.60	N31°	17.06'	W85°	25.87'	360	E02°

Alaska

State/Country	VOR/NDB Name	Ident.	Type	Freq.	Latitude		Longitude		Altitude	Mag Var
	ADAK	NUD	NDB	347.00	N51°	55.01'	W176°	34.01'		
	ADAK	NUD	VOR	113.00	N51°	52.27'	W176°	40.44'	380	E09°
	AMBLER	AMF	NDB	403.00	N67°	06.40'	W157°	51.47'		
	ANCHORAGE	ANC	VOR	114.30	N61°	09.04'	W150°	12.39'	278	E25°
	ANIAK	ANI	NDB	359.00	N61°	35.41'	W159°	35.87'		
	ANNETTE ISLAND	ANN	VOR	117.10	N55°	03.62'	W131°	34.70'	173	E27°
	ANVIK	ANV	NDB	365.00	N62°	38.48'	W160°	11.40'		
	BARROW	BRW	VOR	116.20	N71°	16.40'	W156°	47.28'	39	E25°
	BARTER ISLAND	BTI	NDB	308.00	N70°	07.84'	W143°	38.63'		
	BEAR CREEK	BCC	NDB	212.00	N65°	10.43'	W152°	12.35'		
	BETHEL	BET	VOR	114.10	N60°	47.08'	W161°	49.45'	131	E19°
	BETHEL (LMM)	ET	NDB	344.00	N60°	47.79'	W161°	49.28'		
	BETTLES	BTT	VOR	116.00	N66°	54.30'	W151°	32.15'	646	E27°
	BIG DELTA	BIG	VOR	114.90	N64°	00.26'	W145°	43.02'	1,229	E29°
	BIG LAKE	BGQ	VOR	112.50	N61°	34.16'	W149°	58.02'	160	E25°
	BIORKA ISLAND	BKA	VOR	113.80	N56°	51.56'	W135°	33.07'	239	E28°

State/Country	VOR/NDB Name	Ident.	Type	Freq.	Latitude		Longitude		Altitude	Mag Var
USA/CANADA NAVAIDS										
Alaska	BISHOP	BZP	NDB	331.00	N64°	44.15'	W156°	48.60'		
	BORLAND	HBT	NDB	390.00	N55°	18.93'	W160°	31.10'		
	BROWERVILLE	VIR	NDB	281.00	N71°	16.95'	W156°	47.08'		
	BRUCK (LOM)	BRUC	NDB	387.00	N61°	10.05'	W150°	10.61'		
	BUCKLAND	BVK	NDB	325.00	N65°	58.78'	W161°	08.96'		
	CAIRN MOUNTAIN	CRN	NDB	281.00	N61°	05.95'	W155°	33.13'		
	CAMPBELL LAKE	CMQ	NDB	338.00	N61°	10.26'	W150°	02.86'		
	CAPE LISBURNE	LUR	NDB	385.00	N68°	51.95'	W166°	04.18'		
	CAPE NEWENHAM	EHM	NDB	385.00	N58°	39.35'	W162°	04.54'		
	CAPE ROMANZOF	CZF	NDB	275.00	N61°	47.43'	W165°	58.17'		
	CENTRAL	CEM	NDB	373.00	N65°	34.39'	W144°	47.64'		
	CHANDALAR LAKE	CQR	NDB	263.00	N67°	30.14'	W148°	28.16'		
	CHENA	CUN	NDB	257.00	N64°	50.29'	W147°	29.39'		
	CLAM COVE	CMJ	NDB	396.00	N55°	20.72'	W131°	41.78'		
	COGHLAN ISLAND	CGL	NDB	212.00	N58°	21.56'	W134°	41.96'		
	COLD BAY	CDB	VOR	112.60	N55°	16.04'	W162°	46.45'	98	E17°
	DEADHORSE	SCC	VOR	113.90	N70°	11.95'	W148°	24.97'	49	E31°
	DELTA JUNCTION	DJN	NDB	347.00	N64°	01.41'	W145°	41.20'		
	DILLINGHAM	DLG	VOR	116.40	N58°	59.65'	W158°	33.13'	131	E20°
	DRIFT RIVER	DRF	NDB	368.00	N60°	35.63'	W152°	08.55'		
	DUTCH HARBOR	DUT	VOR	113.90	N53°	54.31'	W166°	32.94'	327	E14°
	DUTCH HARBOR	DUT	NDB	283.00	N53°	54.31'	W166°	32.94'		
	EAGLE	EAA	NDB	519.00	N64°	46.66'	W141°	08.43'		
	EAST KUPURA	ACU	NDB	268.00	N68°	50.40'	W153°	18.95'		
	EIELSON	EAF	VOR	117.00	N64°	34.15'	W147°	00.96'	600	E29°
	ELEPHANT	EEF	NDB	391.00	N58°	10.25'	W135°	15.47'		
	ELFEE (LOM/NDB)	ELFE	NDB	341.00	N55°	17.76'	W162°	47.34'		
	EMMONAK	ENM	VOR	117.80	N62°	47.00'	W164°	29.26'	16	E17°
	ENGLISH BAY	EGY	NDB	374.00	N57°	07.43'	W170°	16.33'		
	EVANSVILLE	EAV	NDB	391.00	N66°	53.59'	W151°	33.82'		
	FAIRBANKS	FAI	VOR	108.20	N64°	48.00'	W148°	00.71'	1,492	E28°
	FAREWELL LAKE	FXW	NDB	412.00	N62°	32.58'	W153°	37.19'		
	FIN CREEK	FNK	NDB	320.00	N69°	29.89'	W147°	35.58'		
	FIVE MILE	FVM	NDB	312.00	N65°	55.02'	W149°	49.83'		
	FORT DAVIS	FDV	NDB	529.00	N64°	29.67'	W165°	18.84'		
	FORT RICHARDSON	FRN	NDB	196.00	N61°	16.58'	W149°	38.93'		
	FORT YUKON	FYU	VOR	114.40	N66°	34.45'	W145°	16.59'	426	E31°
	FOX	FOX	NDB	356.00	N64°	58.14'	W147°	34.79'		
	FREDERICKS POINT	FPN	NDB	372.00	N56°	47.53'	W132°	49.24'		
	GALBRAITH LAKE	GBH	NDB	417.00	N68°	28.74'	W149°	29.91'		
	GALENA	GAL	VOR	114.80	N64°	44.28'	W156°	46.62'	131	E23°
	GAMBELL	GAM	NDB	369.00	N63°	46.92'	W171°	44.20'		
	GLACIER RIVER	GCR	NDB	404.00	N60°	29.92'	W145°	28.47'		
	GLENNALLEN	GLA	NDB	248.00	N62°	11.72'	W145°	28.07'		
	GOLD	OYN	NDB	208.00	N64°	30.77'	W165°	26.00'		
	GRANITE POINT	GRP	NDB	356.00	N60°	57.68'	W151°	20.03'		
	GULKANA	GKN	VOR	115.60	N62°	09.14'	W145°	27.01'	1,548	E28°
	GUSTAVUS	GAV	NDB	219.00	N58°	25.31'	W135°	42.27'		
	HAINES	HNS	NDB	245.00	N59°	12.72'	W135°	25.85'		
	HINCHINBROOK	HBK	NDB	362.00	N60°	23.65'	W146°	05.42'		
	HOMER	HOM	VOR	114.60	N59°	42.57'	W151°	27.40'	1,623	E24°
	HOOPER BAY	HPB	VOR	115.20	N61°	30.87'	W166°	08.07'	160	E16°
	HOTHAM	HHM	NDB	356.00	N66°	54.07'	W162°	33.86'		
	HUSLIA	HSL	VOR	117.40	N65°	42.36'	W156°	22.23'	121	E23°
	ICE POOL	ICW	NDB	525.00	N64°	32.74'	W149°	04.61'		
	IGNEK	CNR	NDB	209.00	N69°	35.68'	W146°	29.71'		
	ILIAMNA	ILI	NDB	328.00	N59°	44.87'	W154°	54.57'		
	IVISHAK	IVH	NDB	379.00	N69°	24.13'	W148°	16.18'		
	JOHNSTONE POINT	JOH	VOR	116.70	N60°	28.85'	W146°	35.95'	45	E27°
	KACHEMAK	ACE	NDB	277.00	N59°	38.47'	W151°	30.00'		
	KENAI	ENA	VOR	117.60	N60°	36.88'	W151°	11.71'	108	E25°
	KING SALMON	AKN	VOR	112.80	N58°	43.48'	W156°	45.12'	78	E21°
	KIPNUK	IIK	VOR	115.90	N59°	56.56'	W164°	02.06'	0	E17°
	KODIAK	ODK	VOR	117.10	N57°	46.50'	W152°	20.38'	131	E23°
	KOTZEBUE	OTZ	VOR	115.70	N66°	53.14'	W162°	32.39'	121	E19°
	KOYUK	KKA	NDB	299.00	N64°	55.91'	W161°	08.87'		
	KUKULIAK	ULL	VOR	117.30	N63°	41.53'	W170°	28.20'	380	E13°
	KULIK LAKE	HCP	NDB	334.00	N59°	01.06'	W155°	36.02'		
	LEVEL ISLAND	LVD	VOR	116.50	N56°	28.06'	W133°	04.98'	98	E28°
	MC GRATH	MCG	VOR	115.50	N62°	57.06'	W155°	36.68'	350	E23°
	MENDENHALL	MND	NDB	332.00	N58°	21.53'	W134°	38.01'		
	MIDDLETON ISLAND	MDO	VOR	115.30	N59°	25.30'	W146°	21.00'	121	E26°
	MINCHUMINA	MHM	NDB	227.00	N63°	53.03'	W152°	18.98'		
	MINERAL CREEK	MNL	NDB	524.00	N61°	07.45'	W146°	21.13'		

State/Country	VOR/NDB Name	Ident.	Type	Freq.	Latitude		Longitude		Altitude	Mag Var
USA/CANADA NAVAIDS										
Alaska	MOSES POINT	MOS	VOR	116.30	N64°	41.79'	W162°	04.27'	13	E19°
	MT EDGECUMBE	IME	NDB	414.00	N57°	02.85'	W135°	22.02'		
	NABESNA	AES	NDB	390.00	N62°	57.94'	W141°	53.29'		
	NANWAK	AIX	NDB	323.00	N60°	23.10'	W166°	12.88'		
	NENANA	ENN	VOR	115.80	N64°	35.39'	W149°	04.37'	1,600	E28°
	NICHOLS	ICK	NDB	266.00	N55°	04.25'	W131°	36.30'		
	NOATAK	OQK	NDB	414.00	N67°	34.31'	W162°	58.42'		
	NOME	OME	VOR	115.00	N64°	29.10'	W165°	15.19'	98	E17°
	NORTH RIVER	JNR	NDB	382.00	N63°	54.46'	W160°	48.71'		
	NORTHWAY	ORT	VOR	116.30	N62°	56.83'	W141°	54.76'	1,177	E30°
	NORTON BAY	OAY	NDB	263.00	N64°	41.76'	W162°	03.77'		
	OCEAN CAPE	OCC	NDB	385.00	N59°	32.61'	W139°	43.68'		
	OLIKTOK	OLI	NDB	329.00	N70°	29.80'	W149°	53.38'		
	OSCARVILLE	OSE	NDB	251.00	N60°	47.47'	W161°	52.36'		
	PETERS CREEK	PEE	NDB	305.00	N62°	19.87'	W150°	05.78'		
	PITSAND	PYC	NDB	290.00	N70°	19.68'	W149°	38.12'		
	POINT HOPE	PHO	NDB	221.00	N68°	20.69'	W166°	47.84'		
	POINT LAY	PIZ	NDB	347.00	N69°	44.06'	W163°	00.81'		
	PORT HEIDEN	PDN	NDB	371.00	N56°	57.24'	W158°	38.93'		
	PRIBLOF	SRI	NDB	399.00	N56°	34.43'	W169°	38.87'		
	PROSPECT	PPC	NDB	340.00	N66°	49.05'	W150°	38.04'		
	PRUDHOE BAY	PUO	NDB	368.00	N70°	14.89'	W148°	23.64'		
	PUNTILLA LAKE	PTI	NDB	397.00	N62°	04.39'	W152°	43.98'		
	PUT RIVER	PVQ	NDB	234.00	N70°	13.38'	W148°	25.03'		
	RAZER (LMM/NDB)	RAZE	NDB	215.00	N58°	41.41'	W156°	40.68'		
	REEVE	SNP	NDB	362.00	N57°	09.09'	W170°	13.52'		
	SALDO (LOM/NDB)	SALD	NDB	400.00	N58°	44.24'	W156°	46.66'		
	SELAWIK	WLK	VOR	114.20	N66°	35.99'	W159°	59.49'	9	E21°
	SHEEP MOUNTAIN	SMU	NDB	221.00	N61°	47.23'	W147°	40.69'		
	SHISHMAREF	SHH	NDB	365.00	N66°	15.48'	W166°	03.14'		
	SISTERS ISLAND	SSR	VOR	114.00	N58°	10.65'	W135°	15.53'	49	E29°
	SITKA	SIT	NDB	358.00	N56°	51.27'	W135°	32.06'		
	SKWENTNA	SKW	NDB	269.00	N61°	57.96'	W151°	12.08'		
	SLATE CREEK	SLX	NDB	280.00	N64°	33.73'	W142°	30.97'		
	SLEETMUTE	SLQ	NDB	406.00	N61°	41.96'	W157°	09.77'		
	SOLDOTNA	OLT	NDB	346.00	N60°	28.49'	W150°	52.73'		
	SPARREVOHN	SQA	VOR	117.20	N61°	05.90'	W155°	38.06'	2,499	E22°
	ST MARYS	SMA	NDB	230.00	N62°	03.50'	W163°	17.49'		
	SUMMIT	UMM	NDB	326.00	N63°	19.68'	W149°	07.84'		
	SUMNER STRAIT	SQM	NDB	529.00	N56°	27.87'	W133°	05.84'		
	TAKOTNA RIVER	VTR	NDB	350.00	N62°	56.81'	W155°	33.43'		
	TALKEETNA	TKA	VOR	116.20	N62°	17.92'	W150°	06.33'	360	E26°
	TANANA	TAL	VOR	116.60	N65°	10.62'	W152°	10.65'	390	E26°
	TIN CITY	TNC	NDB	347.00	N65°	33.92'	W167°	54.53'		
	TOGIAK	TOG	NDB	393.00	N59°	03.83'	W160°	22.45'		
	UMIAT	UMT	NDB	360.00	N69°	22.17'	W152°	08.29'		
	UNALAKLEET	UNK	VOR	116.90	N63°	53.51'	W160°	41.05'	429	E20°
	UTOPIA CREEK	UTO	NDB	272.00	N65°	59.51'	W153°	43.27'		
	WEARR (LOM)	WEAR	NDB	230.00	N64°	53.98'	W147°	42.43'		
	WESSELS	ESS	NDB	260.00	N59°	25.59'	W146°	20.58'		
	WILDWOOD	IWW	NDB	379.00	N60°	35.92'	W151°	12.67'		
	WILEY	IEY	NDB	248.00	N71°	17.12'	W156°	48.50'		
	WOOD RIVER	BTS	NDB	429.00	N58°	59.98'	W158°	32.90'		
	WOODY ISLAND	RWO	NDB	394.00	N57°	46.46'	W152°	19.38'		
	WRANGELL	RGL	NDB	206.00	N56°	29.21'	W132°	23.26'		
	YAKATAGA	CYT	NDB	209.00	N60°	05.17'	W142°	29.32'		
	YAKUTAT	YAK	VOR	113.30	N59°	30.64'	W139°	38.88'	36	E29°
	YUKON RIVER	FTO	NDB	242.00	N66°	34.80'	W145°	12.76'		
Arizona										
	BARD	BZA	VOR	116.80	N32°	46.08'	W114°	36.16'	131	E14°
	BUCKEYE	BXK	VOR	110.60	N33°	27.20'	W112°	49.47'	1,059	E14°
	COCHISE	CIE	VOR	115.80	N32°	02.00'	W109°	45.49'	4,227	E13°
	DOUGLAS	DUG	VOR	108.80	N31°	28.36'	W109°	36.12'	4,159	E13°
	DRAGOO	DAO	NDB	410.00	N31°	35.13'	W110°	20.65'		
	DRAKE	DRK	VOR	114.10	N34°	42.15'	W112°	28.81'	4,959	E14°
	FALCON FIELD	FFZ	NDB	281.00	N33°	27.70'	W111°	43.99'		
	FLAGSTAFF	FLG	VOR	108.20	N35°	08.83'	W111°	40.44'	7,009	E14°
	GILA BEND	GBN	VOR	116.60	N32°	57.37'	W112°	40.45'	790	E14°
	GLENDALE	GEU	NDB	215.00	N33°	31.60'	W112°	17.44'		
	GLOBE	GAZ	NDB	255.00	N33°	21.27'	W110°	39.99'		
	GOLDEN EAGLE	OEG	NDB	413.00	N32°	51.32'	W114°	26.46'		
	GRAND CANYON	GCN	VOR	113.10	N35°	57.62'	W112°	08.76'	6,668	E15°
	KINGMAN	IGM	VOR	108.80	N35°	15.63'	W113°	56.04'	3,407	E15°
	LAKE HAVASU	HII	NDB	364.00	N34°	34.49'	W114°	21.84'		

State/Country	VOR/NDB Name	Ident.	Type	Freq.	Latitude		Longitude		Altitude	Mag Var
USA/CANADA NAVAIDS										
Arizona	LIBBY	FHU	VOR	111.60	N31°	35.43'	W110°	20.56'	4,624	E13°
	NOGALES	ENZ	NDB	394.00	N31°	25.28'	W110°	50.78'		
	NOGALES	OLS	VOR	108.20	N31°	24.89'	W110°	50.93'	3,870	E12°
	PAGE	PGA	VOR	117.60	N36°	55.68'	W111°	27.04'	4,244	E15°
	PEABODY	PBY	NDB	259.00	N36°	28.48'	W110°	24.70'		
	PEACH SPRINGS	PGS	VOR	112.00	N35°	37.48'	W113°	32.66'	4,759	E15°
	PHOENIX	PXR	VOR	115.60	N33°	25.98'	W111°	58.21'	1,180	E12°
	PULLIAM	PUU	NDB	379.00	N35°	08.51'	W111°	40.24'		
	ROBLES	RBJ	NDB	220.00	N32°	04.44'	W111°	21.61'		
	RYAN	RYN	NDB	338.00	N32°	08.30'	W111°	09.69'		
	SAN SIMON	SSO	VOR	115.40	N32°	16.15'	W109°	15.78'	3,598	E13°
	SCOTTSDALE	SDL	VOR	224.00	N33°	37.74'	W111°	54.46'		
	SEDONA	SEZ	NDB	334.00	N34°	49.72'	W111°	48.85'		
	SHOW LOW	SOW	NDB	206.00	N34°	16.03'	W110°	00.49'		
	ST JOHNS	SJN	VOR	112.30	N34°	25.44'	W109°	08.61'	6,838	E12°
	STANFIELD	TFD	VOR	114.80	N32°	53.15'	W111°	54.52'	1,315	E12°
	TUBA CITY	TBC	VOR	113.50	N36°	07.28'	W111°	16.17'	5,044	E15°
	TUCSON	TUS	VOR	116.00	N32°	05.71'	W110°	54.89'	2,669	E12°
	WILLIE	IWA	VOR	113.30	N33°	18.19'	W111°	39.08'	1,371	E13°
	WINDOW ROCK	AWR	NDB	254.00	N35°	39.86'	W109°	04.08'		
	WINSLOW	INW	VOR	112.60	N35°	03.69'	W110°	47.70'	4,910	E14°
	ZUNI	ZUN	VOR	113.40	N34°	57.94'	W109°	09.26'	6,546	E14°
Arkansas	ARKADELPHIA	ADF	NDB	275.00	N34°	03.32'	W93°	06.29'		
	ASH FLAT	AJX	NDB	344.00	N36°	10.83'	W91°	36.39'		
	BAKKY (LOM)	BAKK	NDB	233.00	N36°	11.46'	W93°	09.60'		
	BRIDGE	BDQ	NDB	208.00	N35°	08.35'	W92°	42.74'		
	BRINKLEY	BKZ	NDB	242.00	N34°	52.88'	W91°	10.65'		
	CAMDEN	CDH	NDB	335.00	N33°	36.81'	W92°	46.05'		
	CARTER	CJD	NDB	263.00	N36°	27.67'	W94°	04.16'		
	CLARKSVILLE	CZE	NDB	201.00	N35°	28.15'	W93°	25.41'		
	CONWAY	CWS	NDB	302.00	N35°	05.03'	W92°	25.61'		
	CROSSETT	CRT	NDB	396.00	N33°	10.36'	W91°	53.18'		
	DE QUEEN	DEQ	NDB	281.00	N34°	02.75'	W94°	23.96'		
	DRAKE	DAK	VOR	108.80	N36°	02.57'	W94°	11.85'	1,528	E07°
	DUMAS	DZM	NDB	305.00	N33°	53.06'	W91°	31.88'		
	EL DORADO	ELD	VOR	115.50	N33°	15.36'	W92°	44.63'	229	E07°
	FLIPPIN	FLP	VOR	112.80	N36°	17.97'	W92°	27.50'	780	E03°
	FORREST CITY	FCY	NDB	332.00	N34°	56.46'	W90°	46.41'		
	FORT SMITH	FSM	VOR	110.40	N35°	23.30'	W94°	16.28'	429	E07°
	GILMORE	GQE	VOR	113.00	N35°	20.82'	W90°	28.68'	209	E04°
	GOSNELL	GOJ	VOR	111.80	N35°	57.06'	W89°	56.43'	252	E01°
	HARRISON	HRO	VOR	112.50	N36°	19.09'	W93°	12.79'	1,400	E04°
	HEBER SPRINGS	HBZ	NDB	296.00	N35°	30.86'	W92°	00.66'		
	HICKS	IUI	NDB	299.00	N35°	56.26'	W89°	50.02'		
	HOPE	HPC	NDB	362.00	N33°	43.07'	W93°	38.92'		
	HOSSY (LOM/NDB)	HOSS	NDB	385.00	N34°	25.36'	W93°	11.37'		
	HOT SPRINGS	HOT	VOR	110.00	N34°	28.71'	W93°	05.43'	531	E04°
	INDEPENDENCE CO	INY	NDB	317.00	N35°	41.85'	W91°	47.12'		
	JONESBORO	JBR	VOR	108.60	N35°	52.49'	W90°	35.30'	249	E02°
	LADOS (LOM)	LADO	NDB	418.00	N33°	17.16'	W92°	43.68'		
	LASKY (LOM/NDB)	LASK	NDB	353.00	N34°	40.13'	W92°	18.33'		
	LAWRENCE CO	TNZ	NDB	227.00	N36°	12.33'	W90°	55.39'		
	LITTLE ROCK	LIT	VOR	113.90	N34°	40.65'	W92°	10.83'	239	E05°
	MAGNOLIA	AGO	NDB	266.00	N33°	13.61'	W93°	12.91'		
	MALVERN	MVQ	NDB	215.00	N34°	20.00'	W92°	45.74'		
	MENA	MEZ	NDB	242.00	N34°	32.91'	W94°	12.59'		
	MONTICELLO	MON	VOR	111.60	N33°	33.72'	W91°	42.94'	278	E04°
	MORRILTON	MPJ	NDB	410.00	N35°	07.12'	W92°	55.51'		
	NEWPORT	EWP	NDB	400.00	N35°	38.52'	W91°	10.84'		
	OZARK	OZZ	NDB	329.00	N35°	30.45'	W93°	50.44'		
	PINE BLUFF	PBF	VOR	116.00	N34°	14.80'	W91°	55.57'	209	E04°
	RAZORBACK	RZC	VOR	116.40	N36°	14.78'	W94°	07.28'	1,328	E04°
	RUSSELLVILLE	RUE	NDB	379.00	N35°	15.42'	W93°	05.66'		
	SEARCY	SRC	NDB	323.00	N35°	12.72'	W91°	43.95'		
	SILOAM SPRINGS	SLG	NDB	284.00	N36°	11.35'	W94°	29.31'		
	STUTTGART	SGT	NDB	269.00	N34°	39.87'	W91°	35.50'		
	TECCO (LOM)	TECC	NDB	247.00	N33°	31.44'	W93°	54.36'		
	TEXARKANA	TXK	VOR	116.30	N33°	30.83'	W94°	04.39'	268	E07°
	THOMPSON-ROBBINS	HEE	NDB	251.00	N34°	34.27'	W90°	40.55'		
	TONEYVILLE	TYV	NDB	290.00	N34°	57.14'	W92°	01.16'		
	WALCOTT	PZX	NDB	221.00	N36°	01.80'	W90°	35.81'		
	WALNUT RIDGE	ARG	VOR	114.50	N36°	06.59'	W90°	57.21'	259	E04°
	WARREN	REN	NDB	226.00	N33°	32.82'	W92°	05.75'		
	WEST MEMPHIS	AWM	NDB	362.00	N35°	08.36'	W90°	13.95'		

State/Country	VOR/NDB Name	Ident.	Type	Freq.	Latitude		Longitude		Altitude	Mag Var
USA/CANADA NAVAIDS										
Arkansas	WILCOX	VLX	NDB	348.00	N35°	52.05'	W92°	05.67'		
	WIZER (LOM/NDB)	WIZE	NDB	223.00	N35°	21.25'	W94°	13.02'		
Bahamas										
	BIMINI	ZBB	NDB	396.00	N25°	42.53'	W79°	16.33'		
	BIMINI	ZBV	VOR	116.70	N25°	42.24'	W79°	17.66'	9	W04°
	ELEUTHERA I	ZGV	VOR	112.50	N25°	15.44'	W76°	18.51'	22	W06°
	FREEPORT	ZFP	VOR	113.20	N26°	33.31'	W78°	41.89'	9	W02°
	FREEPORT	ZFP	NDB	209.00	N26°	31.10'	W78°	46.49'		
	FREEPORT/GRAND BA	BHF	NDB	326.00	N26°	34.43'	W78°	39.83'		
	MARSH HARBOUR	ZMH	NDB	361.00	N26°	30.66'	W77°	04.61'		
	NASSAU	ZQA	VOR	112.70	N25°	01.68'	W77°	27.00'	9	W05°
	NASSAU	ZQA	NDB	251.00	N25°	02.41'	W77°	28.21'		
	ROCK SOUND	RSD	NDB	348.00	N24°	53.58'	W76°	10.19'		
	TREASURE CAY	ZTC	NDB	233.00	N26°	44.08'	W77°	17.99'		
	TREASURE CAY	ZTC	VOR	112.90	N26°	44.08'	W77°	22.75'	9	W05°
	WEST END	ZWE	NDB	317.00	N26°	41.00'	W78°	58.99'		
Bermuda										
	BERMUDA	BDA	VOR	113.90	N32°	21.72'	W64°	41.39'	59	W15°
California										
	ABETA (LMM)	ABET	NDB	233.00	N40°	57.87'	W124°	05.92'		
	ALTURAS	ARU	NDB	215.00	N41°	28.31'	W120°	33.44'		
	AMEDEE	AHC	VOR	109.00	N40°	16.07'	W120°	09.11'	4,004	E17°
	ARCATA	ACV	VOR	110.20	N40°	58.88'	W124°	06.49'	190	E17°
	AVENAL	AVE	VOR	117.10	N35°	38.81'	W119°	58.71'	708	E16°
	BECCA (LOM)	BECC	NDB	233.00	N33°	45.39'	W118°	04.64'		
	BIG SUR	BSR	VOR	114.00	N36°	10.87'	W121°	38.52'	4,083	E16°
	BISHOP	BIH	VOR	109.60	N37°	22.61'	W118°	21.99'	4,109	E15°
	BLYTHE	BLH	VOR	117.40	N33°	35.76'	W114°	45.67'	409	E14°
	BOING (LMM)	BOIN	NDB	245.00	N32°	44.39'	W117°	12.95'		
	BRIJJ (LOM)	BRIJ	NDB	379.00	N37°	34.33'	W122°	15.58'		
	CAMARILLO	CMA	VOR	115.80	N34°	12.74'	W119°	05.66'	59	E15°
	CHANDLER	FCH	NDB	344.00	N36°	43.43'	W119°	50.02'		
	CHICO	CIC	VOR	109.80	N39°	47.38'	W121°	50.83'	219	E16°
	CHINA LAKE (NAVY)	NID	NDB	348.00	N35°	41.16'	W117°	41.49'		
	CHUALAR	UAD	NDB	263.00	N36°	29.45'	W121°	28.49'		
	CLOVIS	CZQ	VOR	112.90	N36°	53.05'	W119°	48.90'	360	E15°
	COLUMBIA	CUF	NDB	404.00	N38°	01.85'	W120°	24.82'		
	COMPTON	CPM	NDB	378.00	N33°	53.33'	W118°	14.83'		
	CONCORD	CCR	VOR	117.00	N38°	02.69'	W122°	02.71'	6	E17°
	CRESCENT CITY	CEC	VOR	109.00	N41°	46.77'	W124°	14.45'	49	E19°
	DAGGETT	DAG	VOR	113.20	N34°	57.74'	W116°	34.68'	1,758	E15°
	DEORO (LOM)	DEOR	NDB	210.00	N32°	46.79'	W117°	02.69'		
	EDWARDS	EDW	VOR	116.40	N34°	58.94'	W117°	43.95'	2,355	E15°
	EL MONTE	EMT	NDB	359.00	N34°	05.29'	W118°	01.87'		
	EL NIDO	HYP	VOR	114.20	N37°	13.16'	W120°	24.01'	180	E15°
	EL TORO	NZJ	VOR	117.20	N33°	40.56'	W117°	43.86'	377	E14°
	ESCONDIDO	EKG	NDB	374.00	N33°	09.36'	W117°	05.14'		
	EXECC (LOM)	EXEC	NDB	356.00	N38°	26.98'	W121°	32.77'		
	FELLOWS	FLW	VOR	117.50	N35°	05.58'	W119°	51.93'	3,870	E16°
	FILLMORE	FIM	VOR	112.50	N34°	21.40'	W118°	52.87'	2,200	E15°
	FORT JONES	FJS	VOR	109.60	N41°	26.97'	W122°	48.38'	4,900	E19°
	FORTUNA	FOT	VOR	114.00	N40°	40.27'	W124°	14.07'	400	E19°
	FRIANT	FRA	VOR	115.60	N37°	06.26'	W119°	35.72'	2,377	E17°
	GAVIOTA	GVO	VOR	113.80	N34°	31.87'	W120°	05.46'	2,620	E16°
	GEN WILLIAM J FO	GWF	NDB	282.00	N34°	44.31'	W118°	13.00'		
	GOFFS	GFS	VOR	114.40	N35°	07.86'	W115°	10.58'	3,998	E15°
	GORMAN	GMN	VOR	116.10	N34°	48.24'	W118°	51.68'	4,919	E16°
	GUADALUPE	GLJ	VOR	111.00	N34°	57.14'	W120°	31.28'	141	E16°
	HALOW (LOM/NDB)	HALO	NDB	222.00	N39°	10.16'	W121°	36.59'		
	HANGTOWN	HNW	VOR	115.50	N38°	43.48'	W120°	44.96'	2,601	E17°
	HECTOR	HEC	VOR	112.70	N34°	47.82'	W116°	27.77'	1,849	E15°
	HILAN (LOM)	HILA	NDB	266.00	N36°	43.80'	W119°	38.15'		
	HOMELAND	HDF	VOR	113.40	N33°	46.58'	W117°	11.11'	1,413	E14°
	HUNTER LIGGETT	HGT	NDB	209.00	N35°	56.33'	W121°	09.72'		
	IMPERIAL	IPL	VOR	115.90	N32°	44.93'	W115°	30.51'	-19	E14°
	JORGE (LMM)	JORG	NDB	249.00	N37°	20.93'	W121°	54.89'		
	JOTLY (LOM)	JOTL	NDB	271.00	N37°	49.91'	W121°	08.13'		
	JULIAN	JLI	VOR	114.00	N33°	08.42'	W116°	35.15'	5,559	E15°
	KANAN (LOM)	KANA	NDB	335.00	N38°	02.78'	W122°	02.00'		
	KEARN (LOM)	KEAR	NDB	371.00	N39°	16.55'	W123°	14.42'		
	LAKE HUGHES	LHS	VOR	108.40	N34°	40.97'	W118°	34.61'	5,789	E15°
	LAMPSON	LOP	NDB	217.00	N38°	59.70'	W122°	53.01'		
	LANEE (LOM)	LANE	NDB	400.00	N38°	37.01'	W121°	36.19'		
	LASSN (LOM)	LASS	NDB	367.00	N40°	23.56'	W122°	17.68'		

State/Country	VOR/NDB Name	Ident.	Type	Freq.	Latitude		Longitude		Altitude	Mag Var
USA/CANADA NAVAIDS										
California	LINDEN	LIN	VOR	114.80	N38°	04.47'	W121°	00.23'	259	E17°
	LOMPOC	LPC	NDB	223.00	N34°	39.87'	W120°	27.79'		
	LOS ANGELES	LAX	VOR	113.60	N33°	55.98'	W118°	25.92'	180	E15°
	MAAGG (LMM)	MAAG	NDB	337.00	N33°	41.33'	W117°	51.63'		
	MANTECA	ECA	VOR	116.00	N37°	50.01'	W121°	10.28'	39	E17°
	MARYSVILLE	MYV	VOR	110.80	N39°	05.91'	W121°	34.38'	59	E16°
	MAXWELL	MXW	VOR	110.00	N39°	19.05'	W122°	13.29'	111	E18°
	MC CLELLAN	MCC	VOR	109.20	N38°	40.04'	W121°	24.26'	72	E17°
	MENDOCINO	ENI	VOR	112.30	N39°	03.19'	W123°	16.45'	2,978	E16°
	MERRILL	LFA	NDB	347.00	N41°	59.10'	W121°	38.56'		
	METRE (LOM)	METR	NDB	230.00	N38°	47.68'	W121°	35.97'		
	MISSION BAY	MZB	VOR	117.80	N32°	46.93'	W117°	13.52'	9	E15°
	MODESTO	MOD	VOR	114.60	N37°	37.64'	W120°	57.47'	88	E17°
	MONTAGUE	MOG	NDB	382.00	N41°	43.63'	W122°	28.90'		
	MORRO BAY	MQO	VOR	112.40	N35°	15.13'	W120°	45.57'	1,462	E16°
	MUNSO (LOM)	MUNS	NDB	385.00	N36°	37.24'	W121°	56.31'		
	NEEDLES	EED	VOR	115.20	N34°	45.95'	W114°	28.44'	619	E15°
	NILEY (LOM)	NILE	NDB	385.00	N35°	21.65'	W118°	58.11'		
	NORDE (LOM)	NORD	NDB	327.00	N39°	53.21'	W121°	55.98'		
	OAKLAND	OAK	VOR	116.80	N37°	43.55'	W122°	13.41'	9	E17°
	OCEANSIDE	OCN	VOR	115.30	N33°	14.43'	W117°	25.06'	88	E15°
	OROVILLE	OVE	NDB	212.00	N39°	29.68'	W121°	37.32'		
	PACOIMA	PAI	NDB	370.00	N34°	15.58'	W118°	24.80'		
	PAJAR (LOM/NDB)	PAJA	NDB	327.00	N36°	54.81'	W121°	48.47'		
	PALM SPRINGS	PSP	VOR	115.50	N33°	52.20'	W116°	25.78'	1,600	E13°
	PALMDALE	PMD	VOR	114.50	N34°	37.88'	W118°	03.82'	2,499	E15°
	PANOCHE	PXN	VOR	112.60	N36°	42.92'	W120°	46.72'	2,059	E16°
	PARADISE	PDZ	VOR	112.20	N33°	55.10'	W117°	31.80'	1,430	E15°
	PARKER	PKE	VOR	117.90	N34°	06.11'	W114°	40.92'	1,000	E15°
	PASO ROBLES	PRB	VOR	114.30	N35°	40.34'	W120°	37.62'	819	E16°
	PETIS (LOM/NDB)	PETI	NDB	397.00	N34°	03.38'	W117°	21.95'		
	POGGI	PGY	VOR	109.80	N32°	36.61'	W116°	58.74'	580	E14°
	POINT REYES	PYE	VOR	113.70	N38°	04.78'	W122°	52.06'	1,338	E17°
	POMONA	POM	VOR	110.40	N34°	04.70'	W117°	47.22'	1,269	E15°
	PORTERVILLE	PTV	VOR	109.20	N35°	54.78'	W119°	01.25'	580	E16°
	PRIEST	ROM	VOR	110.00	N36°	08.42'	W120°	39.89'	3,880	E16°
	PROBERTA	PBT	NDB	338.00	N40°	06.84'	W122°	14.24'		
	RED BLUFF	RBL	VOR	115.70	N40°	05.93'	W122°	14.18'	321	E18°
	REDDING	RDD	VOR	108.40	N40°	30.27'	W122°	17.50'	488	E18°
	REIGA (LOM/NDB)	REIG	NDB	374.00	N37°	41.53'	W121°	41.03'		
	RIVERSIDE	RAL	VOR	112.40	N33°	57.12'	W117°	26.95'	780	E15°
	ROMEN (LOM)	ROME	NDB	278.00	N33°	57.89'	W118°	16.67'		
	RORAY (LMM)	RORA	NDB	341.00	N37°	43.28'	W122°	11.64'		
	SACRAMENTO	SAC	VOR	115.20	N38°	26.61'	W121°	33.09'	9	E17°
	SALINAS	SNS	VOR	117.30	N36°	39.82'	W121°	36.19'	78	E17°
	SALYER FARMS	COR	NDB	205.00	N36°	05.08'	W119°	32.72'		
	SAN CLEMENTE	NUC	NDB	350.00	N33°	01.63'	W118°	34.28'		
	SAN FRANCISCO	SFO	VOR	115.80	N37°	37.17'	W122°	22.43'	9	E17°
	SAN JACINTO	SJY	NDB	227.00	N33°	47.69'	W116°	59.95'		
	SAN JOSE	SJC	VOR	114.10	N37°	22.48'	W121°	56.67'	39	E16°
	SAN MARCUS	RZS	VOR	114.90	N34°	30.57'	W119°	46.25'	3,617	E14°
	SAN NICOLAS NAVY	NSI	NDB	203.00	N33°	14.15'	W119°	26.96'		
	SANTA CATALINA	SXC	VOR	111.40	N33°	22.50'	W118°	25.19'	2,089	E15°
	SANTA MONICA	SMO	VOR	110.80	N34°	00.61'	W118°	27.40'	121	E15°
	SANTA ROSA	STS	VOR	113.00	N38°	30.49'	W122°	48.63'	141	E16°
	SANTA YNEZ	IZA	NDB	394.00	N34°	36.35'	W120°	04.56'		
	SAUSALITO	SAU	VOR	116.20	N37°	51.31'	W122°	31.36'	1,039	E17°
	SCAGGS ISLAND	SGD	VOR	112.10	N38°	10.76'	W122°	22.38'	9	E17°
	SEAL BEACH	SLI	VOR	115.70	N33°	46.99'	W118°	03.28'	19	E15°
	SHAFTER	EHF	VOR	115.40	N35°	29.07'	W119°	05.83'	551	E14°
	SHARPE	LRO	NDB	282.00	N37°	49.66'	W121°	16.26'		
	SQUAW VALLEY	SWR	VOR	113.20	N39°	10.81'	W120°	16.17'	8,846	E16°
	SWAN LAKE (LOM/ND	LKA	NDB	257.00	N33°	58.48'	W117°	33.12'		
	THERMAL	TRM	VOR	116.20	N33°	37.68'	W116°	09.61'	-111	E13°
	TRAVIS	TZZ	VOR	116.40	N38°	20.65'	W121°	48.64'	29	E17°
	TWENTYNINE PALMS	TNP	VOR	114.20	N34°	06.73'	W115°	46.19'	1,348	E15°
	VAN NUYS	VNY	VOR	113.10	N34°	13.40'	W118°	29.50'	810	E15°
	VENTURA	VTU	VOR	108.20	N34°	06.90'	W119°	02.97'	1,557	E15°
	VILIA (LOM)	VILI	NDB	220.00	N36°	15.28'	W119°	18.87'		
	VINEE (LMM)	VINE	NDB	253.00	N34°	11.89'	W118°	22.67'		
	VISALIA	VIS	VOR	109.40	N36°	22.03'	W119°	28.93'	259	E16°
	WILLIAMS	ILA	VOR	114.40	N39°	04.26'	W122°	01.63'	49	E18°
	WOODSIDE	OSI	VOR	113.90	N37°	23.55'	W122°	16.87'	2,269	E17°
	WOWAR (LOM)	WOWA	NDB	367.00	N37°	34.38'	W120°	51.30'		

State/Country	VOR/NDB Name	Ident.	Type	Freq.	Latitude		Longitude		Altitude	Mag Var
USA/CANADA NAVAIDS										
Canada, Alberta										
	CALGARY	YYC	VOR	116.70	N51°	06.90'	W113°	52.92'	3,565	E19°
	CALGARY	YC	NDB	344.00	N51°	04.85'	W113°	54.52'		
	EDMONTON	YEG	VOR	117.60	N53°	11.13'	W113°	52.01'	2,555	E21°
	GRANDE PRAIRIE	YQU	VOR	113.10	N55°	10.45'	W119°	01.81'	2,515	E24°
	HAMBURG	B2	NDB	352.00	N57°	22.31'	W119°	47.34'		
	HIGH LEVEL	YOJ	VOR	113.30	N58°	33.22'	W117°	05.63'	0	E26°
	LETHBRIDGE	YQL	VOR	115.70	N49°	38.06'	W112°	40.07'	3,109	E18°
	LETHBRIDGE	QL	NDB	248.00	N49°	36.31'	W112°	53.64'		
	MEDICINE HAT	YXH	VOR	116.50	N49°	57.88'	W110°	48.86'	2,473	E17°
	MEDICINE HAT	XH	NDB	332.00	N50°	00.78'	W110°	47.94'		
	PEACE RIVER	YPE	VOR	117.20	N56°	12.41'	W117°	30.71'	1,925	E24°
	RAINBOW LAKE	YOP	NDB	344.00	N58°	27.40'	W119°	15.10'		
	ROCKY MOUNTAIN	YRM	VOR	114.30	N52°	30.12'	W115°	19.41'	3,542	E21°
	VULCAN	Z5	NDB	274.00	N50°	24.00'	W113°	16.92'		
Canada, British Columbia										
	ABBOTSFORD	XX	NDB	344.00	N49°	00.93'	W122°	29.26'		
	ACTIVE PASS	AP	NDB	378.00	N48°	52.43'	W123°	17.39'		
	ANAHIM LAKE	UAB	NDB	200.00	N52°	22.77'	W125°	10.85'		
	ATLIN	YSQ	NDB	260.00	N59°	37.56'	W133°	40.61'		
	BELLA BELLA	YJQ	NDB	325.00	N52°	11.10'	W128°	06.81'		
	CAMPBELL RIVER	YBL	NDB	203.00	N50°	00.38'	W125°	21.45'		
	CAPE SCOTT	ZES	NDB	353.00	N50°	46.93'	W128°	25.61'		
	CARMI	YXO	NDB	335.00	N49°	29.71'	W119°	05.35'		
	CASTLEGAR	CG	NDB	227.00	N49°	26.82'	W117°	34.50'		
	CHETWYND	F6	NDB	210.00	N55°	41.66'	W121°	32.25'		
	COMOX	QQ	NDB	400.00	N49°	45.23'	W124°	57.48'		
	CRANBROOK	XC	NDB	242.00	N49°	40.96'	W115°	46.98'		
	CRANBROOK	YXC	VOR	112.10	N49°	33.29'	W116°	05.26'	7,583	E20°
	CULTUS	LU	NDB	241.00	N49°	01.27'	W122°	02.97'		
	DAWSON CREEK	DQ	NDB	394.00	N55°	43.66'	W120°	04.10'		
	DEASE LAKE	YDL	NDB	200.00	N58°	27.21'	W129°	59.77'		
	EGG ISLAND	UEM	NDB	207.00	N51°	14.95'	W127°	50.04'		
	ENDERBY	NY	NDB	350.00	N50°	38.99'	W118°	55.51'		
	ENDERBY	YNY	VOR	115.20	N50°	40.67'	W118°	56.32'	6,694	E21°
	ESTEVAN POINT	EP	NDB	373.00	N49°	23.03'	W126°	32.63'		
	FAIRMONT HOT SPRN	D6	NDB	261.00	N50°	19.61'	W115°	52.59'		
	FORT NELSON	YE	NDB	382.00	N58°	47.74'	W122°	43.35'		
	FORT NELSON	YYE	VOR	112.90	N58°	53.50'	W123°	00.96'	2,040	E29°
	FORT SAINT JOHN	YXJ	VOR	114.20	N56°	17.04'	W120°	53.73'	0	E26°
	FORT ST JOHN	XJ	NDB	326.00	N56°	17.06'	W120°	50.68'		
	HELMUT	4D	NDB	364.00	N59°	25.28'	W120°	47.36'		
	HOPE	HE	NDB	245.00	N49°	23.24'	W121°	25.42'		
	HOUSTON	YYD	VOR	114.70	N54°	27.14'	W126°	39.05'	4,188	E25°
	KATHLYN	M9	NDB	240.00	N54°	49.34'	W127°	10.80'		
	KELOWNA	LW	NDB	257.00	N50°	03.64'	W119°	24.98'		
	KITIMAT	ZKI	NDB	203.00	N54°	03.25'	W128°	40.21'		
	LIARD RIVER	ZL	NDB	263.00	N59°	28.10'	W126°	08.60'		
	MACKENZIE	2U	NDB	284.00	N55°	18.29'	W123°	08.24'		
	MASSET	1U	NDB	278.00	N54°	01.89'	W132°	07.63'		
	MCINNES ISLAND	MS	NDB	388.00	N52°	15.68'	W128°	43.39'		
	MILL BAY	MB	NDB	293.00	N48°	40.25'	W123°	32.21'		
	NANAIMO	YCD	NDB	251.00	N49°	07.67'	W123°	52.29'		
	NARAMATA (PENTICT	UNT	NDB	312.00	N49°	35.82'	W119°	36.15'		
	OKANAGAN (PENTICT	ON	NDB	356.00	N49°	20.55'	W119°	34.13'		
	PAPA	P	NDB	350.00	N54°	18.31'	W130°	27.75'		
	PENTICTON	YYF	NDB	290.00	N49°	29.26'	W119°	36.17'		
	PITT MEADOWS	PK	NDB	227.00	N49°	12.69'	W122°	42.86'		
	PORT HARDY	YZT	VOR	112.00	N50°	41.05'	W127°	21.91'	39	E23°
	PORT HARDY	Z	NDB	394.00	N50°	42.87'	W127°	25.56'		
	PORT HARDY	ZT	NDB	242.00	N50°	41.95'	W127°	25.62'		
	POWELL RIVER	YPW	NDB	382.00	N49°	50.20'	W124°	30.08'		
	PRINCE GEORGE	YXS	VOR	112.30	N53°	53.64'	W122°	27.34'	4,050	E24°
	PRINCE GEORGE	XS	NDB	272.00	N53°	49.69'	W122°	39.24'		
	PRINCE RUPERT	PR	NDB	218.00	N54°	15.79'	W130°	25.43'		
	PRINCETON	YDC	VOR	113.90	N49°	22.89'	W120°	22.42'	5,326	E21°
	PRINCETON	DC	NDB	326.00	N49°	28.16'	W120°	31.00'		
	QUESNEL	YQZ	NDB	359.00	N52°	57.63'	W122°	29.16'		
	SANDSPIT	ZP	NDB	368.00	N53°	11.78'	W131°	46.65'		
	SANDSPIT	YZP	VOR	114.10	N53°	15.13'	W131°	48.41'	29	E25°
	SANDSPIT	Z	NDB	248.00	N53°	21.00'	W131°	56.40'		
	SKEENA	TB	NDB	254.00	N54°	28.95'	W128°	35.48'		
	SKOOKUM	SX	NDB	368.00	N49°	57.28'	W115°	47.56'		
	SMITHERS	YD	NDB	230.00	N54°	44.84'	W127°	06.46'		

State/Country	VOR/NDB Name	Ident.	Type	Freq.	Latitude		Longitude		Altitude	Mag Var
USA/CANADA NAVAIDS										
Canada, British Columbia										
	TELKWA (SMITHERS)	TK	NDB	391.00	N54°	40.18'	W126°	59.54'		
	TERRACE	XT	NDB	332.00	N54°	22.43'	W128°	34.98'		
	TOFINO	YAZ	NDB	359.00	N49°	02.88'	W125°	42.35'		
	VANCOUVER	VR	NDB	266.00	N49°	10.37'	W123°	03.42'		
	VANCOUVER	YVR	VOR	115.90	N49°	04.64'	W123°	08.94'	16	E21°
	VICTOR	V	NDB	368.00	N49°	11.48'	W123°	13.18'		
	VICTORIA	YJ	NDB	200.00	N48°	38.64'	W123°	23.96'		
	VICTORIA	YYJ	VOR	113.70	N48°	43.62'	W123°	29.06'	1,967	E21°
	WHITE ROCK	WC	NDB	332.00	N49°	00.20'	W122°	45.01'		
	WILLIAMS LAKE	YWL	VOR	113.60	N52°	14.22'	W122°	10.13'	3,660	E23°
Canada, Manitoba										
	BERENS RIVER	YBV	NDB	370.00	N52°	21.25'	W97°	01.46'		
	BRANDON	YBR	VOR	113.80	N49°	54.59'	W99°	56.74'	1,380	E10°
	BRANDON	BR	NDB	233.00	N49°	54.46'	W100°	04.40'		
	CHURCHILL	YYQ	VOR	114.10	N58°	44.50'	W94°	08.11'	45	E01°
	DAUPHIN	YDN	VOR	116.10	N51°	06.30'	W100°	03.15'	1,023	E10°
	DELTA	UDE	NDB	269.00	N50°	09.98'	W98°	18.43'		
	LANGRUTH	VLR	VOR	112.20	N50°	25.33'	W98°	43.42'	934	E09°
	LYNN LAKE	YYL	VOR	112.60	N56°	51.85'	W101°	04.52'	0	E12°
	PORTAGE	PG	NDB	353.00	N49°	50.33'	W98°	10.83'		
	PORTAGE	YPG	VOR	114.60	N49°	53.98'	W98°	16.01'	0	E07°
	THE PAS	YQD	VOR	113.60	N53°	58.42'	W101°	06.00'	911	E11°
	WINNIPEG	YWG	VOR	115.50	N49°	55.66'	W97°	14.35'	819	E07°
	WINNIPEG	WG	NDB	248.00	N49°	53.94'	W97°	20.95'		
Canada, New Brunswick										
	BATHURST	2F	NDB	382.00	N47°	35.61'	W65°	50.67'		
	CHARLO	CL	NDB	207.00	N48°	00.53'	W66°	26.21'		
	CHATHAM	F9	NDB	530.00	N47°	00.50'	W65°	25.59'		
	FOXTROT	F	NDB	304.00	N46°	02.30'	W64°	46.99'		
	FREDERICTON	YFC	VOR	113.00	N45°	53.68'	W66°	25.13'	52	W21°
	FREDERICTON	FC	NDB	326.00	N45°	55.03'	W66°	35.98'		
	JULIET	J	NDB	397.00	N45°	13.67'	W65°	57.48'		
	LIMA	L	NDB	281.00	N47°	58.40'	W66°	13.41'		
	MIKE	M	NDB	366.00	N46°	06.25'	W64°	47.51'		
	MONCTON	YQM	VOR	117.30	N46°	11.33'	W64°	34.24'	170	W22°
	MONCTON	QM	NDB	224.00	N46°	06.63'	W64°	34.91'		
	POKEMOUCHE	2T	NDB	227.00	N47°	43.07'	W64°	53.37'		
	SAINT JOHN	SJ	NDB	212.00	N45°	23.50'	W65°	49.13'		
	SAINT JOHN	YSJ	VOR	113.50	N45°	24.43'	W65°	52.21'	495	W21°
	ST LEONARD	YSL	NDB	404.00	N47°	12.46'	W67°	52.18'		
Canada, Newfoundland										
	CHANNEL HEAD	CM	NDB	379.00	N47°	34.01'	W59°	09.55'		
	ST JOHNS	UYT	VOR	108.60	N47°	37.63'	W52°	44.89'	491	W24°
	STEPHENVILLE	YJT	VOR	113.10	N48°	34.94'	W58°	40.15'	1,184	W25°
	STEPHENVILLE	JT	NDB	390.00	N48°	32.63'	W58°	45.28'		
	TORBAY	YT	NDB	260.00	N47°	40.17'	W52°	48.50'		
	TORBAY	YYT	VOR	113.50	N47°	29.13'	W52°	51.14'	833	W24°
Canada, Northwest Territories										
	AKLAVIK	YKD	NDB	208.00	N68°	13.62'	W135°	00.58'		
	BAKER LAKE	YBK	VOR	114.50	N64°	19.28'	W96°	06.27'	400	E01°
	CAMBRIDGE BAY	YCB	VOR	112.70	N69°	07.05'	W105°	10.35'	131	E27°
	FORT GOOD HOPE	YGH	VOR	112.30	N66°	14.16'	W128°	37.36'	301	E36°
	FORT LIARD	YJF	NDB	368.00	N60°	14.30'	W123°	27.93'		
	FORT MCPHERSON	ZFM	NDB	373.00	N67°	24.59'	W134°	52.30'		
	FORT SIMPSON	YFS	VOR	117.90	N61°	46.43'	W121°	17.91'	573	E31°
	FT SIMPSON	FS	NDB	375.00	N61°	47.15'	W121°	15.64'		
	HALL BEACH	YUX	VOR	117.30	N68°	46.69'	W81°	14.36'	52	W47°
	INUVIK	YEV	VOR	112.50	N68°	18.48'	W133°	32.90'	262	E38°
	INUVIK	EV	NDB	254.00	N68°	19.56'	W133°	35.56'		
	LAC LA MARTRE	Z3	NDB	304.00	N63°	08.62'	W117°	15.98'		
	NORMAN WELLS	VQ	NDB	326.00	N65°	15.17'	W126°	40.17'		
	NORMAN WELLS	YVQ	VOR	112.70	N65°	15.85'	W126°	43.51'	255	E35°
	TROUT LAKE	7I	NDB	258.00	N60°	26.42'	W121°	14.50'		
	TUKTOYAKTUK	UB	NDB	380.00	N69°	26.06'	W133°	01.03'		
	WRIGLEY	YWY	VOR	113.10	N63°	11.03'	W123°	21.73'	505	E33°
	WRIGLEY	WY	NDB	222.00	N63°	12.77'	W123°	25.76'		
	YELLOWKNIFE	YZF	VOR	115.50	N62°	27.85'	W114°	26.19'	711	E29°
Canada, Nova Scotia										
	ALPHA	A	NDB	201.00	N44°	41.42'	W63°	34.12'		
	AYLESFORD	GF	NDB	341.00	N45°	01.43'	W64°	48.61'		
	DEBERT	8F	NDB	239.00	N45°	25.32'	W63°	27.57'		

State/Country	VOR/NDB Name	Ident.	Type	Freq.	Latitude		Longitude		Altitude	Mag Var
USA/CANADA NAVAIDS										
Canada, Nova Scotia										
	DIGBY	Y9	NDB	220.00	N44°	32.85'	W65°	47.34'		
	GOLF	G	NDB	364.00	N44°	48.13'	W63°	35.37'		
	GREENWOOD	YZX	NDB	266.00	N44°	55.37'	W65°	06.11'		
	HALIFAX	YHZ	VOR	115.10	N44°	55.38'	W63°	24.11'	603	W21°
	ISLE MADAME	W	NDB	304.00	N45°	33.58'	W60°	55.92'		
	JULIET	J	NDB	385.00	N44°	58.00'	W63°	25.62'		
	LIVERPOOL	A9	NDB	330.00	N44°	13.62'	W64°	51.51'		
	PLEASANT LAKE	AC	NDB	230.00	N43°	51.65'	W66°	02.61'		
	PORT HAWKESBURY	PD	NDB	229.00	N45°	39.32'	W61°	16.17'		
	SABLE ISLAND	SA	NDB	374.00	N43°	55.83'	W60°	01.37'		
	SHEARWATER	YAW	NDB	353.00	N44°	36.13'	W63°	26.82'		
	SYDNEY	QY	NDB	263.00	N46°	12.68'	W59°	58.53'		
	SYDNEY	YQY	VOR	114.90	N46°	09.20'	W60°	03.34'	259	W23°
	TRENTON	5Y	NDB	338.00	N45°	36.70'	W62°	37.50'		
	YARMOUTH	YQI	VOR	113.30	N43°	49.50'	W66°	04.95'	163	W20°
	YARMOUTH	QI	NDB	206.00	N43°	47.60'	W66°	07.56'		
Canada, Ontario										
	AMESON	YAN	VOR	112.40	N49°	46.80'	W84°	35.49'	0	W08°
	ARMSTRONG	YYW	NDB	223.00	N50°	18.46'	W89°	01.32'		
	ATIKOKAN	IB	NDB	209.00	N48°	49.51'	W91°	34.65'		
	AYLMER	YQO	VOR	114.20	N42°	42.40'	W80°	53.27'	780	W08°
	BRANTFORD	FD	NDB	207.00	N43°	04.40'	W80°	24.97'		
	BROCKVILLE	3B	NDB	300.00	N44°	42.08'	W75°	41.99'		
	BUTTONVILLE	KZ	NDB	248.00	N43°	56.01'	W79°	19.75'		
	CHAPLEAU	YLD	NDB	335.00	N47°	45.35'	W83°	24.76'		
	CHATHAM	4L	NDB	236.00	N42°	18.73'	W82°	04.66'		
	COEHILL	VIE	VOR	115.10	N44°	39.65'	W77°	53.28'	0	W12°
	DOWNSVIEW	YZD	NDB	356.00	N43°	45.25'	W79°	28.68'		
	DRYDEN	YHD	NDB	413.00	N49°	51.86'	W92°	50.94'		
	EARLTON	YXR	NDB	257.00	N47°	42.75'	W79°	47.42'		
	ELLIOT LAKE	YEL	NDB	276.00	N46°	22.30'	W82°	37.69'		
	FORT FRANCES	YAG	NDB	376.00	N48°	41.38'	W93°	32.34'		
	GERALDTON	YGQ	VOR	114.20	N49°	46.18'	W86°	59.06'	0	W05°
	GIBRALTAR POINT	TZ	NDB	257.00	N43°	36.76'	W79°	23.13'		
	GODERICH	GD	NDB	286.00	N43°	44.78'	W81°	43.84'		
	GOLF	G	NDB	398.00	N42°	14.63'	W83°	02.84'		
	GORE BAY	YZE	NDB	245.00	N45°	55.70'	W82°	36.91'		
	HAMILTON	HM	NDB	221.00	N43°	07.27'	W80°	00.40'		
	HANOVER	S7	NDB	268.00	N44°	09.73'	W81°	03.62'		
	JULIET	J	NDB	236.00	N43°	36.96'	W79°	41.30'		
	KASING	YYU	NDB	341.00	N49°	27.88'	W82°	30.34'		
	KENORA	YQK	NDB	326.00	N49°	47.54'	W94°	25.46'		
	KILLALOE	YXI	VOR	115.60	N45°	39.78'	W77°	36.16'	0	W12°
	KINCARDINE	D7	NDB	350.00	N44°	12.20'	W81°	36.19'		
	KINGSTON	YGK	NDB	263.00	N44°	17.80'	W76°	36.33'		
	KIRKLAND/LAKE ON	YKX	NDB	201.00	N48°	13.62'	W79°	52.18'		
	LIMA	L	NDB	368.00	N43°	37.17'	W79°	32.87'		
	LONDON	U	NDB	201.00	N42°	58.93'	W81°	05.30'		
	LONDON	YXU	VOR	117.20	N43°	02.28'	W81°	08.90'	908	W08°
	LONDON	XU	NDB	383.00	N43°	05.48'	W81°	13.10'		
	MANITOUWADGE	YMG	NDB	219.00	N49°	02.96'	W85°	54.02'		
	MANS	YMS	VOR	114.50	N44°	08.58'	W80°	08.77'	1,682	W09°
	MARATHON	YSP	VOR	115.90	N48°	44.60'	W86°	19.64'	1,200	W05°
	MIDLAND	YEE	VOR	112.80	N44°	34.90'	W79°	47.58'	800	W10°
	MOOSENEE	YMO	VOR	112.90	N51°	17.48'	W80°	36.43'	0	W13°
	MOOSONEE	MO	NDB	224.00	N51°	16.93'	W80°	37.66'		
	MUSKOKA	YQA	NDB	272.00	N45°	02.35'	W79°	16.97'		
	NAKINA	QN	NDB	233.00	N50°	10.80'	W86°	37.74'		
	NORTH BAY	YYB	VOR	115.40	N46°	21.83'	W79°	26.18'	1,220	W11°
	NORTH BAY	YB	NDB	394.00	N46°	23.07'	W79°	28.12'		
	NOVEMBER	N	NDB	347.00	N43°	43.90'	W79°	31.25'		
	OSCAR	O	NDB	344.00	N45°	16.66'	W75°	44.99'		
	OSHAWA	OO	NDB	391.00	N43°	55.24'	W78°	54.01'		
	OTTAWA	OW	NDB	236.00	N45°	21.60'	W75°	33.66'		
	OTTAWA	YOW	VOR	114.60	N45°	26.50'	W75°	53.81'	449	W14°
	PELEE ISLAND	PT	NDB	283.00	N41°	46.76'	W82°	40.19'		
	PEMBROKE	YTA	NDB	409.00	N45°	48.16'	W77°	13.15'		
	PETAWAWA	YWA	NDB	516.00	N45°	53.68'	W77°	16.30'		
	PETERBOROUGH	YPQ	NDB	379.00	N44°	12.78'	W78°	27.48'		
	PICKLE LAKE	YPL	NDB	382.00	N51°	26.51'	W90°	13.33'		
	RED LAKE	YRL	VOR	114.00	N51°	04.28'	W93°	45.71'	1,279	E03°
	RED LAKE	RL	NDB	218.00	N51°	03.65'	W93°	47.08'		
	ROMEO	R	NDB	403.00	N43°	44.30'	W79°	42.18'		

State/Country	VOR/NDB Name	Ident.	Type	Freq.	Latitude		Longitude		Altitude	Mag Var
USA/CANADA NAVAIDS										
Canada, Ontario										
	ROMEO	R	NDB	317.00	N44°	03.17'	W77°	37.60'		
	ROMEO	R	NDB	377.00	N45°	16.10'	W75°	34.41'		
	SARNIA	ZR	NDB	404.00	N42°	56.43'	W82°	14.01'		
	SIERRA	S	NDB	344.00	N46°	41.00'	W80°	44.95'		
	SIMCOE	YSO	VOR	117.35	N44°	14.31'	W79°	10.29'	931	W10°
	SIOUX LOOKOUT	YXL	NDB	346.00	N50°	07.09'	W91°	53.86'		
	SIOUX NARROWS	VBI	VOR	115.20	N49°	28.63'	W94°	02.82'	1,292	E04°
	SMITH FALLS	YSH	NDB	334.00	N44°	54.05'	W76°	00.63'		
	ST CATHERINES	SN	NDB	408.00	N43°	08.81'	W79°	15.28'		
	ST THOMAS	7B	NDB	375.00	N42°	46.25'	W81°	06.34'		
	STIRLING	VQC	VOR	113.50	N44°	23.17'	W77°	43.05'	278	W12°
	SUDBURY	YSB	VOR	112.30	N46°	37.75'	W80°	47.89'	1,118	W10°
	SUDBURY	SB	NDB	362.00	N46°	38.88'	W80°	55.29'		
	TANGO	T	NDB	341.00	N43°	37.67'	W79°	43.87'		
	TANGO	T	NDB	263.00	N48°	23.75'	W89°	13.43'		
	TERRACE BAY	YTJ	NDB	250.00	N48°	47.70'	W87°	09.69'		
	THUNDER BAY	QT	NDB	332.00	N48°	20.80'	W89°	26.02'		
	THUNDER BAY	YQT	VOR	114.10	N48°	15.22'	W89°	26.23'	1,639	W01°
	TIMMINS	YTS	VOR	113.00	N48°	34.32'	W81°	22.19'	0	W10°
	TIMMINS	TS	NDB	212.00	N48°	33.97'	W81°	27.17'		
	TORONTO	YYZ	VOR	113.30	N43°	40.93'	W79°	38.55'	551	W09°
	TRENTON	YTR	NDB	215.00	N44°	11.61'	W77°	24.20'		
	UPLANDS	YUP	NDB	352.00	N45°	13.75'	W75°	29.58'		
	WAPISK	YAT	NDB	260.00	N52°	55.82'	W82°	26.00'		
	WATERLOO	YWT	VOR	115.00	N43°	27.52'	W80°	22.75'	1,069	W08°
	WATERLOO-GUELPH R	K	NDB	335.00	N43°	29.55'	W80°	17.22'		
	WAWA	YXZ	VOR	112.70	N47°	57.03'	W84°	49.37'	0	W06°
	WAWA	XZ	NDB	205.00	N48°	01.30'	W84°	44.82'		
	WIARTON	YVV	VOR	117.70	N44°	44.68'	W81°	06.32'	731	W08°
	WIARTON	VV	NDB	326.00	N44°	41.88'	W81°	10.77'		
	WINDSOR	YQG	VOR	113.80	N42°	14.98'	W82°	49.72'	619	W06°
	WINDSOR	QG	NDB	353.00	N42°	18.76'	W82°	52.11'		
	XRAY	X	NDB	385.00	N43°	44.28'	W79°	34.28'		
	YANKEE	Y	NDB	404.00	N46°	19.82'	W79°	31.48'		
Canada, Prince Edward Island										
	CHARLOTTETOWN	YYG	VOR	114.10	N46°	12.43'	W62°	58.72'	268	W22°
	CHARLOTTETOWN	YG	NDB	347.00	N46°	11.53'	W63°	08.89'		
	GOLF	G 1	NDB	400.00	N46°	20.98'	W63°	06.72'		
	SUMMERSIDE	YSU	NDB	254.00	N46°	23.81'	W63°	52.89'		
Canada, Quebec										
	AMOS	9Q	NDB	291.00	N48°	33.55'	W78°	14.73'		
	BAGOTVILLE	XBG	VOR	111.80	N48°	19.76'	W70°	59.73'	531	W20°
	BAGOTVILLE	YBG	NDB	356.00	N48°	20.03'	W71°	08.75'		
	BAIE-COMEAU	YBC	VOR	117.70	N49°	08.03'	W68°	13.31'	0	W22°
	BAIE-COMEAU	BC	NDB	414.00	N49°	07.06'	W68°	19.56'		
	BEAUCE	VLV	VOR	117.20	N45°	55.50'	W70°	50.75'	0	W18°
	BROMONT	6R	NDB	343.00	N45°	14.43'	W72°	47.67'		
	CHAMPLAIN	BV	NDB	336.00	N46°	52.26'	W71°	16.88'		
	CHARLEVOIX	ML	NDB	392.00	N47°	37.40'	W70°	19.48'		
	CHIBOO	MT	NDB	209.00	N49°	47.97'	W74°	29.72'		
	CHUTE-DES-PASSES	DG	NDB	244.00	N49°	53.87'	W71°	15.23'		
	DRUMMONDVILLE	Y8	NDB	401.00	N45°	50.83'	W72°	23.94'		
	EASTMAIN	ZEM	NDB	338.00	N52°	13.84'	W78°	31.04'		
	FORESTVILLE	FE	NDB	239.00	N48°	44.71'	W69°	06.05'		
	GASPE	GP	NDB	232.00	N48°	46.08'	W64°	23.10'		
	GASPE	YGP	VOR	115.40	N48°	45.78'	W64°	24.27'	108	W24°
	GRINDSTONE	YGR	VOR	112.00	N47°	25.82'	W61°	46.43'	62	W24°
	GRINDSTONE	GR	NDB	370.00	N47°	22.45'	W61°	54.40'		
	HAVRE ST-PIERRE	YGV	NDB	344.00	N50°	15.88'	W63°	39.90'		
	HEATH POINT	HP	NDB	335.00	N49°	05.10'	W61°	42.03'		
	HOTEL	H	NDB	407.00	N45°	33.85'	W73°	20.80'		
	LA TUQUE	YLQ	NDB	289.00	N47°	24.91'	W72°	47.14'		
	LG-4	YFM	NDB	332.00	N53°	42.69'	W73°	42.17'		
	LIMA	L	NDB	284.00	N45°	32.55'	W73°	39.40'		
	MANIWAKI	YMW	NDB	366.00	N46°	12.46'	W75°	57.39'		
	MARS	URX	NDB	269.00	N48°	00.90'	W70°	49.13'		
	MATAGAMI	NM	NDB	218.00	N49°	43.43'	W77°	44.50'		
	MATANE	ME	NDB	216.00	N48°	50.00'	W67°	32.96'		
	MIKE	M	NDB	348.00	N45°	31.43'	W73°	39.25'		
	MIRABEL	YMX	VOR	116.70	N45°	53.30'	W74°	22.54'	0	W15°
	MONT-JOLI	YY	NDB	340.00	N48°	34.00'	W68°	15.51'		
	MONT JOLI	YYY	VOR	115.90	N48°	36.73'	W68°	12.53'	190	W22°
	MONTREAL	UL	NDB	248.00	N45°	27.61'	W73°	50.84'		

State/Country	VOR/NDB Name	Ident.	Type	Freq.	Latitude		Longitude		Altitude	Mag Var
USA/CANADA NAVAIDS										
Canada, Quebec	MONTREAL	YUL	VOR	116.30	N45°	36.93'	W73°	58.25'	200	W16°
	NEMISCAU	K8	NDB	214.00	N51°	41.33'	W76°	08.06'		
	PARENT	YPP	NDB	303.00	N47°	53.36'	W74°	40.33'		
	POINTE-DES-MONTS	TG	NDB	300.00	N49°	18.99'	W67°	22.86'		
	PORT MENIER	PN	NDB	360.00	N49°	50.25'	W64°	23.17'		
	QUEBEC	QB	NDB	230.00	N46°	44.98'	W71°	27.75'		
	QUEBEC	YQB	VOR	112.80	N46°	42.31'	W71°	37.58'	268	W18°
	RIMOUSKI	YXK	NDB	373.00	N48°	28.66'	W68°	30.18'		
	RIVIERE-DU-LOUP	RI	NDB	201.00	N47°	45.81'	W69°	34.68'		
	RIVIERE DU LOUP	YRI	VOR	113.90	N47°	45.45'	W69°	35.38'	0	W20°
	RIVIERE OUELLE	Z8	NDB	347.00	N47°	26.50'	W69°	58.90'		
	ROBERVAL	RJ	NDB	378.00	N48°	32.68'	W72°	17.67'		
	RUOYN	YUY	NDB	218.00	N48°	10.37'	W78°	56.30'		
	SAGUENAY	VBS	VOR	114.20	N48°	01.03'	W71°	15.99'	2,892	W19°
	SEPT-ILES	ZV	NDB	273.00	N50°	12.23'	W66°	09.08'		
	SEPT-ILES	YZV	VOR	114.50	N50°	13.93'	W66°	16.43'	0	W24°
	SHERBROOKE	SC	NDB	362.00	N45°	28.46'	W71°	47.27'		
	SHERBROOKE	YSC	VOR	113.20	N45°	18.98'	W71°	47.28'	1,000	W17°
	ST-FELIX-DE-VALOI	UFX	NDB	260.00	N46°	11.53'	W73°	25.14'		
	ST-HONORE	YRC	NDB	213.00	N48°	32.16'	W71°	09.53'		
	ST BRUNO DE GUIGU	YBM	NDB	230.00	N47°	27.11'	W79°	25.44'		
	ST JEAN	YJN	VOR	115.80	N45°	15.35'	W73°	19.27'	200	W16°
	STE-FOY	OU	NDB	329.00	N46°	46.66'	W71°	17.38'		
	THETFORD MINES	R1	NDB	275.00	N46°	02.73'	W71°	16.07'		
	TROIS-RIVIERES	YRQ	NDB	205.00	N46°	22.15'	W72°	39.90'		
	UNIFORM	U	NDB	201.00	N45°	27.25'	W73°	46.42'		
	VAL-D'OR	VO	NDB	239.00	N48°	03.40'	W77°	47.60'		
	VAL-D'OR	YVO	VOR	113.70	N48°	10.52'	W77°	49.21'	0	W14°
	VICTORIAVILLE	F8	NDB	384.00	N46°	06.63'	W71°	55.62'		
	WAKI	G8	NDB	327.00	N46°	16.10'	W75°	59.73'		
	WASKAGANISH	YKQ	NDB	351.00	N51°	29.22'	W78°	44.68'		
Canada, Saskatchewan										'
	BEECHY	BY	NDB	266.00	N50°	50.51'	W107°	27.58'		
	BROADVIEW	YDR	VOR	117.50	N50°	21.77'	W102°	32.41'	2,013	E12°
	DAFOE	VX	NDB	368.00	N51°	52.38'	W104°	34.18'		
	EMPRESS	YEA	VOR	115.90	N50°	55.58'	W109°	59.34'	2,433	E17°
	ESTEVAN	L7	NDB	395.00	N49°	12.58'	W102°	51.59'		
	LUMSDEN	VLN	VOR	114.20	N50°	40.02'	W104°	53.41'	1,895	E14°
	MOOSE JAW	YMJ	NDB	375.00	N50°	17.50'	W105°	26.36'		
	PRINCE ALBERT	YPA	VOR	113.00	N53°	12.98'	W105°	39.98'	0	E15°
	REGINA	QR	NDB	290.00	N50°	22.18'	W104°	34.38'		
	SASKATOON	YXE	VOR	116.20	N52°	10.86'	W106°	43.18'	0	E16°
	SASKATOON	XE	NDB	257.00	N52°	11.38'	W106°	48.83'		
	SWIFT CURRENT	YYN	VOR	117.40	N50°	17.81'	W107°	41.45'	2,679	E16°
	YORKTON	YQV	VOR	115.80	N51°	15.85'	W102°	28.12'	1,662	E12°
	YORKTON	QV	NDB	385.00	N51°	12.96'	W102°	32.51'		
Canada, Yukon										
	BEAVER CREEK	YXQ	NDB	239.00	N62°	24.52'	W140°	51.69'		
	BURWASH	DB	NDB	341.00	N61°	20.41'	W138°	59.00'		
	DAWSON	DA	NDB	214.00	N64°	01.73'	W139°	10.08'		
	FARO	ZFA	NDB	378.00	N62°	12.71'	W133°	23.21'		
	LABERGE	JB	NDB	236.00	N60°	56.93'	W135°	08.26'		
	LAKESHORE	XG	NDB	338.00	N60°	06.77'	W128°	47.96'		
	MAYO	MA	NDB	365.00	N63°	37.72'	W135°	53.58'		
	OLD CROW	YOC	NDB	284.00	N67°	34.27'	W139°	50.77'		
	ROBINSON	PJ	NDB	329.00	N60°	26.36'	W134°	51.67'		
	ROSS RIVER	YDM	NDB	218.00	N61°	58.40'	W132°	25.61'		
	SHINGE POINT	UA	NDB	226.00	N68°	55.37'	W137°	15.74'		
	TESLIN	ZW	NDB	269.00	N60°	10.66'	W132°	44.20'		
	WATSON LAKE	QH	NDB	248.00	N60°	10.62'	W128°	50.74'		
	WATSON LAKE	YQH	VOR	114.90	N60°	05.18'	W128°	51.46'	2,515	E30°
	WHITEHORSE	XY	NDB	302.00	N60°	46.36'	W135°	06.31'		
	WHITEHORSE	YXY	VOR	116.60	N60°	37.13'	W135°	08.34'	5,284	E30°
	XRAY	X	NDB	353.00	N60°	38.16'	W135°	00.64'		
Caribbean										
	ALEGRE	UPA	NDB	382.00	N22°	22.41'	W78°	46.38'		
	STELLA MARIS	ZLS	NDB	526.00	N23°	34.83'	W75°	15.83'		
	TAMPICO	TAM	VOR	117.50	N22°	17.35'	W97°	51.76'	0	E07°
Colorado										
	AKRON	AKO	VOR	114.40	N40°	09.33'	W103°	10.78'	4,618	E13°
	ALAMOSA	ALS	VOR	113.90	N37°	20.94'	W105°	48.93'	7,527	E13°
	ALTUR (LOM)	ALTU	NDB	362.00	N39°	45.30'	W104°	44.50'		
	ARUBA (LOM/NDB)	ARUB	NDB	373.00	N38°	17.45'	W104°	21.30'		

State/Country	VOR/NDB Name	Ident.	Type	Freq.	Latitude		Longitude		Altitude	Mag Var
USA/CANADA NAVAIDS										
Colorado	BATTEN	BAJ	NDB	392.00	N40°	31.93'	W103°	13.77'		
	BETEE (LMM/NDB)	BETE	NDB	308.00	N39°	45.23'	W104°	52.96'		
	BLUE MESA	HBU	VOR	114.90	N38°	27.12'	W107°	02.38'	8,728	E14°
	BUTTS	FCS	VOR	108.80	N38°	40.84'	W104°	45.41'	5,815	E12°
	CARBONDALE	CQL	NDB	344.00	N39°	24.69'	W107°	09.57'		
	CASSE (LOM/NDB)	CASS	NDB	260.00	N39°	27.11'	W104°	50.74'		
	COLLN (LOM)	COLL	NDB	400.00	N40°	21.79'	W104°	58.28'		
	COLORADO SPRINGS	COS	VOR	112.50	N38°	56.67'	W104°	38.00'	6,927	E13°
	CONES	ETL	VOR	110.20	N38°	02.41'	W108°	15.51'	8,459	E12°
	CORTEZ	CEZ	VOR	108.40	N37°	23.39'	W108°	33.70'	6,218	E14°
	DENVER	DEN	VOR	117.90	N39°	48.75'	W104°	39.64'	5,438	E11°
	DENVER	DEN	VOR	117.00	N39°	48.02'	W104°	53.24'	5,231	E12°
	DOVE CREEK	DVC	VOR	114.60	N37°	48.52'	W108°	55.87'	6,989	E14°
	DURANGO	DRO	VOR	108.20	N37°	09.19'	W107°	44.97'	6,658	E14°
	EAGLE	EGE	NDB	357.00	N39°	38.79'	W106°	54.85'		
	FALCON	FQF	VOR	116.30	N39°	41.40'	W104°	37.25'	5,779	E11°
	FRUITA	RHU	VOR	109.00	N39°	11.03'	W108°	38.31'	4,710	E13°
	GILL	GLL	VOR	114.20	N40°	30.23'	W104°	33.18'	4,910	E13°
	GRAND JUNCTION	JNC	VOR	112.40	N39°	03.57'	W108°	47.55'	7,097	E15°
	GREEY (LOM)	GREE	NDB	348.00	N40°	27.39'	W104°	46.16'		
	HAYDEN	CHE	VOR	115.60	N40°	31.20'	W107°	18.29'	7,229	E14°
	HEGINBOTHAM	HEQ	NDB	404.00	N40°	34.88'	W102°	16.87'		
	HOPKINS	HPL	NDB	375.00	N38°	14.56'	W108°	34.00'		
	HUGO	HGO	VOR	112.10	N38°	48.89'	W103°	37.56'	5,231	E12°
	IRONHORSE	IHS	NDB	335.00	N38°	40.69'	W104°	45.19'		
	JEFFCO	BJC	VOR	115.40	N39°	54.78'	W105°	08.34'	5,733	E11°
	KIOWA	IOC	VOR	117.50	N39°	26.14'	W104°	20.26'	6,169	E13°
	KIT CARSON	ITR	NDB	209.00	N39°	14.77'	W102°	17.02'		
	KREMMLING	RLG	VOR	113.80	N40°	00.15'	W106°	26.54'	9,367	E14°
	LA JUNTA	LHX	NDB	239.00	N38°	02.89'	W103°	37.26'		
	LAMAR	LAA	VOR	116.90	N38°	11.82'	W102°	41.25'	3,949	E12°
	LAPORTE	LQP	NDB	387.00	N40°	34.93'	W105°	02.08'		
	LEADVILLE	LXV	NDB	236.00	N39°	13.47'	W106°	18.90'		
	MEEKER	EKR	VOR	115.20	N40°	04.04'	W107°	55.49'	7,619	E15°
	MERTZ (LOM)	MERT	NDB	302.00	N38°	17.03'	W104°	38.82'		
	MILE HIGH	DVV	VOR	114.70	N39°	53.68'	W104°	37.45'	5,267	E11°
	MONTE VISTA	MVI	NDB	311.00	N37°	31.68'	W106°	02.70'		
	MONTROSE	MTJ	VOR	117.10	N38°	30.38'	W107°	53.95'	5,707	E12°
	PETEY (LOM/NDB)	PETE	NDB	407.00	N38°	41.65'	W104°	42.98'		
	PUEBLO	PUB	VOR	116.70	N38°	17.65'	W104°	25.76'	4,759	E13°
	RED TABLE	DBL	VOR	113.00	N39°	26.36'	W106°	53.68'	11,755	E12°
	RIFLE	RIL	VOR	110.60	N39°	31.68'	W107°	42.96'	5,526	E12°
	SKIPI (LOM)	SKIP	NDB	321.00	N39°	47.51'	W104°	26.05'		
	SNOW	SXW	VOR	109.20	N39°	37.76'	W106°	59.46'	8,058	E12°
	THORNTON	TOT	NDB	281.00	N39°	53.59'	W104°	52.28'		
	THURMAN	TXC	VOR	112.90	N39°	41.89'	W103°	12.89'	4,890	E12°
	TOBE	TBE	VOR	115.80	N37°	15.51'	W103°	36.00'	5,730	E12°
	TRINIDAD	TAD	NDB	329.00	N37°	18.36'	W104°	20.00'		
Connecticut	BRADLEY	BDL	VOR	109.00	N41°	56.45'	W72°	41.31'	160	W14°
	BRIDGEPORT	BDR	VOR	108.80	N41°	09.64'	W73°	07.47'	9	W12°
	CHUPP (LOM)	CHUP	NDB	388.00	N41°	52.63'	W72°	45.97'		
	CLERA (LOM)	CLER	NDB	362.00	N41°	24.15'	W73°	07.18'		
	GROTON	TMU	VOR	111.80	N41°	19.82'	W72°	03.12'	9	W14°
	HARTFORD	HFD	VOR	114.90	N41°	38.46'	W72°	32.85'	849	W13°
	LOMIS (LOM/NDB)	LOMI	NDB	244.00	N41°	38.12'	W72°	37.53'		
	MADISON	MAD	VOR	110.40	N41°	18.83'	W72°	41.53'	229	W13°
	MERIDEN	MMK	NDB	238.00	N41°	30.63'	W72°	49.70'		
	NEW HAVEN	HVN	VOR	109.80	N41°	15.73'	W72°	53.11'	9	W13°
	NORWICH	ORW	VOR	110.00	N41°	33.38'	W71°	59.96'	308	W14°
	PUTNAM	PUT	VOR	117.40	N41°	57.32'	W71°	50.64'	649	W14°
	WATERBURY	TBY	NDB	257.00	N41°	31.75'	W73°	08.63'		
Cuba	VARDER	UVR	NDB	272.00	N23°	05.39'	W81°	22.03'		
District of Columbia	GEORGETOWN	GTN	NDB	323.00	N38°	55.78'	W77°	07.45'		
	POTOMAC	VKX	NDB	241.00	N38°	44.93'	W76°	57.36'		
	WASHINGTON	DCA	VOR	111.00	N38°	51.56'	W77°	02.18'	9	W09°
Delaware	DUPONT	DQO	VOR	114.00	N39°	40.68'	W75°	36.42'	72	W10°
	HADIN (LOM)	HADI	NDB	248.00	N39°	34.86'	W75°	36.83'		
	SMYRNA	ENO	VOR	111.40	N39°	13.89'	W75°	30.95'	9	W09°
	WATERLOO	ATR	VOR	112.60	N38°	48.58'	W75°	12.67'	9	W09°

State/Country	VOR/NDB Name	Ident.	Type	Freq.	Latitude		Longitude		Altitude	Mag Var
USA/CANADA NAVAIDS										
Florida										
	ALLENTOWN (NAVY)	NVK	NDB	368.00	N30°	46.12'	W87°	04.36'		
	ANDREW	AEW	NDB	204.00	N25°	44.12'	W80°	09.80'		
	BROOKSVILLE	BKV	NDB	278.00	N28°	28.42'	W82°	26.99'		
	CAIDY	CYR	NDB	338.00	N30°	53.29'	W84°	09.55'		
	CALOO (LOM)	CALO	NDB	341.00	N26°	30.96'	W81°	56.99'		
	CAPOK (LOM)	CAPO	NDB	360.00	N27°	59.71'	W82°	42.18'		
	CECIL	VQQ	VOR	117.90	N30°	12.78'	W81°	53.45'	68	W03°
	COLLIER CO	CCE	VOR	108.60	N26°	09.20'	W81°	46.68'	9	E00°
	COOK	CKK	NDB	365.00	N25°	47.89'	W80°	20.91'		
	COSME (LOM)	COSM	NDB	368.00	N28°	05.11'	W82°	31.51'		
	CRAIG	CRG	VOR	114.50	N30°	20.33'	W81°	30.59'	39	W03°
	CRESTVIEW	CEW	VOR	115.90	N30°	49.57'	W86°	40.74'	252	E03°
	CROSS CITY	CTY	VOR	112.00	N29°	35.94'	W83°	02.92'	29	W02°
	DELAND	DED	NDB	201.00	N29°	04.05'	W81°	16.45'		
	DINNS (LOM/NDB)	DINN	NDB	344.00	N30°	27.90'	W81°	48.08'		
	EASTPORT	EYA	NDB	357.00	N30°	25.40'	W81°	36.57'		
	FISH HOOK	FIS	NDB	332.00	N24°	32.90'	W81°	47.18'		
	FOLEY	FPY	NDB	254.00	N29°	59.76'	W83°	35.17'		
	FORT LAUDERDALE	FLL	VOR	114.40	N26°	04.48'	W80°	09.14'	9	E00°
	FORT PIERCE	FPR	NDB	275.00	N27°	29.20'	W80°	22.39'		
	GAINESVILLE	GNV	VOR	116.20	N29°	34.33'	W82°	21.75'	59	E01°
	GEIGER LAKE	GGL	NDB	375.00	N28°	35.58'	W80°	48.98'		
	HERLONG	HEG	NDB	332.00	N30°	16.59'	W81°	48.54'		
	HERNY (LOM)	HERN	NDB	221.00	N28°	30.41'	W81°	26.03'		
	JUMPI (LOM)	JUMP	NDB	423.00	N29°	03.38'	W82°	13.38'		
	KEY WEST	EYW	VOR	113.50	N24°	35.14'	W81°	48.03'	9	E01°
	KEYES (LOM)	MI	NDB	248.00	N25°	47.44'	W80°	11.65'		
	KISSIMMEE	ISM	NDB	329.00	N28°	17.36'	W81°	26.05'		
	KNIGHT	TPF	NDB	270.00	N27°	54.50'	W82°	27.25'		
	KOBRA (LOM)	KOBR	NDB	201.00	N30°	51.18'	W86°	32.19'		
	LA BELLE	LBV	VOR	110.40	N26°	49.69'	W81°	23.48'	29	E01°
	LAKE CITY	LCQ	NDB	204.00	N30°	11.11'	W82°	34.71'		
	LAKELAND	LAL	VOR	116.00	N27°	59.17'	W82°	00.83'	131	E01°
	LEE CO	RSW	VOR	111.80	N26°	31.79'	W81°	46.54'	22	W02°
	LYNNE (LOM)	LYNN	NDB	278.00	N30°	19.59'	W85°	46.94'		
	MARATHON	MTH	NDB	260.00	N24°	42.71'	W81°	05.72'		
	MARCO	MKY	NDB	375.00	N25°	59.94'	W81°	40.52'		
	MARIANNA	MAI	VOR	114.00	N30°	47.17'	W85°	07.46'	121	E00°
	MELBOURNE	MLB	VOR	110.00	N28°	06.31'	W80°	38.12'	29	W02°
	MIAMI	MIA	VOR	115.90	N25°	57.80'	W80°	27.63'	9	E00°
	MONRY (LOM)	MONR	NDB	227.00	N25°	51.71'	W81°	00.66'		
	MUFFE (LOM)	MUFF	NDB	336.00	N26°	29.02'	W81°	50.06'		
	NAPLES	APF	NDB	201.00	N26°	09.34'	W81°	46.46'		
	NEW SMYRNA BEACH	EVB	NDB	417.00	N29°	03.26'	W80°	56.46'		
	OCALA REGIONAL/JI	OCF	VOR	113.70	N29°	10.64'	W82°	13.58'	78	E00°
	ORLANDO	ORL	VOR	112.20	N28°	32.56'	W81°	20.10'	111	E00°
	ORMOND BEACH	OMN	VOR	112.60	N29°	18.19'	W81°	06.76'	19	E00°
	PAHOKEE	PHK	VOR	115.40	N26°	46.96'	W80°	41.48'	19	E00°
	PALATKA	IAK	NDB	243.00	N29°	39.16'	W81°	48.69'		
	PALM BEACH	PBI	VOR	115.70	N26°	40.80'	W80°	05.19'	19	W03°
	PANAMA CITY	PFN	VOR	114.30	N30°	12.97'	W85°	40.85'	9	E00°
	PICKENS	PKZ	NDB	326.00	N30°	26.22'	W87°	10.70'		
	PICNY (LOM/NDB)	PICN	NDB	388.00	N27°	51.67'	W82°	32.75'		
	PLANT CITY	PCM	NDB	346.00	N28°	00.14'	W82°	09.40'		
	PLANTATION	PJN	NDB	242.00	N26°	07.93'	W80°	13.13'		
	POMPANO BEACH	PMP	VOR	108.80	N26°	14.88'	W80°	06.50'	19	W03°
	PRAIZ (LOM/NDB)	PRAI	NDB	221.00	N26°	11.53'	W80°	17.90'		
	PUNTA GORDA	PGD	VOR	110.20	N26°	55.00'	W81°	59.47'	22	W03°
	QEEZY (LOM)	TM	NDB	266.00	N25°	38.49'	W80°	30.28'		
	RINGY (LOM)	RING	NDB	245.00	N27°	19.69'	W82°	28.70'		
	RUBIN (LOM/NDB)	RUBI	NDB	356.00	N26°	41.26'	W80°	12.61'		
	SANFORD	SFB	NDB	408.00	N28°	47.09'	W81°	14.60'		
	SARASOTA	SRQ	VOR	115.20	N27°	23.86'	W82°	33.25'	19	W02°
	SATELLITE	SQT	NDB	257.00	N28°	05.96'	W80°	42.05'		
	SAUFLEY	NUN	VOR	108.80	N30°	28.32'	W87°	20.15'	78	E01°
	SEBRING	SEF	NDB	382.00	N27°	27.62'	W81°	20.98'		
	SOYYA	SMY	NDB	329.00	N30°	52.29'	W85°	13.49'		
	ST AUGUSTINE	SGJ	VOR	109.40	N29°	57.48'	W81°	20.29'	9	W04°
	ST PETERSBURG	PIE	VOR	116.40	N27°	54.46'	W82°	41.05'	9	E01°
	TALLAHASSEE	TLH	VOR	117.50	N30°	33.37'	W84°	22.43'	180	E02°
	TAYLOR	TAY	VOR	112.90	N30°	30.27'	W82°	33.17'	141	W03°
	TOMOK (LOM)	TOMO	NDB	263.00	N29°	08.65'	W81°	08.86'		
	TRI CO	BKK	NDB	275.00	N30°	51.09'	W85°	36.07'		
	UNITED	UTX	NDB	405.00	N26°	54.53'	W80°	20.10'		

State/Country	VOR/NDB Name	Ident.	Type	Freq.	Latitude		Longitude		Altitude	Mag Var
USA/CANADA NAVAIDS										
Florida	VENICE	VNC	NDB	206.00	N27°	03.68'	W82°	25.83'		
	VERO BEACH	VEP	NDB	392.00	N27°	39.84'	W80°	25.17'		
	VERO BEACH	VRB	VOR	117.30	N27°	40.70'	W80°	29.37'	19	W04°
	WAKUL (LOM/NDB)	WAKU	NDB	379.00	N30°	19.57'	W84°	21.49'		
	WILLIS	LYZ	NDB	359.00	N30°	58.35'	W84°	31.56'		
	WIREY (LOM)	WIRE	NDB	227.00	N27°	56.12'	W82°	04.54'		
	WYNDS (LOM/NDB)	WYND	NDB	269.00	N29°	40.21'	W82°	10.33'		
	ZEPHYRHILLS	RHZ	NDB	253.00	N28°	13.41'	W82°	09.68'		
Georgia										
	ALCOVY	VOF	NDB	370.00	N33°	37.78'	W83°	46.92'		
	ALMA	AMG	VOR	115.10	N31°	32.19'	W82°	30.48'	200	E00°
	ATHENS	AHN	VOR	109.60	N33°	56.85'	W83°	19.48'	790	E00°
	ATLANTA	ATL	VOR	116.90	N33°	37.74'	W84°	26.10'	1,000	E00°
	BARROW CO	BMW	NDB	404.00	N33°	56.12'	W83°	35.36'		
	BAY CREEK	BEP	NDB	350.00	N32°	27.80'	W83°	45.94'		
	BRUNSWICK	SSI	VOR	109.80	N31°	03.03'	W81°	26.75'	9	W04°
	BULLDOG	BJT	NDB	221.00	N33°	57.08'	W83°	13.17'		
	BULLOCK CO	IBU	NDB	407.00	N32°	24.92'	W81°	39.83'		
	BURKE CO	BXG	NDB	356.00	N33°	02.55'	W82°	00.28'		
	CALHOUN	OUK	NDB	323.00	N34°	24.09'	W84°	55.59'		
	CAMILLA	CXU	NDB	369.00	N31°	12.87'	W84°	14.21'		
	CANTON	DJD	NDB	415.00	N34°	15.14'	W84°	29.25'		
	CARROLLTON	GPQ	NDB	239.00	N33°	33.94'	W85°	07.85'		
	CARTERSVILLE	EVZ	NDB	308.00	N34°	11.98'	W84°	50.61'		
	CATTA (LOM)	CATT	NDB	375.00	N33°	38.80'	W84°	32.53'		
	CHOO CHOO	GQO	VOR	115.80	N34°	57.67'	W85°	09.20'	1,029	E01°
	COFFEE CO	OWC	NDB	390.00	N31°	24.28'	W82°	55.42'		
	COLLIERS	IRQ	VOR	113.90	N33°	42.44'	W82°	09.72'	426	W04°
	COMMERCE	DDA	NDB	244.00	N34°	03.73'	W83°	31.25'		
	CONEY	OHY	NDB	400.00	N31°	59.82'	W83°	51.76'		
	COWETA CO	EQQ	NDB	234.00	N33°	15.40'	W84°	42.76'		
	CULVR	ML	NDB	380.00	N33°	09.10'	W83°	09.57'		
	DONALDSONVILLE	ONG	NDB	352.00	N31°	00.62'	W84°	52.52'		
	DUBLIN	DBN	VOR	113.10	N32°	33.64'	W82°	49.99'	298	W01°
	EASTMAN	EZM	NDB	270.00	N32°	12.84'	W83°	07.52'		
	EMANUEL CO	EEX	NDB	309.00	N32°	40.01'	W82°	27.14'		
	FITZGERALD	SUR	NDB	362.00	N31°	36.77'	W83°	17.44'		
	FLANC (LOM/NDB)	FLAN	NDB	344.00	N33°	45.73'	W84°	38.34'		
	FLOWERY BRANCH	FKV	NDB	365.00	N34°	12.20'	W83°	54.37'		
	FLOYD	OYD	NDB	388.00	N34°	17.92'	W85°	09.84'		
	FOOTHILLS	ODF	VOR	113.40	N34°	41.75'	W83°	17.86'	1,699	E00°
	GREENSBORO	EJK	NDB	397.00	N33°	35.69'	W83°	08.44'		
	GREENVILLE	GEF	VOR	109.00	N30°	33.07'	W83°	46.98'	219	E01°
	GWNET (LOM/NDB)	GWNE	NDB	419.00	N34°	01.19'	W83°	51.76'		
	HABERSHAM	AJR	NDB	347.00	N34°	30.08'	W83°	32.99'		
	HARRIS	HRS	VOR	109.80	N34°	56.58'	W83°	54.94'	3,660	E00°
	HAZLEHURST	AZE	NDB	414.00	N31°	52.81'	W82°	38.84'		
	HOMERVILLE	HOE	NDB	209.00	N31°	03.32'	W82°	46.32'		
	HUNTER	SVN	VOR	111.60	N32°	00.71'	W81°	08.44'	39	W02°
	JEFFI (LOM)	JEFF	NDB	275.00	N31°	13.70'	W81°	32.56'		
	JUMPR (LOM)	JUMP	NDB	219.00	N32°	15.80'	W84°	55.82'		
	KAOLIN	OKZ	NDB	212.00	N32°	57.87'	W82°	50.29'		
	LA GRANGE	LGC	VOR	115.60	N33°	02.94'	W85°	12.37'	790	E01°
	LAWSON	LSF	VOR	111.40	N32°	19.94'	W84°	59.59'	226	E02°
	LINDBERGH	LKG	NDB	242.00	N32°	10.46'	W84°	06.49'		
	LOUVALE	XLE	NDB	407.00	N32°	09.57'	W84°	50.49'		
	MACON	MCN	VOR	114.20	N32°	41.47'	W83°	38.83'	350	E01°
	MAVIS (LOM)	MAVI	NDB	368.00	N32°	07.78'	W81°	19.89'		
	MC DUFFIE	THG	NDB	341.00	N33°	31.67'	W82°	26.30'		
	MC INTOSH	MOQ	NDB	263.00	N31°	49.83'	W81°	30.59'		
	MC KINNON	JUK	NDB	353.00	N31°	09.21'	W81°	23.37'		
	MC RAE	MQW	NDB	280.00	N32°	05.67'	W82°	53.02'		
	METTER	MHP	NDB	432.00	N32°	22.34'	W82°	05.04'		
	MONROE	JNM	NDB	429.00	N33°	44.25'	W83°	43.60'		
	MONTEZUMA	IZS	NDB	426.00	N32°	22.04'	W84°	00.44'		
	MOULTRIE	MGR	VOR	108.80	N31°	04.93'	W83°	48.25'	288	W02°
	ONYUN	UQN	NDB	372.00	N32°	13.39'	W82°	17.89'		
	PATTEN	GTP	NDB	245.00	N30°	57.45'	W83°	49.60'		
	PEACHTREE	PDK	VOR	116.60	N33°	52.53'	W84°	17.92'	970	W02°
	PECAN	PZD	VOR	116.10	N31°	39.31'	W84°	17.58'	278	W02°
	PECAT (LOM/NDB)	PECA	NDB	316.00	N33°	18.03'	W84°	29.18'		
	PICKENS CO	JZP	NDB	285.00	N34°	27.27'	W84°	27.57'		
	PINE MOUNTAIN	PIM	NDB	272.00	N32°	50.57'	W84°	52.34'		
	PRISON	RVJ	NDB	424.00	N32°	03.46'	W82°	09.13'		

State/Country	VOR/NDB Name	Ident.	Type	Freq.	Latitude		Longitude		Altitude	Mag Var
USA/CANADA NAVAIDS										
Georgia	PUTNY (LOM/NDB)	PUTN	NDB	227.00	N31°	27.36'	W84°	16.56'		
	REDAN (LOM/NDB)	REDA	NDB	266.00	N33°	38.72'	W84°	18.67'		
	REGINALD GRANT	RGD	NDB	302.00	N32°	56.22'	W84°	20.42'		
	ROME	RMG	VOR	115.40	N34°	09.75'	W85°	07.16'	1,151	E01°
	RUSKIN	RNQ	NDB	404.00	N31°	14.91'	W82°	24.09'		
	SAVANNAH	SAV	VOR	112.70	N32°	09.63'	W81°	06.75'	9	W01°
	SLOVER	JES	NDB	340.00	N31°	33.14'	W81°	53.23'		
	SOFKE (LOM)	SOFK	NDB	290.00	N32°	38.71'	W83°	42.79'		
	SYLVANIA	JYL	NDB	245.00	N32°	38.94'	W81°	35.62'		
	TIFT MYERS	IFM	VOR	112.50	N31°	25.72'	W83°	29.33'	350	W01°
	TIFTO	TM	NDB	409.00	N31°	21.79'	W83°	26.64'		
	TURKEY CREEK	UPK	NDB	251.00	N32°	29.02'	W83°	00.65'		
	VALDOSTA	OTK	VOR	114.80	N30°	46.82'	W83°	16.78'	200	W02°
	VIENNA	VNA	VOR	116.50	N32°	12.80'	W83°	29.83'	298	E01°
	WASHINGTON-WILKE	IIY	NDB	435.00	N33°	46.49'	W82°	48.79'		
	WAYCROSS	AYS	VOR	110.20	N31°	16.16'	W82°	33.38'	150	E00°
	WHITFIELD	UWI	NDB	400.00	N34°	47.37'	W84°	56.76'		
Hawaii	BRADSHAW	BSF	NDB	339.0	N19°	45.63'	W155°	35.68'		
	EWABE (LOM/NDB)	EWAB	NDB	242.0	N21°	19.49'	W158°	02.93'		
	HILO	ITO	VOR	116.9	N19°	43.28'	W155°	00.65'	22	E11°
	HONOLULU	HNL	VOR	114.8	N21°	18.49'	W157°	55.82'	9	E11°
	KAMUELA	MUE	VOR	113.3	N19°	59.88'	W155°	40.19'	2,669	E11°
	KANEOHE BAY	NGF	NDB	265.0	N21°	27.10'	W157°	45.20'		
	KOKO HEAD	CKH	VOR	113.9	N21°	15.90'	W157°	42.17'	639	E11°
	KONA	IAI	VOR	115.7	N19°	39.26'	W156°	01.48'	49	E11°
	LANAI	LNY	VOR	117.7	N20°	45.86'	W156°	58.13'	1,249	E11°
	LANAI	LLD	NDB	353.0	N20°	46.69'	W156°	57.98'		
	LIHUE	LIH	VOR	113.5	N21°	57.91'	W159°	20.28'	111	E11°
	MAUI	OGG	VOR	114.3	N20°	53.92'	W156°	25.91'	29	E11°
	MOLOKAI	MKK	VOR	116.1	N21°	08.28'	W157°	10.04'	1,420	E11°
	PAHOA	POA	NDB	332.0	N19°	32.46'	W154°	58.33'		
	SOUTH KAUAI	SOK	VOR	115.4	N21°	54.02'	W159°	31.73'	629	E11°
	UPOLU POINT	UPP	VOR	112.3	N20°	12.03'	W155°	50.59'	1,758	E11°
	VALLEY ISLAND	VYI	NDB	327.0	N20°	52.84'	W156°	26.55'		
	WHEELER	HHI	NDB	373.0	N21°	28.48'	W158°	01.84'		
Idaho	BEAR LAKE	BBH	NDB	233.00	N42°	15.14'	W111°	20.02'		
	BOISE	BOI	VOR	113.30	N43°	33.16'	W116°	11.52'	2,869	E17°
	BURLEY	BYI	VOR	114.10	N42°	34.81'	W113°	51.95'	4,227	E18°
	CHALLIS	LLJ	NDB	397.00	N44°	31.16'	W114°	12.93'		
	COEUR D ALENE	COE	VOR	108.80	N47°	46.42'	W116°	49.23'	2,289	E19°
	COUNCIL	CQI	NDB	274.00	N44°	45.09'	W116°	26.57'		
	DONNELLY	DNJ	VOR	116.20	N44°	46.02'	W116°	12.37'	7,297	E19°
	DUBOIS	DBS	VOR	116.90	N44°	05.33'	W112°	12.56'	4,913	E15°
	GRAIN	GVV	NDB	280.00	N45°	56.37'	W116°	13.29'		
	HAILEY	HLE	NDB	220.00	N43°	19.74'	W114°	14.55'		
	IDAHO FALLS	IDA	VOR	109.00	N43°	31.13'	W112°	03.83'	4,719	E15°
	LEENY (LOM)	LEEN	NDB	347.00	N47°	44.57'	W116°	57.66'		
	MALAD CITY	MLD	VOR	117.40	N42°	11.99'	W112°	27.07'	7,327	E17°
	MC CALL	IOM	NDB	363.00	N44°	48.34'	W116°	06.14'		
	MERIDIAN	MPA	NDB	238.00	N43°	35.73'	W116°	34.72'		
	MOUNTAIN HOME	MUO	VOR	114.90	N42°	58.96'	W115°	46.45'	2,988	E18°
	MULLAN PASS	MLP	VOR	117.80	N47°	27.41'	W115°	38.76'	6,097	E20°
	NEZ PERCE	MQG	VOR	108.20	N46°	22.89'	W116°	52.16'	1,718	E20°
	POCATELLO	PIH	VOR	112.60	N42°	52.22'	W112°	39.13'	4,427	E17°
	SALMON	LKT	VOR	113.50	N45°	01.27'	W114°	05.05'	9,256	E18°
	SANDPOE	SZT	NDB	264.00	N48°	17.44'	W116°	33.81'		
	STEELHEAD	HDG	NDB	211.00	N42°	54.97'	W114°	40.45'		
	STRIK (LOM)	STRI	NDB	389.00	N42°	28.71'	W114°	21.25'		
	STURGEON	STI	NDB	333.00	N43°	06.82'	W115°	40.13'		
	SWEDEN	SWU	NDB	350.00	N43°	25.93'	W112°	09.74'		
	TWIN FALLS	TWF	VOR	115.80	N42°	28.79'	W114°	29.36'	4,139	E18°
	TYHEE (LOM)	TYHE	NDB	383.00	N42°	57.82'	W112°	30.98'		
	UCONN (LOM)	UCON	NDB	324.00	N43°	35.86'	W111°	58.86'		
	USTIK (LOM/NDB)	USTI	NDB	359.00	N43°	35.80'	W116°	18.92'		
Illinois	ABRAHAM	AAA	NDB	329.00	N40°	09.60'	W89°	20.26'		
	ALPOS (LOM)	ALPO	NDB	218.00	N38°	51.30'	W89°	56.29'		
	BELLEVILLE	BL	NDB	362.00	N38°	27.80'	W89°	45.38'		
	BELLGRADE	BDD	NDB	254.00	N37°	08.73'	W88°	40.21'		
	BENTON	BEE	NDB	414.00	N38°	00.37'	W88°	55.92'		
	BIBLE GROVE	BIB	VOR	109.00	N38°	55.22'	W88°	28.90'	541	E03°

State/Country	VOR/NDB Name	Ident.	Type	Freq.	Latitude		Longitude		Altitude	Mag Var
USA/CANADA NAVAIDS										
Illinois	BLOOMINGTON	BMI	VOR	108.20	N40°	28.84'	W88°	55.87'	879	E03°
	BRADFORD	BDF	VOR	114.70	N41°	09.58'	W89°	35.27'	810	E00°
	BURNS (LOM)	BURN	NDB	390.00	N40°	39.25'	W91°	07.38'		
	CABBI (LOM)	CABB	NDB	388.00	N37°	52.20'	W89°	14.73'		
	CAIRO	CIR	NDB	397.00	N37°	03.70'	W89°	13.40'		
	CANTON	CTK	NDB	236.00	N40°	33.95'	W90°	04.62'		
	CAPITAL	CAP	VOR	112.70	N39°	53.52'	W89°	37.52'	590	E04°
	CARMI	CUL	NDB	332.00	N38°	05.63'	W88°	07.18'		
	CASEY	CZB	NDB	359.00	N39°	18.31'	W88°	00.11'		
	CENTRALIA	ENL	VOR	115.00	N38°	25.20'	W89°	09.54'	551	E04°
	CHAMPAIGN	CMI	VOR	110.00	N40°	02.07'	W88°	16.56'	751	E03°
	CHICAGO-O HARE	ORD	VOR	113.90	N41°	59.25'	W87°	54.29'	649	E02°
	CHICAGO HEIGHTS	CGT	VOR	114.20	N41°	30.59'	W87°	34.28'	629	E02°
	CIVIC MEMORIAL	CVM	NDB	263.00	N38°	53.53'	W90°	03.37'		
	DANVILLE	DNV	VOR	111.00	N40°	17.62'	W87°	33.43'	698	E02°
	DEANA (LOM/NDB)	DEAN	NDB	350.00	N41°	58.06'	W88°	01.59'		
	DECATUR	DEC	VOR	117.20	N39°	44.24'	W88°	51.38'	698	E03°
	DEKALB	DKB	NDB	209.00	N41°	55.93'	W88°	42.45'		
	DUPAGE	DPA	VOR	108.40	N41°	53.42'	W88°	21.01'	800	E02°
	DWIGHT	DTG	NDB	344.00	N41°	08.00'	W88°	26.08'		
	ELM RIVER	FOA	NDB	353.00	N38°	40.13'	W88°	27.18'		
	ELWIN (LOM)	ELWI	NDB	275.00	N39°	47.43'	W88°	57.22'		
	ERMIN (LOM/NDB)	ERMI	NDB	332.00	N41°	43.14'	W87°	50.18'		
	FREEPORT	FEP	NDB	335.00	N42°	14.73'	W89°	35.15'		
	GALESBURG	GBG	VOR	109.80	N40°	56.23'	W90°	26.06'	760	E03°
	GILMY (LOM)	GILM	NDB	275.00	N42°	06.86'	W89°	05.91'		
	GREENVILLE	GRE	NDB	233.00	N38°	50.05'	W89°	22.33'		
	HARRISBURG/RALEIG	HSB	NDB	230.00	N37°	48.69'	W88°	32.72'		
	HOMER	HMJ	NDB	281.00	N40°	01.58'	W87°	57.18'		
	HUSKK (LOM/NDB)	HUSK	NDB	382.00	N39°	46.38'	W89°	45.59'		
	INDDY (LOM)	INDD	NDB	385.00	N41°	54.28'	W87°	48.36'		
	JACKSONVILLE	IJX	VOR	108.60	N39°	46.58'	W90°	14.32'	613	E02°
	JOCKY (LOM)	JOCK	NDB	257.00	N41°	53.66'	W87°	49.57'		
	JOLIET	JOT	VOR	112.30	N41°	32.78'	W88°	19.10'	593	E02°
	JONNY (LOM)	JONN	NDB	382.00	N37°	50.34'	W88°	58.24'		
	KANKAKEE	IKK	VOR	111.60	N41°	04.46'	W87°	50.98'	616	E00°
	KEDZI (LOM/NDB)	KEDZ	NDB	248.00	N41°	44.49'	W87°	41.37'		
	KEWANEE	EZI	NDB	245.00	N41°	12.06'	W89°	57.55'		
	LAWRENCEVILLE	LWV	VOR	113.50	N38°	46.16'	W87°	35.95'	429	W01°
	LEAMA (LOM)	LEAM	NDB	368.00	N42°	04.15'	W87°	59.44'		
	LITCHFIELD	LTD	NDB	371.00	N39°	09.97'	W89°	40.13'		
	MACOMB	JZY	NDB	251.00	N40°	31.10'	W90°	33.62'		
	MARION	MWA	VOR	110.40	N37°	45.25'	W89°	00.70'	488	E04°
	MATTOON	MTO	VOR	109.40	N39°	28.67'	W88°	17.16'	718	E03°
	METROPOLIS	MIX	NDB	281.00	N37°	11.08'	W88°	45.66'		
	MOLINE	MZV	VOR	114.40	N41°	19.26'	W90°	38.28'	819	E05°
	MOLLI (LOM)	MOLL	NDB	215.00	N41°	26.94'	W90°	37.10'		
	MOUNT CARMEL	AJG	NDB	524.00	N38°	36.72'	W87°	43.56'		
	MT VERNON	VNN	VOR	113.80	N38°	21.71'	W88°	48.43'	554	E02°
	NORTHBROOK	OBK	VOR	113.00	N42°	13.42'	W87°	57.09'	708	E02°
	OLNEY	OLY	NDB	272.00	N38°	43.08'	W88°	10.36'		
	OTTAWA	OIX	NDB	266.00	N41°	21.75'	W88°	51.25'		
	PALESTINE	PLX	NDB	391.00	N39°	00.80'	W87°	38.45'		
	PARIS	PRG	NDB	341.00	N39°	41.90'	W87°	40.45'		
	PEORIA	PIA	VOR	115.20	N40°	40.80'	W89°	47.56'	731	E04°
	PEOTONE	EON	VOR	113.20	N41°	16.17'	W87°	47.46'	688	E02°
	PICKNEYVILLE	PJY	NDB	215.00	N37°	58.50'	W89°	21.78'		
	PITTSFIELD	PPQ	NDB	344.00	N39°	38.45'	W90°	46.80'		
	POCKET CITY	PXV	VOR	113.30	N37°	55.69'	W87°	45.74'	429	E03°
	POLO	PLL	VOR	111.20	N41°	57.93'	W89°	31.45'	839	E03°
	PONTIAC	PNT	VOR	109.60	N40°	49.27'	W88°	44.01'	678	E03°
	QUINCY	UIN	VOR	113.60	N39°	50.87'	W91°	16.73'	708	E05°
	QUINCY (LOM/NDB)	UI	NDB	293.00	N39°	53.21'	W91°	15.21'		
	ROAMY (LOM)	ROAM	NDB	394.00	N42°	03.35'	W88°	00.46'		
	ROBERTS	RBS	VOR	116.80	N40°	34.90'	W88°	09.85'	780	E02°
	ROBINSON	RSV	VOR	108.40	N39°	01.08'	W87°	38.91'	488	E02°
	ROCKFORD	RFD	VOR	110.80	N42°	13.53'	W89°	11.95'	859	E01°
	SALEM	SLO	NDB	400.00	N38°	38.64'	W88°	58.04'		
	SAMSVILLE	SAM	VOR	116.60	N38°	29.11'	W88°	05.14'	541	E03°
	SHELBYVILLE	SYZ	NDB	365.00	N39°	24.40'	W88°	50.62'		
	SPARTA	SAR	NDB	239.00	N38°	08.71'	W89°	42.14'		
	TAFFS (LOM)	TAFF	NDB	414.00	N41°	59.06'	W87°	47.34'		
	TAYLORVILLE	TAZ	NDB	395.00	N39°	32.16'	W89°	19.41'		
	TROY	TOY	VOR	116.00	N38°	44.35'	W89°	55.11'	570	E04°
	TUNGG (LOM/NDB)	TUNG	NDB	356.00	N40°	36.33'	W89°	35.58'		

State/Country	VOR/NDB Name	Ident.	Type	Freq.	Latitude		Longitude		Altitude	Mag Var
USA/CANADA NAVAIDS										
Illinois	VALLEY	VYS	NDB	230.00	N41°	21.28'	W89°	08.88'		
	VANDALIA	VLA	VOR	114.30	N39°	05.62'	W89°	09.74'	603	E04°
	VEALS (LOM)	VEAL	NDB	407.00	N39°	57.97'	W88°	10.94'		
	WAUKE (LOM)	WAUK	NDB	379.00	N42°	27.84'	W87°	48.08'		
	WAYNE CO	FWC	NDB	257.00	N38°	22.80'	W88°	24.58'		
	WHITESIDE	BOZ	NDB	254.00	N41°	42.66'	W89°	47.13'		
	ZEBRE (LOM/NDB)	ZEBR	NDB	347.00	N39°	26.48'	W88°	10.38'		
Indiana										
	AIRPA (LOM)	AIRP	NDB	209.00	N39°	55.52'	W86°	14.30'		
	ANGOLA	ANQ	NDB	347.00	N41°	38.38'	W85°	05.21'		
	BALLL (LOM)	BALL	NDB	365.00	N40°	10.85'	W85°	19.24'		
	BATESVILLE	HLB	NDB	254.00	N39°	20.98'	W85°	15.46'		
	BEDFORD	BFR	NDB	344.00	N38°	50.36'	W86°	26.20'		
	BOILER	BVT	VOR	115.10	N40°	33.36'	W87°	04.15'	751	E01°
	BRINN (LOM)	BRIN	NDB	219.00	N39°	37.03'	W86°	24.47'		
	CAPTAIN	EQZ	NDB	308.00	N38°	52.04'	W85°	58.38'		
	CLAYE (LOM/NDB)	CLAY	NDB	382.00	N39°	03.38'	W86°	35.95'		
	CLIFS (LOM/NDB)	CLIF	NDB	410.00	N39°	19.32'	W85°	49.11'		
	COLFA (LOM)	COLF	NDB	232.00	N39°	39.41'	W86°	11.13'		
	CONNERSVILLE	CEV	NDB	275.00	N39°	41.85'	W85°	08.06'		
	CRAWFORDSVILLE	CFJ	NDB	388.00	N39°	58.85'	W86°	54.94'		
	CULVER	CPB	NDB	391.00	N41°	13.00'	W86°	23.08'		
	EARLE (LOM)	EARL	NDB	401.00	N40°	25.58'	W87°	03.10'		
	EVANSVILLE	PDW	NDB	284.00	N38°	02.40'	W87°	31.85'		
	FERDINAND	FNZ	NDB	239.00	N38°	14.92'	W86°	50.27'		
	FORT WAYNE	FWA	VOR	117.80	N40°	58.74'	W85°	11.28'	800	E00°
	FRANKFORT	FKR	NDB	278.00	N40°	16.23'	W86°	33.76'		
	GARIE (LOM)	GARI	NDB	236.00	N41°	34.34'	W87°	19.62'		
	GIPER	GIJ	VOR	115.40	N41°	46.11'	W86°	19.10'	800	E00°
	GOSHEN	GSH	VOR	113.70	N41°	31.51'	W86°	01.67'	849	E00°
	GREENCASTLE	TVX	NDB	521.00	N39°	42.83'	W86°	48.36'		
	GREENWOOD	HFY	NDB	318.00	N39°	37.96'	W86°	05.44'		
	GRISSOM	GUS	VOR	116.50	N40°	38.69'	W86°	09.10'	810	W02°
	HAPPS (LOM)	HAPP	NDB	331.00	N38°	28.43'	W85°	44.23'		
	HOAGY (LOM)	HOAG	NDB	251.00	N40°	55.83'	W85°	07.17'		
	HOOSIER	OOM	VOR	110.20	N39°	08.63'	W86°	36.78'	849	W02°
	HUNTINGBURG	HNB	VOR	109.20	N38°	15.01'	W86°	57.38'	531	E00°
	HUNTINGTON	HHG	NDB	417.00	N40°	51.33'	W85°	27.85'		
	INDIANAPOLIS	VHP	VOR	116.30	N39°	48.88'	W86°	22.05'	869	E01°
	KNOX	OXI	VOR	115.60	N41°	19.32'	W86°	38.95'	688	E00°
	KOKOMO	OKK	VOR	109.80	N40°	31.66'	W86°	03.48'	829	E00°
	LAREZ (LOM)	LARE	NDB	349.00	N39°	47.18'	W86°	11.77'		
	LOGANSPORT	GGP	NDB	263.00	N40°	42.55'	W86°	22.41'		
	MADISON	IMS	NDB	404.00	N38°	45.65'	W85°	27.63'		
	MARION	MZZ	VOR	108.60	N40°	29.59'	W85°	40.75'	849	W03°
	METROPOLITAN	UMP	NDB	338.00	N39°	56.26'	W86°	03.01'		
	MICHIGAN CITY	MGC	NDB	203.00	N41°	42.42'	W86°	48.99'		
	MISHA (LOM)	MISH	NDB	341.00	N41°	42.34'	W86°	13.14'		
	MUNCIE	MIE	VOR	114.40	N40°	14.23'	W85°	23.64'	941	W03°
	NABB	ABB	VOR	112.40	N38°	35.32'	W85°	38.16'	708	E01°
	NEW CASTLE	UWL	NDB	385.00	N39°	52.79'	W85°	19.13'		
	NORTH VERNON	OVO	NDB	374.00	N39°	02.98'	W85°	36.06'		
	OAKTOWN	OTN	NDB	260.00	N38°	50.75'	W87°	30.41'		
	ORANJ	RRJ	NDB	368.00	N38°	31.67'	W86°	31.66'		
	PORTLAND	PLD	NDB	257.00	N40°	27.21'	W84°	59.01'		
	PULLY (LOM/NDB)	PULL	NDB	266.00	N39°	38.68'	W86°	23.37'		
	RENSSELAER	RZL	NDB	362.00	N40°	56.81'	W87°	11.01'		
	RICHMOND	RID	VOR	110.60	N39°	45.30'	W84°	50.33'	1,134	W03°
	ROCHESTER	RCR	NDB	216.00	N41°	03.90'	W86°	11.41'		
	SEDLY (LOM/NDB)	SEDL	NDB	212.00	N41°	27.06'	W86°	52.65'		
	SHELBYVILLE	SHB	VOR	112.00	N39°	37.95'	W85°	49.45'	810	E01°
	SULLIVAN	SIV	NDB	326.00	N39°	06.81'	W87°	26.80'		
	TELL CITY	TEL	NDB	206.00	N38°	00.85'	W86°	41.41'		
	TERRE HAUTE	TTH	VOR	115.30	N39°	29.33'	W87°	14.94'	610	E02°
	VICCI (LOM)	VICC	NDB	219.00	N38°	07.59'	W87°	26.44'		
	VIDEO (LOM/NDB)	VIDE	NDB	371.00	N40°	04.17'	W85°	30.64'		
	VINCENNES	OEA	NDB	251.00	N38°	41.48'	W87°	33.31'		
	WABASH	IWH	NDB	329.00	N40°	45.81'	W85°	47.86'		
	WASHINGTON	DCY	NDB	212.00	N38°	41.76'	W87°	07.95'		
	WHITE CO	MCX	NDB	377.00	N40°	42.61'	W86°	45.73'		
	WINAMAC	RWN	NDB	335.00	N41°	05.63'	W86°	36.26'		
	WINCHESTER	AWW	NDB	212.00	N40°	10.08'	W84°	55.31'		
	WOLF LAKE	OLK	VOR	110.40	N41°	14.81'	W85°	29.84'	970	W03°
	YINNO (LOM/NDB)	YINN	NDB	245.00	N39°	23.27'	W87°	23.86'		
	ZIONSVILLE	HZP	NDB	248.00	N39°	56.38'	W86°	14.97'		

State/Country	VOR/NDB Name	Ident.	Type	Freq.	Latitude		Longitude		Altitude	Mag Var
USA/CANADA NAVAIDS										
Iowa										
	ALGONA	AXA	NDB	403.00	N43°	04.88'	W94°	16.34'		
	AMES	AMW	NDB	275.00	N41°	59.70'	W93°	37.61'		
	ATLANTIC	AIO	NDB	365.00	N41°	24.23'	W95°	02.77'		
	AUDUBON	ADU	NDB	266.00	N41°	41.41'	W94°	54.59'		
	AUNEY (LOM)	AUNE	NDB	353.00	N41°	41.69'	W90°	39.34'		
	BARRO (LOM)	BARR	NDB	341.00	N42°	30.86'	W94°	18.33'		
	BLOOMFIELD	BEX	NDB	269.00	N40°	44.70'	W92°	25.82'		
	BOONE	BNW	NDB	407.00	N42°	03.25'	W93°	51.18'		
	BURLINGTON	BRL	VOR	111.40	N40°	43.40'	W90°	55.55'	731	E05°
	CARROLL	CIN	NDB	397.00	N42°	02.51'	W94°	47.26'		
	CEDAR RAPIDS	CID	VOR	114.10	N41°	53.25'	W91°	47.14'	869	E05°
	CENTERVILLE	TVK	NDB	290.00	N40°	41.22'	W92°	53.99'		
	CHARITON	CNC	NDB	209.00	N41°	01.00'	W93°	21.71'		
	CHARLES CITY	CCY	NDB	375.00	N43°	04.10'	W92°	36.49'		
	CHUKK	IY	NDB	417.00	N43°	08.03'	W92°	43.69'		
	CINDY (LOM)	CIND	NDB	326.00	N41°	53.14'	W91°	48.14'		
	CLARINDA	ICL	NDB	353.00	N40°	43.60'	W95°	01.64'		
	CLARION	CAV	NDB	387.00	N42°	44.74'	W93°	45.52'		
	CLINTON	CWI	NDB	377.00	N41°	49.72'	W90°	19.65'		
	CORNING	CRZ	NDB	296.00	N40°	59.78'	W94°	45.41'		
	CRESCO	CJJ	NDB	293.00	N43°	21.96'	W92°	07.86'		
	DAVENPORT	CVA	VOR	113.80	N41°	42.50'	W90°	29.01'	760	E04°
	DECORAH	DEH	NDB	347.00	N43°	16.53'	W91°	44.18'		
	DENISON	DNS	NDB	350.00	N41°	59.04'	W95°	22.76'		
	DES MOINES	DSM	VOR	117.50	N41°	26.25'	W93°	38.91'	941	E07°
	DUBUQUE	DBQ	VOR	115.80	N42°	24.08'	W90°	42.54'	1,059	E04°
	EAGLE GROVE	EAG	NDB	302.00	N42°	42.51'	W93°	54.63'		
	ELMWOOD	EMD	VOR	111.00	N42°	06.65'	W92°	54.60'	974	E03°
	EMMETSBURG	EGQ	NDB	410.00	N43°	06.06'	W94°	42.43'		
	ESTHERVILLE	EST	VOR	110.40	N43°	24.54'	W94°	44.66'	1,318	E07°
	FAIRFIELD	FFL	NDB	332.00	N41°	00.66'	W91°	59.31'		
	FLICK (LOM)	FLIC	NDB	513.00	N41°	24.10'	W95°	53.59'		
	FOREM (LOM)	FORE	NDB	344.00	N41°	28.92'	W93°	34.84'		
	FOREST CITY	FXY	NDB	359.00	N43°	14.11'	W93°	37.26'		
	FORT DODGE	FOD	VOR	113.50	N42°	36.66'	W94°	17.69'	1,151	E07°
	GARRISON	VTI	NDB	338.00	N42°	13.30'	W92°	01.21'		
	GREENFIELD	GFZ	NDB	338.00	N41°	19.53'	W94°	26.66'		
	GRINNELL	GGI	NDB	248.00	N41°	42.58'	W92°	43.77'		
	GUTHRIE CENTER	GCT	NDB	518.00	N41°	40.91'	W94°	25.99'		
	HAMPTON	HPT	NDB	230.00	N42°	43.53'	W93°	13.49'		
	HARLAN	HNR	NDB	272.00	N41°	34.74'	W95°	20.43'		
	HAWKEYE	UOC	NDB	524.00	N41°	37.92'	W91°	32.57'		
	HILLZ (LOM)	HILL	NDB	517.00	N41°	45.10'	W90°	23.43'		
	IOWA CITY	IOW	VOR	116.20	N41°	31.13'	W91°	36.79'	770	E05°
	IOWA FALLS	IFA	NDB	368.00	N42°	28.59'	W93°	15.92'		
	JEFFERSON	EFW	NDB	391.00	N42°	00.84'	W94°	20.26'		
	KEOKUK	EOK	NDB	366.00	N40°	27.88'	W91°	26.01'		
	KNOXVILLE	OXV	NDB	284.00	N41°	17.75'	W93°	06.84'		
	LAMONI	LMN	VOR	116.70	N40°	35.80'	W93°	58.05'	1,138	E07°
	LE MARS	LRJ	NDB	382.00	N42°	46.46'	W96°	11.55'		
	LITTLE SIOUX	LTU	NDB	326.00	N43°	07.62'	W95°	07.96'		
	MAPLETON	MEY	NDB	335.00	N42°	10.83'	W95°	47.68'		
	MAQUOKETA	OQW	NDB	386.00	N42°	03.08'	W90°	44.45'		
	MARSHALLTOWN	MIW	NDB	239.00	N42°	06.59'	W92°	55.01'		
	MASON CITY	MCW	VOR	114.90	N43°	05.68'	W93°	19.79'	1,210	E06°
	MERLE (LOM)	MERL	NDB	362.00	N41°	54.16'	W93°	39.54'		
	MONTICELLO	MXO	NDB	397.00	N42°	12.03'	W91°	08.22'		
	MOUNT PLEASANT	MPZ	NDB	212.00	N40°	56.56'	W91°	30.55'		
	MUSCATINE	MUT	NDB	272.00	N41°	21.73'	W91°	08.76'		
	NEWTON	TNU	VOR	112.50	N41°	47.02'	W93°	06.53'	980	E06°
	OELWEIN	OLZ	NDB	260.00	N42°	41.04'	W91°	58.57'		
	ORANGE CITY	ORC	NDB	521.00	N42°	59.48'	W96°	03.63'		
	OSKALOOSA	OOA	NDB	414.00	N41°	13.53'	W92°	29.24'		
	OTTUMWA	OTM	VOR	111.60	N41°	01.74'	W92°	19.55'	819	E06°
	PELLA	PEA	NDB	257.00	N41°	24.31'	W92°	56.59'		
	PERRY	PRO	NDB	251.00	N41°	49.83'	W94°	09.63'		
	PILOT ROCK	CKP	NDB	423.00	N42°	43.93'	W95°	33.18'		
	POCAHONTAS	POH	NDB	314.00	N42°	44.81'	W94°	38.88'		
	PORT CITY	RTY	VOR	108.80	N41°	22.16'	W91°	08.60'	537	E03°
	PRICE (LOM)	PRIC	NDB	382.00	N42°	37.32'	W92°	30.56'		
	PUFF	PUF	NDB	345.00	N43°	21.06'	W94°	44.26'		
	RED OAK	RDK	NDB	230.00	N41°	00.96'	W95°	15.19'		
	ROCK RAPIDS	RRQ	NDB	515.00	N43°	27.06'	W96°	10.68'		
	SAC CITY	SKI	NDB	356.00	N42°	22.54'	W94°	58.86'		

State/Country	VOR/NDB Name	Ident.	Type	Freq.	Latitude		Longitude		Altitude	Mag Var
USA/CANADA NAVAIDS										
Iowa	SALIX (LOM/NDB)	SALI	NDB	414.00	N42°	19.65'	W96°	17.41'		
	SHELDON	DDL	VOR	108.60	N43°	12.72'	W95°	50.03'	1,416	E05°
	SHELDON	SHL	NDB	338.00	N43°	12.84'	W95°	50.03'		
	SHENANDOAH	SDA	NDB	411.00	N40°	45.41'	W95°	24.94'		
	SIBLEY	ISB	NDB	269.00	N43°	22.08'	W95°	45.15'		
	SIOUX CENTER	SOY	NDB	368.00	N43°	07.98'	W96°	11.38'		
	SIOUX CITY	SUX	VOR	116.50	N42°	20.67'	W96°	19.41'	1,079	E09°
	SNORE (LOM)	SNOR	NDB	394.00	N43°	13.95'	W95°	19.65'		
	SPENCER	SPW	VOR	110.00	N43°	09.73'	W95°	12.05'	1,328	E05°
	STORM LAKE	SLB	NDB	227.00	N42°	36.02'	W95°	14.66'		
	SURFF (LOM)	SURF	NDB	308.00	N43°	03.14'	W93°	19.65'		
	UNION CO	UNE	NDB	379.00	N40°	57.42'	W94°	20.76'		
	WAPSIE	IIB	NDB	206.00	N42°	27.13'	W91°	57.05'		
	WASHINGTON	AWG	NDB	219.00	N41°	16.78'	W91°	40.36'		
	WATERLOO	ALO	VOR	112.20	N42°	33.38'	W92°	23.93'	865	E06°
	WAUKON	UKN	NDB	116.60	N43°	16.80'	W91°	32.24'	1,298	E05°
	WEBSTER CITY	EBS	NDB	323.00	N42°	26.47'	W93°	52.15'		
	WEST UNION	XWY	NDB	278.00	N42°	56.63'	W91°	46.94'		
	ZILOM (LOM)	ZILO	NDB	341.00	N42°	19.37'	W90°	35.93'		
Kansas										
	ANTHONY	ANY	VOR	112.90	N37°	09.53'	W98°	10.24'	1,390	E10°
	ATWOOD	ADT	NDB	365.00	N39°	50.31'	W101°	02.70'		
	BABSY (LOM)	BABS	NDB	419.00	N38°	15.09'	W98°	51.35'		
	BEAR CREEK	JHN	NDB	341.00	N37°	38.13'	W101°	44.07'		
	BILOY (LOM/NDB)	BILO	NDB	521.00	N39°	07.22'	W95°	41.22'		
	BOYD	UKL	NDB	245.00	N38°	17.98'	W95°	43.30'		
	CAVALRY	CVY	NDB	314.00	N39°	01.56'	W96°	47.67'		
	CHANUTE	CNU	VOR	109.20	N37°	37.56'	W95°	35.60'	1,079	E05°
	CLAY CENTER	CYW	NDB	362.00	N39°	22.84'	W97°	09.67'		
	COFFEYVILLE	CFV	NDB	212.00	N37°	05.75'	W95°	34.43'		
	CONCORDIA	CNK	NDB	335.00	N39°	33.20'	W97°	39.06'		
	DODGE CITY	DDC	VOR	108.20	N37°	51.03'	W100°	00.33'	2,564	E11°
	DUSTT (LOM)	DUST	NDB	368.00	N38°	44.32'	W94°	53.51'		
	EL DORADO	EQA	NDB	383.00	N37°	46.76'	W96°	48.98'		
	ELKHART	EHA	NDB	377.00	N37°	00.06'	W101°	53.07'		
	EMPORIA	EMP	VOR	112.80	N38°	17.46'	W96°	08.28'	1,220	E08°
	FLORY (LOM)	FLOR	NDB	344.00	N38°	40.89'	W97°	38.70'		
	FORT RILEY	FRI	VOR	109.40	N38°	58.21'	W96°	51.66'	1,239	E06°
	FORT SCOTT	FSK	NDB	379.00	N37°	47.67'	W94°	45.91'		
	FUROR (LOM)	FURO	NDB	526.00	N38°	56.11'	W94°	44.25'		
	GARDEN CITY	GCK	VOR	113.30	N37°	55.14'	W100°	43.50'	2,879	E11°
	GOODLAND	GLD	VOR	115.10	N39°	23.27'	W101°	41.53'	3,650	E12°
	HARVS (LOM)	HARV	NDB	395.00	N38°	08.69'	W97°	16.56'		
	HAYS	HYS	VOR	110.40	N38°	50.85'	W99°	16.60'	2,020	E10°
	HERINGTON	HRU	NDB	407.00	N38°	41.56'	W96°	48.66'		
	HILL CITY	HLC	VOR	113.70	N39°	15.52'	W100°	13.55'	2,689	E11°
	HILYN	HIL	NDB	308.00	N38°	21.54'	W98°	54.17'		
	HUGOTON	HQG	NDB	365.00	N37°	09.81'	W101°	22.48'		
	HUTCHINSON	HUT	VOR	116.80	N37°	59.81'	W97°	56.04'	1,528	E09°
	INDEPENDENCE	IDP	NDB	400.00	N37°	09.60'	W95°	46.33'		
	JOHNSON CO	OJC	VOR	113.00	N38°	50.43'	W94°	44.20'	1,029	E06°
	LARNED	LQR	NDB	296.00	N38°	12.26'	W99°	05.25'		
	LIBERAL	LBL	VOR	112.30	N37°	02.66'	W100°	58.27'	2,889	E11°
	LYONS	LYO	NDB	386.00	N38°	20.83'	W98°	13.62'		
	MANHATTAN	MHK	VOR	110.20	N39°	08.72'	W96°	40.12'	1,059	E06°
	MANKATO	TKO	VOR	109.80	N39°	48.38'	W98°	15.60'	1,879	E10°
	MARYSVILLE	MYZ	NDB	341.00	N39°	51.16'	W96°	38.00'		
	MC DOWELL CREEK	MQD	NDB	391.00	N39°	07.04'	W96°	37.75'		
	MC PHERSON	MPR	NDB	227.00	N38°	20.90'	W97°	41.23'		
	MEADE	MEJ	NDB	389.00	N37°	17.05'	W100°	21.50'		
	MONARCH	MSB	NDB	410.00	N37°	47.48'	W95°	24.89'		
	MORRISON	DBX	NDB	212.00	N39°	45.70'	W97°	02.54'		
	NETTE (LOM)	NETT	NDB	374.00	N38°	46.16'	W99°	15.08'		
	NEWTON	EWK	NDB	281.00	N38°	03.84'	W97°	16.40'		
	NORGE (LOM)	NORG	NDB	517.00	N39°	03.66'	W94°	39.34'		
	NORTON	NRN	NDB	230.00	N39°	51.32'	W99°	53.34'		
	OAKLEY	OEL	NDB	380.00	N39°	06.75'	W100°	48.92'		
	OBERLIN	OIN	NDB	341.00	N39°	49.78'	W100°	32.25'		
	OSWEGO	OSW	VOR	117.60	N37°	09.45'	W95°	12.21'	928	E08°
	OTTAWA	OWI	NDB	251.00	N38°	32.55'	W95°	15.26'		
	PARSONS	PPF	NDB	293.00	N37°	20.28'	W95°	30.52'		
	PHILLIPSBURG	PHG	NDB	368.00	N39°	42.36'	W99°	17.30'		
	PICHE (LOM/NDB)	PICH	NDB	332.00	N37°	34.69'	W97°	27.34'		
	PIEVE (LOM/NDB)	PIEV	NDB	347.00	N37°	49.73'	W100°	43.46'		
	PITTSBURG	PTS	NDB	365.00	N37°	26.53'	W94°	43.59'		

State/Country	VOR/NDB Name	Ident.	Type	Freq.	Latitude		Longitude		Altitude	Mag Var
USA/CANADA NAVAIDS										
Kansas	PRATT	PTT	NDB	356.00	N37°	43.43'	W98°	44.82'		
	REPUBLICAN	RPB	NDB	414.00	N39°	48.79'	W97°	39.49'		
	RIPLY (LOM)	RIPL	NDB	326.00	N38°	53.09'	W95°	34.88'		
	RIVERSIDE	RIS	VOR	111.40	N39°	07.22'	W94°	35.79'	741	E05°
	SAINT FRANCIS	SYF	NDB	386.00	N39°	43.61'	W101°	45.89'		
	SALINA	SLN	VOR	117.10	N38°	55.58'	W97°	37.27'	1,315	E07°
	SALTT (LOM)	SALT	NDB	404.00	N38°	07.41'	W97°	55.60'		
	SAWCY (LOM)	SAWC	NDB	353.00	N37°	05.38'	W97°	02.18'		
	SCOTT CITY	TQK	NDB	256.00	N38°	28.81'	W100°	53.29'		
	SHUGR (LOM/NDB)	SHUG	NDB	414.00	N37°	17.63'	W101°	36.01'		
	STROTHER	SOR	VOR	109.60	N37°	10.24'	W97°	02.39'	1,161	E07°
	TOPEKA	TOP	VOR	117.80	N39°	08.22'	W95°	32.94'	1,069	E05°
	ULYSSES	ULS	NDB	395.00	N37°	35.85'	W101°	22.02'		
	WELLINGTON	EGT	NDB	414.00	N37°	19.43'	W97°	23.37'		
	WHEATFIELD	JDM	NDB	408.00	N39°	30.61'	W101°	02.89'		
	WICHITA	ICT	VOR	113.80	N37°	44.71'	W97°	35.02'	1,469	E07°
Kentucky	AIRBE (LOM/NDB)	AIRB	NDB	293.00	N36°	44.22'	W87°	24.83'		
	BARDSTOWN	BRY	NDB	248.00	N37°	50.86'	W85°	28.99'		
	BEAVER CREEK	BVQ	NDB	260.00	N37°	01.05'	W86°	00.54'		
	BLAYD (LOM/NDB)	BLAY	NDB	242.00	N37°	59.21'	W84°	39.60'		
	BOWLING GREEN	BWG	VOR	117.90	N36°	55.72'	W86°	26.60'	560	E02°
	BOWMAN	BQM	VOR	112.20	N38°	13.81'	W85°	39.88'	541	W01°
	CALLOWAY	CEY	NDB	348.00	N36°	39.78'	W88°	22.07'		
	CENTRAL CITY	CCT	VOR	109.80	N37°	22.94'	W87°	15.82'	478	W01°
	CLAWW (LOM/NDB)	CLAW	NDB	229.00	N38°	05.22'	W85°	45.44'		
	CUMBERLAND RIVER	CDX	NDB	388.00	N36°	59.77'	W84°	40.87'		
	CUNNINGHAM	CNG	VOR	113.10	N37°	00.51'	W88°	50.21'	478	E03°
	ELK SPRING	EKQ	NDB	290.00	N36°	51.37'	W84°	51.17'		
	FALMOUTH	FLM	VOR	117.00	N38°	38.96'	W84°	18.63'	810	W04°
	FARRINGTON	FIO	NDB	263.00	N36°	58.20'	W88°	34.03'		
	FLEMINGSBURG	FGX	NDB	400.00	N38°	32.28'	W83°	44.81'		
	FORT KNOX	FTK	VOR	109.60	N37°	54.44'	W85°	58.37'	741	W01°
	FRANKFORT	FFT	VOR	109.40	N38°	10.94'	W84°	54.51'	800	W03°
	GENEVA	GVA	NDB	224.00	N37°	48.21'	W87°	46.23'		
	GODMAN	GOI	NDB	396.00	N37°	57.52'	W85°	58.59'		
	GOODALL	DVK	NDB	311.00	N37°	34.58'	W84°	45.84'		
	HAZARD	AZQ	VOR	111.20	N37°	23.38'	W83°	15.97'	1,246	W04°
	HIGUY (LOM)	HIGU	NDB	341.00	N37°	38.13'	W87°	09.74'		
	HONEY GROVE	HIX	NDB	356.00	N36°	52.84'	W87°	20.25'		
	HUNTT (LOM)	HUNT	NDB	226.00	N38°	23.94'	W82°	39.24'		
	JETT	JET	NDB	365.00	N38°	12.90'	W84°	49.52'		
	LAANG (LOM)	LAAN	NDB	414.00	N38°	08.69'	W85°	37.99'		
	LEXINGTON	HYK	VOR	112.60	N37°	57.98'	W84°	28.34'	1,039	E00°
	LONDON	LOZ	VOR	116.10	N37°	01.98'	W84°	06.60'	1,249	W03°
	LOUISVILLE	IIU	VOR	114.80	N38°	06.21'	W85°	34.64'	718	E01°
	MAYFIELD	GGK	NDB	401.00	N36°	41.45'	W88°	35.54'		
	MOUNT STERLING	IOB	NDB	210.00	N38°	03.59'	W83°	58.89'		
	MUHLENBERG	GMH	NDB	362.00	N37°	13.62'	W87°	09.55'		
	MYSTIC	MYS	VOR	108.20	N37°	53.64'	W86°	14.67'	790	W01°
	NEW HOPE	EWO	VOR	110.80	N37°	37.90'	W85°	40.55'	961	E01°
	NEWCOMBE	ECB	VOR	110.40	N38°	09.50'	W82°	54.60'	1,069	W02°
	OWENSBORO	OWB	VOR	108.60	N37°	44.61'	W87°	09.95'	400	E01°
	SECO	XYC	NDB	393.00	N37°	45.48'	W84°	01.81'		
	SPRINGFIELD	IKY	NDB	429.00	N37°	38.07'	W85°	14.19'		
	TAYLOR CO	TYC	NDB	272.00	N37°	24.11'	W85°	14.61'		
	TRADEWATER	TWT	NDB	276.00	N37°	27.90'	W87°	56.91'		
	YORK	YRK	VOR	112.80	N38°	38.64'	W82°	58.70'	1,039	W05°
Louisiana	ACADI (LOM/NDB)	ACAD	NDB	269.00	N29°	57.37'	W91°	51.79'		
	ALEXANDRIA	AEX	VOR	116.10	N31°	15.39'	W92°	30.04'	78	E03°
	ANDRA (LOM)	ANDR	NDB	223.00	N31°	23.52'	W92°	10.92'		
	BASTROP	BQP	NDB	329.00	N32°	45.30'	W91°	53.00'		
	CAMPI (LOM/NDB)	CAMP	NDB	407.00	N31°	39.44'	W93°	04.65'		
	DOWNTOWN	DTN	VOR	108.60	N32°	32.39'	W93°	44.47'	180	E07°
	ELM GROVE	EMG	VOR	111.20	N32°	24.00'	W93°	35.70'	160	E07°
	ESLER	ESF	VOR	117.90	N31°	26.84'	W92°	19.31'	193	E04°
	GATOR	GUV	NDB	359.00	N31°	01.69'	W93°	11.09'		
	GRAND ISLE	GNI	NDB	236.00	N29°	11.51'	W90°	04.50'		
	HARVEY	HRV	VOR	112.40	N29°	51.01'	W90°	00.17'	0	E02°
	HODGE	JBL	NDB	256.00	N32°	12.07'	W92°	43.55'		
	HOMER	HMQ	NDB	212.00	N32°	47.40'	W93°	00.04'		
	HOUMA (LOM)	HOUM	NDB	219.00	N29°	39.79'	W90°	39.57'		
	LAKE PROVIDENCE	BLE	NDB	278.00	N32°	49.84'	W91°	11.40'		

State/Country	VOR/NDB Name	Ident.	Type	Freq.	Latitude		Longitude		Altitude	Mag Var
USA/CANADA NAVAIDS										
Louisiana	LEESVILLE	VED	NDB	247.00	N31°	06.14'	W93°	20.51'		
	LEEVILLE	LEV	VOR	113.50	N29°	10.51'	W90°	06.24'	3	E02°
	LINCOLN PARISH	LPZ	NDB	308.00	N32°	30.93'	W92°	37.64'		
	MANSFIELD	MSD	NDB	414.00	N32°	03.86'	W93°	45.86'		
	MANY	MMY	NDB	272.00	N31°	34.27'	W93°	32.49'		
	MARKSVILLE	MKV	NDB	347.00	N31°	05.72'	W92°	04.35'		
	MINDEN	MNE	NDB	201.00	N32°	38.47'	W93°	18.11'		
	MOLLY RIDGE	MRK	NDB	338.00	N32°	24.40'	W91°	46.35'		
	MONROE	MLU	VOR	117.20	N32°	31.01'	W92°	02.16'	78	E03°
	PATTERSON	PTN	NDB	245.00	N29°	42.87'	W91°	20.20'		
	POLK	FXU	VOR	108.40	N31°	06.69'	W93°	13.07'	314	E05°
	SABAR (LOM)	SABA	NDB	219.00	N32°	27.24'	W92°	06.25'		
	SHREVEPORT	SHV	VOR	117.40	N32°	46.28'	W93°	48.59'	190	E07°
	SPRINGHILL	SPH	NDB	375.00	N32°	58.99'	W93°	24.44'		
	TALLULAH	TTT	NDB	344.00	N32°	24.75'	W91°	09.01'		
	TIBBY	TBD	VOR	112.00	N29°	39.86'	W90°	49.74'	9	E02°
	TIGER PASS	VTP	NDB	253.00	N29°	16.30'	W89°	21.46'		
	VENICE	VEC	NDB	263.00	N29°	07.11'	W89°	12.33'		
	WHITE LAKE	LLA	VOR	111.40	N29°	39.79'	W92°	22.41'	39	E04°
	WINNFIELD	IFJ	NDB	402.00	N31°	57.77'	W92°	39.42'		
	ANGER (LOM)	ANGE	NDB	212.00	N30°	36.37'	W90°	25.27'		
	BATON ROUGE	BTR	VOR	116.50	N30°	29.10'	W91°	17.64'	19	E06°
	CARMA (LOM/NDB)	CARM	NDB	353.00	N30°	52.89'	W89°	51.72'		
	DE QUINCY	DQU	NDB	410.00	N30°	26.12'	W93°	28.00'		
	FLORENVILLE	FNA	NDB	371.00	N30°	24.93'	W89°	49.20'		
	HAMMOND	HMU	VOR	109.60	N30°	31.16'	W90°	25.05'	39	E03°
	HAZER (LOM)	HAZE	NDB	356.00	N30°	37.98'	W91°	29.36'		
	IDDER (LOM/NDB)	IDDE	NDB	385.00	N30°	45.12'	W93°	20.08'		
	KEYLI (LOM)	KEYL	NDB	353.00	N30°	11.58'	W93°	15.78'		
	KINTE (LOM/NDB)	KINT	NDB	338.00	N30°	01.51'	W90°	23.99'		
	LAFAYETTE	LFT	VOR	109.80	N30°	11.62'	W91°	59.55'	39	E03°
	LAFFS (LOM)	LAFF	NDB	375.00	N30°	17.35'	W91°	54.47'		
	LAKE CHARLES	LCH	VOR	113.40	N30°	08.49'	W93°	06.33'	19	E07°
	MOSSY (LOM)	MOSS	NDB	418.00	N30°	18.39'	W93°	11.77'		
	NEW ORLEANS	MSY	VOR	113.20	N30°	01.79'	W90°	10.33'	0	E02°
	RUNDI (LOM)	RUND	NDB	284.00	N30°	34.97'	W91°	12.66'		
	SAINT LANDRY	OPL	NDB	335.00	N30°	39.32'	W92°	05.90'		
	SLIDELL	DEF	NDB	256.00	N30°	17.81'	W89°	50.04'		
Maine										
	AUGUSTA	AUG	VOR	111.40	N44°	19.20'	W69°	47.79'	350	W18°
	BANGOR	BGR	VOR	114.80	N44°	50.50'	W68°	52.43'	360	W19°
	BELFAST	BST	NDB	278.00	N44°	24.66'	W69°	00.64'		
	BRACY (LOM/NDB)	BRAC	NDB	399.00	N44°	27.61'	W69°	44.09'		
	BURNHAM	BUP	NDB	348.00	N44°	41.83'	W69°	21.46'		
	DUNNS (LOM)	DUNN	NDB	366.00	N44°	24.65'	W69°	51.64'		
	EASTPORT	EPM	NDB	260.00	N44°	54.75'	W67°	00.73'		
	EXCAL (LOM)	EXCA	NDB	278.00	N46°	36.61'	W68°	01.12'		
	FRENCHVILLE	FVE	NDB	257.00	N47°	16.08'	W68°	15.40'		
	HOULTON	HUL	VOR	116.10	N46°	02.37'	W67°	50.04'	859	W21°
	KENNEBUNK	ENE	VOR	117.10	N43°	25.54'	W70°	36.81'	190	W17°
	LEWIE (LOM)	LEWI	NDB	240.00	N43°	57.82'	W70°	20.14'		
	LINCOLN	LRG	NDB	216.00	N45°	21.38'	W68°	32.21'		
	MACHIAS	MVM	NDB	251.00	N44°	42.27'	W67°	28.69'		
	MILLINOCKET	MLT	VOR	117.90	N45°	35.20'	W68°	30.92'	551	W20°
	MILNOT	LNT	NDB	344.00	N45°	38.91'	W68°	33.01'		
	OLD TOWN	OLD	NDB	272.00	N45°	00.40'	W68°	38.00'		
	ORHAM (LOM)	ORHA	NDB	394.00	N43°	39.14'	W70°	26.46'		
	PRESQUE ISLE	PQI	VOR	116.40	N46°	46.45'	W68°	05.67'	590	W21°
	PRINCETON	PNN	VOR	114.30	N45°	19.75'	W67°	42.25'	400	W21°
	RANGELEY	RQM	NDB	221.00	N44°	56.07'	W70°	45.06'		
	ROLLINS	ESG	NDB	260.00	N43°	13.20'	W70°	49.69'		
	SANFD (LOM)	SANF	NDB	349.00	N43°	20.06'	W70°	50.05'		
	SEBAGO	SZO	NDB	227.00	N43°	54.25'	W70°	46.93'		
	SPRUCEHEAD	SUH	NDB	356.00	N43°	59.86'	W69°	07.05'		
	SQUAW	XQA	NDB	236.00	N45°	31.30'	W69°	40.46'		
	SURRY (LOM/NDB)	SURR	NDB	330.00	N44°	32.33'	W68°	18.42'		
	TOTTE (LOM)	TOTT	NDB	227.00	N44°	43.65'	W68°	42.77'		
	WISCASSET	ISS	NDB	407.00	N43°	58.95'	W69°	38.42'		
Maryland										
	ABERDEEN	APG	NDB	349.00	N39°	32.10'	W76°	06.37'		
	ANDREWS	ADW	VOR	113.10	N38°	48.43'	W76°	51.97'	259	W07°
	BALTIMORE	BAL	VOR	115.10	N39°	10.26'	W76°	39.67'	141	W08°
	CAMBRIDGE	CGE	NDB	257.00	N38°	32.29'	W76°	01.91'		
	COLBE (LOM)	COLB	NDB	278.00	N38°	16.72'	W75°	24.34'		

State/Country	VOR/NDB Name	Ident.	Type	Freq.	Latitude		Longitude		Altitude	Mag Var
USA/CANADA NAVAIDS										
Maryland	CUMBERLAND	CBE	NDB	317.00	N39°	38.88'	W78°	44.84'		
	DAVEE (LOM)	DAVE	NDB	223.00	N38°	39.69'	W77°	06.61'		
	EASTON	ESN	NDB	212.00	N38°	48.28'	W76°	04.16'		
	ELLICOTT	FND	NDB	371.00	N39°	17.24'	W76°	46.62'		
	FORT MEADE	FME	NDB	353.00	N39°	05.07'	W76°	45.59'		
	FREDERICK	FDK	VOR	109.00	N39°	24.73'	W77°	22.50'	298	W08°
	GAITHERSBURG	GAI	NDB	385.00	N39°	10.07'	W77°	09.81'		
	GRANTSVILLE	GRV	VOR	112.30	N39°	38.10'	W79°	03.03'	2,640	W06°
	HAGERSTOWN	HGR	VOR	109.80	N39°	41.86'	W77°	51.34'	560	W07°
	INSTITUTE	IUB	NDB	404.00	N39°	17.22'	W76°	37.51'		
	JEANS (LOM)	JEAN	NDB	219.00	N39°	10.76'	W76°	46.15'		
	KIRBY (LOM)	KIRB	NDB	360.00	N38°	42.04'	W76°	52.21'		
	LANDY (LOM/NDB)	LAND	NDB	407.00	N38°	21.75'	W75°	11.97'		
	MARTIN	MTN	NDB	342.00	N39°	17.98'	W76°	22.80'		
	NOLIN (LOM)	NOLI	NDB	278.00	N39°	43.64'	W77°	35.44'		
	NOTTINGHAM	OTT	VOR	113.70	N38°	42.35'	W76°	44.68'	209	W10°
	OXONN (LOM/NDB)	OXON	NDB	332.00	N38°	45.96'	W77°	01.59'		
	PATUXENT	PXT	VOR	117.60	N38°	17.26'	W76°	24.01'	19	W10°
	PATUXENT RIVER	NHK	NDB	400.00	N38°	17.15'	W76°	24.18'		
	PHILLIPS	PPM	VOR	108.40	N39°	28.00'	W76°	10.27'	39	W09°
	SALISBURY	SBY	VOR	111.20	N38°	20.70'	W75°	30.63'	49	W08°
	SNOW HILL	SWL	VOR	112.40	N38°	03.39'	W75°	27.83'	39	W08°
	WESTMINSTER	EMI	VOR	117.90	N39°	29.70'	W76°	58.71'	819	W08°
	ZOOTE (LOM)	ZOOT	NDB	232.00	N38°	55.17'	W76°	52.28'		
Massachusetts	BARNES	BAF	VOR	113.00	N42°	09.71'	W72°	42.97'	268	W14°
	BEDDS (LOM)	BEDD	NDB	332.00	N42°	28.79'	W71°	23.31'		
	BOGEY (LOM)	BOGE	NDB	342.00	N41°	42.96'	W70°	12.17'		
	BOSTON	BOS	VOR	112.70	N42°	21.44'	W70°	59.37'	19	W16°
	CHESTER	CTR	VOR	115.10	N42°	17.47'	W72°	56.96'	1,600	W13°
	CROW HILL	CLY	NDB	392.00	N42°	15.80'	W71°	46.70'		
	DALTON	DXT	NDB	370.00	N42°	28.25'	W73°	10.21'		
	DICKINSON	DKO	NDB	352.00	N42°	38.76'	W71°	43.61'		
	DUNCA (LOM)	DUNC	NDB	279.00	N42°	16.46'	W71°	01.19'		
	FALL RIVER	FLR	NDB	406.00	N41°	45.33'	W71°	06.72'		
	FITCHBURG	FIT	NDB	365.00	N42°	33.05'	W71°	45.42'		
	GARDNER	GDM	VOR	110.60	N42°	32.75'	W72°	03.49'	1,279	W14°
	GREAT BARRINGTON	GBR	NDB	395.00	N42°	10.97'	W73°	24.24'		
	HAGET (LOM)	HAGE	NDB	402.00	N42°	38.64'	W71°	11.83'		
	HULLZ (LOM)	HULL	NDB	346.00	N42°	18.18'	W70°	55.31'		
	LAWRENCE	LWM	VOR	112.50	N42°	44.42'	W71°	05.68'	298	W15°
	LYNDY (LOM/NDB)	LYND	NDB	382.00	N42°	27.12'	W70°	57.79'		
	MANSFIELD	IHM	NDB	220.00	N42°	00.16'	W71°	11.82'		
	MARCONI	LFV	VOR	114.70	N42°	01.03'	W70°	02.23'	150	W16°
	MARSHFIELD	IMR	NDB	368.00	N42°	05.87'	W70°	40.51'		
	MARTHAS VINEYARD	MVY	VOR	114.50	N41°	23.77'	W70°	36.76'	59	W15°
	MILTT (LOM)	MILT	NDB	375.00	N42°	16.42'	W71°	02.94'		
	NANTUCKET	ACK	VOR	116.20	N41°	16.91'	W70°	01.60'	98	W15°
	NANTUCKET	TUK	NDB	194.00	N41°	16.11'	W70°	10.79'		
	NAUSET	CQX	NDB	279.00	N41°	41.50'	W69°	59.38'		
	NEFOR (LOM)	NEFO	NDB	274.00	N41°	37.29'	W71°	01.05'		
	ORANGE	ORE	NDB	205.00	N42°	33.63'	W72°	12.07'		
	OTIS (LOM)	OTIS	NDB	362.00	N41°	43.96'	W70°	26.45'		
	PALMER	PMX	NDB	212.00	N42°	13.57'	W72°	18.68'		
	PLYMOUTH	FFF	NDB	257.00	N41°	50.84'	W70°	48.16'		
	PROVINCETOWN	PVC	NDB	389.00	N42°	04.13'	W70°	13.41'		
	SHAKER HILL	SKR	NDB	251.00	N42°	27.34'	W71°	10.71'		
	STOGE (LOM)	STOG	NDB	397.00	N42°	07.18'	W71°	07.70'		
	TAUNTON	TAN	NDB	227.00	N41°	52.58'	W71°	01.01'		
	TOPSFIELD	TOF	NDB	269.00	N42°	37.15'	W70°	57.40'		
	WAIVS (LOM)	WAIV	NDB	248.00	N41°	18.67'	W69°	59.20'		
	WESIE (LOM)	WESI	NDB	230.00	N42°	14.90'	W72°	41.77'		
	WESTOVER	CEF	VOR	114.00	N42°	11.85'	W72°	31.57'	245	W14°
Mexico	CHIHUAHUA	CUU	VOR	114.10	N28°	48.49'	W105°	57.49'		E10°
	CIUDAD JUAREZ	CJS	VOR	116.70	N31°	38.16'	W106°	25.58'		E10°
	DEL NORTE	ADN	VOR	115.40	N25°	51.90'	W100°	14.31'		E07°
	DELICIAS	DEL	VOR	113.50	N28°	13.00'	W105°	26.99'		E11°
	HERMOSILLO	HMO	VOR	112.80	N29°	05.71'	W111°	02.93'		E11°
	MATAMOROS	MAM	VOR	114.30	N25°	46.25'	W97°	31.43'		E07°
	MONTERREY	MTY	VOR	114.70	N25°	46.39'	W100°	06.10'		E09°
	NUEVO LAREDO	NLD	VOR	112.60	N27°	26.00'	W99°	34.00'		E09°
	TIJUANA	TIJ	VOR	116.50	N32°	32.06'	W116°	57.03'		E14°

State/Country	VOR/NDB Name	Ident.	Type	Freq.	Latitude		Longitude		Altitude	Mag Var
USA/CANADA NAVAIDS										
Michigan										
	ADRIAN	ADG	NDB	278.00	N41°	52.19'	W84°	04.51'		
	ALMA	AMN	NDB	329.00	N43°	19.40'	W84°	47.11'		
	ALPENA	APN	VOR	108.80	N45°	04.96'	W83°	33.41'	678	W07°
	ALPINE	ALV	NDB	375.00	N45°	00.87'	W84°	48.48'		
	ARTDA (LOM)	ARTD	NDB	206.00	N42°	46.65'	W84°	29.85'		
	AU SABLE	ASP	VOR	116.10	N44°	26.82'	W83°	24.07'	619	W07°
	AUSTN (LOM)	AUST	NDB	371.00	N42°	07.86'	W85°	31.78'		
	BAD AXE	BAX	VOR	108.20	N43°	46.96'	W82°	59.03'	754	W05°
	BATOL (LOM/NDB)	BATO	NDB	272.00	N42°	21.71'	W85°	11.06'		
	BATTLE CREEK	BTL	VOR	109.40	N42°	18.58'	W85°	15.13'	928	W02°
	BERZ	UIZ	NDB	215.00	N42°	39.68'	W82°	57.92'		
	BOYNE FALLS	BFA	NDB	263.00	N45°	10.00'	W84°	55.31'		
	BROWNE	HYX	NDB	385.00	N43°	25.89'	W83°	51.49'		
	CADILLAC	CAD	NDB	269.00	N44°	16.49'	W85°	24.85'		
	CARGL (LOM/NDB)	CARG	NDB	230.00	N42°	21.37'	W82°	57.25'		
	CARLETON	CRL	VOR	115.70	N42°	02.88'	W83°	27.45'	629	W03°
	CHARLEVOIX	CVX	NDB	222.00	N45°	18.18'	W85°	15.88'		
	CLAM LAKE	CXK	NDB	251.00	N44°	53.96'	W85°	14.37'		
	DECKERVILLE	DQV	NDB	378.00	N43°	34.58'	W82°	39.16'		
	DETROIT	DXO	VOR	113.40	N42°	12.78'	W83°	22.00'	636	W06°
	DRUMMOND ISLAND	DRM	NDB	218.00	N46°	00.43'	W83°	44.53'		
	ESCANABA	ESC	VOR	110.80	N45°	43.35'	W87°	05.37'	600	E00°
	FELPS (LOM)	FELP	NDB	206.00	N44°	57.64'	W83°	33.60'		
	FLINT	FNT	VOR	116.90	N42°	57.96'	W83°	44.46'	770	W03°
	GALEY (LOM/NDB)	GALE	NDB	275.00	N47°	06.94'	W88°	24.07'		
	GAYLORD	GLR	VOR	109.20	N45°	00.75'	W84°	42.24'	1,318	W04°
	GRAND RAPIDS	GRR	VOR	110.20	N42°	47.20'	W85°	29.82'	800	W01°
	GRAYLING	CGG	VOR	109.80	N44°	40.89'	W84°	43.73'	1,151	W05°
	GRAYLING	GYG	NDB	359.00	N44°	44.99'	W84°	49.69'		
	GROS CAP	A	NDB	286.00	N46°	30.73'	W84°	36.90'		
	GROSSE ILE	RYS	NDB	419.00	N42°	06.06'	W83°	09.17'		
	GWENN (LOM/NDB)	GWEN	NDB	365.00	N44°	44.07'	W85°	25.75'		
	HARDWOOD	BHW	NDB	236.00	N44°	14.91'	W84°	05.03'		
	HOLLAND	HLM	NDB	233.00	N42°	47.80'	W86°	09.46'		
	HOUGHTON	CMX	VOR	112.80	N47°	10.03'	W88°	28.90'	1,069	W02°
	HOUGHTON LAKE	HTL	VOR	111.60	N44°	21.53'	W84°	39.94'	1,144	W05°
	HOWELL	OZW	NDB	242.00	N42°	38.03'	W83°	59.26'		
	IRON MOUNTAIN	IMT	VOR	111.20	N45°	48.96'	W88°	06.72'	1,128	W02°
	IRONWOOD	IWD	VOR	108.80	N46°	31.93'	W90°	07.54'	1,229	E01°
	JACKSON	JXN	VOR	109.60	N42°	15.55'	W84°	27.51'	1,000	W05°
	JAKSO (LOM)	JAKS	NDB	212.00	N42°	19.06'	W84°	21.93'		
	K I SAWYER	SAW	VOR	116.30	N46°	21.91'	W87°	23.39'	1,170	W03°
	KALAMAZOO	AZO	VOR	109.00	N42°	14.22'	W85°	33.19'	869	W01°
	KEELER	ELX	VOR	116.60	N42°	08.66'	W86°	07.35'	793	E00°
	KNOBS (LOM)	KNOB	NDB	263.00	N42°	53.74'	W85°	22.71'		
	KOLOE (LOM/NDB)	KOLO	NDB	400.00	N46°	19.93'	W84°	32.52'		
	LANSING	LAN	VOR	110.80	N42°	43.04'	W84°	41.86'	879	W05°
	LITCHFIELD	LFD	VOR	111.20	N42°	03.74'	W84°	45.90'	1,039	W01°
	LUDINGTON	LDM	NDB	341.00	N43°	57.79'	W86°	24.57'		
	MADDS (LOM)	MADD	NDB	338.00	N42°	29.68'	W83°	05.59'		
	MALLY (LOM)	MALL	NDB	397.00	N42°	07.60'	W86°	18.80'		
	MANISTEE	MBL	VOR	111.40	N44°	16.32'	W86°	13.77'	619	W01°
	MARQUETTE	MQT	VOR	116.80	N46°	31.73'	W87°	35.12'	1,449	W02°
	MENOMINEE	MNM	VOR	109.60	N45°	10.80'	W87°	38.83'	649	E00°
	MOUNT PLEASANT	MOP	VOR	110.60	N43°	37.40'	W84°	44.70'	760	W02°
	MUSKEGON	MKG	VOR	115.20	N43°	10.15'	W86°	02.36'	659	W01°
	MUSKO (LOM)	MUSK	NDB	219.00	N43°	07.26'	W86°	10.11'		
	NEWBERRY	ERY	VOR	108.20	N46°	18.76'	W85°	27.85'	869	W06°
	OLSTE (LOM)	OLST	NDB	257.00	N43°	27.69'	W84°	10.78'		
	ONTONAGON	OGM	NDB	375.00	N46°	51.01'	W89°	21.90'		
	PECK	ECK	VOR	114.00	N43°	15.35'	W82°	43.07'	810	W07°
	PELLSTON	PLN	VOR	111.80	N45°	37.83'	W84°	39.84'	839	W06°
	PETLI (LOM)	PETL	NDB	269.00	N42°	58.08'	W83°	53.40'		
	PHURN (LOM)	PHUR	NDB	332.00	N42°	50.57'	W82°	35.80'		
	PONTIAC	PSI	VOR	111.00	N42°	42.01'	W83°	31.96'	1,151	W03°
	PULLMAN	PMM	VOR	112.10	N42°	27.92'	W86°	06.35'	639	E00°
	REVUP (LOM)	REVU	NDB	388.00	N42°	07.19'	W83°	25.90'		
	ROGERS CITY	PZQ	NDB	215.00	N45°	24.28'	W83°	49.21'		
	SAGINAW	MBS	VOR	112.90	N43°	31.89'	W84°	04.63'	669	W03°
	SALEM	SVM	VOR	114.30	N42°	24.53'	W83°	35.65'	951	W03°
	SAULT STE MARIE	SSM	VOR	112.20	N46°	24.72'	W84°	18.89'	688	W04°
	SCHOOLCRAFT CO	ISQ	VOR	110.40	N45°	58.59'	W86°	10.44'	678	W01°
	SPENC (LOM)	SPEN	NDB	223.00	N42°	13.19'	W83°	12.20'		

State/Country	VOR/NDB Name	Ident.	Type	Freq.	Latitude		Longitude		Altitude	Mag Var
USA/CANADA NAVAIDS										
Michigan	ST JAMES	SJX	NDB	382.00	N45°	41.60'	W85°	33.51'		
	STURGIS	IRS	NDB	382.00	N41°	48.78'	W85°	26.02'		
	TECUMSEH	TCU	NDB	239.00	N42°	02.16'	W83°	52.83'		
	THREE RIVERS	HAI	NDB	407.00	N41°	57.50'	W85°	35.50'		
	TRAVERSE CITY	TVC	VOR	114.60	N44°	40.07'	W85°	32.99'	908	W02°
	WATERSMEET	RXW	NDB	407.00	N46°	17.29'	W89°	16.72'		
	WEST BRANCH	BXZ	VOR	113.20	N44°	14.55'	W84°	11.00'	803	W06°
	WHITE CLOUD	HIC	VOR	117.60	N43°	34.49'	W85°	42.97'	918	W01°
	WIGGINS	GDW	NDB	209.00	N43°	58.20'	W84°	28.49'		
	YIPPS (LOM)	YIPP	NDB	359.00	N42°	10.45'	W83°	37.29'		
Midway (US)	MIDWAY	NQM	VOR	114.60	N28°	12.01'	W177°	22.86'	13	E09°
Minnesota	AITKIN	AIT	NDB	397.00	N46°	32.84'	W93°	40.51'		
	ALBERT LEA	AEL	VOR	109.80	N43°	40.99'	W93°	22.14'	1,252	E05°
	ALEXANDRIA	AXN	VOR	112.80	N45°	57.50'	W95°	13.95'	1,380	E07°
	ANDRI	AJW	NDB	281.00	N45°	47.50'	W95°	18.32'		
	APPLETON	AQP	NDB	356.00	N45°	13.70'	W96°	00.57'		
	AUSTIN	JAY	VOR	108.20	N43°	34.57'	W92°	55.17'	1,233	E03°
	BABCO (LOM)	BABC	NDB	385.00	N44°	51.40'	W92°	59.06'		
	BAUDETTE	BDE	VOR	111.60	N48°	43.36'	W94°	36.43'	1,079	E04°
	BEMIDJI	BJI	VOR	108.60	N47°	34.55'	W95°	01.48'	1,410	E04°
	BENSON	BBB	NDB	239.00	N45°	19.63'	W95°	39.01'		
	BLUE EARTH	SBU	NDB	332.00	N43°	35.82'	W94°	05.81'		
	BRAINERD	BRD	VOR	116.90	N46°	20.89'	W94°	01.56'	1,249	E06°
	BRECKENRIDGE-WAHP	BWP	NDB	233.00	N46°	14.69'	W96°	36.21'		
	BUNAN (LOM)	BUNA	NDB	371.00	N47°	26.69'	W94°	50.10'		
	CALEDONIA	CHU	NDB	209.00	N43°	35.21'	W91°	29.42'		
	CAMBRIDGE	CBG	NDB	350.00	N45°	33.44'	W93°	15.73'		
	CLOQUET	COQ	NDB	335.00	N46°	41.82'	W92°	30.19'		
	COOK	CQM	NDB	233.00	N47°	49.26'	W92°	41.47'		
	COOK CO	CKC	NDB	358.00	N47°	50.40'	W90°	23.13'		
	CROOKSTON	CKN	NDB	400.00	N47°	50.36'	W96°	36.95'		
	DARWIN	DWN	VOR	109.00	N45°	05.24'	W94°	27.23'	1,128	E07°
	DAWSON-MADISON	DXX	NDB	227.00	N44°	59.04'	W96°	10.75'		
	DETROIT LAKES	DTL	VOR	111.20	N46°	49.53'	W95°	52.91'	1,390	E05°
	DULUTH	DLH	VOR	112.60	N46°	48.12'	W92°	12.17'	1,430	E05°
	ELY	ELO	VOR	109.60	N47°	49.31'	W91°	49.80'	1,489	E04°
	EVELETH	EVM	VOR	108.20	N47°	25.46'	W92°	30.11'	1,380	E05°
	FAIRMONT	FRM	VOR	110.20	N43°	38.75'	W94°	25.35'	1,161	E07°
	FARMINGTON	FGT	VOR	115.70	N44°	37.85'	W93°	10.92'	928	E06°
	FERGUS FALLS	FFM	VOR	110.40	N46°	17.35'	W96°	09.40'	1,190	E05°
	FERGUS FALLS MUNI	FFM	NDB	111.50	N46°	17.44'	W96°	09.87'		
	FLYING CLOUD	FCM	VOR	111.80	N44°	49.54'	W93°	27.40'	898	E06°
	FOSSTON	FSE	NDB	224.00	N47°	35.38'	W95°	46.18'		
	GALEX (LOM)	GALE	NDB	272.00	N47°	07.81'	W93°	28.88'		
	GLENWOOD	GHW	NDB	346.00	N45°	38.65'	W95°	19.10'		
	GOPHER	GEP	VOR	117.30	N45°	08.74'	W93°	22.39'	879	E06°
	GRAND RAPIDS	GPZ	VOR	111.40	N47°	09.81'	W93°	29.31'	1,400	E06°
	HALFWAY	FOW	VOR	111.20	N44°	12.26'	W93°	22.23'	1,098	E06°
	HAMRE (LOM)	HAMR	NDB	337.00	N46°	13.23'	W96°	03.41'		
	HARVI (LOM)	HARV	NDB	260.00	N48°	00.40'	W96°	05.74'		
	HIBBING	HIB	VOR	110.80	N47°	18.09'	W92°	42.24'	1,348	E05°
	HOPEY	PPI	NDB	400.00	N44°	52.38'	W92°	56.53'		
	HUMBOLDT	HML	VOR	112.40	N48°	52.15'	W97°	07.02'	800	E09°
	HUSSK (LOM)	HUSS	NDB	342.00	N45°	28.72'	W93°	58.14'		
	HUTCHINSON	HCD	NDB	209.00	N44°	51.41'	W94°	22.99'		
	INTL FALLS	INL	VOR	111.00	N48°	33.94'	W93°	24.34'	1,180	E06°
	JACKSON	MJQ	NDB	353.00	N43°	38.83'	W94°	59.16'		
	LAREW (LOM)	LARE	NDB	251.00	N46°	27.39'	W94°	01.35'		
	LITTLE FALLS	LXL	NDB	359.00	N45°	56.99'	W94°	20.49'		
	MANKATO	MKT	VOR	110.80	N44°	13.19'	W93°	54.74'	1,020	E07°
	MARSHALL	MML	VOR	111.00	N44°	26.90'	W95°	49.48'	1,180	E08°
	MINGO (LOM)	MING	NDB	329.00	N43°	51.30'	W92°	24.64'		
	MINNEAPOLIS	MSP	VOR	115.30	N44°	52.91'	W93°	13.99'	849	E03°
	MONTEVIDEO	MVE	VOR	111.60	N44°	58.36'	W95°	42.71'	1,033	E05°
	MOOSE LAKE	MZH	NDB	362.00	N46°	24.96'	W92°	48.26'		
	MORA	JMR	NDB	327.00	N45°	53.41'	W93°	16.08'		
	MORRIS	MOX	VOR	109.60	N45°	33.94'	W95°	58.15'	1,131	E05°
	NARCO (LOM/NDB)	NARC	NDB	266.00	N44°	49.54'	W93°	05.48'		
	NEW ULM	ULM	NDB	272.00	N44°	19.07'	W94°	29.88'		
	NODINE	ODI	VOR	117.90	N43°	54.74'	W91°	28.05'	1,279	E04°
	ORR	ORB	NDB	341.00	N48°	01.12'	W92°	51.69'		
	ORTONVILLE	VVV	NDB	332.00	N45°	18.09'	W96°	25.28'		

State/Country	VOR/NDB Name	Ident.	Type	Freq.	Latitude		Longitude		Altitude	Mag Var
USA/CANADA NAVAIDS										
Minnesota	PARK RAPIDS	PKD	VOR	110.60	N46°	53.89'	W95°	04.25'	1,439	E04°
	PINEY PINECREEK	PFT	NDB	342.00	N48°	59.60'	W95°	58.64'		
	PIPESTONE	PQN	NDB	284.00	N43°	59.16'	W96°	17.78'		
	PRINCETON	PNM	NDB	368.00	N45°	33.87'	W93°	36.45'		
	PYKLA (LOM/NDB)	PYKL	NDB	379.00	N46°	50.74'	W92°	21.30'		
	RAIZE (LOM/NDB)	RAIZ	NDB	353.00	N48°	28.88'	W93°	16.68'		
	RED WING	RGK	NDB	248.00	N44°	35.33'	W92°	29.52'		
	REDWOOD FALLS	RWF	VOR	113.30	N44°	28.03'	W95°	07.70'	1,059	E07°
	RIPLEY	XCR	NDB	404.00	N46°	04.71'	W94°	20.59'		
	ROADD (LOM)	ROAD	NDB	360.00	N48°	51.72'	W95°	14.55'		
	ROCHESTER	RST	VOR	112.00	N43°	46.97'	W92°	35.81'	1,380	E05°
	ROSEAU	ROX	VOR	108.80	N48°	51.28'	W95°	41.69'	1,059	E05°
	SCOTT	SCG	NDB	385.00	N48°	15.59'	W92°	28.47'		
	SILVER BAY	BFW	NDB	350.00	N47°	15.03'	W91°	24.84'		
	SPIDA (LOM/NDB)	SPID	NDB	269.00	N46°	50.04'	W94°	58.51'		
	ST CLOUD	STC	VOR	112.10	N45°	32.46'	W94°	03.45'	1,020	E06°
	STAPLES	SAZ	NDB	257.00	N46°	22.93'	W94°	48.29'		
	THIEF RIVER FALLS	TVF	VOR	108.40	N48°	04.16'	W96°	11.18'	1,108	E08°
	TWO HARBORS	TWM	NDB	243.00	N47°	03.13'	W91°	44.67'		
	VAGEY (LOM)	VAGE	NDB	338.00	N44°	49.44'	W93°	18.36'		
	WASECA	ACQ	NDB	371.00	N44°	04.21'	W93°	33.14'		
	WHEATON	ETH	NDB	326.00	N45°	46.99'	W96°	32.81'		
	WILLMAR	ILL	VOR	113.70	N45°	07.05'	W95°	05.43'	1,118	E05°
	WINDOM	MWM	NDB	203.00	N43°	54.56'	W95°	06.54'		
	WINONA	ONA	VOR	111.40	N44°	04.57'	W91°	42.34'	649	E03°
	WONDD (LOM)	WOND	NDB	277.00	N43°	36.96'	W95°	27.67'		
	WORTHINGTON	OTG	VOR	110.60	N43°	38.81'	W95°	34.91'	1,571	E08°
Mississippi										
	ALLEN (LOM)	ALLE	NDB	365.00	N32°	24.75'	W90°	07.17'		
	BAYOU (LOM)	BAYO	NDB	360.00	N30°	29.12'	W89°	09.71'		
	BIGBEE	IGB	VOR	116.20	N33°	29.12'	W88°	30.81'	239	E04°
	BRENZ (LOM/NDB)	BREN	NDB	260.00	N32°	24.78'	W90°	15.67'		
	BROOKHAVEN	BVV	NDB	407.00	N31°	36.47'	W90°	24.61'		
	BROOKLEY	BFM	VOR	112.80	N30°	36.76'	W88°	03.33'	9	E04°
	BRYAN	STF	NDB	281.00	N33°	25.92'	W88°	51.02'		
	CALEDONIA	CBM	VOR	115.20	N33°	38.49'	W88°	26.31'	219	E04°
	CHOCTAW	BCZ	NDB	228.00	N32°	06.85'	W88°	07.28'		
	CLARKSDALE	CKM	NDB	341.00	N34°	17.58'	W90°	30.94'		
	CORINTH	CRX	NDB	338.00	N34°	54.79'	W88°	36.05'		
	EATON	LBY	VOR	110.60	N31°	25.11'	W89°	20.25'	288	E05°
	ELVIS (LOM/NDB)	ELVI	NDB	371.00	N34°	57.21'	W89°	58.42'		
	FERNI (LOM/NDB)	FERN	NDB	413.00	N31°	15.27'	W90°	30.62'		
	FOXWORTH	FOH	NDB	331.00	N31°	17.76'	W89°	49.11'		
	GREENVILLE	GLH	VOR	110.20	N33°	31.41'	W90°	58.97'	131	E04°
	GULFPORT	GPT	VOR	109.00	N30°	24.40'	W89°	04.60'	19	E02°
	HANCO	AYI	NDB	221.00	N30°	27.06'	W89°	27.32'		
	HOLLY SPRINGS	HLI	VOR	112.40	N34°	46.21'	W89°	29.78'	629	E03°
	INDIANOLA	IDL	NDB	284.00	N33°	28.81'	W90°	40.53'		
	JACKSON	JAN	VOR	112.60	N32°	30.44'	W90°	10.05'	360	E05°
	KEWANEE	EWA	VOR	113.80	N32°	22.00'	W88°	27.50'	298	E04°
	KOSCIUSKO	OSX	NDB	269.00	N33°	05.45'	W89°	32.42'		
	LOUISVILLE	LMS	NDB	212.00	N33°	08.62'	W89°	03.65'		
	MARENGO	RZO	NDB	391.00	N32°	24.85'	W88°	00.91'		
	MARKS	MMS	NDB	391.00	N34°	13.97'	W90°	17.38'		
	MC COMB	MCB	VOR	116.70	N31°	18.26'	W90°	15.49'	439	E03°
	MERIDIAN	MEI	VOR	117.00	N32°	22.70'	W88°	48.25'	580	E05°
	METCALF	MTQ	NDB	359.00	N33°	25.52'	W90°	58.92'		
	NATCHEZ	HEZ	VOR	110.00	N31°	37.09'	W91°	17.97'	278	E03°
	NATCHEZ-ADAMS CO	HAH	NDB	388.00	N31°	41.41'	W91°	17.59'		
	OLIVE BRANCH	OLV	NDB	275.00	N34°	58.77'	W89°	47.40'		
	PHILADELPHIA	MPE	NDB	219.00	N32°	47.91'	W89°	07.47'		
	PICAYUNE	PCU	VOR	112.20	N30°	33.67'	W89°	43.82'	68	E05°
	PRENTISS	PJR	NDB	252.00	N31°	35.77'	W89°	54.30'		
	RAYMOND	RYB	NDB	375.00	N32°	18.09'	W90°	24.68'		
	RENOVA	RNV	NDB	272.00	N33°	48.42'	W90°	45.75'		
	SAVOY (LOM/NDB)	SAVO	NDB	356.00	N32°	14.83'	W88°	46.29'		
	SCOBEY	SBQ	NDB	245.00	N33°	53.47'	W89°	52.47'		
	SEMMES	SJI	VOR	115.30	N30°	43.56'	W88°	21.55'	190	E05°
	SIDON	SQS	VOR	114.70	N33°	27.83'	W90°	16.64'	124	E03°
	TALLAHALA	THJ	NDB	346.00	N31°	41.25'	W89°	11.38'		
	TEOCK (LOM)	TEOC	NDB	349.00	N33°	35.51'	W90°	05.06'		
	TUNNG (LOM)	TUNN	NDB	426.00	N34°	23.09'	W89°	37.56'		
	TUPELO	TUP	VOR	109.80	N34°	13.43'	W88°	47.84'	360	E04°
	VERON (LOM)	VERO	NDB	420.00	N34°	10.81'	W88°	46.12'		

State/Country	VOR/NDB Name	Ident.	Type	Freq.	Latitude		Longitude		Altitude	Mag Var
USA/CANADA NAVAIDS										
Mississippi	VICKSBURG	VKS	NDB	382.00	N32°	13.97'	W90°	55.58'		
	WISLE (LOM/NDB)	WISL	NDB	248.00	N30°	45.64'	W88°	18.16'		
Missouri										
	AMAZON	AZN	NDB	233.00	N39°	53.03'	W94°	54.48'		
	BILMART	AOV	NDB	341.00	N36°	58.18'	W92°	40.64'		
	BRENNER	FNB	NDB	404.00	N40°	04.58'	W95°	35.21'		
	BROOKFIELD	BZK	NDB	383.00	N39°	45.85'	W93°	06.54'		
	BUCKHORN	BHN	NDB	391.00	N37°	41.85'	W92°	06.22'		
	BUTLER	BUM	VOR	115.90	N38°	16.32'	W94°	29.29'	888	E07°
	CAHOKIA	CPS	NDB	375.00	N38°	34.64'	W90°	09.96'		
	CAMERON	EZZ	NDB	394.00	N39°	43.75'	W94°	16.32'		
	CAPE GIRARDEAU	CGI	VOR	112.90	N37°	13.65'	W89°	34.34'	341	E04°
	CHARLESTON	CHQ	NDB	208.00	N36°	50.70'	W89°	21.40'		
	CHILLICOTHE	CHT	NDB	375.00	N39°	46.62'	W93°	29.65'		
	COLUMBIA	COU	VOR	110.20	N38°	48.64'	W92°	13.09'	882	E03°
	COOLE (LOM)	COOL	NDB	404.00	N37°	10.81'	W93°	25.02'		
	CUBA	UBX	NDB	380.00	N38°	03.92'	W91°	25.64'		
	DEXTER	DXE	NDB	423.00	N36°	47.27'	W89°	56.44'		
	DOGWOOD	DGD	VOR	109.40	N37°	01.40'	W92°	52.61'	1,600	E06°
	DOTTE (LOM/NDB)	DOTT	NDB	359.00	N39°	13.25'	W94°	44.99'		
	DUTCH (LOM)	DUTC	NDB	248.00	N37°	15.20'	W89°	42.03'		
	EARLI (LOM/NDB)	EARL	NDB	278.00	N36°	40.10'	W90°	19.62'		
	EAVES (LOM/NDB)	EAVE	NDB	227.00	N38°	40.63'	W90°	32.82'		
	EMVILLE	EVU	NDB	317.00	N40°	20.89'	W94°	54.93'		
	FARMINGTON	FAM	VOR	115.70	N37°	40.40'	W90°	14.04'	1,220	E01°
	FESTUS	FES	NDB	269.00	N38°	11.75'	W90°	23.25'		
	FORISTELL	FTZ	VOR	110.80	N38°	41.67'	W90°	58.27'	816	E05°
	FORNEY	TBN	VOR	110.00	N37°	44.54'	W92°	08.34'	1,161	E03°
	GOLDEN VALLEY	GLY	NDB	388.00	N38°	21.53'	W93°	41.08'		
	GUTHRIE	FTT	NDB	317.00	N38°	50.56'	W92°	00.27'		
	HALLSVILLE	HLV	VOR	114.20	N39°	06.81'	W92°	07.69'	918	E06°
	HANNIBAL	HAE	NDB	411.00	N39°	43.63'	W91°	26.90'		
	HIGGINSVILLE	HIG	VOR	110.60	N39°	04.36'	W93°	40.69'	806	E06°
	HUGGY (LOM)	HUGG	NDB	242.00	N39°	18.11'	W94°	51.06'		
	KAISER	AIZ	NDB	272.00	N38°	05.79'	W92°	33.18'		
	KANSAS CITY	MKC	VOR	112.60	N39°	16.76'	W94°	35.48'	1,059	E08°
	KENNETT	TKX	NDB	358.00	N36°	13.73'	W90°	02.17'		
	KENZY (LOM)	KENZ	NDB	344.00	N39°	13.24'	W94°	33.85'		
	KIRKSVILLE	IRK	VOR	114.60	N40°	08.09'	W92°	35.50'	990	E06°
	LEBANON	IEB	NDB	414.00	N37°	34.28'	W92°	39.49'		
	LUNNS (LOM)	LUNN	NDB	344.00	N37°	12.18'	W94°	33.51'		
	MACON	MCM	VOR	112.90	N39°	39.24'	W92°	28.92'	869	E06°
	MALDEN	MAW	VOR	111.20	N36°	33.30'	W89°	54.68'	278	E03°
	MAPLES	MAP	VOR	113.40	N37°	35.44'	W91°	47.31'	1,371	E06°
	MARSHALL	PUR	NDB	371.00	N39°	02.51'	W93°	11.74'		
	MEMORIAL	MEO	NDB	397.00	N38°	33.22'	W92°	04.67'		
	MOBERLY	MBY	NDB	302.00	N39°	27.89'	W92°	25.91'		
	MOUNTAIN VIEW	MNF	NDB	365.00	N36°	59.63'	W91°	42.75'		
	NAPOLEON	ANX	VOR	114.00	N39°	05.72'	W94°	07.73'	879	E07°
	NEOSHO	EOS	VOR	116.60	N36°	50.54'	W94°	26.14'	1,193	E07°
	NEVADA	EAD	NDB	209.00	N37°	51.53'	W94°	18.16'		
	NEW MADRID	EIW	NDB	314.00	N36°	32.18'	W89°	36.10'		
	NOAH	ONH	NDB	515.00	N38°	38.22'	W92°	14.68'		
	OBLIO (LOM/NDB)	OBLI	NDB	338.00	N38°	48.01'	W90°	28.48'		
	PERRINE	PRI	NDB	367.00	N37°	45.90'	W90°	25.75'		
	POINT LOOKOUT	PLK	NDB	326.00	N36°	37.65'	W93°	13.79'		
	POMONA	UNO	NDB	335.00	N36°	52.69'	W91°	54.03'		
	SEDALIA	DMO	NDB	281.00	N38°	42.26'	W93°	10.59'		
	SIKESTON	SIK	NDB	272.00	N36°	53.27'	W89°	33.88'		
	SNOOP (LOM)	SNOO	NDB	326.00	N38°	38.36'	W90°	46.02'		
	SPRING RIVER	LLU	NDB	356.00	N37°	29.22'	W94°	18.61'		
	SPRINGFIELD	SGF	VOR	116.90	N37°	21.35'	W93°	20.04'	1,239	E04°
	ST JOSEPH	STJ	VOR	115.50	N39°	57.63'	W94°	55.51'	1,161	E08°
	ST LOUIS	STL	VOR	117.40	N38°	51.64'	W90°	28.94'	449	E01°
	SULLIVAN	UUV	NDB	356.00	N38°	14.12'	W91°	09.83'		
	SUNSHINE	SHY	VOR	108.40	N38°	02.43'	W92°	36.14'	908	E05°
	TARIO (LOM)	TARI	NDB	260.00	N39°	40.54'	W94°	54.41'		
	TRENTON	TRX	NDB	400.00	N40°	04.81'	W93°	35.58'		
	VICHY	VIH	VOR	117.70	N38°	09.24'	W91°	42.40'	1,108	E06°
	VIERTEL	VER	NDB	347.00	N38°	56.96'	W92°	41.04'		
	WILLARD	ILJ	NDB	254.00	N37°	17.96'	W93°	26.45'		
	ZODIA (LOM)	ZODI	NDB	407.00	N38°	42.99'	W92°	16.10'		
	ZUMAY (LOM)	ZUMA	NDB	404.00	N38°	47.28'	W90°	16.73'		

State/Country	VOR/NDB Name	Ident.	Type	Freq.	Latitude		Longitude		Altitude	Mag Var
USA/CANADA NAVAIDS										
Montana										
	BILLINGS	BIL	VOR	114.50	N45°	48.51'	W108°	37.47'	3,798	E14°
	BOZEMAN	BZN	VOR	112.20	N45°	47.03'	W111°	09.32'	4,427	E18°
	BROADUS	BDX	NDB	335.00	N45°	26.15'	W105°	24.66'		
	CAPITOL	CVP	NDB	317.00	N46°	36.40'	W111°	56.22'		
	CHOTEAU	CII	NDB	269.00	N47°	49.34'	W112°	10.26'		
	CIRCLE	CRR	NDB	245.00	N47°	25.10'	W105°	33.53'		
	CONRAD	CRD	NDB	293.00	N48°	11.13'	W111°	54.84'		
	COPPERTOWN	CPN	VOR	111.60	N46°	01.96'	W112°	44.82'	5,789	E16°
	CUT BANK	CTB	VOR	114.40	N48°	33.89'	W112°	20.59'	3,778	E17°
	DILLON	DLN	VOR	113.00	N45°	14.91'	W112°	32.82'	5,257	E18°
	DRUMMOND	DRU	VOR	117.10	N46°	38.16'	W113°	11.19'	4,149	E17°
	EUREKA	EUR	NDB	392.00	N48°	57.83'	W115°	05.52'		
	FORSYTH	FOR	NDB	236.00	N46°	16.16'	W106°	31.05'		
	GLASGOW	GGW	VOR	113.90	N48°	12.91'	W106°	37.52'	2,279	E14°
	GLENDIVE	GDV	NDB	410.00	N47°	08.00'	W104°	48.28'		
	GREAT FALLS	GTF	VOR	115.10	N47°	26.99'	W111°	24.72'	3,670	E16°
	HAMILTON	HMM	NDB	410.00	N46°	15.41'	W114°	08.05'		
	HARLOWTON	HWQ	NDB	242.00	N46°	26.09'	W109°	49.94'		
	HAUSER	HAU	NDB	386.00	N46°	34.13'	W111°	45.48'		
	HAVRE	HVR	VOR	111.80	N48°	32.42'	W109°	46.19'	2,578	E16°
	HELENA	HLN	VOR	117.70	N46°	36.41'	W111°	57.20'	3,808	E16°
	HORTON	HTN	NDB	320.00	N46°	24.72'	W105°	56.29'		
	JORDAN	JDN	NDB	263.00	N47°	20.00'	W106°	56.28'		
	KALISPELL	FCA	VOR	108.40	N48°	12.84'	W114°	10.55'	2,978	E18°
	KONA	INE	NDB	521.00	N47°	05.66'	W114°	23.80'		
	LEEDS	LDS	NDB	389.00	N48°	32.72'	W109°	41.42'		
	LEWISTOWN	LWT	NDB	353.00	N47°	04.04'	W109°	32.12'		
	LEWISTOWN	LWT	VOR	112.00	N47°	03.17'	W109°	36.37'	4,129	E15°
	LIVINGSTON	LVM	VOR	116.10	N45°	42.14'	W110°	26.54'	4,647	E15°
	MALTA	MLK	NDB	272.00	N48°	21.10'	W107°	53.64'		
	MANNI (LOM)	MANN	NDB	266.00	N45°	52.30'	W111°	17.14'		
	MILES CITY	MLS	VOR	112.10	N46°	22.93'	W105°	57.21'	2,640	E15°
	MILK RIVER	MKR	NDB	339.00	N48°	12.47'	W106°	37.57'		
	MISSOULA	MSO	VOR	112.80	N46°	54.47'	W114°	05.01'	3,197	E17°
	PLENTYWOOD	PWD	NDB	251.00	N48°	47.40'	W104°	31.62'		
	POLSON	PLS	NDB	275.00	N47°	41.74'	W114°	11.27'		
	RED LODGE	RED	NDB	203.00	N45°	14.39'	W109°	15.85'		
	ROUNDUP	RPX	NDB	362.00	N46°	28.83'	W108°	34.04'		
	SAIGE (LOM)	SAIG	NDB	251.00	N45°	51.12'	W108°	41.65'		
	SCOBEY	SCO	NDB	283.00	N48°	48.51'	W105°	26.16'		
	SHELBY	SBX	NDB	347.00	N48°	32.46'	W111°	51.93'		
	SIDNEY	SDY	NDB	359.00	N47°	42.68'	W104°	10.90'		
	SMITH LAKE	SAK	NDB	515.00	N48°	06.49'	W114°	27.67'		
	TARGY (LOM/NDB)	TARG	NDB	415.00	N44°	34.52'	W111°	11.85'		
	TIMBER	BKU	NDB	344.00	N46°	20.87'	W104°	15.37'		
	TRULY	ITU	NDB	371.00	N47°	21.95'	W111°	22.37'		
	WHITEHALL	HIA	VOR	113.70	N45°	51.70'	W112°	10.17'	5,530	E18°
	WOLF POINT	OLF	NDB	404.00	N48°	06.26'	W105°	36.11'		
	YELLOWSTONE	ESY	NDB	338.00	N44°	41.37'	W111°	07.26'		
Nebraska										
	AINSWORTH	ANW	VOR	112.70	N42°	34.14'	W99°	59.37'	2,581	E09°
	ALABY	BVN	NDB	332.00	N41°	43.77'	W98°	03.16'		
	ALLIANCE	AIA	VOR	111.80	N42°	03.33'	W102°	48.26'	3,922	E11°
	ANOKE (LOM)	ANOK	NDB	272.00	N40°	37.56'	W99°	01.53'		
	ANTIOCH	AOQ	NDB	287.00	N42°	00.83'	W102°	46.08'		
	AURORA	AUH	NDB	278.00	N40°	53.54'	W97°	59.83'		
	BEATRICE	BIE	VOR	110.60	N40°	18.08'	W96°	45.27'	1,298	E07°
	BEKLOF	FMZ	NDB	392.00	N40°	35.39'	W97°	34.08'		
	BIG BLUE	BJU	NDB	248.00	N40°	21.81'	W96°	48.77'		
	BROKEN BOW	BBW	NDB	290.00	N41°	26.04'	W99°	38.15'		
	BURWELL	BUB	NDB	362.00	N41°	46.57'	W99°	08.86'		
	CHADRON	CDR	VOR	113.40	N42°	33.52'	W103°	18.72'	4,628	E13°
	CHAPPELL	CNP	NDB	383.00	N41°	04.59'	W102°	27.53'		
	COLUMBUS	OLU	VOR	111.80	N41°	27.00'	W97°	20.44'	1,443	E08°
	COZAD	OZB	VOR	109.00	N40°	52.22'	W100°	00.22'	2,499	E09°
	CRETE	CEK	NDB	420.00	N40°	37.44'	W96°	55.65'		
	CUSTER CO	CUZ	VOR	108.20	N41°	29.03'	W99°	41.34'	2,850	E09°
	DARR	RRX	NDB	326.00	N40°	50.66'	W99°	51.37'		
	DAWES (LOM)	DAWE	NDB	362.00	N42°	45.26'	W103°	10.50'		
	FAIRBURY	FBY	NDB	293.00	N40°	10.60'	W97°	09.95'		
	FREMONT	FET	NDB	311.00	N41°	27.01'	W96°	31.08'		
	GERFI (LOM/NDB)	GERF	NDB	320.00	N41°	22.01'	W95°	57.38'		

State/Country	VOR/NDB Name	Ident.	Type	Freq.	Latitude		Longitude		Altitude	Mag Var
USA/CANADA NAVAIDS										
Nebraska	GERING	GIG	NDB	341.00	N41°	56.66'	W103°	40.97'		
	GORDON	GRN	NDB	414.00	N42°	48.06'	W102°	10.75'		
	GRAND ISLAND	GRI	VOR	112.00	N40°	59.04'	W98°	18.88'	1,840	E07°
	GRANT	GGF	NDB	359.00	N40°	52.25'	W101°	43.82'		
	HARRY STRUNK	CSB	NDB	389.00	N40°	18.25'	W100°	09.46'		
	HASTINGS	HSI	VOR	108.80	N40°	36.27'	W98°	25.77'	1,948	E07°
	HAYES CENTER	HCT	VOR	117.70	N40°	27.24'	W100°	55.41'	3,007	E11°
	HEBRON	HJH	NDB	323.00	N40°	09.02'	W97°	35.26'		
	HOLDREGE	HDE	NDB	396.00	N40°	26.87'	W99°	20.42'		
	IMPERIAL	IML	NDB	283.00	N40°	30.69'	W101°	37.65'		
	KEARNEY	EAR	VOR	111.20	N40°	43.53'	W99°	00.30'	2,128	E10°
	KEHOE (LOM)	KEHO	NDB	380.00	N40°	52.37'	W98°	18.88'		
	KIMBALL	IBM	NDB	317.00	N41°	11.48'	W103°	40.18'		
	LEE BIRD	LED	NDB	375.00	N41°	06.71'	W100°	40.53'		
	LINCOLN	LNK	VOR	116.10	N40°	55.42'	W96°	44.52'	1,371	E09°
	MC COOK	MCK	VOR	116.50	N40°	12.22'	W100°	35.65'	2,568	E11°
	MILLARD	MLE	NDB	371.00	N41°	11.69'	W96°	06.84'		
	NORFOLK	OFK	VOR	109.60	N41°	59.27'	W97°	26.07'	1,538	E08°
	NORTH PLATTE	LBF	VOR	117.40	N41°	02.91'	W100°	44.82'	3,050	E11°
	O NEILL	ONL	VOR	113.90	N42°	28.22'	W98°	41.21'	2,030	E10°
	OMAHA	OMA	VOR	116.30	N41°	10.03'	W95°	44.20'	1,298	E08°
	ORD	ODX	NDB	356.00	N41°	37.42'	W98°	56.87'		
	OSHKOSH	OKS	NDB	233.00	N41°	24.06'	W102°	21.02'		
	PANBE (LOM/NDB)	PANB	NDB	416.00	N41°	04.09'	W100°	34.35'		
	PAWNEE CITY	PWE	VOR	112.40	N40°	12.02'	W96°	12.37'	1,361	E09°
	PLATTE CENTER	PLT	NDB	407.00	N41°	29.79'	W97°	22.90'		
	PLATTSMOUTH	PMV	NDB	329.00	N40°	57.08'	W95°	54.94'		
	POTTS (LOM/NDB)	POTT	NDB	385.00	N40°	44.82'	W96°	45.74'		
	PROSSER	PSS	NDB	338.00	N40°	41.17'	W98°	28.65'		
	RIKKY (LOM)	RIKK	NDB	426.00	N41°	13.17'	W95°	49.07'		
	ROCK CO	RBE	NDB	341.00	N42°	34.41'	W99°	34.66'		
	SCOTTSBLUFF	BFF	VOR	112.60	N41°	53.64'	W103°	28.92'	4,168	E13°
	SEARLE	SAE	VOR	110.20	N41°	07.15'	W101°	46.57'	3,253	E11°
	SEWARD	SWT	NDB	269.00	N40°	51.89'	W97°	06.36'		
	SHAW	HWB	NDB	263.00	N40°	15.90'	W96°	45.42'		
	SIDNEY	SNY	VOR	115.90	N41°	05.80'	W102°	58.98'	4,300	E13°
	TEKAMAH	TQE	VOR	108.40	N41°	45.57'	W96°	10.71'	1,029	E07°
	THEDFORD	TDD	VOR	108.60	N41°	58.90'	W100°	43.14'	3,175	E09°
	TOMMI (LOM/NDB)	TOMM	NDB	305.00	N42°	27.61'	W96°	27.73'		
	VALENTINE	VTN	NDB	314.00	N42°	51.69'	W100°	32.97'		
	WAHOO	AHQ	NDB	400.00	N41°	14.35'	W96°	35.90'		
	WAYNE	LCG	NDB	389.00	N42°	14.15'	W96°	59.15'		
	WHITNEY	HIN	NDB	275.00	N42°	49.72'	W103°	05.62'		
	WILLOW	DWL	NDB	353.00	N40°	52.36'	W100°	04.35'		
	WOLBACH	OBH	VOR	114.80	N41°	22.54'	W98°	21.21'	2,010	E10°
	YORK	JYR	NDB	257.00	N40°	53.85'	W97°	37.02'		
Nevada	BATTLE MOUNTAIN	BAM	VOR	112.20	N40°	34.14'	W116°	55.33'	4,536	E18°
	BEATTY	BTY	VOR	114.70	N36°	48.03'	W116°	44.85'	2,925	E16°
	BOULDER CITY	BLD	VOR	116.70	N35°	59.74'	W114°	51.81'	3,650	E15°
	BULLION	BQU	VOR	114.50	N40°	45.57'	W115°	45.68'	6,458	E17°
	COALDALE	OAL	VOR	117.70	N38°	00.19'	W117°	46.22'	4,798	E17°
	ELY	ELY	VOR	110.60	N39°	17.88'	W114°	50.89'	6,248	E17°
	HAZEN	HZN	VOR	114.10	N39°	30.98'	W118°	59.86'	4,080	E17°
	LAS VEGAS	LAS	VOR	116.90	N36°	04.78'	W115°	09.58'	2,138	E15°
	LOVELOCK	LLC	VOR	116.50	N40°	07.49'	W118°	34.65'	4,782	E16°
	MERCURY	MCY	NDB	326.00	N36°	37.64'	W116°	01.65'		
	MINA	MVA	VOR	115.10	N38°	33.91'	W118°	01.97'	7,858	E17°
	MORMON MESA	MMM	VOR	114.30	N36°	46.15'	W114°	16.64'	2,118	E16°
	MUSTANG	FMG	VOR	117.90	N39°	31.87'	W119°	39.36'	5,940	E16°
	RENO (LMM)	NO	NDB	351.00	N39°	31.17'	W119°	46.15'		
	SOD HOUSE	SDO	VOR	114.30	N41°	24.62'	W118°	01.99'	4,129	E18°
	SPARKS	SPK	NDB	254.00	N39°	41.82'	W119°	46.12'		
	TONOPAH	TPH	VOR	117.20	N38°	01.84'	W117°	02.01'	5,329	E17°
	WELLS	LWL	VOR	114.20	N41°	08.68'	W114°	58.65'	5,903	E17°
	WILSON CREEK	ILC	VOR	116.30	N38°	15.01'	W114°	23.65'	9,315	E16°
	WINNEMUCCA	INA	VOR	108.20	N40°	53.95'	W117°	48.73'	4,296	E16°
	WINNEMUCCA	EMC	NDB	375.00	N40°	57.79'	W117°	50.49'		
New Hampshire	BELKNAP	BLO	NDB	328.00	N43°	32.20'	W71°	32.22'		
	BERLIN	BML	VOR	110.40	N44°	38.00'	W71°	11.16'	1,728	W17°
	CHERN (LOM/NDB)	CHER	NDB	359.00	N42°	49.40'	W71°	36.13'		
	CLAREMONT	CNH	NDB	233.00	N43°	22.15'	W72°	22.26'		

State/Country	VOR/NDB Name	Ident.	Type	Freq.	Latitude		Longitude		Altitude	Mag Var
USA/CANADA NAVAIDS										
New Hampshire	CONCORD	CON	VOR	112.90	N43°	13.18'	W71°	34.52'	708	W15°
	DERRY	DRY	NDB	338.00	N42°	52.19'	W71°	23.82'		
	EPSOM (LOM/NDB)	EPSO	NDB	216.00	N43°	07.12'	W71°	27.14'		
	HANOVER	LAH	NDB	276.00	N43°	42.13'	W72°	10.64'		
	HORNEBROOK	HXK	NDB	281.00	N44°	34.61'	W71°	10.75'		
	KEENE	EEN	VOR	109.40	N42°	47.65'	W72°	17.50'	1,380	W14°
	LEBANON	LEB	VOR	113.70	N43°	40.73'	W72°	12.96'	1,459	W15°
	MAHN	GMA	NDB	386.00	N44°	21.73'	W71°	41.16'		
	MANCHESTER	MHT	VOR	114.40	N42°	52.11'	W71°	22.17'	469	W15°
	PEASE	PSM	VOR	116.50	N43°	05.06'	W70°	49.91'	98	W16°
New Jersey										
	ATLANTIC CITY	ACY	VOR	108.60	N39°	27.35'	W74°	34.57'	68	W10°
	BROADWAY	BWZ	VOR	114.20	N40°	47.90'	W74°	49.30'	1,046	W11°
	CEDAR LAKE	VCN	VOR	115.20	N39°	32.25'	W74°	58.02'	121	W10°
	CHATHAM	CAT	NDB	254.00	N40°	44.45'	W74°	25.78'		
	CHESA (LOM)	CHES	NDB	241.00	N40°	35.61'	W74°	13.79'		
	COLTS NECK	COL	VOR	115.40	N40°	18.70'	W74°	09.58'	121	W11°
	COYLE	CYN	VOR	113.40	N39°	49.03'	W74°	25.89'	209	W10°
	LAKEHURST (NAVY)	NEL	NDB	396.00	N40°	02.68'	W74°	20.14'		
	LIZAH (LOM)	LIZA	NDB	204.00	N40°	36.44'	W74°	13.07'		
	MC GUIRE	GXU	VOR	110.60	N40°	00.57'	W74°	35.77'	121	W11°
	MOREE (LOM)	MORE	NDB	392.00	N40°	52.79'	W74°	20.05'		
	NAADA (LOM)	NAAD	NDB	336.00	N39°	29.89'	W74°	40.34'		
	PALISADES PARK	PPK	NDB	233.00	N40°	49.75'	W73°	58.46'		
	PATERSON	PNJ	NDB	347.00	N40°	56.79'	W74°	09.05'		
	RAINBOW	RNB	NDB	363.00	N39°	25.09'	W75°	08.11'		
	ROBBINSVILLE	RBV	VOR	113.80	N40°	12.14'	W74°	29.70'	249	W10°
	SEA ISLE	SIE	VOR	114.80	N39°	05.72'	W74°	48.01'	9	W09°
	SOLBERG	SBJ	VOR	112.90	N40°	34.98'	W74°	44.50'	190	W10°
	SPARTA	SAX	VOR	115.70	N41°	04.04'	W74°	32.29'	1,410	W11°
	SPEEZ (LOM)	SPEE	NDB	222.00	N39°	54.07'	W75°	05.67'		
	STILLWATER	STW	VOR	109.60	N40°	59.75'	W74°	52.14'	918	W11°
	TETERBORO	TEB	VOR	108.40	N40°	50.92'	W74°	03.73'	9	W11°
	TORBY (LOM)	TORB	NDB	214.00	N40°	48.26'	W74°	07.95'		
	WOODSTOWN	OOD	VOR	112.80	N39°	38.16'	W75°	18.18'	141	W10°
New Mexico										
	ALAMOGORDO	ALM	NDB	341.00	N32°	51.01'	W105°	58.87'		
	ALBUQUERQUE	ABQ	VOR	113.20	N35°	02.62'	W106°	48.97'	5,739	E13°
	ANTON CHICO	ACH	VOR	117.80	N35°	06.70'	W105°	02.39'	5,448	E12°
	ARTESIA	ATS	NDB	414.00	N32°	51.15'	W104°	27.69'		
	BOLES	BWS	VOR	109.60	N32°	49.27'	W106°	00.79'	4,099	E11°
	CAPITAN	CEP	NDB	278.00	N33°	29.39'	W105°	24.26'		
	CARLSBAD	CNM	VOR	116.30	N32°	15.39'	W104°	13.56'	3,250	E12°
	CARLZ (LOM)	CARL	NDB	402.00	N32°	16.00'	W104°	20.31'		
	CHISUM	CME	VOR	116.10	N33°	20.24'	W104°	37.27'	3,768	E12°
	CIMARRON	CIM	VOR	116.40	N36°	29.48'	W104°	52.31'	6,546	E13°
	COLUMBUS	CUS	VOR	111.20	N31°	49.14'	W107°	34.46'	4,008	E12°
	CORONA	CNX	VOR	115.50	N34°	22.02'	W105°	40.68'	6,409	E13°
	COZEY (LOM)	COZE	NDB	251.00	N32°	37.92'	W108°	03.79'		
	DEMING	DMN	VOR	108.60	N32°	16.55'	W107°	36.33'	4,204	E12°
	DOMAN (LOM)	DOMA	NDB	341.00	N35°	33.31'	W106°	08.40'		
	DUDLE (LOM)	DUDL	NDB	308.00	N35°	13.04'	W106°	42.76'		
	FARMINGTON	FMN	VOR	115.30	N36°	44.90'	W108°	05.93'	5,818	E14°
	FLORIDA	FIA	NDB	329.00	N34°	06.01'	W106°	54.03'		
	GALLUP	GUP	VOR	115.10	N35°	28.56'	W108°	52.35'	7,048	E14°
	HAWKE (LOM)	HAWK	NDB	206.00	N32°	13.17'	W106°	50.14'		
	HISAN (LOM)	HISA	NDB	335.00	N34°	21.04'	W103°	10.46'		
	HOBBS	HOB	VOR	111.00	N32°	38.29'	W103°	16.15'	3,660	E11°
	ISLETA	ILT	NDB	247.00	N34°	59.22'	W106°	37.22'		
	LAS VEGAS	LVS	VOR	117.30	N35°	39.45'	W105°	08.13'	6,868	E13°
	LOVINGTON	LGX	NDB	396.00	N32°	56.82'	W103°	24.59'		
	MAXWELL	MXR	NDB	284.00	N36°	42.03'	W104°	32.38'		
	OTTO	OTO	VOR	114.00	N35°	04.33'	W105°	56.16'	6,287	E13°
	PINON	PIO	VOR	110.40	N32°	31.75'	W105°	18.31'	6,579	E12°
	PORTALES	PRZ	NDB	407.00	N34°	09.07'	W103°	24.37'		
	SANTA FE	SAF	VOR	110.60	N35°	32.43'	W106°	03.89'	6,258	E13°
	SILVER CITY	SVC	VOR	110.80	N32°	38.26'	W108°	09.66'	5,418	E13°
	SKI	SKX	NDB	414.00	N36°	27.46'	W105°	40.58'		
	SOCORRO	ONM	VOR	116.80	N34°	20.33'	W106°	49.22'	4,910	E13°
	TAOS	TAS	VOR	117.60	N36°	36.52'	W105°	54.38'	7,858	E13°
	TOPAN (LOM/NDB)	TOPA	NDB	305.00	N33°	21.92'	W104°	26.52'		
	TRUTH OR CONSEQ	TCS	VOR	112.70	N33°	16.95'	W107°	16.83'	4,900	E13°
	TUCUMCARI	TCC	VOR	113.60	N35°	10.92'	W103°	35.91'	4,070	E12°

State/Country	VOR/NDB Name	Ident.	Type	Freq.	Latitude		Longitude		Altitude	Mag Var
USA/CANADA NAVAIDS										
New York										
	ALBANY	ALB	VOR	115.30	N42°	44.83'	W73°	48.19'	275	W13°
	ALPINE	ALP	NDB	245.00	N42°	14.31'	W76°	45.83'		
	AVON	AVN	NDB	344.00	N43°	00.59'	W77°	46.14'		
	BABYLON	BBN	NDB	275.00	N40°	40.34'	W73°	23.06'		
	BETHPAGE	BPA	NDB	248.00	N40°	45.75'	W73°	26.72'		
	BINGHAMTON	CFB	VOR	112.20	N42°	09.44'	W76°	08.18'	1,571	W10°
	BREIT (LOM)	BREI	NDB	400.00	N43°	07.59'	W77°	33.22'		
	BRIDGE	OGY	NDB	414.00	N40°	34.08'	W73°	52.97'		
	BRIEL (LOM)	BRIE	NDB	395.00	N44°	28.61'	W74°	07.44'		
	BUFFALO	BUF	VOR	116.40	N42°	55.74'	W78°	38.78'	731	W08°
	CALVERTON	CCC	VOR	117.20	N40°	55.77'	W72°	47.93'	85	W13°
	CAMBRIDGE	CAM	VOR	115.00	N42°	59.65'	W73°	20.63'	1,489	W14°
	CANARSIE	CRI	VOR	112.30	N40°	36.74'	W73°	53.66'	9	W11°
	CARMEL	CMK	VOR	116.60	N41°	16.80'	W73°	34.88'	688	W12°
	CLAY	CJY	NDB	275.00	N43°	03.16'	W75°	15.86'		
	CONDA (LOM/NDB)	COND	NDB	373.00	N40°	35.20'	W73°	47.97'		
	DE LANCEY	DNY	VOR	112.10	N42°	10.69'	W74°	57.41'	2,558	W11°
	DEER PARK	DPK	VOR	117.70	N40°	47.50'	W73°	18.21'	121	W12°
	DRUM	GTB	NDB	257.00	N44°	04.11'	W75°	44.15'		
	DUNKIRK	DKK	VOR	116.20	N42°	29.43'	W79°	16.44'	678	W07°
	ELMIRA	ULW	VOR	109.65	N42°	05.65'	W77°	01.49'	1,620	W09°
	FRIKK (LOM)	FRIK	NDB	407.00	N40°	46.59'	W73°	28.94'		
	GANSE (LOM)	GANS	NDB	209.00	N43°	15.30'	W73°	36.34'		
	GENESEO	GEE	VOR	108.20	N42°	50.06'	W77°	43.96'	990	W09°
	GEORGETOWN	GGT	VOR	117.80	N42°	47.33'	W75°	49.60'	2,040	W11°
	GLENS FALLS	GFL	VOR	110.20	N43°	20.50'	W73°	36.70'	321	W14°
	GRIMM (LOM)	GRIM	NDB	268.00	N40°	35.84'	W73°	39.44'		
	HALOS (LOM/NDB)	HALO	NDB	269.00	N42°	06.61'	W77°	54.91'		
	HAMPTON	HTO	VOR	113.60	N40°	55.14'	W72°	19.00'	29	W13°
	HANCOCK	HNK	VOR	116.80	N42°	03.78'	W75°	18.97'	2,069	W11°
	HAWKY (LOM)	HAWK	NDB	219.00	N42°	49.03'	W73°	48.50'		
	HESTR (LOM)	HEST	NDB	281.00	N41°	08.72'	W73°	45.98'		
	HUGUENOT	HUO	VOR	116.10	N41°	24.58'	W74°	35.49'	1,298	W11°
	HUNTER	HEU	NDB	356.00	N42°	51.17'	W73°	56.05'		
	ITHACA	ITH	VOR	111.80	N42°	29.70'	W76°	27.58'	1,108	W10°
	JAMESTOWN	JHW	VOR	114.70	N42°	11.31'	W79°	07.27'	1,790	W07°
	JOHNSTOWN	JJH	NDB	523.00	N42°	59.96'	W74°	19.94'		
	KATHI (LOM)	KATH	NDB	329.00	N43°	06.55'	W78°	50.30'		
	KENNEDY	JFK	VOR	115.90	N40°	37.97'	W73°	46.28'	9	W12°
	KINGSTON	IGN	VOR	117.60	N41°	39.92'	W73°	49.33'	580	W12°
	KIRKI (LOM)	KIRK	NDB	242.00	N43°	06.73'	W76°	00.16'		
	KLUMP (LOM)	KLUM	NDB	231.00	N43°	00.01'	W78°	39.04'		
	KRING (LOM)	KRIN	NDB	279.00	N42°	35.08'	W74°	59.18'		
	LA GUARDIA	LGA	VOR	113.10	N40°	47.02'	W73°	52.11'	9	W12°
	LOKKS (LOM)	LOKK	NDB	366.00	N40°	43.73'	W73°	11.41'		
	LORRS (LOM)	LORR	NDB	226.00	N40°	43.51'	W73°	41.58'		
	MASSENA	MSS	VOR	114.10	N44°	54.86'	W74°	43.36'	200	W14°
	MEIER (LOM/NDB)	MEIE	NDB	403.00	N41°	34.55'	W73°	57.92'		
	MISSE (LOM)	MISS	NDB	278.00	N44°	51.24'	W74°	54.94'		
	MONGA (LOM/NDB)	MONG	NDB	359.00	N41°	45.99'	W74°	51.64'		
	NEELY (LOM/NDB)	NEEL	NDB	335.00	N41°	29.15'	W74°	13.68'		
	OGIVE (LOM)	OGIV	NDB	358.00	N44°	42.09'	W75°	21.18'		
	OLDFIELD POINT	OP	NDB	316.00	N40°	58.60'	W73°	07.10'		
	OLEAN	LYS	NDB	360.00	N42°	17.01'	W78°	20.10'		
	ORCHY (LOM)	ORCH	NDB	385.00	N40°	51.98'	W73°	48.21'		
	OTIMS (LOM)	OTIM	NDB	353.00	N41°	26.70'	W74°	17.45'		
	PAWLING	PWL	VOR	114.30	N41°	46.18'	W73°	36.03'	1,249	W12°
	PECONIC	PIC	NDB	339.00	N40°	48.58'	W72°	54.37'		
	PENN YAN	PYA	NDB	260.00	N42°	38.63'	W77°	03.34'		
	PETHS (LOM)	PETH	NDB	332.00	N40°	42.87'	W73°	55.76'		
	PHILMONT	PFH	NDB	272.00	N42°	15.17'	W73°	43.39'		
	PLATTSBURGH	PLB	VOR	116.90	N44°	41.09'	W73°	31.36'	344	W15°
	PLAZZ (LOM)	PLAZ	NDB	204.00	N42°	52.42'	W78°	48.98'		
	PLEIN (LOM/NDB)	PLEI	NDB	329.00	N43°	13.34'	W75°	28.94'		
	POTSDAM	PTD	NDB	400.00	N44°	43.40'	W74°	52.96'		
	ROCHESTER	ROC	VOR	110.00	N43°	07.24'	W77°	40.41'	551	W09°
	ROCKDALE	RKA	VOR	112.60	N42°	27.98'	W75°	14.35'	2,030	W11°
	ROMULUS	RYK	VOR	108.40	N42°	42.78'	W76°	52.93'	636	W10°
	SARANAC LAKE	SLK	VOR	109.20	N44°	23.07'	W74°	12.27'	1,649	W14°
	SENECA	SSN	NDB	208.00	N42°	44.67'	W76°	54.28'		
	SMITE (LOM)	SMIT	NDB	332.00	N42°	06.29'	W75°	53.47'		
	SQUIR (LOM)	SQUI	NDB	400.00	N40°	54.26'	W72°	33.38'		
	STANWYCK	SKU	NDB	261.00	N41°	31.68'	W74°	02.69'		
	SYRACUSE	SYR	VOR	117.00	N43°	09.63'	W76°	12.27'	419	W11°

State/Country	VOR/NDB Name	Ident.	Type	Freq.	Latitude		Longitude		Altitude	Mag Var
USA/CANADA NAVAIDS										
New York	UTICA	UCA	VOR	111.20	N43°	01.59'	W75°	09.87'	1,420	W12°
	VARNA (LOM)	VARN	NDB	266.00	N42°	25.80'	W76°	22.07'		
	WATERTOWN	ART	VOR	109.80	N43°	57.12'	W76°	03.87'	370	W12°
	WELLSVILLE	ELZ	VOR	111.40	N42°	05.37'	W77°	59.97'	2,299	W09°
North Carolina										
	AHOSKIE	ASJ	NDB	415.00	N36°	17.96'	W77°	10.53'		
	AIRLI (LOM)	AIRL	NDB	281.00	N34°	11.47'	W77°	51.97'		
	ALWOOD	AQE	NDB	230.00	N35°	42.41'	W77°	22.31'		
	ANSON CO	AFP	NDB	283.00	N35°	01.44'	W80°	04.98'		
	ASHEE (LOM/NDB)	ASHE	NDB	410.00	N36°	26.03'	W81°	19.31'		
	BARRETTS MOUNTAIN	BZM	VOR	110.80	N35°	52.13'	W81°	14.43'	1,879	W06°
	BENTON	BEZ	NDB	347.00	N34°	05.32'	W78°	51.98'		
	BROAD RIVER	BRA	NDB	379.00	N35°	16.36'	W82°	28.26'		
	BURLINGTON	BUY	NDB	329.00	N36°	02.99'	W79°	28.80'		
	CAMP	CPC	NDB	227.00	N34°	16.31'	W78°	42.83'		
	CAROLINA BEACH	CLB	NDB	216.00	N34°	06.37'	W77°	57.68'		
	CHARLOTTE	CLT	VOR	115.00	N35°	11.41'	W80°	57.10'	731	W05°
	CHERRY POINT MCAS	NKT	NDB	245.00	N34°	50.04'	W76°	48.14'		
	CHOCOWINITY	RNW	NDB	388.00	N35°	30.57'	W77°	06.39'		
	CITY LAKE	CQJ	NDB	266.00	N35°	42.97'	W79°	51.91'		
	CLINTON	CTZ	NDB	412.00	N34°	58.52'	W78°	21.78'		
	COFIELD	CVI	VOR	114.60	N36°	22.37'	W76°	52.29'	68	W09°
	DAVIE	DVZ	NDB	354.00	N35°	54.80'	W80°	27.36'		
	DIXON	DIW	NDB	198.00	N34°	34.11'	W77°	27.17'		
	DOONE (LOM)	DOON	NDB	367.00	N34°	54.75'	W78°	56.38'		
	EDENTON	EDE	NDB	265.00	N36°	01.52'	W76°	33.99'		
	ELIZABETH CITY	ECG	VOR	112.50	N36°	15.45'	W76°	10.53'	9	W07°
	ELIZABETHTOWN	TGQ	NDB	398.00	N34°	31.71'	W78°	30.95'		
	ELLAS (LOM)	ELLA	NDB	261.00	N34°	45.03'	W77°	42.26'		
	FAYETTEVILLE	FAY	VOR	108.80	N34°	59.13'	W78°	52.50'	180	W04°
	FIDDLERS	FIQ	NDB	391.00	N35°	42.61'	W81°	40.27'		
	FIRST RIVER	SLP	NDB	368.00	N35°	15.27'	W81°	35.84'		
	FORT BRAGG	FGP	NDB	393.00	N35°	08.32'	W78°	48.74'		
	GREENSBORO	GSO	VOR	116.20	N36°	02.74'	W79°	58.58'	879	W03°
	GREON (LOM)	GREO	NDB	382.00	N35°	47.81'	W78°	52.96'		
	HARNETT	HQT	NDB	417.00	N35°	25.99'	W78°	40.49'		
	HEMLOCK	BAR	NDB	320.00	N36°	09.20'	W81°	52.79'		
	HUNTSBORO	HXO	NDB	271.00	N36°	18.02'	W78°	37.11'		
	JAMBE (LOM/NDB)	JAMB	NDB	235.00	N35°	46.05'	W77°	57.87'		
	JIGEL	JB	NDB	384.00	N34°	32.75'	W79°	08.30'		
	JNALL	EUU	NDB	251.00	N35°	36.41'	W78°	21.26'		
	KATFI (LOM)	KATF	NDB	362.00	N35°	01.28'	W77°	04.77'		
	KEANS (LOM)	KEAN	NDB	357.00	N35°	31.96'	W82°	35.24'		
	KENAN	DPL	NDB	344.00	N35°	02.85'	W77°	56.73'		
	KINSTON	ISO	VOR	109.60	N35°	22.25'	W77°	33.49'	68	W05°
	LEE CO	EEJ	NDB	428.00	N35°	22.39'	W79°	13.38'		
	LEEVY (LOM/NDB)	LEEV	NDB	350.00	N35°	55.63'	W78°	43.32'		
	LIBERTY	LIB	VOR	113.00	N35°	48.69'	W79°	36.75'	829	W03°
	LINCOLNTON	IZN	NDB	432.00	N35°	32.25'	W81°	05.18'		
	LUMBERTON	LBT	VOR	110.00	N34°	36.64'	W79°	03.28'	124	W06°
	MACKALL	HFF	NDB	278.00	N35°	01.67'	W79°	29.13'		
	MANTEO	MQI	NDB	370.00	N35°	54.91'	W75°	41.70'		
	MARKY (LOM)	MARK	NDB	254.00	N36°	10.02'	W80°	02.13'		
	MAXTN	ME	NDB	257.00	N34°	44.04'	W79°	26.65'		
	MOREHEAD	MRH	NDB	269.00	N34°	43.87'	W76°	39.72'		
	MOUNT AIRY	AXI	NDB	284.00	N36°	27.79'	W80°	33.10'		
	NEW BERN	EWN	VOR	113.60	N35°	04.38'	W77°	02.70'	9	W08°
	NEW RIVER (MARINE	NCA	NDB	356.00	N34°	43.29'	W77°	25.77'		
	PAMLICO	OUC	NDB	404.00	N35°	06.99'	W75°	59.24'		
	PENDY	ACZ	NDB	379.00	N34°	42.97'	W78°	00.21'		
	PERSON (LOM/NDB)	HUR	NDB	220.00	N36°	13.99'	W79°	03.95'		
	PLYMOUTH	PMZ	NDB	221.00	N35°	48.59'	W76°	45.76'		
	POPE (LOM/NDB)	POB	NDB	338.00	N35°	13.61'	W78°	57.26'		
	RALEIGH/DURHAM	RDU	VOR	117.20	N35°	52.35'	W78°	46.99'	429	W04°
	RAPIDS	RZZ	NDB	407.00	N36°	26.45'	W77°	42.49'		
	REENO (LOM)	REEN	NDB	317.00	N36°	04.25'	W80°	10.00'		
	ROBESON	RSY	NDB	359.00	N34°	36.81'	W79°	03.58'		
	ROWAN	RUQ	NDB	211.00	N35°	38.62'	W80°	31.34'	770	W05°
	RUTHERFORD	RFE	NDB	344.00	N35°	20.93'	W81°	57.17'		
	SALISBURY	SRW	NDB	233.00	N35°	40.68'	W80°	30.35'		
	SANDHILLS	SDZ	VOR	111.80	N35°	12.92'	W79°	35.27'	590	W03°
	SILER CITY	TOX	NDB	371.00	N35°	45.69'	W79°	27.73'		
	SIMMONS	FBG	VOR	109.80	N35°	07.99'	W78°	54.99'	239	W07°
	SLAMMER	SIF	NDB	423.00	N36°	22.93'	W79°	45.80'		

State/Country	VOR/NDB Name	Ident.	Type	Freq.	Latitude		Longitude		Altitude	Mag Var
USA/CANADA NAVAIDS										
North Carolina	SNOWBIRD	SOT	VOR	108.80	N35°	47.40'	W83°	03.14'	4,237	W04°
	STALS (LOM)	STAL	NDB	401.00	N35°	14.63'	W77°	41.89'		
	STANLY CO	SWY	NDB	362.00	N35°	24.70'	W80°	09.36'		
	STATESVILLE	SVH	NDB	404.00	N35°	50.94'	W80°	55.58'		
	STONIA	GHJ	NDB	293.00	N35°	11.47'	W81°	09.43'		
	SUGARLOAF MOUNTAI	SUG	VOR	112.20	N35°	24.38'	W82°	16.11'	3,968	W02°
	SWEARING	SEN	NDB	260.00	N35°	46.80'	W80°	17.90'		
	TAR RIVER	TYI	VOR	117.80	N35°	58.60'	W77°	42.22'	68	W05°
	TAWBA (LOM/NDB)	TAWB	NDB	332.00	N35°	47.19'	W81°	18.33'		
	TOMOTLA	TTQ	NDB	335.00	N35°	06.98'	W83°	57.39'		
	TRYON (LOM)	TRYO	NDB	242.00	N35°	09.46'	W81°	01.21'		
	WAYNE (LOM/NDB)	JYN	NDB	208.00	N35°	31.55'	W77°	54.06'		
	WESLEY	TWL	NDB	204.00	N34°	57.17'	W80°	42.31'		
	WILKI (LOM/NDB)	WILK	NDB	209.00	N36°	06.77'	W81°	05.88'		
	WILLIAMSTON	MCZ	NDB	336.00	N35°	51.54'	W77°	10.67'		
	WILMINGTON	ILM	VOR	117.00	N34°	21.09'	W77°	52.46'	19	W07°
	WOODVILLE	LLW	NDB	254.00	N36°	15.78'	W76°	17.86'		
	WRIGHT BROTHERS	RBX	VOR	111.60	N35°	55.23'	W75°	41.81'	9	W08°
	ZEPHYR	ZEF	NDB	326.00	N36°	18.79'	W80°	43.40'		
North Dakota										
	BISMARCK	BIS	VOR	116.50	N46°	45.70'	W100°	39.92'	1,840	E12°
	BOWMAN	BOD	NDB	374.00	N46°	11.10'	W103°	25.72'		
	COLIJ (LOM/NDB)	COLI	NDB	230.00	N46°	41.88'	W100°	38.86'		
	DEVILS LAKE	DVL	VOR	111.00	N48°	06.79'	W98°	54.48'	1,449	E11°
	DICKINSON	DIK	VOR	112.90	N46°	51.59'	W102°	46.40'	2,519	E14°
	FARGO	FAR	VOR	116.20	N46°	45.20'	W96°	51.07'	908	E09°
	GRAND FORKS	GFK	VOR	114.30	N47°	57.29'	W97°	11.12'	839	E09°
	GWINNER	GWR	NDB	278.00	N46°	13.39'	W97°	38.60'		
	HAZEN	HZE	NDB	205.00	N47°	17.91'	W101°	34.86'		
	HETTINGER	HEI	NDB	392.00	N46°	01.02'	W102°	38.93'		
	JAMESTOWN	JMS	VOR	114.50	N46°	55.97'	W98°	40.72'	1,489	E10°
	KENIE (LOM/NDB)	KENI	NDB	365.00	N47°	00.56'	W96°	48.91'		
	MINOT	MOT	VOR	117.10	N48°	15.62'	W101°	17.22'	1,689	E13°
	MOHALL	HBC	NDB	350.00	N48°	45.83'	W101°	32.16'		
	NOSON (LOM)	NOSO	NDB	353.00	N46°	41.28'	W102°	42.73'		
	PARSHALL	PSH	NDB	379.00	N47°	56.16'	W102°	08.22'		
	ROLLA	RLL	NDB	263.00	N48°	52.88'	W99°	36.89'		
	RUGBY	RUG	NDB	212.00	N48°	23.27'	W100°	01.61'		
	SABON (LOM)	SABO	NDB	395.00	N46°	51.77'	W98°	34.84'		
	VALLEY CITY	VCY	NDB	382.00	N46°	52.64'	W97°	54.83'		
	WATFORD CITY	AFD	NDB	400.00	N47°	47.89'	W103°	15.18'		
	WILLISTON	ISN	NDB	275.00	N48°	08.75'	W103°	35.02'		
	WILLISTON	ISN	VOR	116.30	N48°	15.20'	W103°	45.04'	2,371	E12°
	YUSON (LOM)	YUSO	NDB	275.00	N48°	07.09'	W103°	30.69'		
Ohio										
	ADDYS (LOM)	ADDY	NDB	351.00	N39°	07.50'	W84°	40.16'		
	AIRBO (LOM/NDB)	AIRB	NDB	407.00	N39°	29.58'	W83°	44.28'		
	AKRON	ACO	VOR	114.40	N41°	06.47'	W81°	12.09'	1,200	W04°
	AKRON (LOM/NDB)	AKRO	NDB	362.00	N41°	04.18'	W81°	23.24'		
	ALLEN CO	AOH	VOR	108.40	N40°	42.42'	W83°	58.08'	980	W04°
	APPLETON	APE	VOR	116.70	N40°	09.06'	W82°	35.29'	1,361	W06°
	ASHLAND	AAU	NDB	329.00	N40°	57.80'	W82°	15.20'		
	BELLAIRE	AIR	VOR	117.10	N40°	01.02'	W80°	49.03'	1,289	W07°
	BENTON RIDGE	BNR	NDB	209.00	N41°	01.00'	W83°	39.99'		
	BOUTN (LOM/NDB)	BOUT	NDB	230.00	N39°	49.15'	W83°	12.29'		
	BRIGGS	BSV	VOR	112.40	N40°	44.43'	W81°	25.92'	1,229	W04°
	BRUNY (LOM)	BRUN	NDB	315.00	N39°	50.49'	W84°	20.94'		
	BRYAN	BYN	NDB	260.00	N41°	28.78'	W84°	27.96'		
	BUCKEYE	BUD	VOR	109.80	N40°	36.98'	W83°	03.81'	990	W05°
	BURKE LAKEFRONT	BKL	NDB	416.00	N41°	31.73'	W81°	39.78'		
	BURLN (LOM/NDB)	BURL	NDB	321.00	N39°	02.75'	W84°	46.38'		
	CADIZ	CFX	NDB	239.00	N40°	14.20'	W81°	00.78'		
	CAMBRIDGE	CDI	NDB	223.00	N39°	57.83'	W81°	35.28'		
	CASER (LOM)	CASE	NDB	338.00	N39°	44.92'	W82°	32.12'		
	CHARDON	CXR	VOR	112.70	N41°	31.01'	W81°	09.79'	1,328	W05°
	CINCINNATI	LUK	NDB	335.00	N39°	09.55'	W84°	20.52'		
	CINCINNATI	CVG	VOR	117.30	N39°	00.95'	W84°	42.20'	879	E00°
	CINCINNATI-BLUE A	ISZ	NDB	388.00	N39°	14.93'	W84°	23.36'		
	CIRCLEVILLE	CYO	NDB	366.00	N39°	31.38'	W82°	58.78'		
	CLARK CO	CCJ	NDB	341.00	N39°	52.41'	W83°	46.77'		
	COBBS (LOM)	COBB	NDB	253.00	N39°	44.57'	W83°	01.21'		
	COURT HOUSE	CSS	NDB	414.00	N39°	35.96'	W83°	23.52'		
	CUBLA (LOM/NDB)	CUBL	NDB	299.00	N39°	21.20'	W83°	52.53'		
	DAYTON	DQN	VOR	114.50	N40°	00.98'	W84°	23.81'	990	W01°

State/Country	VOR/NDB Name	Ident.	Type	Freq.	Latitude		Longitude		Altitude	Mag Var
USA/CANADA NAVAIDS										
Ohio	DEFIANCE	DFI	NDB	246.00	N41°	20.07'	W84°	25.61'		
	DELAWARE	DLZ	NDB	215.00	N40°	16.68'	W83°	06.54'		
	DON SCOTT	DKG	NDB	348.00	N40°	04.82'	W83°	04.73'		
	DORCH (LOM)	DORC	NDB	212.00	N40°	06.57'	W80°	41.32'		
	DRYER	DJB	VOR	113.60	N41°	21.48'	W82°	09.71'	780	W05°
	EAST LIVERPOOL	EVO	NDB	385.00	N40°	40.58'	W80°	38.31'		
	ENGEL	EZE	NDB	226.00	N41°	29.33'	W81°	43.37'		
	FETCH (LOM)	FETC	NDB	338.00	N41°	12.02'	W80°	35.77'		
	FINDLAY	FDY	VOR	108.20	N40°	57.31'	W83°	45.36'	819	W02°
	FOSTORIA	FZI	NDB	379.00	N41°	11.33'	W83°	23.77'		
	FULER (LOM/NDB)	FULE	NDB	515.00	N40°	04.41'	W83°	11.88'		
	FULTON	USE	NDB	375.00	N41°	36.55'	W84°	07.96'		
	GALLIPOLIS	GAS	NDB	420.00	N38°	50.00'	W82°	09.69'		
	GEORGETOWN	GEO	NDB	219.00	N38°	52.91'	W83°	53.11'		
	GRENS (LOM)	GREN	NDB	272.00	N40°	00.60'	W83°	01.73'		
	HAMILTON	HAO	NDB	260.00	N39°	22.35'	W84°	34.34'		
	HARRI (LOM/NDB)	HARR	NDB	344.00	N41°	20.31'	W81°	57.86'		
	HILLSBORO	HOC	NDB	278.00	N39°	11.08'	W83°	32.54'		
	HOGAF (LMM)	HOGA	NDB	521.00	N41°	34.44'	W81°	28.27'		
	HOOK FLD	HKF	NDB	239.00	N39°	29.92'	W84°	26.84'		
	HUBBARD	HBD	NDB	408.00	N41°	09.17'	W80°	31.83'		
	JEFFERSON	JFN	VOR	115.20	N41°	45.60'	W80°	44.88'	898	W05°
	LAKEFIELD	CQA	NDB	205.00	N40°	28.92'	W84°	33.86'		
	LAKELAND	LQL	NDB	263.00	N41°	40.94'	W81°	22.73'		
	LIMA	LYL	NDB	362.00	N40°	42.27'	W84°	01.39'		
	LONDON	UYF	NDB	284.00	N39°	56.05'	W83°	27.97'		
	LOST NATION	LNN	VOR	110.20	N41°	41.03'	W81°	23.72'	629	W07°
	MADEIRA	MDE	NDB	379.00	N39°	13.35'	W84°	21.33'		
	MANNS (LOM/NDB)	MANN	NDB	372.00	N40°	45.96'	W82°	26.69'		
	MANSFIELD	MFD	VOR	108.80	N40°	52.11'	W82°	35.45'	1,210	W03°
	MARATHON	MAH	VOR	114.90	N41°	00.90'	W83°	39.87'	829	W05°
	MARION	MNN	NDB	201.00	N40°	37.02'	W83°	04.14'		
	MARYSVILLE	MRT	NDB	303.00	N40°	13.60'	W83°	20.97'		
	MIDWEST	MXQ	VOR	112.90	N39°	25.78'	W83°	48.07'	1,049	W04°
	MILLERSBURG	MLR	NDB	382.00	N40°	32.50'	W81°	52.35'		
	NEWARK	HEH	NDB	524.00	N40°	01.55'	W82°	27.81'		
	NEWCOMERSTOWN	CTW	VOR	111.80	N40°	13.75'	W81°	28.58'	1,180	W07°
	ONIDA (LOM)	ONID	NDB	223.00	N39°	34.69'	W84°	19.42'		
	OTTAWA	PDR	NDB	233.00	N41°	01.86'	W83°	58.51'		
	OXFORD	OXD	NDB	282.00	N39°	30.43'	W84°	46.92'		
	PATTERSON	FFO	VOR	115.20	N39°	49.09'	W84°	03.27'	806	W04°
	PEEBLES	PZO	NDB	329.00	N38°	55.27'	W83°	19.61'		
	PICKL (LOM)	PICK	NDB	376.00	N39°	52.85'	W82°	50.16'		
	PORT CLINTON	PCW	NDB	423.00	N41°	31.11'	W82°	52.12'		
	PORTSMOUTH	PMH	NDB	373.00	N38°	46.90'	W82°	50.69'		
	ROSEWOOD	ROD	VOR	117.50	N40°	17.26'	W84°	02.58'	1,079	W05°
	ROSS CO	RZT	NDB	236.00	N39°	26.37'	W83°	01.64'		
	RUSHSYLVANIA	RUV	NDB	326.00	N40°	27.53'	W83°	40.07'		
	SANDUSKY	SKY	VOR	109.20	N41°	26.06'	W82°	39.28'	580	W04°
	SMITHVILLE	SLW	NDB	400.00	N40°	52.50'	W81°	49.99'		
	SPORTYS	PWF	NDB	245.00	N39°	04.60'	W84°	12.92'		
	SPRINGFIELD	SGH	VOR	113.20	N39°	50.18'	W83°	50.69'	1,049	W04°
	STANLEY	VFU	NDB	411.00	N40°	51.75'	W84°	36.82'		
	SUMIE (LOM/NDB)	SUMI	NDB	391.00	N39°	59.17'	W82°	45.26'		
	TABEY (LOM)	TABE	NDB	248.00	N41°	34.14'	W81°	34.41'		
	TIFFIN	TII	NDB	269.00	N41°	05.88'	W83°	12.46'		
	TIVERTON	TVT	VOR	116.50	N40°	27.48'	W82°	07.61'	1,338	W03°
	TOLSON	TSO	NDB	395.00	N40°	33.75'	W81°	04.85'		
	TOPHR (LOM)	TOPH	NDB	219.00	N41°	33.21'	W83°	55.26'		
	UNIVERSITY	UGS	NDB	250.00	N39°	15.43'	W82°	07.56'		
	VERSAILLES	VES	NDB	356.00	N40°	12.37'	W84°	31.36'		
	WATERVILLE	VWV	VOR	113.10	N41°	27.08'	W83°	38.31'	659	W02°
	WEST UNION	AMT	NDB	359.00	N38°	51.35'	W83°	33.82'		
	XENIA	XEN	NDB	395.00	N39°	42.90'	W83°	55.79'		
	YELLOW BUD	XUB	VOR	112.50	N39°	31.60'	W82°	58.66'	688	W05°
	YOUNGSTOWN	YNG	VOR	109.00	N41°	19.85'	W80°	40.48'	1,138	W05°
	ZANESVILLE	ZZV	VOR	111.40	N39°	56.45'	W81°	53.55'	898	W06°
	ZANESVILLE	ZZV	NDB	204.00	N39°	54.37'	W81°	55.15'		
Oklahoma										
	ADA	ADH	VOR	117.80	N34°	48.15'	W96°	40.21'	987	E06°
	ADA	AMR	NDB	302.00	N34°	48.33'	W96°	40.61'		
	ADDMO (LOM)	ADDM	NDB	400.00	N34°	13.93'	W96°	55.98'		
	ALTUS	LTS	VOR	109.80	N34°	39.76'	W99°	16.25'	1,371	E08°
	ALVA	AVK	NDB	203.00	N36°	46.75'	W98°	40.27'		

State/Country	VOR/NDB Name	Ident.	Type	Freq.	Latitude		Longitude		Altitude	Mag Var
USA/CANADA NAVAIDS										
Oklahoma	ANTLERS	AEE	NDB	391.00	N34°	11.50'	W95°	39.11'		
	ARBUCKLE	AUV	NDB	284.00	N34°	09.04'	W97°	07.48'		
	ARDMORE	ADM	VOR	116.70	N34°	12.69'	W97°	10.10'	928	E06°
	BARTLESVILLE	BVO	VOR	117.90	N36°	50.05'	W96°	01.09'	941	E08°
	BLAKI (LOM)	BLAK	NDB	255.00	N36°	14.17'	W97°	05.23'		
	BRISTOW	TZO	NDB	251.00	N35°	46.18'	W96°	25.48'		
	BUFFALO	BFK	NDB	215.00	N36°	51.85'	W99°	37.20'		
	BURNS FLAT	BFV	VOR	110.00	N35°	14.21'	W99°	12.36'	1,781	E08°
	CHICKASHA	OLR	NDB	290.00	N35°	06.26'	W97°	58.30'		
	CLINTON	CLK	NDB	320.00	N35°	32.35'	W98°	56.10'		
	CUSHING	CUH	NDB	242.00	N35°	53.40'	W96°	46.51'		
	DAVIS	MEE	VOR	108.60	N35°	39.79'	W95°	22.06'	610	E06°
	DEWIE (LOM)	DEWI	NDB	201.00	N36°	50.36'	W96°	00.83'		
	DUNCAN	DUC	VOR	111.00	N34°	23.06'	W97°	55.00'	1,088	E09°
	EL RENO	RQO	NDB	335.00	N35°	28.72'	W98°	00.53'		
	ELK CITY	EZY	NDB	241.00	N35°	25.55'	W99°	23.88'		
	FAIRVIEW	FAU	NDB	246.00	N36°	17.10'	W98°	28.67'		
	FOSSI (LOM/NDB)	FOSS	NDB	393.00	N35°	27.03'	W99°	12.08'		
	FREDERICK	FDR	NDB	222.00	N34°	21.22'	W98°	59.18'		
	GAGE	GAG	VOR	115.60	N36°	20.62'	W99°	52.80'	2,430	E10°
	GALLY (LOM/NDB)	GALL	NDB	350.00	N35°	17.70'	W97°	35.31'		
	GARFY (LOM)	GARF	NDB	341.00	N36°	16.50'	W97°	47.44'		
	GLENPOOL	GNP	VOR	110.60	N35°	55.25'	W95°	58.11'	810	E06°
	GUYMON	GUY	NDB	275.00	N36°	42.32'	W101°	30.30'		
	HENRYETTA	HET	NDB	267.00	N35°	24.27'	W96°	00.83'		
	HOBART	HBR	VOR	111.80	N34°	51.99'	W99°	03.80'	1,459	E10°
	HOLDENVILLE	HDL	NDB	411.00	N35°	05.12'	W96°	24.80'		
	HUGO	HHW	NDB	323.00	N34°	02.38'	W95°	32.36'		
	KINGFISHER	IFI	VOR	114.70	N35°	48.31'	W98°	00.23'	1,108	E09°
	LAWTON	LAW	VOR	109.40	N34°	29.77'	W98°	24.78'	1,098	E09°
	LOGAN CO	LCY	NDB	326.00	N35°	50.73'	W97°	24.94'		
	MC ALESTER	MLC	VOR	112.00	N34°	50.96'	W95°	46.93'	819	E08°
	MIAMI	MMW	NDB	317.00	N36°	54.49'	W94°	53.45'		
	MOORELAND	MDF	NDB	284.00	N36°	29.18'	W99°	11.57'		
	MUSKOGEE	MKO	NDB	306.00	N35°	35.69'	W95°	17.23'		
	NORMAN	OUN	NDB	260.00	N35°	14.24'	W97°	28.87'		
	OILLR (LOM)	OILL	NDB	338.00	N36°	05.83'	W95°	53.33'		
	OKMULGEE	OKM	VOR	112.20	N35°	41.58'	W95°	51.95'	764	E08°
	OWASO (LOM/NDB)	OWAS	NDB	375.00	N36°	18.44'	W95°	52.51'		
	PANCK (LOM)	PANC	NDB	383.00	N36°	57.87'	W100°	57.37'		
	PAULS VALLEY	PVJ	NDB	384.00	N34°	42.92'	W97°	13.75'		
	PENO BOTTOMS	AFT	NDB	311.00	N35°	19.36'	W94°	28.45'		
	PIONEER	PER	VOR	113.20	N36°	44.78'	W97°	09.60'	1,059	E06°
	PONCA (LOM/NDB)	PONC	NDB	275.00	N36°	49.50'	W97°	06.03'		
	POST	PFL	NDB	308.00	N34°	36.53'	W98°	24.22'		
	PRAGUE	GGU	NDB	314.00	N35°	31.00'	W96°	43.11'		
	PRESO (LOM)	PRES	NDB	388.00	N35°	45.31'	W95°	56.92'		
	RICH MOUNTAIN	PGO	VOR	113.50	N34°	40.82'	W94°	36.54'	2,699	E04°
	SALLISAW	IQS	NDB	520.00	N35°	23.91'	W94°	47.66'		
	SAYRE	SYO	VOR	115.20	N35°	20.70'	W99°	38.12'	1,990	E10°
	SEMINOLE	SRE	NDB	278.00	N35°	16.30'	W96°	40.48'		
	SHAWNEE	SNL	NDB	227.00	N35°	21.27'	W96°	56.78'		
	STILLWATER	SWO	VOR	108.40	N36°	13.45'	W97°	04.87'	1,020	E07°
	TAHLEQUAH	TQH	NDB	215.00	N35°	55.58'	W95°	00.34'		
	THORP	BCY	NDB	212.00	N36°	45.31'	W102°	32.09'		
	TILGHMAN	CQB	NDB	396.00	N35°	43.33'	W96°	49.11'		
	TINKER	TIK	VOR	115.80	N35°	26.18'	W97°	22.77'	1,282	E07°
	TRAIL	OFZ	NDB	388.00	N34°	46.88'	W98°	24.13'		
	TULOO (LOM/NDB)	TULO	NDB	406.00	N35°	28.28'	W97°	36.32'		
	TULSA	TUL	VOR	114.40	N36°	11.77'	W95°	47.28'	790	E08°
	VANCE	END	VOR	115.40	N36°	20.73'	W97°	55.12'	1,302	E09°
	WAMPA (LOM)	WAMP	NDB	344.00	N34°	47.86'	W95°	49.24'		
	WATONGA	JWG	NDB	299.00	N35°	51.72'	W98°	25.52'		
	WEATHERFORD	OJA	NDB	272.00	N35°	31.80'	W98°	40.23'		
	WEST WOODWARD	OWU	NDB	329.00	N36°	26.05'	W99°	31.44'		
	WILEY POST	PWA	VOR	113.40	N35°	31.97'	W97°	38.83'	1,269	E08°
	WILL ROGERS	IRW	VOR	114.10	N35°	21.51'	W97°	36.55'	1,229	E07°
	WILLIAM POGUE	OWP	NDB	362.00	N36°	10.00'	W96°	09.01'		
	WOODRING	ODG	VOR	109.00	N36°	22.42'	W97°	47.28'	1,151	E08°
Oregon										
	ABATE (LOM)	ABAT	NDB	356.00	N45°	37.81'	W123°	02.74'		
	ASTORIA	AST	VOR	114.00	N46°	09.70'	W123°	52.82'	9	E19°
	BAKER	BKE	VOR	115.30	N44°	50.43'	W117°	48.47'	3,358	E20°
	BODEY (LOM/NDB)	BODE	NDB	411.00	N44°	18.47'	W121°	01.13'		

State/Country	VOR/NDB Name	Ident.	Type	Freq.	Latitude		Longitude		Altitude	Mag Var
USA/CANADA NAVAIDS										
Oregon	CORVALLIS	CVO	VOR	115.40	N44°	29.97'	W123°	17.61'	249	E21°
	DESCHUTES	DSD	VOR	117.60	N44°	15.16'	W121°	18.21'	4,099	E18°
	EMIRE (LOM/NDB)	EMIR	NDB	378.00	N43°	23.68'	W124°	18.61'		
	EUGENE	EUG	VOR	112.90	N44°	07.25'	W123°	13.36'	360	E20°
	FORIS (LOM/NDB)	FORI	NDB	230.00	N45°	41.73'	W118°	43.83'		
	FRAKK (LOM)	FRAK	NDB	260.00	N44°	12.76'	W123°	13.23'		
	GOLD BEACH	GOL	NDB	396.00	N42°	25.07'	W124°	25.40'		
	GOOSE	GOS	NDB	278.00	N42°	09.17'	W120°	24.30'		
	KARPEN	PEN	NDB	201.00	N46°	08.37'	W123°	35.23'		
	KIMBERLY	IMB	VOR	115.60	N44°	38.90'	W119°	42.69'	5,218	E20°
	KLAMATH FALLS	LMT	VOR	115.90	N42°	09.18'	W121°	43.65'	4,086	E17°
	LA GRANDE	LGD	NDB	296.00	N45°	22.34'	W117°	59.57'		
	LAKER (LOM/NDB)	LAKE	NDB	332.00	N45°	32.47'	W122°	27.73'		
	LAKEVIEW	LKV	VOR	112.00	N42°	29.57'	W120°	30.42'	7,458	E19°
	LEWISBURG	LWG	NDB	225.00	N44°	36.81'	W123°	16.23'		
	MC DERMITT STATE	RMD	NDB	204.00	N42°	00.69'	W117°	43.25'		
	MINNE (LOM)	MINN	NDB	383.00	N45°	14.77'	W123°	01.78'		
	NEWBERG	UBG	VOR	117.40	N45°	21.19'	W122°	58.69'	1,439	E21°
	NEWPORT	ONP	VOR	117.10	N44°	34.52'	W124°	03.63'	150	E19°
	NORTH BEND	OTH	VOR	112.10	N43°	24.92'	W124°	10.10'	678	E18°
	ONTARIO	ONO	NDB	305.00	N44°	01.18'	W117°	00.50'		
	PENDLETON	PDT	VOR	114.70	N45°	41.90'	W118°	56.32'	1,554	E20°
	PORTLAND	PDX	VOR	111.80	N45°	35.62'	W122°	36.37'	19	E20°
	PRAHL	PLV	NDB	366.00	N45°	17.00'	W122°	46.25'		
	PUMIE (LOM)	PUMI	NDB	373.00	N42°	27.05'	W122°	54.80'		
	ROGUE VALLEY	OED	VOR	113.60	N42°	28.77'	W122°	54.77'	2,079	E19°
	ROME	REO	VOR	112.50	N42°	35.43'	W117°	52.09'	4,047	E19°
	ROSEBURG	RBG	VOR	108.20	N43°	10.94'	W123°	21.13'	1,318	E20°
	ROSEBURG	RBG	NDB	400.00	N43°	14.11'	W123°	21.48'		
	TURNO (LOM)	TURN	NDB	266.00	N44°	50.85'	W122°	56.99'		
	VIOLE (LMM)	VIOL	NDB	356.00	N42°	23.35'	W122°	52.84'		
	WILDHORSE	ILR	VOR	113.80	N43°	35.58'	W118°	57.30'	4,139	E18°
	WILSON	TKW	NDB	271.00	N45°	29.08'	W123°	51.37'		
Pennsylvania	ALLEGHENY	AGC	VOR	110.00	N40°	16.71'	W80°	02.45'	1,289	W05°
	ALLENTOWN	FJC	VOR	117.50	N40°	43.60'	W75°	27.28'	678	W10°
	ALTOONA	AOO	VOR	108.80	N40°	19.52'	W78°	18.22'	1,630	W07°
	AMBLER	ING	NDB	275.00	N40°	07.55'	W75°	17.10'		
	BARTY (LOM)	BART	NDB	257.00	N41°	16.61'	W75°	46.54'		
	BELLGROVE	BZJ	NDB	328.00	N40°	26.15'	W76°	33.18'		
	BENJE	BHU	NDB	382.00	N40°	22.53'	W79°	16.29'		
	BRADFORD	BFD	VOR	116.60	N41°	47.18'	W78°	37.16'	2,099	W07°
	BRAFO (LOM/NDB)	BRAF	NDB	224.00	N41°	45.26'	W78°	34.41'		
	CAMOR (LOM/NDB)	CAMO	NDB	299.00	N39°	52.96'	W79°	44.68'		
	CARBON	LQX	NDB	339.00	N40°	48.72'	W75°	45.54'		
	CASCADE	CQD	NDB	372.00	N42°	07.15'	W80°	06.27'		
	CASTLE	UCP	NDB	272.00	N41°	01.41'	W80°	24.88'		
	CLARION	CIP	VOR	112.90	N41°	08.77'	W79°	27.47'	1,528	W06°
	CORRY	ORJ	NDB	258.00	N41°	54.75'	W79°	38.90'		
	CRYSTAL LAKE	CYE	NDB	410.00	N41°	12.62'	W75°	49.90'		
	DOYLESTOWN	DYL	NDB	237.00	N40°	20.14'	W75°	07.32'		
	EAST TEXAS	ETX	VOR	110.20	N40°	34.85'	W75°	41.03'	751	W09°
	ELLWOOD CITY	EWC	VOR	115.80	N40°	49.51'	W80°	12.69'	1,220	W08°
	ENOLA (LOM)	ENOL	NDB	204.00	N40°	14.77'	W76°	54.03'		
	ERIE	ERI	VOR	109.40	N42°	01.04'	W80°	17.56'	800	W06°
	ESMER (LOM)	ESME	NDB	349.00	N42°	02.31'	W80°	15.32'		
	FRANKLIN	FKL	VOR	109.60	N41°	26.31'	W79°	51.40'	1,528	W06°
	GOOGL (LOM)	GOOG	NDB	264.00	N40°	14.89'	W75°	26.82'		
	HARRISBURG	HAR	VOR	112.50	N40°	18.13'	W77°	04.17'	1,302	W10°
	HAZLETON	HZL	VOR	109.40	N40°	58.50'	W76°	07.54'	1,708	W09°
	HUMBOLT	HXM	NDB	366.00	N40°	59.31'	W75°	59.81'		
	INDIAN HEAD	IHD	VOR	108.20	N39°	58.45'	W79°	21.50'	2,820	W06°
	INDIANA	INP	NDB	242.00	N40°	37.91'	W79°	03.95'		
	JOHNSTOWN	JST	VOR	113.00	N40°	19.00'	W78°	50.04'	2,279	W06°
	KEATING	ETG	VOR	116.00	N41°	12.89'	W78°	08.56'	2,250	W10°
	LAKE HENRY	LHY	VOR	110.80	N41°	28.54'	W75°	28.95'	2,318	W10°
	LANCASTER	LRP	VOR	117.30	N40°	07.19'	W76°	17.47'	400	W09°
	LATLE (LOM)	LATL	NDB	219.00	N40°	10.69'	W77°	00.34'		
	LEEHI (LOM)	LEEH	NDB	400.00	N40°	35.14'	W75°	32.97'		
	MC KEESPORT	MKP	NDB	287.00	N40°	21.30'	W79°	46.86'		
	MILTON	MIP	VOR	109.20	N41°	01.40'	W76°	39.91'	1,000	W09°
	MODENA	MXE	VOR	113.20	N39°	55.08'	W75°	40.24'	472	W09°
	MONTOUR	MMJ	VOR	112.00	N40°	29.28'	W80°	11.63'	1,200	W06°
	NORTH PHILADELPHI	PNE	VOR	112.00	N40°	04.92'	W75°	00.57'	111	W10°

State/Country	VOR/NDB Name	Ident.	Type	Freq.	Latitude		Longitude		Altitude	Mag Var
USA/CANADA NAVAIDS										
Pennsylvania	PENNRIDGE	CKZ	VOR	108.85	N40°	23.45'	W75°	17.32'	551	W12°
	PENUE (LOM)	PENU	NDB	388.00	N40°	54.61'	W77°	44.50'		
	PHILIPSBURG	PSB	VOR	115.50	N40°	54.97'	W77°	59.56'	2,450	W10°
	PICTURE ROCKS	PIX	NDB	344.00	N41°	16.60'	W76°	42.60'		
	PORTS (LOM)	PORT	NDB	275.00	N40°	59.16'	W78°	08.55'		
	POTTSTOWN	PTW	VOR	116.50	N40°	13.33'	W75°	33.61'	288	W09°
	QUAKERTOWN	UKT	NDB	208.00	N40°	25.48'	W75°	17.84'		
	RAVINE	RAV	VOR	114.60	N40°	33.20'	W76°	35.96'	1,748	W11°
	REVLOC	REC	VOR	110.60	N40°	32.78'	W78°	44.82'	2,338	W09°
	SELINSGROVE	SEG	VOR	110.40	N40°	47.45'	W76°	53.04'	619	W08°
	SHAPP (LOM)	SHAP	NDB	356.00	N40°	18.38'	W75°	56.97'		
	SLATE RUN	SLT	VOR	113.90	N41°	30.76'	W77°	58.20'	2,318	W08°
	ST THOMAS	THS	VOR	115.00	N39°	55.99'	W77°	57.05'	2,338	W07°
	STONEYFORK	SFK	VOR	108.60	N41°	41.71'	W77°	25.19'	1,990	W08°
	STOYSTOWN	SYS	NDB	209.00	N40°	05.14'	W78°	54.99'		
	STROH (LOM/NDB)	STRO	NDB	407.00	N40°	36.88'	W77°	43.07'		
	TIDIOUTE	TDT	VOR	117.60	N41°	42.78'	W79°	25.03'	1,708	W09°
	TRENN (LOM)	TREN	NDB	369.00	N40°	12.76'	W74°	53.90'		
	TYRONE	TON	VOR	114.90	N40°	44.10'	W78°	19.87'	2,630	W07°
	WASHINGTON CO	PNU	NDB	255.00	N40°	08.67'	W80°	09.75'		
	WILKES BARRE	LVZ	VOR	111.60	N41°	16.36'	W75°	41.36'	2,118	W10°
	WILLIAMSPORT	FQM	VOR	114.40	N41°	20.31'	W76°	46.49'	2,089	W09°
	WILLOW GROVE(NAV)	NXX	NDB	388.00	N40°	11.35'	W75°	08.71'		
	YARDLEY	ARD	VOR	108.20	N40°	15.20'	W74°	54.45'	298	W10°
	YORK	EUD	NDB	285.00	N39°	55.20'	W76°	52.65'		
Rhode Island	ARMIN (LOM)	ARMI	NDB	356.00	N41°	48.62'	W71°	21.21'		
	BLOCK ISLAND	BID	NDB	216.00	N41°	09.99'	W71°	34.77'		
	CENTRAL	SFZ	NDB	241.00	N41°	55.14'	W71°	29.31'		
	PROVIDENCE	PVD	VOR	115.60	N41°	43.45'	W71°	25.77'	49	W14°
	RENCH (LOM)	RENC	NDB	335.00	N41°	38.50'	W71°	29.68'		
	SANDY POINT	SEY	VOR	117.80	N41°	10.04'	W71°	34.56'	98	W15°
	WESTERLY	RLS	NDB	264.00	N41°	20.67'	W71°	48.85'		
Russia	ANADYR	KB	NDB	790.00	N64°	44.00'	W177°	44.99'		
	PROVIDENIYA	BC	NDB	320.00	N64°	17.49'	W173°	18.99'		
South Carolina	AIKEN	AIK	NDB	347.00	N33°	39.10'	W81°	40.62'		
	ALCOT (LOM)	ALCO	NDB	335.00	N34°	10.43'	W79°	51.14'		
	ALLENDALE	ALD	VOR	116.70	N33°	00.75'	W81°	17.53'	190	W01°
	ANDERSON CO	AND	NDB	230.00	N34°	29.88'	W82°	42.51'		
	ASHLY (LOM/NDB)	ASHL	NDB	329.00	N32°	58.57'	W80°	05.85'		
	BARNWELL	BNL	NDB	260.00	N33°	15.56'	W81°	22.74'		
	BENNETTSVILLE	BES	NDB	230.00	N34°	37.21'	W79°	43.99'		
	BUSHE (LOM)	BUSH	NDB	233.00	N33°	17.21'	W81°	56.81'		
	CALAB (LOM)	CALA	NDB	267.00	N33°	53.11'	W78°	37.79'		
	CAMDEN	CDN	NDB	263.00	N34°	17.04'	W80°	33.69'		
	CHARLESTON	CHS	VOR	113.50	N32°	53.65'	W80°	02.26'	39	W05°
	CHERAW	CQW	NDB	409.00	N34°	44.51'	W79°	51.93'		
	CHESTERFIELD	CTF	VOR	108.20	N34°	39.02'	W80°	16.49'	560	W03°
	CLEMSON	CEU	NDB	257.00	N34°	40.42'	W82°	53.20'		
	COLUMBIA	CAE	VOR	114.70	N33°	51.43'	W81°	03.22'	409	W02°
	CORONACA	GIW	NDB	239.00	N34°	15.22'	W82°	05.17'		
	DARLINGTON	UDG	NDB	245.00	N34°	26.59'	W79°	53.24'		
	DILLON	DLC	NDB	274.00	N34°	27.00'	W79°	22.13'		
	DORCHESTER CO	DYB	NDB	365.00	N33°	03.67'	W80°	16.63'		
	DYANA (LOM/NDB)	DYAN	NDB	338.00	N34°	41.46'	W82°	26.61'		
	EDISTO	EDS	VOR	111.40	N33°	27.34'	W80°	51.50'	190	W05°
	ELECTRIC CITY	ELW	VOR	108.60	N34°	25.15'	W82°	47.08'	741	E00°
	EMORY	EMR	NDB	385.00	N33°	27.76'	W81°	59.81'		
	ENOREE	EOE	NDB	278.00	N34°	18.69'	W81°	38.15'		
	EVANS	CFY	NDB	420.00	N33°	51.35'	W79°	45.95'		
	FAIRMONT	FRT	NDB	248.00	N34°	54.14'	W81°	59.08'		
	FLORENCE	FLO	VOR	115.20	N34°	13.97'	W79°	39.42'	111	W03°
	FORT MILL	FML	VOR	112.40	N34°	59.34'	W80°	57.28'	649	W02°
	GEORGETOWN	GGE	NDB	242.00	N33°	18.92'	W79°	19.46'		
	GRAND STRAND	CRE	VOR	117.60	N33°	48.82'	W78°	43.47'	19	W03°
	GREENWOOD	GRD	VOR	115.50	N34°	15.09'	W82°	09.24'	629	W01°
	GREER (LOM)	GREE	NDB	287.00	N34°	48.92'	W82°	16.80'		
	HARTSVILLE	HVS	NDB	341.00	N34°	24.42'	W80°	06.91'		
	HORRY	HYW	NDB	370.00	N33°	49.77'	W79°	07.43'		
	JOHNS ISLAND	JZI	NDB	283.00	N32°	42.07'	W80°	00.33'		
	JUDKY (LOM)	JUDK	NDB	521.00	N34°	46.80'	W82°	20.98'		

State/Country	VOR/NDB Name	Ident.	Type	Freq.	Latitude		Longitude		Altitude	Mag Var
USA/CANADA NAVAIDS										
South Carolina	KINGSTREE	CKI	NDB	404.00	N33°	43.06'	W79°	51.30'		
	LAKE KEOWEE	LQK	NDB	408.00	N34°	48.67'	W82°	42.21'		
	LANCASTER	LKR	NDB	400.00	N34°	43.42'	W80°	51.48'		
	LAURENS	LUX	NDB	307.00	N34°	30.49'	W81°	56.98'		
	MANNING	MNI	NDB	381.00	N33°	35.29'	W80°	12.37'		
	MARION	MAO	NDB	388.00	N34°	11.10'	W79°	19.98'		
	MC ENTIRE	MMT	NDB	427.00	N33°	56.14'	W80°	47.93'		
	MONCKS CORNER	MKS	NDB	354.00	N33°	11.45'	W80°	02.00'		
	MURRY (LOM)	MURR	NDB	362.00	N33°	58.03'	W81°	14.68'		
	ORANGEBURG	OYI	NDB	226.00	N33°	25.08'	W80°	54.34'		
	PAGELAND	PYG	NDB	270.00	N34°	44.69'	W80°	20.28'		
	RALLY	UZ	NDB	227.00	N34°	53.40'	W81°	04.85'		
	ROSCOE	RCZ	NDB	375.00	N34°	51.15'	W79°	41.61'		
	SPARTANBURG	SPA	VOR	115.70	N35°	02.01'	W81°	55.62'	908	W02°
	STUCKEY	HEK	NDB	236.00	N33°	43.70'	W79°	31.50'		
	SUMTER	SMS	NDB	252.00	N33°	59.44'	W80°	21.63'		
	UNION CO	UOT	NDB	326.00	N34°	41.04'	W81°	38.54'		
	VANCE	VAN	VOR	110.40	N33°	28.48'	W80°	26.91'	141	W06°
	WALTERBORO	RBW	NDB	221.00	N32°	55.54'	W80°	38.41'		
	WASSA (LOM)	WASS	NDB	335.00	N32°	00.24'	W80°	59.15'		
	WINNSBORO	FDW	NDB	414.00	N34°	18.86'	W81°	06.75'		
	YAUPON	SUT	NDB	233.00	N33°	55.65'	W78°	04.50'		
South Dakota										
	ABERDEEN	ABR	VOR	113.00	N45°	25.04'	W98°	22.12'	1,298	E07°
	BEADY (LOM)	BEAD	NDB	302.00	N44°	26.63'	W98°	20.21'		
	BELLE FOURCHE	EFC	NDB	269.00	N44°	44.15'	W103°	51.54'		
	BLACK HILLS	SPF	NDB	300.00	N44°	29.06'	W103°	47.06'		
	BRITTON	BTN	NDB	386.00	N45°	48.82'	W97°	44.64'		
	BROOKINGS	BKX	VOR	108.80	N44°	18.19'	W96°	48.90'	1,639	E06°
	BUFFALO	BUA	VOR	109.40	N45°	32.75'	W103°	28.57'	3,017	E13°
	CAGUR (LOM)	CAGU	NDB	347.00	N42°	50.61'	W97°	18.12'		
	DUPREE	DPR	VOR	116.80	N45°	04.69'	W101°	42.90'	2,528	E10°
	FLYING T	FTA	NDB	388.00	N43°	23.41'	W103°	26.22'		
	HAND	MKA	NDB	371.00	N44°	31.27'	W98°	57.55'		
	HURON	HON	VOR	117.60	N44°	26.40'	W98°	18.66'	1,298	E10°
	LEMMON	LEM	VOR	111.40	N45°	55.18'	W102°	06.21'	2,568	E13°
	LICAN (LOM)	LICA	NDB	215.00	N44°	48.19'	W97°	09.00'		
	MITCHELL	MHE	VOR	109.20	N43°	46.61'	W98°	02.25'	1,298	E07°
	MOBRIDGE	MBG	VOR	108.60	N45°	33.11'	W100°	21.95'	1,925	E11°
	PHILIP	PHP	VOR	108.40	N44°	03.49'	W101°	39.84'	2,338	E12°
	PIERRE	PIR	VOR	112.50	N44°	23.67'	W100°	09.77'	1,790	E11°
	RANCH (LOM/NDB)	RANC	NDB	254.00	N43°	57.89'	W102°	59.93'		
	RAPID CITY	RAP	VOR	112.30	N43°	58.56'	W103°	00.73'	3,148	E13°
	RENEY (LOM)	RENE	NDB	203.00	N45°	23.15'	W98°	19.69'		
	RIVERBEND	RVB	NDB	407.00	N45°	32.99'	W100°	24.61'		
	ROKKY (LOM/NDB)	ROKK	NDB	245.00	N43°	29.64'	W96°	49.72'		
	SIOUX FALLS	FSD	VOR	115.00	N43°	38.97'	W96°	46.86'	1,571	E09°
	VERMILLION	VMR	NDB	375.00	N42°	45.79'	W96°	56.06'		
	WAGNER	AGZ	NDB	392.00	N43°	03.75'	W98°	17.53'		
	WATERTOWN	ATY	VOR	116.60	N44°	58.78'	W97°	08.50'	1,748	E09°
	WENTWORTH	MDS	NDB	400.00	N44°	00.83'	W97°	05.30'		
	WINNER	ISD	VOR	112.80	N43°	29.27'	W99°	45.68'	2,355	E08°
	YANKTON	YKN	VOR	111.40	N42°	55.10'	W97°	23.09'	1,298	E07°
Tennessee										
	ARNOLD AFS	AYX	VOR	112.50	N35°	23.12'	W86°	05.22'	0	E02°
	AULON (LOM/NDB)	AULO	NDB	287.00	N35°	03.70'	W90°	04.30'		
	BENFI (LOM)	BENF	NDB	353.00	N35°	44.52'	W84°	04.87'		
	BOILING FORK	BGF	NDB	263.00	N35°	10.67'	W86°	04.08'		
	BOOIE (LOM/NDB)	BOOI	NDB	221.00	N36°	23.91'	W82°	29.76'		
	BURWI	ULH	NDB	332.00	N35°	27.69'	W86°	14.50'		
	CLARKSVILLE	CKV	VOR	110.60	N36°	37.32'	W87°	24.75'	541	W01°
	COVINGTON	COO	NDB	326.00	N35°	35.38'	W89°	35.23'		
	DAISY	CQN	NDB	341.00	N35°	09.99'	W85°	09.43'		
	DICKSON	DMZ	NDB	203.00	N36°	07.63'	W87°	25.94'		
	DOBBS (LOM)	DOBB	NDB	304.00	N36°	01.84'	W86°	43.33'		
	DULANEY	DYQ	NDB	263.00	N36°	08.15'	W82°	53.42'		
	DYERSBURG	DYR	VOR	116.80	N36°	01.11'	W89°	19.05'	380	E03°
	ELIZABETHTON	EZT	NDB	275.00	N36°	18.95'	W82°	16.22'		
	GALLATIN	GYN	NDB	214.00	N36°	22.77'	W86°	24.69'		
	GIBSON	TGC	NDB	378.00	N35°	56.05'	W88°	51.05'		
	GILES	GZS	NDB	375.00	N35°	09.08'	W87°	03.48'		
	GRAHAM	GHM	VOR	111.60	N35°	50.03'	W87°	27.10'	770	E03°
	HARDEMAN	BAV	NDB	404.00	N35°	12.85'	W89°	02.52'		
	HARDWICK	HDI	NDB	369.00	N35°	09.22'	W84°	54.34'		

State/Country	VOR/NDB Name	Ident.	Type	Freq.	Latitude		Longitude		Altitude	Mag Var
USA/CANADA NAVAIDS										
Tennessee	HINCH MOUNTAIN	HCH	VOR	117.60	N35°	46.85'	W84°	58.70'	3,040	W02°
	HOLSTON MOUNTAIN	HMV	VOR	114.60	N36°	26.22'	W82°	07.77'	4,319	W04°
	HUNTINGDON	HZD	NDB	217.00	N36°	05.29'	W88°	27.97'		
	HURRICANE	SKN	NDB	256.00	N35°	59.04'	W85°	48.48'		
	HUTCHINS	HEM	NDB	233.00	N35°	59.27'	W85°	35.17'		
	JACKS CREEK	JKS	VOR	109.40	N35°	35.93'	W88°	21.53'	629	E02°
	JACKSBORO	JAU	NDB	204.00	N36°	20.27'	W84°	09.65'		
	JASPER	APT	NDB	382.00	N35°	03.57'	W85°	35.03'		
	JEFFERSON	JXT	NDB	346.00	N36°	06.63'	W83°	28.53'		
	KELSO	TNY	NDB	358.00	N35°	08.04'	W86°	32.52'		
	LAFAYETTE	LFB	NDB	245.00	N36°	30.90'	W86°	03.65'		
	LASCASSAS	MBT	NDB	317.00	N35°	52.35'	W86°	22.76'		
	LAWRENCEBURG	LRT	NDB	269.00	N35°	14.13'	W87°	15.64'		
	LEBANON	LDQ	NDB	414.00	N36°	11.19'	W86°	18.84'		
	LIVINGSTON	LVT	VOR	108.40	N36°	35.07'	W85°	09.99'	1,020	W02°
	LOOSAHATCHIE	LHC	NDB	265.00	N35°	17.07'	W89°	40.28'		
	MADISONVILLE	MNV	NDB	361.00	N35°	32.70'	W84°	22.98'		
	MARK ANTON	DTE	NDB	394.00	N35°	28.91'	W84°	55.85'		
	MAURY COUNTY	PBC	NDB	365.00	N35°	36.49'	W87°	05.48'		
	MC KELLAR	MKL	VOR	112.00	N35°	36.21'	W88°	54.62'	409	E02°
	MC MINN CO	MMI	NDB	242.00	N35°	23.67'	W84°	33.69'		
	MEMPHIS	MEM	VOR	117.50	N35°	03.75'	W89°	58.89'	249	E03°
	MERSY (LOM)	MERS	NDB	394.00	N35°	30.93'	W88°	57.41'		
	MILLINGTON	MIG	NDB	232.00	N35°	16.72'	W89°	55.98'		
	MOCCA (LOM)	MOCC	NDB	299.00	N36°	33.32'	W82°	19.07'		
	MOUNTAIN CITY	JJO	NDB	396.00	N36°	24.99'	W81°	49.45'		
	NALLY DUNSTON	DNT	NDB	343.00	N35°	59.70'	W89°	24.34'		
	NASHVILLE	BNA	VOR	114.10	N36°	08.21'	W86°	41.08'	567	W02°
	NEEDMORE	PED	NDB	221.00	N36°	32.18'	W86°	55.05'		
	OBION	OQZ	NDB	212.00	N36°	17.85'	W88°	59.69'		
	OPERY (LOM/NDB)	OPER	NDB	344.00	N36°	12.23'	W86°	39.16'		
	PINEY GROVE	BPO	NDB	403.00	N36°	32.36'	W84°	28.56'		
	PINHOOK	HHY	NDB	242.00	N35°	13.54'	W88°	12.32'		
	ROGERSVILLE	RVN	NDB	329.00	N36°	27.35'	W82°	53.06'		
	SEWANEE	UOS	NDB	275.00	N35°	12.25'	W85°	53.74'		
	SEWART	SWZ	NDB	391.00	N35°	57.40'	W86°	27.83'		
	SHELBYVILLE	SYI	VOR	109.00	N35°	33.71'	W86°	26.34'	810	W01°
	SIBLEY	SZY	NDB	386.00	N35°	14.21'	W88°	30.96'		
	SNUFF (LOM)	SNUF	NDB	335.00	N36°	31.62'	W87°	23.18'		
	SPAIN	SPQ	NDB	414.00	N35°	12.08'	W90°	03.08'		
	TRAINER	TIQ	NDB	410.00	N36°	14.97'	W88°	24.92'		
	VERONA	LUG	NDB	251.00	N35°	30.02'	W86°	48.58'		
	VOLUNTEER	VXV	VOR	116.40	N35°	54.28'	W83°	53.68'	1,289	W03°
	WARRI (LOM/NDB)	WARR	NDB	209.00	N35°	45.14'	W85°	45.84'		
	WAVERLY	AEY	NDB	329.00	N36°	06.97'	W87°	44.47'		
Texas	ABILENE	ABI	VOR	113.70	N32°	28.88'	W99°	51.80'	1,810	E10°
	ACTON	AQN	VOR	110.60	N32°	26.07'	W97°	39.83'	849	E09°
	ALAMO (LOM/NDB)	ALAM	NDB	368.00	N29°	36.45'	W98°	34.18'		
	ALIBI (LOM/NDB)	ALIB	NDB	281.00	N30°	25.92'	W95°	28.57'		
	ALICE	ALI	VOR	114.50	N27°	44.38'	W98°	01.27'	167	E09°
	AMARILLO	AMA	VOR	117.20	N35°	17.25'	W101°	38.35'	3,548	E11°
	AMASON	CZJ	NDB	341.00	N31°	50.17'	W94°	08.99'		
	AMBASSADOR	ABG	NDB	404.00	N32°	35.12'	W95°	06.77'		
	ANAHUAC	CBC	NDB	413.00	N29°	46.39'	W94°	39.79'		
	ANDRAU	AAP	NDB	269.00	N29°	44.14'	W95°	35.41'		
	ANDREWS	ANR	NDB	245.00	N32°	20.93'	W102°	32.19'		
	ATHENS	AHX	NDB	269.00	N32°	09.55'	W95°	49.81'		
	ATLANTA	ATA	NDB	347.00	N33°	06.22'	W94°	11.42'		
	AUSTI (LOM/NDB)	AUST	NDB	353.00	N30°	14.14'	W97°	37.54'		
	AUSTIN	AUS	VOR	117.10	N30°	17.85'	W97°	42.19'	629	E07°
	BALLINGER	UBC	NDB	239.00	N31°	40.82'	W99°	58.48'		
	BAY CITY	BYY	NDB	344.00	N28°	58.34'	W95°	51.59'		
	BEAUMONT	BPT	VOR	114.50	N29°	56.76'	W94°	00.97'	9	E07°
	BEEVILLE	BEA	NDB	284.00	N28°	22.06'	W97°	47.66'		
	BIG SPRING	BGS	VOR	114.30	N32°	23.13'	W101°	29.02'	2,669	E11°
	BLUE RIDGE	BUJ	VOR	114.90	N33°	16.99'	W96°	21.89'	610	E08°
	BLUIE (LOM)	BLUI	NDB	219.00	N29°	28.47'	W98°	31.11'		
	BONHAM	HJM	NDB	415.00	N33°	36.83'	W96°	10.56'		
	BORGER	BGD	VOR	108.60	N35°	48.42'	W101°	22.92'	3,129	E11°
	BRADY	BBD	NDB	380.00	N31°	10.67'	W99°	19.35'		
	BRASHEAR	BHG	NDB	338.00	N33°	09.50'	W95°	37.09'		
	BRAZOS RIVER	GZV	NDB	280.00	N32°	57.08'	W98°	24.78'		
	BRECKENRIDGE	BKD	NDB	245.00	N32°	44.84'	W98°	53.46'		

State/Country	VOR/NDB Name	Ident.	Type	Freq.	Latitude		Longitude		Altitude	Mag Var
USA/CANADA NAVAIDS										
Texas	BRENHAM	BNH	NDB	362.00	N30°	13.34'	W96°	22.38'		
	BREWSTER CO	BWR	NDB	201.00	N30°	27.59'	W103°	38.77'		
	BRIDGEPORT	BPR	VOR	116.50	N33°	14.26'	W97°	45.98'	888	E09°
	BRONS (LOM)	BRON	NDB	407.00	N33°	02.67'	W96°	52.22'		
	BROOKS CO	BKS	NDB	353.00	N27°	12.42'	W98°	07.28'		
	BROWNFIELD	BFE	NDB	311.00	N33°	10.75'	W102°	11.52'		
	BROWNSVILLE	BRO	VOR	116.30	N25°	55.44'	W97°	22.52'	9	E09°
	BROWNWOOD	BWD	VOR	108.60	N31°	53.55'	W98°	57.44'	1,571	E08°
	BURNET	BMQ	NDB	341.00	N30°	44.34'	W98°	14.23'		
	CADDO MILLS	MII	NDB	316.00	N33°	02.42'	W96°	14.91'		
	CARTHAGE	RPF	NDB	332.00	N32°	10.81'	W94°	17.77'		
	CASH	SYW	NDB	428.00	N32°	58.88'	W96°	04.03'		
	CASTROVILLE	CVB	NDB	338.00	N29°	20.76'	W98°	50.95'		
	CENTER POINT	CSI	VOR	117.50	N29°	55.34'	W99°	12.87'	2,079	E08°
	CHAPARROSA RANCH	CPZ	NDB	385.00	N28°	54.59'	W100°	00.33'		
	CHEROKEE CO	JSO	NDB	263.00	N31°	52.21'	W95°	12.93'		
	CHILDRESS	CDS	VOR	117.60	N34°	22.14'	W100°	17.34'	1,918	E10°
	CLARENDON	CNZ	NDB	281.00	N34°	54.61'	W100°	52.07'		
	COFFI (LOM)	COFF	NDB	242.00	N31°	41.63'	W97°	12.22'		
	COLEMAN	COM	NDB	385.00	N31°	50.47'	W99°	24.36'		
	COLLEGE STATION	CLL	VOR	113.30	N30°	36.29'	W96°	25.23'	370	E08°
	CONIS (LOM)	CONI	NDB	275.00	N32°	46.48'	W96°	46.51'		
	CONOR (LOM/NDB)	CONO	NDB	382.00	N27°	50.07'	W97°	34.59'		
	CORPUS CHRISTI	CRP	VOR	115.50	N27°	54.22'	W97°	26.70'	52	E09°
	CORSICANA	CRS	NDB	396.00	N32°	01.65'	W96°	23.71'		
	COTULLA	COT	VOR	115.80	N28°	27.71'	W99°	07.11'	518	E09°
	COWBOY	CVE	VOR	116.20	N32°	53.41'	W96°	54.23'	449	E06°
	CRAKK (LOM/NDB)	CRAK	NDB	230.00	N32°	30.10'	W93°	52.68'		
	CROSBYTON	CZX	NDB	332.00	N33°	37.42'	W101°	14.30'		
	CROSSROADS	CSZ	NDB	215.00	N32°	03.80'	W95°	57.45'		
	DAISETTA	DAS	VOR	116.90	N30°	11.38'	W94°	38.69'	75	E05°
	DALHART	DHT	VOR	112.00	N36°	05.48'	W102°	32.68'	4,017	E12°
	DALLAS-FT WORTH	DFW	VOR	117.00	N32°	51.95'	W97°	01.68'	560	E08°
	DAVID HOOKS	DWH	NDB	521.00	N30°	07.53'	W95°	33.95'		
	DENISON	DNI	NDB	341.00	N33°	49.44'	W96°	40.18'		
	DEPOO (LOM)	DEPO	NDB	393.00	N25°	59.01'	W97°	30.54'		
	DEVINE	HHH	NDB	359.00	N29°	08.13'	W98°	56.49'		
	DIMMIT CO	DMD	NDB	343.00	N28°	31.43'	W99°	49.52'		
	DURANT	DUA	NDB	359.00	N33°	56.53'	W96°	23.91'		
	DURRETT	DUX	NDB	414.00	N35°	51.79'	W102°	00.77'		
	EAGLE LAKE	ELA	VOR	116.40	N29°	39.76'	W96°	19.01'	190	E08°
	EASTEX	ETO	NDB	201.00	N30°	20.89'	W94°	05.32'		
	EL PASO	ELP	VOR	115.20	N31°	48.95'	W106°	16.91'	4,017	E12°
	ELLINGTON	EFD	VOR	109.40	N29°	36.37'	W95°	09.59'	29	E06°
	EVADALE	EVA	NDB	219.00	N30°	24.27'	W94°	07.62'		
	FALFURRIAS	FFR	NDB	230.00	N27°	28.01'	W98°	24.18'		
	FARLY (LOM/NDB)	FARL	NDB	326.00	N31°	59.27'	W102°	19.50'		
	FLUET (LOM)	FLUE	NDB	421.00	N33°	15.70'	W96°	35.31'		
	FLUFY (LOM)	FLUF	NDB	350.00	N31°	13.13'	W94°	49.50'		
	FORT STOCKTON	FST	VOR	112.80	N30°	57.12'	W102°	58.54'	3,158	E11°
	FOSTR (LOM)	FOST	NDB	226.00	N28°	54.91'	W97°	00.03'		
	FRANKSTON	FZT	VOR	111.40	N32°	04.47'	W95°	31.84'	305	E06°
	FREEP (LOM)	FREE	NDB	263.00	N29°	11.66'	W95°	27.79'		
	GAINES CO	GNC	NDB	344.00	N32°	40.32'	W102°	38.74'		
	GAINESVILLE	GLE	NDB	330.00	N33°	43.12'	W97°	11.91'		
	GALVESTON	GLS	NDB	206.00	N29°	20.03'	W94°	45.37'		
	GARYS (LOM)	GARY	NDB	272.00	N29°	57.54'	W97°	56.93'		
	GEORGETOWN	GUO	NDB	332.00	N30°	41.06'	W97°	40.79'		
	GOODHUE	GDE	NDB	368.00	N30°	04.17'	W94°	12.14'		
	GRAHAM	GHX	NDB	371.00	N33°	09.95'	W98°	29.79'		
	GRAY	GRK	VOR	111.80	N31°	01.97'	W97°	48.82'	980	E07°
	GREGG CO	GGG	VOR	112.30	N32°	25.06'	W94°	45.18'	321	E07°
	GRINDSTONE MTN	GMZ	NDB	356.00	N33°	36.32'	W97°	46.40'		
	GUTHRIE	GTH	VOR	114.50	N33°	46.69'	W100°	20.17'	1,938	E10°
	HAMILTON	MNZ	NDB	251.00	N31°	37.20'	W98°	08.85'		
	HARDIN CO	HRD	NDB	524.00	N30°	20.24'	W94°	15.61'		
	HARLINGEN	HRL	VOR	108.80	N26°	17.47'	W97°	47.59'	49	E09°
	HASKELL	AKL	NDB	407.00	N33°	11.45'	W99°	43.20'		
	HEBBRONVILLE	HBV	NDB	266.00	N27°	21.23'	W98°	44.65'		
	HEMPHILL CO	HHF	NDB	400.00	N35°	53.46'	W100°	24.32'		
	HENDERSON	HNO	NDB	371.00	N32°	11.27'	W94°	51.66'		
	HEREFORD	HRX	NDB	341.00	N34°	51.38'	W102°	19.51'		
	HOBBY	HUB	VOR	117.60	N29°	39.01'	W95°	16.73'	49	E06°
	HONDO	HMA	NDB	329.00	N29°	22.39'	W99°	10.32'		

State/Country	VOR/NDB Name	Ident.	Type	Freq.	Latitude		Longitude		Altitude	Mag Var
USA/CANADA NAVAIDS										
Texas	HOOD	HLR	NDB	347.00	N31°	07.74'	W97°	42.68'		
	HUDSPETH	HUP	VOR	115.00	N31°	34.12'	W105°	22.57'	4,388	E12°
	HULL	SGR	NDB	388.00	N29°	37.94'	W95°	39.36'		
	HUMBLE	IAH	VOR	116.60	N29°	57.41'	W95°	20.74'	88	E08°
	HUMPHREY	HPY	NDB	275.00	N29°	47.45'	W94°	57.31'		
	HUNTSVILLE	UTS	NDB	308.00	N30°	44.44'	W95°	35.45'		
	IDABEL	IBO	NDB	271.00	N33°	54.36'	W94°	50.58'		
	INDUSTRY	IDU	VOR	110.20	N29°	57.36'	W96°	33.73'	419	E08°
	IRESH (LOM/NDB)	IRES	NDB	278.00	N31°	01.44'	W97°	42.48'		
	ISSUE (LOM)	ISSU	NDB	233.00	N32°	48.15'	W97°	01.63'		
	ISSUE (LOM)	ISSU	NDB	233.00	N32°	48.15'	W97°	01.63'		
	JACKSON CO	EDX	NDB	201.00	N29°	00.09'	W96°	35.08'		
	JASPER	JAS	NDB	344.00	N30°	57.27'	W94°	02.01'		
	JECCA	JUG	NDB	388.00	N32°	40.13'	W96°	31.92'		
	JIFFY (LOM)	JIFF	NDB	219.00	N32°	59.74'	W97°	01.77'		
	JUNCTION	JCT	VOR	116.00	N30°	35.88'	W99°	49.05'	2,279	E08°
	KAZOO (LOM)	KAZO	NDB	257.00	N29°	59.77'	W94°	06.37'		
	KEOTE (LOM)	KEOT	NDB	338.00	N29°	25.89'	W98°	52.96'		
	KLEBERG CO	TKB	NDB	347.00	N27°	36.35'	W98°	05.38'		
	KOTTI (LOM)	KOTT	NDB	335.00	N29°	26.74'	W100°	59.32'		
	LA FONDA RANCH	BRX	NDB	269.00	N29°	12.51'	W100°	37.43'		
	LA PRYOR	LKX	NDB	223.00	N28°	55.79'	W99°	51.28'		
	LAKESIDE	LYD	NDB	249.00	N29°	48.98'	W95°	40.65'		
	LAMESA	LSA	NDB	338.00	N32°	45.42'	W101°	54.92'		
	LAMPASAS	LZZ	VOR	112.50	N31°	11.13'	W98°	08.51'	1,289	E08°
	LANCASTER	LNC	NDB	239.00	N32°	34.65'	W96°	43.29'		
	LAREDO	LRD	VOR	117.40	N27°	28.72'	W99°	25.05'	583	E09°
	LAUGHLIN	DLF	VOR	114.40	N29°	21.65'	W100°	46.30'	1,069	E10°
	LEE CO	GYB	NDB	385.00	N30°	10.13'	W96°	58.79'		
	LEONA	LOA	VOR	110.80	N31°	07.44'	W95°	58.07'	350	E08°
	LEROI (LOM)	LERO	NDB	283.00	N31°	44.44'	W97°	04.68'		
	LEVELLAND	LLN	NDB	266.00	N33°	33.33'	W102°	22.51'		
	LITTLEFIELD	LIU	NDB	212.00	N33°	55.15'	W102°	23.19'		
	LLANO	LLO	VOR	108.20	N30°	47.78'	W98°	47.24'	1,200	E08°
	LOCHRIDGE RANCH	LIQ	NDB	335.00	N32°	00.64'	W95°	57.16'		
	LONE STAR	LST	NDB	305.00	N32°	55.67'	W94°	44.59'		
	LUBBI (LOM)	LUBB	NDB	272.00	N33°	39.76'	W101°	43.39'		
	LUBBOCK	LBB	VOR	109.20	N33°	42.30'	W101°	54.84'	3,309	E11°
	LUFKIN	LFK	VOR	112.10	N31°	09.74'	W94°	43.01'	200	E05°
	MAJOR (LOM)	MAJO	NDB	201.00	N33°	09.37'	W96°	03.81'		
	MARATHON	IMP	NDB	388.00	N30°	15.84'	W103°	14.22'		
	MARBE (LOM)	MARB	NDB	379.00	N30°	04.48'	W95°	24.76'		
	MARBLE FALLS	MFS	NDB	403.00	N30°	31.39'	W98°	21.46'		
	MARFA	MRF	VOR	115.90	N30°	17.89'	W103°	57.28'	4,828	E11°
	MC ALLEN	MFE	VOR	117.20	N26°	10.43'	W98°	14.44'	98	E09°
	MELLON RANCH	MNO	NDB	375.00	N28°	16.79'	W97°	12.34'		
	MESQUITE	PQF	NDB	248.00	N32°	48.54'	W96°	31.73'		
	MEXIA	LXY	NDB	329.00	N31°	38.37'	W96°	30.73'		
	MIDLAND	MAF	VOR	114.80	N32°	00.55'	W102°	11.42'	2,850	E11°
	MIDLAND (LMM)	AF	NDB	201.00	N31°	57.05'	W102°	13.53'		
	MILLSAP	MQP	VOR	117.70	N32°	43.57'	W97°	59.84'	888	E09°
	MINERAL WELLS	MWL	NDB	266.00	N32°	47.10'	W98°	03.43'		
	MISSI (LOM)	MISS	NDB	388.00	N26°	15.23'	W98°	18.62'		
	MONAHANS	OHE	NDB	214.00	N31°	34.69'	W102°	54.34'		
	MOUNT PLEASANT	MSA	NDB	381.00	N33°	07.70'	W94°	58.44'		
	MUFIN (LOM/NDB)	MUFI	NDB	365.00	N32°	53.57'	W97°	22.41'		
	NACOGDOCHES	GXD	NDB	391.00	N31°	38.91'	W94°	42.32'		
	NADOS (LOM/NDB)	NADO	NDB	253.00	N31°	29.13'	W94°	43.21'		
	NAVASOTA	TNV	VOR	115.90	N30°	17.34'	W96°	03.51'	242	E08°
	NEW BRAUNFELS	BAZ	NDB	212.00	N29°	42.46'	W98°	02.08'		
	NEWMAN	EWM	VOR	112.40	N31°	57.10'	W106°	16.34'	4,037	E12°
	NIXIN (LOM)	NIXI	NDB	326.00	N29°	59.59'	W95°	12.90'		
	OLD RIP	OIP	NDB	410.00	N32°	23.90'	W98°	48.61'		
	OLNEY	ONY	NDB	272.00	N33°	21.07'	W98°	48.96'		
	ORANGE	ORG	NDB	211.00	N30°	04.21'	W93°	47.69'		
	PALACIOS	PSX	VOR	117.30	N28°	45.86'	W96°	18.37'	19	E08°
	PALESTINE	PSN	NDB	375.00	N31°	46.81'	W95°	42.06'		
	PAMPA	PPA	NDB	368.00	N35°	36.66'	W100°	59.77'		
	PANDE (LOM/NDB)	PAND	NDB	251.00	N35°	08.78'	W101°	48.33'		
	PARIS	PRX	VOR	113.60	N33°	32.54'	W95°	26.89'	508	E07°
	PECOS	PEQ	VOR	111.80	N31°	28.15'	W103°	34.48'	2,620	E11°
	PEKKS (LOM)	PEKK	NDB	405.00	N27°	38.54'	W99°	27.49'		
	PERRYTON	PYX	NDB	266.00	N36°	24.76'	W100°	44.30'		
	PINCK (LOM)	PINC	NDB	257.00	N33°	16.98'	W97°	11.77'		

State/Country	VOR/NDB Name	Ident.	Type	Freq.	Latitude		Longitude		Altitude	Mag Var
USA/CANADA NAVAIDS										
Texas	PLAINVIEW	PVW	VOR	112.90	N34°	05.17'	W101°	47.41'	3,398	E11°
	PLEASANTON	PEZ	NDB	275.00	N28°	57.29'	W98°	31.11'		
	POLLO (LOM)	POLL	NDB	219.00	N33°	44.26'	W101°	49.75'		
	PORT LAVACA	PKV	NDB	515.00	N28°	39.03'	W96°	40.88'		
	POWELL	CGQ	NDB	344.00	N32°	03.84'	W96°	25.68'		
	PYRAMID	PYF	NDB	418.00	N31°	51.76'	W96°	11.84'		
	QUITMAN	UIM	VOR	114.00	N32°	52.82'	W95°	22.00'	518	E08°
	RANDOLPH	RND	VOR	112.30	N29°	31.14'	W98°	17.10'	777	E09°
	REAGAN CO	LUJ	NDB	341.00	N31°	11.55'	W101°	28.12'		
	REDBIRD	RBD	NDB	287.00	N32°	40.61'	W96°	52.26'		
	REESE	RVO	VOR	108.80	N33°	35.80'	W102°	02.64'	3,335	E11°
	REYNOSA	REX	VOR	112.40	N26°	00.69'	W98°	13.99'	0	E07°
	ROBINSON	ROB	NDB	400.00	N31°	30.22'	W97°	04.17'		
	ROCKDALE	RCK	NDB	221.00	N30°	17.01'	W96°	59.01'		
	ROCKPORT	RKP	NDB	391.00	N28°	05.42'	W97°	02.79'		
	ROCKSPRINGS	RSG	VOR	111.20	N30°	00.87'	W100°	17.99'	2,318	E10°
	ROSANKY	RYU	NDB	266.00	N29°	53.74'	W97°	20.26'		
	ROWDY (LOM)	ROWD	NDB	260.00	N30°	29.60'	W96°	20.27'		
	SABINE PASS	SBI	VOR	115.40	N29°	41.20'	W94°	02.27'	9	E07°
	SALT FLAT	SFL	VOR	113.00	N31°	44.88'	W105°	05.20'	3,729	E12°
	SAN ANGELO	SJT	VOR	115.10	N31°	22.49'	W100°	27.29'	1,889	E10°
	SAN ANTONIO	SAT	VOR	116.80	N29°	38.64'	W98°	27.68'	1,161	E08°
	SANDY POINT	SYG	NDB	338.00	N29°	30.16'	W95°	28.09'		
	SANJAC	JPA	NDB	347.00	N29°	40.11'	W95°	04.19'		
	SANTA ELENA	SNE	NDB	260.00	N26°	43.13'	W98°	34.63'		
	SCHOLES	VUH	VOR	113.00	N29°	16.16'	W94°	52.06'	9	E06°
	SCOTLAND	SKB	NDB	344.00	N33°	47.40'	W98°	29.18'		
	SCURRY	SCY	VOR	112.90	N32°	27.87'	W96°	20.24'	436	E08°
	SEBAS (LOM/NDB)	SEBA	NDB	338.00	N26°	18.31'	W97°	39.43'		
	SHAWN (LOM/NDB)	SHAW	NDB	296.00	N33°	54.64'	W98°	27.27'		
	SHEIN (LOM/NDB)	SHEI	NDB	263.00	N29°	54.90'	W99°	00.56'		
	SNYDER	SDR	NDB	359.00	N32°	42.07'	W100°	56.84'		
	SONORA	SOA	NDB	371.00	N30°	34.91'	W100°	38.82'		
	SPOFFORD	PFO	NDB	356.00	N29°	08.71'	W100°	25.65'		
	STAMFORD	TMV	NDB	290.00	N32°	52.11'	W99°	43.98'		
	STARN (LOM/NDB)	STAR	NDB	323.00	N31°	10.06'	W97°	52.69'		
	STINSON	SSF	VOR	108.40	N29°	15.50'	W98°	26.61'	541	E09°
	STONEWALL	STV	VOR	113.10	N30°	12.40'	W98°	42.34'	1,528	E08°
	SULPHUR SPRINGS	SLR	VOR	109.00	N33°	11.91'	W95°	32.55'	478	E08°
	SWEETWATER	SWW	NDB	275.00	N32°	27.68'	W100°	27.95'		
	TEMPLE	TPL	VOR	110.40	N31°	12.55'	W97°	25.49'	708	E09°
	TEXICO	TXO	VOR	112.20	N34°	29.70'	W102°	50.38'	4,057	E11°
	THREE RIVERS	THX	VOR	111.40	N28°	30.31'	W98°	09.06'	265	E08°
	TOMBALL	TMZ	NDB	408.00	N30°	04.41'	W95°	33.33'		
	TOMHI (LOM)	TOMH	NDB	353.00	N32°	17.93'	W99°	40.44'		
	TRAVIS	AVZ	NDB	299.00	N32°	45.61'	W96°	14.95'		
	TRINITY	MHF	VOR	113.60	N29°	32.77'	W94°	44.85'	39	E07°
	TRUAX	NGP	VOR	114.00	N27°	41.17'	W97°	17.68'	19	E06°
	TUSCOLA	TQA	VOR	111.60	N32°	14.14'	W99°	49.00'	2,017	E10°
	TUTTE (LOM)	TUTT	NDB	395.00	N29°	35.34'	W95°	20.42'		
	TYLER	TYR	VOR	114.20	N32°	21.35'	W95°	24.20'	541	E06°
	TYLER (LOM/NDB)	TYLE	NDB	320.00	N32°	24.94'	W95°	28.17'		
	UVALDE	UVA	NDB	281.00	N29°	10.68'	W99°	43.53'		
	VALTR (LOM/NDB)	VALT	NDB	242.00	N31°	51.61'	W106°	19.06'		
	VAN HORN	VHN	NDB	233.00	N31°	03.70'	W104°	47.17'		
	VEELS (LOM)	VEEL	NDB	410.00	N32°	27.33'	W94°	47.85'		
	VICTORIA	VCT	VOR	109.00	N28°	54.01'	W96°	58.73'	131	E06°
	VIVIAN	VIV	NDB	284.00	N32°	51.57'	W94°	00.61'		
	WACO	ACT	VOR	115.30	N31°	39.73'	W97°	16.14'	508	E09°
	WEISER	EYQ	NDB	286.00	N29°	56.03'	W95°	38.45'		
	WHARTON	ARM	NDB	245.00	N29°	15.23'	W96°	09.29'		
	WICHITA FALLS	SPS	VOR	112.70	N33°	59.23'	W98°	35.60'	1,098	E10°
	WILBARGER	VRT	NDB	230.00	N34°	13.55'	W99°	16.75'		
	WINK	INK	VOR	112.10	N31°	52.48'	W103°	14.61'	2,869	E11°
	WINTERS	IEW	NDB	396.00	N31°	57.20'	W99°	59.02'		
	WOOLE (LOM)	WOOL	NDB	356.00	N31°	16.78'	W100°	34.56'		
	YOAKUM	OKT	NDB	350.00	N29°	18.76'	W97°	08.31'		
Utah										
	BLANDING	BDG	NDB	340.00	N37°	31.04'	W109°	29.56'		
	BONNEVILLE	BVL	VOR	112.30	N40°	43.56'	W113°	45.44'	4,218	E17°
	BRIGHAM CITY	BMC	NDB	294.00	N41°	30.96'	W112°	04.67'		
	BRYCE CANYON	BCE	VOR	112.80	N37°	41.35'	W112°	18.23'	9,036	E15°
	CARBON	PUC	VOR	115.50	N39°	36.19'	W110°	45.21'	5,890	E14°
	CEDAR CITY	CDC	VOR	108.60	N37°	47.24'	W113°	04.09'	5,457	E16°

State/Country	VOR/NDB Name	Ident.	Type	Freq.	Latitude		Longitude		Altitude	Mag Var
USA/CANADA NAVAIDS										
Utah	DELTA	DTA	VOR	116.10	N39°	18.13'	W112°	30.33'	4,598	E16°
	DUGWAY	DPG	NDB	284.00	N40°	10.94'	W112°	56.24'		
	FAIRFIELD	FFU	VOR	116.60	N40°	16.49'	W111°	56.43'	7,681	E16°
	HANKSVILLE	HVE	VOR	115.90	N38°	25.00'	W110°	41.98'	4,427	E15°
	KERNN (LOM)	KERN	NDB	338.00	N40°	40.86'	W111°	57.77'		
	LOGAN	LGU	VOR	109.80	N41°	50.65'	W111°	51.92'	4,447	E16°
	LUCIN	LCU	VOR	113.60	N41°	21.77'	W113°	50.43'	4,398	E17°
	MEGGI (LOM)	MEGG	NDB	217.00	N37°	47.47'	W113°	01.28'		
	MILFORD	MLF	VOR	112.10	N38°	21.62'	W113°	00.79'	4,979	E16°
	MOAB	OAB	VOR	109.80	N38°	45.37'	W109°	44.95'	4,569	E15°
	MYTON	MTU	VOR	112.70	N40°	08.69'	W110°	07.65'	5,329	E14°
	OGDEN	OGD	VOR	115.70	N41°	13.44'	W112°	05.89'	4,218	E14°
	PROVO	PVU	VOR	108.40	N40°	12.89'	W111°	43.27'	4,490	E15°
	SAINT GEORGE	OZN	VOR	109.80	N37°	05.28'	W113°	35.50'	2,896	E15°
	SALT LAKE CITY	SLC	VOR	116.80	N40°	51.01'	W111°	58.91'	4,218	E16°
	TOOELE	TVY	NDB	371.00	N40°	36.44'	W112°	20.91'		
	VERNAL	VEL	VOR	108.20	N40°	22.73'	W109°	29.59'	5,339	E15°
Vermont	BURLINGTON	BTV	VOR	117.50	N44°	23.82'	W73°	10.95'	419	W15°
	DYER	DYO	NDB	239.00	N43°	35.03'	W72°	57.68'		
	HERRO (LOM)	HERR	NDB	219.00	N44°	31.94'	W73°	14.97'		
	IRA	IRA	NDB	398.00	N43°	41.52'	W72°	59.15'		
	LYNDONVILLE	LLX	NDB	353.00	N44°	30.25'	W72°	01.75'		
	MONTPELIER	MPV	VOR	110.80	N44°	05.12'	W72°	26.96'	2,079	W16°
	MORRISVILLE-STOWE	JRV	NDB	375.00	N44°	34.72'	W72°	35.24'		
	MOUNT MANSFIELD	VKN	NDB	268.00	N44°	23.19'	W72°	41.61'		
	MOUNT SNOW	VWD	NDB	224.00	N42°	55.65'	W72°	51.84'		
	NEWPORT	EFK	NDB	242.00	N44°	57.17'	W72°	10.64'		
	SPRINGFIELD	SXD	NDB	265.00	N43°	16.19'	W72°	35.17'		
	WHITE RIVER	IVV	NDB	379.00	N43°	33.61'	W72°	27.93'		
	WILLIAMS	MWX	NDB	257.00	N44°	07.23'	W72°	31.09'		
Virginia	ARMEL	AML	VOR	113.50	N38°	56.07'	W77°	28.00'	298	W08°
	ASHEY	LJK	NDB	280.00	N37°	46.39'	W77°	28.78'		
	AZALEA PARK	AZS	NDB	336.00	N38°	00.60'	W78°	31.08'		
	BALES (LOM/NDB)	BALE	NDB	396.00	N36°	35.39'	W79°	55.03'		
	BLACKSTONE	BKT	NDB	326.00	N37°	07.67'	W78°	02.48'		
	BOJAR (LOM/NDB)	BOJA	NDB	385.00	N37°	15.74'	W79°	14.59'		
	BRIDGEWATER	VBW	NDB	241.00	N38°	21.93'	W78°	57.67'		
	BROOKE	BRV	VOR	114.50	N38°	20.17'	W77°	21.16'	121	W09°
	CALLAHAN	CNQ	NDB	379.00	N37°	15.68'	W80°	09.48'		
	CAPE CHARLES	CCV	VOR	112.20	N37°	20.85'	W75°	59.86'	9	W10°
	CASANOVA	CSN	VOR	116.30	N38°	38.47'	W77°	51.93'	446	W06°
	CAVERNS	LUA	NDB	245.00	N38°	41.97'	W78°	28.30'		
	CHASE CITY	CXE	NDB	342.00	N36°	47.49'	W78°	30.05'		
	CHESAPEAKE	CPK	NDB	261.00	N36°	39.98'	W76°	19.47'		
	COGAN	TZ	NDB	364.00	N39°	05.18'	W78°	04.11'		
	CULPEPER	CJR	NDB	252.00	N38°	31.85'	W77°	51.48'		
	DANVILLE	DAN	VOR	113.10	N36°	34.13'	W79°	20.20'	570	W06°
	EMPORIA	EMV	NDB	346.00	N36°	40.96'	W77°	28.93'		
	FARMVILLE	FVX	NDB	367.00	N37°	21.17'	W78°	26.28'		
	FELKER	FAF	NDB	226.00	N37°	08.32'	W76°	37.11'		
	FLAT ROCK	FAK	VOR	113.30	N37°	31.71'	W77°	49.69'	459	W06°
	FORT A P HILL	APH	NDB	396.00	N38°	05.26'	W77°	19.49'		
	FRANKLIN	FKN	VOR	110.60	N36°	42.85'	W77°	00.73'	88	W09°
	GLADE SPRING	GZG	VOR	110.20	N36°	49.50'	W82°	04.74'	4,198	W02°
	GOODWIN LAKE	GDX	NDB	227.00	N38°	57.24'	W77°	49.86'		
	GORDONSVILLE	GVE	VOR	115.60	N38°	00.81'	W78°	09.17'	380	W06°
	HARCUM	HCM	VOR	108.80	N37°	26.92'	W76°	42.68'	9	W07°
	HENRY	PJS	NDB	375.00	N37°	07.96'	W76°	29.59'		
	HILLSVILLE	HLX	NDB	269.00	N36°	45.73'	W80°	49.31'		
	HOPEWELL	HPW	VOR	112.00	N37°	19.73'	W77°	06.95'	68	W06°
	INGLE (LOM)	INGL	NDB	329.00	N36°	50.42'	W76°	15.08'		
	LAWRENCEVILLE	LVL	VOR	112.90	N36°	49.08'	W77°	54.17'	350	W08°
	LINDEN	LDN	VOR	114.30	N38°	51.26'	W78°	12.33'	2,440	W06°
	LONG HOLLOW	LQV	NDB	252.00	N36°	42.42'	W83°	04.44'		
	LOUISA	IQK	NDB	382.00	N38°	01.22'	W77°	51.54'		
	LYNCHBURG	LYH	VOR	109.20	N37°	15.27'	W79°	14.18'	879	W05°
	MECKLENBURG	MBV	NDB	356.00	N36°	41.54'	W78°	03.38'		
	MELFA	MFV	NDB	388.00	N37°	39.36'	W75°	45.49'		
	MONTEBELLO	MOL	VOR	115.30	N37°	54.03'	W79°	06.41'	3,460	W05°
	NORFOLK	ORF	VOR	116.90	N36°	53.51'	W76°	12.02'	19	W07°
	ORANGE	COG	NDB	428.00	N38°	13.14'	W78°	08.50'		
	PETERSBURG	PTB	NDB	284.00	N37°	07.80'	W77°	34.48'		

State/Country	VOR/NDB Name	Ident.	Type	Freq.	Latitude		Longitude		Altitude	Mag Var
USA/CANADA NAVAIDS										
Virginia	PORTSMOUTH	PVG	NDB	241.00	N36°	46.80'	W76°	26.73'		
	PUBBS (LOM/NDB)	PUBB	NDB	392.00	N37°	19.99'	W77°	27.20'		
	PULASKI	PSK	VOR	116.80	N37°	05.26'	W80°	42.77'	2,118	W06°
	RICHMOND	RIC	VOR	114.10	N37°	30.14'	W77°	19.21'	160	W09°
	ROANOKE	ROA	VOR	109.40	N37°	20.60'	W80°	04.22'	3,060	W04°
	SHANNON	EZF	NDB	237.00	N38°	15.92'	W77°	26.91'		
	SOUTH BOSTON	SBV	VOR	110.40	N36°	40.50'	W79°	00.87'	531	W05°
	STAUT (LOM)	STAU	NDB	375.00	N38°	12.10'	W78°	57.43'		
	SUFFOLK	SFQ	NDB	203.00	N36°	40.82'	W76°	36.49'		
	SUZZE (LOM/NDB)	SUZZ	NDB	335.00	N36°	55.25'	W81°	14.54'		
	TECH	TEC	NDB	257.00	N37°	12.46'	W80°	24.71'		
	TILLE (LOM)	TILL	NDB	346.00	N38°	50.83'	W77°	26.26'		
	VINTON	VIT	NDB	277.00	N37°	12.23'	W79°	52.89'		
	WAKEFIELD	AKQ	NDB	274.00	N36°	58.99'	W77°	00.06'		
	WHINE	VJ	NDB	236.00	N36°	44.04'	W81°	56.95'		
	WOODRUM	ODR	VOR	114.90	N37°	19.45'	W79°	58.73'	1,161	W06°
Washington	ABERN (LOM)	ABER	NDB	414.00	N46°	59.26'	W123°	47.86'		
	BATTLEGROUND	BTG	VOR	116.60	N45°	44.86'	W122°	35.49'	249	E21°
	BELLINGHAM	BLI	VOR	113.00	N48°	56.71'	W122°	34.75'	78	E20°
	BENZA (LOM)	BENZ	NDB	338.00	N48°	53.94'	W122°	32.08'		
	CARNEY	CAN	NDB	274.00	N47°	24.63'	W122°	50.32'		
	DEERPARK	DPY	NDB	216.00	N47°	58.06'	W117°	25.58'		
	DONDO (LOM/NDB)	DOND	NDB	224.00	N47°	21.83'	W122°	18.53'		
	DONNY (LOM)	DONN	NDB	371.00	N46°	31.54'	W120°	22.33'		
	DUNEZ (LOM)	DUNE	NDB	331.00	N46°	20.29'	W119°	00.74'		
	ELLENSBURG	ELN	VOR	117.90	N47°	01.46'	W120°	27.50'	1,764	E21°
	ELWHA (LOM/NDB)	ELWH	NDB	515.00	N48°	09.01'	W123°	40.21'		
	EPHRATA	EPH	VOR	112.60	N47°	22.67'	W119°	25.44'	1,249	E21°
	FELTS	SFF	NDB	365.00	N47°	41.16'	W117°	18.70'		
	FRIDAY HARBOR	FHR	NDB	284.00	N48°	31.61'	W123°	01.67'		
	GRAYE (LOM/NDB)	GRAY	NDB	216.00	N47°	09.01'	W122°	36.28'		
	HOQUIAM	HQM	VOR	117.70	N46°	56.82'	W124°	08.95'	9	E19°
	IONE	ION	NDB	379.00	N48°	42.61'	W117°	24.81'		
	KELSO	LSO	NDB	256.00	N46°	09.22'	W122°	54.74'		
	KITSAP	PWT	NDB	206.00	N47°	29.85'	W122°	45.62'		
	KLICKITAT	LTJ	VOR	112.30	N45°	42.81'	W121°	06.05'	3,217	E21°
	LACOMAS	LAC	NDB	328.00	N47°	00.47'	W122°	33.38'		
	LOPEZ ISLAND	OPZ	NDB	356.00	N48°	28.75'	W122°	55.26'		
	MASON CO	MNC	NDB	348.00	N47°	14.90'	W123°	05.19'		
	MCCHORD	TCM	VOR	109.60	N47°	08.85'	W122°	28.50'	278	E22°
	MOSES LAKE	MWH	VOR	115.00	N47°	12.65'	W119°	19.00'	1,177	E18°
	NEAH BAY	EBY	NDB	391.00	N48°	21.45'	W124°	33.37'		
	NOLLA (LOM)	NOLL	NDB	362.00	N47°	37.94'	W122°	23.36'		
	OLYMPIA	OLM	VOR	113.40	N46°	58.29'	W122°	54.11'	200	E19°
	OMAK	OMK	NDB	396.00	N48°	27.20'	W119°	31.00'		
	PAINE	PAE	VOR	110.60	N47°	55.19'	W122°	16.66'	669	E20°
	PARKK (LOM)	PARK	NDB	281.00	N47°	31.94'	W122°	18.41'		
	PASCO	PSC	VOR	108.40	N46°	15.77'	W119°	06.94'	400	E20°
	PELLY (LOM/NDB)	PELL	NDB	408.00	N47°	06.93'	W119°	16.49'		
	PHORT (LOM)	PHOR	NDB	388.00	N47°	40.61'	W117°	27.00'		
	PULLMAN	PUW	VOR	109.00	N46°	40.45'	W117°	13.40'	2,719	E20°
	RENTON	RNT	NDB	353.00	N47°	29.72'	W122°	12.88'		
	RIBOO (LOM)	RIBO	NDB	260.00	N46°	22.22'	W119°	15.54'		
	RITTS (LOM)	RITT	NDB	396.00	N47°	03.16'	W122°	17.32'		
	SEATTLE	SEA	VOR	116.80	N47°	26.12'	W122°	18.57'	341	E22°
	SKAGIT/BAY VIEW	BVS	NDB	240.00	N48°	28.12'	W122°	25.12'		
	SPOKANE	GEG	VOR	115.50	N47°	33.89'	W117°	37.61'	2,758	E21°
	TATOOSH	TOU	VOR	112.20	N48°	17.99'	W124°	37.62'	1,649	E22°
	TOLEDO	TDO	NDB	219.00	N46°	28.56'	W122°	49.01'		
	TRINA (LOM)	TRIN	NDB	353.00	N46°	10.52'	W118°	11.76'		
	WALLA WALLA	ALW	VOR	116.40	N46°	05.21'	W118°	17.55'	1,151	E20°
	WATON (LOM)	WATO	NDB	382.00	N48°	04.56'	W122°	09.23'		
	WENATCHEE	EAT	VOR	111.00	N47°	23.98'	W120°	12.64'	1,220	E19°
	YAKIMA	YKM	VOR	116.00	N46°	34.21'	W120°	26.67'	980	E21°
West Virginia	BECKLEY	BKW	VOR	117.70	N37°	46.81'	W81°	07.40'	2,499	W06°
	BLUEFIELD	BLF	VOR	110.00	N37°	18.38'	W81°	11.65'	2,899	W03°
	BUSHI (LOM/NDB)	BUSH	NDB	346.00	N37°	46.93'	W80°	28.10'		
	CHARLESTON	HVQ	VOR	117.40	N38°	20.98'	W81°	46.19'	1,098	W03°
	CLARKSBURG	CKB	VOR	112.60	N39°	15.19'	W80°	16.07'	1,430	W04°
	CRESAP	RYP	NDB	339.00	N39°	30.14'	W78°	46.34'		
	ELKINS	EKN	VOR	114.20	N38°	54.86'	W80°	05.95'	2,158	W07°
	GUYANDOT	GTC	NDB	293.00	N37°	46.92'	W81°	54.52'		

State/Country	VOR/NDB Name	Ident.	Type	Freq.	Latitude		Longitude		Altitude	Mag Var
USA/CANADA NAVAIDS		-								
West Virginia	HENDERSON	HNN	VOR	115.90	N38°	45.24'	W82°	01.56'	859	W03°
	KESSEL	ESL	VOR	110.80	N39°	13.53'	W78°	59.37'	2,587	W06°
	MARTINSBURG	MRB	VOR	112.10	N39°	23.13'	W77°	50.90'	600	W07°
	MORGANTOWN	MGW	VOR	111.60	N39°	33.40'	W79°	51.62'	2,338	W05°
	NICHOLAS	IJZ	NDB	272.00	N38°	10.50'	W80°	55.19'		
	PARKERSBURG	JPU	VOR	108.60	N39°	26.47'	W81°	22.48'	1,029	W03°
	RAINELLE	RNL	VOR	116.60	N37°	58.51'	W80°	48.39'	3,348	W04°
	RANDOLPH CO	RQY	NDB	284.00	N38°	53.11'	W79°	51.27'		
	VERSI (LOM)	VERS	NDB	388.00	N39°	15.25'	W81°	29.08'		
	WHEELING	HLG	VOR	112.20	N40°	15.59'	W80°	34.11'	1,269	W07°
	WHT SULPHUR SPRNG	SSU	VOR	108.40	N37°	45.83'	W80°	18.09'	3,329	W04°
Wisconsin										
	AMERON	AHH	NDB	278.00	N45°	16.88'	W92°	22.27'		
	ANTIGO	AIG	NDB	347.00	N45°	09.51'	W89°	06.82'		
	ARBOR VITAE	ARV	NDB	221.00	N45°	55.60'	W89°	43.70'		
	ASHLAND	ASX	VOR	110.20	N46°	32.96'	W90°	55.03'	819	E02°
	BADGER	BAE	VOR	116.40	N43°	07.01'	W88°	17.06'	1,079	E02°
	BIG DOCTOR	BXR	NDB	203.00	N45°	49.27'	W92°	21.98'		
	BLACK RIVER FALLS	BCK	NDB	362.00	N44°	15.28'	W90°	50.94'		
	BONG	SUW	NDB	260.00	N46°	41.47'	W92°	06.20'		
	BOULDER JUNCTION	BDJ	NDB	206.00	N46°	08.02'	W89°	39.34'		
	BURBUN	BUU	VOR	114.50	N42°	41.36'	W88°	18.10'	780	W01°
	CALIN (LOM)	CALI	NDB	266.00	N44°	34.14'	W90°	09.05'		
	CAPPY (LOM)	CAPP	NDB	410.00	N42°	50.38'	W87°	54.77'		
	CENTRAL WISCONSIN	HWS	NDB	377.00	N44°	46.61'	W89°	40.73'		
	CLINTONVILLE	CLI	NDB	209.00	N44°	37.12'	W88°	43.99'		
	CODEE (LOM)	CODE	NDB	389.00	N42°	33.61'	W88°	01.73'		
	CUMBERLAND	UBE	NDB	375.00	N45°	30.55'	W91°	58.60'		
	DANCI (LOM)	DANC	NDB	275.00	N44°	45.63'	W89°	47.35'		
	DELLS	DLL	VOR	117.00	N43°	33.05'	W89°	45.81'	1,020	E03°
	DEPRE (LOM/NDB)	DEPR	NDB	332.00	N44°	23.91'	W88°	07.97'		
	EAGLE RIVER	EGV	NDB	341.00	N45°	55.96'	W89°	15.79'		
	EAU CLAIRE	EAU	VOR	112.90	N44°	53.85'	W91°	28.71'	905	E04°
	FALLS	FAH	VOR	110.00	N43°	46.12'	W87°	50.92'	741	W02°
	FAMIS (LOM)	FAMI	NDB	356.00	N44°	26.42'	W88°	14.37'		
	FICHY (LOM)	FICH	NDB	224.00	N44°	45.28'	W87°	26.97'		
	FOND DU LAC	FLD	NDB	248.00	N43°	46.17'	W88°	29.07'		
	GAMIE (LOM)	GAMI	NDB	230.00	N44°	09.74'	W88°	35.09'		
	GREEN BAY	GRB	VOR	115.50	N44°	33.30'	W88°	11.69'	760	E01°
	HARTFORD	HXF	NDB	200.00	N43°	20.88'	W88°	23.78'		
	HAYWARD	HYR	VOR	113.40	N46°	01.14'	W91°	26.78'	1,207	E03°
	HORLICK	HRK	VOR	117.70	N42°	45.47'	W87°	48.85'	659	E01°
	JANESVILLE	JVL	NDB	375.00	N42°	36.90'	W89°	02.47'		
	JANESVILLE	JVL	VOR	114.30	N42°	33.47'	W89°	06.31'	898	E03°
	JUNEAU	UNU	NDB	344.00	N43°	25.81'	W88°	42.04'		
	KENNEDY	ENY	NDB	254.00	N46°	33.17'	W90°	54.87'		
	KENOSHA	ENW	VOR	109.20	N42°	35.94'	W87°	55.90'	731	W02°
	KETTLE MORAINE	LLE	NDB	329.00	N43°	25.53'	W88°	07.78'		
	KICKAPOO	HBW	NDB	251.00	N43°	39.30'	W90°	19.98'		
	KOOKY	AKT	NDB	407.00	N44°	12.95'	W88°	23.93'		
	KOOKY (LOM)	KOOK	NDB	407.00	N44°	12.98'	W88°	24.14'		
	LA CROSSE	LSE	VOR	108.40	N43°	52.56'	W91°	15.36'	649	E02°
	LAKE LAWN	LVV	NDB	404.00	N42°	42.46'	W88°	35.59'		
	LAND O LAKES	LNL	NDB	396.00	N46°	09.41'	W89°	12.55'		
	LONE ROCK	LNR	VOR	112.80	N43°	17.66'	W90°	07.98'	1,184	E00°
	MADISON	MSN	VOR	108.60	N43°	08.69'	W89°	20.38'	859	E03°
	MAGGS (LOM)	MAGG	NDB	239.00	N44°	56.67'	W91°	22.42'		
	MANITOWISH	MHA	NDB	364.00	N46°	07.37'	W89°	52.96'		
	MANITOWOC	MTW	VOR	111.00	N44°	07.70'	W87°	40.79'	649	W02°
	MARSHFIELD	MFI	NDB	391.00	N44°	38.45'	W90°	11.26'		
	MC COY	CMY	NDB	412.00	N43°	56.26'	W90°	38.51'		
	MEDFORD	MDZ	NDB	335.00	N45°	06.32'	W90°	18.52'		
	MERRILL	RRL	NDB	257.00	N45°	11.91'	W89°	42.25'		
	MINDI (LOM)	MIND	NDB	272.00	N44°	00.23'	W91°	15.64'		
	MINERAL POINT	MRJ	NDB	365.00	N42°	53.28'	W90°	13.59'		
	MONAH (LOM/NDB)	MONA	NDB	400.00	N43°	03.75'	W89°	20.75'		
	NECEDAH	DAF	NDB	233.00	N44°	02.04'	W90°	04.95'		
	NEILLSVILLE	VIQ	NDB	368.00	N44°	33.43'	W90°	30.90'		
	NEPCO (LOM)	NEPC	NDB	326.00	N44°	15.59'	W89°	53.27'		
	NEW RICHMOND	RNH	NDB	257.00	N45°	08.83'	W92°	32.00'		
	OCONTO	OCQ	NDB	388.00	N44°	52.55'	W87°	54.74'		
	OSCEOLA	OEO	NDB	233.00	N45°	18.62'	W92°	41.28'		
	OSHKOSH	OSH	VOR	111.80	N43°	59.42'	W88°	33.35'	780	E02°
	PASER (LOM/NDB)	PASE	NDB	206.00	N42°	40.95'	W87°	53.96'		

State/Country	VOR/NDB Name	Ident.	Type	Freq.	Latitude		Longitude		Altitude	Mag Var
USA/CANADA NAVAIDS										
Wisconsin	PHILLIPS	PBH	NDB	263.00	N45°	42.19'	W90°	24.77'		
	PLATTEVILLE	PVB	NDB	203.00	N42°	41.28'	W90°	26.19'		
	POBER (LOM)	POBE	NDB	395.00	N43°	52.42'	W88°	33.45'		
	RHINELANDER	RHI	VOR	109.20	N45°	38.02'	W89°	27.46'	1,590	E02°
	RICE LAKE	RIE	NDB	407.00	N45°	28.77'	W91°	43.24'		
	RICE LAKE	IKE	VOR	110.00	N45°	28.55'	W91°	43.52'	1,134	E02°
	ROCK RIVER	RYV	NDB	371.00	N43°	10.42'	W88°	43.51'		
	RUSK CO	RCX	NDB	356.00	N45°	30.10'	W91°	00.06'		
	SEELEY	SLY	NDB	344.00	N46°	06.61'	W91°	23.02'		
	SHEBB (LOM)	SHEB	NDB	338.00	N43°	50.90'	W87°	46.47'		
	SHELL LAKE	SSQ	NDB	212.00	N45°	43.66'	W91°	55.16'		
	SIREN	RZN	VOR	109.40	N45°	49.22'	W92°	22.47'	987	E02°
	SOLON SPRINGS	OLG	NDB	388.00	N46°	19.02'	W91°	48.83'		
	STEVENS POINT	STE	VOR	110.60	N44°	32.59'	W89°	31.83'	1,108	E02°
	STURGEON BAY	SUE	NDB	414.00	N44°	50.21'	W87°	25.34'		
	TEELS (LOM/NDB)	TEEL	NDB	242.00	N42°	54.54'	W88°	02.46'		
	TIMMERMAN	LJT	VOR	112.50	N43°	06.58'	W88°	02.23'	751	W02°
	TRIBE (LOM)	TRIB	NDB	239.00	N45°	03.69'	W87°	41.75'		
	WAUKESHA	UES	NDB	359.00	N43°	02.68'	W88°	14.11'		
	WAUPACA	PCZ	NDB	382.00	N44°	19.92'	W89°	00.97'		
	WAUSAU	AUW	VOR	111.60	N44°	50.80'	W89°	35.19'	1,210	E02°
	WAUSAU	FZK	NDB	243.00	N44°	55.66'	W89°	37.51'		
	WEST BEND	BJB	VOR	109.80	N43°	25.31'	W88°	07.52'	869	W01°
	WISCONSIN RAPIDS	ISW	NDB	215.00	N44°	21.83'	W89°	50.38'		
	WOODRUFF	RUF	NDB	236.00	N45°	50.07'	W89°	43.82'		
	YANKS (LOM/NDB)	YANK	NDB	260.00	N43°	03.60'	W87°	52.60'		
Wyoming	ANTELOPE	AOP	NDB	290.00	N41°	36.25'	W109°	00.09'		
	BIG PINEY	BPI	VOR	116.50	N42°	34.76'	W110°	06.55'	6,947	E16°
	BOYSEN RESERVOIR	BOY	VOR	117.80	N43°	27.78'	W108°	17.98'	7,547	E16°
	CHEROKEE	CKW	VOR	115.00	N41°	45.34'	W107°	34.91'	7,048	E15°
	CHEYENNE	CYS	VOR	113.10	N41°	12.65'	W104°	46.37'	6,209	E13°
	CODY	COD	VOR	111.80	N44°	37.22'	W108°	57.88'	4,788	E14°
	COWLEY	HCY	NDB	257.00	N44°	54.84'	W108°	26.59'		
	CRAZY WOMAN	CZI	VOR	117.30	N43°	59.98'	W106°	26.14'	4,795	E13°
	DERYK (LOM/NDB)	DERY	NDB	380.00	N44°	16.23'	W105°	31.32'		
	DOUGLAS	DGW	VOR	108.60	N42°	40.56'	W105°	13.57'	4,900	E12°
	DUNOIR	DNW	VOR	113.40	N43°	49.69'	W110°	20.12'	7,717	E15°
	EVANSTON	EVW	VOR	110.00	N41°	16.49'	W111°	01.55'	7,186	E15°
	FORT BRIDGER	FBR	VOR	108.60	N41°	22.70'	W110°	25.44'	7,058	E14°
	GILLETTE	GCC	VOR	114.60	N44°	20.86'	W105°	32.61'	4,332	E12°
	GREYBULL	GEY	NDB	275.00	N44°	30.69'	W108°	04.97'		
	HORSE (LOM)	HORS	NDB	353.00	N41°	08.80'	W104°	40.73'		
	JACKSON	JAC	VOR	108.40	N43°	36.49'	W110°	44.08'	6,428	E15°
	JOHNO (LOM)	JOHN	NDB	375.00	N42°	54.43'	W106°	34.19'		
	KEMMERER	EMM	NDB	407.00	N41°	49.34'	W110°	33.29'		
	KLINT (LOM)	KLIN	NDB	217.00	N43°	00.84'	W108°	18.31'		
	LARAMIE	LAR	VOR	117.60	N41°	20.27'	W105°	43.25'	7,278	E14°
	MEDICINE BOW	MBW	VOR	111.60	N41°	50.73'	W106°	00.25'	6,999	E14°
	MUDDY MOUNTAIN	DDY	VOR	116.20	N43°	05.45'	W106°	16.62'	5,858	E12°
	NEWCASTLE	ECS	VOR	108.20	N43°	52.86'	W104°	18.46'	4,211	E11°
	POWELL	POY	NDB	344.00	N44°	52.00'	W108°	47.17'		
	RAWLINS	RWL	VOR	109.40	N41°	48.28'	W107°	12.25'	6,746	E13°
	RIVERTON	RIW	VOR	108.80	N43°	03.94'	W108°	27.33'	5,539	E16°
	ROCK SPRINGS	OCS	VOR	116.00	N41°	35.41'	W109°	00.91'	6,779	E13°
	SHERIDAN	SHR	VOR	115.30	N44°	50.53'	W107°	03.66'	4,408	E13°
	SINCLAIR	SIR	NDB	368.00	N41°	48.12'	W107°	05.53'		
	TORRINGTON	TOR	NDB	293.00	N42°	03.96'	W104°	09.19'		
	WENZ	PNA	NDB	392.00	N42°	47.82'	W109°	48.20'		
	WORLAND	RLY	VOR	114.80	N43°	57.84'	W107°	57.04'	4,188	E13°

State/Country	VOR/NDB Name	Ident.	Type	Freq.	Latitude		Longitude		Altitude	Mag Var

SOUTH AMERICA/CENTRAL AMERICA/CARIBBEAN REGION NAVAIDS

State/Country	VOR/NDB Name	Ident.	Type	Freq.	Latitude		Longitude		Altitude	Mag Var
Antigua										
	V C BIRD	ANU	VOR	114.50	N17°	07.60'	W061°	47.88'	0	W13°
	V C BIRD	ANU	NDB	351.00	N17°	07.49'	W061°	48.60'		
	V C BIRD	ZDX	NDB	369.00	N17°	09.00'	W061°	46.99'		
Argentina										
	EZEIZA	EZE	VOR	116.50	S34°	49.5'	W058°	32.1'	66	W05°
	EZEIZA	OC	NDB	330.00	S34°	48.3'	W058°	37.8'	66	W05°
	EZEIZA	OC	NDB	330.00	S34°	48.29'	W058°	37.79'	65	
	EZEIZA	C	NDB	305.00	S34°	49.09'	W058°	33.79'	65	
	EZEIZA	A	NDB	237.50	S34°	50.59'	W058°	31.20'	65	
	EZEIZA	OA	NDB	270.00	S34°	53.4'	W058°	30.4'	66	W05°
	GENERAL BELGRANDO	GBE	VOR	115.60	S35°	45.1'	W058°	27.8'	50	W05°
	LA PLATA	PTA	VOR	113.70	S34°	58.6'	W057°	53.8'	69	W05°
	LOBOS	BOS	VOR	114.60	S35°	12.7'	W059°	08.6'	100	W04°
	MORIANO MORENO	ENO	VOR	112.90	S34°	33.8'	W058°	47.4'	105	W05°
	SAN ANTONIO DE ARECO	SNT	VOR	117.70	S34°	13.20'	W059°	25.99'	98	W04°
	SAN FERNANDO	FDO	VOR	114.40	S34°	27.1'	W058°	35.0'	16	W05°
Aruba										
	ARUBA	ABA	VOR	112.50	N12°	30.53'	W069°	56.46'	0	W04°
Ascension Island										
	ASCENSION ISLAND	ASN	NDB	360.00	S07°	56.7'	W014°	24.8'	273	W18°
	ASCENSION AUX	ASI	VOR	112.20	S07°	58.2'	W014°	23.8'	476	W18°
Azores, Portugal										
	LAJES	LM	VOR	112.30	N38°	47.1'	W027°	06.3'	1,855	W14°
	PONTA DELGADA	MGL	NDB	371.00	N37°	44.4'	W025°	35.1'	300	W12°
	PONTA DELGADA	PD	NDB	351.00	N37°	44.1'	W025°	40.5'	187	W12°
	SANTA MARIA	SMA	NDB	323.00	N36°	59.8'	W025°	10.6'	283	W12°
	SANTA MARIA	VSM	VOR	113.70	N36°	57.7'	W025°	10.0'	308	W12°
Bahamas										
	GREAT INAGUA	ZIN	NDB	376.00	N20°	57.58'	W073°	40.64'		
	ROCK SOUND	RSD	NDB	348.00	N24°	53.58'	W076°	10.19'		
	SAN ANDRES	SPP	NDB	387.00	N12°	34.99'	W081°	42.00'		
	STELLA MARIS	ZLS	NDB	526.00	N23°	34.83'	W075°	15.83'		
Barbados										
	ADAMS (GRANTLEY ADAMS INTL)	BGI	VOR	112.70	N13°	04.34'	W059°	29.13'	170	W14°
	ADAMS (GRANTLEY ADAMS INTL)	BGI	NDB	345.00	N13°	04.11'	W059°	29.53'		
Belize										
	BELIZE	BZE	NDB	392.00	N17°	32.2'	W088°	18.4'	12	E03°
	BELIZE	BZE	VOR	114.30	N17°	32.3'	W008°	18.9'	30	E03°
Bermuda										
	BERMUDA	BDA	VOR	113.90	N32°	21.8	W064	41.4	60	W15°
	ST DAVIDS HEAD	BSD	NDB	323.00	N32°	22.0'	W064°	38.9'	20	W15°
Boliva										
	ARICA	ARI	VOR	116.50	S18°	21.9'	W070°	20.7'	191	W04°
	CHARANA	CHA	NDB	310.00	S17°	35.4'	W069°	26.3'	13,320	W02°
	COCHABAMBA	CBA	VOR	112.10	S17°	25.3'	W066°	10.7'	8,365	W04°
	COROICO	CRC	NDB	305.00	S16°	11.5'	W067°	43.2'	6,000	W02°
	LA PAZ	PAZ	VOR	115.70	S16°	30.5'	W068°	13.9'	13,398	W03°
	LA PAZ	R	NDB	330.00	S16°	30.6'	W068°	13.1'	13,398	W03°
	LA PAZ	LPZ	NDB	350.00	S16°	29.7'	W068°	11.0'	13,398	W03°
	SAN BORJA	BOR	VOR	117.50	S14°	55.9'	W066°	44.7'	800	W05°
Brazil										
	AFONSOS	AFS	NDB	270.00	S22°	52.0'	W043°	22.0'	110	W21°
	ANAPOLIS	ANP	VOR	115.40	S16°	15.6'	W048°	59.5'	3,200	W18°
	BRASILIA	BRS	NDB	340.00	S15°	52.2'	W048°	01.3'	3,441	W19°
	BRASILIA	BRS	VOR	115.90	S15°	52.4'	W048°	01.3'	4,035	W19°
	CAMPINA GRANDE	CPG	NDB	230.00	S07°	16.0'	W035°	53.5'	1,642	W22°
	CAXIAS	CAX	NDB	400.00	S22°	45.8'	W043°	20.3'	21	W21°
	CAXIAS	CAX	VOR	113.00	S22°	46.6'	W043°	20.0'	100	W21°
	COCHO	CH	NDB	240.00	S15°	51.6'	W047°	53.1'	3,473	W19°
	FORMOSA	FRM	NDB	210.00	S15°	33.0'	W047°	21.0'	3,166	W19°
	GOIANIA	GOI	VOR	112.70	S16°	37.9'	W049°	12.9'	2,450	W18°
	ILHA	YLA	NDB	330.00	S22°	47.1'	W043°	10.1'	30	W21°
	JOAO PESSOA	JPS	NDB	320.00	S07°	08.5'	W034°	57.1'	212	W22°
	LUZIANIA	LUZ	NDB	400.00	S16°	15.0'	W047°	57.0'	3,347	W15°
	MARICA	MRC	VOR	114.00	S22°	58.0'	W042°	53.5'	16	W21°
	MERITI	IT	NDB	290.00	S22°	49.8'	W043°	21.8'	18	W21°
	MOSSORO	MSS	NDB	275.00	S05°	11.6'	W037°	21.8'	77	W22°

State/Country	VOR/NDB Name	Ident.	Type	Freq.	Latitude		Longitude		Altitude	Mag Var
SOUTH AMERICA/CENTRAL AMERICA/CARIBBEAN REGION NAVAIDS										
Brazil	MOSSORO	MSS	VOR	112.40	S05°	11.8'	W037°	21.9'	75	W22°
	NATAL	NTL	NDB	400.00	S05°	54.1'	W035°	14.8'	167	W22°
	NATAL	NTL	VOR	114.30	S05°	54.5'	W035°	14.9'	167	W22°
	NOVA	NOA	NDB	215.00	S22°	43.3'	W043°	28.1'	164	W21°
	OIAPOQUE	OIA	NDB	340.00	N03°	51.6'	W051°	48.0'	46	W17°
	PAIOL	PP	NDB	415.00	S22°	52.2'	W043°	09.9'	20	W21°
	PIRAI	PAI	VOR	115.00	S22°	27.2'	W043°	50.6'	1,200	W21°
	PORTO	PCX	VOR	114.60	S22°	42.9'	W042°	51.5'	200	W21°
	RASA	IH	NDB	315.00	S23°	03.8'	W043°	08.8'	15	W21°
	SANTA CRUZ	SCR	VOR	113.60	S22°	57.0'	W043°	43.6'	10	W21°
Caicos Islands										
	PROVIDENCIALES	PV	NDB	387.00	N21°	46.63'	W072°	15.65'		
Caymon Islands										
	CAYMAN BRAC	CBC	NDB	415.00	N19°	41.38'	W079°	51.41'		
	GRAND CAYMAN	GCM	VOR	115.60	N19°	17.39'	W081°	22.30'	6	W01°
	GRAND CAYMAN	ZIY	NDB	344.00	N19°	17.00'	W081°	22.99'		
Chile										
	ARTURO MERINO BENITEZ	EL	NDB	205.00	S33°	21.77'	W070°	47.12'	1,554	
	CASABLANCA	CAS	NDB	328.00	S33°	18.6'	W071°	23.9'	600	E06°
	CURICO	ICO	VOR	114.70	S34°	57.90'	W071°	12.80'	698	E07°
	HUECHUN	HUN	NDB	250.00	S33°	02.3'	W070°	48.6'	4,000	E08°
	LO CASTRO	CAS	NDB	220.00	S33°	18.1'	W070°	47.3'	1,549	E05°
	LOS CERRILLOS	SCL	VOR	112.30	S33°	29.9'	W070°	42.1'	1,700	E05°
	QUINTERO	ERO	NDB	384.00	S32°	44.3'	W071°	29.5'	17	E08°
	QUINTERO	ERO	VOR	113.30	S32°	47.5'	W071°	30.9'	17	E08°
	SANTIAGO	AMB	VOR	116.10	S33°	25.2'	W070°	47.0'	1,585	E05°
	SANTO DOMINGO	SNO	VOR	113.70	S33°	39.8'	W071°	36.9'	50	E09°
	TABON	TBN	NDB	288.00	S32°	55.7'	W070°	48.6'	4,000	E08°
	TABON	TBN	VOR	113.90	S32°	55.1'	W070°	50.2'	4,000	E04°
	TONGOY	TOY	VOR	115.50	S30°	16.39'	W071°	28.29'	321	E06°
Colombia										
	AMBALEMA	ABL	NDB	300.00	N04°	47.4'	W074°	46.5'	1,500	W02°
	BARRANQUILLA	BAQ	VOR	113.70	N10°	48.03'	W074°	51.74'	0	W03°
	BARRANQUILLA	BA	NDB	244.00	N10°	48.00'	W074°	52.00'		
	BOGOTA	BOG	NDB	388.00	N04°	50.9'	W074°	19.6'	8,356	W03°
	BOGOTA	DR	NDB	264.00	N04°	43.19'	W074°	09.69'	8,354	
	BOGOTA	ED	NDB	244.00	N04°	46.1'	W074°	13.4'	8,355	W03°
	BOGOTA	BOG	VOR	114.70	N04°	50.9'	W074°	19.6'	10,000	W04°
	EL PASO	EPO	NDB	225.00	N04°	30.0'	N075°	30.0'	10,000	W02°
	GIRARDOT	GIR	VOR	117.30	N04°	11.7'	W074°	52.2'	1,000	W03°
	MARIQUITA	MQU	VOR	116.10	N05°	12.7'	W074°	55.5'	1,531	W03°
	ROMEO	R	NDB	274.00	N04°	40.8'	W074°	06.3'	8,355	W04°
	TECHO	TEH	NDB	284.00	N04°	38.0'	W074°	09.0'	8,500	W04°
	VILLAVICENCIO	VCC	NDB	370.00	N04°	04.09'	W073°	23.10'	898	
	VILLAVICENCIO	VVC	VOR	116.70	N04°	04.0'	W073°	23.1'	900	W04°
	ZIPAQUIRA	ZIP	NDB	294.00	N05°	01.0'	W074°	01.0'	9,000	W03°
Costa Rica										
	BARRA DEL COLORADO	COL	NDB	380.00	N10°	46.0'	W083°	35.3'	10	E01°
	EL COCO	TIO	VOR	115.70	N09°	59.1'	W084°	14.3'	3,500	E03°
	HORCONES	HOR	NDB	260.00	N09°	57.8'	W084°	17.8'	3,000	E03°
	LIBERIA	LIB	VOR	112.80	N10°	35.8'	W085°	32.8'	230	E02°
	LIMON	LIO	VOR	116.30	N09°	57.9'	W083°	01.8'	20	E01°
	PARRITA	PAR	NDB	395.00	N09°	31.1'	W084°	20.3'	100	E02°
Cuba										
	ALEGRE	UPA	NDB	382.00	N22°	22.41'	W078°	46.38'		
	BARACOA	UBA	NDB	212.00	N20°	22.09'	W074°	31.59'	39	
	GERONA	UNG	NDB	412.00	N21°	45.19'	W082°	52.88'		
	GUANTANAMO (US)	UGT	NDB	300.00	N20°	04.80'	W075	09.49'		
	NAVY GUANTANAMO BAY (US)	NBW	VOR	114.60	N19°	54.30'	W075°	11.89'	88	W06°
	MANZANILLO	UMZ	NDB	232.00	N20°	16.13'	W077°	10.08'		
	MOA	UMO	NDB	212.00	N20°	38.30'	W074°	57.29'	39	
	NUEVAS	UNV	VOR	116.30	N21°	23.83'	W077°	13.71'	0	W04°
	NUEVAS	UNV	NDB	256.00	N21°	24.10'	W077°	13.80'		
	SANTIAGO DE CUBA	UCU	VOR	113.30	N19°	58.59'	W075°	49.3'	209	W05°
	SANTIAGO	STG	VOR	114.50	N18°	05.24'	W080°	56.38'	0	E03°
	SIMONES	USR	NDB	315.00	N21°	44.74'	W078°	48.71'		
	VARDER	UVR	NDB	272.00	N23°	05.39'	W081°	22.03'		
Dominica										
	MELVILLE HALL	DOM	NDB	273.00	N15°	32.99'	W061°	17.99'		

State/Country	VOR/NDB Name	Ident.	Type	Freq.	Latitude		Longitude		Altitude	Mag Var
SOUTH AMERICA/CENTRAL AMERICA/CARIBBEAN REGION NAVAIDS										
Dominican Republic										
	CABO ROJO	CRO	VOR	114.30	N17°	56.00'	W071°	38.99'	9	W06°
	PUERTO PLATA	PTA	VOR	115.10	N19°	45.53'	W070°	34.25'	26	W07°
	PUNTA CANA	PNA	VOR	112.70	N18°	33.91'	W068°	21.69'	0	W10°
	PUNTA CAUCEDO	CDO	VOR	114.70	N18°	25.97'	W069°	40.04'	39	W09°
Ecuador										
	AMBATO	AMV	VOR	112.70	S01°	16.9'	W078°	32.6'	8,500	E00°
	ASCAZUBI	ZUI	NDB	290.00	S00°	04.8'	W078°	17.5'	9,000	E00°
	CONDORCOCHA	QIT	VOR	115.30	S00°	02.3'	W078°	30.6'	10,500	E00°
	IPIALES	IPI	VOR	113.60	N00°	51.7'	W077°	40.6'	9,762	E00°
	MONJAS SUR	QMS	VOR	115.00	S00°	13.9'	W078°	28.5'	9,000	E00°
	OLMEDO	OLM	NDB	400.00	N00°	10.0'	W078°	03.5'	7,500	E03°
	QUITO	UIO	NDB	350.00	S00°	10.3'	W078°	28.9'	9,186	E00°
El Salvador										
	AMATE CAMPO	LAN	NDB	331.00	N13°	24.7'	W089°	08.2'	30	E03°
	EL SALVADOR	CAT	VOR	117.50	N13°	26.4'	W089°	02.9'	110	E03°
	ILOPANGO	YSX	NDB	215.00	N13°	42.0'	W089°	07.1'	2,000	E03°
	ILOPANGO	YSV	VOR	114.70	N13°	41.3'	W089°	07.0'	2,052	E03°
	LA AURORA	AUR	VOR	114.50	N14 °	35.0'	W90°	31.6'	4,952	E05°
	LA MESA	LMS	VOR	113.10	N15°	28.3'	W087°	54.5'	88	E03°
Florida										
	FISH HOOK	FIS	NDB	332.00	N24°	32.90'	W081°	47.18'		
	KEY WEST	EYW	VOR	113.50	N24°	35.14'	W081°	48.03'	9	E01°
	MARATHON	MTH	NDB	260.00	N24°	42.71'	W081°	05.72'		
French Guiana										
	ROCHAMBEAU	FXC	NDB	327.00	N04°	49.4'	W052°	21.8'	20	W17°
	ROCHAMBEAU	CYR	VOR	115.10	N04°	48.8'	W052°	22.1'	30	W17°
	ST LAURENT DU MARONI	CW	NDB	283.00	N05°	28.1'	W054°	01.9'	16	W16°
Gran Roque										
	GRAN ROQUE	LRS	VOR	113.10	N11°	56.99'	W066°	40.00'	0	W07°
Guadeloupe										
	POINTE A PITRE	PPR	VOR	115.10	N16°	16.00'	W061°	30.99'	0	W11°
	POINTE A PITRE	AR	NDB	402.00	N16°	17.30'	W061°	37.49'		
	POINTE A PITRE	PPR	NDB	300.00	N16°	15.66'	W061°	31.66'		
Guatemala										
	GUATEMALA	TGE	NDB	375.00	N14°	35.1'	W090°	31.9'	4,952	E05°
	IZTAPA	IZP	NDB	400.00	N13°	56.0'	E090°	44.0'	30	E05°
	LA AURORA	AUR	VOR	114.50	N14°	35.0'	W090°	31.6'	4,952	E05°
	RABINAL	RAB	VOR	116.10	N15°	00.5'	W090°	28.2'	5,000	E05°
	RABINAL	RBN	NDB	313.00	N15°	00.5'	W090°	28.2'	5,000	E05°
	SAN JOSE	SJO	VOR	114.10	N13°	56.0'	W090°	51.1'	21	E05°
Haiti										
	CAP HAITIEN	HCN	VOR	113.90	N19°	43.63'	W072°	11.83'	0	W07°
	CAP HAITIEN	HTN	NDB	288.00	N19°	44.04'	W072°	12.00'		
	OBLEON	OBN	VOR	113.20	N18°	26.23'	W072°	16.48'	0	W07°
	PORT AU PRINCE	PAP	VOR	115.30	N18°	34.58'	W072°	18.26'	111	W07°
	PORT AU PRINCE	HHP	NDB	270.00	N18°	34.58'	W072°	17.21'		
Honduras										
	AMATECAMPO	LAN	NDB	331.00	N13°	24.70'	W089°	08.20'	29	
	LA MESA	LMS	VOR	113.10	N15°	28.29'	W087°	54.49''	88	E03°
	TEGUCIGALPA	TGU	NDB	355.00	N13°	56.78'	W087°	14.86'		
	TONCONTIN	TNT	NDB	405.00	N14°	03.56'	W087°	13.40'		
Jamaica										
	KINGSTON	KIN	VOR	115.90	N17°	58.41'	W076°	53.63'	39	W03°
	KINGSTON	KIN	NDB	360.00	N17°	57.80'	W076°	52.55'		
	MONTEGO BAY	MBJ	VOR	115.70	N18°	29.85'	W077°	55.51'	3	W03°
	MONTEGO BAY	MBJ	NDB	248.00	N18°	30.05'	W077°	55.16'		
Martinique Island										
	FORT DE FRANCE	FOF	VOR	113.30	N14°	35.00'	W060°	59.99'	0	W11°
	FORT DE FRANCE	FXF	NDB	314.00	N14°	35.96'	W061°	05.71'		
Mexico										
	APAN	APN	VOR	114.80	N19°	38.2'	W098°	23.9'	8,000	E07°
	COLIMA	COL	VOR	117.70	N19°	16.3'	W103°	34.7'	1,499	E08°
	COZUMEL	CZM	VOR	112.60	N20°	28.99'	W086°	57.00'	0	E04°
	COZUMEL	CZM	NDB	330.00	N20°	31.41'	W086°	55.89'		
	CUAUTLA	CUA	VOR	116.30	N18°	47.0'	W098°	54.1'	4,400	E07°
	GUADALAJARA	GDL	VOR	117.30	N20°	31.4'	W103°	18.7'	5,012	E08°
	LUCIA	SLM	VOR	116.60	N19°	44.2'	W099°	01.8'	7,500	E07°
	MANZANILLO	ZLO	VOR	116.80	N19°	09.0'	W104°	34.4'	25	E08°

State/Country	VOR/NDB Name	Ident.	Type	Freq.	Latitude		Longitude		Altitude	Mag Var
SOUTH AMERICA/CENTRAL AMERICA/CARIBBEAN REGION NAVAIDS										
Mexico	MATEO	SMO	VOR	112.10	N19°	33.4'	W099°	13.7'	7,900	E08°
	MEXICO CITY	MEX	VOR	115.60	N19°	26.3'	W099°	04.0'	7,339	E08°
	OTUMBA	OTU	VOR	115.00	N19°	41.3'	W098°	46.3'	7,000	E07°
	PACHUCA	PCA	VOR	112.70	N20°	07.9'	W098°	41.1'	7,500	E07°
	PASTEJE	PTJ	VOR	114.50	N19°	38.7'	W099°	47.9'	8,300	E07°
	PLAZA	MW	NDB	370.00	N19°	23.6'	W099°	09.0'	7,333	E08°
	PUEBLA	PBC	VOR	115.20	N19°	09.6'	W098°	22.3'	7,300	E07°
	TEPEXPAN	TPX	NDB	359.00	N19°	36.6'	W098°	57.6'	7,500	E07°
	TEQUIS	TEQ	VOR	113.10	N18°	41.0'	W099°	15.3'	3,300	E07°
	TOLUCA	TLC	VOR	114.30	N19°	21.0'	W099°	34.3'	8,700	E08°
	URUAPAN	UPN	VOR	114.20	N19°	23.7'	W102°	02.4'	5,230	E08°
	ZIHUATANEJO	ZIH	VOR	113.80	N17°	36.2'	W101°	28.6'	10	E08°
Netherlands Antilles										
	CURACAO	PJG	VOR	116.70	N12°	12.01'	W069°	00.59'	0	W07°
	ST MAARTEN	PJM	VOR	113.00	N18°	02.23'	W063°	07.13'	0	W12°
	ST MAARTEN	PJD	NDB	284.00	N18°	02.29'	W063°	07.10'		
	ST MAARTEN	PJM	NDB	308.00	N18°	02.16'	W063°	07.05'		
Panama										
	BOCAS DEL TORO	BDT	VOR	114.90	N09°	20.28'	W082°	15.05'	0	E02°
	DAVID	DAV	VOR	114.30	N08°	23.08'	W082°	26.26'	0	E01°
	FRANCE	FTD	VOR	109.00	N09°	21.66'	W079°	51.95'	0	E00°
	TABOGA ISLAND	TBG	VOR	110.00	N08°	47.13'	W079°	33.61'	0	E01°
	TABOGA ISLAND	TBG	NDB	311.00	N08°	46.99'	W079°	33.99'		
	TOCUMEN	TUM	VOR	117.10	N09°	03.00'	W079°	24.01'	0	E03°
Paraguay										
	ASUNCION	ASU	NDB	360.00	S25°	14.1'	W057°	30.8'	249	W10°
	ASUNCION	VB	NDB	350.00	S25°	16.8'	W057°	31.7'	292	W08°
	ASUNCION	PS	NDB	320.00	S25°	12.80'	W057°	30.80'	291	
	ASUNCION	ST	NDB	340.00	S25°	08.4'	W057°	29.7'	249	W10°
	ASUNCION	VAS	VOR	115.90	S25°	08.39'	W057°	29.69'	298	W10°
	FORMOSA	FSA	VOR	115.60	S26°	12.3'	W058°	13.7'	193	W09°
	PARAGUARI	PRI	NDB	350.00	S25°	36.3'	W057°	08.3'	410	W08°
Peru										
	ASIA	ASI	VOR	115.30	S12°	45.29'	W076°	36.30'	19	E01°
	CHIMBOTE	BTE	VOR	112.50	S09°	08.8'	W078°	31.2'	70	E02°
	LAS PALMAS	LP	NDB	300.00	S12°	13.0'	W077°	01.0'	112	E02°
	LIMA	LIM	VOR	114.50	S12°	00.7'	W077°	07.7'	105	E02°
	LIMA-CALLAO	CH	NDB	248.00	S11°	59.6'	W077°	07.4'	48	E02°
	OYON	YON	NDB	360.00	S10°	39.0'	W076°	46.0'	200	E01°
	PISCO	SCO	VOR	114.10	S13°	44.1'	W076°	12.7'	20	E01°
	SALINAS	SLS	VOR	114.70	S11°	17.6'	W077°	34.1'	20	E02°
	VENTANILLA	JC	NDB	375.00	S11°	55.8'	W077°	08.0'	100	E02°
Puerto Rico										
	BORINQUEN	BQN	VOR	113.50	N18°	29.88'	W067°	06.49'	239	W10°
	DORADO	DDP	NDB	391.00	N18°	28.09'	W066°	24.74'		
	MAYAGUEZ	MAZ	VOR	110.60	N18°	15.38'	W067°	09.06'	19	W10°
	MAYAGUEZ	MAZ	NDB	254.00	N18°	15.22'	W067°	09.14'		
	PATTY (LOM/NDB)	PATT	NDB	330.00	N18°	24.53'	W066°	05.34'		
	PESTE (LOM)	PEST	NDB	241.00	N17°	41.51'	W064°	53.08'		
	PONCE	PSE	VOR	109.00	N17°	59.54'	W066°	31.15'	19	W10°
	SAN JUAN	SJU	VOR	114.00	N18°	26.77'	W065°	59.37'	6	W11°
St. Vincent										
	E T JOSHUA	SV	NDB	403.00	N13°	08.29'	W061°	13.80'		
Trindade (Brazil)										
	ALDEIA	ADA	NDB	345.00	S22°	49.40'	W042°	05.90'	49	W25°
	SANTA CRUZ	SCR	NDB	255.00	S22°	56.90'	W043°	43.59'	9	W25°
Turks										
	GRAND TURK	GTK	VOR	114.20	N21°	26.44'	W071°	08.02'	0	W08°
	GRAND TURK	GT	NDB	232.00	N21°	26.19'	W071°	08.78'		
Venezuela										
	CORO	CRO	VOR	117.30	N11°	24.99'	W069°	41.99'	0	W04°
	MAIQUETIA	MIQ	VOR	114.80	N10°	36.99'	W067°	00.99'	0	W08°
	MAIQUETIA	MIQ	NDB	292.00	N10°	36.99'	W067°	00.99'		
	MARACAIBO	MAR	VOR	115.70	N10°	35.15'	W071°	42.75'	0	W03°
	MARGARITA	MTA	VOR	114.10	N10°	55.41'	W063°	57.66'	0	W11°
	MARGARITA	MTA	NDB	206.00	N10°	55.20'	W063°	57.40'		
	PIARCO	POS	VOR	116.90	N10°	27.86'	W061°	23.61'	59	W12°
	PIARCO	POS	NDB	382.00	N10°	35.65'	W061°	25.58'		
Virgin Islands (US)										
	ST CROIX	COY	VOR	108.20	N17°	44.06'	W064°	42.04'	849	W10°
	ST THOMAS	STT	VOR	108.60	N18°	21.34'	W065°	01.47'	698	W10°

State/Country	VOR/NDB Name	Ident.	Type	Freq.	Latitude		Longitude		Altitude	Mag Var

WESTERN PACIFIC NAVAIDS

Alaska

State/Country	VOR/NDB Name	Ident.	Type	Freq.	Latitude		Longitude		Altitude	Mag Var
	ADAK	NUD	VOR	113.0	N51°	52.27'	W176°	40.44'	380	E09°
	ADAK	NUD	NDB	347.0	N51°	55.01'	W176°	34.01'		
	AMBLER	AMF	NDB	403.0	N67°	06.40'	W157°	51.47'		
	ANCHORAGE	ANC	VOR	114.3	N61°	09.04'	W150°	12.39'	278	E25°
	ANIAK	ANI	NDB	359.0	N61°	35.41'	W159°	35.87'		
	ANNETTE ISLAND	ANN	VOR	117.1	N55°	03.62'	W131°	34.70'	173	E27°
	ANVIK	ANV	NDB	365.0	N62°	38.48'	W160°	11.40'		
	ATLIN	YSQ	NDB	260.0	N59°	37.56'	W133°	40.61'		
	BARROW	BRW	VOR	116.2	N71°	16.40'	W156°	47.28'	39	E25°
	BARTER ISLAND	BTI	NDB	308.0	N70°	07.84'	W143°	38.63'		
	BEAR CREEK	BCC	NDB	212.0	N65°	10.43'	W152°	12.35'		
	BEAVER CREEK	YXQ	NDB	239.0	N62°	24.52'	W140°	51.69'		
	BETHEL	BET	VOR	114.1	N60°	47.08'	W161°	49.45'	131	E19°
	BETHEL (LMM)	ET	NDB	344.0	N60°	47.79'	W161°	49.28'		
	BETTLES	BTT	VOR	116.0	N66°	54.30'	W151°	32.15'	646	E27°
	BIG DELTA	BIG	VOR	114.9	N64°	00.26'	W145°	43.02'	1,229	E29°
	BIG LAKE	BGQ	VOR	112.5	N61°	34.16'	W149°	58.02'	160	E25°
	BIORKA ISLAND	BKA	VOR	113.8	N56°	51.56'	W135°	33.07'	239	E28°
	BISHOP	BZP	NDB	331.0	N64°	44.15'	W156°	48.60'		
	BORLAND	HBT	NDB	390.0	N55°	18.93'	W160°	31.10'		
	BROWERVILLE	VIR	NDB	281.0	N71°	16.95'	W156°	47.08'		
	BRUCK (LOM)	BRUC	NDB	387.0	N61°	10.05'	W150°	10.61'		
	BUCKLAND	BVK	NDB	325.0	N65°	58.78'	W161°	08.96'		
	BURWASH	DB	NDB	341.0	N61°	20.41'	W138°	59.00'		
	CAIRN MOUNTAIN	CRN	NDB	281.0	N61°	05.95'	W155°	33.13'		
	CAMPBELL LAKE	CMQ	NDB	338.0	N61°	10.26'	W150°	02.86'		
	CAPE LISBURNE	LUR	NDB	385.0	N68°	51.95'	W166°	04.18'		
	CAPE NEWENHAM	EHM	NDB	385.0	N58°	39.35'	W162°	04.54'		
	CAPE ROMANZOF	CZF	NDB	275.0	N61°	47.43'	W165°	58.17'		
	CENTRAL	CEM	NDB	373.0	N65°	34.39'	W144°	47.64'		
	CHANDALAR LAKE	CQR	NDB	263.0	N67°	30.14'	W148°	28.16'		
	CHENA	CUN	NDB	257.0	N64°	50.29'	W147°	29.39'		
	CLAM COVE	CMJ	NDB	396.0	N55°	20.72'	W131°	41.78'		
	COGHLAN ISLAND	CGL	NDB	212.0	N58°	21.56'	W134°	41.96'		
	COLD BAY	CDB	VOR	112.6	N55°	16.04'	W162°	46.45'	98	E17°
	DAWSON	DA	NDB	214.0	N64°	01.73'	W139°	10.08'		
	DEADHORSE	SCC	VOR	113.9	N70°	11.95'	W148°	24.97'	49	E31°
	DELTA JUNCTION	DJN	NDB	347.0	N64°	01.41'	W145°	41.20'		
	DILLINGHAM	DLG	VOR	116.4	N58°	59.65'	W158°	33.13'	131	E20°
	DRIFT RIVER	DRF	NDB	368.0	N60°	35.63'	W152°	08.55'		
	DUTCH HARBOR	DUT	VOR	113.9	N53°	54.31'	W166°	32.94'	327	E14°
	DUTCH HARBOR	DUT	NDB	283.0	N53°	54.31'	W166°	32.94'		
	EAGLE	EAA	NDB	519.0	N64°	46.66'	W141°	08.43'		
	EAST KUPURA	ACU	NDB	268.0	N68°	50.40'	W153°	18.95'		
	EIELSON	EAF	VOR	117.0	N64°	34.15'	W147°	00.96'	600	E29°
	ELEPHANT	EEF	NDB	391.0	N58°	10.25'	W135°	15.47'		
	ELFEE (LOM/NDB)	ELFE	NDB	341.0	N55°	17.76'	W162°	47.34'		
	EMMONAK	ENM	VOR	117.8	N62°	47.00'	W164°	29.26'	16	E17°
	ENGLISH BAY	EGY	NDB	374.0	N57°	07.43'	W170°	16.33'		
	EVANSVILLE	EAV	NDB	391.0	N66°	53.59'	W151°	33.82'		
	FAIRBANKS	FAI	VOR	108.2	N64°	48.00'	W148°	00.71'	1,492	E28°
	FAREWELL LAKE	FXW	NDB	412.0	N62°	32.58'	W153°	37.19'		
	FIN CREEK	FNK	NDB	320.0	N69°	29.89'	W147°	35.58'		
	FIVE MILE	FVM	NDB	312.0	N65°	55.02'	W149°	49.83'		
	FORT DAVIS	FDV	NDB	529.0	N64°	29.67'	W165°	18.84'		
	FORT RICHARDSON	FRN	NDB	196.0	N61°	16.58'	W149°	38.93'		
	FORT YUKON	FYU	VOR	114.4	N66°	34.45'	W145°	16.59'	426	E31°
	FOX	FOX	NDB	356.0	N64°	58.14'	W147°	34.79'		
	FREDERICKS POINT	FPN	NDB	372.0	N56°	47.53'	W132°	49.24'		
	GALBRAITH LAKE	GBH	NDB	417.0	N68°	28.74'	W149°	29.91'		
	GALENA	GAL	VOR	114.8	N64°	44.28'	W156°	46.62'	131	E23°
	GAMBELL	GAM	NDB	369.0	N63°	46.92'	W171°	44.20'		
	GLACIER RIVER	GCR	NDB	404.0	N60°	29.92'	W145°	28.47'		
	GLENNALLEN	GLA	NDB	248.0	N62°	11.72'	W145°	28.07'		
	GOLD	OYN	NDB	208.0	N64°	30.77'	W165°	26.00'		
	GRANITE POINT	GRP	NDB	356.0	N60°	57.68'	W151°	20.03'		
	GULKANA	GKN	VOR	115.6	N62°	09.14'	W145°	27.01'	1,548	E28°
	GUSTAVUS	GAV	NDB	219.0	N58°	25.31'	W135°	42.27'		
	HAINES	HNS	NDB	245.0	N59°	12.72'	W135°	25.85'		
	HINCHINBROOK	HBK	NDB	362.0	N60°	23.65'	W146°	05.42'		
	HOMER	HOM	VOR	114.6	N59°	42.57'	W151°	27.40'	1,623	E24°
	HOOPER BAY	HPB	VOR	115.2	N61°	30.87'	W166°	08.07'	160	E16°

State/Country	VOR/NDB Name	Ident.	Type	Freq.	Latitude		Longitude		Altitude	Mag Var
WESTERN PACIFIC NAVAIDS										
Alaska	HOTHAM	HHM	NDB	356.0	N66°	54.07'	W162°	33.86'		
	HUSLIA	HSL	VOR	117.4	N65°	42.36'	W156°	22.23'	121	E23°
	ICE POOL	ICW	NDB	525.0	N64°	32.74'	W149°	04.61'		
	IGNEK	CNR	NDB	209.0	N69°	35.68'	W146°	29.71'		
	ILIAMNA	ILI	NDB	328.0	N59°	44.87'	W154°	54.57'		
	IVISHAK	IVH	NDB	379.0	N69°	24.13'	W148°	16.18'		
	JOHNSTONE POINT	JOH	VOR	116.7	N60°	28.85'	W146°	35.95'	45	E27°
	KACHEMAK	ACE	NDB	277.0	N59°	38.47'	W151°	30.00'		
	KENAI	ENA	VOR	117.6	N60°	36.88'	W151°	11.71'	108	E25°
	KING SALMON	AKN	VOR	112.8	N58°	43.48'	W156°	45.12'	78	E21°
	KIPNUK	IIK	VOR	115.9	N59°	56.56'	W164°	02.06'	0	E17°
	KODIAK	ODK	VOR	117.1	N57°	46.50'	W152°	20.38'	131	E23°
	KOTZEBUE	OTZ	VOR	115.7	N66°	53.14'	W162°	32.39'	121	E19°
	KOYUK	KKA	NDB	299.0	N64°	55.91'	W161°	08.87'		
	KUKULIAK	ULL	VOR	117.3	N63°	41.53'	W170°	28.20'	380	E13°
	KULIK LAKE	HCP	NDB	334.0	N59°	01.06'	W155°	36.02'		
	LEVEL ISLAND	LVD	VOR	116.5	N56°	28.06'	W133°	04.98'	98	E28°
	MC GRATH	MCG	VOR	115.5	N62°	57.06'	W155°	36.68'	350	E23°
	MIDDLETON ISLAND	MDO	VOR	115.3	N59°	25.30'	W146°	21.00'	121	E26°
	MINCHUMINA	MHM	NDB	227.0	N63°	53.03'	W152°	18.98'		
	MINERAL CREEK	MNL	NDB	524.0	N61°	07.45'	W146°	21.13'		
	MOSES POINT	MOS	VOR	116.3	N64°	41.79'	W162°	04.27'	13	E19°
	MT EDGECUMBE	IME	NDB	414.0	N57°	02.85'	W135°	22.02'		
	NABESNA	AES	NDB	390.0	N62°	57.94'	W141°	53.29'		
	NANWAK	AIX	NDB	323.0	N60°	23.10'	W166°	12.88'		
	NENANA	ENN	VOR	115.8	N64°	35.39'	W149°	04.37'	1,600	E28°
	NOATAK	OQK	NDB	414.0	N67°	34.31'	W162°	58.42'		
	NOME	OME	VOR	115.0	N64°	29.10'	W165°	15.19'	98	E17°
	NORTH RIVER	JNR	NDB	382.0	N63°	54.46'	W160°	48.71'		
	NORTHWAY	ORT	VOR	116.3	N62°	56.83'	W141°	54.76'	1,177	E30°
	NORTON BAY	OAY	NDB	263.0	N64°	41.76'	W162°	03.77'		
	OCEAN CAPE	OCC	NDB	385.0	N59°	32.61'	W139°	43.68'		
	OLIKTOK	OLI	NDB	329.0	N70°	29.80'	W149°	53.38'		
	OSCARVILLE	OSE	NDB	251.0	N60°	47.47'	W161°	52.36'		
	PETERS CREEK	PEE	NDB	305.0	N62°	19.87'	W150°	05.78'		
	PITSAND	PYC	NDB	290.0	N70°	19.68'	W149°	38.12'		
	POINT HOPE	PHO	NDB	221.0	N68°	20.69'	W166°	47.84'		
	POINT LAY	PIZ	NDB	347.0	N69°	44.06'	W163°	00.81'		
	PORT HEIDEN	PDN	NDB	371.0	N56°	57.24'	W158°	38.93'		
	PRIBILOF ISLANDS	SRI	NDB	399.0	N56°	34.43'	W169°	38.87'		
	PROSPECT CREEK	PPC	NDB	340.0	N66°	49.05'	W150°	38.04'		
	PRUDHOE BAY	PUO	NDB	368.0	N70°	14.89'	W148°	23.64'		
	PUNTILLA LAKE	PTI	NDB	397.0	N62°	04.39'	W152°	43.98'		
	PUT RIVER	PVQ	NDB	234.0	N70°	13.38'	W148°	25.03'		
	RAZER (LMM/NDB)	RAZE	NDB	215.0	N58°	41.41'	W156°	40.68'		
	REEVE	SNP	NDB	362.0	N57°	09.09'	W170°	13.52'		
	SALDO (LOM/NDB)	SALD	NDB	400.0	N58°	44.24'	W156°	46.66'		
	SELAWIK	WLK	VOR	114.2	N66°	35.99'	W159°	59.49'	9	E21°
	SHEEP MOUNTAIN	SMU	NDB	221.0	N61°	47.23'	W147°	40.69'		
	SHINGE POINT	UA	NDB	226.0	N68°	55.37'	W137°	15.74'		
	SHISHMAREF	SHH	NDB	365.0	N66°	15.48'	W166°	03.14'		
	SISTERS ISLAND	SSR	VOR	114.0	N58°	10.65'	W135°	15.53'	49	E29°
	SITKA	SIT	NDB	358.0	N56°	51.27'	W135°	32.06'		
	SKWENTNA	SKW	NDB	269.0	N61°	57.96'	W151°	12.08'		
	SLATE CREEK	SLX	NDB	280.0	N64°	33.73'	W142°	30.97'		
	SLEETMUTE	SLQ	NDB	406.0	N61°	41.96'	W157°	09.77'		
	SOLDOTNA	OLT	NDB	346.0	N60°	28.49'	W150°	52.73'		
	SPARREVOHN	SQA	VOR	117.2	N61°	05.90'	W155°	38.06'	2,499	E22°
	ST MARYS	SMA	NDB	230.0	N62°	03.50'	W163°	17.49'		
	SUMMIT	UMM	NDB	326.0	N63°	19.68'	W149°	07.84'		
	SUMNER STRAIT	SQM	NDB	529.0	N56°	27.87'	W133°	05.84'		
	TAKOTNA RIVER	VTR	NDB	350.0	N62°	56.81'	W155°	33.43'		
	TALKEETNA	TKA	VOR	116.2	N62°	17.92'	W150°	06.33'	360	E26°
	TANANA	TAL	VOR	116.6	N65°	10.62'	W152°	10.65'	390	E26°
	TIN CITY	TNC	NDB	347.0	N65°	33.92'	W167°	54.53'		
	TOGIAK	TOG	NDB	393.0	N59°	03.83'	W160°	22.45'		
	UMIAT	UMT	NDB	360.0	N69°	22.17'	W152°	08.29'		
	UNALAKLEET	UNK	VOR	116.9	N63°	53.51'	W160°	41.05'	429	E20°
	UTOPIA CREEK	UTO	NDB	272.0	N65°	59.51'	W153°	43.27'		
	WEARR (LOM)	WEAR	NDB	230.0	N64°	53.98'	W147°	42.43'		
	WESSELS	ESS	NDB	260.0	N59°	25.59'	W146°	20.58'		
	WILDWOOD	IWW	NDB	379.0	N60°	35.92'	W151°	12.67'		
	WILEY	IEY	NDB	248.0	N71°	17.12'	W156°	48.50'		
	WOOD RIVER	BTS	NDB	429.0	N58°	59.98'	W158°	32.90'		
	WOODY ISLAND	RWO	NDB	394.0	N57°	46.46'	W152°	19.38'		

State/Country	VOR/NDB Name	Ident.	Type	Freq.	Latitude		Longitude		Altitude	Mag Var
WESTERN PACIFIC NAVAIDS										
Alaska	WRANGELL	RGL	NDB	206.0	N56°	29.21'	W132°	23.26'		
	YAKATAGA	CYT	NDB	209.0	N60°	05.17'	W142°	29.32'		
	YAKUTAT	YAK	VOR	113.3	N59°	30.64'	W139°	38.88'	36	E29°
	YUKON RIVER	FTO	NDB	242.0	N66°	34.80'	W145°	12.76'		
Canada										
	AKLAVIK	YKD	NDB	208.0	N68°	13.62'	W135°	00.58'		
	FARO	ZFA	NDB	378.0	N62°	12.71'	W133°	23.21'		
	FORT MCPHERSON	ZFM	NDB	373.0	N67°	24.59'	W134°	52.30'		
	INUVIK	YEV	VOR	112.5	N68°	18.48'	W133°	32.90'	262	E38°
	INUVIK	EV	NDB	254.0	N68°	19.56'	W133°	35.56'		
	LABERGE	JB	NDB	236.0	N60°	56.93'	W135°	08.26'		
	MASSET	1U	NDB	278.0	N54°	01.89'	W132°	07.63'		
	MAYO	MA	NDB	365.0	N63°	37.72'	W135°	53.58'		
	MENDENHALL	MND	NDB	332.0	N58°	21.53'	W134°	38.01'		
	NICHOLS	ICK	NDB	266.0	N55°	04.25'	W131°	36.30'		
	OLD CROW	YOC	NDB	284.0	N67°	34.27'	W139°	50.77'		
	PAPA	P	NDB	350.0	N54°	18.31'	W130°	27.75'		
	PRINCE RUPERT	PR	NDB	218.0	N54°	15.79'	W130°	25.43'		
	ROBINSON	PJ	NDB	329.0	N60°	26.36'	W134°	51.67'		
	ROSS RIVER	YDM	NDB	218.0	N61°	58.40'	W132°	25.61'		
	SANDSPIT	YZP	VOR	114.1	N53°	15.13'	W131°	48.41'	29	E25°
	SANDSPIT	Z	NDB	248.0	N53°	21.00'	W131°	56.40'		
	SANDSPIT	ZP	NDB	368.0	N53°	11.78'	W131°	46.65'		
	TESLIN	ZW	NDB	269.0	N60°	10.66'	W132°	44.20'		
	TUKTOYAKTUK	UB	NDB	380.0	N69°	26.06'	W133°	01.03'		
	WHITEHORSE	YXY	VOR	116.6	N60°	37.13'	W135°	08.34'	5,284	E30°
	WHITEHORSE	XY	NDB	302.0	N60°	46.36'	W135°	06.31'		
	XRAY	X	NDB	353.0	N60°	38.16'	W135°	00.64'		
Cook Islands, New Zealand										
	AITUTAKI	AI	NDB	320.0	S18°	49.40'	W159°	46.59'		
	RAROTONGA	RG	VOR	113.5	S21°	11.80'	W159°	48.90'	39	E13°
French Polynesia										
	RANGIROA	RAN	VOR	112.3	S14°	56.89'	W147°	40.99'	95	E12°
	TAHITI	TAF	VOR	112.9	S17°	32.89'	W149°	36.10'	0	E12°
Hawaii										
	BRADSHAW	BSF	NDB	339.0	N19°	45.63'	W155°	35.68'		
	EWABE (LOM/NDB)	EWAB	NDB	242.0	N21°	19.49'	W158°	02.93'		
	HILO	ITO	VOR	116.9	N19°	43.28'	W155°	00.65'	22	E11°
	HONOLULU	HNL	VOR	114.8	N21°	18.49'	W157°	55.82'	9	E11°
	KAMUELA	MUE	VOR	113.3	N19°	59.88'	W155°	40.19'	2,669	E11°
	KANEOHE BAY	NGF	NDB	265.0	N21°	27.10'	W157°	45.20'		
	KOKO HEAD	CKH	VOR	113.9	N21°	15.90'	W157°	42.17'	639	E11°
	KONA	IAI	VOR	115.7	N19°	39.26'	W156°	01.48'	49	E11°
	LANAI	LNY	VOR	117.7	N20°	45.86'	W156°	58.13'	1,249	E11°
	LANAI	LLD	NDB	353.0	N20°	46.69'	W156°	57.98'		
	LIHUE	LIH	VOR	113.5	N21°	57.91'	W159°	20.28'	111	E11°
	MAUI	OGG	VOR	114.3	N20°	53.92'	W156°	25.91'	29	E11°
	MOLOKAI	MKK	VOR	116.1	N21°	08.28'	W157°	10.04'	1,420	E11°
	PAHOA	POA	NDB	332.0	N19°	32.46'	W154°	58.33'		
	SOUTH KAUAI	SOK	VOR	115.4	N21°	54.02'	W159°	31.73'	629	E11°
	UPOLU POINT	UPP	VOR	112.3	N20°	12.03'	W155°	50.59'	1,758	E11°
	VALLEY ISLAND	VYI	NDB	327.0	N20°	52.84'	W156°	26.55'		
	WHEELER	HHI	NDB	373.0	N21°	28.48'	W158°	01.84'		
Johnston Atoll (US)										
	APOLLO	APO	NDB	388.0	N16°	43.59'	W169°	32.80'		
	JOHNSTON ATOLL	JON	VOR	111.8	N16°	43.99'	W169°	32.00'	6	E11°
Midway Island (US)										
	MIDWAY	NQM	VOR	114.6	N28°	12.01'	W177°	22.86'	13	E09°
Russia										
	ANADYR	KB	NDB	790.0	N64°	44.00'	W177°	44.99'		
	PROVIDENIYA	BC	NDB	320.0	N64°	17.49'	W173°	18.99'		
Samoa Islands										
	FALEOLO	FA	VOR	113.9	S13°	49.60'	W171°	59.58'	0	E12°
	FALEOLO	FA	NDB	270.0	S13°	49.60'	W172°	01.09'		
	LOGOTALA HILL	LOG	NDB	242.0	S14°	21.52'	W170°	44.86'		
	TONGA	TN	NDB	285.0	S21°	11.09'	W175°	13.09'		
	PAGO PAGO	TUT	VOR	112.5	S14°	20.25'	W170°	42.42'	9	E12°
	PAGO PAGO	TUT	NDB	403.0	S14°	20.21'	W170°	43.08'		
Tonga, Samoa Islands										
	NIUE	NU	NDB	345.0	S19°	04.09'	W169°	54.60'		

State/Country	VOR/NDB Name	Ident.	Type	Freq.	Latitude		Longitude		Altitude	Mag Var

EASTERN AND SOUTHERN PACIFIC NAVAIDS

State/Country	VOR/NDB Name	Ident.	Type	Freq.	Latitude		Longitude		Altitude	Mag Var
Admiralty Islands										
	KAVIENG	KAU	VOR	116.30	S02°	35.39'	E150°	48.89'	0	E07°
Alaska										
	AMCHITKA	NIA	VOR	113.20	N51°	22.52'	E179°	16.44'	272	E06°
	ATTU	ATU	NDB	375.00	N52°	49.73'	E173°	10.81'		
	SHEMYA	SYA	VOR	109.00	N52°	43.09'	E174°	03.72'	78	E03°
	SHEMYA	SYA	NDB	221.00	N52°	43.32'	E174°	03.61'		
Australia										
	AEROPELICAN	PEC	NDB	203.00	S33°	04.09'	E151°	38.80'	29	
	ALICE SPRINGS	AS	NDB	335.00	S23°	47.0'	E133°	52.3'	1,786	E05°
	ALICE SPRINGS	AS	VOR	115.90	S23°	47.7'	E133°	52.6'	1,813	E05°
	AMBERLEY	AMB	NDB	359.00	S27°	39.0'	E152°	43.3'	92	E11°
	ARCHERFIELD	AF	NDB	419.00	S27°	34.3'	E153°	00.9'	63	E10°
	AVALON	AV	VOR	116.10	S38°	03.0'	E144°	27.5'	66	E11°
	AYERS ROCK	AYE	NDB	233.00	S25°	10.50'	E130°	58.40'	1,649	
	BAGOT	BGT	NDB	308.00	S12°	24.5'	E130°	51.3'	96	E04°
	BALLIDU	BIU	NDB	389.00	S30°	35.59'	E116°	46.10'	1,000	
	BALLIDU	BIU	VOR	114.30	S30°	35.7'	E116°	46.7'	1,000	W02°
	BINDOOK	BIK	NDB	206.00	S34°	10.79'	E150°	06.59'	2,899	
	BINDOOK	BIK	VOR	116.80	S34°	10.8'	E150°	06.3'	2,900	E12°
	BOLINDA	BOL	NDB	362.00	S37°	27.8'	E144°	47.8'	432	E11°
	BRISBANE	BN	NDB	302.00	S27°	24.5'	E153°	05.8'	28	E11°
	BRISBANE	BN	VOR	113.20	S27°	22.1'	E153°	08.3'	28	E11°
	CALGA	CAA	NDB	392.00	S33°	24.3'	E151°	10.3'	3,000	E12°
	CAVERSHAM	CVM	NDB	329.00	S31°	52.8'	E115°	58.6'	43	W03°
	CHRISTMAS ISLAND	XMX	NDB	341.00	S10°	25.9'	E105°	41.1'	810	W01°
	CHRISTMAS ISLAND	XMX	VOR	112.40	S10°	25.8'	E105°	41.4'	915	W01°
	CLACKLINE	CKL	NDB	200.00	S31°	41.10'	E116°	33.60'	498	
	COOLANGATTA	CG	NDB	278.00	S28°	10.00'	E153°	29.99'	32	
	COOLANGATTA	CG	VOR	112.30	S28°	10.2'	E153°	30.2'	21	E11°
	COONABARABRAN	CBB	NDB	200.00	S31°	19.79'	E149°	16.00'	1,000	
	COWES	CWS	NDB	275.00	S38°	31.10'	E145°	13.20'	9	
	COWES	CWS	VOR	117.60	S38°	30.6'	E145°	12.7'	10	E11°
	CUDERDIN	CUN	NDB	293.00	S31°	37.6'	E117°	13.4'	300	W02°
	DARWIN	DN	NDB	344.00	S12°	26.0'	E130°	57.6'	96	E04°
	DARWIN	DAR	VOR	113.70	S12°	24.9'	E130°	52.9'	157	E03°
	DARWIN	DN	VOR	112.40	S12°	24.20'	E130°	51.79'	0	E04°
	DUBBO	DU	NDB	251.00	S32°	13.19'	E148°	33.60'	934	
	DUBBO	DU	VOR	114.40	S32°	13.30'	E148°	34.60'	934	E11°
	EAST LAKES	ETL	NDB	218.00	S33°	56.1'	E151°	12.4'	25	E12°
	EILDON WEIR	ELW	VOR	112.30	S37°	12.5'	E145°	50.0'	500	E11°
	EPPING	EPP	NDB	377.00	S37°	40.4'	E145°	01.5'	407	E01°
	ESSENDON	EN	NDB	356.00	S37°	43.7'	E144°	54.6'	282	E10°
	FENTONS HILL	FTH	VOR	115.30	S37°	30.0'	E144°	48.3'	400	E11°
	GERALDTON	GEL	NDB	359.00	S28°	48.00'	E114°	41.99'	144	
	GERALDTON	GEL	VOR	113.90	S28°	47.50'	E114°	42.29'	144	W2°
	GLENFIELD	GLF	NDB	317.00	S33°	59.4'	E150°	58.6'	16	E12°
	GRIFFITH	GTH	NDB	305.00	S34°	16.60'	E146°	03.50'	446	
	GRIFFITH	GTH	VOR	114.80	S34°	15.09'	E146°	03.89'	446	E10°
	GUILDFORD	GFD	NDB	272.00	S31°	56.3'	E115°	56.9'	43	W03°
	HAMILTON	HN	VOR	114.00	S37°	51.09'	E175°	20.30'	170	E20°
	HOWARD SPRINGS	HWS	NDB	257.00	S12°	26.5'	E131°	02.5'	81	E04°
	JACOBS WELL	JCW	VOR	116.50	S27°	45.8'	E153°	20.1'	25	E11°
	KATOOMBA	KAT	NDB	233.00	S33°	42.69'	E150°	17.89'	1,000	
	KILCOY	KCY	NDB	392.00	S26°	55.2'	E152°	34.3'	50	E10°
	KING ISLAND	KII	NDB	332.00	S39°	53.40'	E143°	52.39'	131	
	LARAVALE	LAV	VOR	117.80	S28°	05.5'	E152°	55.4'	600	E10°
	MANGALORE	MNG	VOR	113.20	S36°	53.20'	E145°	11.60'	465	E10°
	MAROOCHYDORE	MC	NDB	380.00	S26°	35.60'	E153°	05.50'	16	
	MAROOCHYDORE	MC	VOR	114.20	S26°	36.0'	E153°	05.4'	15	E11°
	MEADOW	MEA	NDB	230.00	S37°	39.9'	E144°	53.7'	407	E10°
	MELBOURNE	ML	VOR	114.10	S37°	39.7'	E144°	50.4'	412	E11°
	MT GAMBIER	MTG	VOR	117.00	S37°	45.19'	E140°	47.00'	213	E09°
	MT GAMBIER	MTG	NDB	266.00	S37°	45.19'	E140°	46.70'	213	
	MT MCQUOID	MGD	NDB	404.00	S33°	06.80'	E151°	08.30'	200	
	MT MCQUOID	MQD	VOR	117.30	S33°	06.6'	E151°	08.3'	200	E12°
	MT WILLIAM	MWM	NDB	233.00	S37°	17.69'	E142°	36.09'	3,827	
	MUDGEE	MDG	NDB	398.00	S32°	34.00'	E149°	36.89'	1,544	
	MUDGEE	MDG	VOR	112.20	S32°	33.69'	E149°	35.60'	1,544	E11°
	NAREMBEEN	NRB	NDB	227.00	S32°	04.40'	E118°	23.59'	1,000	
	NARRANDERA	NAR	NDB	329.00	S34°	42.40'	E146°	30.49'	472	

State/Country	VOR/NDB Name	Ident.	Type	Freq.	Latitude		Longitude		Altitude	Mag Var
EASTERN AND SOUTHERN PACIFIC NAVAIDS										
Australia	NARRANDERA	NAR	VOR	116.30	S34°	42.19'	E146°	30.90'	472	E10°
	PARKERVILLE	PRL	NDB	352.00	S31°	51.6'	E116°	06.9'	58	W03°
	PEARCE	PEA	NDB	340.00	S31°	39.2'	E116°	01.0'	150	W02°
	PERTH	PH	NDB	400.00	S32°	01.6'	E115°	48.7'	67	W03°
	PERTH	PH	VOR	113.70	S31°	56.8'	E115°	57.5'	87	W03°
	PINGELLY	PIY	NDB	233.00	S32°	32.39'	E117°	04.40'	98	
	PINGEUY	PIY	NDB	233.00	S32°	32.4'	E117°	04.4'	100	W02°
	PLENTY	PLE	NDB	218.00	S37°	43.4'	E145°	06.8'	430	E10°
	REDLAND BAY	RLB	NDB	218.00	S27°	37.0'	E153°	18.5'	15	E11°
	RICHMOND	RIC	NDB	347.00	S33°	35.90'	E150°	46.49'	68	
	ROCKDALE	ROC	NDB	338.00	S37°	35.5'	E144°	49.3'	432	E11°
	ROCKHAMPTON	RK	VOR	116.90	S23°	22.99'	E150°	28.30'	0	E09°
	SCONE	SCN	NDB	209.00	S32°	02.30'	E150°	50.00'	1,000	
	SHELLYS	SLS	NDB	353.00	S34°	42.60'	E150°	00.19'	1,000	
	SIMPSONS GAP	SPG	NDB	362.00	S23°	43.3'	E133°	44.6'	1,786	E05°
	SINGLETON	SGT	NDB	290.00	S32°	33.2'	E151°	15.4'	500	E11°
	STRATHBOGIE	SBG	NDB	413.00	S36°	51.29'	E145°	44.30'	498	
	SYDENHAM	SDM	NDB	266.00	S33°	55.04'	E151°	09.97'	6	
	SYDNEY	SY	VOR	115.40	S33°	56.7'	E151°	10.3'	37	E12°
	TEMPLE BAR	TPB	NDB	352.00	S23°	44.7'	E133°	47.2'	1,786	E05°
	TENNANT CREEK	TNK	NDB	272.00	S19°	38.70'	E134°	10.40'	1,236	
	TENNANT CREEK	TNK	VOR	112.90	S19°	38.2'	E134°	10.8'	1,236	E05°
	THURSDAY ISLAND	HID	NDB	356.00	S10°	35.50'	E142°	17.60'		
	TOWNSVILLE	TL	VOR	114.10	S19°	14.70'	E146°	45.49'	0	E08°
	WALGETT	WLG	VOR	117.60	S30°	01.79'	E148°	07.59'	1,000	E10°
	WALGETT	WLG	NDB	374.00	S30°	01.70'	E148°	06.89'	1,000	
	WALLABY	WAY	NDB	372.00	S23°	52.5'	E134°	01.6'	1,763	E05°
	WEST MAITLAND	WMD	NDB	224.00	S32°	45.39'	E151°	31.90'	75	
	WEST MAITLAND	WMD	VOR	114.60	S32°	45.4'	E151°	31.8'	75	E11°
	WEST PYMBLE	WPB	NDB	254.00	S33°	46.1'	E151°	07.6'	8	E12°
	WILLIAMTOWN	WLM	NDB	365.00	S32°	48.30'	E151°	49.69'	59	
	WILLIAMTOWN	WLM	VOR	113.30	S32°	47.90'	E151°	49.90'	59	E12°
	WOLLONGONG	WOL	NDB	239.00	S34°	33.60'	E150°	47.39'	9	
	WONTHAGGI	WON	NDB	383.00	S38°	28.39'	E145°	37.39'	498	
	WONTHAGGI	WON	VOR	115.90	S38°	28.3'	E145°	37.3'	500	E11°
	YARROWEE	YWE	NDB	389.00	S37°	44.60'	E143°	45.30'	498	
	YARROWEE	YWE	VOR	114.30	S37°	44.4'	E143°	45.2'	500	E11°
	YASS	YAS	NDB	335.00	S34°	49.80'	E149°	02.49'	98	
Borneo	DEN PASAR	OR	NDB	230.00	S08°	44.90'	E115°	10.49'	13	
	MATARAM	GA	NDB	330.00	S08°	33.49'	E116°	05.80'	52	
Caroline Islands	KOSRAE	UKS	NDB	393.00	N05°	21.88'	E162°	58.38'		
	POHNPEI	PNI	NDB	366.00	N06°	58.96'	E158°	12.53'		
	TRUK	TKK	NDB	375.00	N07°	27.31'	E151°	50.24'		
	YAP	YP	NDB	317.00	N09°	29.81'	E138°	05.78'		
Fiji	BAUERFIELD	VLI	VOR	114.30	S17°	39.71'	E168°	14.62'	970	E12°
	MALOLO	AL	NDB	385.00	S17°	49.5'	E177°	23.2'	50	E13°
	MOMI	MI	NDB	364.00	S17°	54.0'	E177°	19.5'	26	E13°
	NADI	NN	NDB	290.00	S17°	47.4'	E177°	25.3'	75	E13°
	NADI	NN	VOR	112.50	S17°	39.3'	E177°	23.7'	75	E13°
	NAUSORI	NA	VOR	112.20	S18°	02.5'	E178°	33.7'	16	E13°
	NAUSORI	NA	NDB	307.00	S18°	02.99'	E178°	33.79'	75	
	NAVAKAI	VK	NDB	405.00	S17°	47.1'	E177°	25.2'	26	E13°
	NAVUA	NV	NDB	281.00	S18°	14.2'	E178°	10.1'	20	E13°
Guam	MT MACAJNA	AJA	NDB	385.00	N13°	27.13'	E144°	44.06'		
	NIMITZ	UNZ	VOR	115.30	N13°	27.18'	E144°	43.85'	659	E02°
Indonesia	BALI	BLI	VOR	116.20	S08°	45.4'	E115°	09.3'	46	E01°
	BEDOK	BED	NDB	232.00	N01°	19.00'	E103°	57.89'	22	
	DEN PASAR	OR	NDB	230.00	S08°	44.9'	E115°	10.5'	12	E01°
	JAYBEE	JB	NDB	400.00	N01°	29.39'	E103°	43.00'	134	
	JOHOR BAHRU	VJR	VOR	112.70	N01°	43.80'	E103°	37.39'	409	W1°
	KONG KONG	KK	NDB	286.00	N01°	31.30'	E103°	59.50'	150	
	MATARAM	GA	NDB	330.00	S08°	33.5'	E116°	05.8'	52	E02°
	PAPA UNIFORM	PU	VOR	115.10	N01°	25.40'	E103°	56.09'	150	E00°
	SINJON	SJ	VOR	113.50	N01°	13.40'	E103°	51.39'	150	E00°
	TANJUNG PINANG	TI	NDB	385.00	S00°	55.00'	E104°	31.99'	36	
	TEKONG	TEK	NDB	259.00	N01°	25.09'	E104°	01.49'	150	

State/Country	VOR/NDB Name	Ident.	Type	Freq.	Latitude		Longitude		Altitude	Mag Var
EASTERN AND SOUTHERN PACIFIC NAVAIDS										
Japan										
	CHINEN	TIC	VOR	114.20	N26°	09.60'	E127°	47.79'	544	W04°
	ERABU	ONC	VOR	113.10	N27°	26.00'	E128°	42.00'	216	W04°
	IWO JIMA	OX	NDB	360.00	N24°	46.89'	E141°	18.29'		
	KUSHIMOTO	KEC	VOR	112.90	N33°	26.79'	E135°	47.70'	150	W06°
	MINAMI DAITO	MD	NDB	405.00	N25°	50.60'	E131°	14.50'		
	MIYAKE JIMA	MJE	VOR	117.80	N34°	07.10'	E139°	29.90'	144	W06°
	MIYAKO JIMA	MYC	VOR	117.50	N24°	47.19'	E125°	17.99'	193	W03°
	MONBETSU	MVE	VOR	110.00	N44°	15.63'	E143°	31.48'	45	W09°
	OKINAWA	OK	NDB	308.00	N26°	06.09'	E127°	39.89'		
Kiribati										
	NAURU	NI	NDB	355.00	S00°	32.69'	E166°	54.99'		
	ROTUMA	RM	NDB	277.00	S12°	29.91'	E177°	02.90'		
Mariana Islands (US)										
	ROTA	GRO	NDB	332.00	N14°	10.21'	E145°	14.24'		
	SAIPAN	SN	NDB	312.00	N15°	06.76'	E145°	42.70'		
Malaysia										
	BATUM	BTM	VOR	116.00	N01°	08.19'	E104°	07.80'	26	E01°
	TEKONG	VTK	VOR	116.50	N01°	24.90'	E104°	01.40'	150	E00°
Marshall Islands										
	BUCHOLZ	NDJ	NDB	359.00	N08°	43.25'	E167°	43.64'		
	MAJURO	MAJ	NDB	316.00	N07°	04.03'	E171°	16.73'		
New Guinea										
	BIAK	BIK	VOR	112.50	S01°	10.90'	E136°	05.10'	0	E03°
New Zealand										
	ALEXANDRA	LX	NDB	386.00	S45°	10.0'	E169°	28.8'	750	E24°
	AUCKLAND	AA	NDB	374.00	S37°	01.3'	E174°	45.6'	15	E20°
	AUCKLAND	AA	VOR	114.80	S37°	00.4'	E174°	48.8'	45	E20°
	AUCKLAND	ZAA	VOR	112.50	S37°	00.49'	E174°	48.39'	19	E19°
	CAPE CAMPBELL	CC	NDB	286.00	S41°	44.1'	E174°	16.3'	50	E21°
	HAMILTON	HN	VOR	113.30	S37°	51.8'	E175°	19.9'	172	E20°
	INVERCARGILL	NV	VOR	112.90	S46°	24.8'	E168°	19.1'	5	E25°
	NEWLANDS	NL	NDB	358.00	S41°	13.8'	E174°	49.7'	40	E22°
	PALMERSTON NORTH	PM	VOR	113.40	S40°	19.2'	E175°	36.9'	148	E20°
	QUEENSTOWN	QN	NDB	362.00	S45°	01.5'	E168°	44.3'	1,175	E24°
	SLOPE HILL	SH	VOR	113.60	S44°	59.2'	E168°	47.0'	1,175	E24°
	SURREY	SY	NDB	350.00	S37°	14.4'	E175°	10.0'	25	E19°
	TITAHI BAY	TY	NDB	234.00	S41°	07.1'	E174°	49.2'	10	E21°
	TORY	TR	VOR	114.60	S41°	11.3'	E174°	21.7'	1,500	E22°
	WAIUKU	WI	NDB	254.00	S37°	16.2'	E174°	48.8'	25	E19°
	WELLINGTON	WN	NDB	298.00	S41°	20.4'	E174°	48.8'	40	E21°
	WELLINGTON	WN	VOR	112.30	S41°	20.3'	E174°	49.0'	40	E22°
	WESTPOINT	OT	NDB	398.00	S37°	03.7'	E174°	36.6'	15	E20°
	WHENUAPAI	WP	VOR	108.80	S36°	47.3'	E174°	37.8'	100	E19°
	WHITFORD	HD	NDB	334.00	S36°	57.0'	E175°	00.9'	23	E20°
Palau										
	KOROR	ROR	NDB	371.00	N07°	21.64'	E134°	32.40'		
Papua New Guinea										
	GIRUA	GUA	VOR	116.50	S08°	44.8'	E148°	15.3'	300	E06°
	GIRUA	GUA	NDB	224.00	S08°	44.8'	E148°	15.3'	300	E06°
	GURNEY	GNY	NDB	1623.00	S10°	18.94'	E150°	22.04'		
	JACKSON	JSN	NDB	380.00	S09°	22.9'	E147°	10.2'	103	E06°
	KIRIWINA	KWA	NDB	287.00	S08°	30.30'	E151°	05.39'		
	KUBUNA	KUB	NDB	1662.00	S08°	41.8'	E146°	45.2'	100	E06°
	KUBUNA	KUB	NDB	662.10	S08°	41.80'	E146°	45.19'	98	
	NADZAB	NZ	VOR	113.60	S06°	34.29'	E146°	43.89'	0	E06°
	PARER	PRE	NDB	395.00	S09°	19.9'	E147°	08.0'	103	E06°
	PORT MORESBY	PY	VOR	117.00	S09°	27.09'	E147°	13.00'	0	E07°
	PORT MORESBY	PY	NDB	368.00	S09°	27.7'	E147°	13.9'	130	E06°
	TAVAI	TVI	NDB	350.00	S09°	43.0'	E147°	28.1'	50	E06°
	WEWAK	WK	NDB	366.00	S03°	34.89'	E143°	40.60'		
Phillipines										
	ALABAT	AL	NDB	247.00	N14°	14.0'	E121°	55.6'	75	E01°
	BALESIN	BAL	VOR	116.90	N14°	26.69'	E122°	02.50'	3	W01°
	CABANATUAN	CAB	VOR	112.70	N15°	27.8'	E120°	58.8'	200	E00°
	JOMALIG	JOM	VOR	116.70	N14°	43.6'	E122°	24.1'	50	W01°
	LIPA	LIP	VOR	115.10	N13°	57.5'	E121°	07.8'	1,220	E00°
	LUBANG	LBG	VOR	117.50	N13°	51.69'	E120°	06.99'	288	E00°
	MANILA	MIA	VOR	113.80	N14°	30.6'	E121°	01.0'	74	W01°
	MANILA	MIA	NDB	389.00	N14°	30.6'	E121°	01.2'	74	W01°

State/Country	VOR/NDB Name	Ident.	Type	Freq.	Latitude		Longitude		Altitude	Mag Var
EASTERN AND SOUTHERN PACIFIC NAVAIDS										
Phillipines	MANILA	OL	NDB	375.00	N14°	32.8'	E121°	5.1'	75	W01°
	RIZAL	RZL	NDB	327.00	N14°	28.0'	E121°	11.1'	75	W00°
	ROSARIO	RS	NDB	285.00	N14°	25.3'	E120°	51.1'	13	W00°
	TACLOBAN	TAC	VOR	115.50	N11°	13.10'	E125°	01.70'	0	E00°
Russia										
	MALKA	WZ	NDB	345.00	N53°	18.99'	E157°	31.99'		
	NIKOLSHOE	UJ	NDB	595.00	N55°	10.99'	E165°	59.00'		
	PETROPAVLOVSK-KAMCHATSKY	Q	NDB	1040.00	N53°	11.4'	E158°	26.5'	131	W06°
	UST-BOLSHERETSK	SD	NDB	907.00	N52°	49.00'	E156°	16.00'		
Soloman Islands										
	BUKA	BUK	NDB	269.00	S05°	26.50'	E154°	40.10'		
	GRACIOSA BAY	GB	NDB	370.00	S10°	43.39'	E165°	46.80'		
	HONIARA	HN	VOR	112.60	S09°	26.57'	E160°	01.20'	0	E09°
Tuvalu, Ellice Islands										
	FUNAFUTI	FU	NDB	340.00	S08°	31.50'	E179°	12.26'		
	NANUMEA	NM	NDB	358.00	S05°	40.30'	E176°	08.20'		
Vanautu, New Hebrides										
	LA TONTOUTA	LTO	VOR	112.90	S22°	00.49'	E166°	12.50'	0	E13°
	SANTO/PEKOA	SO	NDB	412.00	S15°	32.26'	E167°	08.70'		
Wake Island (US)										
	WAKE ISLAND	AWK	VOR	113.50	N19°	17.10'	E166°	37.65'	13	E07°

ASIA NAVAIDS

State/Country	VOR/NDB Name	Ident.	Type	Freq.	Latitude		Longitude		Altitude	Mag Var
Hong Kong										
	CAPE D'AGUILAR	HKG	NDB	338.00	N22°	12.99'	E114°	14.89'	400	W01°
	CHEUNG CHAU	CH	VOR	112.30	N22°	13.3'	E114°	01.7'	330	W01°
	CHEUNG CHAU	CC	NDB	360.00	N22°	12.2'	E114°	01.5'	330	W01°
	HONG KONG INTL'	RW	NDB	377.00	N22°	19.69'	E114°	11.29'	16	W01°
	HONG KONG INTL'	RW	NDB	337.00	N22°	12.2'	E114°	11.3'	15	W01°
	SHA LO WAN	SL	NDB	268.00	N22°	17.59'	E113°	54.30'	400	W01°
	STONECUTTERS	SC	NDB	236.00	N22°	19.3'	E114°	07.8'	400	W01°
	TATHONG POINT	TH	VOR	115.50	N22°	14.4'	E114°	17.2'	500	W01°
	TATHONG POINT	TH	NDB	280.00	N22°	14.5'	E114°	17.1'	500	W01°
	TUNG LUNG	TD	VOR	116.10	N22°	15.0'	E114°	17.4'	500	W01°
India										
	AURANGABAD	AAU	VOR	116.30	N19°	51.8'	E075°	23.6'	1,908	W01°
	BERACHAMPA	BC	NDB	220.00	N22°	42.0'	E088°	42.0'	17	W02°
	BOMBAY	BMB	NDB	396.00	N19°	05.30'	E072°	49.79'	39	W01°
	BOMBAY	CZ	NDB	201.00	N19°	05.31'	E072°	53.73'	39	W01°
	BOMBAY	SC	NDB	345.00	N19°	05.70'	E073°	01.10'	39	W01°
	BOMBAY	BBB	VOR	116.60	N19°	05.1'	E072°	52.5'	40	W01°
	BOMBAY	BB	NDB	265.00	N19°	07.2'	E072°	0.0'		W01°
	CALCUTTA	EA	NDB	323.00	N22°	38.20'	E088°	24.30'	16	W01°
	CALCUTTA	CA	NDB	293.00	N22°	34.99'	E088°	26.59'	16	W01°
	CALCUTTA	UM	NDB	404.00	N22°	40.69'	E088°	27.19'	16	W01°
	CALCUTTA	DU	NDB	385.00	N22°	44.39'	E088°	27.60'	16	W01°
	CALCUTTA	CEA	VOR	112.50	N22°	38.7'	E088°	27.3'	17	W01°
	DAMAN	DMN	VOR	113.30	N20°	26.30'	E072°	51.29'	49	W01°
	DHANBAD	DB	NDB	304.00	N23°	48.70'	E086°	26.20'	16	W01°
	JAMSHEDPUR	JJS	VOR	115.40	N22°	48.7'	E086°	10.2'	500	W02°
	RAJSHAHI	RAJ	VOR	114.60	N24°	26.4'	E088°	37.1'	55	W01°
	SONGADH	SG	NDB	358.00	N21°	10.00'	E073°	33.99'	1,016	
	TARKESHWAR	TK	NDB	390.00	N22°	54.00'	E088°	01.00'	16	
	TRIVANDRUM	TVM	VOR	115.10	N08°	28.39'	E076°	55.60'	42	W03°
Israel										
	BENGURION	BGN	VOR	115.40	N32°	00.8'	E034°	52.4'	125	E03°
	JERUSALEM	IRM	NDB	336.00	N31°	51.90'	E035°	12.90'	2,482	E03°
	JERUSALEM	IRM	NDB	366.00	N31°	51.9'	E035°	12.9'	2,485	E03°
	METZADA	MZD	VOR	115.00	N31°	19.9'	E035°	23.5'	1,247	E02°
	NATANIA	NAT	VOR	112.40	N32°	20.0'	E034°	58.1'	100	E02°
	TEL AVIV	BGN	NDB	309.00	N32°	01.60'	E034°	57.19'	134	E03°
	TEL AVIV	LL	NDB	331.00	N32°	03.8'	E034°	46.2'	125	E03°
Japan										
	AKAN	KQ	NDB	221.00	N43°	08.0'	E144°	08.8'	327	W09°
	AMI	TLE	VOR	116.00	N36°	01.1'	E140°	12.6'	114	W06°
	ARAKAWA	AD	NDB	385.00	N35°	38.8'	E139°	50.7'	13	W07°
Japan	CHOSHI	CVC	VOR	113.60	N35°	43.4'	E140°	48.2'	236	W06°

State/Country	VOR/NDB Name	Ident.	Type	Freq.	Latitude		Longitude		Altitude	Mag Var
ASIA NAVAIDS										
	HACHIJOJIMA	HC	NDB	340.00	N33°	06.59'	E139°	47.69'	16	
	HAMAMATSU	LHE	VOR	110.00	N34°	44.70'	E137°	40.99'	209	W06°
	HANEDA	HME	VOR	109.40	N35°	32.8'	E139°	46.6'	42	W07°
	HANEDA	HME	NDB	337.00	N35°	33.4'	E139°	45.5'	42	W07°
	KISARAZU	KZE	VOR	114.50	N35°	23.9'	E139°	54.7'	38	W07°
	KISARAZU	CL	NDB	200.00	N35°	23.5'	E139°	54.5'	38	W07°
	KOHTOH	KWE	VOR	115.00	N35°	36.3'	E139°	49.1'	78	W07°
	KOWA	XM	NDB	325.00	N34°	44.90'	E136°	55.80'	344	
	KOWA	XMC	VOR	113.50	N34°	42.10'	E136°	57.69'	344	W06°
	KUMAGAYA	AY	NDB	283.00	N36°	09.69'	E139°	18.80'	16	
	KUSHIRO	KSE	VOR	112.50	N43°	01.9'	E144°	12.5'	334	W09°
	KUSHIRO	KS	NDB	194.00	N43°	02.3'	E144°	12.2'	292	W09°
	KUZUMI	KF	NDB	342.00	N35°	49.7'	E140°	19.9'	130	W06°
	MATSUMOTO	MBE	VOR	117.60	N36°	09.19'	E137°	55.39'	2,259	W07°
	MEMANBETSU	TBE	VOR	110.85	N43°	52.9'	E144°	10.2'	132	W09°
	MIYAKEJIMA	MJ	NDB	238.00	N34°	04.09'	E139°	33.89'	1,439	
	MONBETSU	MVE	VOR	110.00	N44°	15.5'	E143°	31.7'	46	W09°
	MORIYA	SNE	VOR	114.00	N35°	55.9'	E139°	59.1'	132	W07°
	NAGOYA	KC	NDB	360.00	N35°	15.39'	E136°	55.19'	75	
	NAGOYA	KCC	VOR	114.20	N35°	15.69'	E136°	55.10'	75	W07°
	NAKASHIBETSU	NSE	VOR	115.60	N43°	34.5'	E144°	57.3'	263	W09°
	OBIHIRO	OBE	VOR	109.65	N42°	43.9'	E143°	13.5'	531	W09°
	ONJUKU	OJC	VOR	115.70	N35°	10.8'	E140°	22.4'	365	W06°
	OSHIMA	XA	NDB	214.00	N34°	41.10'	E139°	24.00'	2,086	
	OSHIMA	XAC	VOR	113.10	N34°	42.49'	E139°	25.00'	2,086	W06°
	OSHIMA AIRPORT	QF	NDB	392.00	N34°	46.90'	E139°	21.60'	2,086	
	SAKURA	TYE	VOR	112.70	N35°	46.80'	E140°	15.99'	98	W07°
	SAKURI	TYE	VOR	112.70	N35°	46.8'	E140°	16.0'	97	W07°
	SAPPORO	SP	NDB	357.00	N43°	10.00'	E141°	19.49'	88	
	SEKIYADO	SYE	VOR	117.00	N36°	00.5'	E139°	50.6'	115	W06°
	TATEYAMA	PQE	VOR	112.50	N34°	56.6'	E139°	53.8'	621	W06°
	TATEYAMA	PQ	NDB	373.00	N34°	59.4'	E139°	52.7'	621	W06°
	TOKACHI	OH	NDB	239.00	N42°	52.8'	E143°	09.7'	275	W09 °
	YAIZU	YZ	NDB	344.00	N34°	49.09'	E138°	17.50'	16	
	YOKOSHIBA	YQ	NDB	256.00	N35°	40.8'	E140°	26.2'	139	W06°
	YOKOSUKA	YU	NDB	249.00	N35°	11.80'	E139°	36.99'	488	
	YOKOSUKA	HYE	VOR	116.20	N35°	15.2'	E139°	35.4'	490	W06°
	ZAMA	DF	NDB	401.00	N35°	34.59'	E139°	22.69'	16	
Korea										
	ANYANG	SEL	VOR	115.10	N37°	24.7'	E126°	55.9'	906	W07°
	ANYANG	SL	NDB	336.00	N37°	24.6'	E126°	55.8'	906	W07°
	KIMPO	OF	NDB	328.00	N37°	36.70'	E126°	43.19'	39	
	KIMPO	SE	NDB	219.00	N37°	36.70'	E126°	43.60'	49	
	KIMPO	FR	NDB	283.00	N37°	34.29'	E126°	46.10'	905	
	KIMPO	EL	NDB	201.00	N37°	34.49'	E126°	46.30'	905	
	KIMPO	KP	NDB	320.00	N37°	32.30'	E126°	48.99'	905	
	KIMPO	KIP	VOR	113.60	N37°	33.2'	E126°	47.8'	40	W07°
	KOREA	0F	NDB	246.00	N37°	36.7'	E126°	43.2'	41	W07°
	KOREA	SE	NDB	219.00	N37°	36.7'	E126°	43.6'	50	W07°
	OSAN	OSN	VOR	114.70	N37°	05.5'	E127°	01.8'	35	W07°
	PYONGTAEK	RE	NDB	381.00	N36°	57.30'	E127°	01.60'	49	
	PYONGTAEK	PTK	VOR	108.20	N36°	58.2'	E127°	01.2'	50	W07°
	SEOUL	KSM	VOR	113.00	N37°	26.2'	E127°	06.5'	100	W07°
	SEOUL	CP	NDB	388.00	N37°	26.1'	E127°	05.9'	100	W07°
Kuwait										
	KUWAIT	WR	NDB	368.00	N29°	18.0'	E047°	55.7'	189	E02°
	KUWAIT	KUA	VOR	115.50	N29°	13.1'	E047°	58.0'	189	E02°
	RAS AL MISHAB	RAS	VOR	116.40	N28°	04.7'	E048°	36.8'	50	E02°
	WAFRA	KFR	VOR	112.00	N28°	37.0'	E047°	57.5'	100	E02°
Maldives										
	MALE	MLE	VOR	114.70	N04°	11.6'	E073°	32.1'	32	W03°
Pakistan										
	CAPE MONZE	KA	NDB	244.00	N24°	49.99'	E066°	40.00'	98	E00°
	GHARO	KF	NDB	296.00	N24°	46.5'	E067°	34.0'	100	E00°
	HYDERABAD	KD	NDB	223.00	N25°	18.0'	E068°	23.0'	130	E00°
	KARACHI	MR	NDB	354.00	N24°	56.0'	E066°	56.0'	35	E00°
	KARACHI	KC	NDB	271.00	N24°	53.6'	E067°	10.0'	100	E00°
	KARACHI	KC	VOR	112.10	N24°	54.6'	E067°	10.6'	120	E00°
	NAWABSHAH	NH	VOR	112.90	N26°	13.0'	E068°	23.2'	120	E00°
People's Republic of China										

State/Country	VOR/NDB Name	Ident.	Type	Freq.	Latitude		Longitude		Altitude	Mag Var
ASIA NAVAIDS										
	KAOHSIUNG	SK	NDB	330.00	N22°	34.77'	E120°	19.06'	29	
	NANHUI	NHW	VOR	114.60	N31°	04.00'	E121°	33.99'	9	W04°
	SHANGHAI	PK	NDB	369.00	N31°	16.89'	E121°	19.39'	9	
	SHANGHAI	CU	NDB	280.00	N31°	14.80'	E121°	19.59'	9	
	SHANGHAI	C	NDB	313.00	N31°	13.30'	E121°	19.80'	9	
	SHANGHAI	B	NDB	257.00	N31°	10.40'	E121°	20.10'	9	
	SHANGHAI	BF	NDB	528.00	N31°	08.90'	E121°	20.29'	9	
	SHANGHAI	WB	NDB	240.00	N31°	07.19'	E121°	20.40'	9	
	SHIKANG	NN	NDB	375.00	N23°	07.60'	E120°	11.59'	49	
Saudi Arabia										
	AL AHSA	HSA	VOR	116.60	N25°	16.7'	E049°	29.0'	576	E02°
	AL KHARJ	AKJ	VOR	117.30	N24°	04.1'	E047°	24.4'	1,479	E02°
	KING KHALID	KIA	VOR	113.30	N24°	53.2'	E046°	45.6'	1,963	E02°
	MAGALA	MGA	VOR	116.30	N26°	13.9'	E047°	16.6'	1,568	E02°
	RIYADH	RIY	VOR	114.50	N24°	43.1'	E046°	43.2'	2,018	E02°
	THUMAMAH	TIH	VOR	113.80	N25°	09.8'	E046°	33.1'	2,076	E02°
Singapore, Malaysia										
	BATUM	BTM	VOR	116.00	N01°	08.2'	E104°	07.8'	25	E01°
	BEDOK	BED	NDB	232.00	N01°	19.0'	E103°	57.9'	22	E00°
	JAYBEE	JB	NDB	400.00	N01°	29.4'	E103°	43.0'	135	W01°
	JOHOR BAHRU	VJR	VOR	112.70	N01°	43.8'	E103°	37.4'	410	W01°
	KONG KONG	KK	NDB	286.00	N01°	31.3'	E103°	59.5'	150	E00°
	PAPA UNIFORM	PU	VOR	115.10	N01°	25.4'	E103°	56.1'	150	E00°
	SINJON	SJ	VOR	113.50	N01°	13.4'	E103°	51.4'	150	E00°
	TANJUNG PINANG	TI	NDB	385.00	N00°	55.0'	E104°	32.0'	36	E01°
	TEKONG	VTK	VOR	116.50	N01°	24.9'	E104°	01.4'	150	E00°
	TEKONG	TEK	NDB	259.00	N01°	25.1'	E104°	01.5'	150	E00°
Sri Lanka										
	BATTICALOA	BAT	VOR	114.60	N07°	42.3'	E081°	40.4'	10	W03°
	COLUMBO KATUNAYAKE	KAT	VOR	112.70	N07°	09.7'	E079°	52.0'	29	W04°
	COLUMBO RATMALANA	RML	VOR	116.70	N06°	49.6'	E079°	53.3'	22	W04°
	KATUNAYAKE	CNL	NDB	315.00	N07°	16.1'	E079°	56.9'	29	W04°
	KATUNAYAKE	ASL	NDB	330.00	N07°	07.5'	E079°	50.5'	29	W04°
	RATMALANA	RM	NDB	350.00	N06°	50.0'	E079°	53.0'	22	W04°
Taiwan										
	GREEN I	GID	VOR	116.90	N22°	40.4'	E121°	28.5'	609	W02°
	HENGCHUN	HCN	VOR	113.70	N21°	55.8'	E120°	50.1'	423	W02°
	HENGCHUN	KW	NDB	415.00	N21°	56.0'	E120°	49.8'	24	W02°
	KAOHSIUNG	CO	NDB	220.00	N22°	34.7'	E120°	17.3'	423	W02°
	SHIKANG	TNN	VOR	113.30	N23°	08.2'	E120°	11.9'	50	W02°
Thailand										
	BANGKOK	BKK	VOR	115.90	N13°	59.7'	E100°	39.2'	36	W01°
	BANGKOK	BK	NDB	293.00	N13°	59.7'	E100°	39.3'	36	W01°
	KORAT	KRT	VOR	113.70	N14°	55.6'	E102°	07.7'	729	W00°
	PRACHIN BURI	PB	NDB	201.00	N14°	06.0'	E101°	22.0'	80	W00°
	RAYONG	RYN	VOR	112.50	N12°	46.70'	E101°	40.89'	59	E00°
	U-TAPHAO	BUT	VOR	110.80	N12°	39.9'	E101°	00.3'	59	W00°
Turkey										
	BEYKOZ	BKZ	VOR	117.30	N41°	07.7'	E029°	08.6'	200	E03°
	CEKMECE	CEK	NDB	328.00	N41°	00.5'	E028°	31.8'	158	E03°
	ISTANBUL	IST	VOR	112.50	N40°	58.1'	E028°	48.5'	171	E03°
	ISTANBUL	ST	NDB	340.00	N41°	03.5'	E028°	48.4'	93	E03°
	ISTANBUL	IS	NDB	396.00	N41°	03.5'	E028°	48.4'	157	E03°
	TEKIRDAG	EKI	VOR	116.30	N40°	57.1'	E027°	25.6'	1,063	E02°
	TOAKAPI	TOP	NDB	370.00	N41°	00.7'	E028°	59.4'	158	E03°
	YALOVA	YAA	VOR	117.70	N40°	34.0'	E029°	22.3'	2,440	E03°
Yemen										
	ADEN	KRY	NDB	400.00	N12°	49.9'	E045°	02.9'	32	E00°
	ADEN	AD	NDB	361.00	N12°	52.2'	E045°	00.3'	32	E00°
	ADEN	KRA	VOR	112.50	N12°	49.8'	E045°	01.5'	32	E00°
	TAIZ	TAZ	VOR	113.60	N13°	42.0'	E044°	08.3'	4,600	E01°

State/Country	VOR/NDB Name	Ident.	Type	Freq.	Latitude		Longitude		Altitude	Mag Var

AFRICA NAVAIDS

Algeria

| | DIJANET | DJA | NDB | 274.00 | N24° | 16.0' | E009° | 26.0' | 3,176 | W02° |
| | DJANET | DJA | VOR | 114.10 | N24° | 16.8' | E009° | 26.9' | 3,176 | W02° |

Ascension Island (UK)

| | ASCENSION AUX | ASI | VOR | 112.20 | S07° | 58.19' | W014° | 23.79' | 475 | W18° |
| | ASCENSION ISLAND | ASN | NDB | 360.00 | S07° | 56.69' | W014° | 24.79' | 272 | |

Canary Islands

	FUERTEVENTURA	FTV	VOR	114.10	N28°	26.9'	W013°	51.6'	79	W10°
	GRAN CANARIA	GDV	VOR	112.90	N28°	04.5'	W015°	25.6'	758	W10°
	GRAN CANARIA	PM	NDB	350.00	N27°	54.49'	W015°	23.59'	75	
	GRAN CANARIA	VR	VOR	115.00	N27°	51.30'	W015°	25.19'	57	W10°
	GRAN CANARIA	TGN	VOR	115.60	N27°	55.29'	W015°	23.29'	757	W10°
	GRAN CANARIA	VR	NDB	365.00	N27°	51.3'	W015°	25.2'	77	W10°
	HIERRO	HR	NDB	376.00	N27°	48.9'	W017°	53.1'	105	W10°
	LA PALMA	BV	VOR	112.40	N28°	36.00'	W017°	45.30'	183	W10°
	LANZAROTE	LT	VOR	113.70	N28°	56.4'	W013°	36.9'	112	W10°
	LANZAROTE	LZR	VOR	115.20	N29°	09.8'	W013°	30.5'	1,762	W10°
	TENERIFE	TFN	VOR	112.50	N28°	32.1'	W016°	16.0'	3,356	W10°
	TENERIFE	FP	NDB	420.00	N28°	29.4'	W016°	22.1'	2,073	W10°
	TENERIFE-SOUTH	TFS	VOR	116.40	N28°	00.1'	W016°	41.2'	115	W10°

Congo

| | BRAZZAVILLE | BZ | VOR | 113.10 | S04° | 14.8' | E015° | 15.9' | 1,106 | W05° |
| | BRAZZAVILLE | BL | NDB | 355.00 | S04° | 18.1' | E015° | 11.7' | 1,106 | W05° |

Egypt

	CAIRO	CAI	VOR	112.50	N30°	09.0'	E031°	25.5'	219	E03°
	CAIRO	CVO	VOR	115.20	N30°	05.5'	E031°	23.3'	372	E03°
	CAIRO	OR	NDB	284.00	N30°	02.6'	E031°	19.3'	382	E03°
	CAIRO	OL	NDB	361.00	N30°	09.4'	E031°	28.7'	375	E03°
	FAYOUM	FYM	VOR	117.30	N29°	25.0'	E030°	21.0'	26	E03°
	MOQUATTAM	MKT	NDB	317.00	N30°	02.7'	E031°	16.5'	190	E03°
	NASAR	NSR	NDB	340.00	N30°	04.7'	E031°	18.9'	190	E03°

Ivory Coast

	ABIDIJAN	AD	NDB	327.00	N05°	16.59'	W003°	55.10'	39	
	ABIDIJAN	PB	NDB	294.00	N05°	14.8'	W003°	57.5'	20	W08°
	ABIDIJAN	AN	NDB	306.00	N05°	20.8'	W003°	53.5'	20	W08°
	ABIDJAN	AD	VOR	114.30	N05°	16.4'	W003°	56.2'	39	W08°
	AFIENDU	IVY	NDB	393.00	N05°	24.5'	W002°	55.0'	40	W08°

Kenya

	ATHI RIVER	TV	VOR	115.50	S01°	30.10'	E037°	01.19'	4,998	W02°
	ATHI RIVER	TH	NDB	329.50	S01°	30.1'	E037°	01.2'	5,000	W02°
	EMBAKASI	AL	NDB	379.00	S01°	22.0'	E036°	56.0'	5,000	W02°
	LODWAR	LW	NDB	338.00	N03°	06.99'	E035°	37.00'	1,715	E00°
	LODWAR	LOV	VOR	114.50	N03°	07.0'	E035°	37.0'	1,715	E00°
	NAIROBI	NI	VOR	113.10	S01°	17.7'	E036°	57.4'	5,247	W02°
	NAIROBI	NO	NDB	278.00	S01°	21.9'	E036°	51.8'	5,327	W02°
	NAIROBI	NI	NDB	283.00	S01°	20.1'	E036°	54.2'	5,327	W02°
	NAKURU	NAK	VOR	115.10	S00°	18.1'	E036°	09.3'	6,270	W01°
	NAROK	NK	NDB	368.00	S01°	06.0'	E035°	51.0'	6,300	W02°
	NGONG	GV	VOR	115.90	S01°	23.6'	E036°	38.2'	5,500	W02°
	NGONG	GG	NDB	315.00	S01°	23.6'	E036°	38.2'	5,500	W02°

Libya

| | GHAT | GHT | NDB | 386.00 | N25° | 11.30' | E010° | 08.30' | 2,394 | W01° |

Madagascar

	ANKAZOBE	TN	NDB	385.00	S18°	18.8'	E047°	06.9'	4,000	W12°
	ANTANANARIVO	TVN	VOR	114.50	S18°	48.1'	E047°	31.1'	4,196	W13°
	IVATO	IA	NDB	364.00	S18°	47.49'	E047°	27.51'	4,113	
	IVATO	NT	NDB	340.00	S18°	49.0'	E047°	36.0'	4,114	W13°
	IVATO	IO	NDB	305.00	S18°	47.0'	E047°	23.6'	4,196	W13°
	MAROMAMY	MMY	NDB	267.00	S18°	48.3'	E049°	01.9'	50	W13°
	MORAMANGA	TE	NDB	371.00	S18°	57.0'	E048°	13.6'	3,000	W13°
	TOAMASINA	MT	VOR	113.10	S18°	07.4'	E049°	23.7'	20	W13°

Morocco

	BEN SLIMANE	CAE	NDB	275.00	N33°	37.0'	W007°	07.0'	600	W05°
	CASABLANCA	CBA	VOR	116.90	N33°	31.4'	W007°	40.7'	358	W06°
	CASABLANCA	NSR	NDB	282.00	N33°	17.0'	W007°	33.5'	656	W06°
	CASABLANCA	NUA	NDB	255.00	N33°	25.9'	W007°	36.7'	656	W06°
	CASABLANCA-MOHAMED	VBRC	VOR	114.00	N33°	17.6'	W007°	33.8'	656	W06°
	DAOUARAT	CSD	NDB	345.00	N32°	56.00'	W008°	02.99'	600	

State/Country	VOR/NDB Name	Ident.	Type	Freq.	Latitude		Longitude		Altitude	Mag Var
AFRICA NAVAIDS										
Morocco	DAQUARTT	CSD	NDB	345.00	N32°	56.0'	W008°	03.0'	600	W06°
	FUERTEVENTURA	FV	NDB	397.00	N28°	22.80'	W013°	51.90'	78	
	RABAT-SALE	RBT	VOR	116.50	N34°	03.2'	W006°	44.9'	325	W06°
Nigeria										
	COTONOU	TYE	VOR	113.30	N06°	21.6'	E002°	23.7'	46	W05°
	IBADAN	IB	VOR	112.10	N07°	20.8'	E003°	58.0'	748	W05°
	IBADAN	IB	NDB	400.00	N07°	26.0'	E003°	55.0'	769	W05°
	LAGOS	LG	VOR	113.70	N06°	42.4'	E003°	19.6'	251	W05°
	LAGOS	LB	NDB	368.00	N06°	35.8'	E003°	18.7'	51	W05°
	LAGOS	LA	NDB	336.00	N06°	36.3'	E003°	03.0'	86	W05°
	OKITIPUPA	OK	NDB	345.00	N06°	30.0'	E004°	50.0'	500	W05°
Seychelles Islands										
	PRASLIN	PRA	VOR	115.70	S04°	18.3'	E055°	42.5'	1,115	W05°
	SEYCHELLES	SEY	VOR	113.10	S04°	40.6'	E055°	32.0'	20	W05°
	SEYCHELLES	SEY	NDB	373.00	S04°	36.9'	E055°	26.5'	10	W05°
South Africa										
	CAPE TOWN	CTV	VOR	115.70	S33°	58.2'	E018°	36.4'	151	W23°
	CAPE TOWN	CT	NDB	400.00	S34°	02.6'	E018°	37.7'	144	W23°
	CAPE TOWN	CB	NDB	462.50	S33°	52.6'	E018°	34.4'	147	W23°
	CAPE TOWN	CA	NDB	282.50	S33°	59.8'	E018°	36.7'	144	W23°
	CLANWILLIAM	CW	NDB	372.50	S32°	11.0'	E018°	53.4'	500	W23°
	GRASMERE	GAV	VOR	115.50	S26°	30.9'	E027°	40.6'	5,000	W17°
	GREYTON	GE	NDB	270.00	S34°	03.4'	E019°	36.2'	300	W23°
	HARTEBEESPOORTDAM	HBV	VOR	112.10	S25°	40.5'	E027°	50.0'	3,800	W16°
	HEIDELBERG	HGV	VOR	116.70	S26°	41.8'	E028°	17.0'	5,000	W16°
	JAN SMUTS	JSV	VOR	115.20	S26°	09.4'	E028°	13.9'	5,558	W16°
	JAN SMUTS	JA	NDB	445.00	S26°	04.6'	E028°	15.6'	5,496	W16°
	JAN SMUTS	JS	NDB	220.00	S26°	12.6'	E028°	12.9'	5,558	W16°
	JAN SMUTS	JL	NDB	250.00	S26°	09.3'	E028°	13.9'	5,558	W16°
	JAN SMUTS	JN	NDB	420.00	S26°	13.3'	E028°	13.8'	5,510	W16°
	JAN SMUTS	JB	NDB	202.00	S26°	02.7'	E028°	15.9'	5,501	W16°
	LANSERIA	LAV	VOR	114.50	S25°	56.6'	E027°	55.3'	4,600	W16°
	MEYERTON	MT	NDB	385.00	S26°	33.4'	E028°	02.0'	5,000	W17°
	NEW LARGO	NL	NDB	367.50	S25°	55.2'	E028°	57.9'	5,000	W16°
	RAND	RAV	VOR	117.70	S26°	14.70'	E028°	09.29'	4,598	W16°
	RAND	RA	NDB	337.50	S26°	22.40'	E028°	14.09'	5,497	
	ROBBEN ISLAND	ZUI	NDB	310.30	S33°	48.9'	E018°	22.5'	50	W23°
	SIR LOWRY'S PASS	SP	NDB	222.50	S34°	08.8'	E018°	56.6'	50	W24°
	VAL	VAL	NDB	345.00	S26°	47.9'	E028°	55.4'	5,200	W18°
	WITBANK	WIV	VOR	113.30	S25°	49.7'	E029°	11.7'	5,078	W16°
	WOLSELEY	WY	NDB	247.50	S33°	24.8'	E019°	11.3'	300	W24°
Sudan										
	KHARTOUM	KIS	NDB	358.00	N15°	40.2'	E032°	33.6'	1,261	E01°
	KHARTOUM	KIN	NDB	335.00	N15°	31.2'	E032°	33.4'	1,261	E01°
	KHARTOUM	KH	NDB	329.00	N15°	38.0'	E032°	33.8'	1,256	E01°
	KHARTOUM	KH	NDB	343.00	N15°	38.00'	E032°	33.00'	1,259	
	KHARTOUM	KTM	VOR	112.10	N15°	35.0'	E032°	33.8'	1,256	E01°
	MEROWE	MRW	VOR	116.00	N18°	24.0'	E031°	49.3'	846	E01°
Zaire										
	KINSHASA	KE	NDB	285.00	S04°	22.10'	E015°	28.40'	1,010	W05°
	KINSHASA	KSA	VOR	115.00	S04°	24.1'	E015°	25.4'	1,055	W05°
	KINSHASA	OK	NDB	340.00	S04°	20.3'	E015°	31.4'	1,010	W05°
	MATADI	MTI	NDB	380.00	S05°	50.00'	E013°	27.99'	1,056	
Zimbabwe										
	BROMLEY	BZ	NDB	284.00	S18°	03.99'	E031°	20.29'	4,998	
	BROMLEY	KU	NDB	363.00	S18°	04.0'	E031°	20.3'	5,000	W09°
	FYDLE	VFY	VOR	114.90	S18°	10.4'	E029°	59.3'	3,800	W07°
	HARARE	VSB	VOR	113.10	S17°	54.4'	E031°	07.1'	4,875	W08°
	HARARE	SI	NDB	330.00	S17°	57.09'	E031°	04.20'	4,792	W08°
	HARARE	OL	NDB	346.00	S17°	59.6'	E031°	01.7'	4,793	W08°
	MAKUMBI	KU	NDB	363.00	S17°	31.40'	E031°	15.50'	4,998	W07°
	MAKUMBI	BZ	NDB	284.00	S17°	31.4'	E031°	15.5'	5,000	W07°
	NORTON	NZ	NDB	373.00	S17°	53.6'	E030°	41.6'	4,500	W09°
	ZISCO	RC	NDB	385.00	S19°	00.8'	E029°	42.7'	4,000	W08°

State/Country	VOR/NDB Name	Ident.	Type	Freq.	Latitude		Longitude		Altitude	Mag Var

EUROPE NAVAIDS

State/Country	VOR/NDB Name	Ident.	Type	Freq.	Latitude		Longitude		Altitude	Mag Var
Austria										
	ABSAM	AB	NDB	313.00	N47°	17.4'	E011°	30.1'	1,905	E00°
	BRUCK	BRK	NDB	408.00	N48°	03.8'	E016°	43.1'	500	E01°
	DESNA	OKF	VOR	113.15	N48°	58.20'	E015°	32.79'	1,594	E00°
	EURACH	EUR	VOR	115.20	N47°	44.2'	E011°	15.0'	2,238	E00°
	FISCHAMEND	FMD	VOR	110.40	N48°	06.3'	E016°	37.8'	624	E01°
	GRAZ	GRZ	VOR	116.20	N46°	57.39'	E015°	26.99'	1,098	E01°
	INNSBRUCK	INN	NDB	420.00	N47°	13.9'	E011°	24.2'	7,000	E00°
	KEMPTEN	KPT	VOR	109.60	N47°	44.8'	E010°	21.1'	2,476	W00°
	KUHTAI	KTI	NDB	413.00	N47°	10.0'	E011°	01.7'	4,000	E11°
	LINZ	LNZ	VOR	116.60	N48°	13.8'	E014°	06.3'	1,150	E01°
	RATTENBERG	RTT	NDB	303.00	N47°	25.9'	E011°	56.4'	3,000	E00°
	RODING	RDG	VOR	114.70	N49°	02.5'	E012°	31.7'	2,124	E01°
	SALZBURG	SBG	VOR	113.80	N48°	00.2'	E012°	53.6'	1,500	E00°
	SALZBURG	SBG	NDB	382.00	N47°	58.1'	E012°	53.7'	1,411	E00°
	SALZBURG	SI	NDB	410.00	N47°	49.2'	E012°	59.3'	1,411	E00°
	SALZBURG	SU	NDB	356.00	N47°	52.8'	E012°	57.0'	1,411	E00°
	SOLLENAU	SNU	VOR	115.50	N47°	52.50'	E016°	17.39'	898	E00°
	STEINHOF	STE	NDB	293.00	N48°	12.7'	E016°	14.9'	600	E01°
	STOCKERAU	STO	VOR	113.00	N48°	25.1'	E016°	01.2'	761	E00°
	VIENNA	WO	NDB	303.00	N48°	08.9'	E016°	27.5'	600	E01°
	VILLACH	VIW	VOR	112.90	N46°	41.8'	E013°	54.9'	6,300	E00°
	WAGRAM	WGM	VOR	112.20	N48°	19.5'	E016°	29.5'	580	E01°
Azores, Portugal										
	LAJES	LAJ	VOR	110.80	N38°	42.79'	W027°	06.99'	1,853	W14°
	LAJES	LM	VOR	112.30	N38°	47.09'	W027°	06.30'	1,853	W14°
	LAJES	TRM	VOR	116.20	N38°	45.59'	W027°	05.60'	170	W14°
	LAJES	GP	NDB	341.00	N38°	47.00'	W027°	06.90'	170	
	PONTA DELGADA	PD	NDB	351.00	N37°	44.10'	W025°	40.50'	186	
	PONTA DELGADA	MGL	NDB	371.00	N37°	44.40'	W025°	35.09'	298	
	SANTA MARIA	VSM	VOR	113.70	N36°	57.69'	W025°	10.00'	308	W12°
	SANTA MARIA	SMA	VOR	323.00	N36°	59.79'	W025°	10.60'	282	
	SANTA MARIA	STA	NDB	240.00	N36°	56.89'	W025°	10.00'	282	
Belgium										
	AFFLIGEM	AFI	VOR	114.90	N50°	54.5'	E004°	08.4'	284	W03°
	BRESSY	BUS	NDB	283.50	N50°	41.7'	E004°	08.4'	200	W04°
	BRUNO	BUN	VOR	110.60	N51°	04.4'	E004°	46.5'	70	W03°
	BRUNO	BUN	NDB	341.50	N51°	04.6'	E004°	46.8'	70	W03°
	BRUSSELS	BUB	VOR	114.60	N50°	54.2'	E004°	32.4'	187	W03°
	BRUSSELS	OB	NDB	293.00	N50°	55.3'	E004°	37.1'	187	W03°
	BRUSSELS	OP	NDB	402.00	N50°	56.4'	E004°	35.6'	187	W03°
	BRUSSELS	OZ	NDB	314.00	N50°	49.7'	E004°	28.1'	187	W03°
	COSTA	COA	VOR	111.80	N51°	20.9'	E003°	21.4'	119	W03°
	DENDER	DEN	NDB	393.00	N50°	52.8'	E004°	01.7'	284	W04°
	DIEKIRCH	DIK	VOR	114.40	N49°	51.7'	E006°	07.9'	1,109	W02°
	DIEKIRCH	DIK	NDB	307.00	N49°	51.7'	E006°	07.9'	1,109	W02°
	HAAMSTEDE	HSD	VOR	115.50	N51°	43.4'	E003°	51.5'	119	W03°
	HULDENBERG	HUL	VOR	117.55	N50°	45.0'	E004°	38.6'	356	W03°
	KLIEN BROGEL	ONT	NDB	431.00	N51°	12.9'	E005°	33.5'	180	W02°
	KOKSY	KOK	VOR	114.50	N51°	05.7'	E002°	39.2'	30	W03°
	LUXEMBOURG	DIK	VOR	114.40	N49°	51.7'	E006°	07.9'	1,109	W02°
	NATTENHEIM	NTM	VOR	115.30	N50°	01.00'	E006°	31.99'	1,348	W02°
	NICKY	NIK	VOR	117.40	N51°	10.0'	E004°	11.1'	119	W03°
	NICKY	NIK	NDB	336.00	N51°	09.8'	E004°	11.4'	119	W03°
	OLNO	LNO	VOR	112.80	N50°	35.2'	E005°	42.7'	811	W02°
	SPIRMONT	SPI	VOR	113.10	N50°	30.9'	E005°	37.5'	966	W02°
Bulgaria										
	RADOVETS	RAD	VOR	112.90	N41°	56.20'	E026°	29.39'	885	W02°
	RADOVETS	RAD	NDB	258.00	N41°	56.10'	E026°	29.60'	118	
Czechoslovakia										
	CHEB	OKG	VOR	115.70	N50°	03.9'	E012°	24.5'	1,594	W01°
	DEJVICE	D	NDB	429.00	N50°	05.17'	E014°	17.77'	1,246	
	HERMSDORF	HDO	VOR	115.00	N50°	55.8'	E014°	22.3'	1,420	E01°
	LIBOC	L	NDB	372.00	N50°	07.23'	E014°	17.39'	1,246	
	NERATOVICE	NER	VOR	108.60	N50°	18.7'	E014°	23.8'	1,222	E00°
	PRAGUE	OKL	VOR	112.60	N50°	06.4'	E014°	13.8'	1,222	E01°
	RAKOVNIK	RAK	NDB	386.00	N50°	05.9'	E013°	41.5'	1,100	W01°
	ROUDNICE	RCE	VOR	117.60	N50°	27.1'	E014°	12.7'	740	E00°
	RUZYNE MIDDLE	PG	NDB	307.00	N50°	02.9'	E014°	22.3'	1,158	E01°
	RUZYNE NORTH	PR	NDB	356.00	N50°	08.7'	E014°	22.1'	1,158	E01°

State/Country	VOR/NDB Name	Ident.	Type	Freq.	Latitude		Longitude		Altitude	Mag Var
EUROPE NAVAIDS										
Czechoslovakia	VLASIM	VLM	VOR	114.30	N49°	42.3'	E015°	04.1'	1,501	E00°
	VOZICE	VOZ	VOR	116.30	N49°	32.0'	E014°	52.6'	2,226	E00°
Denmark										
	AALBORG	AAL	VOR	116.70	N57°	06.29'	E009°	59.79'	32	W01°
	ALMA	ALM	VOR	116.40	N55°	24.7'	E013°	33.6'	249	E00°
	ASTOR	AOR	VOR	113.90	N56°	07.3'	E012°	57.8'	39	E00°
	CODAN	CDA	VOR	114.90	N55°	00.1'	E012°	22.9'	90	E00°
	KASTRUP	KAS	VOR	112.50	N55°	35.5'	E012°	36.9'	28	E00°
	KORSA	KOR	VOR	112.80	N55°	26.4'	E011°	38.0'	136	E00°
	NORA	NOA	VOR	112.60	N56°	06.4'	E012°	14.6'	12	E00°
	ODIN	ODN	VOR	115.50	N55°	34.8'	E010°	39.3'	24	W01°
	RAMME	RAM	VOR	112.30	N56°	28.69'	E008°	11.30'	22	W02°
	SEVDA	SVD	VOR	116.20	N56°	10.2'	E012°	34.6'	39	E01°
	STURUP	SUP	VOR	113.00	N55°	32.1'	E013°	22.9'	249	E01°
	TRANO	TNO	VOR	117.40	N55°	46.5'	E011°	26.4'	12	E00°
	VESTA	VES	VOR	116.60	N55°	36.20'	E008°	18.10'	62	W02°
England										
	BIGGIN	BIG	VOR	115.10	N51°	19.8'	E000°	02.2'	590	W04°
	BOVINGDON	BNN	VOR	113.75	N51°	43.5'	W000°	32.9'	500	W05°
	BROOKMANS PARK	BPK	VOR	117.50	N51°	44.99'	W000°	06.29'	380	W04°
	BURNHAM	BUR	VOR	117.10	N51°	31.0'	W000°	40.2'	183	W05°
	BURNHAM	BUR	NDB	421.00	N51°	31.00'	W000°	40.19'	85	
	CHILTERN	CHT	NDB	277.00	N51°	37.4'	W000°	31.0'	220	W04°
	CLACTON	CLN	VOR	114.55	N51°	50.9'	E001°	09.0'	100	W04°
	COMPTON	CPT	VOR	114.35	N51°	29.5'	W001°	13.1'	498	W05°
	CUMBERNAULD	CBN	NDB	374.00	N55°	58.5'	W003°	58.4'	350	W07°
	DAVENTRY	DTY	VOR	116.40	N52°	10.8'	W001°	06.7'	600	W05°
	DEANCROSS	DCS	VOR	115.20	N54°	43.4'	W003°	20.4'	700	W07°
	DETLING	DET	VOR	117.30	N51°	18.20'	W000°	35.89'	646	W04°
	DOVER	DVR	VOR	114.95	N51°	09.69'	E001°	21.69'	314	W04°
	EPSOM	EPM	NDB	316.00	N51°	19.1'	W000°	22.2'	200	W05°
	GLASGOW	GOW	VOR	115.40	N55°	52.2'	W004°	26.7'	37	W07°
	GLASGOW	AC	NDB	325.00	N55°	48.9'	W004°	32.5'	26	W07°
	GLASGOW	GLG	NDB	350.00	N55°	55.5'	W004°	20.1'	20	W07°
	HEATHROW	OW	NDB	389.50	N51°	27.9'	W000°	34.9'	110	W04°
	HONILEY	HON	VOR	113.65	N52°	21.40'	W001°	39.69'	436	W05°
	LAMBOURNE	LAM	VOR	115.60	N51°	38.7'	E000°	09.2'	200	W04°
	LANDS END	LND	VOR	114.20	N50°	08.09'	W005°	38.20'	800	W7°
	LONDON	LON	VOR	113.60	N51°	29.2'	W000°	27.9'	110	W05°
	LYDD	LYD	VOR	114.05	N50°	59.9'	E000°	52.8'	11	W04°
	MANCHESTER	MCT	VOR	113.55	N53°	21.4'	W002°	15.7'	282	W06°
	MAYFIELD	MAY	VOR	117.90	N51°	00.99'	W000°	07.10'	200	W04°
	MIDHURST	MID	VOR	114.00	N51°	03.2'	W000°	37.4'	200	W05°
	NEW GALLOWAY	NYG	NDB	399.00	N55°	10.60'	W004°	10.00'	111	
	OCKHAM	OCK	VOR	115.30	N51°	18.30'	W000°	26.70'	200	W05°
	PERTH	PTH	VOR	110.40	N56°	26.6'	W003°	22.0'	400	W07°
	POLE HILL	POL	VOR	112.10	N53°	44.6'	W002°	06.1'	1,400	W06°
	SAINT ABBS	SAB	VOR	112.50	N55°	54.4'	W002°	12.3'	760	W06°
	SEAFORD	SFD	VOR	117.00	N50°	45.60'	W000°	07.40'	298	W04°
	SOUTHAMPTON	SAM	VOR	113.35	N50°	57.30'	W001°	20.60'	65	W05°
	SOUTHEND	SND	NDB	362.50	N51°	34.60'	W000°	42.09'	111	
	SOUTHHAMPTON	SAM	VOR	113.35	N50°	57.30'	W001°	20.60'	65	W5°
	STRUMBLE	STU	VOR	113.10	N51°	59.70'	W005°	02.29'	600	W07°
	TALLA	TLA	VOR	113.80	N55°	30.00'	W003°	21.10'	2,784	W07°
	TURNBERRY	TRN	VOR	117.50	N55°	18.80'	W004°	46.99'	600	W07°
	WESTCOTT	WCO	NDB	335.00	N51°	51.09'	W000°	57.59'	111	
	WOODLEY	WOD	NDB	352.00	N51°	27.20'	W000°	52.69'	111	
Finland										
	ANTON	ANT	VOR	113.70	N60°	51.8'	E025°	07.8'	302	E06°
	ESPOO	ESP	NDB	381.00	N60°	14.9'	E024°	48.0'	245	E05°
	FOXTROT	F	NDB	408.00	N60°	16.0'	E025°	02.5'	147	E05°
	HEKA	HEK	NDB	344.00	N60°	15.3'	E025°	29.7'	147	E06°
	HELSINKI	HEL	VOR	114.20	N60°	20.3'	E024°	57.4'	245	E05°
	HOTEL	H	NDB	403.00	N60°	20.25'	E024°	59.81'	167	
	HYVINKAA	HYV	NDB	396.00	N60°	33.2'	E024°	43.1'	151	E05°
	KORSO	KOR	NDB	322.00	N60°	22.3'	E025°	04.3'	149	E05°
	PAKKA	PAK	NDB	368.00	N60°	42.1'	E025°	32.9'	135	E06°
	PIRKKA	PIR	VOR	116.20	N61°	24.60'	E023°	34.89'	449	E05°
	SUNNA	SUA	VOR	116.60	N60°	05.99'	E022°	32.50'	45	E04°
	UNIFORM	U	NDB	371.50	N60°	18.25'	E024°	55.47'	167	
	UTTI	UTT	VOR	114.60	N60°	53.8'	E026°	56.0'	359	E06°
	VIHTI	VTI	VOR	117.00	N60°	27.6'	E024°	14.8'	206	E06°
	ZULU	Z	NDB	291.00	N60°	20.70'	E024°	57.15'	167	

State/Country	VOR/NDB Name	Ident.	Type	Freq.	Latitude		Longitude		Altitude	Mag Var
EUROPE NAVAIDS										
France										
	ABBERVILLE	ABB	VOR	116.60	N50°	08.1'	E001°	51.3'	220	W03°
	ABBEVILLE	ABB	VOR	116.60	N50°	08.09'	E001°	51.29'	219	W03°
	ALENCON	AL	NDB	380.00	N48°	27.0'	E000°	06.8'	479	W04°
	AMBOISE	AMB	VOR	113.70	N47°	25.7'	E001°	03.9'	387	W03°
	AMIENS	GI	NDB	339.00	N49°	50.5'	E002°	29.0'	197	W04°
	ANGERS	ANG	NDB	113.00	N47°	32.2'	W000°	51.2'	187	WO4°
	BEAUVAIS	BVS	VOR	115.90	N49°	26.3'	E002°	09.3'	358	W03°
	BEAUVAIS	BV	NDB	391.00	N49°	29.5'	E002°	01.8'	358	W04°
	BOULOGNE	BNE	VOR	113.80	N50°	37.5'	E001°	54.5'	500	W04°
	BOURSONNE	BSN	VOR	112.50	N49°	11.3'	E003°	03.4'	300	W03°
	BRAY	BRY	VOR	114.10	N48°	24.4'	E003°	17.7'	289	W03°
	BRAY	BRY	NDB	277.00	N48°	24.4'	E003°	17.7'	289	W03°
	CAEN	CAN	VOR	115.40	N49°	10.3'	W000°	27.3'	256	W04°
	CAMBRAI	CMB	VOR	112.60	N50°	13.7'	E003°	09.1'	256	W03°
	CHAMBERY	CBY	VOR	115.40	N45°	53.0'	E005°	45.5'	4,734	W02°
	CHARLES-DE-GAULLE (PARICGN	CGN	VOR	115.35	N49°	01.20'	E002°	30.09'	387	W04°
	CHARLES-DE-GAULLE (PARIPGS		VOR	117.05	N49°	00.00'	E002°	37.50'	387	W03°
	CHARLES-DE-GAULLE (PARIS	CGO	NDB	343.00	N48°	59.3'	E002°	24.1'	387	W04°
	CHARLES-DE-GAULLE (PARIS	CGZ	NDB	370.00	N49°	00.4'	E002°	44.5'	387	W04°
	CHARLES-DE-GAULLE (PARIS	RSO	NDB	364.00	N49°	00.7'	E002°	21.7'	387	W04°
	CHARLES-DE-GAULLE (PARIS	RSY	NDB	356.00	N49°	01.9'	E002°	42.4'	387	W04°
	CHARTRES	CHW	VOR	115.20	N48°	28.8'	E000°	59.3'	730	W04°
	CHATEAUDUN	CDN	VOR	116.10	N48°	03.5'	E001°	23.3'	433	W04°
	CHATEAUDUN	CDN	NDB	359.50	N48°	03.8'	E001°	21.8'	433	W04°
	CHATILLON	CTL	VOR	117.60	N49°	08.3'	E003°	34.7'	673	W03°
	CHIEVERS	CIV	VOR	113.20	N50°	34.5'	E003°	50.1'	221	W03°
	COMPIEGNE	CO	NDB	553.50	N49°	26.1'	E002°	48.4'	315	W04°
	COULOMMIERS	CLM	VOR	112.90	N48°	50.7'	E003°	00.9'	486	W03°
	CREIL	CRL	VOR	109.20	N49°	15.3'	E002°	31.0'	335	W03°
	DEAUVILLE	DVL	VOR	110.20	N49°	18.6'	E000°	18.8'	479	W04°
	DIEPPE	DPE	VOR	115.80	N49°	55.6'	E001°	10.3'	344	W04°
	DIJION	DIJ	VOR	113.50	N47°	16.3'	E005°	05.9'	768	W02°
	EPERNON	EPR	VOR	115.65	N48°	37.5'	E001°	39.3'	300	W03°
	EPINAL	EPL	VOR	113.00	N48°	19.1'	E006°	03.8'	1,086	W02°
	ETAMPES	EM	NDB	295.50	N48°	22.6'	E002°	04.9'	460	W03°
	EVREUX	EVX	VOR	112.40	N49°	01.9'	E001°	13.3'	502	W03°
	L'AIGLE	LGL	VOR	115.00	N48°	47.6'	E000°	32.0'	787	W03°
	LE BOURGET (PARIS)	BT	VOR	108.80	N48°	58.5'	E002°	27.4'	230	W03°
	LE BOURGET (PARIS)	BGW	NDB	334.00	N48°	56.3'	E002°	16.8'	217	W04°
	LE HAVRE	LHO	NDB	346.00	N49°	35.8'	E000°	11.0'	312	W05°
	LE MANS	LM	NDB	326.00	N47°	53.6'	E000°	10.3'	194	W04°
	LUXEUIL	LUL	VOR	117.10	N47°	41.29'	E006°	17.80'	163	W02°
	MARTIGUES	MTG	VOR	117.30	N43°	23.2'	E005°	05.3'	643	W02°
	MELUN	MEL	VOR	109.80	N48°	27.4'	E002°	48.8'	302	W03°
	MELUN	MV	NDB	434.00	N48°	33.2'	E002°	58.7'	302	W04°
	MONTDIDIER	MTD	VOR	113.65	N49°	33.2'	E002°	29.4'	300	W03°
	MOULINS	MOU	VOR	116.70	N46°	42.4'	E003°	38.0'	699	W02°
	NEVERS	NEV	VOR	113.40	N47°	09.2'	E002°	55.8'	587	W03°
	NICE	NIZ	VOR	112.40	N43°	46.19'	E007°	15.30'	2,820	W01°
	ORLEANS	OAN	NDB	385.00	N48°	00.1'	E001°	46.2'	410	W04°
	ORLY (PARIS)	OL	VOR	111.20	N48°	43.8'	E002°	23.3'	306	W03°
	ORLY (PARIS)	OLS	NDB	328.00	N48°	38.8'	E002°	20.8'	292	W04°
	ORLY (PARIS)	ORW	NDB	402.00	N48°	40.4'	E002°	11.0'	292	W04°
	ORLY (PARIS)	OYE	NDB	349.00	N48°	45.2'	E002°	32.4'	292	W04°
	PASSEIRY	PAS	VOR	116.60	N46°	09.9'	E006°	00.0'	1,418	W01°
	PERONNE-ST. QUENTIN	PM	NDB	382.00	N49°	52.1'	E003°	08.2'	292	W03°
	PITHIVIERS	PTV	VOR	116.50	N48°	09.3'	E002°	15.9'	300	W03°
	PONTOISE	PON	VOR	111.60	N49°	05.8'	E002°	02.2'	325	W03°
	RAMBOUILLET	RBT	VOR	114.70	N48°	39.2'	E001°	59.7'	604	W03°
	REIMS	REM	VOR	112.30	N49°	18.7'	E004°	02.8'	335	W03°
	ROLAMPONT	RLP	VOR	117.30	N47°	54.4'	E005°	15.0'	1,490	W02°
	ROUEN	ROU	VOR	116.80	N49°	27.9'	E001°	16.9'	512	W04°
	SATOLAS	LSA	VOR	114.75	N45°	43.6'	E005°	05.7'	820	W02°
	ST PREX	SPR	VOR	113.90	N46°	28.2'	E006°	26.9'	1,252	W01°
	TOUR DU PIN	TDP	VOR	110.60	N45°	29.4'	E005°	26.4'	2,000	W02°
	TOUSSUS	TSU	VOR	108.25	N48°	45.2'	E002°	06.2'	538	W03°
	TROYES	TRO	VOR	116.00	N48°	15.1'	E003°	57.8'	394	W02°

State/Country	VOR/NDB Name	Ident.	Type	Freq.	Latitude		Longitude		Altitude	Mag Var
EUROPE NAVAIDS										
France	TROYES	TY	NDB	320.00	N48°	24.0'	E004°	00.3'	394	W03°
	VILLACOUBLAY	TA	NDB	286.50	N48°	46.3'	E002°	05.4'	581	W03°
	VILLACOUBLAY	TH	NDB	302.00	N48°	46.7'	E002°	22.9'	581	W03°
	VILLACOUBLAY	HOL	NDB	315.00	N48°	43.9'	E001°	49.3'	581	W03°
Germany	ALLERSBERG	ALB	VOR	111.20	N49°	12.9'	E011°	13.4'	1,415	E00°
	ALSIE	ALS	VOR	114.70	N54°	54.4'	E009°	59.7'	65	W01°
	ALSTER	ALF	VOR	115.80	N53°	38.2'	E009°	59.7'	40	W00°
	ANSBACH	ANS	NDB	452.00	N49°	18.5'	E010°	37.9'	451	W00°
	AUGSBURG	AGB	NDB	318.00	N48°	25.5'	E010°	56.0'	1,516	E00°
	AUSBURG	AUG	VOR	115.90	N48°	25.5'	E010°	56.0'	1,542	E00°
	BRUNKENDORF	BKD	VOR	117.70	N53°	02.2'	E011°	32.9'	57	E00°
	DINKELSBUHL	DKB	VOR	117.80	N49°	08.6'	E010°	14.4'	1,720	W00°
	ELBE	LBE	VOR	115.10	N52°	39.4'	E009°	35.8'	4	W00°
	ERDING	ERD	VOR	113.60	N48°	19.6'	E011°	57.3'	1,505	E00°
	ERLANGEN	ERL	VOR	114.90	N49°	39.4'	E011°	09.1'	1,800	E00°
	GEDSER	GES	VOR	113.50	N54°	37.10'	E011°	56.00'	88	E00°
	GLUCKSTADT	GLX	NDB	365.00	N53°	51.1'	E009°	27.3'	320	E00°
	HAMBURG	HAM	VOR	113.10	N53°	41.2'	E010°	12.4'	139	W01°
	HAMBURG	FU	NDB	350.50	N53°	34.6'	E009°	52.6'	77	E00°
	HAMBURG	HAM	NDB	339.00	N53°	40.7'	E010°	05.1'	43	E00°
	HAMBURG	GT	NDB	323.00	N53°	40.7'	E010°	05.1'	53	E00°
	HEHLINGEN	HLZ	VOR	117.30	N52°	21.9'	E010°	47.8'	375	W00°
	HELGOLAND	DHE	VOR	116.30	N54°	11.2'	E007°	54.7'	53	W02°
	HOFENFELS	HFX	NDB	286.00	N49°	13.1'	E011°	51.5'	1,455	W01°
	INGOLSTADT	IGL	NDB	345.00	N48°	44.4'	E011°	38.8'	1,201	E00°
	KARLSPUHE	KRH	VOR	115.95	N48°	59.6'	E008°	35.1'	880	W01°
	KEMPTEN	KPT	VOR	109.60	N47°	44.8'	E010°	21.1'	2,476	W00°
	KLAGENFURT	KFT	VOR	113.10	N46°	35.9'	E014°	33.8'	2,280	E01°
	LANDSBERG	LQ	NDB	448.00	N48°	05.6'	E011°	02.2'	2,044	E00°
	LEINE	DLE	VOR	115.20	N52°	15.1'	E009°	53.1'	362	W01°
	LUBECK	LUB	VOR	110.60	N53°	56.5'	E010°	40.2'	88	W01°
	LUBURG	LBU	VOR	109.20	N48°	54.9'	E009°	20.5'	1,032	W01°
	MAISACH	MAH	VOR	108.40	N48°	15.9'	E011°	18.8'	1,740	E00°
	MENGEN	MEG	NDB	401.00	N48°	03.3'	E009°	22.1'	1,819	W01°
	MICHAELSDORF	MIC	VOR	112.20	N54°	18.4'	E011°	00.4'	20	W00°
	MIKE	MIQ	NDB	426.50	N48°	34.3'	E011°	36.0'	1,545	W02°
	MILLDORF	MDF	VOR	117.00	N48°	14.1'	E012°	20.3'	1,623	E00°
	MOOSBURG	MBG	VOR	117.15	N48°	34.5'	E012°	15.8'	1,597	E00°
	MUNICH	MUN	VOR	112.30	N48°	10.9'	E011°	49.1'	1,756	E00°
	MUNICH	DMN	VOR	116.00	N48°	22.1'	E011°	47.8'	1,384	E00°
	MUNICH	DMS	VOR	108.60	N48°	20.5'	E011°	46.8'	1,416	E00°
	MUNICH	MNE	NDB	358.00	N48°	21.4'	E011°	40.6'	1,486	E00°
	MUNICH	MSE	NDB	385.00	N48°	20.1'	E011°	39.3'	1,486	E00°
	MUNICH	MSW	NDB	400.00	N48°	21.2'	E011°	54.3'	1,486	E00°
	NIENBURG	NIE	VOR	116.50	N52°	37.6'	E009°	22.4'	100	E00°
	NORDLINGEN	NDG	NDB	375.00	N48°	49.8'	E010°	25.2'	1,800	W01°
	OBERPFAFFENHOFEN	OBI	NDB	429.00	N48°	04.9'	E011°	17.2'	1,946	E00°
	OSNABRUCK	OSN	VOR	114.30	N52°	12.09'	E008°	17.20'	98	W01°
	SOLLING	SOG	NDB	374.50	N51°	41.30'	E009°	30.79'	49	
	TANGO	TGO	VOR	112.50	N48°	37.2'	E009°	15.6'	1,213	W01°
	TRANASDINGEN	TRA	VOR	114.30	N47°	41.5'	E008°	26.3'	1,850	W01°
	TRENT	TRT	VOR	108.45	N54°	30.80'	E103°	15.00'	193	E01°
	WALDA	WLD	VOR	112.80	N48°	34.8'	E011°	07.9'	1,374	E00°
	WARBURG	WRB	VOR	113.70	N51°	30.4'	E009°	06.7'	787	W01°
	WESER	WSR	VOR	112.90	N53°	21.0'	E008°	52.6'	33	W01°
	WURZBURG	WUR	VOR	116.35	N49°	43.2'	E009°	56.9'	1,000	W00°
Greece	AIGINA	EGN	NDB	382.00	N37°	45.9'	E023°	25.5'	51	E02°
	ATHENS	ATH	VOR	114.40	N37°	54.1'	E023°	43.8'	51	E02°
	ATHENS	HN	NDB	294.00	N37°	52.1'	E023°	44.8'	51	E02°
	ATHENS	HK	NDB	275.00	N37°	49.2'	E023°	46.4'	51	E02°
	DIDIMON	DDM	VOR	117.20	N37°	28.7'	E023°	13.1'	3,655	E01°
	ELEFSIS	ELF	NDB	418.00	N38°	04.0'	E023°	46.4'	98	E02°
	KARISTOS	KRS	NDB	285.00	N38°	00.8'	E024°	25.1'	50	E02°
	KAVOURI	KVR	NDB	357.00	N37°	48.9'	E023°	45.6'	58	E02°
	KEA	KEA	VOR	115.00	N37°	33.5'	E024°	18.0'	1,388	E02°
	KORINTHOS	KOR	NDB	392.00	N37°	56.0'	E022°	56.0'	50	E02°
	MILOS	MIL	VOR	113.50	N36°	44.7'	E024°	31.1'	12	E01°
	SOUNION	SUN	NDB	319.00	N37°	40.2'	E024°	02.7'	50	E02°
	TANGRA	TNG	NDB	303.00	N38°	20.0'	E023°	43.9'	50	E02°
	TRIPOLIS	TRL	VOR	116.20	N37°	24.3'	E022°	20.5'	2,113	E02°

State/Country	VOR/NDB Name	Ident.	Type	Freq.	Latitude		Longitude		Altitude	Mag Var
EUROPE NAVAIDS										
Hungary										
	GYOR	GYR	VOR	115.10	N47°	39.5'	E017°	43.5'	515	E01°
	GYOR	GYR	NDB	354.00	N47°	39.6'	E017°	43.2'	515	E01°
	IVANKA NORTH	OKR	NDB	391.00	N48°	13.40'	E017°	17.49'	498	
	PUSZTASABOLCS	PTB	NDB	386.00	N47°	08.4'	E018°	45.8'	450	E02°
Iceland										
	ELLIDAVATN	EL	NDB	335.00	N64°	04.9'	W021°	46.3'	200	W21°
	INGO	ING	VOR	112.40	N63°	48.2'	W016°	38.6'	335	W17°
	KEFLAVIK	KEF	VOR	112.00	N63°	59.2'	W002°	36.9'	174	W21°
	KEFLAVIK	KF	NDB	392.00	N63°	59.2'	W022°	36.9'	111	W21°
	KILO	OK	NDB	364.00	N64°	03.0'	W022°	36.3'	163	W21°
	OSCAR-KILO	OK	NDB	364.00	N64°	02.99'	W022°	36.29'	163	
	REYJAVIK	RK	NDB	355.00	N64°	09.1'	W022°	01.8'	45	W21°
	REYKHOLT	RH	NDB	325.00	N64°	39.90'	W021°	17.59'	170	
	SKAGI	SA	NDB	379.00	N64°	18.4'	W021°	58.3'	200	W21°
	SKARDSFJARA	SR	NDB	312.60	N63°	31.0'	W017°	58.9'	335	W18°
	VESTMANNAEY JAR	VM	NDB	375.00	N63°	24.0'	W020°	17.3'	250	W20°
Ireland										
	BALDONNEL	BAL	VOR	115.80	N53°	18.0'	W006°	26.7'	319	W07°
	BELFAST	BEL	VOR	117.20	N54°	39.70'	W006°	13.69'	193	W08°
	BELFAST CITY	HB	VOR	420.00	N54°	36.90'	W005°	52.90'	193	
	CLONMEL	CML	NDB	387.00	N52°	27.2'	W007°	28.8'	500	W08°
	CONNAUGHT	CON	VOR	117.40	N53°	54.8'	W008°	49.0'	707	W09°
	CORK	CRK	VOR	114.60	N51°	50.39'	W008°	29.59'	531	W08°
	CORK	OB	NDB	362.00	N51°	49.29'	W008°	28.80'	531	
	DUBLIN	DUB	VOR	114.90	N53°	29.99'	W006°	18.40'	163	W08°
	DUBLIN	OE	NDB	316.00	N53°	25.80'	W006°	25.69'	163	
	DUBLIN	OP	NDB	397.00	N53°	24.80'	W006°	08.29'	163	
	GARRISTOWN	GAR	NDB	407.00	N53°	31.7'	W006°	26.8'	242	W08°
	GLASGOW	GOW	VOR	115.40	N55°	52.19'	W004°	26.69'	36	W07°
	ISLE OF MAN	IOM	VOR	112.20	N54°	04.0'	W004°	45.7'	573	W07°
	KILLINEY	KLY	NDB	378.00	N53°	16.2'	W006°	06.3'	242	W08°
	MACHRIHANISH	MAC	VOR	116.00	N55°	25.79'	W005°	38.99'	75	W08°
	RUSH	RSH	NDB	326.00	N53°	30.7'	W006°	06.6'	242	W08°
	SHANNON	SHA	VOR	113.30	N52°	43.29'	W008°	53.09'	52	W08°
	STRUMBLE	STU	NDB	400.00	N52°	00.49'	W005°	01.00'	600	
Italy										
	AJACCIO	AJO	VOR	114.80	N41°	46.2'	E008°	46.5'	2,142	E00°
	ALGHERO	ALG	VOR	113.80	N40°	27.7'	E008°	14.7'	1,447	W00°
	ALGHERO	ALG	NDB	382.00	N40°	35.2'	E008°	15.8'	1,447	W00°
	BASTIA	BTA	VOR	114.15	N42°	34.4'	E009°	28.5'	36	E00°
	BOLSENA	BOL	NDB	327.00	N42°	37.00'	E012°	03.09'	2,082	
	BOLSENA	BOL	VOR	114.40	N42°	37.1'	E012°	02.9'	2,082	E01°
	CAMPAGNANO	CMP	VOR	111.40	N42°	07.4'	E012°	22.9'	1,442	E01°
	CAMPAGNANO	CMP	NDB	301.50	N42°	07.49'	E012°	22.80'	1,443	
	CARBONARA	CAR	NDB	402.00	N39°	06.29'	E009°	30.89'	167	
	CARBONARA	CAR	VOR	115.10	N39°	06.7'	E009°	30.5'	167	W00°
	CIAMPINO	CMP	NDB	412.00	N41°	51.9'	E012°	33.7'	341	E01°
	ELBA	ELB	VOR	114.70	N42°	43.8'	E010°	23.8'	1,338	E00°
	FIUMICINO	FN	NDB	421.00	N41°	54.7'	E012°	14.0'	14	E01°
	FIUMICINO	FW	NDB	345.00	N41°	52.8'	E012°	11.9'	8	E01°
	FIUMICINO	FE	NDB	354.00	N41°	49.8'	E012°	21.1'	7	E01°
	FROSINONE	FRS	NDB	371.00	N41°	38.6'	E013°	17.4'	632	W01°
	GUIDONIA	GUI	NDB	388.00	N42°	00.00'	E012°	44.39'	45	
	OSTIA	OST	VOR	114.90	N41°	48.2'	E012°	14.3'	46	E01°
	OSTIA	OST	NDB	321.00	N41°	48.3'	E012°	14.2'	46	E01°
	PESCARA	PES	VOR	115.90	N42°	26.1'	E014°	11.1'	70	E01°
	PISA	PIS	VOR	112.10	N43°	40.6'	E010°	23.5'	39	W02°
	PONZA	PNZ	VOR	114.60	N40°	54.7'	E012°	57.5'	684	E01°
	PRATICA DI MARA	PRA	NDB	339.00	N41°	40.8'	E012°	27.2'	135	E01°
	SARONNO	SRN	VOR	113.70	N45°	38.7'	E009°	01.3'	814	W01°
	SORRENTO	SOR	NDB	426.00	N40°	34.90'	E014°	20.00'	1,653	
	SORRENTO	SOR	VOR	112.20	N40°	34.9'	E014°	20.1'	1,653	E01°
	TARQUINIA	TAQ	VOR	111.80	N42°	12.9'	E011°	44.0'	76	E01°
	TARQUINIA	TAQ	NDB	312.00	N42°	12.80'	E011°	43.80'	55	
	TEANO	TEA	VOR	112.90	N41°	17.8'	E013°	58.2'	3,289	E01°
	TEANO	TEA	NDB	316.00	N41°	17.69'	E013°	58.18'	3,289	E01°
	TORINO	TOP	VOR	114.50	N44°	55.49'	E007°	51.69'	865	W01°
	URBE	URB	NDB	285.00	N41°	56.7'	E012°	29.4'	55	E01°
Netherlands										
	STAD	STD	NDB	386.00	N51°	44.49'	E004°	14.60'	183	

State/Country	VOR/NDB Name	Ident.	Type	Freq.	Latitude		Longitude		Altitude	Mag Var
EUROPE NAVAIDS										
Norway										
	AMBLA	AMA	NDB	303.00	N61°	10.80'	E007°	16.80'	163	
	ASKOY	ASK	NDB	360.00	N60°	25.39'	E005°	10.79'	163	
	BRATTA	BTA	NDB	336.00	N60°	02.89'	E005°	18.10'	163	
	FLESLAND	FLE	VOR	114.50	N60°	18.0'	E005°	12.9'	189	W04°
	OMASTRAND	OMA	NDB	326.00	N60°	13.0'	E005°	59.1'	189	W05°
	SOLA	SOL	VOR	114.20	N58°	52.59'	E005°	38.20'	62	W03°
Norway	VOLLO	VOO	VOR	114.85	N60°	32.9'	E005°	07.8'	189	W04°
	VOLLO	VOL	NDB	391.00	N60°	32.2'	E005°	06.8'	189	W04°
Poland										
	KARNICE	KRN	VOR	117.80	N51°	56.8'	E020°	26.8'	584	E03°
	LODZ	LDZ	VOR	112.40	N51°	48.0'	E019°	39.5'	820	E03°
	PIASECZNO	PNO	VOR	112.90	N52°	03.5'	E021°	03.7'	364	E02°
	PIASECZNO	PNO	NDB	330.00	N52°	03.20'	E021°	03.89'	364	
	PRZYSUCHA	TMS	NDB	488.00	N51°	21.4'	E022°	38.0'	364	E02°
	SIEDLCE	SIE	VOR	114.70	N52°	09.7'	E022°	12.1'	364	E03°
	WARSAW	OKE	VOR	113.40	N52°	10.3'	E020°	57.7'	381	E02°
	WARSAW	WAG	NDB	336.00	N52°	12.7'	E020°	48.5'	381	E02°
	WARSAW	W	NDB	361.00	N52°	08.5'	E020°	59.4'	351	E02°
	WARSAW	WAO	NDB	412.00	N52°	05.9'	E021°	01.7'	362	E02°
	WARSAW	WAG	NDB	375.00	N52°	10.6'	E020°	56.1'	362	E02°
	ZABOROWEK	WAR	VOR	114.90	N52°	15.6'	E020°	39.5'	381	E02°
Portugal										
	ARRUDA	LAR	NDB	382.00	N38°	59.59'	W009°	02.19'	373	
	BEJA	BEJ	VOR	115.80	N38°	07.8'	W007°	55.5'	620	W06°
	CAPARICA	CP	NDB	389.00	N38°	38.50'	W009°	13.19'	373	
	ESPICHEL	ESP	VOR	112.50	N38°	25.4'	W009°	11.1'	648	W06°
	FATIMA	FTM	VOR	113.50	N39°	39.9'	W008°	29.5'	676	W05°
	LISBON	LO	NDB	401.00	N38°	51.10'	W009°	05.79'	373	
	LISBON	LIS	VOR	114.80	N38°	53.2'	W009°	09.7'	1,112	W06°
	MONTE REAL	MTL	NDB	336.00	N39°	54.39'	W008°	52.90'	373	
	SINTRA	SRA	VOR	112.10	N38°	49.8'	W009°	20.3'	440	W06°
Russia										
	ANADYR	KB	NDB	790.0	N64°	44.00'	W177°	44.99'		
	BOROVOYE	JK	NDB	816.00	N54°	40.00'	E082°	37.00'	364	E09°
	BRATSK	BRT	VOR	113.60	N56°	22.3'	E101°	41.1'	1,700	W01°
	BUZHAROVO	AR	NDB	1,080.00	N55°	59.0'	E036°	48.0'	627	E11°
	IVANOVSKOYE	UM	NDB	405.00	N55°	52.00'	E036°	54.99'	626	
	KOLYVAN	GV	NDB	660.00	N55°	19.00'	E082°	42.99'	364	E09°
	KOSTINO	KN	NDB	642.00	N56°	18.0'	E037°	43.0'	627	E08°
	LEGOSTAYEVO	OC	NDB	320.00	N54°	37.99'	E083°	49.00'	364	E09°
	MALKA	MK	NDB	345.00	N53°	19.40'	E157°	31.99'	131	
	MATVEYEVSKY	EB	NDB	1,170	N54°	56.00'	E083°	05.00'	364	E10°
	NIKOLSHOE	UJ	NDB	595.00	N55°	10.99'	E165°	59.00'		
	NOVOSIBIRSK	RO	NDB	310.00	N55°	00.19'	E082°	33.79'	360	E09°
	NOVOTRYSHKINO	KD	NDB	715.00	N55°	11.00'	E082°	23.99'	344	E10°
	OPALIKHA	KS	NDB	565.00	N55°	50.0'	E037°	16.0'	620	E08°
	ORENBURG	L	NDB	843.00	N51°	47.79'	E055°	29.39'	383	
	ORENBURG	LM	NDB	415.00	N51°	47.79'	E055°	32.10'	383	
	PETROPAVLOVSK-KAMCHATSK	PR	NDB	535.00	N53°	06.90'	E158°	29.49'	131	
	PETROPAVLOVSK-KAMCHATSKY	Q	NDB	1040.00	N53°	11.4'	E158°	26.5'	131	W06°
	PRETORIIA	PO	NDB	730.00	N52°	15.0'	E054°	19.0'	730	E10°
	PROVIDENIYA	BC	NDB	320.0	N64°	17.49'	W173°	18.99'		
	SAVELOVO	SW	NDB	285.10	N56°	22.0'	E037°	26.0'	627	E08°
	SHEREMETYEVO	MR	VOR	114.60	N55°	57.7'	E037°	20.9'	656	E08°
	SHEREMETYEVO	N	NDB	770.00	N55°	57.90'	E037°	22.49'	626	E08°
	SHEREMETYEVO	AD	NDB	700.00	N55°	59.2'	E037°	30.09'	626	E08°
	SHEREMETYEVO	B	NDB	770.00	N55°	58.70'	E037°	27.90'	626	E08°
	SHEREMETYEVO	M	NDB	338.00	N55°	57.99'	E037°	22.40'	626	E08°
	SHEREMETYEVO	BW	NDB	380.00	N55°	59.09'	E037°	30.60'	619	E08°
	TALMENKA	TM	NDB	988.00	N53°	48.00'	E083°	31.99'	364	
	UST-BOLSHERETSK	UB	NDB	907.00	N52°	49.00'	E156°	16.00'	131	
	UST-BOLSHERETSK	SD	NDB	907.00	N52°	49.00'	E156°	16.00'		
	ZAELTSOVSKY	PG	NDB	860.00	N55°	05.00'	E082°	53.99'	364	
	ZHELTOIE	VL	NDB	5.10	N51°	38.00'	E056°	35.99'	1,003	E10°
Scotland										
	ABEERDEN	AOS	NDB	377.00	N57°	16.10'	W002°	14.70'	600	
	ABERDEEN	ADN	VOR	114.30	N57°	18.59'	W002°	15.90'	600	W07°
	ABERDEEN	AQ	NDB	336.00	N57°	08.29'	W002°	24.19'	600	
	ABERDEEN	ATF	NDB	348.00	N57°	04.69'	W002°	06.29'	600	
	BENBECULA	BEN	VOR	114.40	N57°	28.70'	W007°	21.90'	98	W09°
	GLASGOW	AC	NDB	325.00	N55°	48.90'	W004°	32.49'	36	

State/Country	VOR/NDB Name	Ident.	Type	Freq.	Latitude		Longitude		Altitude	Mag Var
EUROPE NAVAIDS										
Scotland	GLASGOW	GLG	NDB	350.00	N55°	55.49'	W004°	20.10'	36	
	STORNOWAY	SWY	NDB	669.50	N58°	17.20'	W006°	20.69'	98	
	STORNOWAY	STN	VOR	115.10	N58°	12.40'	W006°	10.99'	98	W09°
	SUMBURGH	SBH	NDB	351.00	N59°	52.99'	W001°	17.60'	85	
	SUMBURGH	SUM	VOR	117.35	N59°	52.80'	W001°	17.09'	85	W07°
	TIREE	TIR	VOR	117.70	N56°	29.60'	W006°	52.49'	36	W09°
Spain	ALCOBENDAS	ACD	NDB	417.00	N40°	35.2'	W003°	40.5'	2,375	W05°
	ARBACON	ARN	NDB	291.00	N40°	57.9'	W003°	07.3'	3,000	W04°
	BAGUR	BGR	VOR	112.20	N41°	56.9'	E003°	12.6'	1,066	W02°
	BARAHONA	BAN	VOR	112.80	N41°	19.5'	W002°	37.7'	3,717	W04°
	BARAJAS	AA	NDB	355.00	N40°	27.09'	W003°	32.36'	1,997	
	BARAJAS	MA	NDB	390.00	N40°	24.1'	W003°	29.3'	1,933	W04°
	BARAJAS	BJ	NDB	308.00	N40°	26.9'	W003°	33.7'	1,949	W04°
	BARAJAS	RS	NDB	326.00	N40°	23.4'	W003°	33.6'	1,959	W04°
	BARAJAS	MD	NDB	369.00	N40°	33.5'	W003°	33.7'	1,936	W04°
	BARCELONA	QUV	VOR	114.30	N41°	17.8'	E002°	05.2'	23	W02°
	BARCELONA	AA	NDB	355.00	N41°	17.30'	E002°	03.10'	22	
	BARCELONA	QA	NDB	338.00	N41°	16.0'	E001°	59.2'	23	W02°
	CALAMOCHA	CMA	VOR	116.00	N40°	52.09'	W001°	17.79'	3,115	W04°
	CAMPO REAL	CPL	VOR	114.50	N40°	19.5'	W003°	22.3'	2,585	W04°
	CASTEJON	CJN	VOR	115.60	N40°	22.4'	W002°	32.7'	3,488	W04°
	COLMENAR VIEJO	CNR	VOR	117.30	N40°	38.7'	W003°	44.3'	2,684	W05°
	DOMINGO	DGO	VOR	112.60	N42°	27.2'	W002°	52.8'	2,126	W04°
	GETAFE	GE	NDB	421.00	N40°	12.0'	W003°	50.6'	2,200	W04°
	LERIDA	LRD	NDB	404.00	N41°	33.3'	E000°	39.0'	705	W03°
	MAELLA	MLA	VOR	112.10	N41°	07.9'	E000°	10.0'	1,184	W03°
	NAVAS DEL REY	NVS	NDB	432.00	N40°	22.2'	W004°	14.9'	3,400	W05°
	REUS	RES	VOR	114.20	N41°	09.0'	E001°	10.1'	272	W02°
	SABADELL	SBD	NDB	367.00	N41°	31.2'	E002°	06.3'	463	W02°
	SOMOSIERRA	SMA	NDB	350.00	N41°	08.2'	W003°	34.7'	4,000	W04°
	TOLEDO	TLD	VOR	113.20	N39°	58.2'	W004°	20.2'	1,936	W04°
	TORRALBA DE ARAGON	TRL	NDB	335.00	N41°	56.5'	W000°	30.5'	600	W03°
	TORREJON	TJZ	VOR	115.10	N40°	28.6'	W003°	28.0'	1,956	W04°
	VILLANUEVA	VNV	NDB	380.00	N41°	12.7'	E001°	42.4'	293	W02°
	VILLATOBAS	VTB	VOR	112.70	N39°	46.8'	W003°	27.4'	2,400	W04°
	ZAMORA	ZMR	VOR	117.10	N41°	31.90'	W005°	38.29'	2,092	W05°
Sweden	BACKA	BAK	VOR	112.70	N57°	33.30'	E011°	58.79'	318	E00°
	DUNKER	DKR	VOR	116.80	N59°	12.49'	E017°	00.89'	141	E02°
	MANTOR	MNT	VOR	114.00	N58°	23.3'	E015°	17.0'	187	E01°
	MANTOR	MNT	VOR	114.00	N58°	23.30'	E015°	17.00'	186	E01°
	RONNE	ROE	VOR	112.00	N55°	04.00'	E014°	45.70'	68	E02°
	SKAVASTA	NW	NDB	364.00	N58°	47.10'	E016°	46.99'	111	
	SKAVASTA	PEO	NDB	398.00	N58°	47.8'	E017°	02.9'	139	E01°
	SKAVASTA	NW	NDB	364.00	N58°	47.1'	E016°	47.0'	112	E01°
	SVEDA	SVD	VOR	116.20	N56°	10.20'	E012°	34.59'	39	E01°
	TROSA	TRS	VOR	114.30	N58°	56.3'	E017°	30.3'	187	E02°
	VASSEN	VSN	VOR	115.30	N58°	18.30'	E015°	42.79'	26	E02°
	VEDBY	VEY	VOR	116.90	N56°	08.90'	E013°	13.20'	26	E00°
Switzerland	FRIBOURG	FRI	VOR	110.85	N46°	46.7'	E007°	13.5'	1,955	W01°
	GENEVA	GVA	VOR	114.60	N46°	15.3'	E006°	08.0'	1,377	W01°
	GLAND	GLA	NDB	320.00	N46°	24.6'	E006°	14.7'	1,352	W01°
	HOCHWALD	HOC	VOR	113.20	N47°	28.1'	E007°	40.0'	2,430	W01°
	LES EPLATURES	LPS	NDB	403.00	N47°	05.09'	E006°	47.70'	1,400	
	NICE	NIZ	VOR	112.40	N43°	46.2'	E007°	15.3'	2,822	W01°
	ZURICH	ZUE	VOR	110.50	N47°	35.6'	E008°	49.1'	1,730	W00°
Turkey	BEYKOZ	BKZ	VOR	117.30	N41°	07.69'	E029°	08.60'	200	E03°
	BEYKOZ	BKZ	NDB	432.00	N41°	07.69'	E029°	08.60'	157	
	BIGA	BIG	VOR	116.90	N40°	17.09'	E027°	21.99'	170	E02°
	CEKMECE	CEK	NDB	328.00	N41°	00.49'	E028°	31.79'	157	
	ESKISEHIR	ESR	NDB	372.00	N39°	48.99'	E030°	31.30'	157	
	ISTANBUL	ST	NDB	340.00	N40°	57.69'	E028°	47.90'	91	
	ISTANBUL	IS	NDB	396.00	N41°	03.50'	E028°	48.40'	157	
	ISTANBUL	IST	VOR	112.50	N40°	58.10'	E028°	48.50'	170	E03°
	MESTA	MES	VOR	117.60	N38°	15.19'	E025°	54.20'	1,167	E02°
	TEKIRDAG	EKI	VOR	116.30	N40°	57.10'	E027°	25.59'	1,062	E02°
	TEKIRDAG	EKI	NDB	360.00	N40°	57.10'	E027°	25.59'	157	
	TOPKAPI	TOP	NDB	370.00	N41°	00.70'	E028°	59.40'	157	
	YALOVA	YAA	VOR	117.70	N40°	33.99'	E029°	22.30'	2,440	E03°
	YALOVA	YAA	NDB	305.00	N40°	33.99'	E029°	22.30'	157	
	YESILKOY	ES	NDB	380.00	N40°	57.69'	E028°	48.59'	91	

State/Country	VOR/NDB Name	Ident.	Type	Freq.	Latitude		Longitude		Altitude	Mag Var

NORTH ATLANTIC NAVAIDS

Azores, Portugal

State/Country	VOR/NDB Name	Ident.	Type	Freq.	Latitude		Longitude		Altitude	Mag Var
	LAJES	LM	VOR	112.30	N38°	47.1'	W027°	06.3'	1,855	W14°
	PONTA DELGADA	MGL	NDB	371.00	N37°	44.4'	W025°	35.1'	300	W12°
	PONTA DELGADA	PD	NDB	351.00	N37°	44.1'	W025°	40.5'	187	W12°
	SANTA MARIA	SMA	NDB	323.00	N36°	59.8'	W025°	10.6'	283	W12°
	SANTA MARIA	VSM	VOR	113.70	N36°	57.7'	W025°	10.0'	308	W12°

Canada, Newfoundland

	DEER LAKE	YDF	VOR	113.30	N49°	14.0'	W057°	12.80'	470	W25°
	GANDER	YQX	VOR	112.70	N48°	54.0'	W054°	32.10'	600	W25°
	GANDER	QX	NDB	280.00	N48°	57.9'	W054°	40.10'	496	W25°
	GOOSE	YYR	VOR	117.30	N53°	19.2'	W060°	17.70'	92	W28°
	GOOSE	Y	NDB	212.00	N53°	16.5'	W060°	31.10'	160	W26°
	GOOSE	YR	NDB	257.00	N53°	20.3'	W060°	31.10'	153	W28°
	RIGOLET	JC	NDB	396.00	N54°	10.6'	W058°	26.10'	40	W30°
	TORBAY	YT	NDB	260.00	N47°	40.2'	W052°	48.50'	461	W24°

Canada, Quebec

	BAIE-COMEAU	YBC	VOR	117.70	N49°	08.03'	W068°	13.31'	0	W22°
	HAVRE ST-PIERRE	YGV	NDB	344.00	N50°	15.88'	W063°	39.90'		
	HEATH POINT	HP	NDB	335.00	N49°	05.10'	W061°	42.03'		
	POINTE-DES-MONTS	TG	NDB	300.00	N49°	18.99'	W067°	22.86'		
	PORT MENIER	PN	NDB	360.00	N49°	50.25'	W064°	23.17'		
	SEPT-ILES	YZV	VOR	114.50	N50°	13.93'	W066°	16.43'	0	W24°
	SEPT-ILES	ZV	NDB	273.00	N50°	12.23'	W066°	09.08'	0	W24°

England

	DOVER	DVR	VOR	114.95	N51°	09.69'	E001°	21.69'	314	W04°
	LANDS END	LND	VOR	114.20	N50°	08.09'	W005°	38.20'	800	W07°
	LONDON	LON	VOR	113.60	N51°	29.20'	W000°	27.90'	111	W05°
	POLE HILL	POL	VOR	112.10	N53°	44.59'	W002°	06.10'	1,400	W06°
	SOUTHHAMPTON	SAM	VOR	113.35	N50°	57.30'	W001°	20.60'	65	W05°
	STRUMBLE	STU	VOR	113.10	N51°	59.70'	W005°	02.29'	600	W07°

Faeroe Islands, Denmark

	MYGGENAES	MY	NDB	337.00	N62°	06.39'	W007°	35.10'	0	
	AKRABERG	AB	NDB	381.00	N61°	23.60'	W006°	40.10'	0	

Greenland

	FREDERIKSHAB	FH	NDB	331.00	N61°	59.79'	W049°	39.09'	0	
	GODTHAB	NK	NDB	273.00	N64°	40.8'	W051°	22.70'	281	W37°
	GODTHAB	QT	NDB	258.00	N64°	20.7'	W051°	35.20'	281	W37°
	GODTHAB	GH	NDB	314.00	N64°	10.9'	W051°	45.30'	281	W37°
	KOOK ISLANDS	KU	NDB	298.00	N64°	04.30'	W052°	01.09'	0	
	KULUSUK	DA	NDB	377.00	N65°	34.30'	W037°	12.69'	114	
	KULUSUK	KK	NDB	283.00	N65°	31.80'	W037°	09.39'	114	
	PRINS CHRISTIAN SUND	OZN	NDB	372.00	N60°	03.50'	W043°	09.79'	0	
	SIMIUTAQ	SI	NDB	279.00	N60°	41.10'	W046°	35.99'	0	
	SONDRE STROMFJORD	SF	NDB	382.00	N66°	58.09'	W050°	56.89'	163	
	SUKKERTOPPEN	ST	NDB	310.00	N65°	25.19'	W052°	54.49'	0	

Iceland

	ELLIDAVAIN	EL	NDB	335.00	N64°	04.9'	W021°	46.30'	200	W21°
	INGO	IN	NDB	316.00	N63°	48.09'	W016°	38.60'	334	
	INGO	ING	VOR	112.40	N63°	48.2'	W016°	38.60'	335	W17°
	KEFLAVIK	KEF	VOR	112.00	N63°	59.2'	W022°	36.90'	174	W21°
	KEFLAVIK	OK	NDB	364.00	N64°	02.99'	W022°	36.29'	170	
	KEFLAVIK	KF	NDB	392.00	N63°	59.2'	W022°	36.90'	111	W21°
	KILO	OK	NDB	364.00	N64°	03.0'	W022°	36.30'	163	W21°
	REYJAVIK	RK	NDB	355.00	N64°	09.1'	W022°	01.80'	45	W21°
	SKAGI	SA	NDB	379.00	N64°	18.4'	W021°	58.30'	200	W21°
	SKARDSFJARA	SR	NDB	312.60	N63°	31.0'	W017°	58.90'	335	W18°
	VESTMANNAEY JAR	VM	NDB	375.00	N63°	24.0'	W020°	17.30'	250	W20°

Ireland

	BELFAST	BEL	VOR	117.20	N54°	39.70'	W006°	13.69'	193	W08°
	BELFAST CITY	HB	NDB	420.00	N54°	36.90'	W005°	52.90'	193	
	CORK	CRK	VOR	114.60	N51°	50.39'	W008°	29.59'	531	W08°
	CORK	OB	NDB	362.00	N51°	49.29'	W008°	28.80'	531	
	DUBLIN	DUB	VOR	114.90	N53°	29.99'	W006°	18.40'	163	W08°
	DUBLIN	OE	NDB	316.00	N53°	25.80'	W006°	25.69'	163	
	DUBLIN	OP	NDB	397.00	N53°	24.80'	W006°	08.29'	163	
	GLASGOW	GOW	VOR	115.40	N55°	52.19'	W004°	26.69'	36	W07°
	MACHRIHANISH	MAC	VOR	116.00	N55°	25.79'	W005°	38.99'	75	W08°
	SHANNON	SHA	VOR	113.30	N52°	43.29'	W008°	53.09'	52	W08°
	STRUMBLE	STU	NDB	400.00	N52°	00.49'	W005°	01.00'	600	

State/Country	VOR/NDB Name	Ident.	Type	Freq.	Latitude		Longitude		Altitude	Mag Var
NORTH ATLANTIC NAVAIDS										
Scotland										
	ABEERDEN	AOS	NDB	377.00	N57°	16.10'	W002°	14.70'	600	
	ABERDEEN	ADN	VOR	114.30	N57°	18.59'	W002°	15.90'	600	W07°
	ABERDEEN	AQ	NDB	336.00	N57°	08.29'	W002°	24.19'	600	
	ABERDEEN	ATF	NDB	348.00	N57°	04.69'	W002°	06.29'	600	
	BENBECULA	BEN	VOR	114.40	N57°	28.70'	W007°	21.90'	98	W09°
	GLASGOW	AC	NDB	325.00	N55°	48.90'	W004°	32.49'	36	
	GLASGOW	GLG	NDB	350.00	N55°	55.49'	W004°	20.10'	36	
	STORNOWAY	SWY	NDB	669.50	N58°	17.20'	W006°	20.69'	98	
	STORNOWAY	STN	VOR	115.10	N58°	12.40'	W006°	10.99'	98	W09°
	SUMBURGH	SBH	NDB	351.00	N59°	52.99'	W001°	17.60'	85	
	SUMBURGH	SUM	VOR	117.35	N59°	52.80'	W001°	17.09'	85	W07°
	TIREE	TIR	VOR	117.70	N56°	29.60'	W006°	52.49'	36	W09°

AIRPORT DIRECTORY

FS 5.1 CD contains 341 airports around the world, but the FS 5.1 floppy disk version has only the default 107 airports that existed in the previous FS 5.0 version. Since the FS 5.1 CD version includes 234 new airports, facilities, and hundreds of new VOR/NDB Navaids for the rest of the world, it is well-worth paying more for it so you can enjoy navigating and visiting over 118 new countries and states.

Location	City	Airport Name	Ident.	Latitude	Longitude	ILS Runway & Freq.	ATIS Freq.
AFRICA							
Azores	SANTA MARIA	SANTA MARIA	LPAZ	N36° 58' 24"	W25° 10' 18"	18 - 110.3	118.1
Canary Island	GRAN CANARIA	GRAN CANARIA	GCLP	N27° 55' 48"	W15° 23' 06"	03L - 109.9	118.6
Egypt	CAIRO	CAIRO INTL	HECA	N30° 07' 18"	W31° 24' 18"	05 - 109.9	122.6
						23R - 110.3	
						23L - 109.5	
Ivory Coast	ABIDJAN	PORT BOUET	DIAP	N05° 15' 06"	W03° 55' 42"	21 - 110.3	118
Kenya	NAIROBI	NAIROBI JOMO KENYATTA	HKNA	S01° 19' 06"	E36° 55' 36"	06 - 110.3	118.7
Madagascar	ANTANANARIVO	IVATO	FMMI	S18° 47' 42"	E47° 28' 36"	11 - 109.5	118.1
Morocco	CASABLANCA	MOHAMED V	GMMN	N33° 22' 00"	W07° 35' 00"	35 - 109.9	118.5
Nigeria	LAGOS	MURTALA	DNMM	N06° 34' 30"	E03° 19' 06"	01L - 109.3	123.8
						09R - 109.3	
Seychelles	SEYCHELLES	SEYCHELLES INTL	FSIA	S04° 40' 18"	E55° 31' 24"	31 - 110.3	118.3
South Africa	CAPE TOWN	D.F. MALAN	FACT	S33° 58' 06"	E18° 36' 18"	01 - 110.3	118.1
						19 - 109.1	
	JOHANNESBURG	JAN SMUTS	FAJS	S26° 08' 00"	E28° 14' 36"	03R - 109.1	118.1
						03L - 110.3	
						21L - 109.9	
Sudan	KHARTOUM	KHARTOUM	HSSS	N15° 36' 00"	E32° 33' 30"	18 - 110.9	119.2
						36 - 110.3	
Zaire	KINSHASA	N'DJILI INTL	FZAA	S04° 23' 06"	E15° 27' 00"	24 - 110.3	118.1
Zimbabwe	HARARE	HARARE INTL	FVHA	S17° 55' 54"	E31° 05' 36"	05 - 110.3	118.1
ASIA							
Christmas Island	CHRISTMAS IS.	CHRISTMAS ISLAND	YPXM	S10° 27' 00"	E105° 41' 24"		122.8
Hong Kong	HONG KONG	HONG KONG INTL	VHHH	N22° 19' 06"	E114° 12' 00"	31 - 109.9	128.2
India	BOMBAY	BOMBAY	VABB	N19° 05' 30"	E72° 52' 00"	27 - 110.3	126.4
	CALCUTTA	CALCUTTA	VECC	N22° 39' 12"	E88° 27' 00"	01R - 109.9	126.4
						19L - 110.3	
Indonesia	DEN PASAR	BALI INTL	WRRR	S08° 45' 00"	E115° 10' 00"	27 - 110.3	126.2
Israel	TEL AVIV	TEL AVIV BEN GURION	LLBG	N32° 00' 36"	E34° 52' 36"	12 - 110.3	132.5
						26 - 108.7	
Japan	KUSHIRO	KUSHIRO	RJCK	N43° 02' 18"	E144° 11' 48"	17 - 108.9	118.5
	TOKYO	TOKYO INTL (HANEDA)	RJTT	N35° 32' 54"	E139° 46' 30"	22 - 111.7	128.8
						33 - 110.9	
						34 - 110.1	
Korea	SEOUL	KIMPO INTL	RKSS	N37° 33' 18"	E126° 48' 00"	14R - 110.1	126.4
						14L - 109.9	
						32R - 110.7	
Kuwait	KUWAIT	KUWAIT INTL	OKBK	N29° 13' 24"	E47° 58' 06"	15L - 110.1	118.3
						33R - 110.5	
						33L - 109.5	
Maldives	MALE	MALE INTL	VRMM	N04° 11' 30"	E73° 32' 00"	36 - 108.7	118.1
Pakistan	KARACHI	QUAID-E-AZAM INTL	OPKC	N24° 56' 06"	E67° 09' 00"	25R - 109.7	126.7
Philippines	MANILA	NINOY AQUINO INTL	RPMM	N14° 30' 42"	E121° 00' 54"	06 - 109.1	126.4
						24 - 109.9	
People's Republic of China	SHANGHAI	HONGQIAO	ZSSS	N31° 11' 54"	E121° 20' 00"	18 - 110.3	118.1
						36 - 110.3	
Saudi Arabia	RIYADH	KING KHALID INTL	OERK	N24° 57' 48"	E46° 42' 30"	15L - 109.5	118.6
						15R - 110.5	
						33L - 110.1	
						33R - 109.1	

Location	City	Airport Name	Ident.	Latitude	Longitude	ILS Runway & Freq.	ATIS Freq.
Singapore	SINGAPORE	CHANGI	WSSS	N01° 21' 36"	E103° 59' 30"	02R - 108.3	128.6
						02L - 110.9	
						20R - 108.9	
						20L - 109.7	
Sri Lanka	COLOMBO	KATUNAYAKE	VCBI	N07° 10' 48"	E79° 53' 00"	22 - 110.3	118.7
Taiwan	KAOHSIUNG	KAOHSIUNG INTL	RCKH	N22° 34' 36"	E120° 20' 36"	09L - 108.3	127.8
Thailand	BANGKOK	BANGKOK INTL	VTBD	N13° 54' 54"	E100° 36' 30"	21R - 109.3	126.4
Yemen	ADEN	ADEN INTL	OYAA	N12° 49' 42"	E45° 01' 54"		118.7

EUROPE

Location	City	Airport Name	Ident.	Latitude	Longitude	ILS Runway & Freq.	ATIS Freq.
Austria	INNSBRUCK	INNSBRUCK	LOWI	N47° 15' 42"	E11° 20' 42"	08 - 109.7	126.02
						26 - 111.1	
	SALZBURG	SALZBURG	LOWS	N47° 47' 42"	E13° 00' 12"		
	ST JOHANN	SAINT JOHANN	LOIJ	N47° 31' 18"	E12° 27' 00"		
	SCHARDING	SCHARDING	LOXX	N48° 24' 00"	E13° 27' 00"		
	VIENNA	SCHWECHAT	LOWW	N48° 06' 42"	E16° 34' 18"	11 - 108.1	118.72
						16 - 108.5	
						29 - 109.7	
						34 - 108.1	
	ZELL AM SEE	ZELL AM SEE	LOWZ	N47° 17' 36"	E12° 47' 18"		
Belgium	BRUSSELS	BRUSSELS NATIONAL	EBBR	N50° 54' 06"	E04° 29' 18"	02 - 109.9	132.47
						25R - 108.9	
						25L - 110.3	
Czech	PRAGUE	RUZYNE	LKPR	N50° 06' 06"	E14° 15' 42"	24 - 109.1	122.15
						31 - 109.5	
Denmark	COPENHAGEN	KASTRUP	EKCH	N55° 37' 06"	E12° 39' 04"	04R - 109.3	122.85
						04L - 110.5	
						12 - 109.9	
						22R - 110.9	
						22L - 109.5	
						30 - 108.9	
Finland	HELSINKI	VANTAA	EFHK	N60° 19' 00"	E24° 58' 00"	04 - 111.3	135.7
						15 - 109.1	
						22 - 110.3	
France	AMIENS	GLISY	LFAY	N49° 52' 24"	E02° 23' 24"		
	BEAUVAIS	TILLE	LFOB	N49° 27' 18"	E02° 06' 54"		
	CAMBRAI	NIERGNIES AB	LFYG	N50° 08' 36"	E03° 15' 54"		
	CHATEAUDUN	CHATEAUDUN AB	LFOC	N48° 03' 30"	E01° 22' 48"		
	DEAUVILLE	ST GATIEN	LFRG	N49° 21' 48"	E00° 09' 54"		
	JOIGNY	JOIGNY	LFGK	N47° 59' 42"	E03° 23' 30"		
	LE HAVR	OCTEVILLE	LFOH	N49° 32' 06"	E00° 05' 24"		119.5
	LE MANS	ARNAGE	LFRM	N47° 57' 00"	E00° 12' 12"		
	PARIS	CHARLES DEGAULLE	LFPG	N49° 00' 36"	E02° 32' 54"	10 - 108.7	128
						28 - 109.1	
						09 - 110.1	
						27 - 110.7	
	PARIS	LE BOURGET	LFPB	N48° 58' 18"	E02° 26' 36"		120
	PARIS	ORLY	LFPO	N48° 43' 30"	E02° 22' 54"	07 - 108.5	126.5
						26 - 109.5	
						02L - 110.3	
						25 - 110.9	
	PERONNE-ST. QUENTIN	PERONNE-ST. QUENTIN	LFAG	N49° 52' 12"	E03° 01' 48"		
	PERSAN-BEAUMONT	PERSAN-BEAUMONT	LFPA	N49° 10' 00"	E02° 18' 48"		
	PONTOISE	CORMEILLES-EN-VEXIN	LFPT	N49° 05' 54"	E02° 02' 30"		
	REIMS	CHAMPAGNE AB	LFSR	N49° 18' 42"	E04° 03' 06"		
	ROUEN	BOOS	LFOP	N49° 23' 30"	E01° 11' 06"		
	ST ANDRE DE L'EURE	ST ANDRE DE L'EURE	LFFD	N48° 53' 54"	E01° 15' 00"		
	TOUSSUS-LE-NOBLE	TOUSSUS-LE-NOBLE	LFPN	N48° 45' 06"	E02° 06' 48"		
	TROYES	BARBEREY	LFQB	N48° 19' 18"	E04° 01' 06"		
Germany	AALEN-HEIDENHEIM	ELCHINGEN	EDTA	N48° 46' 42"	E10° 16' 00"		
	ARNBRUCK	ARNBRUCK	EDYB	N49° 07' 36"	E12° 59' 12"		
	AUGSBURG	AUGSBURG	EDMA	N48° 25' 36"	E10° 56' 00"		118.22
	DEGGENDORF	DEGGENDORF	EDMW	N48° 49' 54"	E12° 52' 54"		
	DONAUWORTH-GENDERKINGEN	DONAUWORTH-GENDERKINGEN	EDMQ	N48° 42' 12"	E10° 51' 06"		
	EGGENFELDEN	EGGENFELDEN	EDME	N48° 23' 48"	E12° 43' 30"		
	FURSTENZELL	FURSTENZELL	EDMF	N48° 30' 48"	E13° 20' 54"		
	GIENGEN / BRENZ	GIENGEN / BRENZ	EDGI	N48° 38' 12"	E10° 13' 00"		
	GUNZENHAUSEN	REUTBERG	EDMH	N49° 06' 48"	E10° 47' 00"		
	HAMBURG	HAMBURG	EDDH	N53° 37' 54"	E09° 59' 24"	05 - 110.5	124.27
						15 - 111.1	
						23 - 111.5	
	JESENWANG	JESENWANG	EDMJ	N48° 10' 30"	E11° 07' 36"		122.42

Location	City	Airport Name	Ident.	Latitude	Longitude	ILS Runway & Freq.	ATIS Freq.
	LANDSHUT	LANDSHUT	EDML	N48° 30' 48"	E12° 02' 12"		
	LEUTKIRCH	UNTERZEIL	EDYL	N47° 51' 36"	E10° 00' 54"		
	MINDELHEIM	MATTSIES	EDMN	N48° 06' 36"	E10° 31' 30"		
	MUHLDORF	MUHLDORF	EDMY	N48° 16' 48"	E12° 30' 24"		
	MUNICH	MUNICH	EDDM	N48° 21' 18"	E11° 47' 18"	26L - 108.3	118.37
						25R - 108.7	
						08L - 110.3	
						08R - 110.9	
	NORDLINGEN	NORDLINGEN	EDNO	N48° 52' 24"	E10° 30' 24"		
	OBERPFAFFENHOFEN	OBERPFAFFENHOFEN	EDMO	N48° 04' 54"	E11° 17' 06"		
	REGENSBURG	OBERHUB	EDYR	N49° 08' 36"	E12° 05' 00"		
	STRAUBING	WALLMUHLE	EDMS	N48° 54' 06"	E12° 31' 12"		
	VILSHOFEN	VILSHOFEN	EDMV	N48° 38' 12"	E13° 11' 48"		
	VOGTAREUTH	VOGTAREUTH	EDYV	N47° 56' 48"	E12° 12' 24"		
Greece	ATHENS	ATHENS	LGAT	N37° 53' 48"	E23° 43' 42"	33R - 110.3	123.4
Iceland	KEFLAVIK	KEFLAVIK	BIKF	N63° 59' 06"	W22° 36' 18"	11 - 109.5	118.3
						20 - 110.3	
Ireland	DUBLIN	DUBLIN	EIDW	N53° 25' 54"	W06° 15' 12"	10 - 108.9	124.52
						16 - 111.5	
						28 - 108.9	
Italy	ROME	FIUMICINO	LIRF	N41° 48' 42"	E12° 15' 12"	16R - 110.3	118.7
						16L - 108.1	
						25 - 109.7	
						34L - 108.9	
						34R - 109.3	
Norway	BERGEN	FLESLAND	ENBR	N60° 17' 36"	E05° 13' 12"	18 - 109.9	125.25
						36 - 110.5	
Poland	WARSAW	OKECIE	EPWA	N52° 09' 60"	E20° 58' 06"	11 - 109.9	118.3
						33 - 110.3	
Portugal	LISBON	LISBON	LPPT	N38° 46' 24"	W09° 08' 00"	03 - 109.1	118.1
						21 - 109.5	
Russia	MOSCOW	SHEREMETYEVO	UUEE	N55° 58' 18"	E37° 24' 54"	07R - 109.1	126.37
						25L - 110.5	
	ORENBURG	ORENBURG CENTRAL	UWOO	N51° 47' 48"	E55° 27' 24"	08 - 109.9	128
						26 - 109.3	
Spain	BARCELONA	BARCELONA	LEBL	N41° 17' 54"	E02° 04' 48"	07 - 110.3	118.65
						25 - 109.5	
	MADRID	BARAJAS	LEMD	N40° 28' 34"	W03° 33' 36"	18 - 109.3	118.25
						33 - 109.9	
						36 - 110.3	
Sweden	STOCKHOLM	SKAVSTA	ESKN	N58° 47' 26"	E16° 54' 24"	09 - 111.3	127.7
						27 - 111.9	
Switzerland	GENEVA	COINTRIN	LSGG	N46° 14' 24"	E06° 06' 36"	05 - 110.9	125.72
						23 - 109.9	
Turkey	ISTANBUL	ISTANBUL ATATURK	LTBA	N40° 58' 36"	E28° 48' 54"	06 - 110.3	128.2
						18 - 111.1	
						36 - 108.1	
United Kingdom	GLASGOW	GLASGOW	EGPF	N55° 52' 18"	W04° 25' 54"	05 - 110.1	118.8
						23 - 110.1	
	LONDON	HEATHROW	EGLL	N51° 28' 36"	W00° 27' 36"	09R - 109.5	133.7
						09L - 110.3	
						27R - 110.3	
						27L - 109.5	

SOUTH AMERICA

Location	City	Airport Name	Ident.	Latitude	Longitude	ILS Runway & Freq.	ATIS Freq.
Argentina	BUENOS AIRES	EZEIZA INTL-MINISTRO PISTARINI	SAEZ	S34° 49' 06"	W58° 32' 12"	11 - 110.1	119.1
						35 - 108.7	
Bolivia	LA PAZ	KENNEDY INTL	SLLP	S16° 30' 36"	W68° 10' 54"	09R - 110.3	118.3
Brazil	BRASILIA	BRASILIA INTL	SBBR	S15° 51' 42"	W47° 54' 42"	11 - 110.3	127.8
						29 - 109.3	
	NATAL	AUGUSTO SEVERO	SBNT	S05° 54' 30"	W35° 14' 54"		118.7
	RIO DE JANEIRO	RIO DE JANEIRO INTL-GALEAO	SBGL	S22° 48' 42"	W43° 15' 00"	10 - 109.3	127.6
						15 - 110.3	
						28 - 111.5	
Chile	SANTIAGO	ARTURO MERINO BENITEZ INTL	SCEL	S33° 23' 24"	W70° 47' 06"	17 - 110.3	132.1
Columbia	SANTAFE DE BOGATA	ELDORADO INTL	SKBO	N04° 42' 24"	W74° 08' 30"	12 - 109.9	118.1
Ecuador	QUITO	MARISCAL SUCRE INTL	SEQU	S00° 08' 18"	W78° 29' 06"	35 - 110.5	118.1
French Guiana	CAYENNE	ROCHAMBEAU	SOCA	N04° 49' 06"	W52° 21' 42"	08 - 110.3	118.1
Guatemala	GUATEMALA CITY	LA AURORA INTL	MGGT	N14° 34' 54"	W90° 31' 42"		
Paraguay	ASUNCION	ASUNCION-SILVIO PETTIROSSI INTL	SGAS	S25° 14' 06"	W57° 31' 00"	20 - 109.5	118.1
Peru	LIMA-CALLAO	JORGE CHAVEZ INTL	SPIM	S12° 01' 06"	W77° 06' 42"	15 - 109.7	118.1

Location	City	Airport Name	Ident.	Latitude	Longitude	ILS Runway & Freq.	ATIS Freq.

NORTH AMERICA - UNITED STATES

Location	City	Airport Name	Ident.	Latitude	Longitude	ILS Runway & Freq.	ATIS Freq.
Alabama	HUNTSVILLE	HUNTSVILLE INTL-CARL T JONES FIELD	HSV	N34° 38' 21"	W86° 45' 56"	18L - 111.9 18R - 109.3 36L - 108.5	121.25
	MONTGOMERY	DANNELLY FIELD	MGM	N32° 17' 58"	W86° 23' 26"	10 - 109.9 28 - 108.5	124.42
Alaska	ADAK ISLAND	ADAK ISLAND	NUD	N51° 52' 54"	W176° 38' 48"	23 - 108.9	
	ANCHORAGE	ANCHORAGE INTL	ANC	N61° 10' 11"	W149° 58' 42"	06R - 111.3 06L - 109.9 Loc only	118.4
	BARROW	WILEY POST-WILL RODGERS MEMORIAL	BRW	N71° 17' 07"	W156° 45' 57"	06 - 109.1	123.6
	FAIRBANKS	FAIRBANKS INTL	FAI	N64° 48' 09"	W147° 51' 05"	01L - 109.1 19R - 110.3	124.4
	UNALASKA	UNALASKA	DUT	N53° 53' 54"	W166° 32' 42"		122.6
Arizona	GRAND CANYON	GRAND CANYON	GCN	N35° 57' 08"	W112° 08' 49"	03 - 108.9	124.3
	PHOENIX	PHOENIX SKY HARBOR INTL	PHX	N33° 26' 27"	W112° 00' 31"	08R - 108.3 26R - 111.75	124.3
Arkansas	LITTLE ROCK	ADAMS FIELD	LIT	N34° 43' 45"	W92° 13' 45"	04L - 110.3 22L - 110.7 22R - 110.3	125.65
California	ALAMEDA	ALAMEDA NAS/NIMITZ FIELD	NGZ	N37° 27' 46"	W122° 19' 00"		
	AVALON	CATALINA ISLAND	AVX	N33° 24' 17"	W118° 24' 57"		
	CARLSBAD	MC CLELLAN-PALOMAR	CRQ	N33° 07' 41"	W117° 16' 49"		
	CHICO	CHICO MUNI	CIC	N39° 47' 44"	W121° 51' 27"		
	CHINO	CHINO	CNO	N33° 58' 29"	W117° 38' 12"		
	COLUMBIA	COLUMBIA	O22	N38° 01' 50"	W120° 25' 02"		
	COMPTON	COMPTON	CPM	N33° 53' 25"	W118° 14' 32"		
	CONCORD	BUCHANAN FIELD	CCR	N37° 59' 14"	W122° 03' 29"		124.7
	CORONA	CORONA MUNI	L66	N33° 53' 51"	W117° 36' 09"		
	CROWS LANDING	CROWS LANDING NALF	NRC	N37° 24' 36"	W121° 06' 38"		
	EL MONTE	EL MONTE	EMT	N34° 05' 09"	W118° 02' 05"		
	FALLBROOK	FALLBROOK COMMUNITY AIR PARK	L18	N33° 21' 16"	W117° 14' 57"		
	FRESNO	CHANDLER DOWNTOWN	FCH	N36° 43' 57"	W119° 49' 09"		121.35
	FRESNO	FRESNO AIR TERMINAL	FAT	N36° 46' 34"	W119° 42' 58"		
	GARBERVILLE	GARBERVILLE	O16	N40° 05' 11"	W123° 48' 52"		
	HALF MOON BAY	HALF MOON BAY	HAF	N37° 30' 49"	W122° 29' 59"		
	HAWTHORNE	HAWTHORNE MUNI	HHR	N33° 55' 22"	W118° 20' 06"		
	HAYWARD	HAYWARD AIR TERMINAL	HWD	N37° 39' 37"	W122° 07' 21"		
	LA VERNE	BRACKETT FIELD	POC	N34° 05' 31"	W117° 46' 50"		
	LITTLE RIVER	LITTLE RIVER	O48	N39° 15' 43"	W123° 45' 13"		
	LIVERMORE	LIVERMORE MUNI	LVK	N37° 41' 37"	W121° 49' 13"		
	LODI	LODI	1O3	N38° 12' 10"	W121° 16' 11"		
	LODI	KINGDOM AIRPARK	O20	N38° 05' 32"	W121° 21' 23"		
	LOS ANGELES	LOS ANGELES INTL	LAX	N33° 57' 02"	W118° 24' 59"	06L - 108.5 24R - 108.5 07R - 109.9 07L - 111.1 25R - 111.1 06R - 111.7 25L - 109.9 24L - 111.7	133.8
	MARYSVILLE	YUBA COUNTY	MYV	N39° 05' 54"	W121° 34' 07"		
	MERCED	MERCED MUNI-MACREADY FIELD	MCE	N37° 17' 05"	W120° 30' 49"		
	MODESTO	MODESTO CITY	MOD	N37° 37' 30"	W120° 57' 06"		
	MONTEREY	MONTEREY PENINSULA	MRY	N36° 35' 12"	W121° 50' 20"		
	MOUNTAIN VIEW	MOFFETT FIELD NAS	NUQ	N37° 25' 02"	W122° 02' 51"		
	NOVATO	HAMILTON (AFB)	NZZ	N38° 03' 34"	W122° 30' 28"		
	OAKLAND	METRO OAKLAND INTL	OAK	N37° 43' 39"	W122° 12' 48"	11 - 111.9 27R - 109.9 29 - 108.7	128.5
	OCEANSIDE	OCEANSIDE MUNI	L32	N33° 13' 04"	W117° 21' 07"		
	ONTARIO	ONTARIO INTL	ONT	N34° 03' 24"	W117° 36' 09"	08L - 109.7 26L - 109.7 26R - 109.7	
	OROVILLE	OROVILLE MUNI	OVE	N39° 29' 20"	W121° 37' 23"		
	PALO ALTO	PALO ALTO	PAO	N37° 27' 39"	W122° 06' 53"		
	PLACERVILLE	PLACERVILLE	PVF	N38° 43' 27"	W120° 45' 11"		
	PORTERVILLE	PORTERVILLE MUNI	PTV	N36° 01' 46"	W119° 03' 45"		122.8
	RED BLUFF	RED BLUFF MUNI	RBL	N40° 09' 03"	W122° 15' 08"		
	RIVERSIDE	RIVERSIDE MUNI	RAL	N33° 57' 07"	W117° 26' 36"		
	SACRAMENTO	SACRAMENTO METRO	SMF	N38° 41' 43"	W121° 34' 48"		
	SACRAMENTO	SACRAMENTO EXEC	SAC	N38° 30' 41"	W121° 29' 43"		

Location	City	Airport Name	Ident.	Latitude	Longitude	ILS Runway & Freq.	ATIS Freq.
	SALINAS	SALINAS MUNI	SNS	N36° 39' 43"	W121° 36' 31"		
	SAN CARLOS	SAN CARLOS	SQL	N37° 30' 44"	W122° 14' 50"		
	SAN DIEGO	SAN DIEGO INTL					
		LINDBERGH FIELD	SAN	N32° 44' 00"	W117° 11' 22"	09 - 110.9	134.8
	SAN FRANCISCO	SAN FRANCISCO INTL	SFO	N37° 37' 07"	W122° 22' 32"	19L - 108.9	118.85
						28L - 109.55	
						28R - 111.7	
						LDA: 28R - 110.75	
	SAN JOSE	REID-HILLVIEW	RHV	N37° 19' 59"	W121° 49' 09"		
	SAN JOSE	SAN JOSE INTL	SJC	N37° 21' 40"	W121° 55' 52"		126.95
	SANTA ANA	JOHN WAYNE AIRPORT-					
		ORANGE COUNTY	SNA	N33° 40' 29"	W117° 52' 09"	19 - 108.3	126
						19R - 111.75	
	SANTA BARBARA	SANTA BARBARA MUNI	SBA	N34° 25' 39"	W119° 50' 31"	07 - 110.3	127.8
	SANTA MONICA	SANTA MONICA MUNI	SMO	N34° 00' 56"	W118° 27' 04"		119.15
	SANTA ROSA	SONAMA COUNTY	STS	N38° 30' 32"	W122° 49' 00"		
	SOUTH LAKE TAHOE	LAKE TAHOE	TVL	N38° 53' 37"	W119° 59' 43"		
	STOCKTON	STOCKTON METRO	SCK	N37° 53' 36"	W121° 14' 10"		
	TORRANCE	ZAMPERINI FIELD	TOA	N33° 48' 13"	W118° 20' 21"		
	TRUCKEE	TRUCKEE-TAHOE	TRK	N39° 39' 12"	W120° 08' 09"		
	VAN NUYS	VAN NUYS	VNY	N34° 12' 48"	W118° 29' 22"	16R - 111.3	118.45
	VISALIA	VISALIA MUNI	VIS	N36° 19' 07"	W119° 23' 34"		
	WATSONVILLE	WATSONVILLE MUNI	WVI	N36° 56' 03"	W121° 47' 30"		
	WILLOWS	WILLOWS-GLENN COUNTY	WLW	N39° 30' 58"	W122° 12' 54"		
Colorado	DENVER	DENVER INTL	DVX	N39° 50' 26"	W104° 42' 19"	07 - 111.55	125.6
						08 - 108.9	
						16 - 111.1	
						17R - 108.5	
						25 - 111.55	
						26 - 108.9	
						34 - 111.1	
						35R - 110.15	
						17L - 110.15	
						35L - 108.5	
	DENVER	STAPLETON INTL	DEN	N39° 45' 33"	W104° 52' 29"	26L - 110.3	124.45
						35L - 110.7	
						35R - 109.3	
						08R - 110.3	
						17L - 109.3	
						36 - 111.9	
						18 - 111.9 Loc only	
	TELLURIDE	TELLURIDE REGIONAL	TEX	N37° 57' 13"	W107° 54' 30"		123
Connecticut	BRIDGEPORT	IGOR I. SIKORSKY					
		MEMORIAL	BDR	N41° 09' 41"	W73° 07' 33"		119.15
	CHESTER	CHESTER	3B9	N41° 23' 02"	W72° 30' 21"		
	DANBURY	DANBURY MUNI	DXR	N41° 22' 14"	W73° 28' 59"		
	DANIELSON	DANIELSON	5B3	N41° 49' 11"	W71° 54' 03"		
	HARTFORD	HARTFORD-BRAINARD	HFD	N41° 44' 01"	W72° 39' 12"		
	MERIDEN	MERIDEN MARKHAM MUNI	MMK	N41° 30' 31"	W72° 49' 46"		
	NEW HAVEN	TWEED-NEW HAVEN	HVN	N41° 15' 49"	W72° 53' 15"		
	OXFORD	WATERBURY- OXFORD	OXC	N41° 28' 53"	W73° 08' 08"		
	WILLIMANTIC	WINDHAM	IJD	N41° 44' 41"	W72° 10' 39"		
	WINDOSOR LOCKS	BRADLEY INTL	BDL	N41° 56' 18"	W72° 40' 47"		
Delaware	WILMINGTON	NEW CASTLE COUNTY	ILG	N39° 40' 43"	W75° 36' 09"	01 - 110.3	118.3
Florida	JACKSONVILLE	JACKSONVILLE INTL	JAX	N30° 29' 59"	W81° 41' 16"	07 - 110.7	125.85
						13 - 108.9	
						25 - 109.1 Loc only	
	MIAMI	MIAMI INTL	MIA	N25° 48' 04"	W80° 17' 07"	09L - 110.3	119.15
						09R - 110.9	
						12 - 108.9	
						27R - 109.1	
						27L - 109.5	
						30 - 111.7 Loc only	
	ORLANDO	ORLANDO INTL	MCO	N28° 25' 18"	W81° 17' 44"	17 - 111.75	121.25
						18R - 111.9	
						35 - 110.5	
						36R - 110.7	
	TALLAHASSEE	TALLAHASSEE REGIONAL	TLH	N30° 23' 29"	W84° 20' 37"	27 - 111.9	119.45
						36 - 110.3	
Georgia	ATLANTA	THE WILLIAM B. HARTSFIELD	ATL	N33° 38' 58"	W84° 25' 27"	08L - 109.3	125.55
						08R - 109.9	
						09L - 110.5	
						26L - 108.7	
						26R - 110.1	
						27L - 108.5	
						27R - 111.3	
						09R - 108.9	

Location	City	Airport Name	Ident.	Latitude	Longitude	ILS Runway & Freq.	ATIS Freq.
Hawaii	HONOLULU	HONOLULU INTL	HNL	N21° 19' 26"	W157° 54' 54"	08L - 109.5 04R - 110.5 LDA: 26L - 109.1	127.9
Idaho	BOISE	BOISE AIR TERMINAL/ GOWEN FIELD	BOI	N43° 33' 57"	W116° 13' 27"	10R - 108.5	123.9
Illinois	BLOOMINGTON/ NORMAL	BLOOMINGTON/ BLOOMINGTON/L	BMI	N40° 28' 51"	W88° 55' 42"		
	CHAMPAIGN/URBANA	UNIVERSITY OF ILLINOIS-WILLARD	CMI	N40° 02' 23"	W88° 16' 55"	32L - 109.1	124.8
	CHICAGO/AURORA	AURORA MUNI	ARR	N41° 46' 19"	W88° 28' 00"		
	CHICAGO	CHICAGO MIDWAY	MDW	N41° 47' 14"	W87° 45' 03"		132.75
	CHICAGO	CHICAGO O'HARE INTL	ORD	N41° 59' 24"	W87° 54' 01"	32L - 108.95 14R - 109.75 04R - 110.1 09L - 110.5 27R - 110.5 32R - 110.75 09R - 111.1 27L - 111.1 04L - 111.3 22R - 111.3 22L - 110.1 14L - 110.9	135.4
	CHICAGO	LANSING MUNI	3HA	N41° 32' 19"	W87° 31' 48"		
	CHICAGO	MERRIL C. MEIGS		N41° 52'	W87° 36'		127.35
	CHICAGO/ SCHAUMBURG	SCHAUMBURG AIR PARK	06C	N41° 59' 21"	W88° 06' 06"		
	CHICAGO	WEST DUPAGE	DPA	N41° 54' 02"	W88° 15' 04"		
	DANVILLE	VERMILION COUNTY	DNV	N40° 12' 01"	W87° 35' 39"		
	DWIGHT	DWIGHT	DTG	N41° 08' 02"	W88° 26' 35"		
	FRANKFORT	FRANKFORT	C18	N41° 28' 39"	W87° 50' 25"		
	GIBSON CITY	GIBSON CITY MUNI	C34	N40° 29' 29"	W88° 16' 00"		
	JOLIET	JOLIET PARK DISTRICT	JOT	N41° 31' 06"	W88° 10' 30"		
	KANKAKEE	GREATER KANKAKEE	IKK	N41° 04' 12"	W87° 50' 36"		
	MONEE	SANGER	C56	N41° 22' 39"	W87° 40' 43"		
	MORRIS	MORRIS MUNI JAMES R. WASHBURN FIELD	C09	N41° 25' 31"	W88° 25' 07"		
	NEW LENOX	HOWELL-NEW LENOX	1C2	N41° 28' 46"	W87° 55' 20"		
	PAXTON	PAXTON	1C1	N40° 26' 56"	W88° 07' 39"		
	PLAINFIELD	CLOW INTL	1C5	N41° 41' 45"	W88° 07' 45"		
	CHICAGO/ ROMEOVILLE	LEWIS UNIVERSITY	LOT	N41° 36' 22"	W88° 05' 10"		
	URBANA	FRASCA FIELD	C16	N40° 08' 42"	W88° 12' 01"		
Indiana	INDIANAPOLIS	INDIANAPOLIS INTL	IND	N39° 43' 28"	W86° 17' 14"	05L - 109.3 05R - 111.15 14 - 110.5 23R - 110.9 32 - 110.5 23L - 111.75	124.4
Iowa	SIOUX CITY	SIOUX GATEWAY	SUX	N42° 24' 01"	W96° 23' 09"	13 - 111.3 31 - 109.3	119.45
Kansas	GREAT BEND	GREAT BEND MUNI	GBD	N38° 20' 50"	W98° 51' 26"	35 - 111.9 Loc only	122.8
	TOPEKA	PHILIP BILLARD MUNI	TOP	N39° 04' 05"	W95° 37' 22"	13 - 110.7	118.7
Kentucky	LOUISVILLE	STANDIFORD FIELD	SDF	N38° 10' 23"	W85° 44' 13"	01 - 110.3 19 - 111.3 29 - 109.1	118.15
Louisiana	NEW ORLEANS	NEW ORLEANS INTL/ MOISANT FIELD	MSY	N29° 59' 36"	W90° 15' 13"	01 - 111.7 10 - 109.9 28 - 109.9	127.55
Maine	PORTLAND	PORTLAND INTL JETPORT	PWM	N43° 38' 41"	W70° 18' 42"	11 - 109.9 29 - 109.9	119.5
Maryland	BALTIMORE	BALTIMORE-WASHINGTON INTL	BWI	N39° 10' 25"	W76° 39' 56"	10 - 109.7 15R - 111.7 28 - 109.7 15L - 111.95 33R - 111.95 33L - 111.7	127.8
Massachusetts	BOSTON	GENERAL E.L.LOGAN INTL	BOS	N42° 22' 05"	W71° 00' 33"		135
	MARTHA'S VINEYARD	MARTHA'S VINEYARD	MVY	N41° 23' 30"	W70° 36' 48"	24 - 108.7	126.25
	SOUTHBRIDGE	SOUTHBRIDGE MUNI	3B0	N42° 06' 03"	W72° 02' 14"		
Michigan	GRAND RAPIDS	KENT COUNTY INTL	GRR	N42° 53' 24"	W85° 31' 41"	08R - 108.3 26L - 109.7	127.1
	MARQUETTE	MARQUETTE COUNTY	MQT	N46° 32' 04"	W87° 33' 31"	08 - 110.5	123

Location	City	Airport Name	Ident.	Latitude	Longitude	ILS Runway & Freq.	ATIS Freq.
Minnesota	DULUTH	DULUTH INTL	DLH	N46° 50' 32"	W92° 10' 56"	09 - 110.3	124.1
						27 - 108.7	
	MINNEAPOLIS	MINNEAPOLIS-SAINT-PAUL INTL	MSP	N44° 53' 08"	W93° 13' 10"	04 - 109.3	135.35
						11L - 110.7	
						11R - 110.3	
						29L - 110.3	
						29R - 109.9	
						22 - 110.5	
Mississippi	JACKSON	ALLEN C. THOMPSON FIELD	JAN	N32° 19' 02"	W90° 04' 21"	15L - 110.5	121.5
						15L - 110.5	
Missouri	KANSAS CITY	KANSAS CITY INTL	MCI	N39° 18' 28"	W94° 43' 30"	01 - 110.5	128.35
						09 - 109.7	
						19R - 109.1	
						19L - 109.55	
	ST LOUIS	LAMBERT INTL	STL	N38° 45' 05"	W90° 22' 09"	12L - 108.9	120.45
						12R - 109.7	
						24 - 110.3	
						30R - 111.3	
						30L - 111.5	
						LDA: 30L - 110.55	
						LDA: 12L - 110.1	
Montana	BILLINGS	LOGAN INTL	BIL	N45° 48' 30"	W108° 32' 51"	09L - 110.3	126.3
	GREAT FALLS	GREAT FALLS INTL	GTF	N47° 28' 46"	W111° 22' 07"	03 - 111.3	126.6
Nebraska	LINCOLN	LINCOLN MUNI	LNK			17R - 111.1	118.5
						35L - 109.9	
Nevada	LAS VEGAS	MC CARRAN INTL	LAS	N36° 05' 30"	W115° 09' 38"	25L - 111.75	125.6
						25R - 110.3	
	MINDEN	DOUGLAS COUNTY	MEV	N39° 00' 01"	W119° 45' 10"	16R - 110.9	
	RENO	RENO CANNON INTL	RNO	N39° 29' 46"	W119° 46' 04"	16R - 110.9	124.35
	RENO	RENO/STEAD	4SD	N39° 39' 35"	W119° 52' 54"		122.8
	TONOPAH	TONOPAH	TPH	N38° 03' 44"	W117° 05' 00"		123
New Hampshire	BERLIN	BERLIN MUNI	BML	N44° 34' 29"	W71° 10' 32"		122.7
	MANCHESTER	MANCHESTER	MHT			35 - 109.1	119.55
New Jersey	ATLANTIC CITY	ATLANTIC CITY INTL	ACY	N39° 27' 25"	W74° 34' 48"	13 - 109.1	120.3
New Mexico	ALBUQUERQUE	ALBUQUERQUE INTL	ABQ	N35° 01' 59"	W106° 37' 03"	08 - 111.9	118
	SANTA FE	SANTA FE CO. MUNI	SAF	N35° 37' 03"	W106° 05' 17"	02 - 111.7	128.55
New York	FARMINGDALE	FARMINGDALE/REPUBLIC	FRG	N40° 43' 45"	W73° 24' 51"		
	ISLIP	ISLIP / LONG ISLAND MAC ARTHUR	ISP	N40° 47' 43"	W73° 06' 12"		
	NEW YORK CITY	JOHN F. KENNEDY INTL	JFK	N40° 38' 07"	W73° 46' 30"		128.72
	NEW YORK CITY	LA GUARDIA	LGA	N40° 46' 38"	W73° 52' 38"		
	WHITE PLAINS	WHITE PLAINS/ WESTCHESTER COUNTY	HPN	N41° 03' 56"	W73° 42' 28"		
North Carolina	RALEIGH/DURHAM	RALEIGH DURHAM INTL	RDU	N35° 53' 02"	W78° 47' 24"	05L - 109.1	123.8
						05R - 109.5	
						23L - 108.5	
						23R - 111.7	
North Dakota	BISMARCK	BISMARCK MUNI	BIS	N46° 46' 04"	W100° 44' 31"	13 - 111.5	119.35
						31 - 110.3	
	GRAND FORKS	GRAND FORKS INTL	GFK	N47° 57' 08"	W97° 10' 34"	35L - 109.1	119.4
Ohio	CINCINNATI	CINCINNATI MUNI- LUNKEN FIELD	LUK	N39° 06' 15"	W84° 25' 17"	20L - 110.9	120.25
	COLUMBUS	PORT COLUMBUS INTL	CMH	N39° 59' 27"	W82° 52' 38"	10L - 109.1	124.6
						10R - 108.7	
						28L - 108.7	
Oklahoma	OKLAHOMA CITY	WILEY POST	PWA	N35° 32' 03"	W97° 38' 49"	17L - 108.7	132.75
	OKLAHOMA CITY	WILL ROGERS WORLD	OKC	N35° 23' 49"	W97° 36' 23"	17R - 110.7	125.85
						35R - 110.9	
	TULSA	TULSA INTL	TUL	N36° 11' 43"	W95° 53' 13"	18L - 109.7	124.9
						18R - 111.1	
						36R - 110.3	
Oregon	PORTLAND	PORTLAND INTL	PDX	N45° 35' 21"	W122° 36' 25"	10R - 109.9	128.35
						28R - 111.3	
						20 - 108.9 Loc only	
Pennsylvania	PHILADELPHIA	PHILADELPHIA INTL	PHL	N39° 51' 51"	W75° 15' 25"	09R - 109.3	133.4
						17 - 108.75	
						09L - 108.95	
						27R - 109.3	
						27L - 109.3	
	PITTSBURGH	PITTSBURGH INTL	PIT	N40° 29' 21"	W80° 13' 32"	10L - 111.7	127.25
						10R - 108.9	
						28L - 108.9	
						32 - 111.3	
						28R - 111.7	
Puerto Rico	SAN JUAN	LUIS MUNOZ MARIN INTL	SJU	N18° 26' 38"	W66° 00' 05"	08 - 110.3	125.8
						10 - 109.7	

Location	City	Airport Name	Ident.	Latitude	Longitude	ILS Runway & Freq.	ATIS Freq.
Rhode Island	BLOCK ISLAND	BLOCK ISLAND STATE	BID	N41° 10' 05"	W71° 34' 40"		
	PROVIDENCE	THEODORE FRANCIS GREEN STATE	PVD			05R - 109.3 23L - 109.3 34 - 111.5	124.2
South Carolina	CHARLESTON	CHARLESTON AFB/INTL	CHS	N32° 54' 09"	W80° 02' 24"	15 - 109.7 33 - 108.9	124.75
	HILTON HEAD	HILTON HEAD	49J	N32° 13' 27"	W80° 41' 50"	21 - 111.3	123
South Dakota	RAPID CITY	RAPID CITY REGIONAL	RAP	N44° 03' 00"	W103° 03' 28"	32 - 109.3	118.7
	SIOUX FALLS	JOE FOSS FIELD	FSD	N43° 34' 57"	W96° 44' 38"	21 - 111.1 03 - 109.9	126.6
Tennessee	MEMPHIS	MEMPHIS INTL	MEM	N35° 03' 29"	W89° 58' 14"	09 - 109.5 18L - 108.3 18R - 109.9 27 - 108.7 36L - 108.9 36R - 110.5	127.75
	NASHVILLE	NASHVILLE INTL	BNA	N36° 07' 01"	W86° 40' 51"	02L - 109.9 02R - 111.75 20L - 109.35 31 - 109.7 20R - 111.3 LDA: 02C - 110.75	135.67
Texas	DALLAS-FORT	DALLAS/FORT WORTH INTL	DFW	N32° 54' 13"	W97° 00' 40"	13R - 109.5 17L - 110.3 17R - 111.35 18R - 111.9 31R - 110.9 35L - 111.35 36L - 111.9 36R - 110.55 18L - 110.55 35R - 110.3	135.5
	HOUSTON	HOUSTON INTERCONTINENTAL	IAH	N29° 59' 36"	W95° 20' 24"	08 - 109.7 09 - 110.9 14L - 111.9 27 - 110.9 32R - 111.9 26 - 109.7	124.5
	SAN ANTONIO	SAN ANTONIO INTL	SAT	N29° 31' 51"	W98° 27' 43"	03 - 109.7 12R - 110.9 30L - 110.9	118.9
	WACO	TSTC WACO	CNW	N31° 38' 23"	W97° 04' 23"	17L - 110.7	124
Utah	SALT LAKE CITY	SALT LAKE CITY	SLC	N40° 46' 46"	W111° 58' 01"	17 - 111.5 34 - 109.5 35 - 110.1 16 - 110.7	124.75
Vermont	BURLINGTON	BURLINGTON INTL	BTV	N44° 28' 07"	W73° 09' 07"	15 - 110.3	123.8
Virginia	NORFOLK	NORFOLK INTL	ORF	N36° 53' 44"	W76° 11' 55"	05 - 109.1 23 - 109.1	127.15
	RICHMOND	RICHMOND INTL (BYRD FIELD)	RIC	N37° 30' 27"	W77° 19' 37"	02 - 110.9 16 - 110.7 34 - 110.7	119.15
Washington	ALDERWOOD	MARTHA LAKE MANOR	S13	N47° 51' 48"	W122° 14' 12"		
	ARLINGTON	ARLINGTON MUNI	S88	N48° 09' 31"	W122° 09' 47"		
	AUBURN	AUBURN MUNI.	S50	N47° 19' 44"	W122° 13' 30"		
	BREMERTON	BREMERTON NATIONAL	PWT	N47° 29' 33"	W122° 45' 44"		
	EVERETT	EVERETT/SNOHOMISH COUNTY (PAINE FIELD)	PAE	N47° 54' 08"	W122° 16' 17"	16R - 109.3	
	MONROE	FIRST AIR FIELD	WA38	N47° 52' 19"	W121° 59' 33"		
	OLYMPIA	OLYMPIA	OLM	N46° 58' 12"	W122° 54' 05"		
	PORT ORCHARD	PORT ORCHARD	0S8	N47° 25' 59"	W122° 39' 44"		124.4
	PORT ANGELES	WILLIAM R. FAIRCHILD INTL	CLM	N48° 07' 07"	W123° 29' 56"		134.15
	PUYALLUP	PIERCE COUNTY-THUN FIELD	1S0	N47° 06' 14"	W122° 17' 13"		
	RENTON	RENTON MUNI	RNT	N47° 29' 35"	W122° 12' 56"		
	SEATTLE	BOEING FIELD/KING COUNTY INTL	BFI	N47° 32' 00"	W122° 18' 13"	13R - 110.9	127.75
	SEATTLE	SEATTLE-TACOMA INTL	SEA	N47° 26' 50"	W122° 18' 28"	34R - 110.3 16R - 111.7 34L - 111.7	118
	SHELTON	SANDERSON FIELD	SHN	N47° 14' 00"	W123° 08' 51"		
	SNOHOMISH	HARVEY FIELD	S43	N47° 54' 20"	W122° 06' 02"		
	SPANAWAY	SHADY ACRES	WA61	N47° 04' 13"	W122° 22' 15"		
	SPANAWAY	SPANAWAY	S44	N47° 05' 12"	W122° 25' 53"		
	SPOKANE	FELTS FIELD	SFF	N47° 40' 58"	W117° 19' 26"		120.55
	TACOMA	TACOMA NARROWS	TIW	N47° 16' 04"	W122° 34' 41"		

Location	City	Airport Name	Ident.	Latitude	Longitude	ILS Runway & Freq.	ATIS Freq.
West Virginia	HUNTINGTON	TRI-STATE/MILTON J FERGUSON FIELD	HTS	N38° 21' 47"	W82° 33' 16"	12 - 109.9 30 - 108.7	125.2
Wisconsin	MILWAUKEE	GENERAL MITCHELL FIELD	MKE	N42° 56' 40"	W87° 53' 42"	01L - 110.3 07R - 111.5 19R - 110.3 25L - 111.5	126.4
	OSHKOSH	WITTMAN REGIONAL	OSH	N43° 59' 23"	W88° 33' 13"	36 - 110.5	125.8
Wyoming	CHEYENNE	CHEYENNE	CYS	N41° 09' 20"	W104° 48' 24"	26 - 110.1	134.42
	JACKSON	JACKSON HOLE	JAC	N43° 36' 23"	W110° 44' 17"	18 - 109.1	122.8

NORTH AMERICA (outside USA)

Location	City	Airport Name	Ident.	Latitude	Longitude	ILS Runway & Freq.	ATIS Freq.
Belize	BELIZE CITY	PHILIP S W GOLDSON INTL	MZBZ				
Canada, Alberta	CALGARY	CALGARY INTL	CYYC	N51° 06' 48"	W114° 01' 12"	16 - 109.3 28 - 110.9 34 - 111.5	127.2
	EDMONTON	EDMONTON INTL	CYEG	N53° 18' 36"	W113° 34' 48"	02 - 110.3 12 - 109.9 30 - 109.1	128
Canada, British Columbia	VANCOUVER	VANCOUVER INTL	CYVR	N49° 11' 42"	W123° 11' 00"	08 - 109.5 12 - 111.1 26 - 110.7	124.6
Canada, Newfoundland	GANDER	GANDER INTL	CYQX	N48° 56' 24"	W54° 34' 06"		124.8
	GOOSE BAY	GOOSE	CYYR	N53° 19' 12"	W60° 25' 36"	04 - 109.5 08 - 110.3 13 - 109.9	128.1
Canada, Ontario	TORONTO	PEARSON INTL	CYYZ	N43° 40' 36"	W79° 37' 48"	06R - 109.1 06L - 109.7 15 - 110.5 24R - 111.5 24L - 109.3 33 - 110.3	133.1
Costa Rica	SAN JOSE	JUAN SANTAMARIA INTL	MROC	N09° 59' 36"	W84° 12' 42"	07 - 109.5	118.6
Cuba	GUANTANAMO BAY NAS	LEEWARD POINT	MUGM	N19° 54' 24"	W75° 12' 24"		126.6
El Slavador	SAN SALVADOR	ILOPANGO INTL	MSSS	N13° 41' 30"	W89° 07' 00"		118.3
Greenland	GODTHAB	GODTHAB	BGGH	N64° 11' 30"	W51° 41' 00"	24 - 110.3	119.1
Jamaica	MONTEGO BAY	SANGSTER INTL	MKJS	N18° 30' 00"	W77° 55' 00"		127.9
Mexico	MEXICO CITY	LIC BENITO JUAREZ INTL	MMMX	N19° 26' 06"	W99° 04' 18"	05R - 109.1 23L - 109.7	127.7
	ZIHUATENEJO	IXTAPA-ZIHUATANEJO INTL	MMZH	N17° 36' 06"	W101° 27' 36"		118.3

OCEANA

Location	City	Airport Name	Ident.	Latitude	Longitude	ILS Runway & Freq.	ATIS Freq.
Australia	ALICE SPRINGS	ALICE SPRINGS	YBAS	S23° 48' 30"	E133° 54' 06"	12 - 109.9	118.3
	BRISBANE	BRISBANE INTL	YBBN	S27° 23' 12"	E153° 07' 00"	01 - 109.5 19 - 110.1	125.5
	DARWIN	DARWIN INTL	YPDN	S12° 25' 00"	E130° 52' 30"	29 - 109.7	133.1
	MELBOURNE	MELBOURNE INTL	YMML	S37° 40' 30"	E144° 50' 30"	16 - 109.7 27 - 109.3	132.7
	PERTH	PERTH INTL	YPPH	S31° 56' 30"	E115° 57' 54"	21 - 109.5 24 - 109.9	123.8
	SYDNEY	KINGSFORD SMITH INTL	YSSY	S33° 56' 30"	E151° 10' 18"	07 - 109.9 16 - 109.5 34 - 110.1	127.6
Fiji Island	NADI	NADI INTL	NFFN	N17° 45' 18"	E177° 26' 48"	02 - 109.9	119.1
Guam	GUAM	AGANA NAS	PGUM	N13° 28' 54"	E144° 47' 36"	06L - 110.3	118.1
Johnston Atoll	JOHNSTON ATOLL	JOHNSTON ATOLL	PJON	N16° 43' 48"	W169° 32' 06"		122.8
Midway Island	MIDWAY ISLAND	MIDWAY NAF	PMDY	N28° 11' 36"	W177° 23' 42"		126.2
New Zealand	AUCKLAND	AUCKLAND INTL	NZAA	S37° 00' 36"	E174° 47' 30"	05 - 110.3 23 - 109.9	127.8
	QUEENSTOWN	QUEENSTOWN	NZQN	S45° 01' 18"	E168° 44' 12"		118.1
	WELLINGTON	WELLINGTON INTL	NZWN	S41° 19' 42"	E174° 48' 18"	16 - 110.3 34 - 109.9	126.9
Papua New Guinea	PORT MORESBY	JACKSONS INTL	AYPY	S09° 26' 36"	E147° 13' 00"	14L - 110.1 32R - 109.5	128
Wake Island	WAKE ISLAND	WAKE ISLAND	PWAK	N19° 16' 54"	E166° 38' 12"		128

NAVIGATIONAL MAPS

With the advent of FS 5.1 CD's new worldwide airport facilities, the Flight Simulator pilot can now fly around the world and refuel as needed. But in order to navigate, it is important to have navigational maps that plot the VOR/NDB Navaids, as well as airport locations. The next section includes maps for the USA/Canada region and the world, so you can see the locations of these types of navigational and refueling facilities. However, due to space considerations, each map only displays the VOR/NDB names, not the frequencies or course headings between stations. In order to use these maps, you'll need to look up the Navaid's name in the previously listed Navaid database and then find its frequency, latitude/longitude, and magnetic variation. Then, using the techniques demonstrated in Chapter 12, you can figure out the magnetic bearing between any two VOR/NDB stations.

The Navaid map for the USA, which plots only the VOR stations, is divided into 34 smaller maps. You can see the territory each map covers by consulting Figure B.1. Thus, for example, consulting Figure B.1, you can see that California is covered by Maps 1, 2, and 3, while New York and Massachusetts are covered by Map 33. Hawaii and Alaska are plotted separately in Figure B.2 and Figure B.3 respectively.

The following regions each have a separate map:

- North Atlantic Ocean
- Europe (with separate country maps showing greater detail below)
    United Kingdom
    Sweden/Finland
    France
    Spain
    Germany
    Italy
    Denmark/Norway
    Greece/Turkey
- Africa
- Asia
- Eastern and southern Pacific Ocean
- Western Pacific Ocean
- Australia   ·
- South America
- Central America/Caribbean Ocean

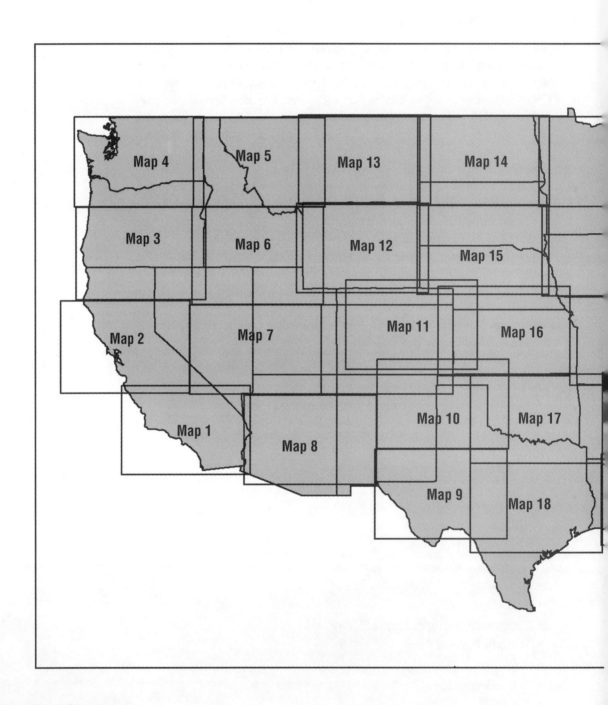

Figure B.1 USA map index

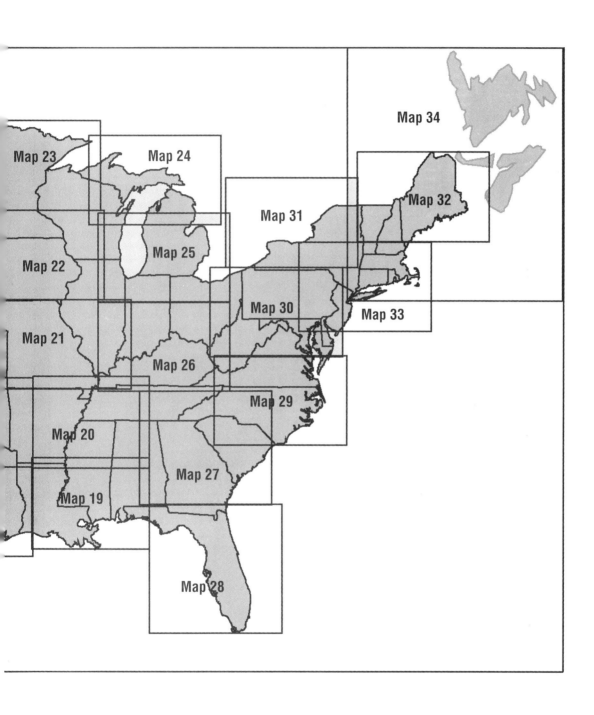

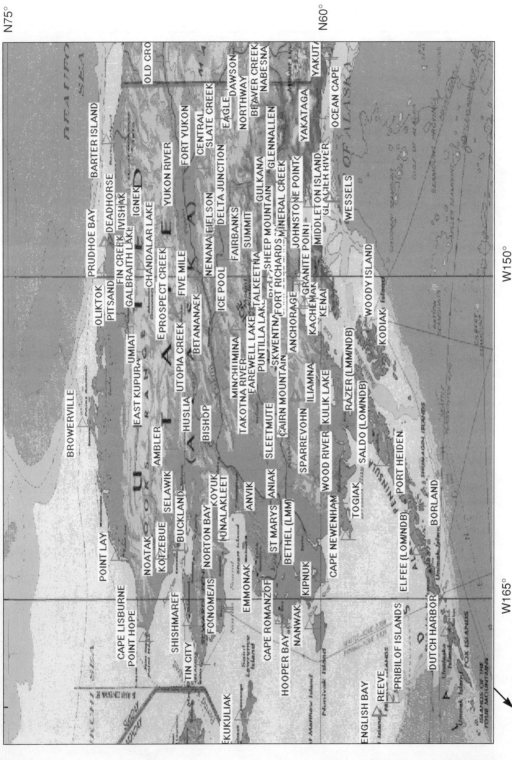

To Adak Amchitka Shemya and Attu

Figure B.2 Alaska

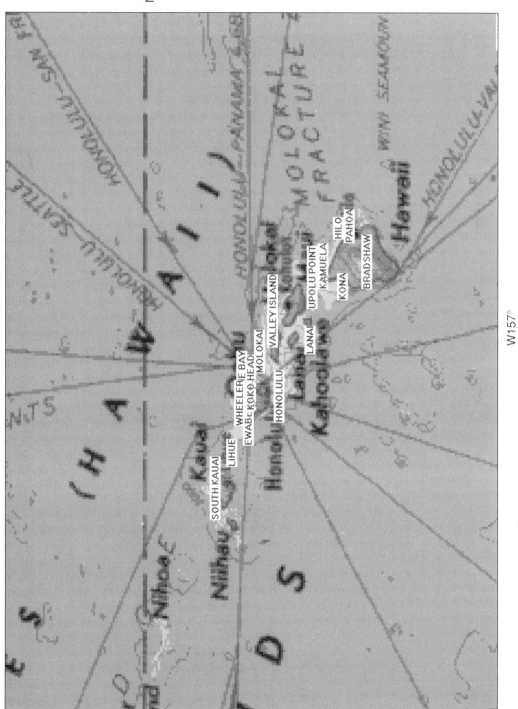

Figure B.3 Hawaii

MAP 1

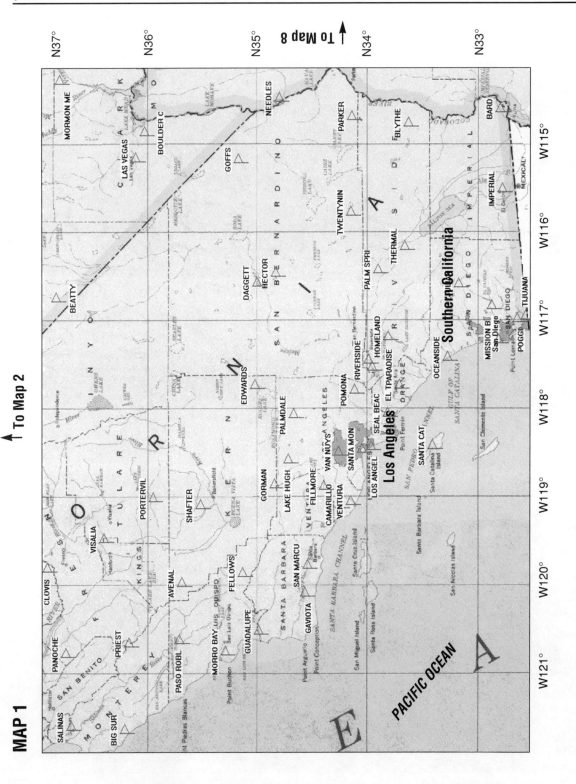

To Map 2 →

To Map 8 ↑

N37°
N36°
N35°
N34°
N33°

W115°
W116°
W117°
W118°
W119°
W120°
W121°

MORMON ME

LAS VEGAS

BOULDER C

NEEDLES

PARKER

BLYTHE

BARD

MEXICALI

IMPERIAL

GOFFS

TWENTYNIN

THERMAL

PALM SPRI

Southern California

SAN DIEGO

TIJUANA

POGGI

MISSION B
San Diego

OCEANSIDE

HOMELAND

EL TPARADISE

RIVERSIDE

BEATTY

DAGGETT

HECTOR

SAN BERNARDINO

INYO

EDWARDS

PALMDALE

POMONA

SEAL BEAC

SANTA MON

LOS ANGEL

Los Angeles

SANTA CAT

Santa Catalina
Island

PACIFIC OCEAN

SAN
CLOVIS

VISALIA

PORTERVIL

SHAFTER

GORMAN

LAKE HUGH

FILLMORE

VAN NUYS

CAMARILLO

VENTURA

SANTA BARBARA

SAN MARCU

GAVIOTA

GUADALUPE

PASO ROBL

MORRO BAY

FELLOWS

AVENAL

PRIEST

PANOCHE

SALINAS

BIG SUR

SEQUOIA

TULARE

KINGS

KERN

SAN BENITO

MONTEREY

SAN LUIS OBISPO

MAP 2

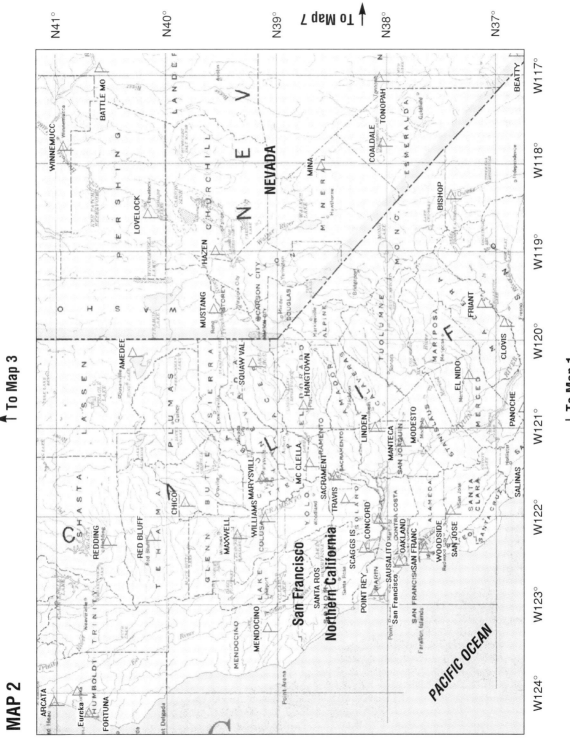

MAP 3

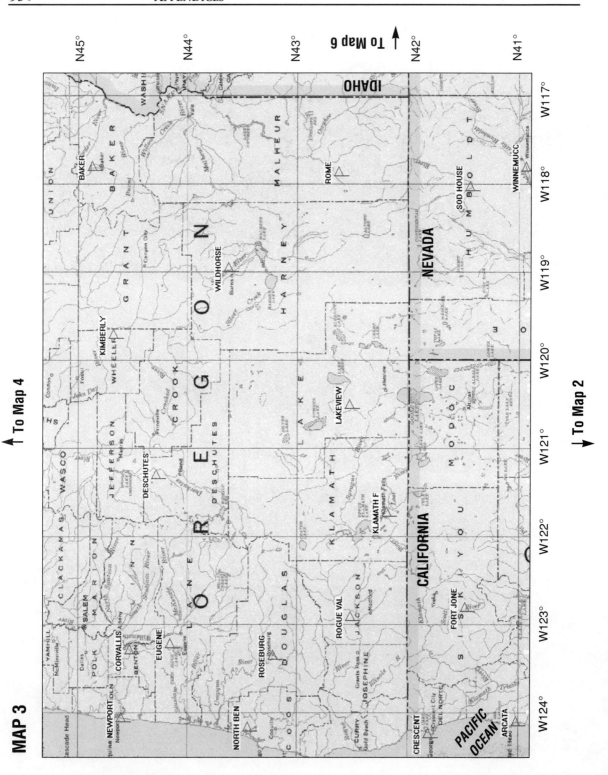

↑ To Map 4

↑ To Map 6

↓ To Map 2

N45°
N44°
N43°
N42°
N41°

W117°
W118°
W119°
W120°
W121°
W122°
W123°
W124°

IDAHO

NEVADA

CALIFORNIA

OREGON

PACIFIC OCEAN

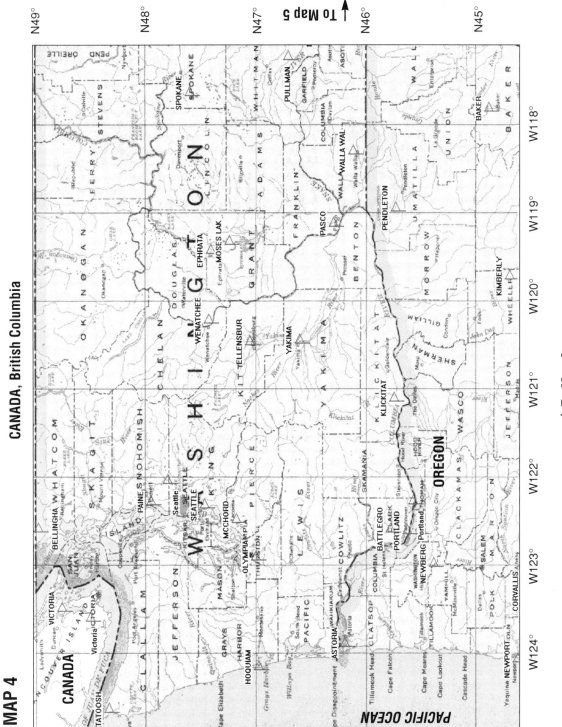

MAP 5

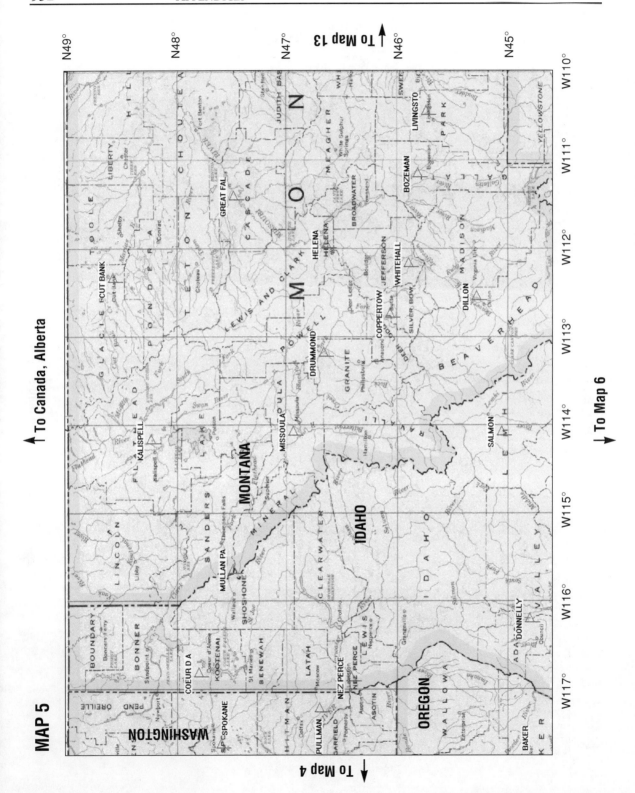

↑ To Canada, Alberta

↑ To Map 13

→ To Map 6

↓ To Map 4

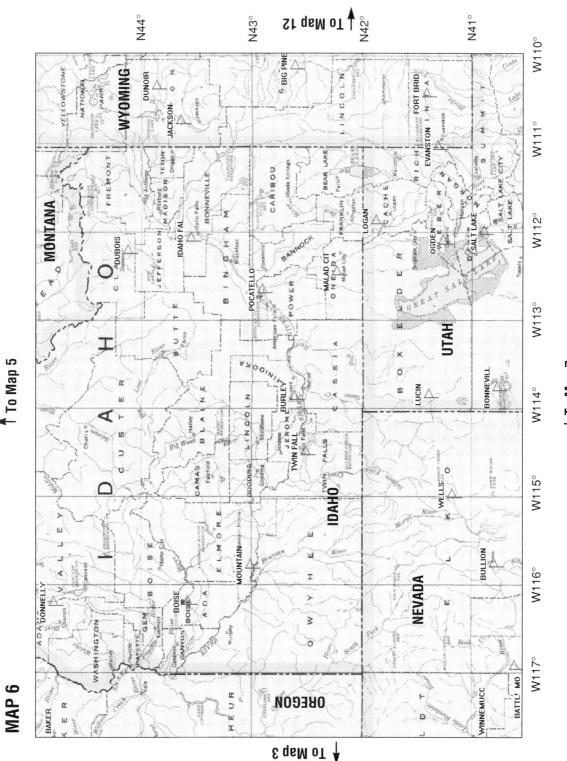

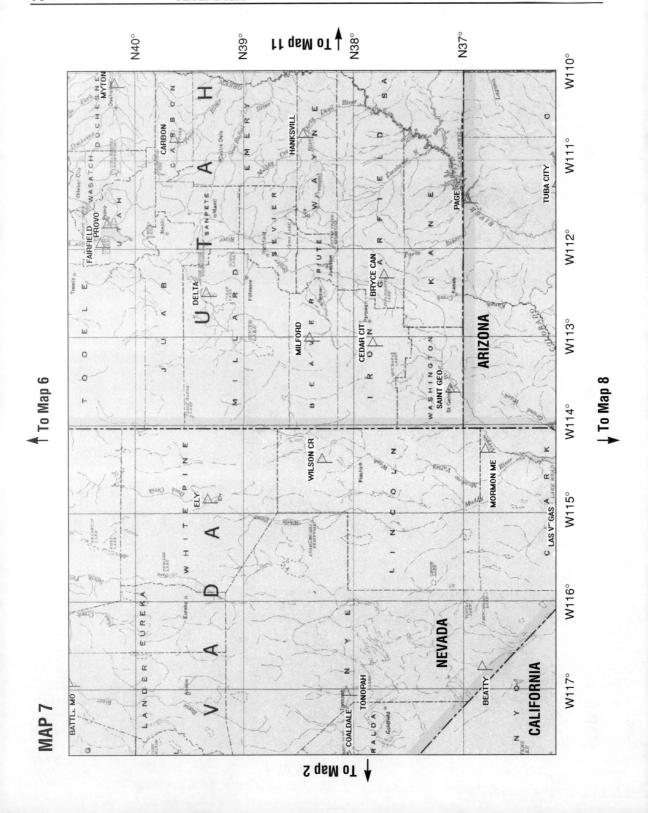

MAP 7

To Map 6

To Map 11

To Map 8

To Map 2

N40°
N39°
N38°
N37°

W110°
W111°
W112°
W113°
W114°
W115°
W116°
W117°

UTAH
NEVADA
ARIZONA
CALIFORNIA

MYTON
DUCHESNE
CARBON
HANKSVILL
PROVO
FAIRFIELD
SANPETE
DELTA
MILFORD
BRYCE CAN
CEDAR CIT
WASHINGTON
SAINT GEO
PAGE
TUBA CITY
WILSON CR
ELY
MORMON ME
BEATTY
COALDALE
TONOPAH
BATTLE MO

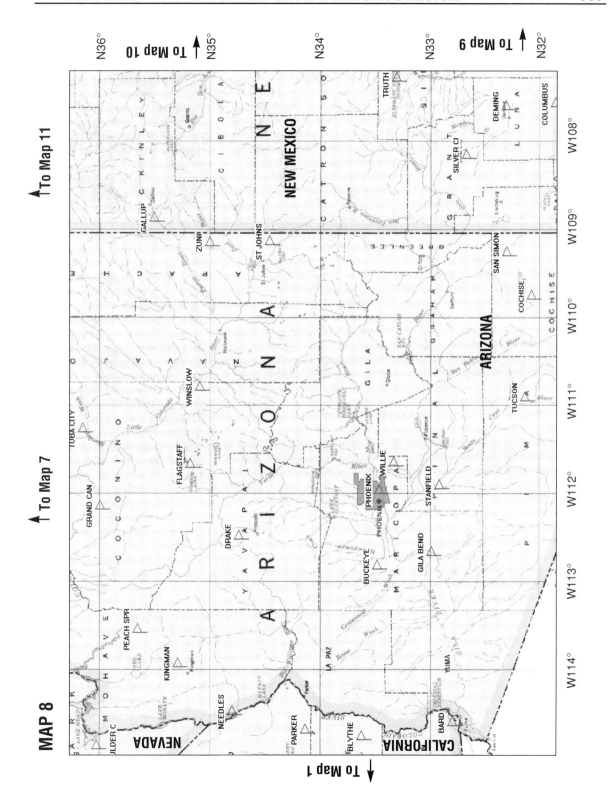

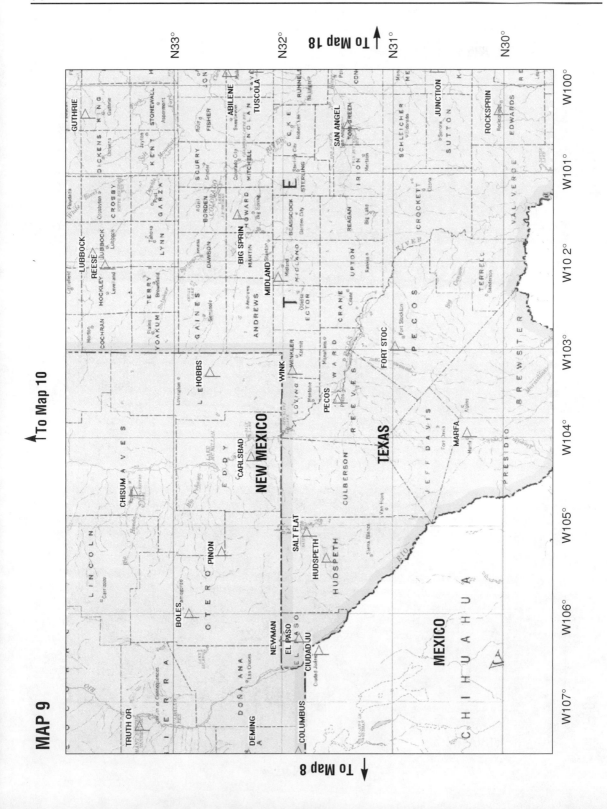

MAP 9

↑To Map 10

↓ To Map 8

↑ To Map 18

MAP 10

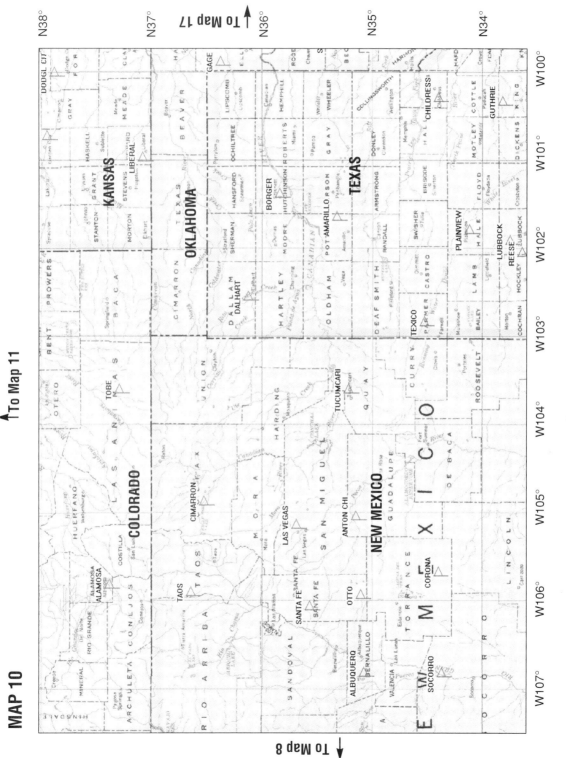

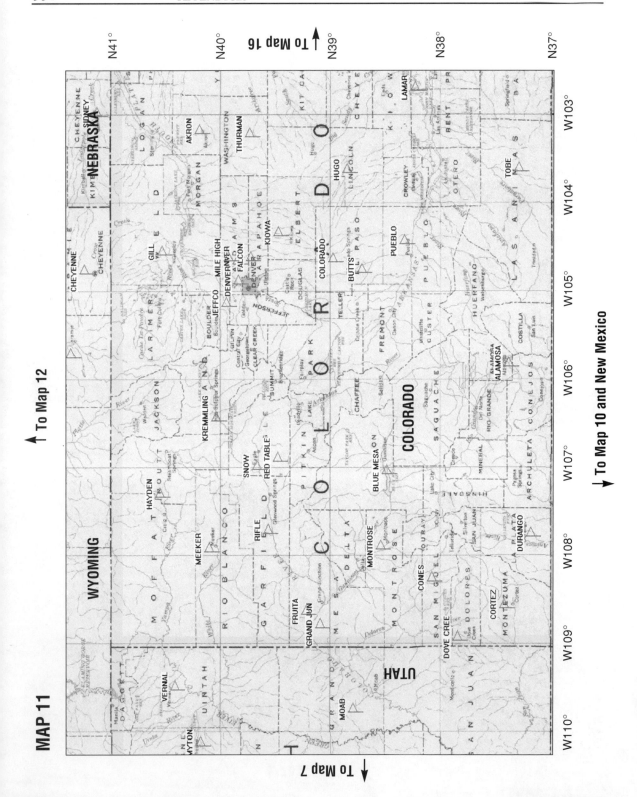

MAP 11

↑ To Map 12

↑ To Map 16

↓ To Map 7

↓ To Map 10 and New Mexico

N41°
N40°
N39°
N38°
N37°

W103°
W104°
W105°
W106°
W107°
W108°
W109°
W110°

WYOMING

UTAH

NEBRASKA

COLORADO

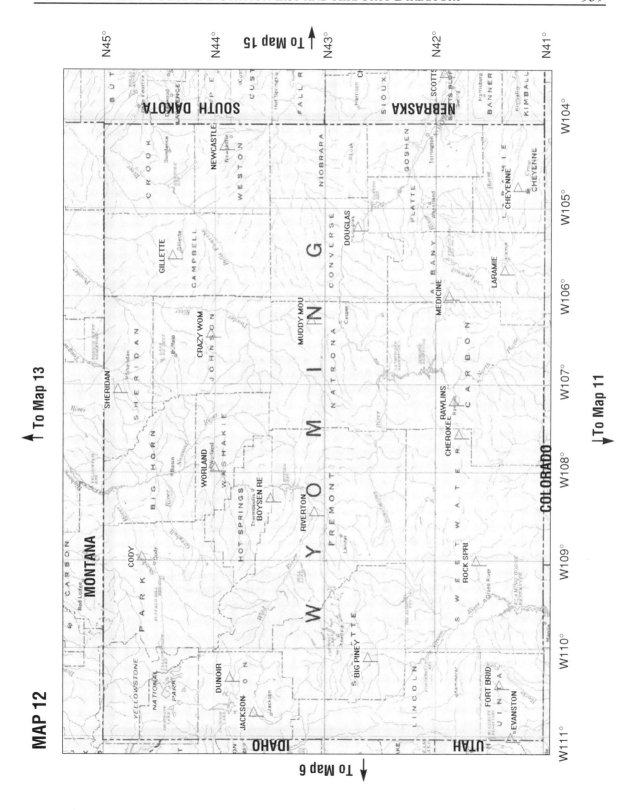

MAP 12

MAP 13

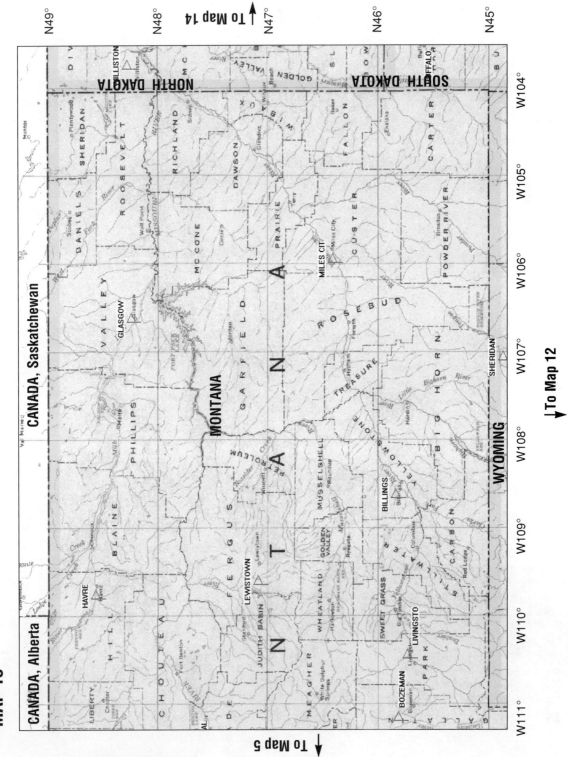

To Map 14

To Map 12

To Map 5

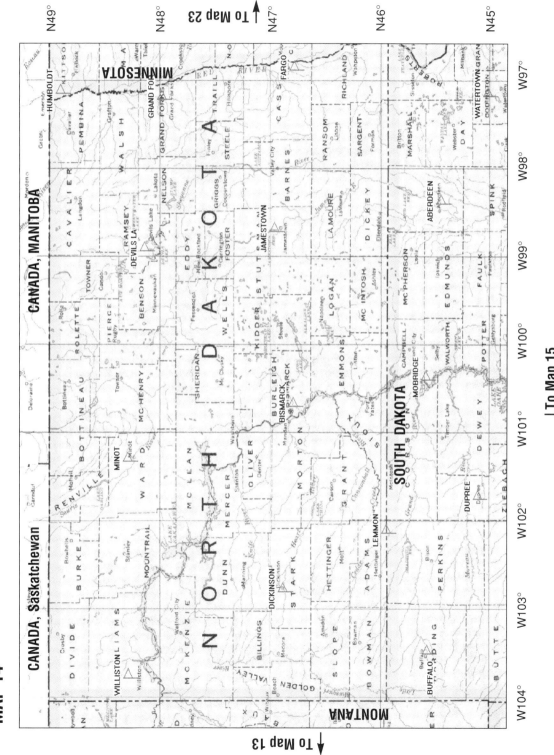

MAP 14

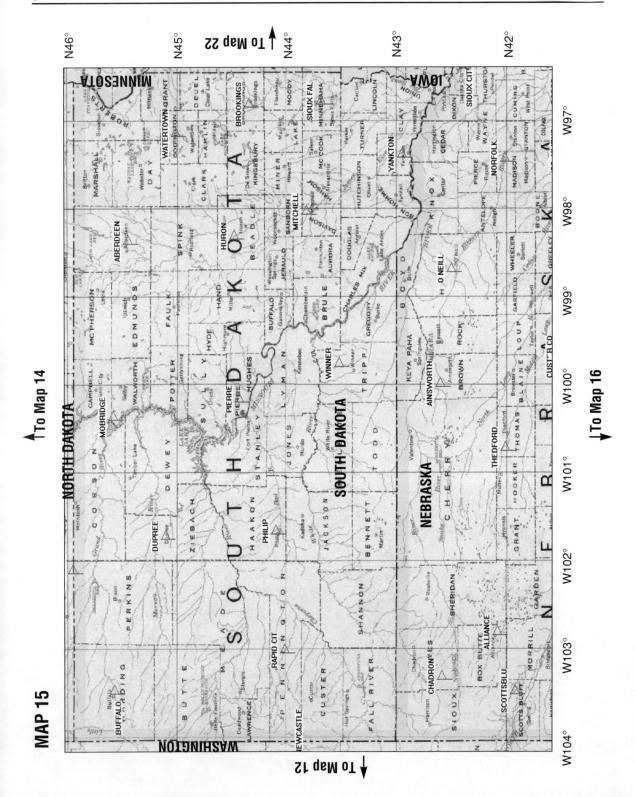

MAP 15

To Map 14

To Map 22

To Map 16

To Map 12

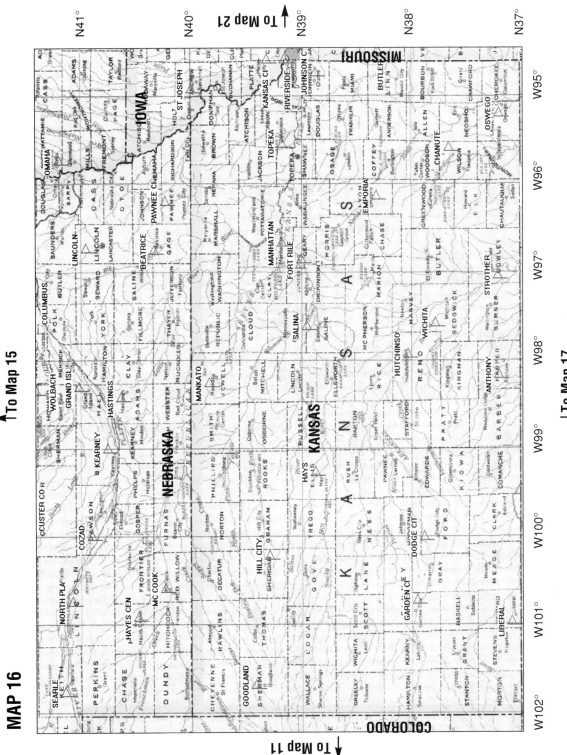

MAP 16

↑To Map 15

↓To Map 17

↑To Map 21

↓To Map 11

MAP 17

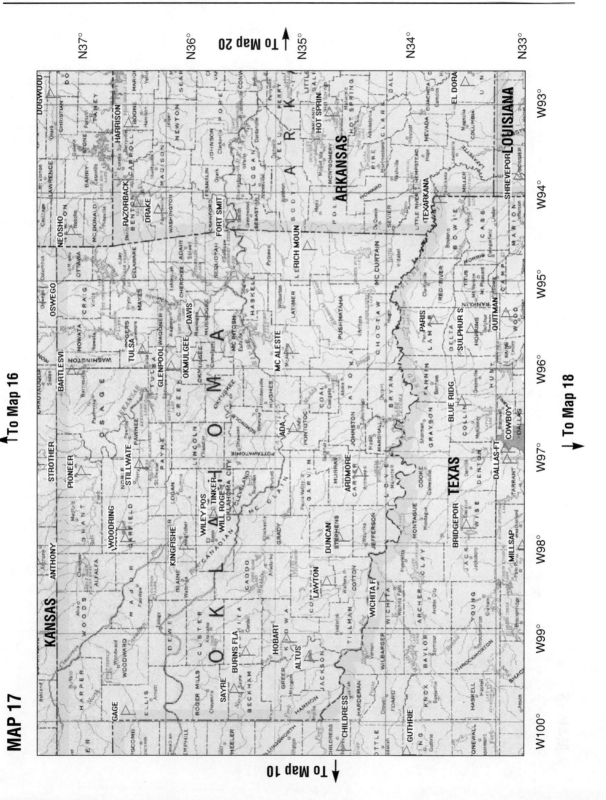

To Map 16

To Map 20

To Map 18

To Map 10

N37°

N36°

N35°

N34°

N33°

W100° W99° W98° W97° W96° W95° W94° W93°

KANSAS

OKLAHOMA

TEXAS

ARKANSAS

LOUISIANA

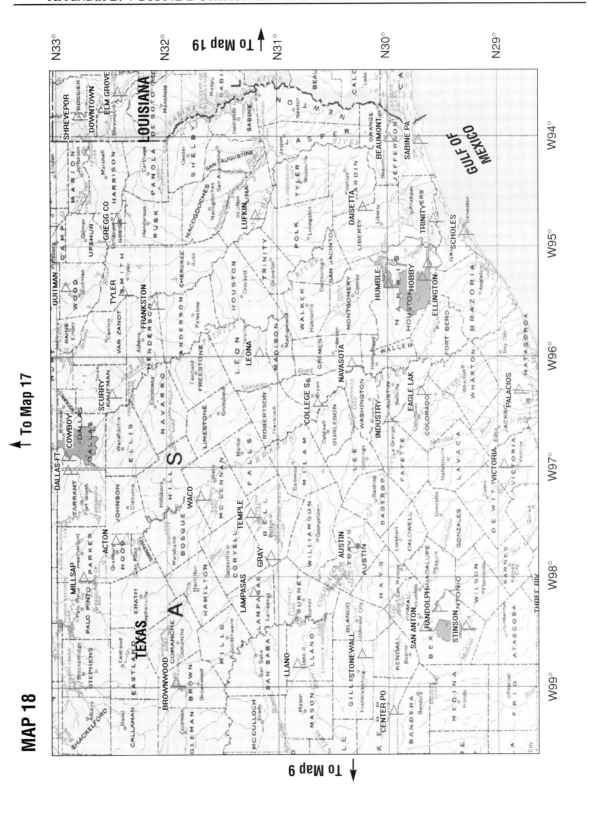

MAP 18

MAP 19

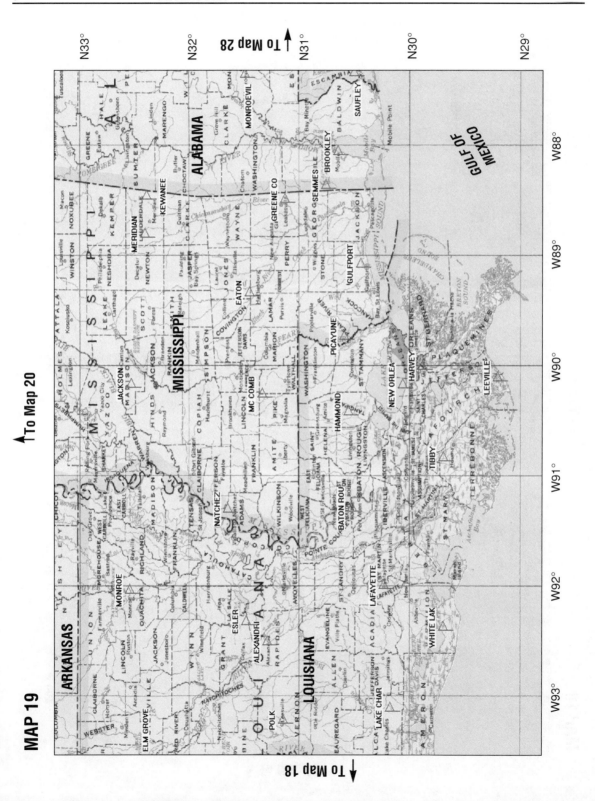

↑ To Map 20

↑ To Map 28

↓ To Map 18

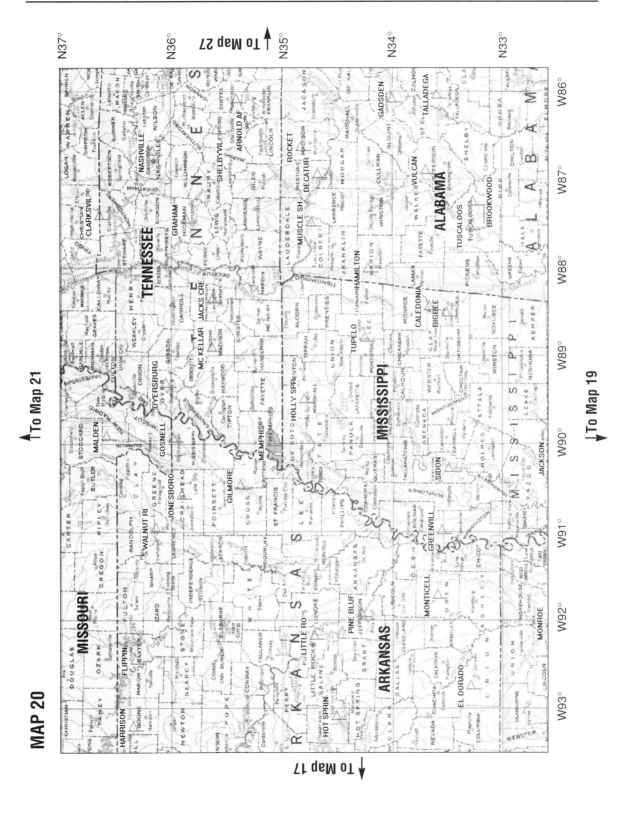

To Map 26
To Map 22
To Map 20
To Map 16

MAP 21

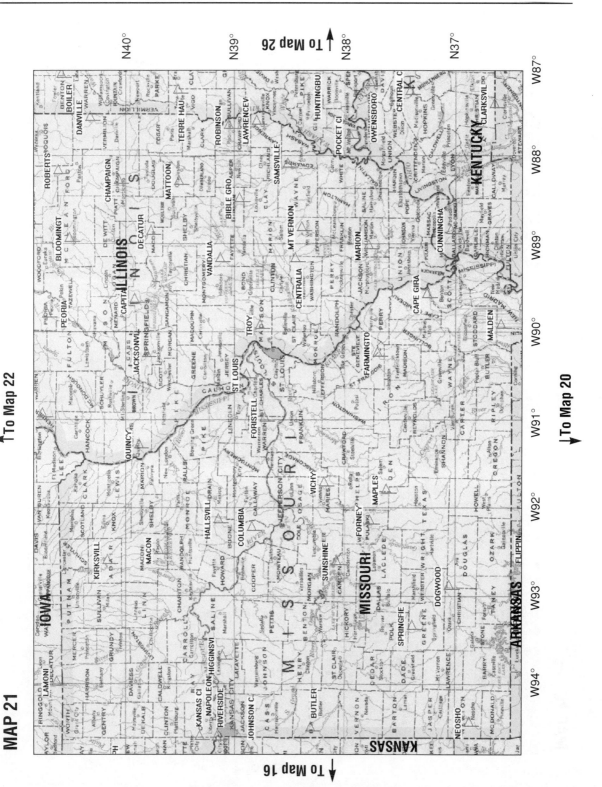

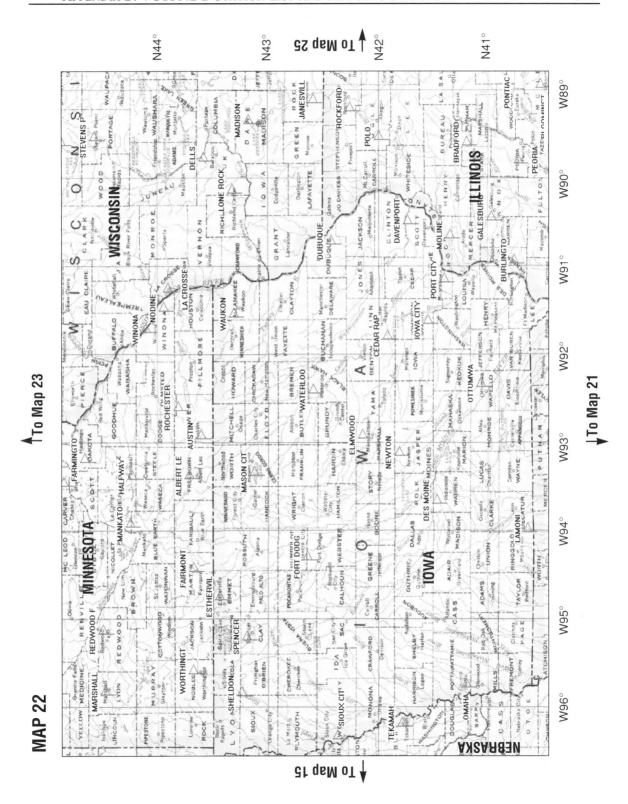

MAP 22

MAP 23

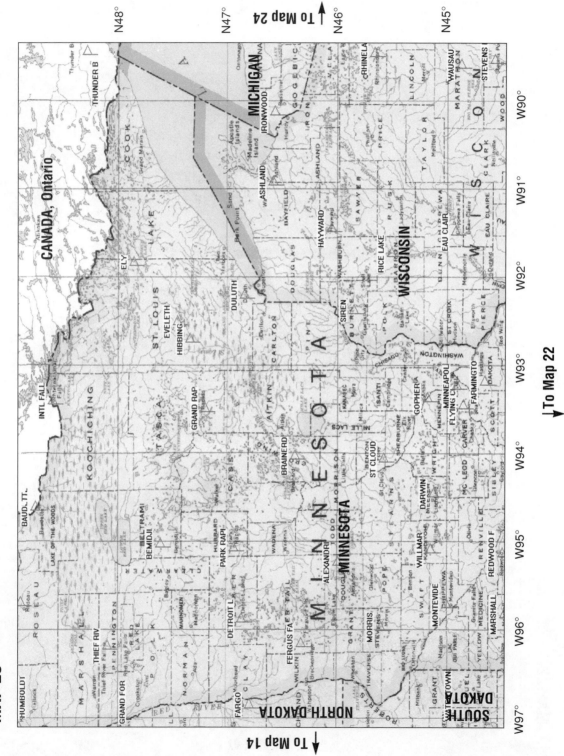

To Map 14 ↓

↑ To Map 24

↓ To Map 22

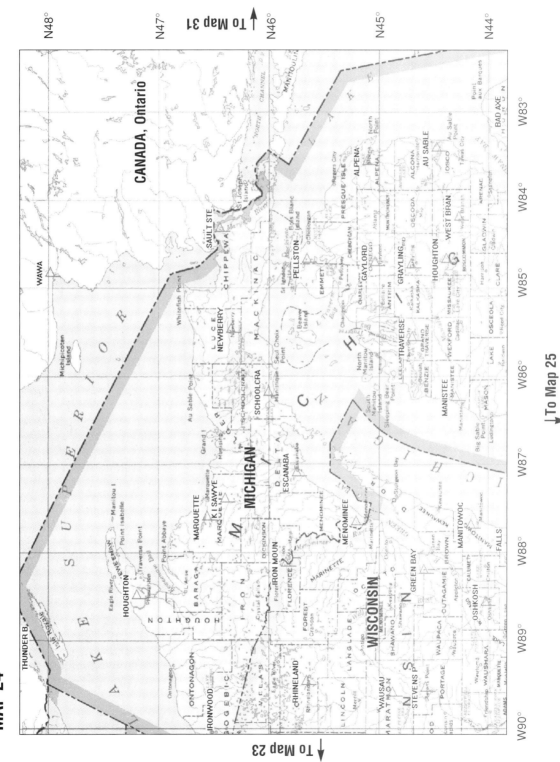

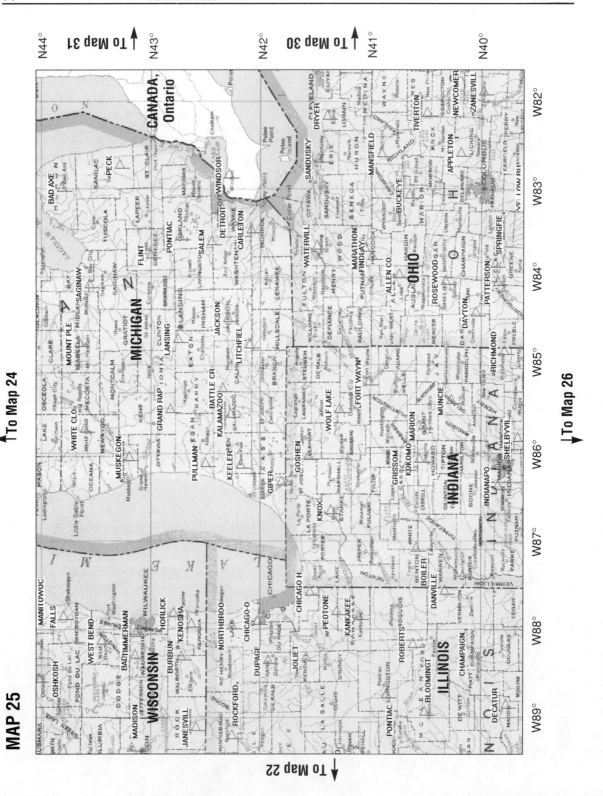

MAP 25

↑To Map 24

To Map 26↓

↑To Map 31

↑To Map 30

↓To Map 22

N44° N43° N42° N41° N40°

W82° W83° W84° W85° W86° W87° W88° W89°

CANADA, Ontario

MICHIGAN

WISCONSIN

INDIANA

ILLINOIS

OHIO

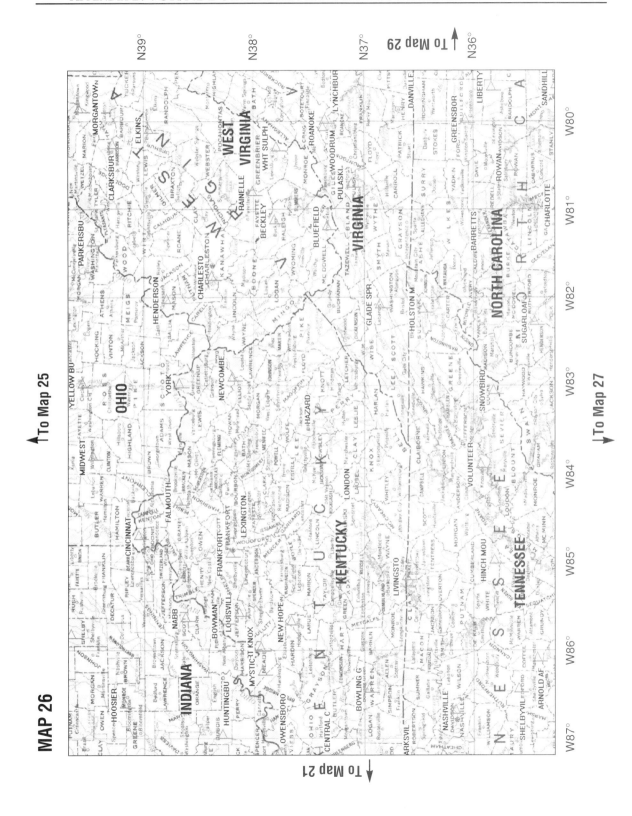

MAP 26

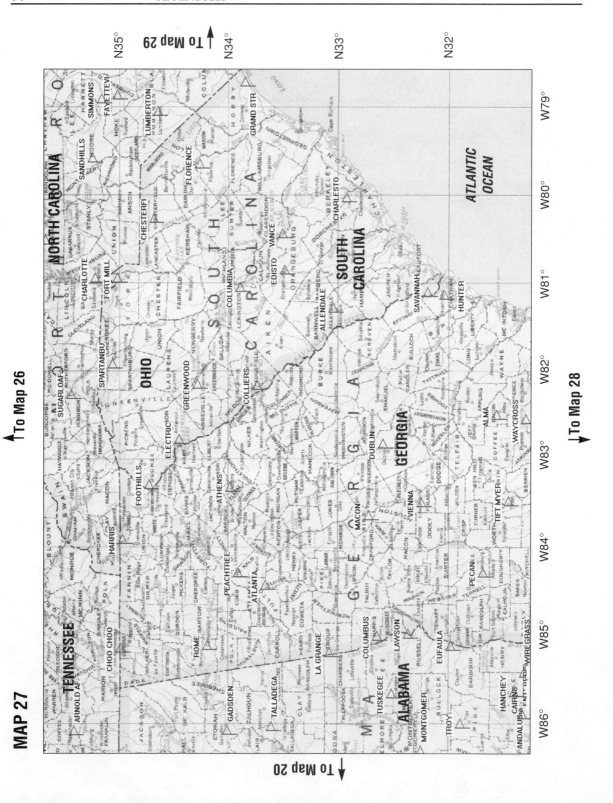

MAP 27

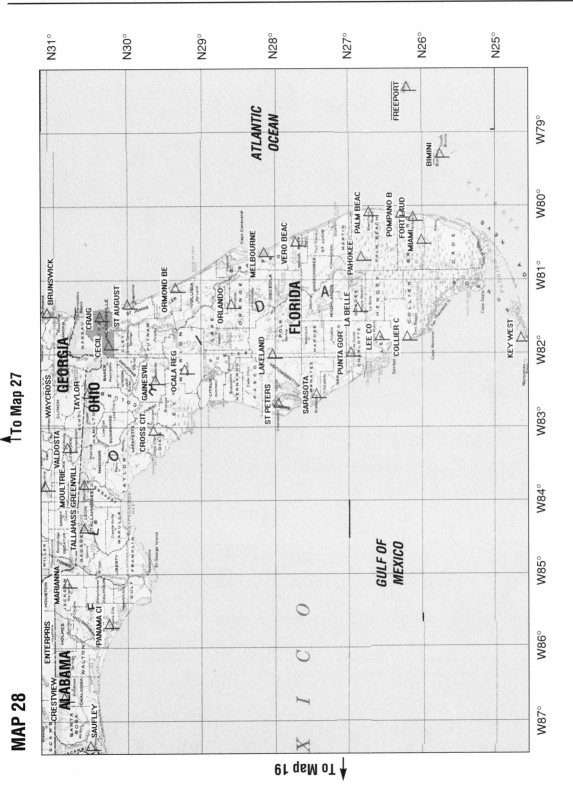

MAP 28

↑To Map 27

↓To Map 19

↑ To Map 30

MAP 29

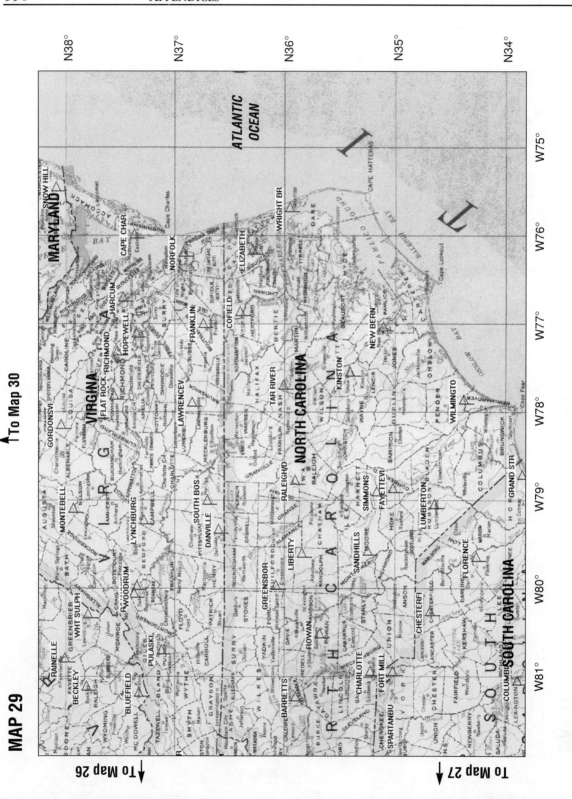

↓ To Map 26

↓ To Map 27

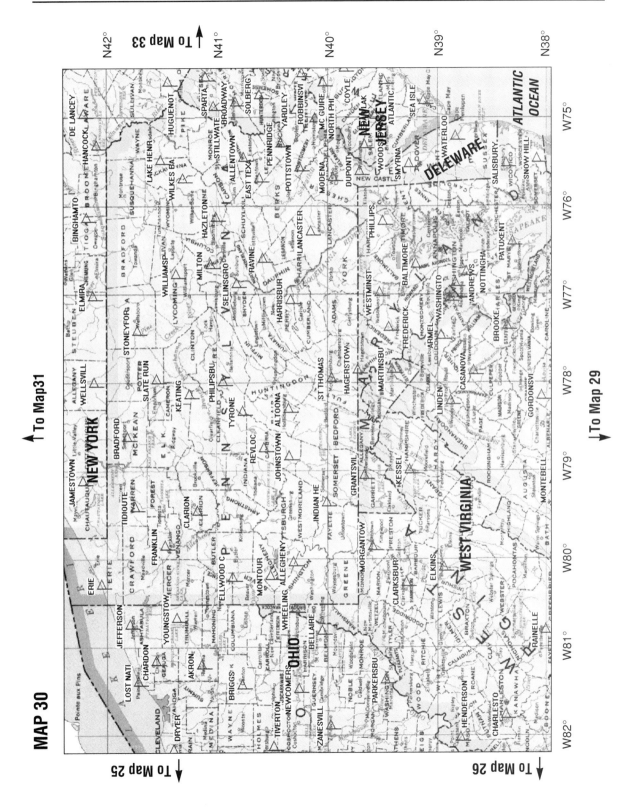

MAP 30

To Map31

To Map 33

To Map 25

To Map 26

To Map 29

N42°
N41°
N40°
N39°
N38°

W82°
W81°
W80°
W79°
W78°
W77°
W76°
W75°

MAP 31

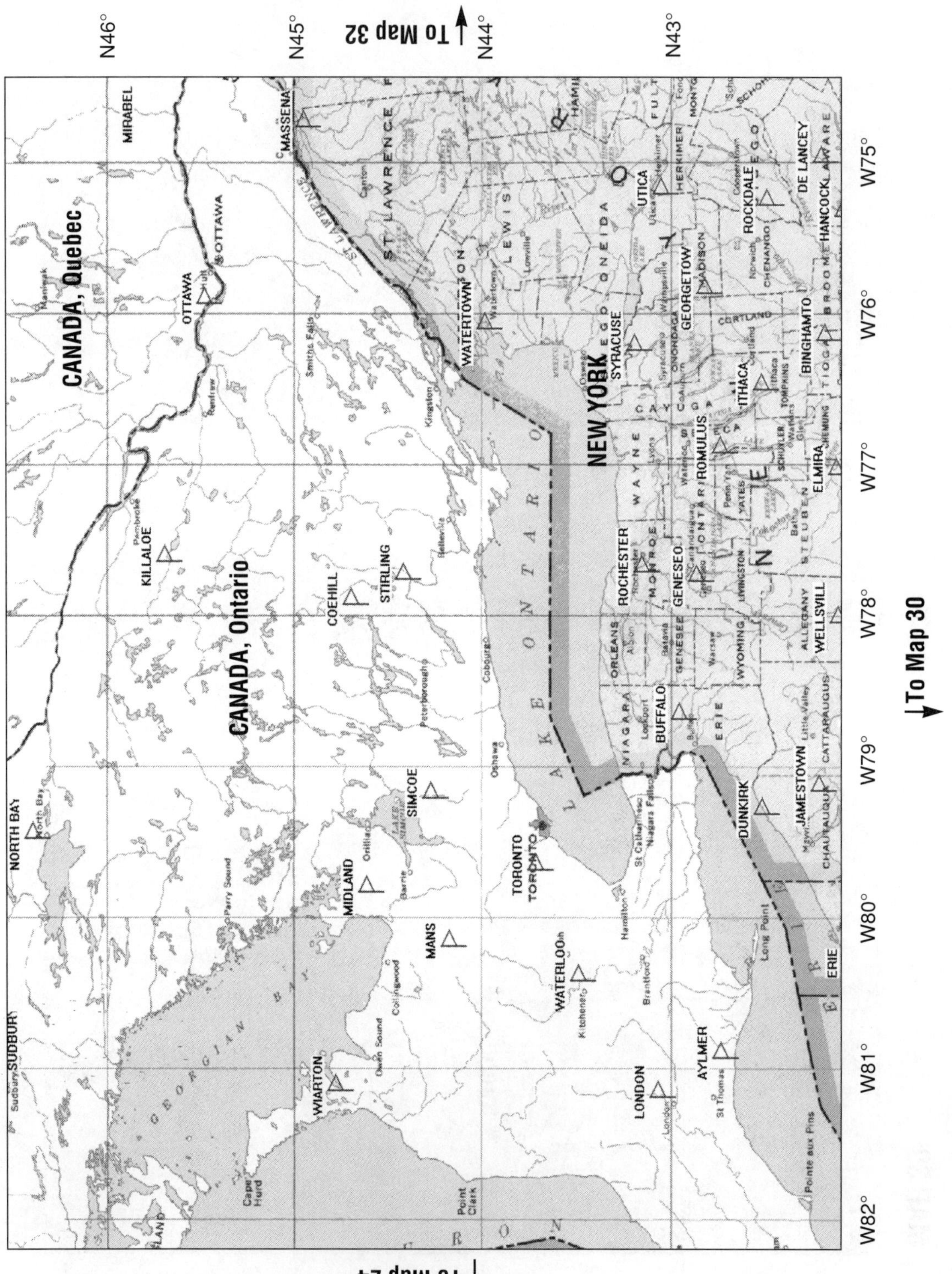
N46°
N45°
N44°
N43°
To Map 32
To Map 24
To Map 30
W82°
W81°
W80°
W79°
W78°
W77°
W76°
W75°
CANADA, Quebec
CANADA, Ontario
NEW YORK
MIRABEL
OTTAWA
MASSENA
KILLALOE
COEHILL
STIRLING
NORTH BAY
SUDBURY
SIMCOE
MIDLAND
TORONTO
MANS
WATERLOO
WIARTON
LONDON
AYLMER
WATERTOWN
SYRACUSE
UTICA
GEORGETOW
MADISON
ROCKDALE
DE LANCEY
HANCOCK
BINGHAMTO
ITHACA
ROMULUS
ELMIRA
ROCHESTER
GENESEO
WELLSVILL
BUFFALO
DUNKIRK
JAMESTOWN
ERIE
L A K E   O N T A R I O
G E O R G I A N   B A Y

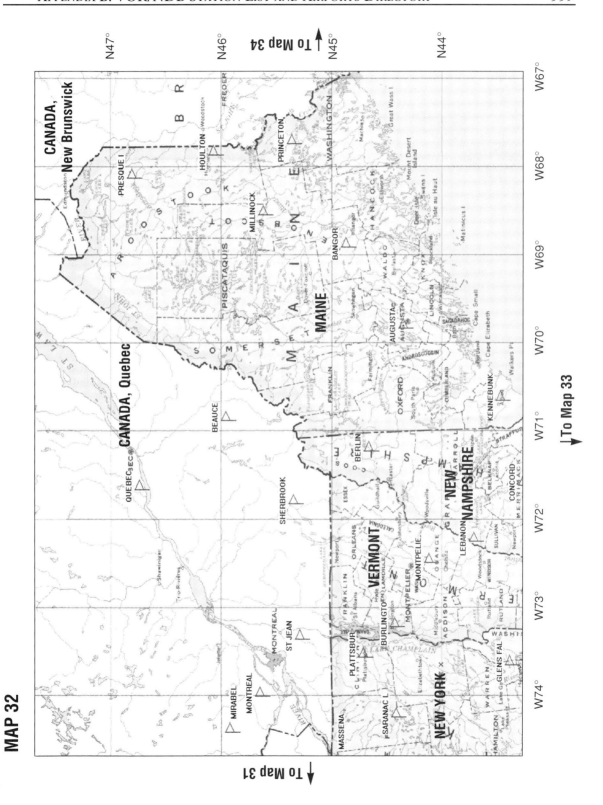

MAP 32

To Map 34

To Map 31

To Map 33

MAP 33

To Map 31

To Map 32

To Map 30

To Map 30

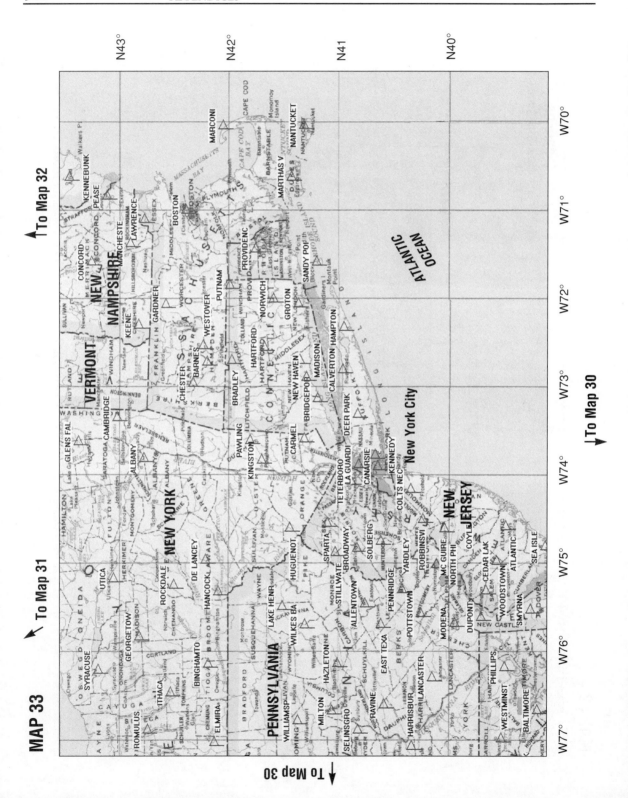

N43°

N42°

N41

N40°

W77° W76° W75° W74° W73° W72° W71° W70°

VERMONT

NEW HAMPSHIRE

NEW YORK

PENNSYLVANIA

NEW JERSEY

MASSACHUSETTS

CONNECTICUT

ATLANTIC OCEAN

New York City

North Atlantic Provinces of Canada

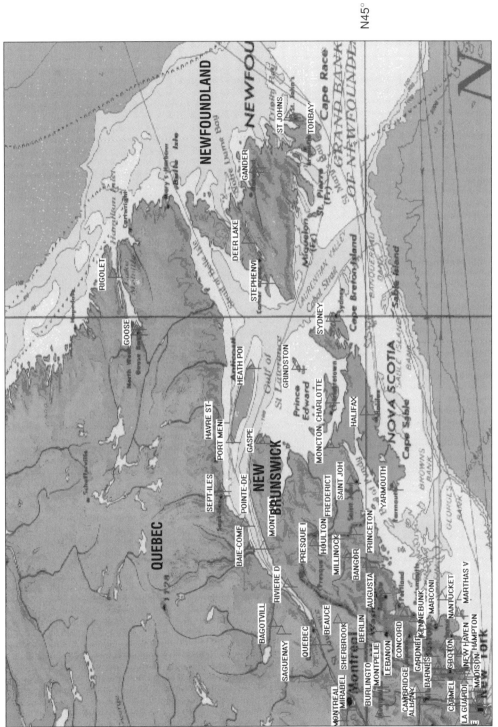

↑ To Map 32

North Atlantic

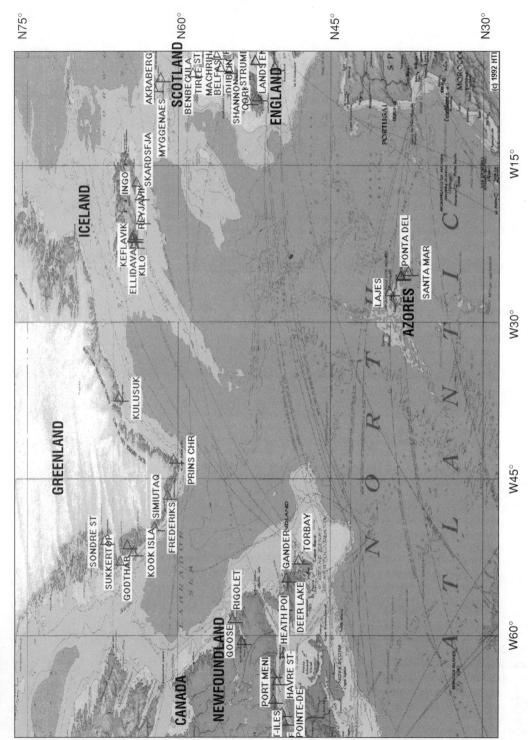

Europe

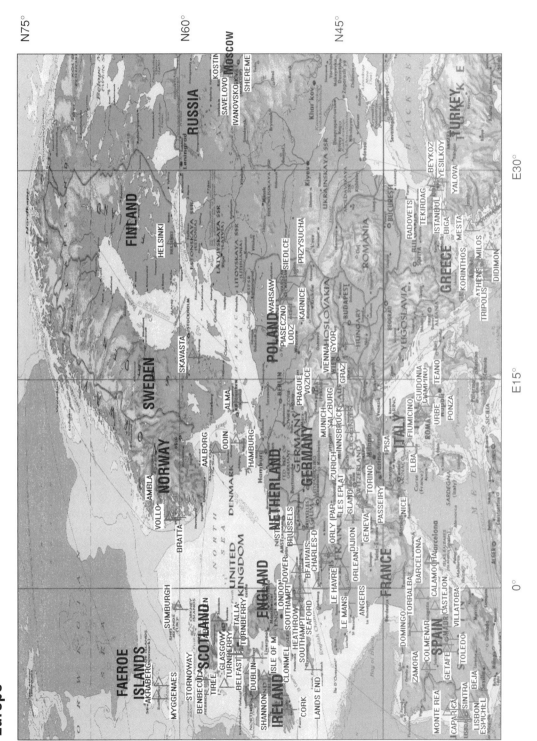

United Kingdom

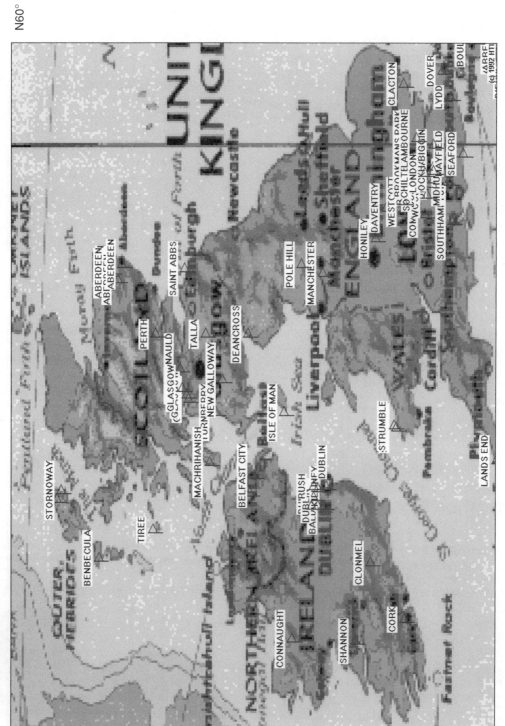

N60°

0°

(c) 1992 HTI

Sweden and Finland

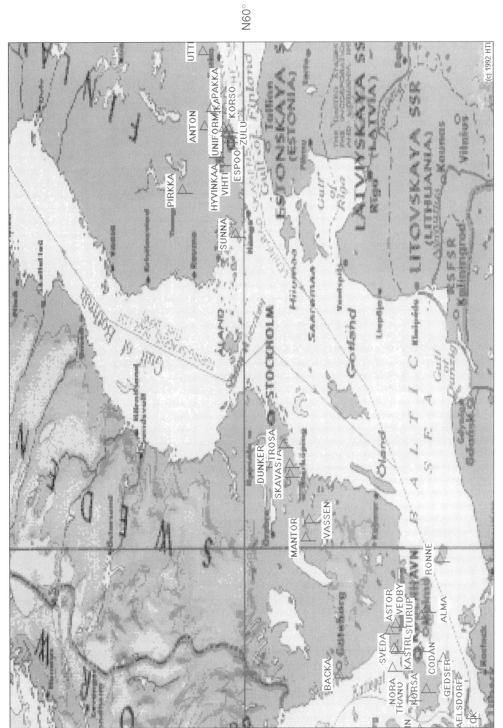

France

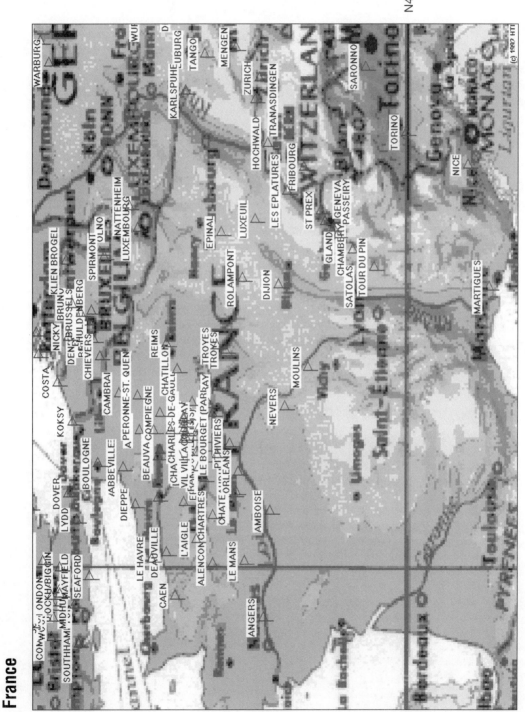

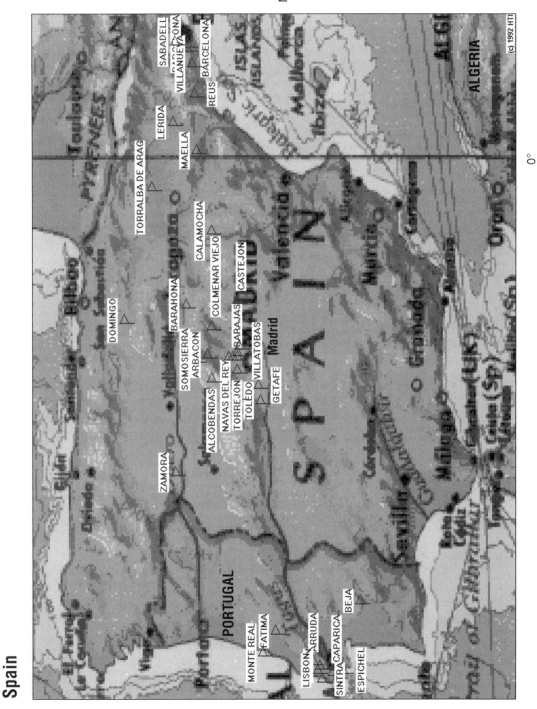

Spain

Germany

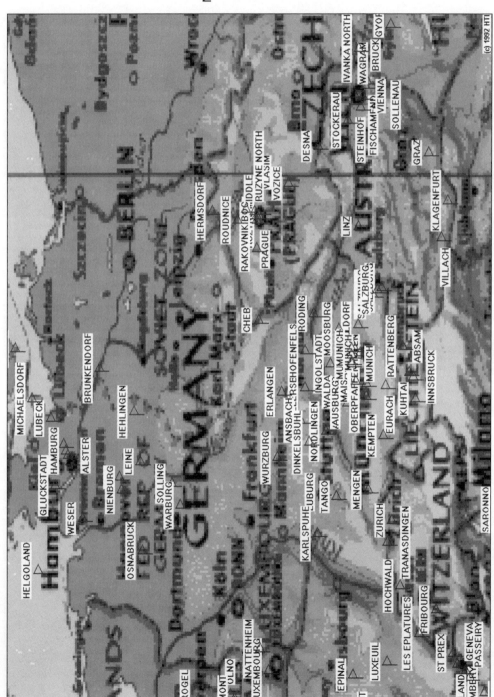

N51°

E15°

(c) 1992 HTI

Italy

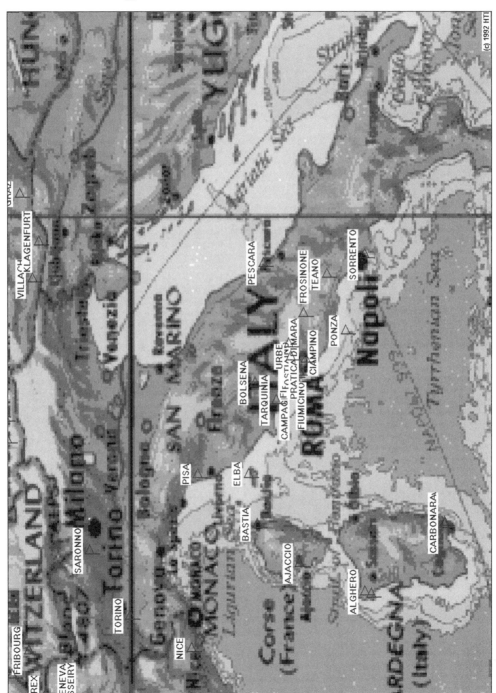

Denmark and Norway

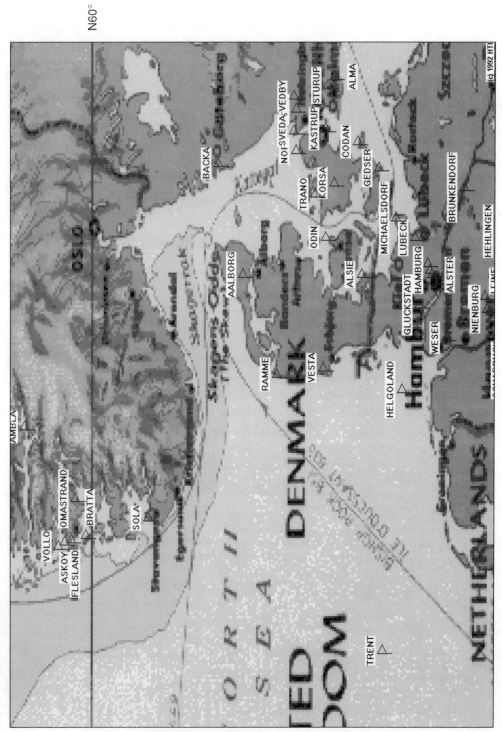

N60°

E7°

(c) 1992 HTI

Greece and Turkey

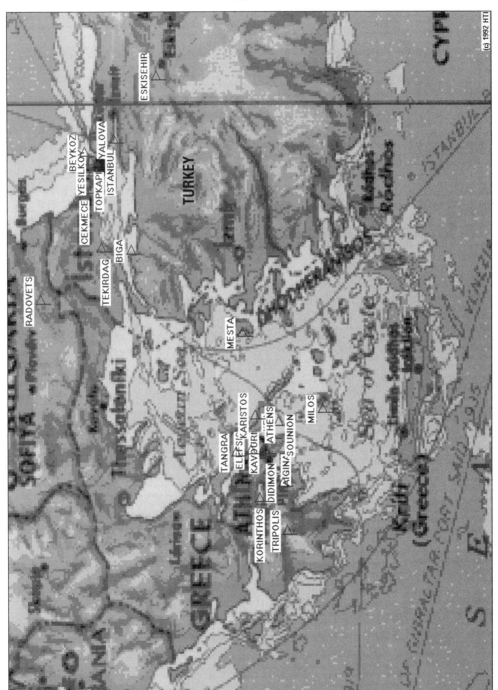

Africa

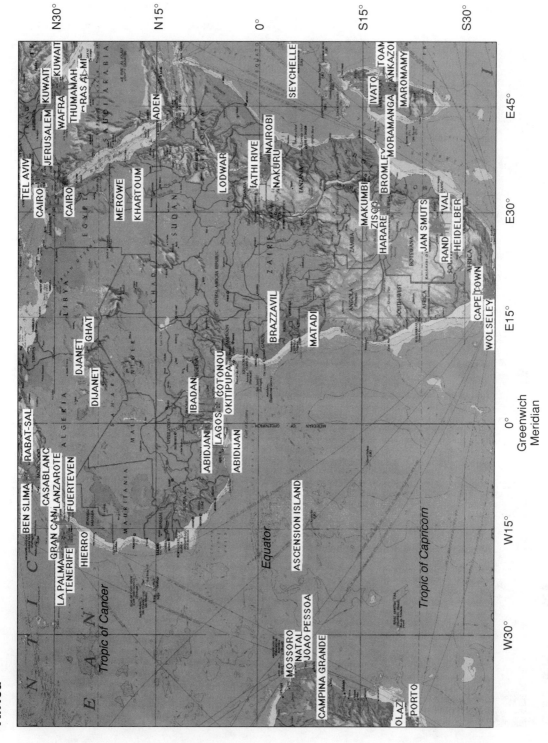

Asia

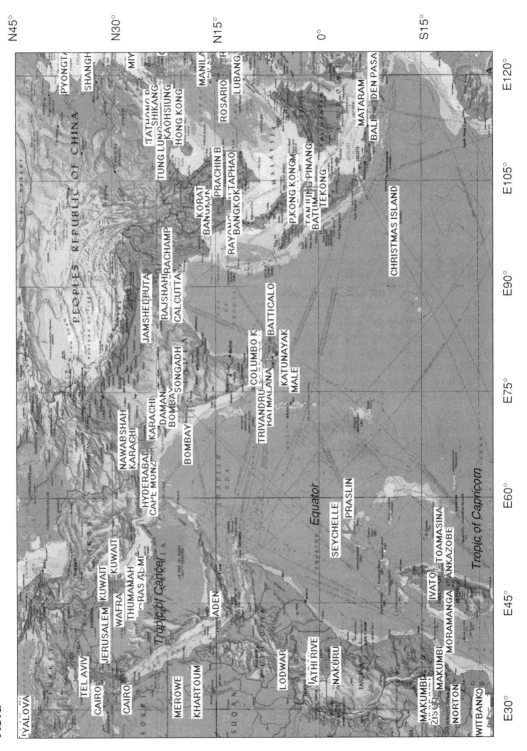

Eastern and Southern Pacific

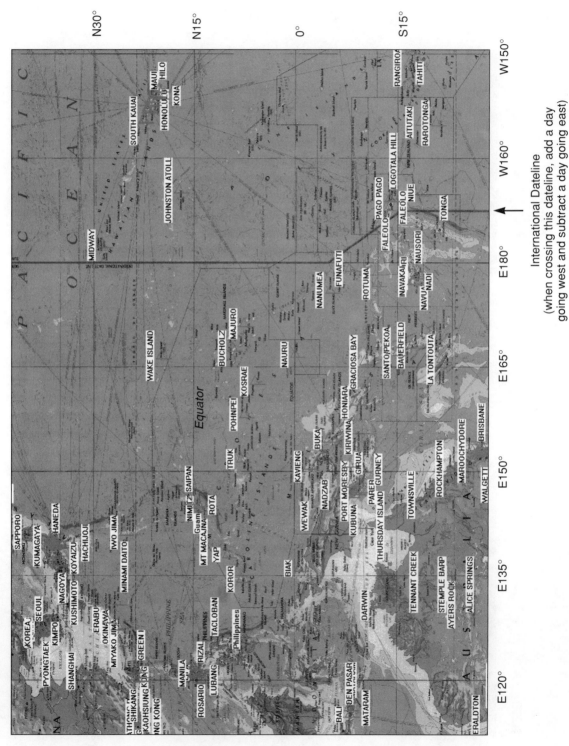

International Dateline
(when crossing this dateline, add a day
going west and subtract a day going east)

Western Pacific

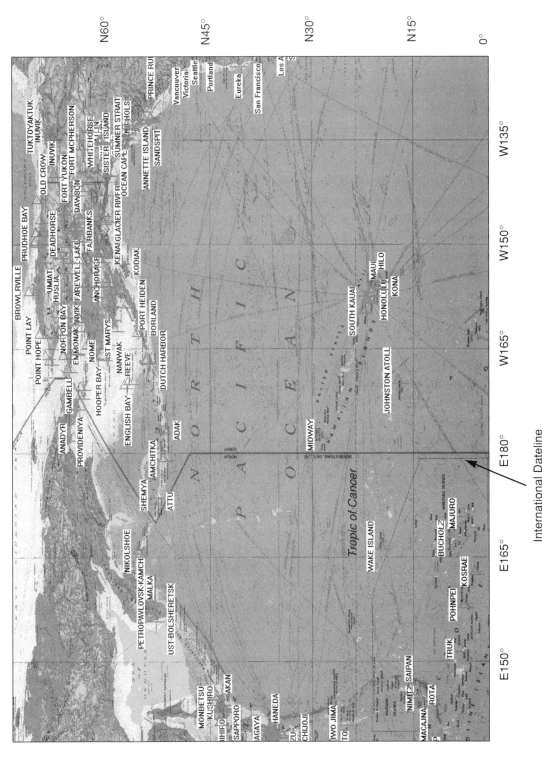

International Dateline
(when crossing this dateline, add a day
going west and subtract a day going east)

Australia

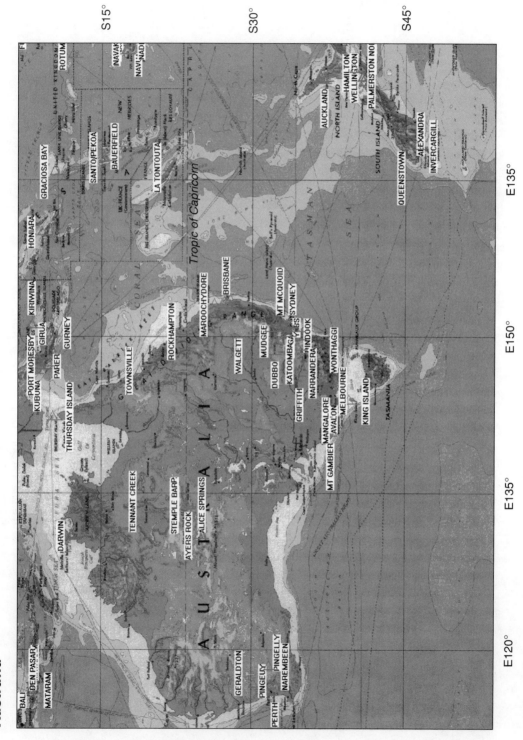

S15°

S30°

Tropic of Capricorn

S45°

E120°

E135°

E150°

E135°

BALI
DEN PASAR
MATARAM

GRACIOSA BAY

SANTO/PEKOA
BAUERFIELD

LA TONTOUTA

NAVAK
NAVI/NAD
ROTUM

UNITED KINGDOM

NEW HEBRIDES

FRANCE

UK-FRANCE (Condominium)

HONIARA

KIRIWINA
GIRUA
GURNEY

PORT MORESBY
KUBUNA
PARER

THURSDAY ISLAND

TOWNSVILLE

ROCKHAMPTON

MAROOCHYDORE
BRISBANE

MT MCQUOID
SYDNEY
PINDOOK
KATOOMBA
NARRANDERA
WONTHAGGI
MELBOURNE
KING ISLAND

WALGETT
MUDGEE
DUBBO
GRIFFITH
MANGALORE
AVALON
MT GAMBIER

AUCKLAND
NORTH ISLAND

HAMILTON
WELLINGTON
PALMERSTON NO

SOUTH ISLAND

QUEENSTOWN

ALEXANDRA
INVERCARGILL

TASMANIA

AUSTRALIA

TENNANT CREEK

STEMPLE BARP
AYERS ROCK
ALICE SPRINGS

DARWIN

GERALDTON
PINGEUX
NAREMBEEN
PERTH

CORAL SEA

TASMAN SEA

South America

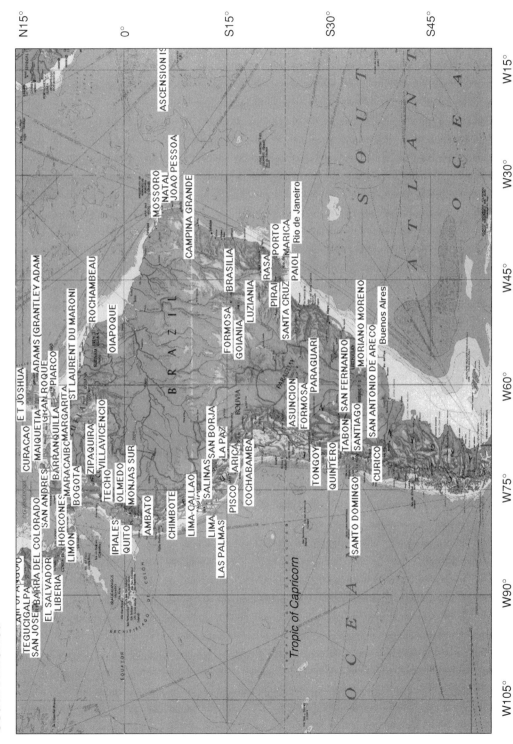

Central America and Caribbean

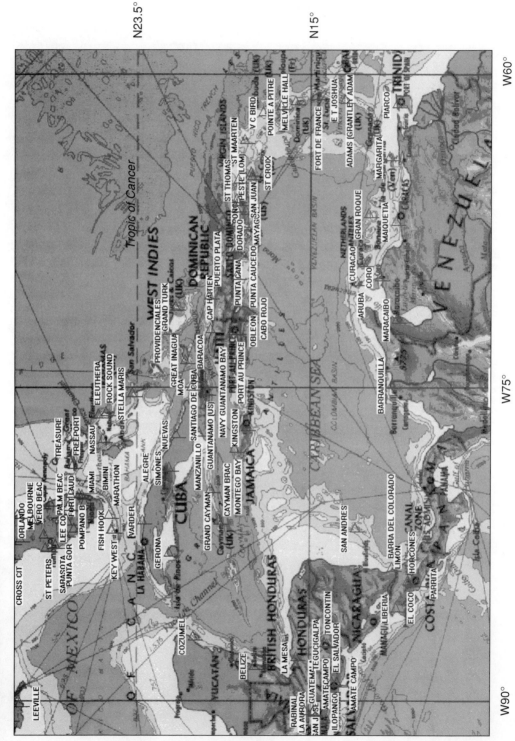

APPENDIX

C

Keyboard Summary

This appendix summarizes all the keyboard functions in *Flight Simulator 5.1.* In many cases, some program functions can be accessed only by multiple keystrokes. In those instances, you will see two key identifiers presented side by side. For example, to shift your view direction from the front to the rear, you would use the following keystrokes: [Shift] [8]. This would mean that you must press and hold the [Shift] key down and then press [8] on the numeric keypad. Whenever you see a number key identified, it is always assumed to be a *numeric keypad number, not one of the numbers on the main keyboard.* For some functions, the number keys on the main keyboard are used; for example, if you wanted to increase a single engine throttle on the Learjet you would press [E] [1] (on the main keyboard) or [E] [2] (on the main keyboard) followed by [9] on the numeric keypad. To avoid confusion, always press the number keys on the numeric keypad, unless otherwise told.

On the other hand, whenever you see [+] or [−], it is assumed that you must press the keys that are located on the main keyboard, not the numeric keypad.

Note that for FS5.1, there are some new auto-pilot keyboard shortcuts, as well as a jet fuel flow restart keyboard command for the Learjet.

FUNCTION KEYS ON THE MAIN KEYBOARD

KEY	FUNCTION
[A]	Set ADF Radio: Press [A] for first digit, [A] [A] for second digit, [A] [A] [A] for third digit, followed by [+] or [−].
[B]	Calibrate Altimeter

KEY	FUNCTION
C	Set COM Radio Frequency: Press C followed by + or − for integer portion; press C C followed by + or − for fractional portion.
D	Calibrate Directional Gyro
E	Engine Control. Press E 1 (on the main keyboard) for Left Engine 1; Press E 2 for right engine 2; or Press E 1 2 for both Engines followed by 9 (numeric keypad) to increase throttle, or 3 (numeric keypad) to decrease throttle.
F	DME Radio Control. Press F 1 (on the main keyboard) for DME 1, or F 2 for DME 2, followed by + to toggle between readout of speed toward station in knots (KTS) or distance in nautical miles (NM)
G	Landing Gear Up/Down
H	Carburetor Heat On/Off
I	Smoke/Spray On/Off
J	Jet Starter Switch On/Off: Press J 1 (on the main keyboard) for left engine 1, or J 2 for right engine 2, followed by + or −.
K	Calibrate Joystick
L	All Lights On/Off. For instrument lights only, press Shift L . For landing lights, press Ctrl L .
M	Magnetos On/Off. Press M followed by + or −.
N	NAV Radio Control. Set NAV Radio Frequency. For NAV 1 Radio, press N 1 (on the main keyboard) followed by + or − for integer portion; Press N N followed by + or − for fractional portion. For NAV 2 Radio, press N 2.
O	Strobe On/Off
P	Pause/Resume Flight
Q	Sound On/Off
R	Rate of Simulation: Press R followed by + or −.
S	Cycle through Cockpit, Tower, and Spot View
T	Transponder. Press T (first digit), T T (second digit), T T T (third digit), T T T T (fourth digit), followed by + or −.
U	Move EGT Bug Needle. Press U + to increase or U − to decrease.

KEY	FUNCTION
V	VOR OBI Course Selector. Press V 1 (on the main keyboard) for OBI 1, or V 2 for OBI 2, followed by + or −. Shift + or Shift − adjusts in 10° increments.
W	Enlarge active window to full screen (toggle key).
X	Land Me
Y	Enter Slew Mode (toggle key)
Z	Autopilot On/Off
Shift Z	Display Latitude/Longitude Coordinates
Ctrl Z	Autopilot Altitude Lock On
Backspace	Normal 1X Magnification
Tab	Switch Between Instrument Sub Panels.
Shift Tab	On Cessna, switches between VOR 2 and the ADF Indicator. On the Learjet, switches between VOR 1, VOR 2, and ADF Indicator.
Esc	Turn Menu Bar On/Off
Num Lock	Map View. Press Num Lock twice to close
Ctrl Print Screen	Reset Situation
Ctrl C	Exit Flight Simulator
Ctrl Break	Go to MS-DOS Prompt
.	Brakes On/Off and Release Parking Brakes
Ctrl .	Parking Brake On
;	Save Situation
	Bring Selected or Active Window to Top
?	Spoilers (Learjet)/Dive Brake(Sailplane) On/Off
+	Zoom In. For fine zoom in, press Shift +
−	Zoom Out. For fine zoom out, press Shift −
[	View 3-D View Window 1. Press [[to close
]	View 3-D View Window 2. Press]] to close
\	Stop Recording a Video, or Stop Maneuver Analysis
Spacebar	Close Open Menu. Also, Formation Flying Catch Up.
Ctrl Spacebar	Catch Up With Flying Companion while in Dual-player Mode (First make sure you are both on the ground, or both in the air, otherwise the simulation crashes).
0 (on main keyboard)	Send Message to Flying Companion while in Dual-player Mode (For the first message, click on the Send Message button in Dual-Player Dialog Box; thereafter use 0).

The Following Keys are on the Numeric Keypad:

KEYPAD	FUNCTION
1	Elevator Trim Up (Nose Up)
2	Elevator Up (Nose Up)
3	Decrease Throttle
4	Bank Left (Left Ailerons)
5	Center Ailerons & Rudder
6	Bank Right (Right Ailerons)
7	Elevator Trim Down (Nose Down)
8	Elevator Down (Nose Down)
9	Increase Throttle
0	Left Rudder (only in uncoordinated flight mode) or Steer Left while Taxiing
Enter	(on numeric keypad) Right Rudder (only in uncoordinated flight mode) or Steer Right while Taxiing

FUNCTION KEYS ON THE ENHANCED KEYBOARD (FUNCTION KEYS ON TOP)

If you are using an enhanced 101 keyboard with the function keys on the top row, use the following keys to perform the operations listed:

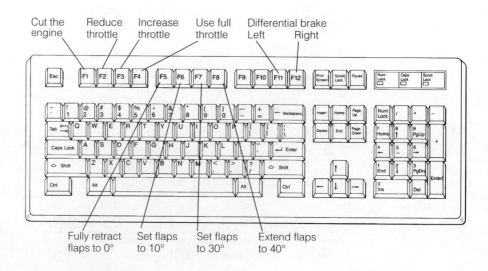

Figure C.1
Function keys on the top row of the keyboard

FUNCTION KEY	FUNCTION
F1	Cut Throttle
F2	Decrease Throttle One Step
F3	Increase Throttle One Step
F4	Full Throttle
F5	Flaps Fully Retracted (0°)
F6	Flaps 10°
F7	Flaps 30°
F8	Flaps 40°
F11	Left Differential Brake
F12	Right Differential Brake

FUNCTION KEYS ON THE STANDARD KEYBOARD (FUNCTION KEYS ON SIDE)

If you are using a standard keyboard, with the function keys on the left side of the keyboard, use the following keys to perform the operations listed:

FUNCTION KEY	FUNCTION
F1	Flaps Fully Retracted (0°)
F2	
F3	Flaps 10°
F4	Full Throttle
F5	Flaps 20°
F6	Increase Throttle One Step
F7	Flaps 30°
F8	Decrease Throttle One Step
F9	Flaps 40°
F10	Cut Throttle
F11	Left Differential Brake
F12	Right Differential Brake

Flap Controls	Key (Function Keys on Top)	Key (Function Keys on Left)
Flaps Retracted		
0°	F5	F1
10°	F6	F3
20°		F5
30°	F7	F7
40°	F8	F9

FLIGHT CONTROLS ON THE NUMERIC KEYPAD

The following keyboard functions for the numeric keypad allow you to set your flight controls:

CONTROL		KEY
Ailerons		
	Left	4
	Center	5
	Right	6
Elevator		
	Nose up	2
	Nose down	8
Elevator trim		
	Nose up	1
	Nose down	7
Rudder		
	Left	0
	Center	5
	Right	Enter (on numeric keypad)

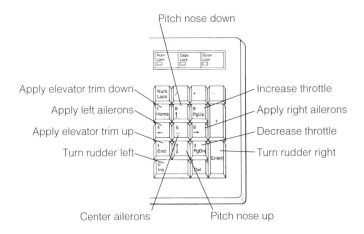

Figure C.2
Flight controls on the numeric keypad

ENGINE CONTROLS

The following keys and key combinations control your engines:

CONTROL	KEY (FUNCTION KEYS ON TOP)	KEY (FUNCTION KEYS ON LEFT)
Throttle		
Increase a step	9	9
Decrease a step	3	3
Cut	F1	F10
Decrease a step	F2	F8
Increase a step	F3	F6
Full	F4	F4
Propeller Control		
Increase	Ctrl 9	Ctrl 9
Decrease	Ctrl 3	Ctrl 3
Cut	Ctrl F1	Ctrl F10
Decrease	Ctrl F2	Ctrl F8
Increase	Ctrl F3	Ctrl F6
Full	Ctrl F4	Ctrl F2

CONTROL	KEY (FUNCTION KEYS ON TOP)	KEY (FUNCTION KEYS ON LEFT)
Mixture Control		
Increase	`Ctrl` `Shift` `9`	`Ctrl` `Shift` `9`
Decrease	`Ctrl` `Shift` `3`	`Ctrl` `Shift` `3`
Cut	`Ctrl` `Shift` `F1`	`Ctrl` `Shift` `F10`
Decrease	`Ctrl` `Shift` `F2`	`Ctrl` `Shift` `F8`
Increase	`Ctrl` `Shift` `F3`	`Ctrl` `Shift` `F6`
Full	`Ctrl` `Shift` `F4`	`Ctrl` `Shift` `F2`
EGT Bug Needle		
Move Needle Forward	`U` `+`	`U` `+`
Move Needle Back	`U` `−`	`U` `−`
Jet Engine Shutdown	`Ctrl` `Shift` `F1`	`Ctrl` `Shift` `F1`
Jet Starter	`J` `+` or `J` `−`	`J` `+` or `J` `−`

NAVIGATION COMMUNICATION KEYS

Certain keys or key combinations control navigation and communication functions, as is shown in the following list:

KEY COMBINATION	FUNCTION
`A` `+`	Set first digit of ADF Radio (ADF Radio must be activated first)
`A` `A` `+`	Set second digit of ADF radio
`A` `A` `A` `+`	Set third digit of ADF radio
`C` `+`	Set integer portion of COM Radio frequency
`C` `C` `+`	Set fractional portion of COM Radio frequency
`F` `1` (on main keyboard) `+`	DME 1 Radio control toggle between readout of speed toward station in knots (KTS) or distance in nautical miles (NM)
`F` `2` (on main keyboard) `+`	DME 2 Radio control toggle between readout of speed toward station in knots (KTS) or distance in nautical miles (NM)
`N` `1` `+`	Set integer portion of NAV 1 Radio frequency

KEY COMBINATION	FUNCTION
[N] [N] [1] [+]	Set fractional portion of NAV 2 Radio frequency
[N] [2] [+]	Set integer portion of NAV 2 Radio frequency
[N] [N] [2] [+]	Set fractional portion of NAV 2 Radio frequency
[T] [+]	Set first digit of Transponder Squawk Code
[T] [T] [+]	Set second digit of Transponder Squawk Code
[T] [T] [T] [+]	Set third digit of Transponder Squawk Code
[T] [T] [T] [T] [+]	Set fourth digit of Transponder Squawk Code

For the above list of keyboard combinations, you can substitute [−] for the [+] to reduce the frequency setting.

AUTO-PILOT KEYS

FS 5.1 now includes special auto-pilot keyboard shortcuts, so you don't have to constantly use the pull down menus for frequently used auto-pilot tasks. To turn the auto-pilot on or off, you can click the auto-pilot status indicator on the instrument panel, or you can press [Z]. Also, from the Nav/Com menu, you can select Auto-pilot and a dialog box will open allowing you to access all the auto-pilot functions.

KEY COMBINATION	AUTO-PILOT FUNCTION
[Z]	Toggle auto-pilot on or off.
[Ctrl] [V]	Level the wings.
[Ctrl] [T]	Maintain present pitch and bank attitude.
[Ctrl] [Z]	Lock to present altitude.
[Ctrl] [A]	Lock to an ILS tuned on NAV 1 for a landing. Aircraft flies the glide slope and localizer descent profile for the selected ILS runway.
[Ctrl] [N]	Lock to a VOR Radial tuned on NAV 1.
[Ctrl] [H]	Lock to your current magnetic course heading.
[Ctrl] [O]	Lock to the ILS Localizer (but not the glide slope) tuned on NAV 1 for a landing.
[Ctrl] [B]	Lock to a back course of a ILS Localizer tuned on NAV 1. This allows you to approach the runway from the opposite end for a landing.

VIEW KEYS

Certain keys or key combinations control viewing functions (from the numeric keypad), as is shown by the following:

VIEW DIRECTION	FUNCTION
Front	[Shift] [8]
Rear	[Shift] [2]
Left	[Shift] [4]
Right	[Shift] [6]
Left front	[Shift] [7]
Right front	[Shift] [9]
Left rear	[Shift] [1]
Right rear	[Shift] [3]
Down	[Shift] [5]
Pan up	[Shift] [Backspace]
Pan down	[Shift] [Enter]
Pan left	[Shift] [Ctrl] [Backspace]
Pan right	[Shift] [Ctrl] [Enter]
Straight and Level (No Pan)	[Scroll Lock]

Other Viewing Keys

KEY COMBINATION	FUNCTION
[S]	Cycle through Cockpit, Tower, and Spot View
[Shift] [S]	Reverse cycle through Cockpit, Tower, and Spot View
[W]	Maximize currently active window to full screen
[+]	Zoom in
[Shift] [+]	Fine Zoom in
[−]	Zoom out
[Shift] [−]	Fine Zoom out
[Backspace]	1× Normal Magnification
[[]	Open 3-D View Window 1. Press [[] [[] to Close.
[]]	Open 3-D View Window 2. Press []] []] to Close.

Key Combination	Function
[Num Lock]	Bring up Map Window, or select Map Window for zooming in or out: Press [Num Lock] [+] to zoom in, or [Num Lock] [−] to zoom out). Press [Num Lock] twice to close.

SLEWING CONTROLS

Slewing is a special nonflight mode that allows you to quickly move from point to point in the *Flight Simulator* world. In addition to actually moving the aircraft in three dimensions (called translation), you can also reorient the plane to any attitude (called rotation).

The slewing controls will work only when you enter slew mode. To enter and exit slew mode, press [Y].

Slewing Translation

The following keys allow you to move the aircraft in three dimensions:

Slew Translation	Key (Function Keys on top)	Key (Function Keys on Left)
Up or Down in Altitude		
Up Slowly	[Q]	[Q]
Up Quickly	[F4]	[F2]
Down Slowly	[A]	[A]
Down Quickly	[F1]	[F10]
Freeze	[5]	[5]
Forward & Backward		
Forward	[8]	[8]
Backward	[2]	[2]
Freeze	[5]	[5]
Sideways		
Left	[4]	[4]
Right	[6]	[6]
Freeze	[5]	[5]

Slewing Rotation

The following keys allow you to reorient the aircraft's pitch, bank (roll), and heading:

SLEW ROTATION	KEY (FUNCTION KEYS ON TOP)	KEY (FUNCTION KEYS ON LEFT)
Pitch		
Nose up slowly	9 (on main keyboard)	9 (on main keyboard)
Nose up fast	F5	F1
Freeze	F6	F5
Nose down fast	F8	F9
Nose down slowly	0 (on main keyboard)	F7
Bank (Roll)		
Left	7	7
Right	9	9
Freeze	5	5
Heading (Yaw)		
Left	1	1
Right	3	3
Freeze	5	5

Other Slewing Functions

Other slewing functions include the following:

| Z | Toggle Position Display Between On/Off/Latitude-Longitude/North-East Coordinate Systems |
| Spacebar | Reset Aircraft Orientation so that it is level: |

	Heading:	North
	Pitch:	0°
	Bank:	0°

MOUSE CONTROLS

The mouse can act as a flight control in *Flight Simulator*. By pressing the right mouse button, the cursor will disappear and the mouse can be rolled left or right, backwards or forwards, to affect the yoke controls. To exit mouse yoke control, simply press the right mouse button once again.

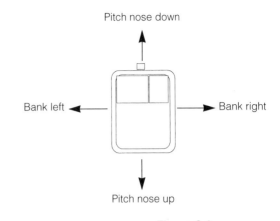

Figure C.3
Mouse movements affect flight controls (first press right mouse button so cursor disappears)

MOUSE MOVEMENT (FIRST PRESS RIGHT MOUSE BUTTON SO CURSOR DISAPPEARS)	FUNCTION
Forward	Pitch Nose Down (Elevator Down)
Backward	Pitch Nose Up (Elevator Up)
Left	Bank Left (Set Left Aileron & Rudder)
Right	Bank Right (Set Right Aileron & Rudder)

In addition, if you hold down the left mouse button while moving the mouse, you can control the throttle and brakes.

MOUSE MOVEMENT WHILE HOLDING LEFT MOUSE BUTTON DOWN	FUNCTION
Forward	Increase Throttle
Backward	Decrease Throttle
Left	Apply Brakes
Right	Release Brakes

Figure C.4
Mouse functions for controlling engine and brakes

Using the Mouse in Slew Mode

While in slew mode, the mouse can also be used to move the plane. First enter slew mode by pressing Ⓨ. Then, to activate the mouse, press the right mouse button so that the mouse pointer disappears. To move forward, move the mouse forward; to move backward, move the mouse backward. To rotate the plane left or right, roll the mouse left or right, but notice that the plane is merely rotating in place and not moving from its present posi-

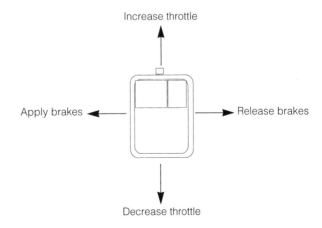

tion. To stop all motion, click the left mouse button. To make the mouse pointer reappear, click the right mouse button.

USING THE VIDEO RECORDER

The following keystrokes will work only when you are recording videos by using the Video Recorder command under the Options menu.

KEY	FUNCTION
[\]	Stop Recording a Video
[6] (on main keyboard)	Record at a 1 Second Interval
[7] (on main keyboard)	Record at a 5 Second Interval
[,]	Insert Messages During Playback
[Esc]	Stop Playback

Bibliography

How to Order These Books and Publications

Many of the aviation books and publications listed in this bibliography can be ordered directly from:

> The Aviator Store
> 7201 Perimeter Road South
> Seattle, WA 98108
> Their toll free USA telephone number is 800-635-2007.

Books

Bowditch, Natheniel. *The American Practical Navigator: An Epitome of Navigation.* Bethesda, Maryland: Defense Mapping Agency Hydrographic/Topographic Center, U.S. Government, 1995.

Broadbent, Stephen. *Jane's Avionics 1987-88.* New York: Jane's Publishing Inc., 1988.

—— *Cessna 1986 Turbo Skylane RG Information Manual.* Wichita, Kansas: Cessna Aircraft Company, 1985.

Conns, Keith. *The LORAN, GPS & NAV/COM Guide.* Templeton, California: Butterfield Press, 1992.

Conway, Carle. *The Joy of Soaring: A Training Manual.* Hobbs, New Mexico: The Soaring Society of America, 1989.

—— *Federal Aviation Regulations/Airman's Information Manual FAR/AIM 1993.* ASA-93-FR-AM-BK. Renton, Washington: Aviation Supplies & Academics, Inc., 1993.

——*Federal RadioNavigation Plan 1992.* DOT-VNTSC-RSPA-92-2/DOD-4650.5. Washington, D.C.: U.S. Department of Transportation and Department of Defense, 1992.

——*Flight Training Handbook.* AC-61-21A. Washington, D.C.: U.S. Department of Transportation, Federal Aviation Administration, 1980.

Hobbs, Richard R. *Marine Navigation 2: Celestial and Electronic.* Second Edition. Annapolis: Naval Institute Press, 1981.

——*Instrument Flying Handbook.* AC-61-27C. Washington, D.C.: U.S. Department of Transportation, Federal Aviation Administration, 1980.

Lambert, Mark. *Jane's All the World's Aircraft 1991-92.* Alexandria, Virginia: Jane's Information Group, 1992.

——*Microsoft Flight Simulator 5.1 Pilot's Handbook.* Bellingham, Washington: Microsoft Press, 1995.

Rider, Paul R. *Plane and Spherical Trigonometry.* New York: The Macmillan Company, 1942.

Porter, Donald J. *Learjets.* Blue Ridge Summit, Pennsylvania: Tab Books, 1987.

Serway, Raymond A. *Physics For Scientists & Engineers with Modern Physics.* Third Edition. San Francisco: Saunders College Publishing, 1990.

Pamphlets

Cost of Operation: Learjet 35A. Wichita, Kansas: Learjet Inc.

Learjet 35A. Wichita, Kansas: Learjet Inc.

Mission Planning Guide: Learjet 35A. Wichita, Kansas: Learjet Inc.

Optional Equipment Description & Pricing: Learjet 35A. Wichita, Kansas: Learjet Inc.

The Schweizer 2-32 Sailplane Flight-Erection-Maintenance Manual. Elmira, New York: Schweizer Aircraft Corp.

Specification & Description: Learjet 35A. Wichita, Kansas: Learjet Inc.

U.S. Department of Commerce, National Oceanic and Atmospheric Administration, National Ocean Service. *Aeronautical Charts and Related Products.* Riverdale, Maryland. 1993.

Articles

Collins, Richard L. "Skylane Round Robin." *Flying Magazine* (November 1979): 77-83.

MacKay, Robert. "Microsoft's Flight Simulator 5.0." *MicroWINGS Magazine,* vol. 1, no. 3 (August 1993): 12-15.

Navin, Patrick. "GPS Update." *InFlight Aviation News Monthly* (June 1993): 54-55.

North, David M. "Learjet 60 Stakes Claim in Corporate Market." *Aviation Week & Space Technology* (June 28, 1993): 38-43.

Schiff, Barry. "Skyregs Review: Controlled Airspace." *AOPA Pilot Magazine* (February 1985): 44-47.

Maps and Sectionals

Flight Simulator is best enjoyed if you have the real navigational maps pilots use. The Federal Government's National Oceanic and Atmospheric Administration (NOAA) agency publishes all the maps you might need to use. They have a free catalog, called the *Aeronautical Charts and Related Products*, which lists all the maps they publish and their prices.

How to Order Maps and Aeronautical Sectionals from NOAA in Maryland

To order the NOAA map catalog, contact the NOAA at:

> NOAA Distribution Branch, N/CG33
> National Ocean Service
> Riverdale, MD 20737-1199
> Telephone and Fax orders are also accepted by the
> NOAA Distribution Branch:
> General Information and Individual Orders 301-436-6990
> Fax Orders 301-436-6829

Ordering Maps For Overnight Delivery

Although you can order aviation maps directly from the NOAA, if you are in a big hurry and can't wait several weeks for your maps to arrive (which is typical when ordering federal government documents), you can order maps for overnight delivery from:

> Aviation Publications Services
> 1327 Maiden Lane, P.O. Box 400
> Del Mar, CA 92014-0400
> Telephone   619-755-1190
> Fax   619-755-5910
> Toll Free   800-869-7453 (for orders only)

Aviation Publications Services has a huge selection of worldwide aeronautical maps in stock, and can answer any questions you might have about the maps you decide to order.

Types of Maps

There are several different kinds of maps that the NOAA publishes. They are listed as follows:

- Visual Flying Rules (VFR) Terminal Area Charts
- Sectional Aeronautical Charts
- Enroute Low Altitude Victor Airway Maps
- Instrument Flying Rules (IFR) Enroute High Altitude Jet Airway Maps
- Department of Defense (DOD) Global Route Maps

Sectional and VFR Terminal Area Charts

Visual Flying Rules (VFR) Terminal Area Charts are maps that show the area immediately surrounding the city's major airports. They include landmarks, airspace obstruction information, lakes, dams, rivers, roads, large buildings, as well as VOR/NDB stations. The Terminal Area Charts also show the runway orientations, so you know where to head your airplane when landing. Basically, you use the Terminal Area Chart to plan your final approach to the airport. The Terminal Area Charts that are most useful for Flight Simulator include the following:

- Los Angeles Terminal Area Chart
- San Francisco Terminal Area Chart
- Seattle Terminal Area Chart
- Chicago Terminal Area Chart
- New York Terminal Area Chart

Sectional Aeronautical Charts show terrain and topographical features as well as VOR/NDB stations. However, they cover a much larger region than the Terminal Area Charts. Here is a listing of the charts used for Flight Simulator's main US scenery areas:

- Los Angeles Sectional
- San Francisco Sectional
- Seattle Sectional
- Chicago Sectional
- New York Sectional

Figure D.1 shows the Sectional and VFR Terminal Area charts for the United States, Hawaiian Islands, Puerto Rico, and the Virgin Islands. If you want to see which chart you need to get for your area, consult this figure and find the rectangle that covers the area you want to fly in. The dots on the figure represent VFR Terminal Area Charts, while the rectangular areas are the Sectional Charts.

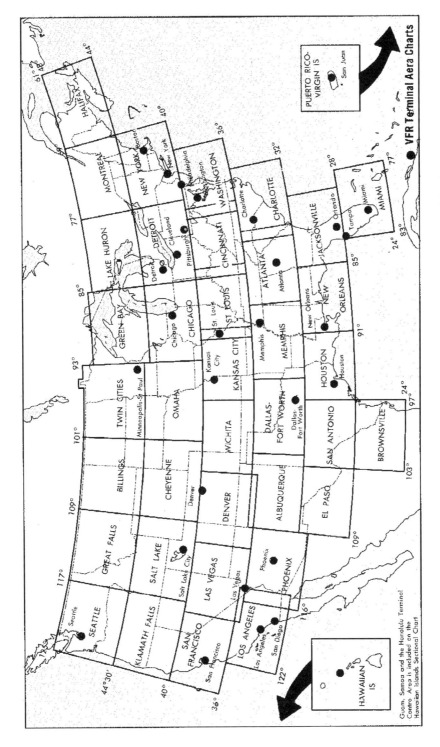

Figure D.1: Sectional aeronautical and VFR terminal area charts for the United States, Hawaiian Islands, Puero Rico, and the Virgin Islands. Use this Figure to decide which maps you want to order from the NOAA.

Enroute Low Altitude Charts

The Low Altitude Victor Airway Charts show only VOR/NDB stations and the air routes for flights that take place below 18,000 feet. No geographical or topographical information is included. Some of the more popular of these charts are listed as follows:

- L-1/L-2: Covers the West Coast of the US,except for Santa Barbara down to Los Angeles.
- L-3: Covers Santa Barbara to San Diego, California eastward to Arizona.
- L-19: Covers east coast of Florida.
- L-27/L-28: Covers East Coast of US from Georgia to New York.
- L-11/L-23: Covers the area around Chicago.
- L-13: Covers the area around Dallas-Ft. Worth.

Figure D.2 shows the available Enroute Low Altitude Charts for the United States you can order from the NOAA.

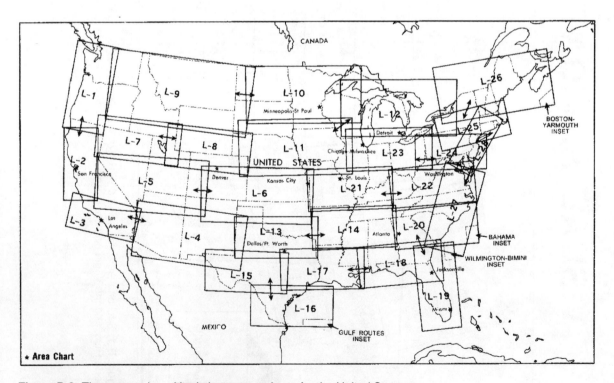

Figure D.2: The enroute low altitude instrument charts for the United States that you can order from the NOAA.

IFR Enroute High Altitude Charts

The Instrument Flying Rules (IFR) High Altitude Jet Airway Maps do not include geographical or topographical features. They only include the air routes and the VOR/NDB stations. They are to be used for flights above 18,000 feet. If you get all three of the following "H" charts, you will have a navigational map of the entire United States:

- Northwest H-1/Northeast H-3 IFR Enroute High Altitude US Chart: Covers the northern USA. west from the northern California coast to the New York coast.
- Southwest H-2/Southeast H-4 IFR Enroute High Altitude US Chart: Covers the southern USA. west from southern California to the northern Florida coast.
- H-5/South H-6/East IFR Enroute High Altitude US Chart: Covers southern Texas to southern Florida, and east coast of the USA.

Figure D.3 shows the coverage area for the Enroute High Altitude Charts that you can order from the NOAA.

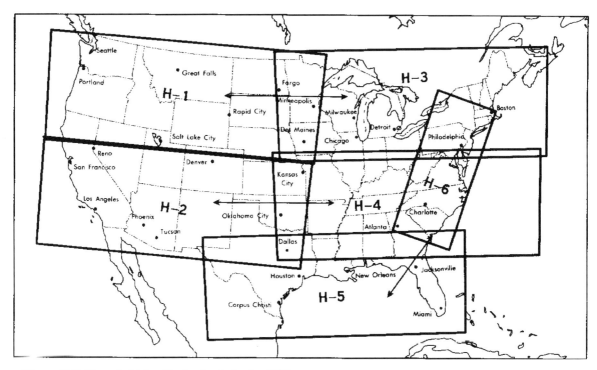

Figure D.3: Enroute high altitude charts for the USA

Transoceanic Department of Defense Global Route Charts

For transoceanic flights you will need these charts:

- Pacific, Australasia, and Antarctica: Twenty charts printed back to back, accordian folded. Shows VOR/NDBs and principal waypoints over oceanic routes. Includes magnetic course bearing information. Highly recommended. See Figure D.4 for coverage area.

- Caribbean and South America High Altitude: Six high altitude charts printed back to back, accordian folded. Shows VOR/NDBs and magnetic course bearing information. See Figure D.5 for coverage area.

- Europe, North Africa, and Middle East High Altitude: Fourteen charts printed back to back, accordian folded. Shows VOR/NDBs and magnetic course bearing information. See Figure D.6 for coverage area.

- Africa High and Low Altitude: Four charts printed back to back, accordian folded. Shows VOR/NDBs and magnetic course bearing information for Mid-Africa and South Africa. See Figure D.7 for coverage area.

- North Atlantic Route Chart: Covers the US and Canadian Eastern

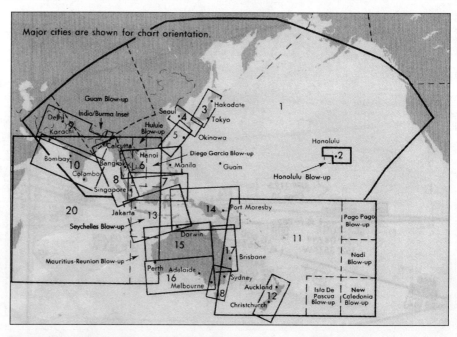

Figure D.4: Department of Defense (DOD) Pacific, Australasia, and antarctica charts available from NOAA

Seaboard, the Caribbean region, Bermuda, Cuba, Venezuela, Greenland, Iceland, England, Ireland, Azores, Spain, Morroco, Western Sahara, down to Dakar, Africa. Includes principal VOR/NDB stations, and latitude/longitude waypoints for the main air corridors for the North and Mid-Atlantic Ocean regions. Unfortunately, this chart does not include magnetic course bearing information.

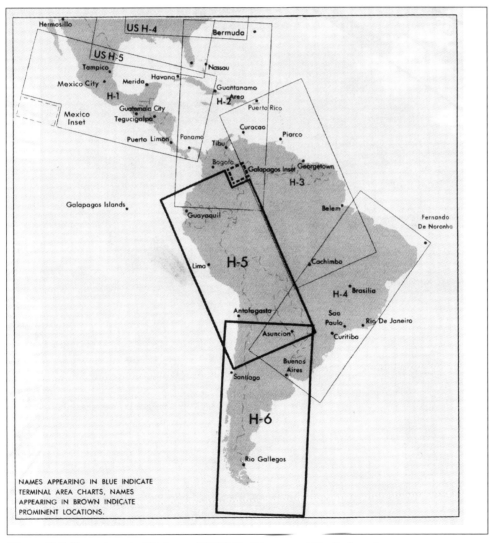

Figure D.5: Department of Defense (DOD) Caribbean and South America high altitude charts available from NOAA

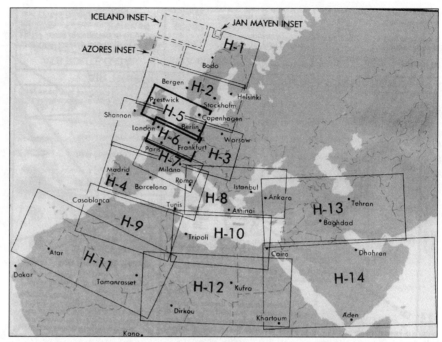

Figure D.6: Department of Defense (DOD) Europe, North Africa, and Middle East high altitude available from NOAA

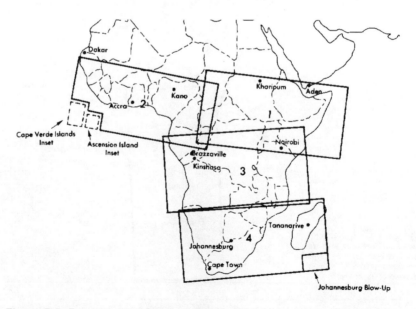

Figure D.7: Department of Defense (DOD) Africa high and low altitude charts available from NOAA

Index

It's coming! —"WAKA-WAKA
WAKA-WAKA"—That relentless
chomping sound is getting closer
closer every second.—"WAKA-WA
WAKA-WAKA"—It's eating the d
all around me.— "WAKA-WAK
WAKA"— I can't get away!—"
WAKA-WAKA"—There's n
place to hide! It's PacM

Pac-Man™ **was** here.

Relive those carefree and
exciting days when every
quarter burned a hole in your
pocket. **Microsoft**® **Return of
Arcade** puts you in command
of four hot arcade classics—
replicated exactly for the PC!

Pac-Man™ **is** here.

Pac-Man™
Be quick, be fearless. Chomp
away on the dots and avoid
those four relentless ghosts,
level after level!

Pole Position
Ladies and gentlemen, start your
engines! Pole Position is a thrill a
minute behind the wheel.

Galaxian™
Head for deep space and get the
bugs out of it! The better you do, the
more threatening the swarms of
invaders become.

Dig-Dug™
Use your skill and daring to
burrow your way to survival.
You're going to dig it!

Microsoft®

WHERE DO YOU WANT TO GO TODAY?™

*Catch the new wave of classic arcade action
blasting into Windows*® *95.*

© 1995 Microsoft Corporation. All rights reserved.
Microsoft is a registered trademark and *Where do you want to go today?* is a trademark of Microsoft
Corporation. Windows is a registered trademark of Microsoft Corporation for its Windows operating
system products. Dig-Dug, Galaxian, and Pac-Man are trademarks of Namco Corporation.

"Map clip art? Bite your tongue Bernice.
They're ready-to-use, digitized, full-color,
mosaiced, geo-referenced, USGS raster maps."

Sure! MAPS. RASTER

Finally, map data with all the right buzz words needed by today's highly specialized GIS spatial data market. Whether your area of study is 2 miles or 200 miles, Sure!MAPS® RASTER map sets will make a world of information work for you. Information like lakes, parks, buildings, freeways, radio towers, water tanks, golf courses, terrain contours and more.

Sure!MAPS RASTER is a series of digitized, mosaiced, geo-referenced USGS raster maps that can be imported into most popular software packages. Packages from companies like ESRI, AutoDesk, Intergraph, MapInfo, ERDAS, Genasys, PCI, Adobe and others who provide raster capable systems. The included viewer software lets you choose the area to incorporate into your application, extract the map data from the map set CD-ROM and write it to a designated directory. Output map files can be imported by any software application supporting TIF, BMP or TGA file formats.

Sure!MAPS RASTER map sets are based on 1:24K, 1:100K and 1:250K USGS topographic maps. The 1:100K and 1:250K map sets cover the entire US and the 1:24K map sets cover more than 60 US metropolitan areas. We can also custom scan other USGS quads or your proprietary maps.

Sure!MAPS RASTER. For detailed, easy-to-use map data, there's nothing faster. Just ask Bernice's friend Helen. Or call us at 800-828-3808. We'd be happy to chat with you.

HORIZONS TECHNOLOGY, INC.®

1:250,000 scale

1:100,000 scale

1:24,000 scale

Horizons Technology, Inc. 3990 Ruffin Rd. San Diego, CA 92123 • 800-828-3808, FAX (619) 565-1175 • http://www.horizons.com

© 1995 Horizons Technology, Inc. Sure!MAPS is a registered trademark of Horizons Technology, Inc. All other product names are trademarks of their respective companies.